Type Right!

A Complete Program for Business Typewriting

Gertrude S. Altholz
Former Head, Department of Secretarial Studies
Midwood High School, New York City

Delores S. Cotton
Head, Business Education Department
Henry Ford High School, Detroit

Vito C. Metta
Assistant Supervisor, Business and Office Education
Cleveland Public Schools

A Pitman Book Fearon Pitman Publishers, Inc., Belmont, California

Typewriting Consultant: Herbert L. Becker

Editorial Director: Louis P. Prete
Cover and Text Designer: Eleanor Mennick
Illustrators: Mary Burkhardt, Judith McCarty,
   Eleanor Mennick
Photographers: Lynda Gordon, Thomas Tracy

ISBN-0-8224-2128-3
Library of Congress Catalog Card Number: 78-73160
Printed in the United States of America
1.9876554321

TYPE RIGHT! is designed and written for teachers who are on the front line—facing students day in and day out. It is a new book, but it makes no claims to any revolutionary breakthroughs in typewriting instruction. Its contents are based on tried and tested methods and materials proven through years of classroom use in its forerunner, *Modern Typewriting Practice.*

TYPE RIGHT! is a complete instructional program from basic keyboard operation to applied business typewriting. It contains voluminous material for a full two-year course. Not only is there an abundance of exercise material stressing all kinds of on-the-job applications, but, in addition, two complete sections are devoted entirely to drill material —so necessary for the development of speed and accuracy.

Organization

The text is organized into five main sections. Section One introduces the keyboard. The material in this section is presented in 39 *units,* each designed for one classroom period. To accommodate differences in student achievement, 12 of the 39 units provide either review or skill development material to be used at the teacher's discretion.

Sections Two and Three present the main body of instructional matter. Section Two emphasizes the personal, everyday uses of typewriting; Section Three emphasizes the vocational applications. Both sections are organized into *topics* that each focus on a single subject, such as *horizontal centering, crowding and spreading, manuscript typing, preparing form letters,* and so forth. Topics are arranged in clusters of related learning, and within each cluster the topics are presented in a progression of difficulty. It is not intended that all topics be used in the same sequence as they appear in the text, nor that all exercises in any one topic be done at one time. To achieve variety, the teacher should feel free to move about the text according to class needs and course objectives. The topical organization facilitates this freedom of movement because all exercises that focus on a particular skill or new learning can be found in the same place.

Section Four, *Work Experience Simulations,* consists of 15 projects that simulate on-the-job applications of the learnings presented in Sections Two and Three. The projects are arranged in order of increasing complexity. The first projects may be started early in Section Three; the latter ones, at its conclusion. The skills required for each project are clearly stated at the beginning of the project.

Section Five, *Supplementary Practice Exercises,* contains a wealth of drills and timed writings. These are provided for concentrated effort in developing speed and accuracy, for remediation, and for the measurement of speed and accuracy. This material should be interwoven at regular intervals throughout the teaching of Sections Two and Three. It may also be used during the last part of Section One.

Language Arts

With the increased use of transcribing machines and electronic typewriters, language arts has become an important aspect of advanced typing instruction. Special emphasis has been given to developing the typist's ability to find and correct misspelled words, errors in punctuation, and other types of language problems that occur in copy to be typed. Two 100-word spelling lists, detailed rules of punctuation, and rules for typing numbers and abbreviations are included for students' reference and review. Exercises with a language arts emphasis are integrated into several topics and are grouped at the end of the topic for easy identification. To help students locate errors in uncorrected copy, clues in the form of "editing alerts" are given in many of the language arts exercises.

Exercise Materials

An abundance of exercise material accompanies each topic. Exercises are presented in a variety of formats that become progressively more challenging. The first exercises that students type are usually presented in typewriter type and arranged as finished copy should appear. Afterward, exercises are presented (1) in book type, arranged or unarranged; (2) in handwriting; and (3) in rough draft, both typed and handwritten. The exercises with a language arts emphasis are also presented in different formats that demand more and more of the student's ability to read copy for accuracy and make the appropriate corrections. Many of the exercises in Section Three are copy-counted in standard five-stroke words so that they may be used for timed production practice.

Models

Whenever a new learning is presented, an annotated typewritten model accompanies the instruction. Models are numbered consecutively throughout the text and are listed separately after the table of contents for easy reference.

Clarity of Instructions

The instructions that accompany each exercise or group of exercises are written in simple language that all students can understand. For ease of reading, the instructions are given in short phrases rather than running sentences wherever possible. All instructions are visually different from exercise copy to facilitate differentiation between the two.

Supporting Materials

A comprehensive teacher's manual is available separately. It contains suggestions for teaching each of the topics in the text, together with guidelines for the use of the exercise materials. Also included are suggested course outlines for a one-year and a two-year course.

A daily lesson plan guide is available, upon request, to teachers who have adopted *Type Right!* for classroom use. The guide contains a series of 300 lesson plans that outline specific suggestions for the content of each lesson.

Working papers consisting of letterhead stationery, envelope forms, invoice forms, legal documents, and other forms needed for the completion of exercises in Sections Three and Four are also available. Use of working papers during the second year of typewriting is recommended for more realistic practice.

CONTENTS

SECTION ONE Introduction to the Keyboard

SECTION TWO Typing for Everyday Use

SECTION THREE   Typing for Vocational Use

SECTION FOUR   Work Experience Simulations

SECTION FIVE   Supplementary Practice Exercises

MODELS

SELECTED ILLUSTRATIONS

SPECIAL INDEX

This index is provided to facilitate the location of specific *drills* (for speed, accuracy, and technique development), *exercises* of a special nature, and *timed writings*.

PARTS OF THE TYPEWRITER

MANUAL

1 Cylinder or platen
2 Cylinder knobs
3 Paper guide
4 Paper bail
5 Paper guide scale
6 Paper table or paper rest
7 Paper release

8 Line space regulator
9 Margin set
10 Printing point indicator
11 Aligning scale and card holder
12 Variable line spacer
13 Automatic line finder

14 Touch control
15 Ribbon control
16 Carriage
17 Carriage return lever
18 Carriage release
19 Carriage scale

a PBX operator usually receives all incoming 195
calls. In a large office, callers may be able to 205
dial individual offices directly, without going 214
through the central switchboard operator. 222

Telephone company operators are most 230
often called when a person needs their help in 239
order to place a call or to find a number. Most 249
central office operators deal most of the time 258
with long distance calls. They obtain the infor- 268
mation needed to complete the call, make the 277
required connections, and record the details of 286
each call for billing. Directory assistance opera- 296
tors help callers who need local or out-of-town 306
numbers.   SI 1.52 308

5

310 Words

One of the world's most important economic 9
minerals is coal. The first users of coal of whom 19
we have any record were the Anglo-Saxons. They 28
burned lignite, a form of soft coal, as early as the 38
ninth century. In the late seventeenth century, 48
coal was discovered in the United States along 57
the Illinois River. Soon afterward a bed was 66
found near Richmond, Virginia, but mining did 75
not start there until fifty years later. By the mid- 86
nineteenth century, coal was being mined on a 95
scale so great that it was of major importance 104
in shaping the industrial life of our nation. Among 114
its largest users were the railroads that were 123
beginning to crisscross the land. 129

Coal is of vegetable origin. It forms when the 139
vegetable matter decomposes and is subjected to 149
great water pressure, forcing it to give off gases. 159
This process, when carried on for thousands of 168
centuries, leaves nothing but pure carbon. 176

There are two principal kinds of coal: hard 186
coal or anthracite, and soft coal or bituminous. 196
There are also grades of coal softer than bitu- 205
minous. Anthracite was formed under greater 214
pressure than bituminous, and, thus, it has more 224
carbon and less moisture. It is also generally 233
found deeper in the earth. Supplies of anthracite 243
are much scarcer than soft coals; bituminous is 252
the most plentiful of all. 257

Anthracite is used mainly for home heating, 267
since it produces almost no smoke when it burns. 277
Bituminous is used for heating, too. More im- 286
portant, however, it can be used for fuel in 295
power plants that generate electricity from 304
steam—thus conserving our oil.   SI 1.53 310

6

331 Words

All of us expect Mother Earth to support us, 10
to provide us with food and drink, and to supply 20
us with the other materials we require. We are 29
meeting our needs by using not only the pro- 38
ductivity of the earth but also its great surplus 48
of capital that has been accumulated during past 58
ages. Generation after generation, this capital 68
becomes less, as we consume it for our needs. 77

We can reasonably expect the productivity 86
of Mother Earth to continue as long as human 95
beings exist. If we take care of the land, it will 105
always provide us with the food necessary for 114
life. But the land may be overworked to such 123
an extent that it loses its fertility. We must allow 134
it to rest for a while so that its fruitfulness will 144
be restored, and we must develop better methods 153
of farming so that the land will not be depleted. 163

The needs of primitive people were few. 172
They gathered food from the land and the waters. 182
Nature replaced whatever they consumed. Even- 191
tually, however, people began to find the capital 201
that the earth contained. In the course of time, 211
iron was discovered; then coal, oil, and other 220
materials. People learned how to use these to 229
develop greater comfort and more safety for 238
themselves. More and more uses were rapidly 247
found for the capital resources of the earth. 256

There is, however, one aspect of this story 266
that demands serious attention. We are using 275
up the capital that nature took many millions 284
of years to build. We can grow more food, but 293
we cannot replace iron, coal, or oil. We shall 302
have to manufacture substitutes for many nat- 312
ural products that cannot be replaced, and at the 322
same time reduce our reliance on such products. 331

SI 1.51

ELECTRIC

1	Cylinder or platen	12	Variable line spacer
2	Cylinder knobs	13	Automatic line finder
3	Paper guide	14	Touch control (not on most electric machines)
4	Paper bail	15	Ribbon control (not visible in machine below)
5	Paper guide scale	16	Carriage (not on an element machine)
6	Paper table or paper rest (not on machine shown here)	18	Carriage release (not on an element machine)
7	Paper release	19	Margin pitch scale
8	Line space regulator	20	Impression control
9	Margin set	21	On-off control
10	Printing point indicator	22	Return key
11	Aligning scale and card holder	23	Index key (element machine only)
		24	Typing element (element machine only)

ELEMENT MACHINE

huge size. Most of them have a strong attach- 64
ment to the places in which they live. Nonetheless, 74
New Yorkers love their city. 79

New York, with its varied social and business 89
life, is a symbol of America. The city is so enor- 99
mous that the average person does not appreciate 109
all its many attractions. Some find their affec- 119
tions stirred by Greenwich Village. Others enjoy 129
the activity of the Great White Way, the center 138
of the theatrical world. Some people prefer the 148
wide expanse of Park Avenue. Some enjoy the 157
quiet and beauty of Central Park. Some are moved 167
by the many activities of the harbor, with its 176
stately vessels and its busy tugboats. Others are 186
comfortable in the financial district. Still others 196
are attracted to the exclusive shops, with their 206
dazzling window displays. 211

Seen from a height in the darkness of a 220
velvety summer night, New York is a city of 229
magic. The vista enjoyed from a window high 238
above Manhattan is breathtaking. Decked with 247
patterns of glittering light, the giant city, bounded 258
by two mighty rivers, lies quiet and content, all 268
its shabbiness hidden in a violet haze, all its noise 279
thinned to a faint murmur. Here and there, 288
only moving lights suggest the ceaseless activity 298
going on below.   SI 1.49   301

3

309 Words

Many of the natives of the South Sea Islands 10
still live as primitive people must have lived. 19
They have no idea of personal ownership of 27
property; everything they have is shared. They 37
have no houses and spend their days and nights 46
in the open. One interesting fact about them is 56
that until very recently, they had never seen any 66
form of written language. One can imagine how 76
surprised they were when they first encountered 86
visitors to their islands who could read and 95
write. 96

A health officer relates the following experi- 106
ence. One afternoon, as he was typing in his 115
room, several of the islanders entered. They came 125
nearer and nearer to him, finally touching the 134

paper and the typewriter. The sudden appear- 143
ance of the tiny black characters on the piece 153
of white paper was something entirely unknown 162
to them and beyond their understanding. Even- 171
tually, he had to stop working, clear an area 180
around the typewriter, and show them what he 189
was doing. 191

With the assistance of a boy who understood 201
a little English, he explained that writing is like 211
talking. The marks on the paper were words. But 221
nobody understood what he was attempting to 230
say. He then tried to demonstrate to his listeners 240
more clearly what he meant. He wrote a note to 250
an officer on his ship requesting him to give a 260
blanket to the boy he sent with the message. 269
After the boy had left, he told the islanders what 279
he had written. The boy came back shortly with 289
the blanket. The people were amazed. They called 299
the signs talk marks and wanted to learn how to 309
make them.   SI 1.45   311

4

308 Words

Even though millions of telephone calls are 10
direct-dialed each day, almost everyone makes 19
some calls that cannot be made without help 28
from an operator. For instance, you may want 37
to reverse the charges on a long distance call, 46
or you may want to find out what a call will cost. 56
Perhaps you need a number that you cannot 64
find in the phone book. In each case, you will 73
need to dial the operator for help. The operator 83
may also be used to call the police or fire depart- 93
ment in an emergency, or to arrange a confer- 102
ence call which will allow three or more people 111
in different places to talk to each other at the 121
same time. 123

These and many other services are supplied 132
by two groups of operators—those at switch- 141
boards in the phone company's office and those 150
at private branch exchange (PBX) switchboards. 159
Both types of operators may insert and remove 168
plugs attached to cords, or they may make use 177
of keys to connect callers. In a small office, 186

(Continued on next page)

How the Parts Function

1. CYLINDER or PLATEN   The large roller around which the paper turns.
2. CYLINDER KNOBS   Located at both ends of the cylinder and used to turn the cylinder.
3. PAPER GUIDE   Guides the left edge of the paper as it is inserted into the typewriter.
4. PAPER BAIL   The bar with small rubber rollers that holds the paper against the cylinder.
5. PAPER GUIDE SCALE   Indicates the number of typing spaces on a given width of paper, shows the position of the paper, and serves as the scale for setting the paper guide.
6. PAPER TABLE or PAPER REST   The plate on which the unused portion of the paper rests.
7. PAPER RELEASE   Used to straighten or remove the paper.
8. LINE SPACE REGULATOR   The lever that sets the machine for single, double, or triple line spacing.
9. MARGIN SET   Used to set the points at which the writing line begins and ends.
10. PRINTING POINT INDICATOR   Points to the position on the carriage or cylinder scales at which the type will strike the paper.
11. ALIGNING SCALE   Used for locating the writing line when the paper is reinserted and for "fine tuning" the horizontal or vertical position of the paper.
12. VARIABLE LINE SPACER   Usually located in the left cylinder knob, it releases the line spacing mechanism to allow the cylinder to turn freely and to set a new writing line.
13. AUTOMATIC LINE FINDER   The lever that disengages the line spacing mechanism temporarily, but which, when restored, returns the paper to its original alignment.
14. TOUCH CONTROL   Adjusts the resistance of the keys to the force with which you strike them; the higher the number on the control, the harder it is to strike the keys.
15. RIBBON CONTROL   The button or lever that controls the position of the ribbon when a key is struck. Three positions are usually available: (1) the position in which the top half of the ribbon is used to make a black ink impression; (2) the position in which the lower half of the ribbon is used to make a red ink impression; and (3) the position for cutting stencils, in which the mechanism that lifts the ribbon is disengaged so that no ink impression is made.
16. CARRIAGE   On a typebar machine, the entire top moving section that carries the paper.
17. CARRIAGE RETURN LEVER   Used to return the carriage to the far right and advance the paper to the next writing line.
18. CARRIAGE RELEASE   Used for moving the carriage freely from side to side.
19. CARRIAGE SCALE or MARGIN PITCH SCALE   Used for counting spaces, selecting margin stops, and locating the midpoint of the paper.
20. IMPRESSION CONTROL   On an electric typewriter, used to set the force with which the typebar or element strikes the paper.
21. ON-OFF CONTROL   On an electric typewriter, used to turn the power on and off.
22. RETURN KEY   Automatically returns the carriage to the far right on an electric typebar machine; on an element machine, it returns the element to the left margin; on both machines, it also advances the paper to the next writing line.
23. INDEX KEY   Advances the paper to the next line without returning to the left margin.
24. TYPING ELEMENT   The small globe that moves from the left to the right of the paper and types the characters.

INTRODUCTION TO YOUR TYPEWRITER

How to Center the Carriage

1. Hold the cylinder knob (2)* and with the same hand firmly depress the carriage release (18) near it, as shown in the illustration at the left.
2. Move the carriage left or right and bring it to a stop near the center of the carriage scale (19).
3. Disengage the carriage release and the carriage will remain centered.

*Numbers in parentheses refer to the numbered parts of the typewriter shown in the diagrams on pages 1 and 2.

37

291 Words

An important factor in the success of a busi- 10
ness is the personality of the man or the woman 19
who manages it. 22

Vital to success in business is the ability to 32
get along with people and inspire confidence. 41
The owner of a business must establish a friendly 51
relationship with customers and with employees. 60
A moment of reflection will bring to your mind 69
men and women who have attracted customers 77
by their warm personalities, their tact, their cour- 87
tesy, their understanding. You will recall others 97
who have driven customers away by being abrupt 106
and unobliging. A person can be pleasant even 116
when refusing a request. 121

Another factor that contributes to business 131
success is responsibility in money matters. The 141

store owner has a financial obligation to both 150
employees and creditors. Before the business 159
can clear a profit, the payroll must be met and 168
bills must be paid as they become due. 176

Finally, to achieve success, the owner of a 186
business must enjoy the work enough to spend 195
many hours at it willingly. Every day, important 205
decisions will need to be made, and they will 214
need to be made wisely. And the owner must 223
be a good organizer and a good manager, too, 232
so that the business will operate at maximum 241
efficiency. For instance, buying must be geared 251
to customer demand; and finances must be man- 260
aged so that cash is available to meet payments 269
on time. 271

Business is a great adventure. To the person 281
who has the right qualities, it will bring success. 291

SI 1.60

OVER 300 WORDS   These timed writings range in syllabic intensity from 1.45 to 1.53.

1

300 Words

Over a century ago, a game known as town- 9
ball, the ancestor of baseball, was very popular 19
in New England. It was played on a square field. 29
At each corner of the field was a post that was 38
used as a base. To win, a team had to make one 47
hundred runs. As years passed, the game was 56
modified until it assumed the form that we rec- 65
ognize as baseball. 69

During the Civil War, the soldiers in camp 78
found recreation in playing baseball. At the con- 88
clusion of the fighting, when the soldiers returned 98
to their homes in every area of the United States, 108
they carried the game with them, until it became 118
a national sport. At first, many kinds of teams 128
competed; then clubs were organized; still later, 138
the clubs were combined into the leagues of the 147
present day. 149

There are two major leagues and several 158
minor leagues. The clubs of the major leagues, 167
the National and the American, compete in sched- 177
uled games from April until October. The winning 187

clubs in these leagues then compete in the final 197
series of games for the national championship. 206

The leagues play according to rules estab- 215
lished by a national association, the head of which 225
is the national commissioner of baseball. He has 235
the authority to issue final decisions about any 245
matter in dispute. 249

Interest in baseball has spread from the 258
United States to many other areas in the world. 267
The game is now enjoyed in almost every coun- 276
try. Fans in other countries follow with intense 286
interest the games played by the two major leagues 296
in the United States.   SI 1.47   300

2

301 Words

Most visitors to New York City inform us 9
that they would not like to make it their perma- 19
nent dwelling place. Some of them, coming from 28
small towns with tree-shaded houses set back 37
from the street on green lawns, find the city 46
too crowded. Others become overwhelmed by its 55

(Continued on next page)

How to Insert the Paper

1. See that the paper guide (3) is set to correspond to zero on the carriage scale (19) and the paper guide scale (5).
2. Place your paper at the left of the machine. Pick up the paper with your left hand as shown in the illustration below.
3. Rest the paper lightly against the paper table (6) along the line where the paper table and the cylinder (1) meet.
4. With your right index and middle fingers above and your right thumb below, grasp the right cylinder knob (2) and turn it quickly to bring the paper into position, as shown in the illustration below.
5. Place the paper bail (4) over the paper to hold it flat against the cylinder.

How to Straighten the Paper

1. If the paper is not straight, use the paper release (7) to loosen the paper. Then raise the paper bail (4) and straighten the paper. You can align the edge of the sheet with the aligning scale (11) or the paper guide scale (5), or you can match the left and right edges of the paper as shown in the drawing to the left.
2. Restore the paper release and place the paper bail back against the paper.

How to Remove the Paper

1. Pull the paper release (7) toward you and remove the paper.
2. Restore the paper release to its normal position.

How to Set Line Spacing

Typewritten lines may be single-, double-, or triple-spaced. Some typewriters also provide for $1\frac{1}{2}$ and $2\frac{1}{2}$ line spacing.

The line space regulator (8) controls the vertical spacing between lines. When it is set at 1, the cylinder advances one line when the carriage is returned. This results in *no* blank lines between lines of type.

When the line space regulator is set at 2, there is *one* blank line between lines of type.

When the line space regulator is set at 3, there are *two* blank lines between lines of type.

Single Spacing	Double Spacing	Triple Spacing
Single Spacing		
Single Spacing	Double Spacing	
		Triple Spacing
	Double Spacing	
		Triple Spacing

34

229 Words

In most large organizations—and in many small ones—there are receptionists to greet people and provide them with information. It is the receptionist's job to determine the nature of each caller's business. The receptionist then sends the caller to the proper office, or else contacts that office by telephone to arrange for an appointment. In different types of organizations, receptionists have somewhat different duties. In a hospital clinic, the receptionist must direct each patient to the proper waiting room; in a beauty shop, he or she must make an appointment or accompany the customer to the operator's booth; and in a large defense plant, it may be part of the receptionist's job to provide the caller with an identification card and an escort to the proper office.

Some receptionists also keep records showing the name of each caller, the reason for the visit, the time, and the person to whom the caller was referred.

If receptionists have some time when they are not occupied with callers, they often handle other office tasks. They may receive and route telephone calls, sort and open mail, file, or keep books. SI 1.56

35

252 Words

Advertising appeals are planned according to the group to be reached, or according to the particular kind of response desired.

Good advertisements are designed to fit the particular class of readers for whom they are intended. When a producer advertises a product, the prospective buyer could be a wholesaler, a retailer, or a consumer. The appeal in each case would be different. A circular letter sent to a retailer might emphasize the advantage of taking a sales agency for the goods. It might offer to help create a demand by preparing window displays, or by supplying free samples to customers. On the other hand, an advertisement to a consumer might show how a product can be used, what its qualities are, and where it can be obtained.

Good advertisements vary also according to sales methods used. For example, when a drug manufacturer advertises a patent medicine to create a demand for it at the drugstore, the name of the remedy is brought repeatedly before the public. If, on the other hand, an advertiser wants to persuade people to buy a product by mail, the advertisement stresses prompt action. In the former case, the object is to make the name of the product well known; in the latter case, it is to secure an immediate sale. SI 1.58

36

264 Words

In small firms, stock clerks may do the same jobs as receiving clerks, shipping clerks, and inventory clerks; but in large firms, stock clerks may be responsible for only one of these functions.

The duties of stock clerks also depend on the products they handle. For example, stock clerks working with foods or drugs must maintain proper temperature and humidity conditions. Stock clerks responsible for large construction items may be required to do a lot of walking and climbing to keep track of the condition and quantity of that stock.

Stock clerks usually receive and unpack incoming goods, and check the items for quality and quantity. They sometimes make minor repairs or adjustments. They also report spoiled or damaged goods and process any papers needed for obtaining replacements or credit.

Stock clerks store goods in bins, on the floor, or on shelves, according to the plan of their stockroom. They may organize and mark items with identifying codes, letters, figures, or prices so that inventories may be located quickly and easily. Stock clerks must always keep a record of what enters and leaves the stockroom. They may prepare inventory reports to show what stock is on hand. In addition, stock clerks sometimes order supplies, and they may label, pack, crate, and address goods for delivery. SI 1.51

How to Figure Margin Stops

Two sizes of type are commonly found on typewriters today. The smaller size, called *elite*, contains twelve characters to the inch. The larger size, called *pica*, contains ten characters to the inch.

Typing paper that is 8½ inches wide has space for 102 elite characters or 85 pica characters on a line. Dividing each of these numbers by two gives the center point of the horizontal scale—51 for elite, 42½ for pica. For convenience, these numbers are rounded to 50 and 42 respectively.

To figure margin settings so that the left and right margins on the page will be equal, imagine a vertical line down the center of the page. One-half of the typed material should be to the left of the line, and one-half to the right. Use this principle to determine margin stops for a 40-space line as follows:

1. Divide the number of spaces in the line in half (40 ÷ 2 = 20). This means there will be 20 characters on each side of the center point.
2. Determine the left margin by subtracting 20 from the center point.

   ELITE   50 − 20 = 30   Left margin is 30.
   PICA   42 − 20 = 22   Left margin is 22.

3. Determine the right margin by adding 20 to the center point. Then add an additional 5 spaces to allow the margin bell to ring before the point where the line should end.

   ELITE   50 + 20 + 5 = 75   Right margin is 75.
   PICA   42 + 20 + 5 = 67   Right margin is 67.

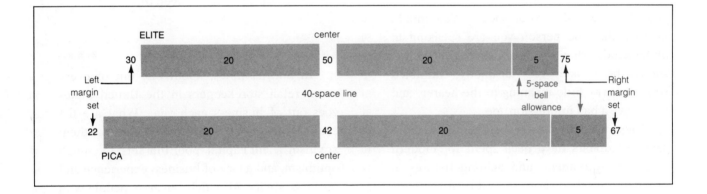

How to Set Margin Stops

SPRING-SET MACHINES   To set the left margin, press or pull the left set key, move the carriage to the desired position, and release the set key. To set the right margin, follow the same procedure, using the right set key.

SLIDING-SET MACHINES   To set the left margin, press or push the left margin stop and move it to the desired position on the scale. Set the right margin stop the same way.

KEY-SET MACHINES   Some typewriters have a margin reset key on the keyboard. To set the left margin, first pull the carriage all the way to your right. Then press the margin reset key and hold it down as you space forward (or backward) to reach the point at which you want the margin set. Then release the key and the left margin will be set. To set the right margin, first pull the carriage to your left. Then press the margin reset key and hold it down as you space forward (or backward) to reach the point at which you want the margin set. Release the key.

better way to make the trip. Instead of going to 236
the most crowded part of the train, they learn by 246
experience which part is least crowded and go 255
there. They may use a slower but more comfort- 264
able mode of transportation, even though they 273
may have to walk a little farther or pay a double 283
fare. Measures like these are worth the effort 293
in order to start the day right. SI 1.41 299

Selections 31–37, SI Range 1.51–1.60

31

205 Words

Good speech is a mark of good training and 10
good manners. It stamps the speaker as one 19
qualified to deal intelligently with persons and 29
with situations. 32

If you would be understood by others, you 41
should be careful of your speech. You should 50
be sure that the person you are speaking to 59
understands what you are saying. Your words 67
should be spoken very distinctly. Mumbled 75
words convey little meaning to the hearer, and 84
they leave a bad impression, too. 91

There are many business offices where thou- 101
sands of dollars have been spent for modern 110
furniture, equipment, and lighting fixtures in 119
order to impress visitors favorably. All this ex- 129
penditure of money may be wasted if a recep- 138
tionist stationed in such a costly setting fails to 149
make a favorable impression on a caller. The 158
receptionist, or any other employee in charge 167
of the outer office, should have good manners 176
and good speech. This means not only choosing 185
words carefully, but pronouncing them clearly 194
and distinctly, in a tone that is cordial and 203
courteous. SI 1.57 205

32

212 Words

Every telephone user should be familiar 9
with the information provided in the front pages 19
of the telephone directory. These pages give 28
valuable pointers on practically every kind of 37
telephone service. They tell, for instance, how 47

to make local and long-distance calls; what the 57
rates are to many points; how to make emergency 67
calls; and how to call the telephone company 76
regarding repairs, problems in service, and busi- 86
ness matters. These pages also explain how to 95
use the directory itself. 100

You should always look first in the directory 110
for correct telephone numbers. If you cannot 119
find the desired number, you may then dial di- 128
rectory assistance according to the directions 137
given on the first page of the directory. You will 147
find it a great timesaver to keep at hand a special 157
list of the numbers that you frequently call. A 167
list of this kind will be an easy reference and 177
will prevent the confusion and delay that may 186
be caused if you rely on your memory. On re- 195
quest, the telephone company will supply you 204
with a booklet in which to keep this list. SI 1.55 212

33

226 Words

In normal times, about one out of every 9
seven retail storekeepers in the United States 18
goes out of business each year. What are the 27
causes of failure among retailers? Some of them 37
are insufficient capital, poor markets, too much 47
optimism, and a lack of business experience and 57
business ability. Although business people who 66
fail in years of depression often attribute their 76
failure to conditions in general, such depressions 86
are not usually the chief cause. 92

A person who invests a fair amount of his 101
or her own capital in a business has a much bet- 111
ter chance of surviving than one who begins with 121
a large proportion of borrowed capital. There is 131
danger in borrowing too much. An analysis of 140
failures in retail stores shows a definite relation- 150
ship between the lifespan of a retail store and 160
the amount of capital invested by the owner. 169
From this evidence, it is safe to say that the owner 180
should invest his or her own funds to the extent 190
of at least 50 percent of the required capital. 200
However, the business will probably be on a 209
sounder financial footing if the owner invests 218
at least 75 percent of the funds required. SI 1.59 226

Introduction to the Keyboard

now have some form of air control. The desire 37
for comfort and the effect that the quality of the 47
air has on some products account for the great 56
growth in methods of air control. 63

Many materials must be kept at a certain 72
temperature—articles in storage, for instance, 81
such as butter or eggs or fruit. In other cases, a 91
certain temperature must be maintained during 100
the manufacturing process as, for instance, dur- 110
ing the cooling process in the making of chocolate 120
candy bars. 122

A second reason for the great growth in air 132
conditioning is the human factor. Better air 141
means better health for workers. Owners of 150
stores have found that money spent on installing 160
a system of air conditioning is well spent, for it 170
leads to more trade; customers who are comfort- 180
able in a store spend a longer time there, and 189
buy more goods. In schools, the air in the rooms 199
must be kept moving at a desired rate and a cer- 209
tain temperature must be maintained so that 218
conditions will be best for learning. 225

Lately, new designs for buildings are being 235
used that take advantage of natural air flow and 245
temperature gradations, depending on the local 254
climate. In this way, we are learning to rely less 264
on powered systems of air conditioning that use 274
too much energy. SI 1.50 277

29

281 Words

On his second voyage to America, Columbus 9
found native boys playing games with high- 17
bouncing balls that were made of a strange sub- 26
stance. This substance was rubber. He took a 35
few of these curios back to Spain with him and 45
presented them to the queen. During the next 54
three centuries, explorers brought back to Europe 64
various rubber articles made by the American 73
Indians, including capes, hats, shoes, bowls, 82
and bottles. Traders returned home with small 91
amounts of crude rubber. 96

Many efforts were made during those early 105
years to adapt rubber to the needs of the civilized 115
world. It is believed that the discovery of the 125
method on which present-day rubber manufac- 134
ture is based was the result of a happy accident. 144

Charles Goodyear, a poor inventor, had been 154
experimenting with rubber for years. The story 164
goes that he went to bed one evening, forgetting 174
to remove from contact with a hot stove a sample 184
of rubber-sulfur compound that he had smeared 193
on a piece of cloth. In the morning, he found 202
this sample charred like leather and marvelously 212
changed. It was no longer sticky, but dry and 221
firm. Heat or cold no longer affected it. Its 231
strength had increased. Goodyear found that, 240
by just changing the proportion of sulfur in the 250
mixture, he could make a substance as flexible 259
or as hard as he desired. This was the beginning 269
of the process which later came to be known as 278
vulcanization. SI 1.50 281

30

299 Words

Some individuals begin the day's work as if 10
the whole world and its troubles were resting on 20
their shoulders. They arrive at the office in the 30
morning low in spirit, or in a surly mood that 39
requires several hours to wear off. By noontime 49
they seem to become normal, and only then is it 58
possible to approach them with assurance of 67
receiving a cordial response. 73

In the office, this type of person may lower 83
the general high standard of business efficiency. 93
Such attitudes may leave their imprint on the 102
work of those nearby. This is especially true when 112
the duties of a group of workers are so related 121
that the office routine depends on the coopera- 130
tion of every member of the group. 137

These morning moods are usually only a 146
matter of habit, perhaps caused by a hasty break- 156
fast or no breakfast at all, or by jostling in the 166
subway or trying to beat the deadline at the time 176
clock. Remove the cause, and the symptoms will 186
disappear. Many office workers have solved such 196
problems sensibly. If the cause is lack of food, 206
they get up earlier so they can eat breakfast. If 216
the cause is discomfort in traveling, they find a 226

(Continued on next page)

Unit 1

Before you begin to type, check your typewriter and make the necessary adjustments for margins, line spacing, and so on, as outlined in each unit. Then check your posture to be sure your position at the typewriter is correct and comfortable.

Machine Adjustments

1. Ribbon indicator on blue or black.
2. Line space regulator on 1 for single spacing.
3. Paper guide set at 0 so left edge of paper is also at 0 on the carriage scale.
4. Margin stops set at 30 and 75 (elite) or 22 and 67 (pica) for a 40-space line.

Position for Typing

POSTURE Sit about eight inches from the typewriter with your feet on the floor and your body bent *slightly* forward.

FINGERS AND THUMBS Curve your fingers, with the tips of the left hand on the *A S D F* keys, and those of the right hand on the *J K L ;* keys. These eight keys are called the **home** keys. The fingers will be referred to by the home keys on which they rest; for example, *A* finger, *S* finger, *L* finger, *Semi* (semicolon) finger, and so on. Keep both thumbs resting lightly on the space bar at the bottom of the keyboard.

But he had an idea. He would go to America 105
and fight. He would help the Americans become 114
free from their ruler. 118

So Tadeusz Kosciuszko came to America. 127
The Revolutionary Army made him captain of 135
an engineers corps. Because he was brave and 144
wise, Tadeusz was soon a colonel. By the end 153
of the Revolution, he was a general. 160

Americans loved the young Polish soldier 169
who had helped them become free. They gave 178
him money. The new United States government 187
made him a citizen, and also gave him 500 acres 196
of wooded land near what is now Columbus, 205
Ohio. But General Kosciuszko was sad. The 214
Americans were now free, but Poland was not. 223
He loved America, but he loved Poland, too. He 232
had to go back to his home. He now had enough 241
money and experience to help him fight for the 251
freedom of Poland, his native land.   SI 1.46   258

26

263 Words

If you are a typist today, you may not fully 10
realize how fortunate you are to have a machine 19
that is a masterpiece of mechanical efficiency. 28
Your typewriter is as different from the first 38
writing machine as the streamlined locomotive 47
is from the first "iron horse." 53

You would find your daily tasks much harder 63
if you had to do your work on one of the early 72
writing machines. One model looked like a toy 81
piano. It turned out letters after a fashion, but the 92
operator broke no speed records. Even stranger 102
was a later model that was worked with one 110
thumb and printed words letter by letter on a 119
long, narrow roll of paper tape. 125

Before 1874, when the first practical type- 135
writer was put on the market in this country, 144
hundreds of patents were issued. Many inventors 154
played with the idea of a machine that would 163
replace writing by hand. The first record of a 173
writing machine is found in the files of the British 183
Patent Office in London. It briefly mentions a 192
device made early in the eighteenth century, but 202
no model has been found. 207

Several thousand patents have been issued 216
by the U.S. Patent Office to inventors who helped 227
speed the day of the modern typewriter. And the 237
end is not yet in sight. Manufacturers are con- 247
stantly trying to turn out machines that will make 257
the job of typing still simpler.   SI 1.46   263

27

264 Words

Few of us pay much attention to the old 9
proverb, "Never put off until tomorrow what 18
you can do today." Many of us seem, in fact, to 28
live by this rule in reverse and never do today 38
what we can put off until tomorrow. Letters re- 48
main unanswered; bills are not paid promptly; 57
the car waits patiently for the time when we shall 67
get around to cleaning it. 72

We have two stock excuses for such behav- 81
ior—lack of time and a poor memory. Neither 90
one of these, however, really holds true. Even 100
the busiest of us wastes a great deal of time; 109
and we never forget what we really want to 117
remember—a party or a pleasure trip or any- 126
thing else that is fun. The things we put off 135
usually involve doing what we do not enjoy or 144
making decisions we would rather not face. 152

What, then, is the solution? We must start 162
out by facing the fact that all our excuses are 172
without any basis. We should then decide which 181
of our neglected duties, though perhaps not en- 190
joyable in the doing, would yield the most sat- 199
isfying results for us. We should apply ourselves 209
first to the task we have decided upon, without 219
worrying about the others. If we attend to each 229
chore in turn during our spare time, we shall 238
find our efforts rewarded by a sense of accom- 247
plishment. Before too long, we shall easily 256
be able to keep up with our obligations.   SI 1.41   264

28

277 Words

In modern building construction, air en- 9
gineering has become very important. Most large 19
buildings and shops, as well as many homes, 28

(Continued on next page)

ARMS, ELBOWS, WRISTS   Keep the upper arms and elbows near the body. The forearms and the hands should be parallel to the slant of the keyboard. Do not arch the wrists, but do not let them touch the machine.

Striking the Keys

1. Hit the key sharply, exactly in the center, and release it immediately. Do not push the key or linger on it.
2. Strike the keys evenly—with even timing and with the same amount of force. Keep your fingers curved.
3. Move your hands and arms as little as possible; almost all movement should be in the fingers.

Striking the Space Bar

While keeping the fingers on the home keys, strike the space bar sharply with the right thumb. Make it bounce off the space bar.

Returning the Carriage

MANUAL MACHINE

1. Keeping your eyes on the printed copy, raise your left hand to the carriage return lever, palm down, fingers close together, index finger pressing against the carriage return lever. Keep your right hand in position on the home keys.
2. Return the carriage quickly to the beginning of the next line.
3. Immediately return your left hand to its typing position on the home keys.

ELECTRIC MACHINE

1. Extend the *Semi* finger to the return key.
2. Tap the key lightly.
3. Return the finger to the home position.

Putting it All Together

You're now ready for a trial run. Insert a sheet of paper into the typewriter and get ready to type the lines shown at the bottom of the page.

1. Check your position and posture.
2. Place your fingertips on the home keys as shown in the diagram at the left.
3. Relax, and don't worry about making errors.

Type each line as it appears below. Think and say each letter as you type it. Try not to look at the keyboard unless you lose your home key position.

fff jjj fff jjj ff jj fj jf fjf fjf jff	Return
fff jjj fff jjj ff jj fj jf fjf fjf jff	Return twice
ddd kkk ddd kkk dd kk dk kd kdk kdk kdd	Return
ddd kkk ddd kkk dd kk dk kd kdk kdk kdd	Return twice
sss lll sss lll ss ll sl ls lsl lsl lss	Return
sss lll sss lll ss ll sl ls lsl lsl lss	Return twice
fdsa jkl; fdsa jkl; fdsa jkl; fdsa jkl;	Return
asdf ;lkj asdf ;lkj asdf ;lkj asdf ;lkj	Return

Turn the page and begin the practice lines for this unit.

filled by checking incoming shipments against 160
the original orders and the accompanying bills 169
of lading or invoices. They also check to see 179
whether the merchandise in each shipment has 188
arrived in good condition. Receiving clerks re- 198
cord all incoming shipments and do the clerical 207
work required for damaged and lost shipments. 216
Routing shipments—to the proper departments 225
of the company, to sections of the warehouse, 234
or to the stockroom—also may be part of their 243
regular duties, especially in smaller companies. 253

SI 1.53

23

261 Words

Not long ago, I became of age. To mark the 9
occasion, my father suggested that I open a 18
checking account at a bank, and he presented 27
me with a check to give the venture a good start. 37
He made it clear that it was my responsibility 46
to keep the bank account alive. 52

To open a checking account, I had to sign 61
my name on a card. I believe bank tellers are 70
expected to know the signatures of many regular 80
depositors of their bank; but if necessary, they 90
can refer to the specimen signature. I received 100
a checkbook when I opened the account. In my 109
checkbook I record the deposits I make in addi- 118
tion to recording the checks I issue. Once each 128
month, the bank sends me a statement of my 137
account. In this way, I can check that the bank's 147
records and my records are in agreement. 155

I felt very important the first time I wrote a 165
check, which was made payable to myself. The 174
bank teller was very polite. I have since made 184
a few deposits and have written a number of 193
checks. 194

I learned a great deal about banking practice 204
by having a bank account of my own. I do not 213
need to carry much money with me now. I know 222
that my money is quite safe in the bank—safer 231
than it would be in my pocket. Besides, I have 241
a record of important payments I make and 249
a receipt for each payment in the form of a can- 258
celed check. 261

SI 1.36

24

256 Words

I was part of a once-large family, but only 10
six of us were left—four boys and two girls, all 20
born on the Lower East Side. In the Ukraine, 29
before the turn of the industrializing and ravag- 39
ing century, eight others had been borne by my 48
stolid mother. They had died in infancy in those 58
times of easy dying. But we, Americans all, were 68
tougher, burlier, hardier, and better fed. We were 78
another set of health statistics. We had more 87
possibilities, if less of God. My father, with his 97
stern, fatherly hand, tried to give us, with the 107
bread my mother baked and the wine he made, 116
the guided spiritualism of a man who was as 125
Old Testament as Moses. 130

As children, we were American from the 139
start. But to our parents we were always Jews, 148
never Americans. Our Jewishness came out with 157
the preparation for the Sabbath. It meant going 167
to the baker with a ten-pound iron pot filled with 177
meat and vegetables, the cholent. There the pot 190
remained for twenty-four hours, baking slowly. 199
I would go back there after Saturday's morning 208
service, to take the hot pot back home for the 217
best meal of the week. My mother blessed the 226
challah, the Sabbath bread, my father blessed 238
the wine, and all of us turned to the steaming 247
cholent awaiting the pot's exotic revelations. 256

SI 1.44

25

258 Words

The young Polish soldier, Tadeusz Kos- 9
ciuszko (pronounced Kosh-oo-shko), read the 18
news. The thirteen colonies of America were 27
fighting with Great Britain. They wanted to be 36
independent. They wanted to be free. That was 45
just what Kosciuszko wanted for his country. 54
He wanted Poland to be free from its rulers— 63
Prussia and Russia. But what could he do? He 72
was just a young man, and he had little fighting 82
experience. He had no money to buy guns and 91
powder for an army. 95

(Continued on next page)

Line spacing: single
Line length: 40
Type each line as shown.
Double-space after
each pair of lines.

Home Key Location

Check your typing position.

1 `fff  jjj  fff  jjj  fff  jjj  fjf  jfj  fjj  ffj`
2 `fff  jjj  fff  jjj  fff  jjj  fjf  jfj  fjj  ffj`

Keep your fingers curved—
tips resting lightly on the
home keys.

3 `ddd  kkk  ddd  kkk  ddd  kkk  dkd  kdk  dkk  ddk`
4 `ddd  kkk  ddd  kkk  ddd  kkk  dkd  kdk  dkk  ddk`

5 `sss  lll  sss  lll  sss  lll  sls  lsl  sll  ssl`
6 `sss  lll  sss  lll  sss  lll  sls  lsl  sll  ssl`

Strike the keys sharply
and release them quickly.

7 `aaa  ;;;  aaa  ;;;  aaa  ;;;  a;a  ;a;  a;;  aa;`
8 `aaa  ;;;  aaa  ;;;  aaa  ;;;  a;a  ;a;  a;;  aa;`

9 `asdf  ;lkj  asdf  ;lkj  asdf  ;lkj  asdf  ;lkj`
10 `asdf  ;lkj  asdf  ;lkj  asdf  ;lkj  asdf  ;lkj`

Word and Phrase Practice

Eyes on copy!

11 `as ask; as ask; all all all; sad sad sad`
12 `as ask; as ask; all all all; sad sad sad`

13 `fad fad fad; lad lad lad; fall fall fall`
14 `fad fad fad; lad lad lad; fall fall fall`

15 `add add add; dad dad dad; asks asks asks`
16 `add add add; dad dad dad; asks asks asks`

17 `ask dad lad; ask dad lad; alas lass alas`
18 `ask dad lad; ask dad lad; alas lass alas`

Can't remember the
location of a key? Use
the keyboard chart.

19 `ask a lad; all lads add; a fad; a flask;`
20 `a salad; as dad asks; a lad falls; alas;`

are also useful. You should have sturdy shoes 180
and a pair of rubbers. Another useful item is a 190
passport case that will fit into your purse or in- 200
side coat pocket. 203

It is wise to plan your packing carefully. 213
Sometimes it is difficult to find the things you 223
need while traveling abroad. And often they are 233
very expensive. SI 1.39 236

20
236 Words

We like to think that we can make new 8
things. The simple truth, however, is that we 17
actually can make nothing; we just change the 26
forms of materials that already exist. Still, we 36
can do many amazing things by making those 44
changes. 46

For instance, a sculptor takes marble from a 56
quarry and shapes it into a beautiful statue. A 66
farmer places seeds in the ground to grow the 75
plants needed for food. A shipbuilder puts to- 85
gether wood and metal to build ships that sail 94
the high seas. A well driller digs deep into the 104
earth and removes oil millions of years old to 113
run machines and heat buildings. An engineer 122
changes the course of a river in order to store 132
drinking water, irrigate farmlands, and turn 141
waterpower into the electricity needed to run 150
factories. An inventor develops instruments that 160
transmit sounds and pictures through the air 169
around the world. 172

We do not possess the magic of making 180
something from nothing, but we can combine 188
and use in different ways the materials drawn 197
from the earth, the air, and the sea. In so doing, 208
we accomplish wonders that are almost beyond 217
belief. These changes would not be possible with- 227
out our imagination, ingenuity, and skill. SI 1.48 236

21
245 Words

Years ago, when canvas was scarce, artists 9
painted over the works of other artists. Discov- 19
eries have been made of many old masterpieces 28
hidden in this way. 32

When there is a suspicion that a valuable 41
painting has been covered over, an expert goes 50
to work. First, the surface varnish is removed 60
and the back of the canvas is cleaned. The canvas 70
is then studied under ultraviolet lights and by 79
X ray. If it is found that a picture has indeed 89
been painted on top of another one, the next 98
step is to determine the origin of the first work. 108
To do this, the paint on the surface is loosened 118
with alcohol and a sample pigment is chipped off 120
the painting underneath. This is then matched 137
up with samples of pigments used by well-known 147
artists of the time, who had mixed their own dis- 157
tinctive paints. 160

When the identity of the artist has been 169
learned, the work of restoration starts, one sec- 179
tion at a time. The chemicals used for this de- 189
pend on the condition of the canvas and on the 198
kind of paint to be cleaned from the surface. 207
Such work requires the steadiest of eyes and 216
hands in order to avoid damage to the original 225
painting. The reward of all this careful and 234
painstaking work is the reappearance of a lost 243
work of art. SI 1.40 245

22
253 Words

Shipping and receiving clerks keep track of 10
the goods transferred from place to place by 19
business firms. Before shipments are sent out 28
from a company, shipping clerks check to be 37
sure that the orders have been correctly filled. 47
They prepare the shipping forms, look up freight 57
and postal rates, record the weight and cost of 66
each shipment, and check to see that it is prop- 76
erly addressed. They also keep records of the 85
date and other details about each shipment. 94
Sometimes shipping clerks requisition mer- 102
chandise from the firm's stockroom, wrap and 111
pack the shipment, and direct its loading onto 120
company trucks. 123

Receiving clerks do similar work when ship- 133
ments reach their companies. They find out 142
whether their firm's orders have been correctly 151

(Continued on next page)

Unit 2

Line spacing: single
Line length: 40
Type each line twice.
Double-space after
each pair of lines.

Warmup

Every time you *think* where the key is, you learn its location better.

1 fff jjj ddd kkk sss lll aaa ;;; fff jjj;

2 as ask all sad fad lad dad fall add alas

3 asks a lad; a sad lass; dad falls; flask

New Key Location

D finger **E**

Return finger to home position after striking **e**.

4 ded ded led led see see fed fed fee fee

5 sell sell deal deal seek seek jell jell

6 seal seal lake lake safe safe fake fake

J finger **U**

Return finger to home position after striking **u**.

7 juj juj sue sue due due use use dud dud

8 dull dull full full suds suds used used

9 dusk dusk fuse fuse dual dual juke juke

Word and Phrase Practice

10 sea sea elk elk elf elf use use due dues

11 self self duel duel fell fell jell jells

12 fall due; sue us; used less; sell seeds;

13 a deal; led us; dusk falls; a sleek elk;

Supplementary Practice

Sometimes when you strike a key before the preceding one is released, the keys will clash or jam. To avoid this, use a quick release—don't press the keys; snap them! To release jammed keys, gently pull the one nearest you first.

14 jade jade seas seas fade fade fuel fuels

15 skull skull deaf deaf sulk sulk eel eels

16 sell a desk; asks us; used a jade flask;

17 a safe deal; a dead leaf; use less fuel;

18 fell due; a deaf lass; sell a used desk;

circuit in the air, returning to the point from 140
which it started. When the performer throws 149
several boomerangs in rapid succession, the il- 158
lusion of a flock of birds in flight is created. 168
Because of the peculiar property the boomerang 177
possesses of traveling in a circle, we have come 187
to apply the term boomerang to anything we do 200
that backfires on us; for example, something 209
that is meant to harm another but that results 218
only in injury to ourselves.   OI 1.42   224

17   229 Words

If you are flying at an elevation of six or 10
seven miles, you are at the level of the highest 20
clouds. There, the tiny drops of water that form 30
the clouds are frozen into very fine snow crys- 39
tals. Approximately two miles below this level, 49
the swiftest winds are blowing. There, the clouds 59
appear to be most numerous, and they are 67
twisted and stretched into their most feathery 77
configurations. 80

The clouds from which most of the precipi- 89
tation falls are usually at a height of two to three 99
miles. These clouds may have a spread of less 108
than half a mile, but they often have a height 117
of four or five miles. In the tropics, such clouds 127
reach even higher than this, for they may extend 137
as much as nine miles from top to bottom. 145

A fog is actually a cloud on the earth. An 155
observer flying above the fog gazes upon a mag- 165
nificent scene—mile after mile of snow-white, 174
fleecy billows of down. Pilots understand the 183
truth of the saying that every cloud has a silver 193
lining. From below, clouds may look black with 202
the threat of an approaching storm; from above, 212
they seem transformed into silver by the reflec- 222
tion of sunlight on their white tops.   SI 1.37 229

18   233 Words

Have you considered the advantages of 8
wearing contact lenses? Millions who must use 17
corrective lenses are now wearing them instead 26
of glasses. 28

Contact lenses are thin, curved, plastic discs, 38
smaller than a dime, that are worn under the eye- 48
lids. They cause no discomfort once the wearer 58
becomes accustomed to them—and most people 67
become adjusted to them quickly. The new "soft" 77
contact lenses take even less time to become 86
adjusted to than the "hard" lenses. 93

Contact lenses are not visible to others; so 103
people who feel self-conscious wearing glasses 112
feel more at ease with the lenses. In some types 122
of work where wearing glasses is a source of 131
danger, contact lenses eliminate the hazard. 140
Athletes also use contact lenses to avoid possible 150
injury from glasses. And people who have had 159
cataracts removed from their eyes see much bet- 169
ter with the lenses than with glasses. 177

Contact lenses are durable, and they do not 187
harm the eyes. They do not "steam up" when the 196
temperature turns from cold to warm, as glasses 206
do. Frequent changes in prescription are gener- 216
ally not necessary; but if vision does change, 225
the lenses in use can often be modified. SI 1.50 233

19   236 Words

Here are some suggestions about the bag- 9
gage to take along on the trip we at Travel Time 19
have planned for you. 23

In the first place, try to reduce the amount 33
of your luggage as much as possible. Take a fairly 43
large suitcase and an overnight bag. The suitcase 53
should not be too large to carry in an emer- 62
gency. Use the overnight bag so that you will 71
not have to open the suitcase if you spend only 81
one night in a place, and so that you may keep 90
conveniently together the articles you need every 100
day. Choose baggage that is light in weight, with 110
lock and key, and label it clearly with your name 120
and address. 122

As for clothing, choose slacks and shirts that 132
will not crush easily and that will not need laun- 142
dering too frequently. Use undergarments that 151
you can launder yourself, if necessary. A light- 161
weight coat, a raincoat, and a folding umbrella 171

(Continued on next page)

Line spacing: single
Line length: 40
Type each line twice.
Double-space after
each pair of lines.

Warmup

Release keys quickly to avoid jamming keys.

1 ded ded juj juj ded ded juj juj ded jujj
2 led led use use due due sue sue see sees
3 fall due; fed elk; asks us; used a fuse;

New Key Location

F finger **R**

Return finger to home position after striking **r**.

4 frf frf jar jar are are far far red red
5 dark dark real real jars jars rule rule
6 erase ruler dresses refuse dread reader

K finger **I**

Return finger to home position after striking **i**.

7 kik kik rid rid lid lid kid kid did did
8 rail rail fill fill jail jail life life
9 silk kill ails ride fail like slid side
10 lid file risk jeer refill residue field

Word and Phrase Practice

Move your hands and arms as little as possible.

11 ill ill sir sir fur fur air air err err;
12 jerk jerk fear fear; side side sale sale
13 fell ill; real full; dark reds; liked us
14 lead us; desk file; a risk; all did less
15 a real sale; fearful fun rides; deaf ear

Supplementary Practice

If you finish early, practice lines 16–20 and repeat if time permits.

16 red red air air rid rid fir fir lie lard
17 slur skid sail kiss free sulk deaf skull
18 is rude; real jade; all rules; dull life
19 a deed; is filed; less skill; fill a jar
20 a full skid; refuse all risks; red sails

became popular for making the sheerest of hose, 58
since it is as elastic and strong as it is fine. 68

Thousands of useful articles have been made 78
from this synthetic, which was unknown not so 87
long ago, but which has since swept the world. 96
Fabrics, fishing lines, cords for stringing beads, 106
sewing thread, bristles for brushes of all kinds, 116
string for tennis rackets, tents, watch bands, pen 126
tips, tires, rugs, bearings, and gears are just a very 137
few of them. Many beautiful products, such as 146
lace, are also manufactured from nylon. 154

Progressive manufacturers are still experi- 164
menting with nylon and finding many new appli- 173
cations for it. The public continues to be amazed 183
at the ever-increasing number of uses to which 192
it is being put. And there are still so many unex- 202
plored fields where nylon may yet prove to be of 212
great value. SI 1.50 214

14

216 Words

You must love justice, and demand it for all, 10
if you would be a true American. You must love 19
equality, and be willing to grant it to all, if you 29
would be a true American. You must love free- 38
dom, not only for yourself, but freedom for all, 48
if you would be a true American. 54

You must be willing to recognize talent, and 64
to help to give it an opportunity to develop, if 74
you would be a true American; not merely the 83
talent that your children and mine may chance 92
to possess, but also the talent of the humblest 101
among us. 103

As a true American, you must practice toler- 113
ance, tolerance of others' religious convictions, 123
tolerance of their social and economic convic- 132
tions, tolerance of their political convictions. You 143
are not a true American, whether you are native- 153
born or foreign-born, if you would deny another 162
the rights that you demand for yourself. 170

As a true American, you must be willing to 180
share—no, demand to share—all the rights and 189
privileges that this free country gives you. You 199
ask them not only for yourself and for your 208
family, but for everyone, everywhere. SI 1.49 216

15

219 Words

To possess an open mind is to possess some- 10
thing of real worth as we go through life. Because 20
of it, we shall discover much to interest us and to 30
give us pleasure. An open mind means that we 39
are willing to change an opinion if there are good 49
reasons for the change. It means that we are will- 59
ing to consider novel ideas, however strange they 69
may at first seem to be. 74

I am afraid that most of the opinions we hold 84
are the result of general custom rather than the 94
outcome of our own considered thought and 102
observation. Too many people accept an idea 111
only because it has always been accepted. They 121
see no reason for change. That is why improve- 130
ments in living conditions and in industrial con- 140
ditions do not come to pass as quickly as we 149
might desire. We hold fast to what is familiar, 159
and we fear to move forward into something 167
that we do not know. 171

We all want life to be richer and happier. 181
If this happy state of affairs is to come about, 191
we must view facts with clear eyes and judge 200
them not according to set opinions, but accord- 209
ing to their merit. Let us each keep an open mind. 219

SI 1.38

16

224 Words

The natives of Australia use a weapon called 10
a boomerang. It is a piece of hardwood, curved 19
like a crescent, with a flat surface on one side and 30
a curved surface on the other. It is used as a 39
weapon of war or as a weapon of the hunt or even 49
as a means of amusement. The skillful boomer- 58
ang thrower can throw the weapon so that it will 68
travel in a curved line up or down, or to the left 78
or to the right. It can be thrown a great distance, 88
high into the air, and it can be made to circle a 98
selected spot. 101

In exhibitions of boomerang throwing, the 110
feat most interesting to the spectator is the throw- 120
ing of the boomerang so that it makes a complete 130

(Continued on next page)

Unit 4

Line spacing: single
Line length: 40
Type each line twice.
Double-space after
each pair of lines.

Warmup

Return the carriage quickly
without looking up.

1 frf juj ded kik ark ark lie lie due due
2 far far jar jar did did rid rid ill ill
3 is like; did less; is killed; real sale

New Key Location

F finger **T**

Return finger to home
position after striking **t**.

4 ftf ftf sat sat tea tea lit lit its its
5 just just last last jest jest rate rate
6 take take feet feet date date fret fret

J finger **H**

Return finger to home
position after striking **h**.

7 jhj jhj had had his his hit hit her her
8 this this hurt hurt shut shut heat heat
9 that that halt halt half half fish fish
10 thus thus hark hark dish dish here here

Word and Phrase Practice

Keep wrists low, but not
touching the frame of the
machine. Don't hump
your wrists.

11 sets sets hill hill fret fret task tasks
12 talk talk shirt shirts faith faith three
13 dread shark teeth that jut; half a shelf
14 he hurried; just tell her; fast as usual

Supplementary Practice

15 hid hid jut jutted let let she the these
16 tide tide just just task tasks shut shut
17 the dim shuttered hut; red thread skirts
18 safer at last; a head taller; three feet

as its good, its sorrows as well as its joys? Or do 154
we want the story to take us away from the real 164
world and into a dream world, to show us life 173
as it might be in an ideal society? 180

Our answers to all these questions will de- 189
pend partly on the purpose for which we read 198
and partly on our frame of mind at the time. If 208
we read with no set purpose in mind, we shall 217
probably like best those books that tell a story. 227
If we are seeking knowledge, or if we enjoy 236
beauty of expression, our choice can be made 245
from a wider field—science, history, travel, po- 255
etry, music, art, and more. Whatever type of 264
book we choose, we can find a quiet joy in read- 274
ing that will enrich our lives through the years. 284

SI 1.34

11

296 Words

The Indian rope trick is one of the most 9
puzzling things in the world. It has existed for 19
ages—travelers to India hundreds of years ago 28
reported seeing it. We are not sure of how this 38
trick is done. The man who performs the trick 47
takes a long rope and throws one end of it into 57
the air. It unwinds and unwinds until the end 66
is high up in the air. Some say that the end can 76
go so far that it is out of sight. Then a small boy 87
climbs up the rope and disappears at the top. 96

Some explain this as a trick of the mind. 105
People think they see what they are told they 114
see. For example, tie a cork to a long black cotton 124
thread, trail it quickly across the carpet in a dim 135
light, and make it disappear behind some article 145
of furniture, crying out, "Look, a mouse!" Most 155
people will then believe that they have seen a 164
mouse. 165

A story is told of a man who was walking a 175
few steps behind a native of Bhutan. The native 185
suddenly turned and cried out a warning about a 194
snake. The traveler thought he saw a large snake 204
glide quickly past his foot, and he jumped back. 214
Then the native laughed and explained that there 224
was really no snake. He went over to the long 233
grass at the side of the road and picked up an 242

ordinary walking stick. He had skillfully used 252
the stick to make the traveler imagine that he 261
had seen a snake. 265

In the same way, we may be led to imagine 275
we have seen things that really do not exist. In 285
this may lie the explanation of the Indian rope 295
trick. 296

SI 1.26

Selections 12–30, SI Range 1.36–1.50

12

213 Words

The successful operation of a business re- 9
quires accurate and up-to-date records of its 18
financial affairs. Some say that they cannot af- 28
ford the time to bother with records. This is a 38
mistaken idea. It is not shared by the bank and 48
the tax collector, and they have the power to 57
enforce their ideas—the bank when you need 66
a loan, and the tax collector when your income 75
tax figures are checked. Poor accounting can 84
prove to be costly. 88

Moreover, records must be kept and used in 97
the interest of good business management. For 106
instance, records show whether or not a business 116
is yielding a profit, whether there are ample 125
funds for new equipment, and whether credit 134
sales should be reduced or expanded. Even for 143
the simplest business, a record is needed of its 153
cash receipts and payments, its purchases on 162
credit, and its sales to charge customers. 170

The account books may be very simple, 178
but the records must be adequate to meet the 187
owner's needs in trading with creditors and cus- 197
tomers, in dealing with the bank, and in prepar- 207
ing reports to the government. SI 1.49 213

13

214 Words

Nylon is produced, by means of a series of 9
chemical changes, from several natural mate- 18
rials: coal, air, water, petroleum, agricultural by- 29
products, and natural gas. From these can be 38
spun strands of yarn finer than a hair. Nylon first 48

(Continued on next page)

Unit 5

Line spacing: single
Line length: 40
Type each line twice.
Double-space after
each pair of lines.

Warmup

Type evenly and calmly.

1 eat eat see see did did his his red red
2 tree tree fail fail that that just just
3 silk silk lake lake read read hill hill

Word Practice

Strike and release keys in one motion.
Make quick, sharp strokes.

4 did did rid rid jar jar far far lid lid
5 kid kid ill ill red red use use all all
6 led led are are due due sat sat had had
7 his his hit hit has has her her ate ate
8 she she the the hut hut jut jut jet jet
9 rail rail fill fill jail jail kill kill
10 dark dark risk risk fell fell real real
11 shriek fresher rather faith three heard

Phrase Practice

Too many errors?

Try the following:
• Concentrate on each reach.
• Use the keyboard chart when in doubt.
• Practice, practice, practice.

12 red silk; that tall tree; sell this desk
13 fried fish; a fast jet; read that letter
14 just rule; these hard tests; their third

Supplementary Practice

15 life life like like sure sure jell jells
16 sets sets half half hill hill tall tall;
17 desk desk head head left left fast fast;
18 just heard that she hid her head at last

Typing Skill Checkup

Goal: To type lines 19–20 (70 strokes) in 1 minute. Eyes on copy. Two or more tries.

19 he fled just as the fire hit the jailer;
20 she said the desk file is safe ■

country, I hung a bell around her neck to keep 244
bears away from her. Incidentally, the bell kept 254
the bears away from me, too. SI 1.30 260

8

273 Words

Suppose a friend said to you, "What differ- 10
ence does it make whether or not you do your 19
schoolwork well? In a few years, you will be out 29
in the working world. That will be the time for 39
you to begin doing your work well." Would you 48
believe such a statement? 53

If so, you would be making a very serious 62
mistake. It is certainly true that the nature of 72
your work will change when you get out of 80
school. You will not be reading the textbooks 89
that you are reading today. Your daily routine 99
will be different in many ways. Your habits, how- 109
ever, will probably be about the same. Habits are 119
not likely to change once they are firmly fixed; 129
and habits decide the pattern of your life. 138

Suppose that during your school years you 148
develop the habit of dependability. When you 157
say you will do something, you make certain it 166
is done. When you have work to do, you apply 175
yourself to it and allow nothing to interfere with 185
its completion. You plan to work first and play 195
later. These habits will probably remain with you 205
throughout life. 208

If, on the other hand, during your school 217
career you keep coming late repeatedly, or if 226
you fail again and again to complete your work 235
at the time it is due, you are building a fixed habit 246
that will probably be a handicap to you through 256
the years that lie ahead. Heed that proverb, "As 266
the twig is bent, so the tree grows." SI 1.33 273

9

273 Words

As soon as we saw the old house, we wanted 9
to own it. Every consideration of common sense 18
was against the idea. The house had none of the 28
modern conveniences that make life so much 36
easier. It was badly in need of repair, and we 46
would have to spend a good part of our savings 55

to make it habitable. It was miles from town, 64
and there was no good road leading to it. This 73
would mean difficulty in getting service people 83
to come out our way. Even the weather was 91
against it; records showed that rain fell in that 101
area much of the year, and in the winter the 110
snows were very deep. 114

We understood all this, and we tried to tell 124
ourselves that this was not the place for us. Yet 134
there was something about the old house that 143
reached out to us and urged us to take it on. It 153
was a charming house, beautifully situated on a 163
small piece of land with water on three sides. 172
To the south was a river running into the sea. 181
To the west and north was the sea itself. This 191
was not the open sea, rough and troubled, but a 200
small arm of it with enough motion in the water 209
to keep it fresh. A feeling of peace and a quiet 219
loveliness lingered about the whole place, and 228
we longed to become part of it. 234

In spite of all our misgivings, we purchased 244
the old house. And we have lived in it for many 254
years. As we had hoped when we first saw it, we 264
had found the haven we had been searching for. 273

SI 1.26

10

284 Words

Most of us look forward to getting a good 9
new book and finding the leisure hours to read 18
it. As we open the book, what do we hope to find 28
in its pages? Are we planning to read the book 38
simply to enjoy the story it tells? Are we trying 48
to increase our knowledge of some particular 57
subject? Are we seeking beauty in the language 66
of the book and in the writer's expression of 75
his or her thoughts? Sometimes, one or another 85
of these purposes is uppermost in our minds. 94
At other times, we read for a combination of 103
purposes. 105

If we are reading just for the story, what 114
kind of story do we hope the book will tell? Do 124
we want a picture of life as it is, showing us its 134
sordid side as well as its beauty, its evil as well 144

(Continued on next page)

Unit 6

Line spacing: single
Line length: 40
Type each line twice.
Double-space after
each pair of lines.

Warmup

Keep fingers curved; use a snappy stroke.

1 fed fled sled dust just rust fuss trust;
2 jeer fear dear hear rear dash sash trash
3 fee feet tree free kill hill till skill;

New Key Location

F finger **G**

4 fgf fgf leg leg egg egg keg keg get get
5 girl girl glad glad glue glue huge huge
6 digs digs tags tags high high jugs jugs

J finger **Y**

7 jyj jyj day day gay gay yet yet key key
8 they they rays rays year year yard yard
9 eyes eyes fray fray yell yell fury fury
10 jury jury says says stay stay easy easy

Word and Phrase Practice

Strive for smooth, steady typing.

11 yeast yeast hurry hurry judge judge flag
12 great great agree agree early early tray
13 a great hurry; the girls agree; they try
14 safety first; is easily hurt; great risk

Supplementary Practice

15 glad glad keg keg just just gay gay jugs
16 gray gray yield yield fight fight steady
17 slight delays; she left early yesterday;

Typing Skill Checkup

Goal: To type lines 18–19 (75 strokes) in 1 minute. Two or more tries. Do not look at the keys.

18 he had a great idea later that day; take
19 the three full tall jars after dark ■

5

249 Words

The strand of cotton that we cut from a spool (10) and deftly thread through the eye of a needle (19) is the product of one of the greatest industries (29) in the world—the cotton industry. (36)

We may see cotton growing first in the fields (46) of our own southern states; or we may trace it to (56) Egypt, where a plant very similar to our cotton (65) plant grows. The seeds are sown in February or (74) March, and within ten days the green shoots are (84) up. Before the middle of June, the plants have (93) grown well and are covered with showy yellow (102) or purple flowers. These quickly fall, and in their (113) place appears the fruit, which contains the seeds. (123) Around the seeds are many downy fibers—cotton (132) in its first stage. (136)

These fibers must be separated from the (145) seeds, a task that was once performed by hand. (154) Today it is done by the cotton gin, a machine that (164) tears the cotton away from the seeds. Then the (174) cotton is tightly packed by machine into bales (183) weighing approximately 500 pounds each. (191)

Most of this product is spun into yarn, and (201) most of the yarn is made into cotton materials. (210) The cotton on our spools of thread is more dif- (219) ficult to make. When the little strands of cotton (229) have been spun into yarn, two or three strands (238) are twisted together, doubled, and wound onto (247) bobbins. SI 1.32 (249)

6

252 Words

Right now, the one thing we all seem to want (9) is more energy—energy to warm our homes, en- (19) ergy to run our factories and automobiles, energy (29) to do many other things for us. And we are not (39) sure that America has enough energy supplies to (48) meet our needs for the next century. So we are (58) thinking again of coal, of which there is still an (68) enormous supply. (71)

Unfortunately, coal is a dirty fuel. So some (81) companies are designing and building factories (90) to make clean coal. Clean coal? Yes, you know (100) what coal is. It is black and it burns with a hot (110) fire for a long time. When you touch a piece of (120) coal, your hands get black and dirty. (127)

That kind of dirt is only the surface of the (137) coal, and it won't hurt your hands too much. You (147) just have to wash it off. The real dirt in coal (157) comes out only when it burns. When coal burns, (167) it gives off a black smoke, much of which con- (176) sists of waste chemicals that are lost in the smoke. (187) If you breathe this smoke, it is harmful to your (197) lungs. (198)

When coal is cleaned, these chemicals are (207) removed before the coal is burned, to prevent (216) them from being wasted. They can be used to (225) produce plastics, insulation, and other useful (235) things. Thus, coal is not only turned into clean (245) energy, but we get extra use from it. SI 1.29 (252)

7

260 Words

When you go on a camping trip into the (9) mountains and forests of British Columbia, it's (18) a good idea to have a pack pony to carry your (27) equipment. Distances between settlements are (36) often so immense that you cannot carry with you (45) all the supplies you will require on the journey. (55)

Before I set out on my trip, therefore, my (64) first task was to locate a suitable pony. Any pony (74) would not do; it had to be a very gentle one. I (84) had seen packs thrown off by ponies, with the (93) result that frying pans, eggs, and sugar were (102) hurled to the four winds, and I wanted to avoid (111) that. Moreover, I required a pony that was not (121) too tall. I am short and I did not want to carry (131) a ladder with me in order to place the pack on (140) the pony's back. In addition, the pony had to be (150) easily led and acquired at little cost. (158)

It took me a week to locate the right pony— (168) a little dark brown mare with a white stripe on (178) her nose. There were a few slight misunderstand- (188) ings when we began, but by the end of another (197) week, we knew each other well. A strong friend- (207) ship had even developed between us. I did dis- (217) cover that there was one thing she did not like, (227) and that was a bear. When we were in bear (235)

(Continued on next page)

Unit 7

Line spacing: single
Line length: 50
Type each line twice.
Double-space after
each pair of lines.

Warmup

Start using a 50-space line:
25–80 (elite), 17–72 (pica).

Semi finger RIGHT SHIFT

1 just just adjust adjust yield yield shield shield

2 leak leak health health fight fight fright fright

3 sure sure surely surely ready ready steady steady

New Key Location

To capitalize a letter typed by a lefthand finger, hold down the right shift key with the semicolon finger and strike the letter.

4 fFf FfF fFf Fred Fred sSs SsS sSs Sue Sue Sue Susy

5 dDd DdD dDd Duke Duke rRr RrR rRr Red Red Red Ruth

To capitalize a letter typed by a righthand finger, hold down the left shift key with the A finger and strike the letter.

A finger LEFT SHIFT

6 jJj JjJ jJj Jay Jay Jay lLl LlL lLl Luke Luke Luke

7 kKk KkK kKk Kurt Kurt iIi IiI iIi Ida Ida Ida Iris

8 UuU Utah; AaA Arthur; HhH Harris; RrR Ray; EeE Ed;

9 GgG Gary; YyY Yale; TtT Terry; EeE Elsie; JjJ Jed;

L finger ⬤

Space twice after a period at the end of a sentence; once after a period in an abbreviation.

10 l.l l.l; Dr. Dale; I like Dr. Dale. I use a rake.

11 I like his sister Judy. I shall see her Saturday.

12 This is her Easter gift. Ask her if she likes it.

Word and Phrase Practice

13 gay gray hard guard rest gay gray hard guard rest.

14 ask task star start date ask task star start date.

15 a jagged edge; shall start early; right after dark

16 a great desire; the usual results; straight ahead;

2

235 Words

I have recently been making a list of all the things that I wouldn't have missed. It has been fun—something like going through a lot of old photographs and choosing some to put into an album. My list has grown and grown. The more I think about my life, the more my mind seems to scamper from one thing to another—from Scotland to China, from this year and last year to my boyhood days, backward and forward, forward and backward.

Many of the things on my list consist of the first time I did something—the first time I rode a bicycle, my first day at school, the first speech I gave, the first time I had a book published. There was a thrill in all of them.

From my college days, I remember very vividly the times when I went home for the holidays. I remember my home and all that it stood for—the familiar front door, the rooms that seemed so small and cozy in contrast to the large, bare classrooms and halls. I remember, too, returning from the noise and mud and pain of war to the same room and the same bed in which I had slept as a child.

It is good, in the busy life of the present, to pause occasionally and recall happy experiences of the past. SI 1.26

3

248 Words

Wild animals wage a continual struggle against one another, and only the most crafty of them survive. The small creatures of the countryside are masters of disguise and concealment. Every meadow and every wood has its share of small creatures; yet how seldom we see them! Our eyes, of course, are not often trained to see. And we make a good deal of noise as we walk, thus giving the alarm to hundreds of pairs of ears.

It is mainly because our wild creatures know where and how to hide that they are so seldom seen. When they hear noisy human beings coming, they do not start dashing about; if they did, we should certainly see them. They do not hide, as we should do, behind a tree or a bush; they stand dead still at the least sound.

Some wild creatures change their color with the seasons of the year. Many others choose a background with coloring similar to their own, so that they may escape notice. A toad sits on a mossy stone where it will not be seen. A bat hangs like a cobweb from a beam. The deer stands still and relies on the background to hide him. By covering our faces and hands and dressing in drab clothes, we can become nearly as invisible as the wild creatures, increasing our chances of spotting them. SI 1.31

4

247 Words

My friend Jack is a fox terrier. He is really not my best friend, but he thinks he is, which amounts to much the same thing. I am not his master, and I do not want to take him away from his owner; but his idea is that I am his master and that I want him very much.

I blame myself for having made the first advances, although nothing came of them then except a growl. I met him in his master's house, where I was paying a visit. After we had looked at each other for about a minute, I spoke a few kind words to him, and he growled. I thought he was a surly dog and paid no more attention to him that day.

About a week later, when I again visited his master, I learned that Jack had had a serious accident. I saw him lying there, a very sick dog indeed. He allowed me to stroke him, opening one eye very slightly.

For some time, I did not see Jack at all. Then, as I was taking a walk one evening, I saw his head poking out of a hedge. I said hello to him, and that was enough. He followed me on my walk, and he has been walking with me ever since. He does not really walk with me—he races around me and then away from me and back. I played with him out of sympathy at first, but now I belong to him completely. SI 1.23

Sentence Practice

Depress the shift key firmly. Hold it down until *after* the letter key is struck. Then release it quickly and return finger to the home key.

17 Dr. Kessel left Friday. Dr. Harris is still here.

18 Judge Stark is late. I regret that he is delayed.

19 Art asked the judge. There is just a little left.

20 Sue is ready. Ray is glad. Guy trusts Les fully.

Unit 8

Line spacing: single
Line length: 50
Type each line twice.
Double-space after
each pair of lines.

Warmup

Two spaces after a period at the end of a sentence; one space after an abbreviation.

1 dust rust fire tire high dust rust just tire right

2 the large shelf; the high shelf; the ledge is high

3 Dr. Glaskel liked the test. Jeff says it is easy.

New Key Location

S finger W

4 sws sws we we we saw saw was was way way jaws jaws

5 why why sew sew what what wait wait were were were

6 walk walk with with wish wish dew dew where always

Semi finger P

7 ;p; ;p; up up gap gap put put apt apt pay pay paid

8 lap lap pass pass swap swap park park ape ape whip

9 paid paid lip lip peep peep reply reply deep depth

10 prepare prepare happy happy party party flap slept

Leave one space after a comma.

K finger ,

11 k,k k,k I wish, had tried, after all, if she will,

12 I will get full details, as Lee said, late Friday.

13 Please, Phil, wait a little while with that reply.

14 We like the way it was settled. Keep it up, Kate.

Each, too, has a unique and ancient heritage 70
in both oral and written poetry. In Japan, written 81
poetry first appeared at the end of the 700's 90
There are more than 4,000 poems from that pe- 99
riod. The poems deal mainly with life in the 108
emperor's court, rather than with the life of the 118
common people. But like most Japanese poetry, 127
the poems deal with the closeness of the people 137
to nature. SI 1.52 139

34

159 Words

Money is the lifeblood of business. The lack 10
of it has brought failure to thousands of business- 20
people who had everything else they needed— 29
personality, courage, willingness to work hard, 38
ability, and experience. 43

This does not mean that you must, before 52
starting a business, amass all the money that you 62
will need. Most businesses finance their opera- 72
tions by borrowing funds from time to time. 81

To obtain a loan for a business operation, 90
a manufacturer or merchant must show that he 99
or she is a good risk. The bank's cash funds come 109
from the deposits of other people, and so the 118
banker must be quite sure that the borrower 127
will pay back the loan. The banker is influenced 137

most by the past record of the applicant, either 147
as a responsible employee or as a successful 156
business person. SI 1.53 159

35

183 Words

When great machines began to do the work 9
formerly done by work animals and hand labor, 18
many people found themselves unemployed. As 27
a result, they were violently opposed to the new 37
machinery, and they attempted to destroy it. 46
In the course of time, however, the use of ma- 55
chines greatly increased the number of people 64
employed. 66

Modern industry has been built upon meth- 75
ods of mass production, which were made pos- 84
sible by machinery. Mass production has put 93
many articles within the reach of everybody and 103
raised our standard of living. Luxuries of past 113
eras have now become commonplace goods. 121

Books are an excellent example of the ad- 130
vantages of mass production. When books had 139
to be written by hand, they were rare works of 149
art that only a very few people could afford. 158
Now books, as well as newspapers and maga- 166
zines, are published by the thousands, and nearly 176
everybody can afford to buy them. SI 1.57 183

200 TO 300 WORDS

The following timed writings are arranged in three groups according to the syllabic intensities of the individual selections.

Selections 1–14, SI Range 1.23–1.34

1

207 Words

A walk on the beach can be full of interest 10
every step of the way. To begin with, it is along 20
the seashore that we can best sense the great 29
wonder of creation. The sea is older than any- 38
thing else in the world. It has always been there 48
and—just think of it—it has always been in mo- 58
tion. The motion of the sea that attracts your 67
eyes, the noise of it that fills your ears, existed 77
thousands and thousands of years before anyone 86

walked the earth and wondered where the sea 95
had come from. Stop and think about the roar 104
of the ocean going on for thousands of years 113
before there were any people on the earth to hear 123
it. How grand, but how lonely it must have been! 133

Then think about the sands. Take up a hand- 143
ful of dry sand, and it runs through your fingers 153
like powder. Go near the waves where the sand 162
is wet, and you will see in it tiny grains of various 173
colors. Once the sands were shells and stones. 182
The sea has ground them into fine particles. 191
Every year the stones on the beach grow smaller 201
as the ocean wears them away. SI 1.23 207

Figuring Your Speed

In the lessons from now on you will be taking timed writings; that is, you will be typing for a set period of time and trying to reach a better speed, with control, than in previous attempts.

In figuring typing speed, every five strokes (spaces included) are counted as one word. To assist you in figuring the number of words you typed, a cumulative word count is shown at the end of each line. Immediately below the timed writing is a word scale that shows the word count at various points throughout a line.

For example, suppose you typed the following for 1 minute:

Word count

15 Yes, Pat liked the first test. It was truly easy. 10

16 As a result, he was paid   15

    1| 2| 3| 4| 5| 6| 7| 8| 9| 10|

If you completed both lines, you would have typed 15 words (10 + 5) a minute. If you had typed only to the word "a" in line 16, you would have typed 11 words (10 + 1) per minute (wpm).

Typing Skill Checkup

Goal: To type 17 wpm. Two or more tries.

Don't worry about errors, but try to keep them to a minimum.

15 Yes, Pat liked the first test. It was truly easy. 10

16 As a result, he was paid Friday. He left Tuesday. 20

17 If Wiley will study a little harder, he will pass. 30

SI 1.30

    1| 2| 3| 4| 5| 6| 7| 8| 9| 10|

Unit 9

Line spacing: single
Line length: 50
Type each line twice.
Double-space after
each pair of lines.

Warmup

Strike each key with equal force.

1 kit wit fit jut; day gay way play; art start parts

2 law raw paw thaw; wide pride jury; we three agreed

3 See if Dr. Kyle is here. If he is, I shall start.

should be on as small a scale as possible. Otherwise lower prices will force markdowns and losses. In a rising market, on the other hand, enough goods must be bought to meet competition. The buyer, however, should not yield to the temptation of speculating and overloading. 93 101 111 120 130 138

In the second place, the buyer must purchase only needed merchandise and not be influenced by high-pressure sales talks, clever advertising, or attractive displays. If he or she buys because the salesperson is persuasive rather than because the goods fill a need, the unwanted stock will prove a burden. 147 156 165 175 185 195 SI 1.47 200

Selections 29–35, SI Range 1.52–1.59

29
92 Words

We need to understand ourselves and others. The observance of holidays, whether or not they are religious, is one way in which people keep their culture alive. You may understand the world better, and be able to accept the differences in others, if you study these holidays. 10 19 29 38 47 56

Some American holidays have brought together customs from many lands. By studying these holidays, you will see how our culture is made up from the contributions of many peoples. 65 74 83 92

SI 1.59

30
112 Words

Meteoroids are celestial bodies, possibly associated with comets, that move through space with velocities up to 40 miles per second. When they reach the earth's atmosphere, they are vaporized by the heat caused by the friction of their passage into the atmosphere, and then they are seen as meteors. 10 19 29 38 48 57 60

An unusual number of meteors in a short period of time is called a meteor shower. Meteors are popularly known as falling stars or shooting stars. While most of them are consumed, a few fall to the earth as fused metal or stone and are called meteorites. 69 79 89 98 108 SI 1.54 112

31
119 Words

Our natural environment is formed from chemical elements which join in different ways to form minerals, rocks, soils, water, air, and organic matter. In past years, this natural environment has been much changed by the effects of chemical pollution, at least in some regions. Some of the chemical pollutants might be beneficial to human and animal health, and some might be neutral, but many of them are harmful. The task now is to remove pollutants from the environment, and to prevent further pollution. The task will be difficult and expensive. But in the long run it will pay for itself. 9 18 27 37 46 56 65 74 84 93 102 112 SI 1.55 119

32
136 Words

Bookkeeping and accounting workers keep a daily financial history of a business. Records of business dealings, such as the sale or purchase of merchandise, are kept in books called journals or ledgers. 9 19 29 38 41

In most small firms, one general bookkeeper does all the recording, analysis, and other accounting work. Large firms may have many bookkeeping and accounting clerks, each specializing in one or two kinds of accounting work. 51 60 68 77 87

Bookkeeping and accounting workers also file, answer the telephone, use adding, calculating, and bookkeeping machines, and prepare and mail bills. Some also do payroll work. They record and write checks, too, but they usually do not sign them. 96 106 114 124 133 SI 1.55 136

33
139 Words

The history of Japanese Americans is in many ways similar to that of Jewish and Afro-Americans. As a people, each has cultural roots that go far into the past. Each has experienced both power and oppression. Each has suffered rejection in our country where all, it is said, are free and equal. 9 18 28 38 47 57 60

(Continued on next page)

New Key Location

A finger

Q

4 aqa aqa aqa quit quit quit equal equal quiet quiet
5 quart quart quart quite quite quite quay quay quay
6 Quality quart jade jars; requires quiet; was equal

L finger

O

7 lol lol lol old old old low low low told told talk
8 does does does words words words quote quote quote
9 Follow the quay as far as it goes or you will pay.

Sentence Practice

Eyes on copy!

10 Fill this quart jar with water for yourself, Ross.
11 Take a ferry for your trip; a ride is quite short.
12 High quality paper is required for work like this.
13 Let us show you how to get a profit without risks.

Capital Practice

To avoid "flying" capitals (capitals that are above the line), hold the shift key down firmly and release it promptly after the letter has been struck.

14 Delaware, DE; Georgia, GA; Hawaii, HI; or Ohio, OH
15 Joe, Walt, Pete, Roy, Si, or Kate will go to Utah.
16 Laura will take quite a trip to Italy this August.
17 Fred left for Hawaii Friday. George will go also.
18 You should go to Quail Hill or Key Largo Thursday.

    1| 2| 3| 4| 5| 6| 7| 8| 9| 10|

REVIEW

Unit 10

Line spacing: single
Line length: 50
Type each line twice.
Double-space after
each pair of lines.

Do not let your fingers slant or slouch. Keep the correct alignment as shown above.

Warmup

1 your your equip jugs tour poor quote foul owl jowl
2 At her request, he took Dorothy to the Ford Hotel.
3 George refused our request to pay us what he owes.

has the judgment to know which papers may be 86
released or which requests should be ignored. 95

A career as a secretary can give you great 105
personal rewards. Your work day and the con- 114
ditions about you could be pleasant. Your office 124
is likely to be a comfortable one. If you work 134
in a big office, you will meet many people and 143
make new friends. Your work can put you in 152
touch with men and women of achievement in 161
many fields.   SI 1.36 163

25   163 Words

A great many people still think that a secre- 10
tary is a kind of machine who turns out perfect 19
letters from nine to five. Some use the title to 29
mean one who is employed as a stenographer or 38
clerk in an office. It is true that typing and short- 49
hand are two of the basic skills of the secretary, 59
but it is also true that a secretary's duties cover 69
a much wider area than those of a typist, stenog- 79
rapher, or file clerk. 83

The secretary, as we use the term today, 92
often does this kind of work, but he or she is 101
much more like an assistant to an executive. The 111
secretary often knows a great deal about many 120
of the confidential matters relating to the com- 130
pany's business. Knowing how to use this infor- 140
mation helps avoid delays and clears the decks 149
for the "boss" in a score of other ways through- 159
out the working day.   SI 1.44 163

26   175 Words

It is hard to realize that there ever was a time 10
when a typewriter was not a necessary piece of 20
equipment in every business office. At first, the 30
greatest appeal a typewritten letter had was the 40
ease with which it could be read. In the early 49
days, typed material did not always look attrac- 59
tive; but it was legible. Misstruck characters and 69
strikeovers were common. 74

Because everyone expected these faults in a 84
typewritten letter, form letters were sent out 93
purposely with such errors, in order to give the 103

impression that the letter was especially written 113
for the individual to whom it was addressed. 122
Today an employer demands that a typist do 130
work that measures up to a high standard of 139
performance. Typed work must meet three re- 148
quirements: It must be done quickly; it must 157
be accurate; and it must be well arranged so that 167
it makes a good impression on the reader. SI 1.50 175

27   188 Words

The choice of a line of business calls for 9
good judgment. You should select a field that 18
you know, and one that is growing or for which 27
there is a steady demand. Sometimes it is pos- 37
sible to provide some service that does not exist 47
but for which there is a real need. For example, 57
one person thought of a service for supplying 66
box lunches to factory workers—something new, 75
something needed. Now there are many trucks 84
that carry food to workers in districts with few 94
eating places. 97

You might go into business producing in 106
wholesale quantities some article of food that 115
you prepare especially well and that is not al- 125
ready on the market. You might have some spe- 134
cial training of which you can make use. There 144
are other considerations to be kept in mind 153
when choosing a business. You should know the 162
amount of capital you require and the amount 171
available. And you must be careful not to enter 181
a field that is already overcrowded.   SI 1.43 188

28   200 Words

The buyer for a store must use a buying plan. 9
The following practices related to planned buy- 19
ing have stood the test of time. 25

In the first place, the buyer should make 34
purchases often, so that fresh stock is always on 44
hand. This practice will also prevent stock from 54
running out and will avoid the need for a heavy 64
investment at any one time. In a falling market— 74
that is, when prices are going down—purchases 83

(Continued on next page)

Skill Building

4 I said it was quite easy.   5
5 They will go to see the house.   6
6 He would like to see the jail yard.   7
7 We felt that we really had to look hard.   8
8 It is a pleasure to supply you with the help.   9
9 While she was out, two people were here to see it. 10

Double-Letter Word Practice

10 pp supports ll Stella ss assure pp supply equipped
11 gg suggest ff Jeffrey ll really ee agreed oo goods
12 ll shall rr ferries ss passed tt Seattle gg ragged
13 rr hurry ll equally ee freed oo shooter dd ladders

Typing Skill Checkup

Goal: To type 17 wpm.

14 Rudolf or Pat will go to Dallas this week. Walter 10
15 hopes to go with his sister. They look forward to 20
16 the trip with great pleasure.   SI 1.24 26

    1   2   3   4   5   6   7   8   9   10

Unit 11

Line spacing: single
Line length: 50
Type each line twice.
Double-space after each pair of lines.

Warmup

1 old old, quell quell; top top, quit quite; jog jog
2 why why lip lip reply reply walks walks pays pays;
3 Dr. Starr offered us the property at a low figure.

20

142 Words

Students frequently do poor work in school because they do not know how to develop good study habits. Trying to read or do homework while you are watching television or listening to the latest recording by your favorite singers is not studying.

When questioned about the problem of studying, one student replied, "I don't need a course in how to study; I need a course in how to stop watching television." The solution is really very simple. Just turn off the television set, put one foot in front of the other, and keep moving until you find a quiet place. Then go to work! This is the first and probably the most important step in getting started. You can't be attentive to two things at one time. SI 1.46

21

149 Words

Printing is a good business. It is an honorable and respectable kind of work. It has prepared many for high stations in life. It has its own inspiring traditions and legends. The printer must have a knowledge of almost everything under the sun—mechanics, language, color, salesmanship. There is no end to the skills required, because the printer is brought into contact with all other trades and professions.

Whether it be a reading primer or a college textbook, a handbill or a newspaper, a ticket or a poster, a folder or a magazine, a box label or a legal document—its message is told to the world by means of the printed word. In this modern age, no business or other organized activity could get far without the art of the printer. SI 1.49

22

153 Words

Once you are in the business world, you will learn many things that are not to be found in books. When you meet people at close range in the office, you tend to get deeper insight into human nature. And the longer you are engaged in business, the more respect you will have for the dignity of labor.

You will soon learn the importance of spending wisely the money that you earn and of making good use of your leisure time. You will learn that your rate of progress depends on your own efforts. You will learn to accept tasks that are boring and even unpleasant, and to face, at times, unreasonable attitudes that your employer may take. In short, you will learn to adapt yourself to other people and to deal intelligently with any situation that may arise. SI 1.37

23

156 Words

Today we have a greater amount of leisure time than any of our ancestors enjoyed. We work fewer hours a day and fewer days a week than they did. What are we doing with all this free time? The wonderland of nature is ever ready to welcome us. The world, with its treasure of books, art, music, drama, and science, is before us.

Do we make full use of libraries, museums, art galleries, and parks? Do we go to concerts and to the theater? Do we spend part of our free time in outdoor sports, such as hiking, swimming, playing tennis or golf, and fishing? The range of recreations is wide enough to enable every one of us to satisfy our own tastes and indulge in our pet hobbies.

Many people who started out collecting stamps and coins as a hobby, have now made a business of it. SI 1.42

24

163 Words

One secretary may type a great volume of letters in one day, while another may type just a few. At any rate, there is very little that is like a machine about the work. There is no machine with the tact to soothe the ruffled feelings of an important caller who must cool her heels while an equally important one overstays his time with the boss. When the boss is absent, no machine

(Continued on next page)

Alternate Hands Practice

Goal: To speed up finger movements.

4 the for rug did she due got fit eye fork also duty

5 lap oak dot pry pal the girl held for she got paid

6 sit with tight quake tutor shelf world their digit

Tabulator Key or Bar

The tabulator makes the carriage move 5, 10, 20, or any number of spaces in one motion. It is faster to use the tabulator to make an indention for a paragraph than to strike the space bar five times. To set a tab stop, follow this procedure:

1. Clear all the tab stops previously set, by moving the carriage to the extreme left. As you hold the tab clear key down, pull the carriage all the way to the right.
2. Set the new stops by moving the carriage to the desired positions. Press the tab set key for each stop needed.
3. Test the new stops by moving the carriage to the extreme right. Hold down the tabulator bar or key until the carriage stops; then release the tabulator bar or key. Repeat. Does the carriage stop at the points desired?

Paragraph Practice

Set a tab stop for a 5-space paragraph indention.

At your own speed, type the first paragraph with no more than 3 errors. If you succeed, move to the second paragraph. Otherwise, retype the first paragraph. Continue the same way on the following paragraphs.

7   We feel that our request is justified, as you 10

8 had agreed to pay. Please pay what you owe today. 20

9   Perhaps you would prefer to write the reports 10

10 yourself. If so, please go ahead after four days. 20

11   If you require a supply of household goods, I 10

12 will gladly help you to prepare your orders today. 20

13   The store is large. It is well equipped with 10

14 all sorts of supplies for those who like hardware. 20

15   I should like to suggest that you let us fill 10

16 all your orders for leather goods. Just write us. 20

SI 1.29

Supplementary Practice

17 Without further delay, they paid all that he owed.

18 Joe took a short trip last April for that purpose.

19 We hope the sale of the house will yield a profit.

20 History supports this theory; perhaps it is right.

21 Philip was glad that his star pupil got the award.

Typing Skill Checkup

Take two or more 1-minute writings on this paragraph.

Goal: Speed–18 wpm
      Error limit–3

22   If she swore to a false report, she is guilty 10

23 of perjury. It is quite justified that she should 20

24 go to jail.

SI 1.27 **22**

1 | 2 | 3 | 4 | 5 | 6 | 7 | 8 | 9 | 10 |

15

114 Words

Fruit-bearing trees can be important parts of 10
a landscape plan. Whether planted in a row to 19
mark borders or grouped orchard-style or set 28
out as specimen plantings, they enhance the gar- 38
den year after year. They add to the value of your 48
property, too. 51

Because fruit trees usually last a long time, it 62
is important to choose the best trees when you 71
are buying. A nursery, garden center, or land- 81
scape specialist can give advice on the different 91
varieties and on the best places for planting 99
them. These sources can also give advice for 109
proper planting and upkeep. SI 1.44 114

16

130 Words

The word <u>Halloween</u> is short for All Hallow 13
Even, the evening before All Hallows' Day, or All 23
Saints' Day. Halloween was meant to be a reli- 33
gious time. But our celebration comes from old 42
customs of people who believed in ghosts, 50
witches, and goblins. 54

People all over the world are afraid some- 63
times. They look for sources to explain their fear. 74
For example, people once thought that gods in 83
the sky threw lightning at the earth. In the same 93
way, people thought up ghosts, witches, and gob- 103
lins. If an animal died, they believed that a witch 113
or goblin made it happen. They were afraid, but 123
at least they had an explanation. SI 1.38 130

17

133 Words

Banks will make certain kinds of loans; 9
other loans will not be made, either because they 19
are barred by law or because they are considered 29
unsound. In general, banks prefer not to make 38
loans for a long period without return payments 47
at regular intervals. In fact, they usually require 58
loans to be repaid within a short time, except 67
loans on land and buildings. Banks often ask 76
for security for a loan—even from very large 85
companies. 87

As a rule, a bank wants to know the purpose 97
of a loan, to help in deciding whether or not to 107
grant it. This information also helps the bank fix 117
the length of time for the loan, as well as the 127
amount of security required. SI 1.40 133

18

140 Words

Jewish-Americans have a holiday called 9
Hanukkah. Hanukkah is the celebration of the 18
victory of Judas Maccabaeus. Judas and his 27
small band of patriots defeated the Syrians in 36
165 B.C. But before the Syrians left the land of 46
Israel, they destroyed the Jewish temple. 54

When the Jews built a new temple on the 63
ruins of the old one, a strange thing happened. 73
As the workmen were clearing stones from the 82
floor of the temple, they found a jar of holy oil. 92
The holy oil was used for the burning of the 101
Eternal Light in the temple. The jar they found 111
held enough oil for only one day's light. For some 121
reason, the oil burned for eight days and nights. 131
So Hanukkah lasts for eight days and nights. 140

SI 1.43

19

144 Words

It seems just a few years ago that many 9
Americans spoke up and demanded an early end 18
to the problem of air pollution. But the air re- 28
mains foul, and the struggle to clean it goes on 38
endlessly, with little progress that we can see 47
or smell. 49

People once moved to the suburbs to get 58
clean air, but there is no place there to hide any- 68
more. Many surrounding communities are as 76
polluted as the central cities and as hazardous 86
to health, even though the pollutants may be 95
invisible. 97

Now there is talk of minimizing clean air 106
standards, of easing enforcement so that more 115
coal can be burned as an answer to the energy 124
shortage. This could delay our goal of clean air 134
for quite a few years. There are no easy answers. 144

SI 1.40

Unit 12

Line spacing: single
Line length: 50
Type each line twice.
Double-space after
each pair of lines.

Warmup

Sit up straight. Keep your wrists low and your elbows loosely at your sides.

1 jagged jaws; please pleasure; quire require, fires
2 Kurt took a trip west last April for that purpose.
3 Louis, please write us if you require further aid.

New Key Location

D finger **C**

4 dcd dcd dcd cat cat cat car car car jack jack lack
5 call call call each each each case case case space
6 quick quick quick reduce reduce reduce clear clear

F finger **V**

7 fvf fvf fvf eve eve eve vat vat vat save save save
8 have have have give give give very very very prove
9 vivid vivid vivid velvet velvet velvet valve valve
10 We have to leave quickly for the drive over there.

Leave 2 spaces after a question mark at the end of a sentence.

Semi finger **?**
and
A finger
to shift

11 ;?; ;?; ;?; Who called? Did he go? Where is she?
12 What have you to say? What does that prove, Carl?
13 How did you do it, Vi? Will Dr. Davis drive over?
14 Shall I do it today? Do you prefer check or cash?
15 We provide delivery service. Could that help you?

Skill Building

- Select a sentence you feel you can complete twice in 1 minute. Take a 1-minute writing.
- If you don't complete the sentence twice or you make more than 3 errors, select a shorter sentence.
- If you complete a sentence twice easily, select a longer one.

16 Are we required to do it?   5
17 Work for quick, sharp strokes.   6
18 Sit up, erect; type without pauses.   7
19 Try to strike each key with equal force.   8
20 You will type well if you practice regularly.   9
21 Do strive to reach for the key with little effort. 10

       1   2   3   4   5   6   7   8   9   10

10

171 Words

Perhaps the best way to give you an impression of the sport of sand yachting is to take you on an imaginary trip along the beach on a glorious summer day. As a pleasant breeze blows off the sea, we travel over ground where probably no one has been before. The sails are pulled in, and the big wheels are coasting over the hard sand. The first sensation is one of surprising speed, with a complete absence of noise or vibration.

As we gain speed, you may have your first misgivings as you see the windward front wheel leave the ground. A glance at the speedometer shows that we are moving at forty miles an hour. When you consider that the fastest racing yacht has never exceeded half this speed, you realize how fast a sand yacht is. There is absolute silence, except for the sound of the wheels splashing through the puddles left by the receding tide.

SI 1.33

11

189 Words

A few minutes spent at the end of every workday in caring for your typewriter will keep it in good operating condition.

First, clean the type with a short brush that has straight bristles. To dislodge ribbon ink and other dirt, use a jabbing motion. Finish by wiping the type with several thicknesses of cloth wrapped around the brush, using a side-to-side motion. You may also use a plastic cleaner, which is rolled back and forth over the type. It should be kneaded after each use, so that it will absorb the dirt it has picked up.

Second, use a long-handled brush to clean the frame, keys, key levers, typebars, and carriage. Move the carriage right and left to reach underneath. Then brush the back.

To finish up, clean the surface under the machine. (If it is fastened, put paper under it while performing the first two steps.) Center the carriage, so no one will bump it and throw it off its rail; then cover the machine. SI 1.34

12

99 Words

America began as a land of immigrants, who came from the lands of their birth to make new homes in this country. People from lands all over the world now call America their home. From their native lands, they have brought their old customs and traditions.

The customs and traditions of groups of people are called their culture. The cultures of many countries have mixed to make up America. You might call America a multicultural society. It is a land made up of many groups of people.

SI 1.43

13

100 Words

You will often have occasion to use your typing skills to write letters. Aim to make your letters attractive, so that they will make a good impression on the readers.

In business and in personal life, letters often serve as important records. If there is a dispute about the terms of a transaction, for instance, a letter may be brought out of a file to provide the evidence to settle it. It is, therefore, essential that the contents of a letter be accurate, complete, and clearly set forth. SI 1.47

14

108 Words

There was one main difference between slavery as it existed in Africa and the "peculiar institution" as it came about in the United States.

The slave in African life was a status symbol— a sign of the wealth and position of the owner. People could not afford to own slaves unless they were already wealthy. Therefore, they could not become wealthy on the basis of labor done by slaves. In the southern United States, the economy was based on the free labor supplied by slaves; and through their slaves, owners could amass wealth. SI 1.48

Unit 13

Line spacing: single
Line length: 50
Paragraph indention: 5
Type each line twice.
Double-space after each pair of lines

Warmup

Leave 2 spaces after a question mark.

Return the carriage quickly.

1 wave waves; vest request; serves service; discover
2 voice rejoice juices quick plaque grace face facts
3 The price is high. Could you, perhaps, reduce it?

New Key Location

S finger X

4 sxs sxs sxs tax tax tax fox fox fox exit exit exit
5 flax flax flax fix fix fix lax lax lax sex sex sex
6 expect expect expect sox sox sox sixth sixth sixth

J finger M

7 jmj jmj jmj my my my me me me am am am mix mix mix
8 firm firm firm arm arm arm may may may times times
9 came came cave dam dam dam same same game fame jam
10 Who came? What time was it? May they expect you?

F finger B

No space is left after the period in an abbreviation when a semicolon or comma follows.

11 fbf fbf fbf box box box bad bad bad lab lab lab be
12 bake bake bake job job job bid bid bid mob mob mob
13 back back back tub tub tub blue blue blue beam big
14 Mrs. Butler expects a reply by mail this February.
15 September is abbreviated to Sept.; Friday, to Fri.

Typing Skill Checkup

Two or more 1-minute writings.

Goal: Speed—19 wpm
Error limit—3

16   For today, try to put aside worries or doubts 10
17 you may have about yourself. Have thoughts about 20
18 success. Start each day with thoughts of success. 30
SI 1.32

19   I require good quality paper for these works. 10
20 I would like to order it today. Perhaps you would 20
21 prefer that I wait for your approval.   SI 1.35 27

1| 2| 3| 4| 5| 6| 7| 8| 9| 10|

5

113 Words

I live in my car. I drive it everywhere. But this week I am leaving it home. There is nothing wrong with my car. But rush-hour traffic keeps getting worse, and the cost of driving keeps going up.

So last week I made a decision. I'd leave my car in the garage for a week and give public transportation a chance. After all, I am the public. It has been an experience. Instead of watching the brakelights of the car in front of me, I get a chance to look at some scenery for a change, or to read a newspaper, or just to relax and not think about anything. SI 1.28

6

121 Words

We live in what we regard as a very advanced state of culture. We seldom recall that each age must have seemed just as advanced to those who lived in it. We look back on the life led by people a hundred years ago, and we wonder how they were able to get along.

On the other hand, is it not just as likely that in a hundred years from now, new generations, in their turn, will look back on us and, in the light of their increased comforts, think our present way of life incomplete? We have no way to know what new discoveries and inventions may entirely change the standards of living in the future.

SI 1.29

7

128 Words

The world pays everyone in his or her own coin. If you smile, the world smiles at you in return; if you frown, you will be frowned at. If you sing, you will be invited into musical company; if you think, you will be sought by thinkers. If you love the world and truly seek for the good that is in it, you will have loving friends, and nature will pour into your lap the wealth of the earth. If you blame and criticize, you will be blamed and criticized by your fellows.

Every seed brings forth after its kind. Mistrust brings mistrust, and confidence brings confidence. Malice is paid with malice, and love is paid with love. SI 1.26

8

142 Words

It was a cold midwinter evening. Four friends sat near the fire for warmth and comfort. They had enjoyed a good dinner, and now they were ready to spend the rest of the evening in pleasant company. One of them turned on the radio. They listened to a short talk about people who were out of work and about others who were employed at wages that were too low to support them and their families.

The little company of four was moved by the troubles that beset some of their neighbors. When the radio program came to a close, the four friends began to discuss what might be done to provide for the needs of their less fortunate neighbors. The next morning, the Mutual Aid Society of our town was born. SI 1.33

9

169 Words

It has long been the custom for people, on the first day of April, to play friendly tricks on each other. The origin of this is unknown. According to one version, people are sent on fruitless errands in memory of the mistake Noah made on the first of April when he sent the dove from the ark before the flood had eased up.

Another version traces the custom to a Roman tale. A mother, hearing the echo of her daughter's voice calling her, went in search, guiding herself by the echo. This, of course, was a fool's errand.

Another story says the custom began in France. Formerly the New Year came at the end of March. The height of the holiday occurred on the first of April, when people made visits and gave gifts. When the New Year was changed to the first of January, the custom was kept up as a joke, with mock visits and gifts. SI 1.34

Unit 14

Line spacing: single
Line length: 50
Paragraph indention: 5
Type each line twice.

Warmup

Remember to double-space after each pair of lines.

1 job move love above; same came blame; rough slough
2 Dec., ox fox box, whim make bake; me my myself mix
3 You will get a job if you prepare yourself for it.

New Key Location

A finger **Z**

4 aza aza aza lazy lazy lazy zoo zoo zoo seize seize
5 zeal zeal zeal size size size zero zero zero seize
6 jazz jazz jazz, raze raze raze, dazed dazed dazed;
7 quiz quiz quiz; zebra zebra zebra; doz. doz. doz.;

J finger **N**

8 jnj jnj jnj no no no net net net on on on ten tens
9 pen pen pen zone zone zone new new new men men men
10 oxen oxen oven been been been many many many dozen
11 Dr. Dorfs ordered a dozen copies of the new books.

Up and Down Reach Practice

Make reaches between the third and the first row without having your fingers pause on the home row.

12 ice ice ice mud mud mud sum sum sum curb curb curb
13 much much much debt debt debt must must must nerve
14 jump jump jump curve curve curve funny funny funny
15 sun sunny numb number brow brown unbend unbendable
16 I must quickly select the clothes to pack my bags.

Typing Skill Checkup

Take two or more 1-minute writings.

Goal: Speed—20 wpm
Error limit—3

17   Stop and think back over your past. What are 10
18 the things you have done at home, at school, with 20
19 friends that you enjoyed doing? What you like can 30
20 enable you to recognize careers worth exploring.   40

SI 1.32

| 1 | 2 | 3 | 4 | 5 | 6 | 7 | 8 | 9 | 10 |

Group 5 TIMED WRITINGS

The selections in this group serve two purposes. They can be used (1) to help you develop greater speed and accuracy, and (2) to test your progress toward the attainment of these goals.

Before you select the copy for your timed writings, decide what your goal is. If you want to increase speed, select easy copy. If your goal is to improve accuracy, select difficult copy.

Syllabic intensity (S.I.) is one measure that can be used to rate the difficulty of a timed writing. Material that has a syllabic intensity of from 1.45 to 1.50 is considered to be of average difficulty. For building speed, select copy that has a syllabic intensity in the lower ranges (1.20 to 1.35). For improving accuracy, select copy that has a syllabic intensity in the higher ranges (above 1.50). For *measuring* speed and accuracy, select copy of average difficulty.

Use a 70-space line and double spacing.

UNDER 200 WORDS

The following timed writings are arranged in three groups according to the syllabic intensities of the individual selections.

Selections 1–11, SI Range 1.26–1.34

1

91 Words

A group of us were discussing our jobs, and 10
the talk turned to the subject of tact. We all 19
agreed that tact is one of the important qualities 29
that lead to a successful career. Then we tried to 39
describe what tact means. Someone said that 48
tact is not so much what you say, but how you say 58
it. I said that since it comes from a Latin word 68
meaning touch, it suggests a sensitive touch that 78
works with human nature, not against it. The 87
group accepted this.   SI 1.26   91

2

97 Words

Few things taste better than sweet, juicy 9
fruit picked fresh from your own trees. 17

The wide variety of fruit trees you can have 27
in your own yard will bring you other joys, too. 37
Planting and caring for the trees will give you 46
healthy exercise. Their colorful blooms in spring 56
will please your eyes. And in the warm summer 65
months, your trees will provide cool shade. 74

Fruit trees provide healthful food and offer 84
all the benefits of a green and natural environ- 94
ment. Grow some!   SI 1.30   97

3

101 Words

Not too long ago, when the first airplanes 9
were built, some people shook their heads and 18
said that man was not meant to fly. But human 27
skill soon mastered the air, just as once it had 37
mastered the land and the sea. The first small 46
airplanes rose only a few feet in the air and flew 56
slowly over short distances. Modern airplanes 65
rise many thousands of feet and fly around the 74
world in hours. Some are supersonic and move 83
faster than the speed of sound. The impossible of 93
yesterday is the commonplace of today.   SI 1.30   101

4

109 Words

Throughout the world, people seem to have 10
always felt the need to tell the time of year. In 20
most regions, time was told by the changes in the 30
moon or the changes in the seasons of winter, 39
spring, summer, and fall. 44

The moon passes through its changes from 53
new moon to new moon in twenty-eight days. 61
It goes from a bright circle in the sky, to a little 72
slice of light, to no light at all. Then it goes back 83
to a bright circle. Native Americans reckoned 93
their time of year by these changes in the moon, 103
which they called the Night Sun.   SI 1.20   109

Unit 15

Line spacing: single
Line length: 50
Paragraph indention: 5
Type each line twice.

Warmup

Spacing review:
- Two spaces follow a period or a question mark at the end of a sentence.

1 men ten mind dent envy rent open went enjoy manner
2 zeal zest haze fix tax next quit quiz quote mosque
3 Shall I exchange these gloves? Size six is small.
4 We must sell them now. Tomorrow will be too late.

Up and Down Reach Practice

- One space follows a comma, a semicolon, and a period when used in an abbreviation.

5 sum sum sum deny deny deny sung sung sung fund fun
6 zinc verb live myth uncle exert winds begin breaks
7 Mr. Zed must be present, or else they cannot vote.
8 Judy denied that any amount of the funds was lost.
9 He could not play; music never came easily to him.

Alternate Hands Practice

Type lines 10–18 twice. Then take two or more 1-minute writings: If your goal is speed, select lines 13 and 14 for your copy; if your goal is accuracy, select any line from 15 to 18 for your copy.

10 so is to if me of or to he am go am by is us to do
11 but an man sit eye got dig may dog fur did tie sue
12 down also lake auto city keys make firm hand worms
13 The women may go with Susie to help with the work.
14 An auditor paid for an ornament and got it for us.

Alphabetic Sentence Practice

Keep your wrists low!

15 A brown fox quickly jumps over the big, lazy dogs.
16 Joe packed five boxes of frozen quail in my trunk.
17 Quick, Jay, fix my two big zinc valves which drip.
18 The six brave women do quick flying trapeze jumps.

Tabulator Review

- Clear all tab stops.
- Set new stops 5, 10, 15, and 20 spaces to the right of the left margin.
- Begin line 19 at the left margin.
- Use the tab bar or key to indent the other lines.

19 Just put some zip in your work; use sharp strokes.
20   As you hit the keys, do not move your elbows.
21   Learn how to throw the carriage quickly.
22   Never rest your wrist on the frame.
23   Sit up straight when you type.

17   It's easy to save, if you save regularly. If you deposit the same amount   16
with us each month—say $50—we pay not only your regular 5¼% interest   30
but also a ½% bonus at the end of each year. When you bank with us,   44
your money earns <u>extra</u> interest! Call at our local branch, 114 North   60
Wabash Avenue (at Butterfield Street).   68

18   Henry Bolton of Cleveland, Ohio, reported to the police today that his   15
wife's jewels had been stolen. He said that the jewels, valued at $3,200,   30
were taken from a wall safe in his home. They included a pearl necklace   44
valued at $1,500; a diamond and ruby ring, $900; and an emerald and   57
diamond brooch, $800. The ring was inscribed, "H. B. to L. B.—   70
6/14/66."   72

19   We have just published our handy pocket edition of <u>A Citizen's</u>   18
<u>Guide to The City</u>, size 5½″ × 3¼″. It contains 124 pages of informa-   39
tion about our city—its public buildings, restaurants, hotels, theaters,   54
transit lines—and costs only 95¢. A similar guide, size 10″ × 7½″, has   68
been selling for $2.50.   73

20   Oliver & Martin advertised in this morning's <u>Daily Examiner</u> for a   20
stenographer, giving the following particulars: salary, $166; 40-hour   34
week; good working conditions. The applicant must be at least 20 years   48
of age and must have a minimum of two years' experience. Applicants   62
should apply at the Horn Building, 106 Flag Street (Room 849).   74

21   BERNARD & FRENCH stores rugs on its premises at a charge of   13
3% of the appraised value. A minimum charge of $7.50 is made for rugs   27
9′ × 12′ or smaller. Small rugs are accepted as scatter rugs in groups of   42
four, at a $9 minimum for the group. In addition, the store offers a   56
cleaning service—80¢ per square foot for domestic rugs and 90¢ per   69
square foot for Oriental rugs.   75

22   At the low cost of only $5 a month, our life insurance policy pays up to   15
$5,500 to your beneficiary if death is due to natural causes. Death   28
benefits are increased for loss of life due to (1) an automobile or bus   42
accident or (2) an accident while traveling in a train or in an airplane.   56
Our policies are issued to men and women, ages 21 to 60 years. Don't   70
delay! Write for full information TODAY!   78

23   NOTICE IS HEREBY GIVEN that the twentieth annual meeting of   13
stockholders of the Regal Gas & Electric Corporation will be held on   27
Monday, November 25, at 2:30 p.m., for (1) the election of directors   41
and (2) the transaction of all other business that may properly come   55
before the meeting. Stockholders who do not expect to attend are urged   69
to <u>sign and return the enclosed proxy</u>.   90

Unit 16

Line spacing: single
Line length: 50
Paragraph indention: 5
Type each line twice.

Warmup

Type evenly and smoothly.

1 jaw car coal yard want, high stands; quick markets
2 It gives us pleasure to forward seven sample jars.
3 Six dozen boxes burned. Frequently zero boxes do.

Up and Down Reach Practice

Make reaches to top and bottom rows without stopping to return to home keys.

4 fund face pony menu fume lump lung hymn muff erect
5 twice check human broad count voice lunch no brain
6 I continue to serve my country every chance I get.
7 You must understand that I expect you much sooner.

Alternate Hands Practice

Try to type short words as a whole instead of letter by letter. Think or say the word; type it.

8 to do the, to do that, to do the, to do work, goal
9 and the, and then, and this, and that, and did, so
10 It is his duty to do the work as well as possible.
11 Down the lane is an old office in which she works.

Corrective Practice

Lines 12–15 reinforce the locations of **o** and **i** so that errors in confusing these keys can be reduced.

12 oil into iron omit noise obvious involve inclusion
13 folio obtain occasion indication invoice imitation
14 Importing more oil is going to increase inflation.
15 We will obtain action tonight at the union office.

Alphabetic Paragraph

Take two or more 2-minute writings.

Goal: Speed–20 wpm
Error limit–5

To obtain your speed, divide the total number of words you typed by 2.

16   There   is   a   time   for   everything;   and   this   is   the   10
17 time   to   buy   a   new   car.   You   will   certainly   be   amazed   21
18 at   our   attractive   offer   on   your   present   car.   Just   31
19 examine   our   stock   of   new   models.   We   have   never   seen   41
20 their   equal.   We   look   forward   to   seeing   you.   SI 1.33   50

| 1 | 2 | 3 | 4 | 5 | 6 | 7 | 8 | 9 | 10 |

9 Our accident insurance policy costs you only 9½¢ a day. Isn't the protection it gives you well worth that amount? Read what Ms. Ellen Burgess writes: "I have received your check for $225 in payment of my claim on policy #4110. I certainly appreciate your prompt settlement."

14
28
42
56

10 ACKNOWLEDGMENTS: The picture on the cover, entitled "The Open Door," appears through the courtesy of White & Lyons Studios. The cartoon, "Good News," (page 69) is printed by special permission of the Women's Club. We are indebted to Mr. John O'Connor for the photographs on pages 28, 30, and 74.

12
25
39
52
59

11 The opening performance of Smoke Screens received favorable reviews (with one exception), and the star, Claudine O'Hare, was highly praised by all the critics. As a result, at seven o'clock last night, a Standing Room Only sign was posted at the box office.

18
32
51
60

12 Kearny & Bell, a manufacturer of children's sweaters, has rented 6,750 square feet of floor space (75 feet by 90 feet) on the 14th floor of the Lincoln Building, 2834 Clinton Street. They are paying a monthly rental of $3,375. The lease runs for five years, with the option of a five-year renewal.

14
29
43
58
60

13 On March 1, Cromwell & Company had on hand orders amounting to $68,000—40% more than a year ago—with prospects of an additional increase by April 1. Ms. Yates (in charge during Mr. Cromwell's absence) was very much pleased with the report.

13
39
53
61

14 A family group (husband, wife, and children under 18 years of age) can obtain a policy for $1,200 a year. The policy covers hospital bills of $200 a day per person, up to a maximum of 40 days a year. The Insurance Dealers' Association rates our company "AA—excellent." Write for additional information—you can't lose!

15
31
45
59
65

15 LISTEN BEFORE YOU DIAL. The old saying, "Look before you leap," might well be changed to "Listen before you dial." For with telephone lines crowded with calls—especially during business hours—you may have to wait a little longer than usual before you hear the steady hum-m-m of the dial tone—the signal that means, "You may now dial!"

12
25
39
52
65
67

16 The Lewis & Haley Toy Shop is conducting a word-building contest. The following sign is displayed in the window: "Prizes of $25, $15, and $10 to the girls or boys who prepare the longest lists of words, four letters or more, using the letters in Lewis Haley Toys. Come inside for a circular giving details."

15
29
44
65
68

Line spacing: single
Line length: 50
Paragraph indention: 5
Type each line twice.

Warmup

1 jets yet keg zoo been being veal vile pen park far
2 What size? Who came next? Did Fred quit quickly?
3 He can do the job, but he should go with them now.

    1   2   3   4   5   6   7   8   9   10

Margin Release and Double Spacing

To type beyond the point where the right margin locks, press the margin release key. This must be done each time the margin locks.
To double-space material (each typed line will have a blank line above and below), set the line-space regulator on 2.

Semi finger
or **A** finger [MAR REL]

Set line-space regulator on 2. Set a tab for paragraph indentions. Type lines 4–12 line for line. Each time the carriage locks, use the margin release key to complete the line. (Your copy will not have an even right margin.)

4   The next time our family goes camping, we will take our
5 new camper bus. It is a good way to relax. It is the most
6 versatile and comfortable vehicle ever made, as well as the
7 most civilized. You can quote me on that.
8   You can go anywhere in comfort. It has everything,
9 including the kitchen sink. In fact, it also has an icebox,
10 a water pump, closets, and a dining table, plus room enough
11 for beds for two adults and a child. It is quite an
12 enjoyable way to go on a carefree vacation.

Corrective Practice

Lines 13–17 reinforce the locations of **r** and **t** so that errors in confusing these keys can be reduced.

Goal: Try to type line 16 or 17 twice in 1 minute with not more than 2 errors.

13 rot tar rate tear rust trap rent later ratio water
14 trip rest hurt repeat trade report right term tree
15 great there third rebate tenure thereafter theater
16 Try to rotate tires at intervals for better tread.
17 The rate the rat traps were returned was terrible.

    1   2   3   4   5   6   7   8   9   10

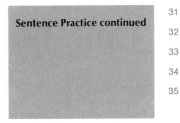

31	You have paid $450; the balance ($300) is due on September 18.	12
32	Bob's mark on his first test was 65%; his mark today was 79%.	24
33	We expect to leave at 8:45 a.m. and to return about 6:30 p.m.	36
34	Jeanne Landsman & Company has leased Rooms 127, 129, and 131.	48
35	A year's subscription to the magazine <u>Leisure Time</u> costs $8.	65

1 | 2 | 3 | 4 | 5 | 6 | 7 | 8 | 9 | 10 | 11 | 12 |

PARAGRAPH PRACTICE

Choose a paragraph that contains the number of words that you can type in either 1 or 2 minutes. Then practice that paragraph until you can type it at near your normal rate.

PARAGRAPH PRACTICE

Note that underscored words in these paragraphs have been given triple value in the word counts at the right.

70-space line.

1   James sang "Ol' Man River" in a deep, rich voice. In response to the   15
applause of the audience, he sang, as an encore, "When Twilight's Here"   29
(his own composition).   33

2   Instead of a #2½ can, the child brought home a #2 can of Hill's   14
tomatoes. She had bought it at the R & S Grocery and had paid 59¢ for   28
it, which was 10¢ more than the usual price.   37

3   The new Copeland set (model #16) is known as the "three-in-one"—   14
television, radio, and phonograph. We give a year's guarantee with each   28
set; a small sum purchases a second year's service insurance.   40

4   Here's a spray that's guaranteed to protect woolens against moths.   14
Buy <u>now</u>, before the moths do any damage. ANTIMOTH sells at 95¢ a   28
pint, $1.45 a quart, $4.35 a gallon. A special sprayer sells at 89¢.   42

5   The corporation's records show that 96% of its 58,000 shares are held   15
by stockholders with addresses in the United States and only 4% are held   29
by stockholders with addresses in foreign countries (chiefly England).   43

6   Colored bulbs for lamps are of three types: (1) natural colored glass,   15
(2) glass-coated outside, and (3) glass-coated or enameled inside. Bulbs   30
may be clear or frosted. Bulbs frosted on the inside absorb only 1% or 1½%   45
of the light.   48

7   The farmer ordered three #6 spades at $5.75 and a #41 hoe at $4.50.   14
He said, "I can use more tools than I can afford to buy. I'm hoping for a   29
sale in the spring (or possibly in the early summer) when I can buy at prices   44
that I can afford."   48

8   The Federal Power & Light Company plans to open another branch   13
office (their fourth) near Detroit, Michigan. They are at present looking   28
for suitable quarters. They require from 80,000 to 90,000 square feet of   43
floor space at a monthly rental of about $97,000.   53

Line spacing: single
Line length: 50
Paragraph indention: 5
Type each line twice.

Warmup

Strike the keys with a quick, light movement.

1 just equal; five copies; size six; too much ground

2 night flight bright quaint acquaint joke woke yoke

3 Mr. Foy; above zero; below zero; tax expert; What?

    1   2   3   4   5   6   7   8   9   10

New Key Location

The hyphen is used to connect parts of a compound word, like *up-to-date*, and to divide a word at the end of a line. (Word division is explained in Unit 39.)
Two hyphens typed in succession are used to make a dash. Leave no space before, between, or after typing hyphens.

Semi finger

4 ;-; ;-; a self-made man; fifty-two weeks in a year

5 ;--; ;--; a set-back--no defeat; strike three--out

6 Mrs. Day needs twenty-one change-of-address cards.

7 I hate to ask--you know me--but we need your help.

8 Pins, needles, thread--the store has many notions.

9 Her son-in-law had the right-of-way on the street.

10 We gave that know-it-all a good send-off Saturday.

Up and Down Reach Practice

11 opener opener music music curb curb once once much

12 expect expect noisy noisy cent cent verb verb debt

13 In May the fare was raised from five cents to ten.

14 Tommy expects to travel to France and Switzerland.

Corrective Practice

Lines 15–18 reinforce the locations of **m** and **n** so that errors in confusing these keys can be reduced.

15 men men mine mine minor minor mind mind manner man

16 money money numbers numbers manage manager mariner

17 For a nominal sum, we can maintain numerous names.

18 Many minors are mailing money to merchant marines.

Group 4 NUMBERS AND SPECIAL CHARACTERS

SENTENCE PRACTICE

To overcome hesitation in typing numbers and special characters, practice these sentences a few minutes each day. Note that some symbols that would ordinarily be spelled out as words, appear as symbols here in order to provide practice on those keys.

SENTENCE PRACTICE

Note that underscored words in these sentences have been given triple value in the word counts at the right.

65-space line.

#		
1	The MORGAN SCHOOL admits children from 3½ to 12 years of age.	12
2	Boys and girls (10 to 14) are admitted—annual tuition, $825.	24
3	Dr. Sumner treated the semiconscious woman at Kramer's store.	36
4	The committee from Local #92 met with the mayor at 9 o'clock.	48
5	What a relief to hear the announcement: "Meeting adjourned!"	60
6	Thomas R. O'Neill (1875–1947) is the author of A Winter's End.	17
7	Pamphlet #1026 contains 39 pages of Mrs. Janus' prize recipes.	29
8	Mr. Horn's exhibit of 19th-century prints will open on June 6.	41
9	Dickens' BLEAK HOUSE will play at the Star Theater July 11–19.	53
10	The committee's report was called "Vocational Training Today."	65
11	"How can they say such a thing!" exclaimed Randolph indignantly.	15
12	Stoner & Co. allows a 10% discount on bills paid within 30 days.	28
13	In a two-year period, shipments increased from 89 to 4760 tons.	41
14	The Thrift Club's motto was: "A penny saved is a penny earned."	54
15	John's address is Room 108, Hotel Clayton, 293 West 45th Street.	67
16	Hill & Co. called bonds #841 to #940 inclusive for redemption.	12
17	Only 1.06% of those who had been inoculated had flu that year!	24
18	The news bulletin (an AP dispatch) was broadcast at 10:45 p.m.	36
19	"My best offer is $3.75 a yard—that's final!" said the buyer.	50
20	Swan & Bergere offers solid investments yielding 7½% interest.	62
21	Mr. Webb paid $1,250 for an Oriental rug measuring 7 by 9 feet.	13
22	At yesterday's hearing, the prisoner cried: "I am not guilty!"	29
23	Their hourly rate of pay ($5.85) is 18½¢ more than last year's.	41
24	The bank's slogan was: "Save now so that you may spend later."	54
25	The first prize (a $75 bond) was awarded to a 26-year-old woman.	67
26	Our net profit this year is 20% less than in 1978, our best year.	13
27	The steamship East Lynn, which sailed on May 9, is due on May 24.	29
28	Today's cash surrender value of insurance policy #9146 is $9,750.	42
29	The art book (a new edition in 18 chapters) is very well 'written.	55
30	We offer a prize of $50 for the best poem entitled "Happy Homes."	68

1 | 2 | 3 | 4 | 5 | 6 | 7 | 8 | 9 | 10 | 11 | 12 | 13 |

Typing Skill Checkup

Take two or more
2-minute writings.

Goal: Speed–21 wpm
Error limit–5

To obtain your speed,
divide the total number
of words you typed by 2.

```
19     As a young worker, you will be trading your      10
20  time and energy and skills for wages--for money.     19
21  Working is really your way of paying the employer    29
22  for all the wages he pays you.                       35
23     Wages help determine the place you live, the      45
    clothes you wear, and the food you eat.    SI 1.30   53
     1│   2│   3│   4│   5│   6│   7│   8│   9│  10│
```

SKILL DEVELOPMENT   # Unit 19

Line spacing: single
Line length: 50
Paragraph indention: 5

Warmup

Type each line twice and
double-space after each
pair of lines.

```
1  ice ice run run curb curb zinc zinc next next much
2  They will deny; care-free week; seven-page article
3  Is my service satisfactory?  Yes, it is excellent.
    1│   2│   3│   4│   5│   6│   7│   8│   9│  10│
```

Typing from Script Practice

Set margins for a 40-space
line.

4 *I must pack all the clothes in my trunk.*
5 *In April the fare was raised five cents.*
6 *He expects to travel to Spain and Italy.*

Speed Paragraphs

Use these paragraphs for
1- and 2-minute writings.

Push for a new level of
speed by applying the
proper typing techniques
learned in earlier units.

```
1     Here are a few hints on the use of the phone     10
   when customers call.  Answer the call at once and   20
   start by giving the name of your company.  In this  30
   way you save time.                        SI 1.18   33
2     Always use a pleasant tone of voice.  Speak      10
   clearly, so that whoever is at the other end can    19
    1│   2│   3│   4│   5│   6│   7│   8│   9│  10│
```

(Continued on next page)

MOVING FROM BANK TO BANK

In this drill, you will get additional practice in making long reaches. Reach from the first to the third bank of keys, and from the third to the first, without stopping to return to the home keys.

1 my fun face pony menu fume lump lung hymn muff erect thumb break 13
2 twice check human broad count voice lunch brain pound broil round 26
3 brick elect price under since brush bring humor found bread uncle 39
4 enemy force place sound clung brass piece doubt music ounce amuse 52
5 forbid chance harbor Sunday record junior affect mutual numeral 65

6 amount barber branch immune hunger recent advice murmur central 13
7 recent lumber sprung ground tumble select autumn success account 26
8 receive breathe laundry science mystery counsel subject brought 39
9 economy certain observe brother connect balance perfect country 52
10 service advance destiny maximum because harmony precede proceed 65

11 We expect to continue manufacturing brass plumbing until August. 13
12 We have recently had an opportunity to effect certain economies. 26
13 I assume that you will respect my advice and check the account. 39

14 I remained at the office until six trying to balance the account. 13
15 I found it necessary to obtain insurance on my new car at once. 26
16 No doubt your brother will volunteer to connect our large radio. 39
17 Under the circumstances, this place will serve as my art studio. 52

18 The sound of the tuning of the musical instruments was annoying. 13
19 My uncle expects to succeed in paying off the debt by December. 26
20 They have recently had great success by using a special process. 39
21 Unless we deny the rumor at once, it is certain to affect prices. 52
22 We shall continue to serve our government at every opportunity. 65

23 The office manager found that a number of changes were necessary. 13
24 The laundry announced a slight reduction in price for the summer. 26
25 You must understand that they expect all of you to be punctual. 39
26 My brother and I spent all last summer on a farm in the country. 52
27 Since you have brought up the subject, you must face the truth. 65
28 We have found the lumber we received yesterday of poor quality. 78

29 The balance of his account shows he is too heavily in debt to us. 13
30 The junior partner told the clerk to issue a summons immediately. 26
31 I have no doubt that she will object to the amount of the bill. 39
32 With our new process, we can produce a hundred copies a minute. 52
33 I have found a great difference in the number of copies produced. 65
34 I have checked my count twice, and my answer is certainly correct. 78

1 | 2 | 3 | 4 | 5 | 6 | 7 | 8 | 9 | 10 | 11 | 12 | 13 |

understand what you are saying. When the person   29
who is wanted is not in, offer to take a message.   39

SI 1.35

3   If you are able to take care of a matter, do   10
it yourself. Be brief and clear. When the other   20
person talks on and on, try to find your chance to 30
bring the talk to an end without being too abrupt. 40
End on a cordial note, so as to leave a friendly   49
impression.

SI 1.23 51

4   All of our employees must stamp a time clock   10
when they arrive in the morning and when they go   19
at the close of the day. In this way, we have a   29
record of the number of days and hours each worker 39
has worked. We need this record when we make up   49
our payroll at the end of the week.

SI 1.15 56

Eyes on copy!

5   If you are a good typist, you can always be   10
sure of finding work. There is a great demand for 20
good typists in the business office. You may not   29
use your typing skill for a long time; but once it 39
is learned, you can easily regain your speed. It   49
will then be a simple matter for you to get a job   59
you want.

SI 1.19 61

    1| 2| 3| 4| 5| 6| 7| 8| 9| 10|

SKILL DEVELOPMENT   # Unit 20

Line spacing: single
Line length: 50
Paragraph indention: 5

Warmup

Type each line twice.

1 sun sun any any verb verb seize seize yield yields
2 full-time workers; part-time work; Is he a member?
3 What is the amount of discount on the list prices?

    1| 2| 3| 4| 5| 6| 7| 8| 9| 10|

ALTERNATING HAND WORDS

In this drill, each word contains letters typed by alternating hands. This arrangement of letters permits you to type faster than your normal rate. Use this drill whenever you have reached a barrier in your speed and cannot break into new, higher levels.

ALTERNATING HAND WORDS
65-space line.

1 and big man for end pay six air own cut sir the may but sit did 13
2 girl work make turn coal name them such hand duty when down paid 26
3 than both pair town sign land firm with half city goal also held 39
4 corn dish rich hang lake melt ivory eight shake panel shelf field 52
5 right usual spend laugh world slept quake chair shape panel fight 65
6 their sight rifle slant burns civic bushel chapel embody formal 78
7 social handle dismay quench sleigh profit enamel island emblems 91
8 visual penalty auditor problems entitle ancient memento signals 104
9 quantity neighbor chairman ornament busybody amendment proficient 117

1 | 2 | 3 | 4 | 5 | 6 | 7 | 8 | 9 | 10 | 11 | 12 | 13 |

DOUBLE LETTERS

When you strike the same key twice in succession, use equal force each time. To do this, be sure that you release the key before making the second stroke.

DOUBLE LETTERS
65-space line.

1   good beef deep roof cool miss wood ebbs need soon adds door odds 13
2   steep annul cheer feels fully alley annex spool apply berry stood 26
3   sweep allow tooth arrow essay utter troop error asset flood witty 39
4   steel annoy bloom offer added broom carry ditto upper occur funny 52
5   follow common manner supply horror matter appeal errand assistant 65
6   accept afford beggar teller winner ballot effect alleged borrower 78
7   little coffee summer occupy lesson vacuum cotton piazza attentive 91

8   accent canned affair differ dagger sullen effort wallet schooling 13
9   attack attach appear barrel tissue assert arrive attend excessive 26
10 bazaar robber stucco sudden suffer access esteem waffle illogical 39
11 rubbing succeed account address fifteen taffeta suggest trolley 52
12 baggage swallow million ammonia current vanilla suppose appoint 65
13 collect stammer shipped support command channel apparel connect 78
14 approve correct dresser affects planned battery possess proceed 91

15 terrible assemble allotted tomorrow dissolve blizzard occasional 13
16 announce applause surround opposite pressure currency procession 26
17 accuracy struggle alliance commerce druggist collapse biannually 39
18 different efficient aggravate beginning immediately surrendered 52
19 dismissal committee necessary attribute accommodate predecessor 65
20 supplement correspond expression accumulate remittance bookkeeper 78
21 abbreviate commission disappoint appreciate difficulty challenged 91

1 | 2 | 3 | 4 | 5 | 6 | 7 | 8 | 9 | 10 | 11 | 12 | 13 |

Typing from Script Practice

Use a 40-space line for lines 4, 5, and 6.

4 *We organized committees to represent all.*

5 *Barbara made a brief but adequate reply.*

6 *I am paid in full; I expect delivery now.*

Alphabetic Paragraphs

Use these paragraphs for 1- and 2-minute writings.

Concentrate on the reaches that are difficult for you.

1   Have you a picture you would like us to take   10
and exhibit in our gallery of modern art? We try   20
to invite only artists whose work is recognized by 30
well-known judges of art as superior in quality.   39
SI 1.45

2   Here at Green Meadow Inn, vacation dreams do   10
come true. If you want relaxation, you may enjoy   20
quiet, lazy hours stretched out beneath big sunny   29
skies. If you prefer activity, you may prefer to   39
swim, fish, or play tennis and golf.   SI 1.41 46

3   Pay all your bills with a personalized check.   10
Our special checking account saves you time and a   20
lot of money. You receive a monthly statement of   30
deposits and withdrawals. Your canceled checks   39
are a record of your major expenses.   SI 1.49 46

4   All authorized employees of our company must   10
carry a card showing their name and their picture. 20
We expect them to show this card upon request. We 30
are justified in refusing to admit persons who say 40
they work for us but will not identify themselves. 50
SI 1.50

Return the carriage rapidly without looking up.

5   On this, our fiftieth anniversary as a large   10
organization, we wish to express our thanks to the 20
many good friends who patronize our service. We   29
hope you will join us in celebrating this event on 39
next Saturday. We shall be happy to mail you two   49
tickets upon your request.   SI 1.51 54

   1 | 2 | 3 | 4 | 5 | 6 | 7 | 8 | 9 | 10 |

Letter Y

1   any why boy only play body story party young system employ beyond   13

2   They always carry completely equipped bags of the best quality.   13

3   I have really not yet had an opportunity to pay you the money.   12

4   Early in the day, he is generally busy getting the mail ready.   12

5   Every time you give us an order, you are in a hurry for delivery.   13

6   We have a supply of gray yarn at the factory ready for delivery.   13

7   We are very sorry it is necessary to reduce your supply of coal.   13

8   The youthful style of this dress is typical of the stock we buy.   13

9   Everybody is fully aware of the necessity of an early delivery.   13

10   The lawyer says he does not yet know why you had to pay so much.   13

Letter Z

1   zone size dozen seize prize razor hazard realize citizen organize   13

2   We realize that they were not authorized to seize the property.   13

3   The organization offered a dozen prizes for the best suggestions.   13

4   We must familiarize the public with the two sizes of our razors.   13

5   We recognize the great power of an organization of this size.   12

6   The citizens were puzzled by his zeal and amazed at his energy.   13

7   The authorized agents in this zone sold dozens of these razors.   13

8   We realize the size is wrong, but we are puzzled about the error.   13

9   An organization of this size must systematize all its records.   12

10   The citizens asked the officials to recognize their organization.   13

    1 | 2 | 3 | 4 | 5 | 6 | 7 | 8 | 9 | 10 | 11 | 12 | 13 |

LEFT- AND RIGHT-HAND WORDS

Each word in this drill is made up of letters typed entirely by either the left hand or the right hand. Left-hand and right-hand words alternate. Use this drill to strengthen fingers of each hand.

LEFT-HAND AND RIGHT-HAND WORDS
65-space line.

1   red you war him tax ill set lip bad oil get joy was pin are mop   13

2   safe look case noon rest upon were pull grew kill best lion read   26

3   text July rate milk dear only feet join date lump fact link card   39

4   poppy trade imply state onion serve pupil exact union brave hilly   52

5   regret million exceeded opinion career minimum addressed monopoly   65

6   plump estate uphill baggage poplin steadfast pumpkin afterwards   78

    1 | 2 | 3 | 4 | 5 | 6 | 7 | 8 | 9 | 10 | 11 | 12 | 13 |

Unit 21

Line spacing: single
Line length: 60
Paragraph indention: 5
Type each line twice.

Warmup

Start using a 60-space line: 20–85 (elite), 12–77 (pica).

1 middle–aged, forget–me–not, first–class, up–to–date check–up
2 How quickly were the jackets sent? We shipped them express.
3 Jose––and three men––did not see Van at the end of the path.

　1　2　3　4　5　6　7　8　9　10　11　12

New Key Location

A finger　**1**

If your machine has no **1** key, use the small **l**.

4 aqa aqa aqa aql aql aql ala ala ala alla alla alla
5 zone 1, 1 television, 1 jet plane, 1 taxi, 1 quart
6 The sheik has 11 wives, and 11 planes and 11 cars.

F finger　**4**

7 frf frf frf fr4 fr4 fr4 f4f f4f f4f f44f f44f f44f
8 area 4, 4–point grade average, 4 players, 4 houses
9 Mabel is 4 years of age. Her brother Frank is 14.

Number Practice

Hold your hands directly over the home keys; avoid slanting your fingers.

10 1 and 4; 4 and 11; 14 and 1; 1 and 14; 114 and 1; 1 and 114;
11 These 114 men won 144 prizes in five days in the 11th month.
12 I need 11 or 44 blue, 4 or 14 white, 141 or 414 red, 4 pink.

Corrective Practice

Lines 13–16 reinforce the locations of **a** and **s** so that errors in confusing these keys can be reduced.

13 as safe said seal soap ages scale shape staff state assassin
14 stake areas arise swear space spare speak small smash arrest
15 atlas answer assure standards special adjust surpass assault
16 After the assault, an assassin was arrested by small squads.

Alphabetic Paragraph

Take two or more 1-minute writings.

Goal: Speed–23 wpm
Error limit–2

　　　Are you looking for a luxury apartment? If so, apply to 12
our authorized agency. The homes we offer, equipped with the 24
best modern improvements, are just what you will like.　SI 1.50　35

　1　2　3　4　5　6　7　8　9　10　11　12

Letter V

1 even very have move drive voice leave every serve provide improve   13

2 We see your point of view and shall be governed by your advice.   13
3 Whenever it is to our advantage to leave, we will move to Denver.   13
4 On several occasions, we have been able to give you this service.   13

5 We believe, moreover, that we can save several hundred dollars.   13
6 We take advantage of every opportunity to improve our service.   12
7 My visit to the governor evidently proved to be a very good move.   13

8 We advise you to give us an order for our new improved varnish.   13
9 We believe you must have received delivery early in November.   12
10 We have, however, investigated their service very carefully.   12

Letter W

1 low own way away view wish power owing where toward follow window   13

2 We know who wrote the letter, and we will answer the complaint.   13
3 A few of the workers went away without waiting for an interview.   13
4 It would be well worth our while to watch them work tomorrow.   12

5 The lawyer wants to know how much power is wasted in this way.   12
6 We know that we owe you the money, but you must wait awhile.   12
7 We would be willing to make an allowance on the damaged pillows.   13

8 Within the next two weeks, we will install a powerful new motor.   13
9 Deposits which are made now will draw interest at seven percent.   13
10 While you were away last week, I did whatever work was necessary.   13

Letter X

1 tax six box next exit exist exact exert extra mixed luxury except   13

2 We expect to send six boxes of canned goods by express next week.   13
3 He explained that he wished to exchange the sixty wax candles.   12
4 She examined the electric fixtures on display at the exposition.   13

5 We ordered textbooks containing the maximum number of exercises.   13
6 Next week we shall begin recording extra charges on index cards.   13
7 She expressed the opinion that we should expand our export market.   13

8 The expert explained that expensive luxuries were subject to tax.   13
9 We expect to be extremely busy with income tax reports next week.   13
10 The extra fixtures were forwarded by express in two large boxes.   13

1 2 3 4 5 6 7 8 9 10 11 12 13

Unit 22

Line spacing: single
Line length: 60
Paragraph indention: 5
Type each line twice.

Warmup

Use firm, sharp, brisk strokes.

1 enjoy enjoys enjoyed; quick quickly; offices official; saves
2 expect expert express; seize prizes realizes; sack Jack back
3 He applied 4 times--in 14 days. Give him 1 day and 4 hours.

|1 |2 |3 |4 |5 |6 |7 |8 |9 |10 |11 |12 |

New Key Location

F finger **5**

4 ftf ftf ft5f ft5f ft5f ft5f f5f f5f f55f f55f f55f
5 Code 5, 5 slips, 5 men, 5 dollars, 5 boys, 5 girls
6 He lives at 5 Park Avenue and works 5 blocks away.

K finger **8**

7 kik kik ki8k ki8k ki8k ki8k k8k k8k k88k k88k k88k
8 8 seconds 8 minutes 8 hours 8 days 8 weeks 8 years
9 An airplane flew the route in 8 hours, 18 minutes.

Number Practice

10 1 and 4; 5 and 8; 14 and 55; 11 and 4; 15 and 88; 15 and 18;
11 On May 5, the 18 women boarded Flight 85 and flew 584 miles.
12 The 15 boys and 8 girls had a picnic at a park 8 miles away.

Corrective Practice

Lines 13–16 reinforce the locations of **e** and **i** so that errors in confusing these keys can be reduced.

13 tie lie ice edit emit irate edible either elicit ignite nice
14 indeed earlier easiest eligible eminent engineer inefficient
15 Efficient service and delicious food are our chief concerns.
16 The eminent engineers said that the evidence was sufficient.

Alphabetic Paragraph

Take two or more 1-minute writings.

Goal: Speed–23 wpm
Error limit–2.

17   Wreckers will attack an abandoned building at 58 Smythe 12
18 Street next Friday. A wrecking company at 814 Wharton Place 24
19 has just received a permit to raze the property. SI 1.50 34

|1 |2 |3 |4 |5 |6 |7 |8 |9 |10 |11 |12 |

Letter S

1   was his set also last wise sweet start trust person answer custom   13

2   I must express my personal disapproval of his course of action.   13
3   First consider the cost before starting to act on her suggestion.   13
4   It is impossible to please this customer; he refuses to listen.   13

5   The advertisement in the last issue caused a sharp rise in sales.   13
6   This store sells shoes, slippers, and socks at reasonable prices.   13
7   Perhaps he considers it advisable to ship these goods by express.   13

8   I assure you that the suggestion is the subject of careful study.   13
9   For several reasons we suspect his answer is not an honest one.   13
10   We wish you would test our service to see how satisfactory it is.   13

Letter T

1   put get art list both test built doubt after health commit better   13

2   It is about time for you to stop trying to control every detail.   13
3   I doubt whether conditions will be any better in the near future.   13
4   Thank you for taking the trouble to investigate the situation.   12

5   The president thought their objections were of little importance.   13
6   After missing the train, they returned from the station together.   13
7   In order not to waste time, ship twenty additional bolts at once.   13

8   If it is not too much trouble, please wait until next Tuesday.   12
9   We operate the factory at great cost and with many difficulties.   13
10   Part of the time was spent in pointing out the faults in style.   13

Letter U

1   out cut buy much your upon about trust usual summer bought future   13

2   Unless your products improve, we must close our account with you.   13
3   Under the circumstances, you should have no serious difficulty.   13
4   He thought that you do not carry enough insurance on your house.   13

5   You will be surprised to see how much better our results are now.   13
6   Unless you have a discount card, we must charge our usual price.   13
7   Let us support the young folk in their drive for a building fund.   13

8   We trust that you can furnish us with double the number of tubes.   13
9   During the summer, we usually offer wonderful values in furs.   12
10   The usual business circular could be drawn up in about an hour.   13

1   2   3   4   5   6   7   8   9   10   11   12   13

Unit 23

Line spacing: single
Line length: 60
Paragraph indention: 5
Type each line twice.

Warmup

Use a sharp, bounce-off stroke on the space bar.

1 banks rank; nests jest quest; size prizes; carry marry Jerry
2 If they flee to prevent the exams, she may go to Washington.
3 48 kilograms, 15 grams, 85 liters, 41 centimeters, 58 quarts

   1   2   3   4   5   6   7   8   9   10   11   12

Margin Release Key Practice

Before typing lines 4–7 change the margin settings for a 50-space line. Use the margin release to complete each line.

4 Under the circumstances, this place will serve as my studio.
5 The office manager found a number of changes were necessary.
6 My brother and I spent last summer on a farm in the country.
7 Tom realized very quickly that jumping was excellent for us.

Tabulator Key Practice

	Left margin 30	First tab 45	Second tab 60
8	bad	worse	worst
9	good	better	best
10	much	more	most
11	little	less	least

Clear previous tabs. Set left margin at 30 and tab stops at 45 and 60. Type **across** rows 8–11, not down the columns.

Number Practice

Did you remember to reset your margins for a 60-space line?

12 He assigned us pages 8 and 15 in our math book for homework.
13 She scored 48 and 55 on the seventh series of English tests.
14 He made 8 home runs in 14 different games during the season.
15 See page 14 in Pamphlet 18 for old—but less costly—models.

Alphabetic Paragraph

Take two or more 2-minute writings.

Goal: Speed–23 wpm
Error limit–4

16   When you are in Europe, make sure you visit Switzerland, 12
17 famous for its majestic snow-clad mountains. Our agency will 24
18 provide up-to-date, luxurious quarters, with the skill born 36
19 of experience. When you travel on Sky-Line Airways, you will 48
20 enjoy both safety and comfort. We have never had an accident. 61

SI 1.50

   1   2   3   4   5   6   7   8   9   10   11   12

Letter P

1 pay cap lip deep hope open place cheap speak employ report people 13

2 What we plan to do depends on what happens at the open meeting. 13
3 These samples represent only part of our complete line of paints. 13
4 The present policy of the company prevents our accepting returns. 13

5 We expect a special shipment of paper the latter part of April. 13
6 Our shop hopes to supply superior products at popular prices. 12
7 Our report on the property is based on the opinion of our expert. 13

8 We expect prompt payment for purchases when bills are presented. 13
9 We simply cannot depend on a cheap product to serve our purpose. 13
10 They probably plan to put these imported platters on special sale. 13

Letter Q

1 quite quote equal quick equip liquid inquire frequent acquainted 13

2 I question whether it is worth quoting on so small a quantity. 12
3 Consequently, we requested a large quantity of new equipment. 12
4 A quart of the liquid is required to wax the equipment properly. 13

5 We frequently find it necessary to submit quotations quickly. 12
6 An inquiry into her qualifications proved her equal to the task. 13
7 He inquired about the quantity and the quality of the stock. 12

8 In consequence, we can quote values you cannot equal anywhere. 12
9 We frequently require several months to get adequate equipment. 13
10 Six and a quarter yards are not quite adequate for the quilt. 12

Letter R

1 air are nor care part burn cover front large direct master rather 13

2 The experiment proves that direct advertising is worth the cost. 13
3 Whenever there is serious trouble, they try to win our support. 13
4 We cannot grant further credit before you pay the previous bill. 13

5 Certainly our course is clear; we must look for other markets. 12
6 Unless we approve his report, the treasurer will surely resign. 13
7 Our ready-to-wear winter dresses have been reduced for clearance. 13

8 In March we distributed samples of our product from door to door. 13
9 Under the circumstances, we regret we cannot accept your order. 13
10 As a rule, we try not to censor articles appearing in our paper. 13

1 2 3 4 5 6 7 8 9 10 11 12 13

Unit 24

Line spacing: single
Line length: 60
Paragraph indention: 5
Type each line twice.

Warmup

1 tax, lax, axes, vex, exists, zeal, zone, zero, zinc, buzzard

2 Math is fun——4 and 4 is 8; 5 less 1 is 4; and 8 less 4 is 4.

3 What did Mr. Gant say? He said he will consider my request.

4 Jorge and Bob did not get their pay for walking off the job.

| 1 | 2 | 3 | 4 | 5 | 6 | 7 | 8 | 9 | 10 | 11 | 12 |

Alternate Hands Sentence Practice

To develop speed, type smoothly and continuously.

5 She is busy with her work, but is to go to town for the bow.

6 His wish is to go to the city to talk to the man about gold.

7 He may wish to bus them if and when they go to work for her.

Alphabetic Sentence Practice

Goal: To type lines 8–10 with no more than 2 errors.

8 Yesterday, Jo quietly picked six zippers from the woven bag.

9 Please pack my boxes with five dozen jugs of liquid varnish.

10 Jack Farming realized the big, yellow quilts were expensive.

Number Practice

11 1 and 4; 51 and 8; 11 and 4 and 5; 48 and 1; 15 and 8; 4 and

12 a house 15 years old; less than 48 hours; 45 gallons of milk

13 They ordered 18 quilts, but they liked only the 5 blue ones.

14 The accident occurred on July 18. He returned on August 14.

15 Our bill dated November 5 covered your purchase of 48 cases.

Typing Skill Checkup

Take a 2-minute writing on lines 16–21. If you make 4 errors or less, practice lines 5–7. If you make more than 4 errors, practice lines 8–10. Then take two more 2-minute writings. Compare with the first timing.

Goal: Speed—24 wpm
Error limit—4

16   Office jobs are found everywhere—not just downtown in 12

17 cities and towns, but in the country, too. Every business— 24

18 no matter whether it is in the city or whether it is in the 36

19 country—needs office workers. 42

20   And when you are looking for a job, do not skip any place 54

21 because it does not seem like an ordinary business.   SI 1.36 64

| 1 | 2 | 3 | 4 | 5 | 6 | 7 | 8 | 9 | 10 | 11 | 12 |

Letter M

1   met arm rim firm time warm admit limit mimic moment number common   13

2   I remember many remarks he made that seemed strange at the time.   13
3   It is important to have most of the motors completed by tomorrow.   13
4   We may, for example, employ more people in autumn than in summer.   13

5   The company has adopted a modern, improved method of manufacture.   13
6   You must take as much time as you need to match the material.   12
7   Inform him that the men will meet me at the same time tomorrow.   13

8   It may be as much as a month or more before we hear from them.   12
9   Remember that our firm will meet a great deal of competition.   12
10   I recommend this as a modern home, with a good plumbing system.   13

Letter N

1   man not win mean sign turn learn round train within reason nation   13

2   It is my opinion that we need not be concerned about competition.   13
3   Your answers to our questions were neither frank nor friendly.   12
4   Since the situation has changed, I want to reconsider the plan.   13

5   I cannot understand why he did not engage in that discussion.   12
6   It is now nearly a month since we sent the prints on approval.   12
7   The president did not know that the money had been spent.   11

8   Many men have obtained personal or business loans at this bank.   13
9   Kindly notify them that I cannot obtain the information sooner.   13
10   The purchase of savings bonds is a sound financial investment.   12

Letter O

1   for you too work stop move motor short could ought profit dollar   13

2   The road to town has been closed on account of flood conditions.   13
3   Only this afternoon I discovered another error in your accounts.   13
4   I doubt whether the property would altogether suit your purpose.   13

5   We shall, of course, continue to employ some people all year round.   13
6   If you cooperate, we can dispose of our old stock without loss.   12
7   Everyone knows that the spot remover we recommend is a good one.   13

8   You acknowledge that you owe the amount shown on the invoice.   12
9   You owe it to yourself to take advantage of this opportunity.   12
10   Our colored cotton is sold at notion counters in most stores.   12

1   2   3   4   5   6   7   8   9   10   11   12   13

Unit 25

Line spacing: single
Line length: 60
Paragraph indention: 5
Type each line twice.

Warmup

Return the carriage without looking up.

1 box boxes; size sizes; dozen dozens; checks checked; wrecked
2 These 154 new fliers flew 58 planes at the 18th annual show.
3 The man cut up the six gray furs just the way you had asked.

    1| 2| 3| 4| 5| 6| 7| 8| 9| 10| 11| 12|

New Key Location

L finger **9**

4 lol lol lol lo9 lo9 lo9 191 191 191 1.19 1.19 1.19
5 9 cents; 9 nickels; 9 dimes; 9 quarters; 9 dollars
6 All of the meetings will be held on July 19, 1991.

Semi finger **0**

7 ;p; ;p; ;p; ;p0 ;p0 ;p0 ;0; ;0; ;0; ;00; ;00; ;00;
8 10 whites 40 blues 50 greens 80 browns 100 oranges
9 After 50 men gave 100 talks in 90 days, they quit.

Number Practice

Be careful of slanting reaches.

10 10 and 40; 50 and 80; 90 and 100; 10 and 80; 40 and 50 and 9
11 The skillful athletes lost only 15 of their 94 tennis games.
12 The 18 students drove 549 miles in one day and 498 the next.

Skill Building

wpm twice in 30 sec.

Use lines 13–20 for 30-second writings to develop speed. Select the line you feel you can complete twice in 30 seconds. If you type it more than twice, select a longer line on the next try. If you do not complete the selected line twice, pick a shorter line. Continue this procedure on successive tries.

13 I wish to burn it down.   18
14 Wrap these for the women.   20
15 Get the right form to sign.   22
16 When both men land, we may go.   24
17 The bank ought to use a new form.   26
18 The man made a big hit in the city.   28
19 They will go there today if they can.   30
20 It is their duty to do this work for me. 32

    1| 2| 3| 4| 5| 6| 7| 8|

Letter J

1 joy job jar just jump join judge major juice object junior injury   13

2 The majority of the men have no objection to joining the group.   13
3 The judge instructed the jury to deal justly with both parties.   13
4 On account of this prejudice, he misjudged the junior partner.   12

5 He rejected the offer of an adjustment for personal injuries.   12
6 The major object of the demonstration is to combat prejudice.   12
7 Subject to her approval, I will pay interest in January and July.   13

8 These jars contain jams and jellies judged worthy of prizes.   12
9 He jumped and struck his hand, injuring the joint of his finger.   13
10 The junior class joined us to celebrate this joyous jubilee.   12

Letter K

1 ask sky oak book knew week black drink check market thanks remark   13

2 He knew the background of the kind of people to whom he spoke.   12
3 The sick man was too weak to take anything but a drink of tea.   12
4 I will not keep the blankets, as there is no market for them now.   13

5 She would like us to make another attempt to take stock next week.   13
6 We know that our stock of cookbooks will be sold within a week.   13
7 First, I should like to thank the speaker for her kind remarks.   13

8 Kindly ask the clerk whether this skirt material will wrinkle.   12
9 The driver of the truck was asked to take the milk to market.   12
10 I shall go back to the bank at two o'clock to make a deposit.   12

Letter L

1 law fly let rule talk will while until value follow public simple   13

2 We told you it would be difficult to sell the lot at full price.   13
3 We should all be capable of living together in a friendly world.   13
4 The doctor told Len he could get well and live to be an old man.   13

5 It is likely that the usual quality will no longer be available.   13
6 It finally developed that the buildings were sold to a realtor.   13
7 The delicious flavor of our apple jelly appeals to all children.   13

8 Let me call Nell on the telephone and tell her about the deal.   12
9 We will not offer it for sale unless the quality is excellent.   12
10 We cannot possibly deliver the coal until early in the fall.   12

1   2   3   4   5   6   7   8   9   10   11   12   13

Unit 26

Line spacing: single
Line length: 60
Paragraph indention: 5
Type each line twice.

Warmup

Strike each key with equal force.

1 view reviews reviewed; acquit acquires acquaint; lacks likes
2 pay way—next text—daze haze graze—juice June—sings swing
3 The first 89 people received 89 prizes at the 140th meeting.
4 Who is Gale Perog? Who is Aimee Robbuff? Are they seniors?

  1   2   3   4   5   6   7   8   9   10   11   12

New Key Location

S finger   **2**

5 sws sws sws sw2 sw2 sw2 s2s s2s s2s s22s s22s s22s
6 2 cows 2 pigs 2 dogs 2 cats 2 sheep 2 bats 2 birds
7 Today 12 boys and 2 girls won prizes in 22 events.

J finger   **7**

8 juj juj juj ju7 ju7 ju7 j7j j7j j7j j77j j77j j77j
9 7 towns 7 cities 7 counties 7 countries 7 planets;
10 In 1987, 7 astronauts may travel 77 million miles.

Number Practice

11 1 and 2; 4 and 5; 7 and 8; 9 and 10; 7 and 2; 5 and 7 and 12
12 Ship it March 27 to 72 West Kinney Street, Newark, NJ 07102.
13 Please check the orders numbered 127–172, as well as 90–101.
14 Change the address from 75 Huron Street to 987 River Street.
15 His committee will meet on Thursday, August 14, in Room 180.

Corrective Practice

Lines 16–19 reinforce the locations of **s** and **d.**

16 sad dash sand skid dust suds sedan reside salad seduce squid
17 seldom sledge smudge soldier solid speed daisy debris design
18 Sidney should send the dress goods to the designers Tuesday.
19 The slender sardine looks delicious with the salad and soda.

  1   2   3   4   5   6   7   8   9   10   11   12

Letter G

1 big ago get sign gave page large again begin danger figure regret 13

2 The engineer regarded crossing the bridge as far too dangerous. 13
3 We ought to begin making arrangements for our regular meeting. 12
4 During the morning, they agreed among themselves to charge less. 13

5 The judge thought that the paper ought to be signed that night. 13
6 We generally get a great many packages that contain glassware. 12
7 The eggs are packed in large cartons for shipping to groceries. 13

8 I shall be glad to go again, as the house shows signs of neglect. 13
9 We thought that the girls might get along very well together. 12
10 The messenger gave both packages to a guard, who signed for them. 13

Letter H

1 who had why help both show happy which north method should though 13

2 When the weather permits, the ship will sail to the north shore. 13
3 Though he saw how the accident happened, he did not wish to sign. 13
4 I should be happy to help him, but I do not have the right size. 13

5 We happen to have on hand a hundred reams of heavy white paper. 13
6 These three boxes should be sent to the branch office by freight. 13
7 Each of these machines is worth more than a thousand dollars. 12

8 They themselves wish him to investigate the theft thoroughly. 12
9 Neither of these chairs is worth as much as the man is charging. 13
10 He will show you how to use the polish to obtain a high luster. 13

Letter I

1 oil sit air live idea fine field issue begin differ winter engine 13

2 The firm provided quick repair service by a skilled mechanic. 12
3 If you do not require an immediate answer, I can get his opinion. 13
4 I should like to renew this insurance policy, if it is possible. 13

5 I received a bit of reliable information about his activities. 12
6 If I had any such intention, I have long since given up the idea. 13
7 In my opinion, he is responsible for providing us with an office. 13

8 You might have informed him of the difference in selling price. 13
9 This paint may be high in price, but it is worth the difference. 13
10 It is impossible to find a safe investment that will yield more. 13

1   2   3   4   5   6   7   8   9   10   11   12   13

Alphabetic Paragraph

Type lines 20–24 once. Practice three times all phrases in which you typed a word incorrectly. Then take two 2-minute writings.

Goal: Speed–24 wpm
Error limit–4

20 When you get a chance, relax and read about the trials 12
21 and work of Christopher Sholes, the printer who invented the 24
22 first typewriter.   Reading the story will not quicken your 35
23 pulse, but it will make you admire the vision and zeal of this 48
24 man.   Just why did he desire to help his fellows communicate? 60

SI 1.35

| 1| 2| 3| 4| 5| 6| 7| 8| 9| 10| 11| 12|

Unit 27

Line spacing: single
Line length: 60
Paragraph indention: 5
Type each line twice.

Warmup

Type continuously, not hurriedly.

1 causes because; insures insured insurance; respects inspects
2 How could 24 men and 25 women use up 178 tickets in 19 days?
3 This is a matter on which I am unable to express an opinion.

| 1| 2| 3| 4| 5| 6| 7| 8| 9| 10| 11| 12|

New Key Location

D finger **3**

4 ded ded ded de3 de3 de3 d3d d3d d3d d33d d33d d33d
5 3 letters 3 words 3 phrases 3 sentences 3 chapters
6 33 divided by 3 is eleven.   133 minus 133 is zero.

J finger **6**

7 j6j j6j j6j j66j j66j j66j j67j j67j j67j j67j j6j
8 6 balls; 6 tennis balls; 6 baseballs; 6 golf balls
9 East 6th Street becomes Highway 66 at Main Street.

Number Practice

10 we 23 yew 632 try 546 pop 090 writ 2485 riot 4895 peep 0330;
11 to 59 wry 246 ewe 323 pup 070 tire 5843 rout 4975 purr 0744;
12 Deliver these 2 packages May 9 to 7860 45th Avenue by 3 p.m.

Letter D

1 and had red side hard food spend field under second around indeed   13

2 Although the day was cold, windows and doors were left wide open.   13
3 He was told that his credit depended on his keeping his word.   12
4 You should provide for your old age by building up a fund now.   12

5 We find the goods were shipped yesterday, according to schedule.   13
6 Dine and dance at the Roadside House every Saturday and Sunday.   13
7 We should like to have a hundred dresses delivered immediately.   13

8 Edna needs a dictionary so that she can look up difficult words.   13
9 The goods you ordered were forwarded Tuesday for delivery today.   13
10 The dealer was driving a red sedan that she planned to deliver.   13

Letter E

1 new she let cent near week weigh after never beyond people before   13

2 They spent a little more money than they had intended to invest.   13
3 Competition in this business is keen, but I believe I can meet it.   13
4 If the machine breaks, we must finish sewing the dress by hand.   13

5 It appears certain that some change in their system will be made.   13
6 I believe that we had better let her see the letter we received.   12
7 A great deal of money was needed to get the necessary equipment.   13

8 Early yesterday morning, we sent a telegram rejecting the offer.   13
9 You need never for one moment fear that we shall overcharge you.   13
10 Perhaps you expect prices to rise, but I believe they will fall.   13

Letter F

1 far off few left self half often after chief inform profit effect   13

2 Left to himself for a few hours, he finally found a solution.   12
3 We are satisfied with the offer, for we consider the figure fair.   13
4 We are fully aware of how difficult it is to effect this change.   13

5 In the future, find out first how much you can afford to pay.   12
6 We were informed a few days ago that the first half is finished.   13
7 If you feel sure the fund is sufficient, get gifts for all four.   13

8 Keep them fully informed of all efforts to confirm the facts.   12
9 First of all, I refuse to allow friendship to affect my decision.   13
10 In fact, you will often find it profitable to offer free samples.   13

1 | 2 | 3 | 4 | 5 | 6 | 7 | 8 | 9 | 10 | 11 | 12 | 13 |

Corrective Practice

Lines 13–16 reinforce the locations of **r** and **e.**

13 are wear read more beer dear rather rebel recent eager refer

14 effort enroll enter exert repeat recede rotate celery ordeal

15 Their remarks about the irresponsible engineer were correct.

16 Request three large pears there before they refuse to serve.

Word and Phrase Practice

Think and type the short words as a whole.

17 an so us we or me the you our his may she and this them wish

18 my do am if it is in to by now her him for out that like who

19 it is, to do, to go, to do it, if he is, it is to, if it is,

20 and if the, if we go, for it, for me, and did it, and if he,

21 It will still pay you to do a job as well as it can be done.

    1   2   3   4   5   6   7   8   9   10   11   12

Unit 28

Line spacing: single
Line length: 60
Paragraph indention: 5
Type each line twice.

Warmup

1 forms forgets forever; others another mother brother; dreams

2 taxes wax; boys joy; oak cloak; queer steer; tone zone; live

3 Mr. Polk ordered 3 dozen—or 36—6 oz. bottles of champagne.

4 Learn to return the carriage quickly, with eyes on the copy.

    1   2   3   4   5   6   7   8   9   10   11   12

New Key Location

The # sign stands for the word *number* if it precedes a numeral, and the word *pound*, or *pounds,* if it follows a numeral. Leave no space between the # sign and the numeral that precedes or follows it.

***D* finger; right shift**

5 ded ded ded d3d d3d d3d d#d d#d d#d #3 #4 #5 6# 7#

6 Serial #314; Flight #67; Claim ticket #34; Gate #9

7 If you want pinto beans, buy a few 1# or 5# sacks.

Letter A

1   has car pay coal yard want trade stand shall market happen regard   13

2   A few days ago, we again advertised a sale of coats and capes.   12

3   We attempted to ascertain the reason for the failure of the bank.   13

4   All the repairs had been made, and the car was ready for delivery.   13

5   About a month ago, we called attention to a small balance due us.   13

6   A sale of heavy aluminum ware was announced last Saturday.   12

7   We are glad to be able to announce these great savings today.   12

8   I can assure you that the quality is as good as it has ever been.   13

9   It gives us great pleasure to forward several samples of paper.   13

10   Each patient is given the same careful attention as in the past.   13

Letter B

1   cab buy big able both best above doubt about number object become   13

2   Our object is to establish better business relations between us.   13

3   I doubt whether they can possibly publish the book by September.   13

4   Both buildings burned, but they are probably not a total loss.   12

5   Avoid trouble by careful inspection before you buy bargains.   12

6   It will probably be impossible to bring him back before December.   13

7   The fabric of which the blue blouse was made was thin but strong.   13

8   His bank balance was low, but he believed it would be sufficient.   13

9   My brother Ben thought it best to subscribe to the building fund.   13

10   When we publish the book, we shall probably use a brown binding.   13

Letter C

1   act can cut much once each piece force touch school record direct   13

2   I can credit your account or send you a check for the difference.   13

3   The fact is that cheap products do not give satisfactory service.   13

4   The company carried accident insurance on all trucks and cars.   12

5   Once we reach a decision, it is difficult to change our course.   13

6   We offer a choice of attractive lace curtains in white and cream.   13

7   The case has become so difficult that we scarcely expect to win.   13

8   The inspector recommended no change except a new concrete cover.   13

9   The fact is the company cannot give this service free of charge.   13

10   Once officers are elected, we let them exercise complete control.   13

1   2   3   4   5   6   7   8   9   10   11   12   13

F finger;
right shift **$**

8 frf frf frf f4f f4f f4f f$f f$f f$f $4.00; $34.00;

9 costs $4; a bill for $41; pay him $67; pay her $68

10 Do not pay more than $8 for the concert on May 16.

Leave no space between the % sign and a number.

F finger;
right shift **%**

11 ftf f5f f5f f5f f5%f f5%f f5%f f%f f%f f%f 45% 35%

12 5% tax; a profit of 15%; 10% discount; reduced 25%

13 The discount was 20%. The finance charge was 12%.

Corrective Practice

Lines 14–16 reinforce the locations of **v** and **b**.

14 brave bevel verb adverb beaver vibrant beloved believe blvd.

15 Beverly verbal beloved brevity visible proverb vagabond bevy

16 I believe Beverly drank lots of potent beverages in Bavaria.

Alternate Hands Practice

For speed, keep your wrists and arms almost motionless.

17 paid also duty city envy when name fork make lamb held girls

18 firm spent right shape gowns widow auditor blame chair risks

19 social ancient haughty visible bicycle thrown dismal emblems

Typing Skill Checkup

Type lines 20–23 once. Practice three times all the phrases in which you typed a word incorrectly or which caused you to stumble. Then take two 2-minute writings.

Goal: Speed–25 wpm
Error limit–4

20 When you buy the things you need, you may sometimes buy 12

21 unwisely, but you will almost always get something of value 24

22 for your money. For example, you may buy too much junk food 36

23 and not get enough meat and vegetables. SI 1.33 44

| 1| 2| 3| 4| 5| 6| 7| 8| 9| 10| 11| 12|

REVIEW

Unit 29

Line spacing: single
Line length: 60
Paragraph indention: 5
Type each line twice.

Warmup

1 tire hires quires; ever never; towns down gowns; flame blame

2 except expects; lights night bright; wave knave brave; fines

3 July 6, 9 boxes of #7 size jars were sent--50% of the order.

4 Employ quick wrist and hand motions to return your carriage.

| 1| 2| 3| 4| 5| 6| 7| 8| 9| 10| 11| 12|

Group 3 REMEDIAL DRILLS

LETTERS AND PUNCTUATION MARKS

These drills provide material for corrective practice on each letter of the alphabet and on punctuation marks. If you often make errors in typing a particular letter or punctuation mark, or if you slow down in striking a particular key, practice the appropriate drill. *Use a 70-space line.*

Comma		
	1 You want a comfortable home, good food, and time for recreation.	13
	2 I set out at once, making my way slowly, carefully, over the ice.	13
	3 In another ten years, in fact, we shall be firmly established.	12

Semicolon		
	1 The neighborhood was poor; the house was old; the room was small.	13
	2 The family is gone; the old house is closed; now all is quiet.	12
	3 The change has been beneficial for us; it has also helped you.	12

Question Mark		
	1 Is he the right man for a position of so much responsibility?	12
	2 What qualities make a good leader? Does this woman possess them?	13
	3 Why did the account not balance? What mistake had he made?	12

Colon		
	1 I need the following information: name, date, age, file number.	13
	2 I have only one question to ask: Why are you so eager for the change?	13
	3 His reasoning was as follows: he had never meant to stay there.	13

Exclamation Point		
	1 How slowly they moved! At what cost was each step forward taken!	13
	2 Oh, you have let them go without me! Stop them! Call them back!	13
	3 I looked for one rare stamp—I found three! What a surprise!	12

Dash		
	1 You and I have a great heritage—the heritage of a free democracy.	13
	2 The piano was very, very large—too large to fit into the room.	13
	3 That method—trial and error—was the only one he had ever tried.	13
	4 I promise—and you can believe me—that I will be there at noon.	13

Parentheses		
	1 We rose bright and early (or at any rate, early) that morning.	12
	2 That is the main purpose (perhaps the only purpose) of his visit.	13
	3 They referred to the house (our house) as their legal property.	13

1 | 2 | 3 | 4 | 5 | 6 | 7 | 8 | 9 | 10 | 11 | 12 | 13 |

Capital Practice

Avoid raised or lowered capitals by depressing the shift key firmly; striking the letter; quickly releasing the shift key.

5 Shirley and Betty-Lou took the Southland Express to Raleigh.

6 Mr. and Mrs. Herrera bought tickets to the Houston Symphony.

7 Jack leased his red car from U-Drive-Em Rents last Saturday.

8 Lorna told her Aunt Carole that Uncle Victor was at the bar.

9 The thirst for fuel has taken drillers to Idaho and Wyoming.

Hyphen and Dash Practice

10 one-half; hit-skip; back-to-school; mid-Pacific; well-suited

11 fifteen-mile limit; up-to-date equipment; cross-country race

12 His brother-in-law was selected vice-president--would I lie?

13 Their devil-may-care attitude was obvious--no self-reliance.

14 Ms. River was well-intentioned, I think--but he thought not.

Number and Symbol Practice

15 I have only $1.30, but I need a 5# bag of the sugar on sale.

16 Did you save 10% of $79.50 you earned last week for college?

17 I want a 10# sack of #1 potatoes and a 3# box of #2 raisins.

18 Every payday, I pay 2% as city taxes and 4% for state taxes.

Alphabetic Sentences

In lines 19–23, type each line until you type it perfectly.

19 One day the quick brown foxes jumped over all the lazy dogs.

20 Max and Francis quickly vowed to seize the good job opening.

21 Every exam with puzzling questions baffled Jackie as always.

22 A jovial workman quickly fixes the blue azalea planting box.

23 The squad has asked Jim to give a box of candies as a prize.

Corrective Practice

Lines 24–28 reinforce the locations of **f** and **g**.

24 fog fig gift golf gulf flag frogs foggy feign forgo frontage

25 figure fixing filing forget frigid godfather gainful gratify

26 lifelong kingfish graft forge filling infringe fudge gainful

27 Four fleeing firebugs took a foreign flight across the gulf.

28 Forgive him if he again forgot to give the gift to Mr. Ferg.

```
 1|    2|    3|    4|    5|    6|    7|    8|    9|   10|   11|   12|
```

Speed Paragraph

Type lines 29–33 once. Then take two or more 2-minute writings.

Goal: Try to break your wpm record. Ignore errors this one time only.

29   All look to the time when they can do just as they like 12

30 to do. Some like to read books, some like to go in the woods 24

31 to hunt and fish. Some like to hike or take part in sports. 36

32 Then there will be times when all you want to do is rest, and 48

33 this may be a wise thing to do.   SI 1.00 54

Cum.
Words Words

shade of the maple; however, realizing there was work to be done,   26   86
he jumped up quickly.   30   90

39 The junior partner authorized a well-qualified older member of the   13   103
firm to vote in her place by giving him her proxy for the stock   26   116
which they held jointly.   31   121

40 At the inquiry Monday night, the janitor was somewhat hazy as to   13   134
whether the fire started on the stairway next to the elevator or in   26   147
the book closet opposite.   31   152

41 The house next door was small, containing five rooms and bath; but   13   13
it took our fancy because it had an adjoining garage, a wide piaz-   26   26
za, and a quaint rock garden.   32   32

42 At the banquet, the hotel served an appetizer, jellied consomme,   13   45
roast chicken and gravy with potatoes and green peas, a mixed salad,   26   58
ice cream and cake, and coffee.   32   64

43 When the bookkeeper asked him for two assistants to investigate   13   77
fully all delinquent accounts, whatever their size, the owner ob-   26   90
jected because of the expense involved.   34   98

44 Make both speed and accuracy your objectives, because both are re-   13   111
quired of the expert typist, and everybody must recognize that each   26   124
has little value without the other.   33   131

45 Although the four sisters did not like to relinquish their claim   13   144
to the jewels, they realized that the next move would probably be   26   157
a court action that they could not win.   34   165

46 The even ticking of the clock could be heard quite clearly in the   13   13
silence that followed his explanation, when the people realized   26   26
the grave injustice the man had suffered.   34   34

47 Most of the people were accustomed to the luxuries of civilization   13   47
and found difficulty in relinquishing them and making the adjust-   26   60
ments necessary to life in a barren wilderness.   35   69

48 Try this gentle soap, which is kind to your hands and yet so effec-   13   82
tive that you will get many hours of lazy enjoyment and relaxation,   26   95
because you will finish your washing so quickly.   36   105

49 In addition to an excellent stock of canned goods, jellies, dairy   13   118
products, breads, and cakes, the grocer had the equipment to carry   26   131
frozen meats and vegetables, if he wished to do so.   36   141

50 The production of large quantities of canned and frozen foods has   13   154
stabilized the market and made many vegetables and fruits, former-   26   167
ly seasonal luxuries, just as available in winter as in summer.   38   179

1 | 2 | 3 | 4 | 5 | 6 | 7 | 8 | 9 | 10 | 11 | 12 | 13 |

Unit 30

Line spacing: single
Line length: 60
Paragraph indention: 5
Type each line twice.

Warmup

1 excel excellent; over cover quiver; life wife knife; special

2 January in Phoenix; April in Kalamazoo; October in Cleveland

3 Lou and Marge did not get all their pay for the one day off.

Call-the-Throw Practice

wpm in 15 sec.

Take several 15-second writings. Your teacher will call "Return" at the end of each 15-second interval. Change sentences until you find the one you can complete as time is called. Then take several 1-minute writings on that sentence.

4	He said it is very easy to do.	24
5	I can show you how to do that well.	28
6	The man will pay him now for all he did.	32
7	That was a happy day when she was able to go.	36
8	She was right and we shall type all this work now.	40
9	Time is on the side of those who plan their work fully.	44

| 1 | 2 | 3 | 4 | 5 | 6 | 7 | 8 | 9 | 10 | 11 |

Corrective Practice

Lines 10–12 reinforce the locations of **w** and **e.**

10 we wet ewe were wade weep weak well where wager waste wallet

11 water elbow endow write waiver winter wrench weather whoever

12 Where were the new winter sweaters they wanted on Wednesday?

Lines 13–15 reinforce the locations of **d** and **e.**

13 die dear dent deep date head lead debt dance feed dread edit

14 bed debit damage danger deaden debate credit edible expedite

15 Mildred developed a different method of dealing with delays.

Phrase Practice

Think and type the word.

16 if he, if an, if so, on it, if it, if I, to be, to do, in it

17 or if, or to, as it, will be, or not, we were, so we, on the

18 to see, in the, ask us, to the, at this, he will, by the way

Typing Skill Checkup

Type lines 19–22 once. Then take two or more 1-minute writings.

Goal: Speed–26 wpm
Error limit–2

19   As a citizen, it is your duty to learn something about 12

20 your environment.   Someday you will be the adult members of 23

21 your towns and cities.   As voters you will make many choices 35

22 which will affect your surroundings.   SI 1.49 43

| 1 | 2 | 3 | 4 | 5 | 6 | 7 | 8 | 9 | 10 | 11 | 12 |

		Cum.
	Words	Words

26 Tomorrow the judge will issue an order authorizing an investiga- — 13 — 13
tion of the bankruptcy and an exhaustive inquiry into the charges — 26 — 26
of perjury. — 28 — 28

27 To meet household expenses, the lawyer and his wife have a joint — 13 — 41
account at the Zenith Bank that requires only one signature for — 26 — 54
withdrawals. — 28 — 56

28 The next day when she saw the market quotations on copper and zinc, — 13 — 69
she discovered why her first bid on the job had been so eagerly — 26 — 82
accepted. — 28 — 84

29 Although averse to high taxes, the citizens demand many services — 13 — 97
and public works; they forget that these projects require heavy — 26 — 110
expenditure. — 28 — 112

30 We realize that to get the maximum benefit from the lectures, we — 13 — 125
must make further inquiries into several phases of the subject with- — 26 — 138
out delay. — 28 — 140

31 In this zone there was a produce farm, with very fertile soil, ad- — 13 — 13
joining the railroad and extending an equal distance on each side of — 26 — 26
the brook. — 28 — 28

32 To the best of my knowledge, the president authorized the reporters — 13 — 41
to quote him as saying that a state of civil war had existed since — 26 — 54
January. — 28 — 56

33 The speaker eulogized the candidate as a highly qualified liberal — 13 — 69
and explained that the accusations against him were merely evi- — 26 — 82
dences of jealousy. — 30 — 85

34 The lawyer recognized the right of the judge to make the decision — 13 — 98
of acquittal, but he took exception to the way she arrived at her — 26 — 111
conclusions. — 29 — 114

35 The entire civilized world rejoiced when, after six years, the war — 13 — 127
was ended and men could go back to their families and a life of — 26 — 140
peace and quiet. — 29 — 143

36 She quoted examples of how the two firms had saved money on the — 13 — 13
work by increasing production, by undertaking projects jointly, and — 26 — 26
by good organization. — 30 — 30

37 In the window of the flower shop next door, there was a beautiful — 13 — 43
display of azaleas, jonquils, violets, and other spring flowers in — 26 — 56
a small rock garden. — 30 — 60

38 The boy would have preferred to relax, stretched out lazily in the — 13 — 73

| 1 | 2 | 3 | 4 | 5 | 6 | 7 | 8 | 9 | 10 | 11 | 12 | 13 |

(Continued on next page)

Line spacing: single
Line length: 60
Paragraph indention: 5
Type each line twice.

Warmup

1 tone bone zone known zinc; coin joins; ox fox proxy; qualify

2 1 vat 2 mat 3 bat 4 jam 5 van 6 gun 7 fun 8 low 9 Joe 10 hoe

3 Thinking words rather than letters will help increase speed.

    1   2   3   4   5   6   7   8   9   10   11   12

New Key Location

Leave a space before and after the sign & (ampersand).

J finger; left shift   **&**

4 juj juj juj j7j j7j j7j j7&j j7&j j7&j j&j j&j j&j

5 James & Conklin; Payner & Russell; Hatter & Lipton

6 Sims & Weld are featuring their fifty-dollar hats.

Leave no space between the parentheses and the material they enclose.

L finger; left shift   **(**

Semi finger; left shift   **)**

7 lol lol 191 191 1(1 1(1 ;p; ;p; ;0; ;0; ;); ;); ( )

8 (1) one (2) two (3) three (4) four (5) five (6) six

9 Carl is (1) a good typist, and (2) a fine wrestler.

10 Ship four microwave ovens (price $379.98 less 10%).

The Shift Lock

Use the shift lock when you wish to type a series of capital letters. To return to small letters, strike the shift key to release the lock.

A finger   **LOCK**

SHIFT

11 Use the shift lock when you want to stress A WORD OR PHRASE.

12 I was minding my own business when--CRASH--the picture fell.

13 Capital letters are sometimes used for book titles--IVANHOE.

Corrective Practice

Lines 14–17 reinforce the locations of **o** and **l.**

14 low oil only foul loyal allow close colon alone novel pillow

15 lot pilot couple balloon conceal formal hollow lovely double

16 toll locale payroll prolong propel outlay absolute pollution

17 Once a pilot and balloonist, he is now in pollution control.

    1   2   3   4   5   6   7   8   9   10   11   12

Cum.
Words Words

12 The president, who spoke next, appealed to all citizens to avoid · 13 · 38
quarrels that might easily lead to prejudice and bad feelings. · 25 · 50

13 The firm gave her an exquisite jeweled watch valued at four hun- · 13 · 63
dred and fifty dollars as a prize for submitting the best sketch. · 25 · 75

14 The pewter box, which had a design of oblique lines, contained over · 13 · 88
a dozen keys, but none of them exactly fitted the jewel case. · 26 · 101

15 In our July sale we featured exceptional values in garments of all · 13 · 114
sizes, in black or light colors, superior in quality and design. · 20 · 127

16 Faced with many perplexing problems on this puzzling question, the · 13 · 13
directors held several sessions last week to discuss the subject. · 26 · 26

17 When the excitement of the quarrel was over, the guard had only a · 13 · 39
hazy recollection of the specific remarks to which he had objected. · 26 · 52

18 In the open square adjoining the exchange, an outdoor market was · 13 · 65
organized, at which articles of various types were bartered and · 26 · 78
sold. · 27 · 79

19 The most puzzling feature of his reckless perjury during the exam- · 13 · 92
ination at the inquest was that there seemed to be no motive for · 26 · 105
it. · 27 · 106

20 If you freeze the vegetables until you require them next month, · 13 · 119
they will keep as well as if they had been purchased just before · 26 · 132
using. · 27 · 133

21 After the two organizations were joined and an extra dividend was · 13 · 13
declared, the market quotation rose to nearly double the former · 26 · 26
price. · 27 · 27

22 He will be glad to know our branch is fully equipped to handle his · 13 · 40
export shipments just as soon as we receive the authorization from · 26 · 53
him. · 27 · 54

23 The teacher explained that by seizing every opportunity to practice · 13 · 67
and by using effective technique we can enjoy improved typewrit- · 26 · 80
ing skills. · 28 · 82

24 In our judgment, both the salve and the powder are excellent for · 13 · 94
the treatment of eczema, and they are backed by our unqualified · 26 · 107
guarantee. · 28 · 109

25 The objective of advertisements of this kind is to familiarize the · 13 · 122
public with the fine quality of goods produced by our exclusive · 26 · 135
process. · 28 · 137

| 1 | 2 | 3 | 4 | 5 | 6 | 7 | 8 | 9 | 10 | 11 | 12 | 13 |

(Continued on next page)

Typing Skill Checkup

Type lines 18–26 once. Practice three times all the phrases in which you typed a word incorrectly. Take a 2-minute writing.

Goal: Speed–26 wpm
Error limit–4

18   Being well dressed but poorly groomed is something like   12

19 putting a beautiful photo into an ugly frame—the total effect   24

20 is poor. When you choose your clothing, you hope to make your-   37

21 self as attractive and appropriately dressed as your budget   49

22 will allow.   51

23   Now, to set these clothes off to the best advantage, you   63

24 must be certain that all the other parts of your grooming are   75

25 the best possible. As a matter of fact, careful grooming, even   88

26 more than proper clothes, will make you an attractive person.   100

SI 1.39

1 | 2 | 3 | 4 | 5 | 6 | 7 | 8 | 9 | 10 | 11 | 12 |

Unit 32

Line spacing: single
Line length: 60
Paragraph indention: 5
Type each line twice.

Warmup

1 Thirteen women work for the chairperson of the bicycle firm.

2 The lazy man worked diligently because he expects something.

3 His novel (QUIET JOVE, published by Vos & Zap) did not sell.

1 | 2 | 3 | 4 | 5 | 6 | 7 | 8 | 9 | 10 | 11 | 12 |

New Key Location

There is no space before or after an apostrophe within a word.

Manual: *K* finger;
    left shift
Electric: *Semi* finger

M4 kik k8k k8k k'k k'k k'k it's, don't, Mary's, Tom's

E4 ;'; ;'; ;'; can't, don't, doesn't, Ed's, Kennedy's

5 Nine 5's; three 6's; four 2's; five 3's; seven 4's

6 I've been wanting to see your Dad's new power saw.

(Continued on next page)

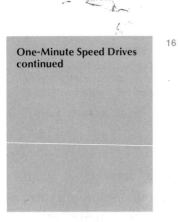

One-Minute Speed Drives continued

16 We must make things; we must be active. Our energy must have an outlet.   14

The human race would die of boredom if we could not find work to do.   28

The industrial world satisfies these needs in part; but it becomes less   42

and less satisfactory as the power of machines displaces human labor.   56

A reduction in the number of working hours gives time for other activi-   70

ties in which we can find satisfaction after our main wage-earning   84

work is done. Such activities give us a chance to do things for sheer   98

pleasure.   100

1 | 2 | 3 | 4 | 5 | 6 | 7 | 8 | 9 | 10 | 11 | 12 | 13 | 14 |

ALPHABETIC SENTENCES

Each of these sentences contains every letter of the alphabet. Type them at a rate that is slower than your best speed. This will help you concentrate more closely on the difficult reaches and improve your accuracy. You may use these sentences periodically for 1- or 2-minute writings to check yourself on the number of errors you make per minute.

ALPHABETIC SENTENCES

65-space line.

		Words	Cum. Words
1	The pink grapefruit was of excellent quality, very juicy and sweet,	13	13
	but small in size.	17	17
2	The citizens openly rejoiced when their brave king and queen re-	13	30
	turned from exile after many years.	20	37
3	This inexpensive bleach makes clothing a dazzling white; try it	13	50
	and judge its quality for yourself.	20	57
4	Jack took a taxicab after the party, since the warm drizzle had	13	70
	quickly changed to a heavy, chilly rain.	21	78
5	A knife or a razor which is made of flexible steel of good quality	13	91
	should never be used to pry open a jar.	21	99
6	Prizes were given for the best experiment described in the quar-	13	13
	terly journal, which the workshop published.	22	22
7	As the visitor was too busy to make up his own speech, he quoted	13	35
	exactly the major part of a magazine article.	22	44
8	The young executive and his wife had a party on the Queen Elizabeth	13	57
	just as the huge vessel was about to embark.	22	66
9	I know that the beef and the veal are of excellent quality, as the	13	79
	cattle grazed on the rich pastures adjoining my farm.	24	90
10	The adjoining room was equipped with parquet flooring, bronze elec-	13	103
	tric fixtures, a brick fireplace, and heavy storm windows.	25	115
11	I realize that the janitor, who has previously had experience as	13	13
	a carpenter, will unquestionably make good use of his skills.	25	25

1 | 2 | 3 | 4 | 5 | 6 | 7 | 8 | 9 | 10 | 11 | 12 | 13 |

(Continued on next page)

Leave two spaces after an exclamation point at the end of a sentence, one space if within a sentence.

A finger; right shift, **!** *or* type a period; backspace once and type an apostrophe.

7 I shall return! Don't give up the ship! Help me!

8 Suddenly, KAWUMP! went the cannon. It was scarey!

9 What a beautiful day! Let's enjoy it in the park!

The backspace key is used to move the carriage or element back toward the left margin. For instance, you would depress the backspace key to go back and fill in a letter that was omitted. Another use of the backspace key is in centering words or phrases horizontally on a line.

Center the three lines below following this procedure:

1. Move the carriage to the center of your paper (42 or 50).
2. Spell out each line to be centered silently to yourself and backspace once for every two letters or spaces. Ignore a single letter left over.
3. Begin to type at the point where you finished backspacing.

Semi finger **BK SP**

10   John S. Farley

11   17100 Harvard Ave.

12   Philadelphia, PA 19144

Centering Practice

Center each line following the procedure outlined in Steps 1, 2, and 3.

13   You are Cordially Invited

14   to attend

15   the Typing Awards Assembly

16   Thursday, June 12

17   at 11 a.m.

18   in the

19   Main Auditorium

20   Freemont Unified High School

Typing Skill Checkup

Type each paragraph (lines 21–25 and 26–30) once. Use double spacing. Practice three times all the phrases in which you typed a word incorrectly. Take a 2-minute writing on each paragraph.

Goal: Speed–26 wpm
Error limit–4

21   Over 70 years ago the Wright brothers made history with   12
22 the first airplane flight ever to be made. In all, the plane   24
23 was off the ground for 13 seconds and traveled a little more   36
24 than 100 feet before it crashed into the sand, but a human   48
25 had flown for the first time in a flying machine.   SI 1.25   58

26   In southern California, there is a turkey ranch that has   12
27 some interesting office jobs. You might think that office   24
28 workers would not be needed in a place like that. But there   36
29 are typists, order clerks, billing clerks, and payroll clerks,   48
30 to mention a few. The ranch is a good place to work.   SI 1.35   59

1   2   3   4   5   6   7   8   9   10   11   12

10 There are always people among us who would rather turn their eyes to the 14
future than look at what is good in the present. Tomorrow, next week, 28
next year, life will be wonderful; and so they forget about today. How- 42
ever, if they do not get some small pleasure from each day as it comes 56
along, it is probable that they will never find it in the days ahead. 70

11 We believe it will interest you to learn that during the three years of 14
our existence as an association, the number of our members has increased 28
from less than one hundred at the end of the first month to nearly three 42
thousand at the present time. As a direct result of the wide support 56
that the public has given us, we have been able to effect great improve- 70
ments in our servicing. 75

12 The time may come when some countries will find it difficult to get 14
enough electricity to meet all their needs because they depend upon coal 28
to produce it, and their supply of coal is limited. In other countries, 42
however, water power is used to produce electricity. There, the supply 56
should last forever, for as long as water continues to fall from high 70
ground to low ground, electricity can be produced. 80

13 Boys and girls are full of interest in life; and for this reason, they 14
have a questioning attitude. The questions that they ask are chiefly 28
of three types. In the first place, they ask questions about the world 42
around them and about human nature. Secondly, they ask questions that 56
have to do with their relationships with other people. Finally, they 70
ask questions about their work and what they will have to do to make a 84
living. 85

14 Ms. Brown had a business appointment in Chicago Monday afternoon. The 14
plane that she took early in the morning was scheduled to make the trip 28
in less than two hours, but it took more than two days. About an hour 42
after leaving, the plane was forced down by bad weather conditions. As 56
the weather did not improve, the passengers finally had to cover the 70
rest of the distance by railroad. Ms. Brown arranged by telephone for 84
a change in her appointment. 90

15 Throughout its past and up to the present time, Wall Street has main- 14
tained its position as a business and financial center. Wall Street 28
will always be a short and narrow canyon. The sweeping changes are in 42
its skyline, as bigger and taller buildings have replaced the old, small, 56
bulging buildings with their carved and gilded domes. Yes, the bankers, 70
the underwriters, the big stock exchanges, all have their roots dug in 84
and around Wall Street, and all are here to stay forever. 95

1 2 3 4 5 6 7 8 9 10 11 12 13 14

Unit 33

Line spacing: single
Line length: 60
Paragraph indention: 5
Type each line twice.

Warmup

Move your hands and arms as little as possible; use a finger movement.

1 Jovial Peggy dances badly to mazurkas with that quiet Felix.

2 You must stay awake and work to make those dreams come true.

3 Jot down a list of 11 friends to come to the party August 9.

| 1 | 2 | 3 | 4 | 5 | 6 | 7 | 8 | 9 | 10 | 11 | 12 |

New Key Location

To underscore a word or phrase, first type the word or words to be underscored. Then return to the first letter by backspacing or moving the carriage back by hand. When underscoring a few letters, use the shift key; otherwise, use the shift lock. Use a continuous line to underscore a series of words.

Manual: *J* finger
left shift
Electric: *Semi* finger;
left shift

M4 j6j j6j j6j j_j j_j j_j; do it <u>now</u>; it's <u>very</u> hot!

E4 ;p; ;p; ;p; ;_; ;_; ;_; so <u>sorry</u>; the <u>London Times</u>

5 This coverage is <u>for a lifetime</u>--not just till 65!

6 Have they started reading <u>The Adventures of Zorro</u>?

7 Please put your <u>name</u> and <u>address</u> on the blue card.

The asterisk may appear before or after a word. Leave no space between the asterisk and the word.

Manual: *Semi* finger;
left shift
Electric: *K* finger;
left shift

M8 ;-; ;-*; ;-*; ;*; ;*; credited*; her recent novel*

E8 kik k8k k8k k*k k*k k*k Ford V-8*, famous*, meter*

9 An (*) may be used to call attention to footnotes.

10 For 8 days nothing happened on the Eastern Front.*

11 Use ** for a second footnote. I like her books.**

Leave no space between quotation marks and the material they enclose.

Manual: *S* finger;
right shift
Electric: *Semi* finger;
left shift

M12 sws sw2s s2s s2s s"s s"s s""s "Oh yes, of course!"

E12 ;"; ;"; ;"; "Strike three, you're out!" he called.

13 The stock's "high" and "low" is in today's <u>Herald</u>.

14 "Go back at once--there's danger ahead!" he cried.

15 Anne wrote an essay entitled "My Happiest Moment."

ONE-MINUTE SPEED DRIVES

Select the passage you feel you can type in 1 minute. If you complete it before time is called, select a longer one for the next writing. Continue this way for several 1-minute writings until you find the one you can complete—or almost complete—as time is called.

ONE-MINUTE SPEED DRIVES

70-space line.

1   Too much importance should not be attached to these figures, since it   14
    is not possible to make an accurate estimate at this time.   25

2   This is the second annual meeting of the company, and I know that you   14
    will be very happy to learn that the report I am about to make is a fa-   28
    vorable one.   30

3   The woman wrote a few words on a piece of paper and rang a bell. A girl   14
    appeared, took the paper without saying a word, and returned in a short   28
    time with a heavy load of books.   35

4   We want to make it easy for the person with a small income to own his or   14
    her own home. For this reason, we are willing to grant a loan up to   28
    sixty percent of the value of any house that you wish to buy.   40

5   It is much harder to avoid censure than to gain applause; for applause   14
    may be earned by one great or wise action, but a person must pass his   28
    or her whole life without saying or doing one wrong or foolish thing to   42
    escape censure.   45

6   The iron and steel industry is one of the basic industries of this coun-   14
    try, with a great influence on many others. For this reason, business   28
    people everywhere watch for reports on the wage and price changes in the   42
    big companies that make iron and steel.   50

7   Much of the craze for amusements is due to the fact that people are not   14
    able to live easily with just themselves. They do not know how to oc-   28
    cupy their time if they happen to have a spare hour; so they look around   42
    eagerly to see what they can purchase in the form of amusements.   55

8   How fast should you type? It is fairly certain that you can and should   14
    type much faster than you are able to do now. Much of the speed you at-   28
    tain during this course will depend upon your desire to improve and upon   42
    your typing form and style. Now is the time to renew your effort to   56
    increase typing speed.   60

9   The storm burst upon us with its great fury. It was all we could do to   14
    stand up against it. The night was pitch dark and very cold. Deep down   28
    below us, we could hear the thunder of the surf upon the rocks, but we   42
    could see no sign of the vessel for which we had come to search. Per-   56
    haps the storm had already torn her to pieces.   65

    1   2   3   4   5   6   7   8   9   10   11   12   13   14

Typing Skill Checkup

Type each paragraph (lines 16–19 and 20–24) once. Use double spacing. Practice three times all the phrases in which you typed a word incorrectly. Take two 2-minute writings on lines 20–24.

Goal: Speed–27 wpm
Error limit–4

16   I used to make up boxes of strawberries in an Ann Arbor 12
17 store in 1978.   Each box contained 560 to 567 grams of straw- 24
18 berries in a liter box, approximately 12 cm × 12 cm × 7 cm. 36
19 The berries were zesty and would nicely serve 4 or 5 persons. 48
SI 1.33

20   As you gain knowledge about the environment, you may find 12
21 that you would like to work at a job dealing with plant life. 25
22 Landscape companies, greenhouse operators, florists, nurseries, 37
23 and the parks all employ people who are interested in working 49
24 at jobs that are helping to preserve our environment.   SI 1.55 60

    1   2   3   4   5   6   7   8   9   10   11   12

Unit 34

Line spacing: single
Line length: 60
Paragraph indention: 5
Type each line twice.

Warmup

1 Quietly pack all the crates with five dozen blue gift boxes.
2 We all think it would help if we have you talk to our child.
3 After May 1, Stock Nos. 37 and 38 will no longer be carried.
4 "I can't decide if 1984* or Jaws** is the best," said Marge.

    1   2   3   4   5   6   7   8   9   10   11   12

New Key Location

Leave 2 spaces after a colon, except in indicating time.

Semi finger; left shift

5 ;; ;:; ;:; two aims: accuracy and speed; example:
6 Items to be ordered: soap, towels, powder, brush.
7 The movie, Wizard, will be shown at 7:15 and 9:45.
8 Quotations were as follows: 90 at $50; 10 at $47.

(Continued on next page)

THIRTY-SECOND SPEED DRIVES

Use these sentences for 30-second writings. Remember to double the word count to get *wpm*. If, for example, your goal is 32 *wpm*, choose two sentences from the group numbered 1–5; for a goal of 40 *wpm*, choose two sentences from those numbered 11–15.

		Words
1	Let me see. She may go in a day or two.	8
2	Buy the set. We will need it this week.	8
3	Try some, and let me hear from you soon.	8
4	Do not go. He lives very far from here.	8
5	We are no longer free to act as we wish.	8
6	The man said that he is ready to start today	9
7	Ask for an exchange. You got the wrong size.	9
8	If they must go, they ought to leave at once.	9
9	I shall act as soon as he gives his approval.	9
10	I am very sorry that we are out of that size.	9
11	Thank you for your prompt attention to our letter.	10
12	The sale ended; so you must pay the regular price.	10
13	Please inform us in the near future of your plans.	10
14	We shall send you a check on the second, as usual.	10
15	The women object to the systems in use at present.	10
16	We note what you say. The idea seems to be a good one.	11
17	There is very little chance of getting any other color.	11
18	We hope to learn from the hospital about her condition.	11
19	He expects to receive a supply by the end of next week.	11
20	I brought this matter to your attention seven days ago.	11
21	This is a matter on which I am unable to express an opinion.	12
22	I shall give you a full account of the work that I am doing.	12
23	The question is whether I can make any profit at that price.	12
24	Everybody knows that words have power for good and for evil.	12
25	If you desire more details, we shall be glad to supply them.	12
26	We must be ready to act at once when the time for action arrives.	13
27	In all they said and all they did, they were moved by one motive.	13
28	We are glad to learn you have so high an opinion of our products.	13
29	We can assure you of our prompt attention to all customer orders.	13
30	The new machines have reduced our costs and increased our output.	13
31	No one fights reform so much as someone who stands most in need of it.	14
32	I made application a while ago, but I have not received any answer yet.	14
33	I would like to make you see that this change is a very desirable one.	14
34	So often we allow our emotions to get the better of our good judgment.	14
35	The fact is that we are too slow. We will let you know in a few days.	14

1 | 2 | 3 | 4 | 5 | 6 | 7 | 8 | 9 | 10 | 11 | 12 | 13 | 14 |

Semi finger

Leave 1 space between a whole number and a fraction made with the slant.

9 The sum of 5/8 and 7/8 is 1 1/2. Is that correct?

10 ;/; ;/; 1/2 and 1/3 and 1/4 and 1/5 and 1/6; 7 3/8

11 Contact them at 216/845-2630 any day after 10 a.m.

Semi finger;
left shift
for +

Leave a space on either side of both the plus sign and the equal sign.

12 ;=; ;=; ;+; ;+; 2 + 3 = 5; 4 + 6 = 10; 7 + 8 = 15;

13 He wrote the equation "(a + b + c/d) = e" quickly.

14 I know A = L + C is the basic accounting equation.

Three-Minute Timed Writing

Take a 3-minute writing on lines 15–23. If you make 3 errors or less, practice the speed drills, lines 24–26. If you make more than 3 errors, practice the accuracy drills, lines 27–29. Take another 3-minute writing and compare the results with your first timing.

Goal: Speed–27 wpm
Error limit–4

15   We live in what we regard as a very advanced state of   12

16 civilization. We seldom remember that each age must have   21

17 seemed just as advanced to the people who lived in it. We   33

18 look back at the life led by people a hundred years ago and   44

19 wonder how they found it possible to live.   53

20   On the other hand, is it not just as likely that in a   64

21 hundred years from now new generations, in their turn, will   77

22 look back upon us and, in the light of their increased com-   88

23 forts, consider our present way of life incomplete?   SI 1.33   99

| 1 | 2 | 3 | 4 | 5 | 6 | 7 | 8 | 9 | 10 | 11 | 12 |

Speed Drills

24 we in as age who led by it in to for as our on from way upon

25 do not in the in what at the in it to live of our as a is it

26 live very that each must just look they take part hand their

Accuracy Drills

27 advanced civilization remember possible comfort conveniences

28 hundreds generations increased inventions present incomplete

29 I regard too advanced is responsible to control a suggestion

Number and Symbol Practice

30 The title of Ian Brume's essay was "2 Against 20."

31 Joe Dru, an end, ran for 4 touchdowns (135 yards).

32 Interest charged on a $5,000 loan is 10% (not 9%).

33 I want a copy of the book, <u>Run & Hide</u> (Cat. #136).

34 The "bid" price was $98, with 9% annual interest.*

35 The problem was easy: 49 + 6 + 24 + 8 + 19 = 106.

36 Rowe & Baron advertised in <u>Time</u> (the May 1 issue).

TEN-SECOND SPEED DRIVES

Select a sentence you feel you can type in 10 seconds. If you complete the sentence before time is called, select a longer sentence for the next writing. Continue this way for several 10-second writings until you find the one you can complete just as time is called. (To improve your carriage return, the teacher may call the carriage return at 10-second intervals for 1 minute.)

TEN-SECOND SPEED DRIVES

70-space line.

		wpm in 10 sec.
1	I will try to come over at nine.	39
2	We wish you would tell them now.	39
3	Get her team to work like yours.	39
4	The show was a big hit in the city.	42
5	My car may be in the garage a week.	42
6	We can plan on your taking one pie.	42
7	They wish to have the bill paid today.	46
8	In the next few days we shall send it.	46
9	He does not plan to give a large gift.	46
10	I suddenly noticed a woman in the window.	49
11	Perhaps it is too early to make a report.	49
12	I had to stop in the office on the sixth.	49
13	If you agree with us, we shall act at once.	52
14	You asked me to try to get you two tickets.	52
15	Two seats are yours, in back of third base.	52
16	We are very sorry that we are out of that size.	56
17	It may be just what we require for our project.	56
18	Thank you for inviting me to stop at the plant.	56
19	We shall send you a check on the first, as usual.	59
20	I wish to thank you for the party you had for us.	59
21	We are glad to hear that you have both recovered.	59
22	Reginald refused our request to pay us what he owes.	62
23	We will purchase several vases, if you allow credit.	62
24	Mr. Soo expects you to reply to his inquiry by mail.	62
25	There is very little chance of getting a better price.	65
26	They hope you will notice the progress they have made.	65
27	I found that he did not bring up the subject of price.	65
28	She could not repair the broken box; so she sent it back.	68
29	If you are a good typist, you can always be sure of work.	68
30	The men in the club believe they should offer their help.	68
31	They want to purchase the land by the old dam, if they can.	71
32	The first step in any operation is to review all the steps.	71
33	They may make a big profit if they reinvest the money soon.	71
34	They spent most of their money for an audit of their business.	74
35	This is the plan they told us to follow for touring the plant.	74
36	They do not wish to continue without hearing from their banks.	74

Line spacing: single
Line length: 60
Paragraph indention: 5
Type each line twice.

Warmup

1 Next week Hank will buy twenty dozen pies for his busy shop.
2 The woman is to go to town and then make six signs for them.
3 1 2 3 4 5 6 7 8 9 10 11 12 13 14 15 16 17 18 19 20 21 22 23.

    1｜   2｜   3｜   4｜   5｜   6｜   7｜   8｜   9｜ 10｜ 11｜ 12｜

New Key Location

Leave no space between a number and the ¢ sign.

Manual: ***Semi*** finger ¢
Electric: ***J*** finger;
left shift

M4 ;¢; ;¢; Candy bars are priced at 15¢, 20¢ and 25¢.
E4 j6j j6j j¢j j¢j Bread prices rose from 49¢ to 56¢.
5 He paid 10¢ but charged me 28¢ and Susan 10¢ more.
6 I think that 56¢ is a lot; 38¢ is more reasonable.

Leave a space before and after the @ sign.

Manual: ***Semi*** finger; @
left shift

Electric: ***S*** finger;
right shift

M7 ;@; ;@; The sign @ is used to bill--3 pounds @ $5.
E7 sws s2s s@s s@s 78 bushels of potatoes @ $12 a bu.
8 The bill included 4 roses @ 96¢ and 3 shrubs @ $5.
9 Save 11¢ on Swiss cheese, selling regularly @ 30¢.

Leave no space between a whole number and the signs ½, ¼. Leave 1 space after the ½, ¼ when a word follows.

Semi finger ½
Semi finger ¼
left shift

10 ;½; ;½; 9½¢ a pound; 4½" thick; 8½' long; 7½' wide
11 ;¼; ;¼; 12¼ inches; 30¼ feet; 61¼ yards; 87¼ miles
12 Bill us for 20¼ dozen knives and 30½ dozen spoons.

Double Letter Practice

13 equal equally whip whipping zigzag zigzagged visual visually
14 ton tonnage sum summarize run runner quit quitter let letter
15 zip zipper hop hopping over overrule net netting kid kidding
16 infer inferring off office less lesser fun funny lap lapping

    1｜   2｜   3｜   4｜   5｜   6｜   7｜   8｜   9｜ 10｜ 11｜ 12｜

32 In the long run, we shall all suffer if farmers cannot make a decent living.   15

33 During the next three years, we hope to make a considerable amount of money.   30

34 The directors have considered this matter carefully, but they have no ideas.   45

35 We suggest that when you again make your calls, you pay this dealer a visit.   60

36 There is no truth in the rumor that the manager of this company will resign.   75

37 When you listen at noon to a broadcast from London, it is late afternoon there.   16

38 Again we appeal to our staff to join the effort to reach our quota in this drive.   32

39 We have been compelled to limit production because we cannot get enough material.   48

40 An efficient road system is essential to the well being and growth of our nation.   64

41 His attention was suddenly attracted to a door on the opposite side of the house.   80

| 1 | 2 | 3 | 4 | 5 | 6 | 7 | 8 | 9 | 10 | 11 | 12 | 13 | 14 |

Group 2 SPEED AND ACCURACY DRILLS

These practice drills and timed writings are designed to increase your speed and improve your accuracy. Use them as directed by your teacher or as independent practice whenever time permits. To get the greatest benefit from your practice, set a goal for each drill you type and always observe the rules of good technique. Check yourself on these points:

1. *Maintain a good posture.* Sit back in the chair and lean slightly forward. Your body should be about 8 to 10 inches from the typewriter, both feet on the floor.
2. *Keep your eyes on the copy.* Don't look up when you return the carriage.
3. *Strike the keys quickly and sharply.* Try to strike and release each key with one motion.
4. *Type with rhythm.* Allow your fingers to speed up on short, easy words and phrases. Allow your fingers to slow down when typing more difficult words and letter combinations.
5. *Choose a speed goal.* See if you can add another 3 *wpm* to your existing rate on a 1-minute writing.
6. *Set an accuracy goal.* Set a limit of 1 error for each alphabetic sentence. If you make more than 1 error, repeat the sentence.

Corrective Practice

Lines 17–20 reinforce the locations of **i** and **u**.

17 suit unit input build bruise audit union suite tuition until
18 juice buried caution illusion causing uplift council utilize
19 busiest required auditors burial circuit injuries continuity
20 The council was cautious, requiring only qualified auditors.

| 1 | 2 | 3 | 4 | 5 | 6 | 7 | 8 | 9 | 10 | 11 | 12 |

SKILL DEVELOPMENT

Unit 36

Line spacing: single
Line length: 60
Paragraph indention: 5

Sentence Practice

Accuracy is the mark of a good typist.

1 Marty gave my excited boy quite a prize for his clever work.
2 The four women she got from the firm can solve the problems.
3 We are very pleased with the work that you have done for us.

| 1 | 2 | 3 | 4 | 5 | 6 | 7 | 8 | 9 | 10 | 11 | 12 |

Paragraph Practice

1   I invested $900 in the bonds offered by Stone & Tuttle.   12
This is an excellent, safe investment, with a yield of $8\frac{1}{4}\%$.   24

2   In Thursday morning's <u>Press</u>, Hansen & Sons advertised   14
#2 cans of tomatoes at 55¢ each--regularly 69¢.   23

3   Frank & Peabody announce a sale of women's "Easy-Tread"   12
shoes, sizes $4\frac{1}{2}$ to $7\frac{1}{4}$. The sale will continue all week.   23

4   The huge machine (Heavy Duty Model #84) contained more   12
than $1\frac{1}{4}$ tons of steel. Yet it worked with great precision.   24

5   She read in this morning's <u>Clarion</u> that as a result of   15
the tie-up, 28 trains were late. Some of the trains were   26
delayed as much as 45 minutes.   32

6   Tracy & Staten announce that they plan to publish a new   12
edition of Harrington's <u>The Story of Radio and Television</u> in   37
one volume. A two-volume edition was published in 1972.   48

| 1 | 2 | 3 | 4 | 5 | 6 | 7 | 8 | 9 | 10 | 11 | 12 |

(Continued on next page)

SENTENCE PRACTICE

These sentences may be used for developing greater keyboard fluency. They may also be used as 1-minute writings for speed forcing. Practice aimed at helping you to break out of your existing speed level may cause you to make more errors, but don't let this bother you. As you get accustomed to typing at a new level, your errors should decrease.

SENTENCE PRACTICE

70-space line. Double spacing.

Words

1 We are no longer free to act as we wish.   8
2 The repair shop said it would not start.   16
3 We shall be happy to serve him any time.   24
4 If they must go, they should go tonight.   32

5 Thank you for your attention to this problem.   9
6 As the sale is over tomorrow, you must hurry.   18
7 They will agree that quality must come first.   27
8 In the future, please inform us of your aims.   36

9 We expect to learn more about the matter tomorrow.   10
10 We assure you that we process all orders promptly.   20
11 We all know that words have a great deal of power.   30
12 This is a matter on which I have a strong opinion.   40

13 I am sorry that I will no longer require your services.   11
14 I will give you a full account of the progress we make.   22
15 We must be ready to act when the time for action comes.   33
16 Those machines have reduced costs and increased output.   44

     1 | 2 | 3 | 4 | 5 | 6 | 7 | 8 | 9 | 10 | 11 |

17 We are glad to learn that you have so high an opinion of us.   12
18 I made an application a while ago, but I have not heard yet.   24
19 Often people allow their emotions to get the better of them.   36
20 I should like to make it clear that the change is desirable.   48
21 No one fights reform so bitterly as people who need it most.   60

22 I am sure that you will be surprised by the results of this test.   13
23 Audiences will find jokes amusing only when they are in the mood. 26
24 People are often judged by their words rather than by their acts. 39
25 The rain stopped quickly and the skies were clear for the parade. 52
26 If delivery is not made by Friday, we shall not accept the goods. 65

27 Hour after hour, the goldfish swim about in their calm world of water. 14
28 Monday was sunny, with no sign of the storm through which we had come. 28
29 We all want to protect our personal liberty and keep our country free. 42
30 The glow of the setting sun clearly outlined the barn against the sky. 56
31 On one side, the slope is gentle; on the other, there is a steep drop. 70

     1 | 2 | 3 | 4 | 5 | 6 | 7 | 8 | 9 | 10 | 11 | 12 | 13 | 14 |

(Continued on next page)

7   Our #7 notebook comes in smooth cowhide in three colors   12
(charcoal, ginger, and red). It has ½-inch rings in either   24
a 2- or 3-ring style. The price is $7.98--plus a 6% tax.   35

8   A 17-jewel Latham watch (Model #3) is guaranteed water-   12
proof--that is, as long as the crystal is unbroken and the   24
case is not opened. Buy one for only $79.95, plus 5½% tax!   36

9   On June 3, the training ship LINCOLN ended a 4,000-mile   12
cruise, with 276 cadets aboard for before-the-mast training.   24
When the ship docked at Pier #8, a crowd of about 500 rela-   36
tives and friends awaited the cadets' arrival.   45

10   Here's a chance to buy personal stationery of the best   12
quality at a great saving. You get 200 envelopes (3½ inches   24
by 6¼ inches) and a 125-sheet writing tablet for only $4.98.   36
This price includes imprinting a 3-line name and address.   47

1 | 2 | 3 | 4 | 5 | 6 | 7 | 8 | 9 | 10 | 11 | 12 |

SKILL DEVELOPMENT

Unit 37

Line spacing: single
Line length: 60
Paragraph indention: 5
Type each line twice.

Sentence Practice

Work toward accuracy
and speed.

1 Send it to us if they do not want to spend the money for it.
2 She may pay the men to fix her car, but it still won't work.
3 She owes it to you to try to write or to type up her report.

1 | 2 | 3 | 4 | 5 | 6 | 7 | 8 | 9 | 10 | 11 | 12 |

Paragraph Practice

1   If you are interested in debating, I invite you to join   12
a club which we expect to organize. We shall meet Friday at   24
3:15 in Room #217. Mr. Raeburn will be our faculty advisor.   36

2   Save 6¢ on each container of Goldberg's cottage cheese,   12
selling regularly @ 69¢. Buy one or more now, dated June 9.   24
You'll be amazed at such superior quality at so low a price!   36

1 | 2 | 3 | 4 | 5 | 6 | 7 | 8 | 9 | 10 | 11 | 12 |

(Continued on next page)

	A	B	C
4	all of them	as soon as	please ship
	one of these	as soon as we can	please send us
	a few of those	as soon as possible	please let me hear
5	we are not	now and then	just now
	we are not able	again and again	not just yet
	we shall not be able	more and more	just in time
6	as much as	I hope you will	some time today
	as well as	I think you are	some time next week
	as we have seen	I know you will be	in the morning
7	once more	on sale	for this reason
	many more	sale price	any other reason
	more or less	special sale	within reason
8	at some time	I am glad	I have received
	some time ago	glad to hear	you will receive
	at the same time	I am very sorry	we have just received
9	in a year	out of the way	we regard this
	in a few days	out of town	with regard to
	a few days ago	not very long ago	we regret that
10	so much	they wish to know	in all sizes
	very much	should like to know	large sizes only
	much more than	should be glad to hear	a very large number
11	let us hear	please accept	I do not doubt
	I have not said	please write us	without any doubt
	we have not seen	please let me know	there is little doubt
12	of this kind	in reply to	good enough
	in this way	in your reply	whether or not
	in every way	a prompt reply	whether you can
13	next week	quite a few	your request
	next month	quite certain	your account
	during the week	not quite ready	charge account
14	on hand	I suggest that	your attention
	on the one hand	may we suggest that	special attention
	on the other hand	should like to suggest	as early as possible
15	six weeks ago	express charge	at your service
	about six weeks	free of charge	in question
	six months ago	without charge	in addition to

3   Do you have vacation plans? If not, take a luxury trip   12
on our well—equipped jets to Bermuda, Nassau, and Jamaica.   24
Round trip fares are as low as $125. We guarantee you'll   35
love the lazy, carefree week you'll spend on these islands.   47

4   When Alfred was sixteen years old, he inherited $75,000   12
from his father. The will included the following provision: 24
that until Alfred reaches the age of twenty—seven, the money   36
was to be invested in AAA bonds and/or government securities.   48

5   He began dictating the contract as follows: "AGREEMENT   12
made on the fifth day of May, 1978, between Arthur Lewis, of   24
Cincinnati, Ohio (hereinafter called the SELLER), and Bonnie   36
Dix, of Dayton, Ohio (hereinafter called the PURCHASER)."   47

6   Tonight will be Ms. Whalen's 250th performance as Laura   12
in Polk's play, "Happy New Year!" Next week the play moves   24
from the Washington Theatre to the Columbus, on 39th Street.   36
The play's success led the producer to plan for a long run.   48

7   We offer household appliances at very low prices. Our   12
"special" for this month is an L & R washer, reduced from a   24
list price of $269 to $199——you save $70! You can save even   36
more by presenting the enclosed card, which offers you an   47
additional 5% discount. Hurry——this offer ends soon.   58

003240

    1| 2| 3| 4| 5| 6| 7| 8| 9| 10| 11| 12|

SKILL DEVELOPMENT   # Unit 38

Line spacing: single
Line length: 60
Paragraph indention: 5

Sentence Practice

Aim for an even shade in
copy. Use more force on
weaker fingers.

1 The helpful men held the forms for them to sign their names.
2 The job requires extra pluck and zeal from all young people.
3 Ms. McCreery teaches English as well as typing at Lowe High.
4 Let us show you how to do this work a new way and save time.

    1| 2| 3| 4| 5| 6| 7| 8| 9| 10| 11| 12|

Six-Letter Words continued	7	better	divide	happen	office	should
	8	bought	dollar	indeed	people	simple
	9	change	during	inform	person	street
	10	charge	effect	insure	please	strong
	11	common	either	letter	profit	supply
	12	course	employ	little	rather	system
	13	credit	enough	market	reason	toward
	14	custom	except	matter	record	within

SEVEN-LETTER WORDS	1	account	control	hundred	present	special
Left margin at 15. Single spacing.	2	another	country	improve	product	station
	3	balance	deliver	inquire	provide	subject
	4	because	develop	machine	purpose	success
	5	believe	example	measure	quality	suggest
	6	between	express	morning	receive	thought
	7	brought	forward	neither	regular	through
	8	certain	further	nothing	require	weather
	9	company	general	perfect	service	whether
	10	connect	however	perhaps	several	without

LONGER WORDS	1	attention	consider	pleasure	question
Left margin at 20. Single spacing.	2	business	gentlemen	position	straight
	3	complete	important	possible	thousand
	4	condition	interest	probably	together

PHRASE PRACTICE

Practice the following phrases several times until you can type them rapidly, without thinking of the individual letters in each word.

PHRASE PRACTICE		A	B	C
Type these phrases in groups of three as directed by your teacher.	1	to us to be to do it	by the way in the way in the past	from them from that time from time to time
	2	if it is if he is if you will	you sent us he must be they must do	on your part to take part on the part of
	3	to be sure we feel sure you may be sure	agree with you you will agree that we have agreed that	our letter in this letter no longer than

(Continued on next page)

Paragraph Practice

Note: Underscored words are given triple value in the word counts in these paragraphs.

1   My hobby is traveling. I haven't really traveled yet—— 12
except to and from school, and to the lake during the sum- 24
mer. I'd like to visit Spain. I'm quite good at Spanish; I 36
have just won <u>first</u> <u>prize</u>, a medal which I shall always keep 52
and treasure. 54

2   Tonight, John, Hazel, and I went to see "Sink or Swim" 12
at the Roxy Theater. The performance was quite delightful. 24
<u>Don't</u> miss it! Tickets are available at prices ranging from 38
$4.20 to $8.60. Theater parties of twenty-five or more are 50
allowed a 20% discount. 54

3   More than 250 delegates are expected at the campus of 12
the University of Iowa from May 9-11 for this year's meeting 24
of the Phi Beta Kappa Council. A dinner will be held at the 36
final session, at which Dr. John Frazier will speak. 46

4   Mr. Zims always pays his rent promptly. A few days ago 12
he received a notice from his landlords, Linden & Son, say- 24
ing that the rent was late. He was not worried or anxious, 36
because he had the canceled check, #345, proving he had paid 48
$225——the full amount owed. 53

5   We have two slogans used to discourage jaywalking and 12
hazards due to careless driving. For <u>pedestrians</u>, the 27
slogan is: "Cross at green, not in between!" For <u>drivers</u>, 41
it's: "Drive carefully; the life you save may be your own!" 53
These simple requests should be obeyed without exception. 64

6   One 17-year-old boy was captain and driver of a four- 12
person bobsled team that made a record run. After a week's 24
practice together, the four (all under 18) made the twenty- 36
five dangerous turns on Lake Placid's bobsled run at speeds 48
of over 70 miles an hour. They plan to enter a race for a 59
$500 prize. 61

7   In 1977, one 465,000-pound generator went by rail from 12
New York to Florida. It was mounted on a 16-wheel steel car 24
weighing 88,720 pounds——which made a total weight of nearly 36
277 tons. 38

8   This whole unit was 13 feet high, 12 feet wide, and 27 12
feet long. It can meet the needs of over 450,000 homes—— 24
or of a community of over a million people. 32

1 | 2 | 3 | 4 | 5 | 6 | 7 | 8 | 9 | 10 | 11 | 12 |

14	case	form	just	mean	rate	sure	west
15	cent	free	keep	meet	read	take	what
16	city	from	kind	mind	real	talk	when
17	cold	full	knew	mine	rest	tell	whom
18	come	gave	know	miss	road	than	will
19	copy	girl	land	more	room	that	wish
20	cost	give	last	most	rule	them	with
21	date	good	late	move	safe	then	word
22	dear	grow	lead	much	said	they	work
23	door	half	left	must	sale	this	year
24	down	hand	less	name	same	time	your

FIVE-LETTER WORDS

Left margin at 15. Single spacing.

1	about	could	labor	place	spent	until
2	above	cover	large	plain	stand	usual
3	after	doubt	learn	point	start	value
4	again	dress	least	power	state	voice
5	agree	drink	leave	price	still	waste
6	along	drive	light	quick	store	water
7	among	early	might	quite	story	weigh
8	begin	equal	money	reach	teach	where
9	black	every	month	ready	thank	which
10	board	field	never	right	their	while
11	break	final	night	round	there	whole
12	bring	first	north	serve	these	whose
13	build	force	offer	shall	thing	woman
14	carry	found	often	short	think	women
15	cause	front	order	since	third	world
16	cheap	fully	other	small	those	worth
17	check	great	ought	sound	today	would
18	clean	happy	paper	south	trade	write
19	clear	house	party	speak	trust	wrong
20	color	issue	piece	spend	under	young

SIX-LETTER WORDS

Left margin at 20. Single spacing.

1	affect	degree	expect	method	regard
2	amount	demand	family	minute	regret
3	answer	depend	figure	modern	report
4	appear	desire	follow	nation	result
5	become	detail	friend	number	return
6	before	direct	future	object	second

(Continued on next page)

Unit 39

Line spacing: single
Line length: 60
Paragraph indention: 5

Warmup

Eliminate waste motions and increase your speed.

1 You must return the coupon if you want to get a cash refund.

2 All of the goods damaged by the fire will be placed on sale.

3 Max and Charles did not receive pay, but Joe did pay Lizzie.

Keeping the Right Margin Even

The right margin of a typewritten page should be kept as even as possible. In the preceding units, you have typed from copy in which the length of the line was set. In this unit, you will decide for yourself when to begin a new line.

The warning bell on your machine will ring as you approach the end of a line. On most typewriters the bell will ring about 9 spaces before the carriage locks. Find out where the bell rings on your typewriter. If you were to type until the carriage locked, you would exceed your right margin by 5 spaces. A good rule is to try to end each line within 3 to 6 spaces after you hear the bell.

In this diagram, the margins are set at 20 and 85 for a 60-space line. The warning bell might ring at 74, 75, 76, or 77—depending on the model of the typewriter.

Avoid using the margin release. If you type up to the margin stop very often, you will have lines that are too long and this will make the right margin of your page uneven. To achieve an attractive margin, you may have to divide a word at the end of some lines. In such cases, observe the following word division rules.

Dividing Words at the End of a Line

1. Divide a word between syllables. EXAMPLES: **con·tain, trans·act, sci·ence.** When in doubt, consult a dictionary or a word division manual.

2. As a rule, divide a word between double consonants. However, if a word is derived from a word ending in a double consonant, divide after the second consonant.
   EXAMPLES: **bet·ter, run·ning;** but **tall·est, add·ing.**

3. Never divide a word of one syllable. EXAMPLES: **through, please, shipped.**

4. Never divide a word so that either part of the word contains only one letter.
   EXAMPLES: the first syllable of **along, enough, unite;** the last syllable of **wealthy, radio, city.**

5. Avoid dividing a word if, as a result, a syllable of only two letters would be separated from the rest of the word. EXAMPLES: the first syllable of **accept, endorse;** the last syllable of **rested, lovely, also.**

(Continued on next page)

Group 1 FLUENCY DRILLS

WORD PRACTICE

When you read, your eyes see whole words rather than the individual letters that make up the words. Skilled typists apply the same principle in typing. They type each word as a whole, rather than as a series of individual letters.

Type each of these words as a unit (a word-whole), without thinking of the individual letters. When you come to the longer words, you may find it helpful to use syllables or letter groups as typing units. *Type lines across, not down, in columns. Space once after each word.*

TWO-LETTER WORDS

Left margin at 30. Single spacing.

1	an	be	he	it	of	to
2	am	by	if	me	on	up
3	as	do	in	my	or	us
4	at	go	is	no	so	we

THREE-LETTER WORDS

Left margin at 25. Single spacing.

1	act	ask	far	law	oil	saw	try
2	add	bad	few	let	old	say	two
3	age	big	for	low	one	see	use
4	ago	boy	get	man	our	set	was
5	air	but	has	may	out	she	way
6	all	buy	had	men	owe	sir	who
7	and	can	her	met	own	sit	why
8	any	car	him	new	pay	six	yes
9	are	day	his	not	put	the	yet
10	arm	end	how	now	run	too	you

FOUR-LETTER WORDS

Left margin at 15. Single spacing.

1	able	each	hard	life	near	seem	told
2	also	east	have	like	need	seen	true
3	away	easy	head	line	next	send	turn
4	back	even	hear	list	note	sent	upon
5	bank	ever	help	live	once	shop	very
6	best	face	here	long	only	show	view
7	blue	fact	high	look	open	side	wait
8	body	fall	hold	lose	over	size	walk
9	book	fear	home	love	part	some	want
10	both	feel	hope	made	pass	soon	week
11	call	find	hour	make	plan	sort	well
12	came	food	idea	many	play	stop	went
13	care	foot	into	mark	poor	such	were

(Continued on next page)

6. Never divide figures, contractions, or abbreviations.
   EXAMPLES: **$3,000,000, C.O.D., 8:30 a.m.**
7. Divide compound words only at the point after the hyphen.
   EXAMPLES: **cross-examination, above-mentioned.**
8. Avoid dividing proper names. EXAMPLES: **William, Tuesday, Hudson.**
9. Do not separate a title from the name that it precedes. EXAMPLES: **Mr. Miller, Dr. Evans.**
10. Do not divide a date. EXAMPLE: **July 4, 1776.**
11. Do not divide the last word in a paragraph or the last word on a page.
12. Avoid dividing a word at the end of a line on three or more lines in a row.

Word Division Practice

The following paragraphs give practice in listening for the warning bell and in dividing words. Set margins for a 60-space line and type the paragraphs on a full sheet, using single spacing. Strive for an even right margin.

If the warning bell rings at the beginning of a long word, look for a good place in the word to hyphenate it.

1   Geothermal energy—the heat that is stored several thousand feet below the earth's surface—is undoubtedly a significant store for future generations. In the western states, where energy is plentiful, subterranean heat has not been tapped to any extent in this century.

2   Paper as we know it today, made from fiber pulp, originated with the Chinese. In the first century they made paper from such materials as silk and old linen. For several centuries the secret of this art lay locked within the borders of China.

3   In deciding upon a career from among the many opportunities available, a person has several factors to consider. A person's talent and education, of course, are two primary factors. No one can hope to gain success in an area in which he or she has little ability or no training.

4   A factor that contributes to business success is responsibility in money matters. Those who operate business firms have a financial obligation to their employees and to their creditors. To meet a payroll every week and to pay bills when they become due are good tests of financial responsibility.

If the warning bell rings at the end of a word, type the next word, but be prepared to hyphenate it if it is long.

5   The flag should be displayed on all days when the weather permits—especially on legal holidays and other special occasions—on official buildings when in use, in or near polling places on election days, and in or near schools when in session. Citizens may fly the flag at any time they wish.

6   Those students who seek an employable skill upon graduation from high school should seriously consider what a business education program has to offer. Many business courses provide a skill sufficient for a student to qualify for positions at an entry level in business offices, retail establishments, and manufacturing plants.

Supplementary Practice Exercises

Typing for Everyday Use

Task 4

Mr. Clark has made some additions and corrections to the customer mailing list. However, he is relying on you to check it thoroughly and to type it in good style. As a first step, prepare an index card for each customer and arrange the cards in alphabetical order by customer name.

CUSTOMER MAILING LIST, (Revised _____*(insert date)*_____)

Dr. Edwin L. Harman, PH.D.
745 Bedford Road
Albany, NY 12208
463-1266

LePetite Salon
New Center Bldg.
3423 Linden Blvd.
Brooklyn, New York
922-9702

Nate Leone & Sons, Inc.
707 Willow Road
Long Island City, NY *11102*
427-7650

Walt Mullins & Associates *Rd*
Brookline Building
815 S. John Daley *375-1677*
Mount Vernon, New York 10542

Jentzen-Miller Co.
158 State
Albany, *NY 12207*
347-7434
Mr. Zahn O. ~~Fascher~~ *Fisher*
500 Lexington
NY, NY 10016
 # 628-3527

Mrs. Zeline ~~Fisher~~ *Fischer*-Brooks
~~*Fischer*~~ ~~Fisher~~-Brooks Fashions
13756 Livernois
Buffalo, NY 14213 *342-6177*

The Mullins Clothes Closet
125 W. Grand
Rochester, NY *14614*
532-3502

H. F. Jensen Boutique
17322 Harper Street
Rochester, *14630*
(722-1799)

Leo's Custom Shoppe
20916 Woodbine Avenue
Syracuse, New York 13204
532-0357

Jennie's Designs
5436 Cheyenne
Bronx, N. Y. 10466
788-1532

Kozak Distributors
3041 Griffin
Buffalo 14202
855-3723

Task 5

From the index cards prepared in Task 4, type a revised customer mailing list in tabulated form. Be sure to mark it *revised*, and include the date on which you revised it. Then duplicate copies of the list for enclosure with the memo prepared in Task 3.

Task 6

Assemble all the materials prepared in Tasks 1–5, including envelopes as required, in a manner suitable for presentation and/or signature.

PART 1

KEYBOARD SKILL BUILDING

Topic 1 TECHNIQUE PRACTICE

You can improve both your speed and accuracy by developing better typing techniques. For example, training yourself to hold the shift key all the way down will eliminate capital letters that hang above the line. Returning the carriage without looking up will avoid the time wasted when you have to find your place again in the copy.

The drills in this unit give you practice material for improving your technique in operating different parts of the typewriter. Practice these drills frequently. You can use them at the beginning of a period for warmup or at the end of the period whenever you have a few minutes to spare.

CARRIAGE RETURN

A quick, smooth carriage return will add to your typing speed.

Drill 1

CALL-THE-THROW DRILLS

Select the sentence that will require you to type a little faster than your normal rate. The drill will last for 1 minute with your teacher calling the throw at the end of either a 20-second or 30-second interval. If you finish the sentence before the call, wait until the call to throw the carriage so that everyone returns at the same time. Change sentences after each 1-minute writing until you find the one you can complete just as the throw is called.

65-space line. Single spacing.

		wpm in 20 sec.	30 sec.
1	We wish you would tell him how.	19	12
2	Get her team to work like yours.	19	13
3	Larry will send you a check soon.	20	13
4	My car may be in the garage a day.	20	14
5	We can plan on your taking one boy.	21	14
6	He wishes to have the bill paid now.	22	14
7	In the next few days I shall send it.	22	15
8	He does not plan to give a large gift.	23	15
9	Maybe it is too early to make a report.	23	16
10	Try a few and let me hear from you soon.	24	16
11	I had to stop in the office on the sixth.	25	16
12	Marian filed an application some time ago.	25	17
13	You asked me to try to get you two tickets.	26	17
14	I am very sorry that we are out of that pie.	26	18
15	We wish to sign the note and send it to them.	27	18

1 | 2 | 3 | 4 | 5 | 6 | 7 | 8 | 9 |

(Continued on next page)

sure that she will be very pleased to hear of the admirable job you did for us.

I have the printers assurance that the catalog will be ready within 2 wks. I will see that you receive a copy as soon as its ready.

Yours Truly
EJC

Copy to Alice Kelty~
Rm. 412

Task 3

Mr. Clark drafted the following memo but he forgot to include the subject line. You are to supply one. Use today's date. Be alert for errors and correct them as you type. Prepare interoffice envelopes for delivery as follows: Wilson, Room 1370; Brownlee, Room 1375; Hall, Room 1381; Thompson, Room 1411.

```
TO:  Spencer Wilson
     Walter Brownlee
     Victoria Hall
     Alfreda Thompson

FROM:  EJC
```

Our new catalog for the upcoming fashion season is just about ready. It has many new features that will add much to its value for our customers.

This year instead of mailing the catalogs as we have done in the pass, we are going to try a new approach suggested by James Ellis our sales rep for the northwest District. Each representative will personally deliver the catalogs to the customers and explain to them ideas we have for advertising our products. I am therefore calling a meeting of all sales representatives on Mon. of next week, ____(insert date)____. At that meeting we will discuss our proposed new plan of catalog delivery.

I am enclosing a copy of the revised mailing list of costumer's who will receive catalogs.

		wpm in 20 sec.	30 sec.
16	The money is due and I can pay it if you wish.	28	18
17	We are very sorry that we are out of that size.	28	19
18	In the future, send their money to them by wire.	29	19
19	We shall send you a check on the first, as usual.	29	20
20	I wish to express my thanks for the time she gave.	30	20
21	Charles refused our request to pay us what he owes.	31	20
22	He will purchase several vases, if you allow credit.	31	21
23	Mr. Mack expects you to reply to his request by mail.	32	21
24	There is very little chance of getting a better price.	32	22
25	I found that she did not bring up the subject of costs.	33	22
26	He could not read the type on the map; so I returned it.	34	22
27	If you are a good typist, you can always be sure of work.	34	23
28	She may go there today if she can get them to go with her.	35	23
29	They do not own the land by the high dam, but they rent it.	35	24
30	Send it to us if they do not want to spend the money for it.	36	24
31	If they desire more details, we shall be glad to supply them.	37	24
32	They spent half of their money for an audit of their business.	37	25
33	Some of them felt that the man did not know how to do the work.	38	25
34	I can assure you of our prompt attention to all customer orders.	38	26

1 | 2 | 3 | 4 | 5 | 6 | 7 | 8 | 9 | 10 | 11 | 12 | 13 |

TAB MECHANISM

Learn to use the tab key or bar without pausing before or after.

Drill 2
TABULATOR

Type the columns of words at the right across each line.

Left margin at 10. Single spacing. Tab stops at 20, 30, 40, 50, 60, and 70.

it	is	to	if	by	an	am
the	for	and	did	due	the	for
is	if	by	to	an	me	it
for	the	did	and	did	for	the
is	if	by	it	is	if	to
and	did	the	did	and	the	for

Drill 3
TABULATOR

Practice smooth, quick indentions on the short paragraphs to the right and following.

60-space line. Single spacing. 5-space paragraph indention.

1   Less than a hundred years ago, humans made their first   12   12
attempt to fly with an airplane.   18   18

2   Many people responded by shaking their heads and saying   12   30
that we were never meant to fly.   18   36

3   In time, people became skillful with air travel just as   12   48
they had become so with travel by water.   20   55

1 | 2 | 3 | 4 | 5 | 6 | 7 | 8 | 9 | 10 | 11 | 12 |

(Continued on next page)

by its new format. In addition to the usual attractive layouts of our past catalogs it offers informative predictions of fashion trends for thecoming year.

Instead of simply mailing the catalog to you we are trying a new procedure this year which I am sure you will appreciate. Our sales representative in your area will deliver a copy to you personlaly. And discuss with you several advertising plans we have made to help increase your sales of our products.

The representative will call you within a few days to make an appointment. If you need assistance before then, please do not hesitate to contact our office.

Sincerely

Type this letter to Mr. Arthur Melbourne, 156 Second Avenue, New York, NY 10014. Use today's date. Be alert to correct errors in spelling, punctuation, grammar, and style. Make a carbon copy of the letter for the person indicated.

Dear Mr. Melbourne

Thank you for your help in the preparation of our catalog for the new fashion season.

I have seen a mock up of the catalog and I am extremely satisfied with its appearance. I especially liked the new page format that you designed as well as the excellent photos. In addition your idea to include a section to forcast fashion trends for the next year adds greatly to the value of the catalog.

Miss Alice Kilty our head Fashion Consultant recomended that we use your services. I'm

(Continued on next page)

Drill 3 continued

4   You can become whatever you want to be. You can make 12 12
yourself into almost any kind of person. 20 20

5   In the future, please make sure that you get a receipt 12 31
from the person to whom you make the delivery. 21 41

6   I am pleased to be able to tell you that the financial 12 52
position of this company is a very strong one. 21 62

7   As we expect to be very busy next month, we should ap- 12 74
preciate it if you would give us your order now. 22 83

8   All office workers should know how to consult reference 12 12
books in order to get the information they need. 22 22

9   When you apply by mail for a position as typist, it is 12 33
advisable to typewrite your letter of application. 22 43

10   We should be grateful if you would consider this offer 12 55
at once and let us have your decision within a few days. 23 66

11   We suggest you increase the size of your order so that 12 78
you may take advantage of the special discount we offer. 23 89

12   We are pleased to inform you that we plan to open a new 12 12
branch of our store in your neighborhood within six weeks. 24 24

13   They hope to complete the new plant early next year, and 12 36
to have the machines in full production before the beginning 24 48
of fall. 26 50

14   Since tomorrow is going to be sunny, why don't we go on 12 62
a picnic? We can pack a basket of cheese, sausages, bread, 24 74
and brownies. 26 76

15   In choosing a place to live, people usually consider the 12 12
advantages for their children. They prefer neighborhoods 24 24
with good schools. 27 27

16   Experts haggle over precise definitions, but most agree 12 39
word processing is basically the use of automated equipment 24 51
to manipulate words. 28 55

17   A bank offers you the convenience of taking care of all 12 67
your financial needs, both business and personal, at one con- 24 79
venient location. 27 82

1 | 2 | 3 | 4 | 5 | 6 | 7 | 8 | 9 | 10 | 11 | 12 |

(Continued on next page)

District 2

Luke L. Page, 191 Snow, Dearborn, Michigan, 48110, (313) 321-7662

Ann G. Smith, 2885 Joplin, Detroit, Mich. 48235, (313) 435-6172

Selden Fogel, 8230 Roylat Avenue, Pontiac, MI 48011, (313) 226-1734

R. Patrice Adams, 7634 Edmore, Ann Arbor, 48131, (313) 839-1377

Joan Adamson, 3421 Waterloo, Adrian, Mich. 49221, (313) 567-5564

District 3

Chas. Jos. Harvey, 850 Lincoln, Lansing, MI 48917, (517) 482-5213

Lynn T. Holt, 1976 Riveria Drive, Marshall, Mi. 49068 (616) 351-7044

Rita A. Maier, 3232 Alden St., Flint, MI 48517, (313) 882-9736

John L. Phillips, 2182 Ladue, Saginaw, Mich. 48604, (517) 349-4864

Rex E. Ray, #2 Biscay Way, Grand Rapids, MI 49540, (616) 339-9183

Task 5

Address envelopes as required for Tasks 2 and 3. Assemble all the
typed materials from Tasks 1–4 in a suitable manner for presentation
to Miss Ackroyd for her approval and/or signature.

Project C-3

SKILLS COVERAGE
1. Typing business letters
2. Applying English language skills
3. Typing interoffice memos
4. Preparing multiple carbon copies
5. Preparing envelopes
6. Preparing interoffice envelopes
7. Typing index cards
8. Alphabetizing names
9. Typing a tabulated mailing list
10. Utilizing different duplicating
   processes

You are employed in the office of Mr. E. Jackson Clark, President of Fashion House, Inc., 504 Fifth
Avenue, New York, NY 10036. This company is a manufacturer-wholesaler of women's clothing and
sells to retail stores all over the country. You have been given the following tasks to complete for
Mr. Clark as soon as possible.

Task 1

In the following sales letter, Mr. Clark asks you to include the
company name in the signature block. Watch for errors in spelling,
punctuation, grammar, and style, and correct them as you type.
Duplicate enough copies of the letter to send to the customers in
the mailing list you will prepare in Task 5.

Dear Special Customer

   Our new FASHION HOUSE catalog for the up coming season will
soon be off the press. I am certain you will be pleasantly surprised

(Continued on next page)

Drill 3 continued

18 If you have any more trouble with your stereo after we 12 12
return it to you, please let us know and we shall make any 24 24
necessary adjustments. 28 28

19 For millions of industrial workers, the time clock is a 12 40
way of life. It checks the attendance of employees and it 24 52
records the hours they work. 29 57

20 When you have decided on a career goal and the path that 12 69
leads to it, you have really settled on a way of looking at 24 81
life, a blueprint for living. 30 87

21 We have acknowledged the receipt of their order but have 12 12
advised them that we cannot make shipment until we complete 24 24
our investigation of their financial standing. 33 33

22 If you cultivate an agreeable personality, you will not 12 45
only become a happier person but you will also find friends 24 57
and co-workers more helpful in whatever you do. 33 66

1 | 2 | 3 | 4 | 5 | 6 | 7 | 8 | 9 | 10 | 11 | 12 |

Drill 4

TABULATOR

Type your name and today's date three times across as shown at the right.

Left margin at 15. Single spacing. 5 spaces between columns.

1 *Your name*   *Your name*   *Your name*
2 *Your name*   *Your name*   *Your name*
3 *Your name*   *Your name*   *Your name*

4 *Today's date*   *Today's date*   *Today's date*
5 *Today's date*   *Today's date*   *Today's date*
6 *Today's date*   *Today's date*   *Today's date*

BACKSPACE KEY

Operate the backspace key without looking up.

Drill 5

BACKSPACE KEY

Remember that to center a line horizontally, start at the center of your paper and backspace once for every 2 letters or spaces in the line. Center horizontally all the lines at the right.

Double spacing.

SOME INTERESTING OCCUPATIONS
TS
Graphic Artist
Tour Guide
Soil Conservationist
Forester
Copywriter
Computer Analyst
City Planner
Surveyor
Travel Agent

Task 3

Type this interoffice memo to the sales representatives in District 1. Correct any errors in spelling, punctuation, grammar, and style. Use today's date. Duplicate enough copies for each of the representatives in the district. (See Task 4 below.)

TO: District 1, Sales Reps
FROM: Diana Ackroyd, Michigan Sales Director
SUBJECT MCA Convention

The Michigan Cosmetology Association is holding it's convention next month at the Waterford Inn in Alpena, Michigan. The convention will run for 3 days beginning Friday, ___*(insert date)*___, 19--. As usual, our co. will set up a booth to display our products.

The exhibit will have to be staffed by X̶X̶X̶X̶X̶ our District 1 representives on Fri. & Sat. from 8:30a.m. to 4:30 p.m. and on Sunday from 8:30 to 12 o'clock noon. I have asked Joyce Digue to prepare a schedule of coverage, assigning each rep to the booth for a 4-hr period. She will make personel contact with the other District 1 reps to finalize the arrangements for the coverage. If any of you will be unavailable for booth coverage, Joyce will request asisstance from Reps in Dist. 2 & 3.

Task 4

Prepare a mailing list of the sales representatives in the three districts under Miss Ackroyd's supervision. Alphabetize the names within each district, and use an attractive, easy-to-read style. Correct any obvious errors.

CLAIRAINE HAIR AND BEAUTY PRODUCTS, INC.

Sales Representatives, Districts 1, 2, and 3

District 1

Thomas A. McLain, 44 e. Roanoke Avenue, Bellaire, Michigan 49615, (616) 661-2347

John L. Diaz, 132 Newport, Petoskey, Mich. 49770, (616) 381-1109

Joyce M. Digue, 205 W. Longwood, Alpena, MI 49707, (517) 821-9266

Robert G. Ander, 25245 Five Mile Road, Traverse City, MI. 49684, (616) 872-3553

Mary K. Brode, 435 Dover, Gaylord, Michigan 48935, (517) 731-3456

(Continued on next page)

Drill 6

BACKSPACE KEY

Type the sentences at the right. Immediately after typing each italicized word, backspace, spelling out each letter in the word as you do so. Then underscore each letter in the word—no more, no less (Each underscored word is given triple word count.)

65-space line. Double spacing.

1 I cannot be your *friend* and your flatterer, too. 12 12
2 This is the *first* annual meeting of the company. 12 24
3 Let your elbows hang loosely *close* to your body. 12 36
4 Learn to return your carriage *without* looking up. 13 49
5 The visitor was *too* busy to make up his *own* speech. 13 62

6 The spoken word is *more* powerful than the written word. 13 13
7 Our agents inform us that *you* wish to take out a policy. 12 25
8 The average life of a paper bill is less than *two years*. 14 39
9 You understand, of course, that *we shall* expect payment. 14 53
10 The *pink* grapefruit from Florida is of excellent quality. 13 66

11 Consciously listen for the *bell* for an even right margin. 13 13
12 *You* have probably seen the announcement in the newspapers. 13 26
13 The train was *crowded* with students returning from school. 14 40
14 A *great* variety of evergreens are used as Christmas trees. 14 54
15 Our profits for the past year have reached a *new* high mark. 13 67

16 In order to type *speedily*, keep the arms almost motionless. 15 15
17 We are sending you full particulars as to *sizes* and *prices*. 16 31
18 As a rule we require a deposit of at least *half* the amount. 13 45
19 When typing, your fingers are *never* straight but kept curved. 14 59
20 A man will never change his *mind* if he has no *mind* to change. 15 74

1 2 3 4 5 6 7 8 9 10 11 12

Drill 7

BACKSPACE KEY

When composing a rough draft at the typewriter, it is faster to X-out an incorrect word or phrase than to erase it. As you type the paragraphs at the right, X-out each word that you type incorrectly. (Use the backspace key to reach the point to begin X-ing.) Then type the correct word following the one you have crossed out.

60-space line. Double spacing. 5-space paragraph indention.

1 A recent survey of eight hundred banks revealed that during the past 14
five years there was a great increase in the number of banks having 28
employee pension plans. The study covered two-thirds of all bank workers 36
in the United States. 40

2 For years scientists and laymen alike have wondered about what makes 14
some whales and dolphins suddenly strand themselves on the beach. One 28
theory is that environmental conditions in the water interfere with the 42
natural sonar system used by these creatures to navigate, and that they 56
confuse direction. 60

3 Children should be encouraged to form the habit of saving a small sum 15
every week until they reach a definite goal. They should then be guided to 29
select wisely the item they want to buy and helped to make the purchase. In 44
this way they will receive training both in keeping money and spending their 59
savings wisely. 62

(Continued on next page)

achieve. Your beauty school customers will be happy smiling, and satisfied.

I am enclosing a mailing list of our sales reps in this state. Any of these well trained professionals will be pleased to present you with our descriptive brochure & to demonstrate some of the many uses of our products. They will come to your school or — if you prefer meet with you at the annual convention of the Mich. Cosmetology Assn.

As I'm sure you are aware this year's convention will be held next month in Alpena Mich. at the Waterford Inn. Be sure to visit our exhibit in Room 2133. We will be handing out distributing free samples of our new products which you are certain to find useful.

Sincerely

D. A.

Mich. Sales Dir.

Task 2

Send a copy of the letter prepared in Task 1 to each of the following customers. Fill in today's date, and address each letter individually. Provide an appropriate salutation on each letter.

1 Mrs. Edward Boyd, Boyd's World of Beauty College, 232 Maine, Detroit, MI 48236

2 Mr. Cecil R. Prince, Star Institute of Hair Designing, 1533 Wildemere, Marshall, MI 49068

3 Mr. Alfred K. Woods, Michigan School of Beauty, 486 Maple, Bloomfield Hills, MI 48013

4 Mrs. Janice McKean, Northern Academy of Cosmetology, 13667 Woodstock, Petoskey, MI 49770

5 Miss Alice Dean, Excelsior School of Hairstyling, 1429 Crescent Drive, Saginaw, MI 48604

4   Many students have found that most of their homework and other   13
notes that were typed may be kept until they need to be reviewed. This is not   29
always true of handwritten notes that tend to blur and fade, and which may   43
have been written without thought of saving them for another day.   56

5   Important characteristics of successful real estate salespersons include   15
a pleasing personality, honesty, and a neat appearance. Dealing with pros-   30
pective customers requires maturity and tact as well as enthusiasm for the   45
job. Agents also should have a good memory for names and faces and for   59
business details such as prices and zoning regulations.   69

6   Some years ago a man had the idea that we should all begin our day   14
earlier in the summer than in the winter. From this idea grew the plan of   24
daylight saving time. The proposal to move the hands of the clock ahead in   43
the early spring and to move them back in the fall was one of those obvious   58
yet daring suggestions that rarely occurs to anybody.   69

7   Many people still think that a secretary is a kind of machine that turns   15
out perfect work from nine to five. Some people use the title to mean one   30
who is employed as a stenographer or clerk in an office. Typing and   43
shorthand are two basic secretarial skills, but the duties of a secretary cover   59
a much wider range than the work of such office workers as typists,   72
stenographers, or file clerks.   78

8   Salespeople who travel try to make calls at the time most convenient to   15
their customers. Frequently, they spend their evenings and weekends writ-   30
ing reports and planning itineraries. However, some salespeople are able to   45
schedule their time off when they want it. When on business trips, sales-   59
people are reimbursed for expenses such as transportation, food, and   72
lodging. Some companies provide a car or pay a mileage allowance to those   87
who use their own cars.   91

SHIFT KEY

Depress the shift key firmly when you type a capital letter. Release it quickly after the letter is struck.

Drill 8
SHIFT KEY

Type each of the sentences at the right.

70-space line. Single spacing.

1 J. W. Fisher ran for Attorney General of Florida.   10 10
2 Daryl called Caroline and invited her to the dance.   10 20
3 Business declined in June but will be better in July.   11 31
4 The next sales meeting will be held in May in Hawaii.   11 41
5 George Landers was elected Senator of North Carolina.   11 52

   · 1 2 3 4 5 6 7 8 9 10 11

(Continued on next page)

just now catching up on the correspondence he left for copmletion.

I am enclosing an announcement of themeeting with a reservation form on the lower half. When we receive the completed form we will send your tickets by return mail. A stamped self addressed envelope is enclosed for your convenence in returning the reservation form.

Your long time membership in our organisation, and your active participation in all it's functions, are appreciated.

Sincerely yours

Task 5

Assemble all the materials prepared in Tasks 1–4 for presentation to Mr. Downing for his approval or reference. Include all necessary envelopes, carbon copies, and enclosures.

Project C-2

SKILLS COVERAGE
1. Typing form letters
2. Applying English language skills
3. Typing interoffice memos
4. Utilizing a duplicating process
5. Filling in form letters
6. Typing a mailing list
7. Alphabetizing names

You are employed in the office of Miss Diana Ackroyd, Michigan Sales Director for Clairaine Hair and Beauty Products, Inc., 11372 Palmer Road, Detroit, MI 48220. Miss Ackroyd is responsible for communicating with the owners of beauty schools in the area. She also supervises the company's sales representatives in three districts in the state.

The Michigan Cosmetology Association convention is planned for the last weekend of next month, and Miss Ackroyd needs your help in notifying both her representatives and the beauty school owners. The following tasks are to be completed for her approval and signature as soon as possible.

Task 1

Type this form letter on a stencil and duplicate copies for use in Task 2. Be alert for errors in spelling, punctuation, grammar, and style. Correct the errors as you type the letter. Note the enclosure. Leave room for the date line, the inside address, and a salutation.

Our exciting new line of Clairaine Products will help your students do the proffessional kind of work they are ~~aiming to~~ striving to

(Continued on next page)

6   Did you see the new Sphinx motorcycle at Norton Motors?   11   11
7   I heard that a new Burger Shack is opening on Arrow Lane.   11   22
8   Last year we vacationed in Miami; this year, in San Francisco.   12   34
9   Worldwide Products will open a new warehouse in New Jersey.   12   46
10 Ms. Zuchs plans to visit Zaire, Egypt, and Libya this summer.   12   58

11 Tom R. Busher was promoted to Assistant Vice President today.   12   12
12 A benefit show will be given for the United Appeal of Dayton.   12   24
13 John Forbes is no longer City Council President as of Friday.   12   36
14 Lake Tahoe is located on the border of California and Nevada.   12   48
15 The Princess Inn Hotel in Quebec City is a nice place to stay.   12   60

16 Our bank has twenty branch offices covering England and Canada.   13   13
17 Our employees plan to give blood to the Red Cross next Wednesday.   13   26
18 You can buy annuities from the International Mutual Fund in Peoria.   13   39
19 The training director will hold the seminars in the Ocean View Room. 14   52
20 Tom McBride of the Accounting Department was transferred to Montreal. 14   66

21 You can get some of the best land buys from Richey Land Co. in Ocala. 14   14
22 The Sleepy Hollow Club is having its annual Christmas Show on Tuesday. 14   28
23 Investment advice is available at Thompson, Garafoli, and Sweeney, Inc. 14   42
24 James Ford Rhodes High School won the state meet in Toledo last year. 14   56
25 Interest rates are lower at the Credit Union than at Holmes State Bank. 14   70

26 Hale Brothers will be open on Friday, which is Martin Luther King Day. 14   14
27 Trade between Israel and Europe's Common Market will be increasing. 14   28
28 Ida and Randy are going to New Orleans for the Mardi Gras in February. 14   42
29 We shall send you the latest prices no later than Tuesday or Wednesday. 14   56
30 Amy and Bob wrote letters to colleges in Denver, Dallas, and San Diego. 14   70

1   2   3   4   5   6   7   8   9   10   11   12   13   14

Drill 9
SYMBOL PRACTICE

This drill will give you practice in typing numbers and the more commonly used symbols that require the use of the shift key.

60-space line. Single spacing. 5-space paragraph indention.

1   A business card is usually $3\frac{1}{2}'' \times 2''$ (though some people use larger sizes).   16   16

2   Will you telephone Mr. Berry and let me know if lunch on Tuesday is convenient?   17   33

3   Somewhere along the line someone has "goofed" in the shipment of your purchases.   17   50

4   Last year I earned 9% interest on some bonds, and only 6% dividends on my stocks.   17   67

5   The ANNUAL STOCKHOLDERS' REPORT for the Benson Division was completed last week.   17   83

1   2   3   4   5   6   7   8   9   10   11   12   13   14

(Continued on next page)

Task 3

Design an attractive form for the announcement of the luncheon meeting. Two original-looking copies are needed. Correct any errors in spelling, punctuation, grammar, and style.

THE PITTSBURGH MUSICIAN'S CREDIT UNION CORDIALLY INVITES YOU TO ATTEND ITS 48th ANNUAL MEETING AND LUNCHEON, SATURDAY, _____*(insert date)*_____, AT THE REYNOLDS HOUSE, 25300 WEST TEN MILE ROAD, PITTSBURGH, PENN-SYLVANIA.   Luncheon at 12 o'clock noon ($4.50), Speaker and Meeting after luncheon

Please detach & return the bottom part of this form to purchase luncheon tickets.

Enclosed is $_____ for _____ tickets (limit 2 per member) for the PMCU Anual Luncheon Meeting at the ~~XXXXX~~ Reynolds House.

Member Name _____   Address_____

City _____   State _____   ZIP Code _____

Credit Union Account No _____

Send no cash.   Send checks or money orders only, payable to Pitts-burgh Musicians' Credit Union.

Task 4

During Mr. Downing's absence, you received a telephone call from Mr. Lawrence Brown, inquiring about the luncheon meeting. You follow up on the conversation by drafting the letter shown below. As you type the letter, pay close attention to errors in spelling, punctuation, grammar, and style. Mr. Brown's address is shown at the right. Send the letter under your own name and make a copy for Mr. Downing's reference.

Mr. Lawrence Brown
377 E. Grant Street
Pittsburgh, PA 15219

Dear Mr. Brown

   SUBJECT: PMCU Luncheon Reservations

   Please accept our apologies for the delay in sending you a copy of the announcement of our annual luncheon meeting. Mr. Downing's
                                           created a
unexpected absence from the office has ~~XXXXXXXXXXX~~ back-log, and I'm

(Continued on next page)

6   My letter to the Credit Department (outlining your proposal) apparently went astray.   18   18

7   Will you be kind enough to give us information (in confidence) about June's qualifications?   19   37

8   Here's to you—Marion and John! Congratulations on becoming the proud parents of a boy!   18   55

9   Endicott is out with a new paint called COLONIAL WHITE which sells for only $8 a gallon!   18   73

10   Will you please, at your earliest convenience, give me a Dun & Bradstreet report on them?   19   92

11   For the sanity of your accounting department (as well as ours), we shall invoice ten times a year.   20   20

12   The ATTUNED EAR, a magazine for music listeners, places the accent on quality instead of quantity.   20   41

13   The Phoenix Savings & Loan has increased the interest rate from 5.5% to 5.75% effective July 8.   19   60

14   The so-called "coffee break," a firmly established custom in millions of offices, takes many forms.   21   81

15   I've just been notified by our accounting department that your refund of $50 will be mailed tomorrow.   21   102

16   Our new copier, which we purchased for $1,545, gives us a range of copy sizes from 5½″ × 8½″ to 11.7″ × 17″.   22   22

17   Companies have rules about points of behavior that could properly be called etiquette (promptness, for example).   23   45

18   The price for the entire group of concerts will be $76 (plus the usual 10% entertainment tax), or a total of $83.60.   24   69

19   The enclosed Request Card entitles you to a free copy of Bulletin #72, HOME GARDENING AND CANNING FOR THE HOMEMAKER.   24   93

20   Will you send your letter of recommendation to Ms. Nancy Kelso at Adams & Bilsky, 22 Park Place, Austin, Texas 78710?   24   117

21   We must now call a halt to any further purchases until the balance shown on the enclosed statement ($3,460.00) is paid.   25   25

22   I realize that a simple "thank you" isn't very much, but I hope you'll understand that it comes from the bottom of my heart.   26   50

23   Should you pick up an extension telephone and discover you've interrupted a conversation, quickly say, "I'm sorry," and hang up.   26   77

24   If you'd like to receive the newsletter every month, just drop me a note and I'll put your name on our regular mailing list—no charge, of course!   30   107

1 | 2 | 3 | 4 | 5 | 6 | 7 | 8 | 9 | 10 | 11 | 12 | 13 | 14

to disappoint Mr. Downing's friend, but you have specific instructions to limit ticket sales to two per member. You tactfully explain the situation to Mr. Lewiston. He then asks that you take a message for Mr. Downing. Mr. Lewiston wishes Mr. Downing to call him at his office at 327-3459, Extension 114, before 3:30 p.m. on the day Mr. Downing returns to the office.

Task 2

The letter below is to be sent to Mr. Irwin Ferrette, the scheduled speaker for the luncheon meeting. His address is shown at the right. The letter was prepared hurriedly by Mr. Downing, who trusts your ability to find and correct errors in spelling, punctuation, grammar, and style. Send a copy of the letter to the public relations director, Ms. Jane Byer. Her office is in Room 132A of your building.

Executive Hotel
237 Park Avenue
New York, NY 10039

Dear Irwin

Our Public Relations Director Ms. Jane Byer has informed me that you have accepted our invitation to speak at our cr. union's annual luncheon meeting. As you know its being held on Sat. ___(insert date)___. For your convenience, I am enclosing a copy of the announcement of the meeting, which gives all the details as to time + place.

I understand that you will arrive in Pittsburgh on Eastern Airlines Flight 284 Friday evening before the luncheon. I will plan to meet your plane and take you to your hotel. Ms. Byer has arranged acommodations for you at the Squire's Inn. I will pick you up at your hotel at eleven thirty o'clock Sat. morning to drive you to the Reynolds House where the luncheon meeting is being held.

I look forward to seeing you, and to renewing our debate on the foremost Wagnerian sopranos.

Yours sincerly

Drill 10

SHIFT LOCK

Type each line *across*. Use the shift lock for the state abbreviations. Release the lock immediately after each use without taking your eyes from the copy.

Left margin at 15; tab stops at 35 and 50. Double spacing.

1	Denver	CO	80201
2	Las Vegas	NV	89101
3	Miami	FL	33139
4	Mobile	AL	36601
5	Topeka	KS	66601
6	Memphis	TN	38101
7	Lincoln	NE	68501
8	Baltimore	MD	21215
9	Milwaukee	WI	53228
10	Boston	MA	02138
11	Salem	OR	97302
12	Pittsburgh	PA	17109
13	Mobile	AL	36608

MARGIN RELEASE

Learn to use the margin release smoothly, without hesitation.

Drill 11

RELEASING THE RIGHT MARGIN

As you type the paragraphs at the right, end each line exactly as it appears in the printed copy. Use the margin release when necessary.

Margins at 20 and 85. Single spacing. 5-space paragraph indention.

1   We are sorry that we cannot guarantee early delivery. We have 13
none of these parts in stock. As soon as we get a complete supply 27
from the factory, we shall fill your order. 35

2   If we do not hear from you before October 10, we shall assume 13
that you are no longer interested in our plan and we shall feel free 27
to make a similar offer to some other agent. 36

3   An ice cap that averages five thousand feet in thickness now 13
covers the Antarctic region. Millions of years ago, however, this 26
region had a mild climate and a rich vegetation. 36

4   I found myself in a large room, in which there were several 13
long tables. These were occupied by a number of men who were read- 26
ing and taking notes. The room was quiet, except for a rustle now 39
and then as a reader turned a page. 46

5   Our function is to manufacture and to sell electric equipment 13
of all kinds. If we are to be equal to that task, we must be ready 27
to meet every demand that will be made on us as a result of new 39
inventions and improved facilities. 46

6   Division of labor in modern methods of production has come to 13
be an accepted practice. One worker may be employed all day, year 26
after year, in sewing buttons on coats; other workers may make one 40
small part of a machine day in and day out. 48

1 2 3 4 5 6 7 8 9 10 11 12 13

ADVANCED INTEGRATED PROJECTS

The material to be typed in these projects is similar to that in Series B. These projects, however, are longer and more complicated, and they require more independent thinking and planning. All the copy is presented in draft form so that it closely resembles the copy given to typists in an actual office setting. Much of the material contains errors that the typist is expected to find and correct. These errors test the student's ability to apply the rules of punctuation, capitalization, spelling, and style presented in Section 2, Part 6 and Section 3, Part 1.

Project C-1

SKILLS COVERAGE
1. *Typing business letters*
2. *Applying English language skills*
3. *Centering vertically and horizontally*
4. *Preparing envelopes*
5. *Handling telephone calls*
6. *Taking telephone messages*

You are working in the office of Mr. J. D. Downing, Board Chairman of the Pittsburgh Musicians' Credit Union (PMCU), 7480 Duquesne Avenue, Pittsburgh, PA 15218. One of your employer's responsibilities is to plan and coordinate the credit union's annual luncheon meeting. This year, the meeting will be held on the Saturday three weeks from today's date. Mr. Downing is going to be out of the office for a few days, and he leaves several clerical tasks to be completed for his approval and signature upon his return.

Task 1

From the information in the paragraph below, create and type the script of a telephone conversation as you imagine it might develop. Use proper telephone answering techniques and manners. Then type a telephone message for Mr. Downing, giving him a report of the conversation. Use plain paper if no message form is available.

Mr. Ralph Lewiston, a personal friend of Mr. Downing, calls and asks to speak to him. When you explain that Mr. Downing is away from the office for a few days, Mr. Lewiston asks for five tickets to the annual luncheon meeting. This creates a dilemma for you. You do not want

(Continued on next page)

To begin each paragraph,
depress the margin release
and backspace 5 spaces into
the left margin. Make your
line endings the same as
those in the printed copy.

60-space line. Single spacing.

1 There were dozens of little boys in the main street of the town. When
a tourist came near them, they would run up with palms outstretched,
crying for a coin.

2 The employees in this department deserve a special tribute for the very
fine way in which they have all worked. Through their unfailing
efforts they have maintained the desired production.

3 As you will see in our report, we have enough contracts to keep our plant
in full operation for several months. Our facilities may be fully
employed throughout the year.

4 In relation to body size, the eyes of small animals are much larger as a
rule than are the eyes of human beings. On the other hand, with
large animals the opposite is true.

5 The ship was seaworthy, but she was slow under sail. As it was important
to reach our destination, it was necessary to use the engines more
than expected.

6 It has been said that young people lack a sense of purpose. I believe
that they very definitely have purposes, but those purposes are not
apt to be the same as those of adults.

Topic 2 SPEED PRACTICE

Select practice lines from the drills in this topic as directed by your teacher. Follow the
technique hints given with each drill. As your technique improves, your speed will
improve.

WORDS

Read, think, and type the short, easy words and phrases as a whole instead of thinking
of them letter by letter.

Directions:
*Type each line twice. 60-
space line. Single spacing.
DS after each pair of lines.*

1 it we or my is us by so of up as be in go if at on to an do 12
2 he in be no go on if at to an do ox or we it is us by so of 24
3 she too ask buy run ago two can end its may get one got eye 35

4 old lot and due how but not now use boy hay her way try for 12
5 out let pay cot day sir own and has new big the any who off 24
6 some here work paid mail such able duty well they your send 35

| 1 | 2 | 3 | 4 | 5 | 6 | 7 | 8 | 9 | 10 | 11 | 12 |

(Continued on next page)

The outline of the speech Mr. Suroyal plans to give at the NABE luncheon is shown below. Type the outline in standard outline form. (To review procedures for typing outlines, refer to page 151.)

BUILDING OFFICE SKILLS

I.   Learning Basic Skills First
   A.   Crawling as Preliminary to Walking
   B.   Typing as Preliminary to Other Office Skills

II. Skills Required for Office Work
   A.   Basic Skills
      1.   Typing skills
      2.   Language skills
         a.   Listening
         b.   Speaking
         c.   Reading
         d.   Writing
   B.   Complementary Skills
      1.   Personal/social skills
         a.   Dealing with co-workers
         b.   Dealing with supervisors
         c.   Dealing with the public
      2.   Management skills
         a.   Planning and organizing work
         b.   Setting priorities
         c.   Making decisions

III. Office Functions Requiring Learned Skills
   A.   Simple Functions Related to Language Skills
      1.   Answering telephones
      2.   Filing papers
      3.   Typing correspondence
      4.   Understanding and following directions
   B.   More Complex Functions Related to Communication Skills
      1.   Originating correspondence
      2.   Using reference works
      3.   Listening to criticism or complaints
      4.   Resolving day-to-day problems

IV. Need for Learning Communication Skills in School
   A.   To Qualify For a Rewarding Job
   B.   For Survival on the Job
   C.   To Increase Chances of Promotion

V.   Implications of Word Processing Equipment for Communication Skills

Words continued

7 list this just glad more bill very much note like last with   12
8 make what must city will know them name next have good sent   24
9 half soon time made envy line part hand fork wish same been   35

10 right chain until going wrote other cover write sorry early   12
11 would first above taken books check favor these delay claim   24
12 about could again mouth small thank stock three money short   35

    1 | 2 | 3 | 4 | 5 | 6 | 7 | 8 | 9 | 10 | 11 | 12 |

PHRASES

Curve your fingers directly over the keys. Use a snappy stroke—strike and release the key in one motion.

Directions:

Type each line twice. 60-space line. Single spacing. DS after each pair of lines.

1 it is, to go, to do, by us, to it, of us, to us, is it, he is   12
2 to do, he is, by it, to go, or if, is to, if it, if he, is he   24
3 to do this, of the, to do that, by the, to do the, to do work   37
4 if the, with them, to do such, and the, with both, with which   49

5 for them, and then, of them, and this, for the, and that was   12
6 and did, and them, and for, by them, and work, they wish for   24
7 they wish, and they, and wish, to them, and shows, got there   36
8 and do, of the, and name, that man, and both, for their good   48

9 with the, to make, with them, when it, with both, and is the   12
10 for them, and their, with me, and they, with that, they make   24
11 did make, for the, did work, for they, and so, for which the   36
12 and if, the big, and if they, go to the, they make, to their   48

13 if they take, as it is, of our, she owns, if they show those   12
14 all of them, one of these, one of our men, as soon as we can   24
15 a few of those, as soon as, we are not, now and then, for he   36
16 as soon as you are, we have been, here and there, as much as   48

17 please send us, by the way, in the past, from them, we asked   12
18 from that time, in this letter, you sent us, he must be here   24
19 you will agree that, to take part, not later than, she feels   36
20 I feel sure, if you agree with us, for a long time, to do so   48

21 as she said, it was done, when it is ready, in the beginning   12
22 around the world, during the week, so to speak, to the right   24
23 if possible, and we quote, last name first, give and receive   36
24 jumps the gun, return a call, join the group, every so often   48

    1 | 2 | 3 | 4 | 5 | 6 | 7 | 8 | 9 | 10 | 11 | 12 |

introduce some of our new products, and this, I hope, will lead to increased interest in our company's exhibit.

I am enclosing a copy of my proposed intinerary for your information and reference.

Exercise 2

Type the itinerary for Mr. Suroyal's trip to New York as outlined below. Remember to make an extra copy for enclosure with the memo to Mr. Dryer.

Itinerary

L. M. Suroyal

April 1–4, 19—

WEDNESDAY, April 1

7 p.m. EST	Leave Cleveland, American Airlines Flight 274, Hopkins Airport.
8:40 p.m. EST	Arrive New York, LaGuardia Airport. Confirmed accommodations at Gotham City Hotel; 280 East 48th Street; Telephone: (212) 988-1072.

THURSDAY, April 2

9 a.m.	Formal opening of NABE Convention, Dewey Auditorium, Gotham City Hotel.
12 noon	Presentation at luncheon, Empire Room.
3 p.m.	At company's exhibit. Make final arrangements for our hospitality hour.
6 p.m.	Hospitality Hour, Suite 3478.

FRIDAY, April 3

12 noon	Luncheon meeting with our exhibit staff.
7 p.m.	Formal banquet of convention.

SATURDAY, April 4

12 noon	Closing luncheon of convention.
3:30 p.m. EST	Leave New York, LaGuardia Airport, American Airlines Flight 208.
4:50 p.m. EST	Arrive Cleveland, Hopkins Airport.

MONDAY, April 6

	In office.

SENTENCES

Maintain a good posture. Sit erect, with feet on the floor and body bent slightly forward. Keep the upper arms and the elbows near the body. Let the forearms and wrists slant upward to the machine. Do not hump or arch the wrists; on the other hand, do not let them touch the machine.

Directions:
Take a series of 30-second timed writings on lines 1–20. Explore a new level of typing by reaching for two words more than your regular 1-minute rate. (To figure wpm on a 30-second writing, double the total words you typed.)

60-space line. Double spacing.

1 Both of them may rush to the ancient city for the festivals. 12
2 Elaine wants to move from the crowded town into the country. 24
3 When my best friend Robert asked for help, I gave it to him. 36
4 Those who are masters of themselves are the leaders in life. 48

5 Those who have climbed to the top often began at the bottom. 12
6 We never know the worth of water till the well runs too dry. 24
7 The name of the firm they own is to the right of the window. 36
8 Many schools now offer a placement service to some students. 48

9 The judge made sure the lady got just what she ought to get. 12
10 People take more vacations in the summer than in the winter. 24
11 He did the work of five men today, and this is not his duty. 36
12 At the end of the year the firms gave each employee a bonus. 48

13 I had the form with me when I took down the name of the man. 12
14 We wish you would please send us a copy of your fall prices. 24
15 This is the first time we have been able to make our quotas. 36
16 I was happy to find your name was listed in the top quarter. 48

17 There will be many price changes before the end of the year. 12
18 We promise to press just the tip of each finger when typing. 24
19 Eyes on the road at all times; do not drive at a high speed. 36
20 We received notice that a second meeting would be held soon. 48

1 | 2 | 3 | 4 | 5 | 6 | 7 | 8 | 9 | 10 | 11 | 12 |

ONE-MINUTE SPEED DRIVES

Keep eyes on copy, not only while you type, but also when you return the carriage.

Directions:
Use these sentences for 1- or 2-minute timed writings. For additional selections, use the Supplementary Practice section at the end of this book.

60-space line. Double spacing. 5-space paragraph indention.

1   The history of humanity, both in the far past and in the 12
recent past, is largely a history of war.   SI 1.40 20

2   The extremely mild weather that we have enjoyed this 11
spring has had a favorable effect on our business.   SI 1.50 21

3   Our new pen writes as smoothly and naturally as a pencil. 12
The more you use it, the better you will like it.   SI 1.27 22

1 | 2 | 3 | 4 | 5 | 6 | 7 | 8 | 9 | 10 | 11 | 12 |

(Continued on next page)

6 Mr. Conrad D. Boyd, Goodwill Hardware, 942 New Street, St. Paul, MN 55116

7 Mr. Louis F. Swarthmore, 709 West Tenth Street, St. Paul, MN 55107

8 Miss Barbara Krantz, 721 McKibbin Street, St. Paul, MN 55115

9 Mr. Leonard D. Nielson, 494 Wellman, St. Paul, MN 55103

10 Dr. Eugene M. Ryan, School of Medicine, Stillwell University, St. Paul, MN 55118

11 Mr. Robert A. Ostmann, Jr., 195 S. Chatsworth, St. Paul, MN 55103

12 Dr. Valerie J. Clappison, 2852 Colby Avenue, St. Paul, MN 55101

Exercise 5

Prepare 12 self-addressed No. 6 envelopes to be used as enclosures with the letters typed in Exercise 3. The envelopes should be addressed to the Children's Club.

Project B-7

This project covers:
1. Interoffice memo
2. Itinerary
3. Outline for a speech

Review the general directions on page 394 before you begin.

Exercise 1

The typewritten draft of the memo below contains three spelling errors and one comma error. Find and correct the errors as you type the memo.

SUBJECT: Itinerary for Proposed Trip   DATE: March 19, 19--

TO: C. V. Dryer, District Director

FROM: L. M. Suroyal, Manager, Educational Marketing Division

As we discussed prevously, I have been invited to be the

luncheon speaker on April 2 at the annual convention of the Nation-

al Association of Business Educators in New York City. I think

that you will agree that my presence at this convention will give

me an exellent opportunity to make friends for our company.

My topic "Building Office Skills" should be of great interest

to those who attend. During my talk, I will have an opportunity to

(Continued on next page)

4   One of our objectives should be to offer employment to 12
all people who wish to work and who are able to do so. SI 1.30 23

5   One day during the summer we noticed that the trim lawn 12
was no longer trim and that weeds were appearing in the paths. 24
SI 1.26

6   People have learned to fly. Parting company with their 12
friend the horse, they've sailed high into the sky with the 24
eagle. SI 1.27 25

7   As he walked along he noticed, at the side of the road, 12
a few stones that marked the foundation of what had once been 24
a house. SI 1.15 26

8   We are taking the matter up with the clerk who waited on 12
you and wish to assure you that you will have no further cause 25
for   complaint. SI 1.22 27

    1   2   3   4   5   6   7   8   9   10   11   12

Beginning with paragraph 9, your typed lines will not end at the same point as those shown in the text. Listen for the warning bell to alert you that you are approaching the end of your line.

9   In the spring the garden was a beautiful picture. The tulips were 14
a mass of bright colors, red and yellow. The lawn became a soft green. 28
SI 1.31

10 Within the next few weeks, we plan to place on the market a new 13
type of motor, which will undoubtedly find a ready sale both at home 26
and abroad. SI 1.28 28

11 We regret to have to inform you that work on your order is being 14
delayed because Bob cannot obtain delivery of the materials that we 27
need for it. SI 1.50 29

12 A business of our standing is under an obligation to do every- 13
thing in its power to preserve its proper share of the export trade in 27
the next two years. SI 1.40 31

13 It has become the custom in recent years at our open meetings 13
to make a few remarks in regard to general business conditions, as 26
well as those in our own field. SI 1.39 32

14 The spoken word is more powerful than the written word. Today 13
the spoken word is not limited by space or time, because we have the 27
radio and we can make recordings. SI 1.42 34

    1   2   3   4   5   6   7   8   9   10   11   12   13

(Continued on next page)

Exercise 2

This letter was dictated by Gerald T. Horner, Chairman of the Fund-Raising Committee for the St. Paul Children's Club. Supply the salutation and complimentary closing. Determine paragraphing.

October 2, 19— / Mr. Harvey N. Nugent / Nugent Paints / 815 Forge Street / St. Paul, MN 55112 / I wish to thank you on behalf of the Children's Club for the advertisement you placed in the program of our Annual Sports Show. This year, through the support of all our area advertisers, we will again be able to provide many unfortunate young people of St. Paul with assistance ranging from food and clothing to college scholarships. We hope that you will be able to attend a performance of the sports show. We shall be happy to send you a complimentary ticket if you will let us know which performance you would like to attend. If you wish additional tickets, please use the enclosed order form. We will see that your order is filled promptly.

Exercise 3

Type this form letter, which was prepared by Edith W. Wise, Director of the Children's Club. Determine paragraphing. Duplicate 12 copies of the letter for use in Exercise 4.

October 3, 19— / Dear Friend / At this time every year, the Children's Club of St. Paul begins to make plans for its Annual Sports Show. The main objective of the club is to improve the lives of the needy children in this city by providing them with milk and other foods, clothing, and medical and dental care. We sponsor several youth clubs, too, and every summer, we send hundreds of children to a camp where they stay for a week. In recent years, we have also been able to offer scholarships to several institutions of learning. The Annual Sports Show provides the major part of the funds for these activities, and we hope you will help us by attending. We are sure that this year's show has something for everyone to enjoy. We are enclosing a scale of ticket prices with an attached order form. Please fill in the form and mail it to us with your check in the self-addressed envelope. / Cordially

Exercise 4

Type address labels from the mailing list below for envelopes in which to mail the form letters prepared in Exercise 3.

1 Ms. Catherine Ives, 66 Newton Avenue, St. Paul, MN 55107

2 Mrs. Rona Willis, 254 Central Avenue, St. Paul, MN 55110

3 Mr. Samuel F. Jeffries, 52 Kingsbridge Street, St. Paul, MN 55103

4 Mrs. Flora Cuneo, Sunrise House, 175 Henry Street, St. Paul, MN 51123

5 Dr. Howard Fishbein, 505 Buckminster Building, 291 Stapleton Plaza, St. Paul, MN 55101

(Continued on next page)

15   I have placed a lot of stress on the important problems facing us 14
because I believe that our course of action must be decided in rela- 28
tion to the facts that I have presented.   SI 1.40 37

16   To those of us who spend their lives in the light of open spaces, 14
it may be strange to think that there are men who spend a large part 28
of their lives moving about under the ground.   SI 1.14 37

17   I am sending you two lists of books that I recommend. The 13
lists have several divisions, each containing a group of books of one 27
type, for example, books of adventure, books on sports.   SI 1.36 38

18   Nothing here seems to change. The river still runs over its bed 14
of stones, just as it has been doing for many years. The house is the 28
same as ever. Even the people do not seem to change.   SI 1.21 39

19   The average price of most stocks has fallen considerably during 14
the past several months, but the experts say prices will rise again in 28
a week or two. As a matter of fact, some are up already.   SI 1.39 39

20   Reading is one of the cheapest and yet one of the most profitable 14
of pleasures. It may even be enjoyed without cost in a public library. 28
Reading offers a storehouse of pleasure which need never end.   SI 1.45 40

21   Many boys and girls of high school age spend a great deal of time 14
thinking about which college they should enter. It seems to me that 28
the first question they should decide is whether to go to college at all. 43
    SI 1.23

22   All of us have met people who will conceitedly explain to anyone 14
who will listen how to manage the finances of this country, and then 28
they will try to borrow a dollar or two to keep them until the next 41
payday.   SI 1.39 42

23   A Frenchman once said that, although the people of other nations 14
could not be expected to agree that France is the greatest nation in 28
Europe, it was enough that they all allowed the French nation to claim 42
second place.   SI 1.39 44

24   Once Daisy, our dog, finds a trail, she will follow it no matter 14
how many other paths cross it—unless it enters a body of water. Since 28
water carries no scent, she has to try to pick up the trail again on the 42
other side.   SI 1.29 44

1   2   3   4   5   6   7   8   9   10   11   12   13

Project B-6

This project includes the preparation of:
1. Order form with duplicated copies
2. Business letter
3. Form letter with duplicated copies
4. Address labels
5. Self-addressed envelopes

Review the general directions on page 394 before you begin.

Exercise 1

Prepare a ticket order form from the information given below.
Then duplicate 13 copies to use as enclosures in Exercises 2 and 3.

CHILDREN'S CLUB

318 Central Avenue

St. Paul, MN 55106

Scale of Prices—Annual Sports Show

Evenings: November 15, 16, and 17, 19—

Matinees: November 15 and 16, 19—

	Matinee	Evening
Orchestra, rows 1 to 15	$7.00	$8.00
Orchestra, rows 16 to 30	5.50	6.50
Mezzanine	4.50	5.50
Balcony, rows 1 to 3	3.00	4.00
Balcony, rows 4 to 10	2.50	3.50

_ _

Detach here and return order form below with your check.

TO: Children's Club   DATE: _____

     318 Central Avenue

     St. Paul, MN 55106

Please send me tickets for your Annual Sports Show as indicated below:

a) _____ tickets @ $ _____ for the matinee performance on November _____

b) _____ tickets @ $ _____ for the evening performance on November _____

If tickets are not available for the date or performance requested, my

second choice is: _____

Name _____

Street _____

City, State _____ ZIP _____

Telephone _____

THREE-MINUTE SPEED DRIVES

There are times in your practice work when you should try to break through your speed level. You should do this when you have gained control and can't seem to type at a higher rate of speed. When this happens, forget errors temporarily and concentrate on typing at a new high rate. Each time you hit a new high in your speed, the slower rates will become more natural and your control will return.

Directions:
Use the paragraphs at the right for 3-minute writings. For additional selections, refer to the Supplementary Practice section at the end of this book.

60-space line. Double spacing. 5-space paragraph indention.

1   The paper used for printing paper money of the United   12
States is supplied by a firm that has a secret process for   23
producing a kind of paper that nobody can counterfeit. Only   36
the owner of the mill knows the secret of the process. He   48
received it from his father; he will pass it on to his child.   59
SI 1.39

2   The electric typewriter has made things so much easier   12
that it is hard to understand why the busy typist wishes to   24
use a manual. The finished work always is so much neater.   35

Many more clear copies may be made by just regulating a   47
control for the number of copies that you want. The copies   59
produced will all be clear.   SI 1.43   64

3   The state plans to take over part of your land in order   12
to widen the state road which runs past it. The enclosed map   24
shows the part which the state intends to acquire. We shall   36
send a representative from our department shortly to confer   48
with you. She will arrange by next week to adjust your claim   60
for an amount satisfactory to you and to the state.   SI 1.32   70

4   I have your letter and the map on which you have marked   12
the part of my property which the state plans to acquire in   24
order to widen the present state road. I shall make a careful   36
study of the map so that I may be in a position to talk the   48
matter over with your representative when she comes. Please   60
ask her to telephone and let me know when she will call at my   72
home.   SI 1.25   73

5   Two weeks ago I sent you an order, with check enclosed,   12
for a dozen linen guest towels, listed in your catalog at ten   24
dollars a dozen. I said that I prefer the towels in tan with   36
red border; but that if you do not have these, I would accept   48
them in orange. Since then I have not heard from you. Will   60
you please send the towels promptly or write or call me and   72
explain the delay.   SI 1.22   76

1   2   3   4   5   6   7   8   9   10   11   12

(Continued on next page)

This letter is a reply to Mr. Kahn's letter in Exercise 1. It is written by Rupert C. Pennington, District Sales Manager. Supply the salutation and complimentary closing for this letter. Date the letter August 14, 19—, and send it to the attention of Mr. Kahn at the address shown at the right. Send a copy to Ms. C. L. Trenton, Sales Representative, Suite 326, Danville Bank Building, Danville, VA 24541.

Danville Area Vocational Center
2935 Grover Road
Danville, VA 24541

~~We are~~ *I am* sending you under separate cover our illustrated catalog, which gives descriptions and prices for *all* our folding auditorium chairs.

~~I believe that you will find~~ model No. 28372, *shown on* page 65, ~~espe-cially~~ *appears to be especially* suitable for your purposes. The cahirs are luxuriously padded, with armrests between them. They are easily folded and unfolded in a single movement to allow for *quick and compact* storage. Since they have no nuts, bolts, or scres, ~~unnecessary~~ *costly* manpower is not ~~wasted in moving the chairs;~~ *required to assemble and disassemble them.* ¶ Generally, we require a shipping time of fifteen days after receipt of an order.

A copy of this letter is being forwarded to our sales representative in your area, ~~Ms. C. L.~~ *Constance* Trenton, so that she can follow through on your inquiry. Her office is located in the Danville Bank Bldg. in your city. You ~~will~~ *can expect to* hear from her this week to arrange ~~for~~ a convenient time to meet ~~with you~~ to discuss your order.

Thank you for giving us the oportunity to serve you.

Compose a letter from Constance L. Trenton to Albert T. Kahn. Date it September 1, 19—, and include the following information, using your own words:

a. Thank Mr. Kahn for placing an order for 600 folding auditorium chairs. (He placed the order after you suggested that he visit the office to see showroom samples.)

b. Tell him that his order has been put on rush and that the shipment should arrive within ten days.

c. Thank him for his business and ask him to call Ms. Trenton if he does not receive a confirmation copy of the shipping order in the next day or two.

6 This morning we received a telegram from our factory, 12
telling us that there will be a slight delay in shipping the 24
two clocks that you ordered. We regret this delay very much, 36
but it is due to conditions beyond our control. We hope that it 48
will not cause you any trouble. We have instructed the fac- 60
tory to send the shipment to you as soon as possible. It will 72
be shipped by express at our expense. SI 1.37 79

7 It is easier to find fault with the world as it is than 12
to set the world straight. There is no doubt that many of our 24
complaints are well founded; but our duty lies not so much in 36
finding fault with the world as in trying to make the world 48
what it ought to be. If we gave our best strength all day 60
long to setting the world straight, we should not be so likely 72
to sit up far into the night complaining of what is wrong with 84
it. SI 1.15 85

8 Throughout our lives we are spending time. We can go 12
through a day now and then without breaking into our store of 24
money, but we cannot live at all without using some of our 36
store of time. Minute by minute we are spending our time, 48
and the way in which the minutes are spent makes up our way 60
of living. If we let the days slip idly by, we are likely to 72
lead incomplete lives. If we spend our time wisely, we shall 84
lead happy and productive lives. SI 1.25 90

9 Typists who wish to build up their speed should use copy 12
that is easy to type and simple to read. Also, the copy should 25
contain words that they can type at a high rate. 35

Many words should be typed as though they were just one 47
unit, for this is what typists must do when they want to raise 59
their rates to a new high. Some words may be hard to type 71
even though they are short words and the typist should try to 83
stroke such words at a pace slow enough to write without mis- 95
takes. SI 1.14 96

10 We went into the village grocery. It was not a large 12
place; in fact, it was only twelve feet square; but it was 24
filled with a variety of good things. There were hams and sides 36

| 1 | 2 | 3 | 4 | 5 | 6 | 7 | 8 | 9 | 10 | 11 | 12 |

(Continued on next page)

This letter was dictated by Lila Stallworth, Supervisor of the Customer Service Department. Determine paragraphing. Note the itemized list.

Mrs. Alice Gardiner / 1482 Bay Road / Milwaukee, WI 53217 / Dear Mrs. Gardiner / Thank you for trusting your fur coat to us for summer storage. We are certain you will be satisfied with our service. At your request, our fur experts have completed an examination of your coat, and they have found it in need of the following repairs: 1. The buttons and the fur around them are worn and should be replaced. 2. The edge of the right cuff is frayed and a new piece of fur should be substituted. 3. The fur lacks luster and would be greatly improved by our Hollanderizing treatment. This gives new life to furs that have received years of wear. It removes grime from beneath the surface and restores natural oils. If you wish the repairs to be made, we shall be happy to give you a quotation. We urge you to have the work done, as it will prolong the life of your beautiful coat. / Sincerely

Project B-5

This project covers the preparation of:
1. Business letter
2. Letter with special notation
3. Letter composed from notes

Review the general directions on page 394 before you begin.

Exercise 1

This letter was written by Albert T. Kahn, Purchasing Agent for Danville Area Vocational Center. Supply the salutation and complimentary closing. Date the letter August 9, 19—, and send it to the address shown at the right.

Institutional Furniture Suppliers
62 Myrtle Street
Richmond, VA 23222

We are in need of approximately six hundred ~~seats~~ *auditorium chairs* for a dining-forum area in ~~a~~ *our* new building. We are ~~interested in purchasing~~ *looking for portable* chairs ~~which are portable~~ *used for different* since the area will be ~~multi~~ purpose*s*. The chairs should be *of a type that can be* easily assembled and disassembled, and *they* should fold quickly for storage. We would prefer *a model that has* ~~chairs with an~~ interlocking padded arm rest*s* between every two ~~seats~~ *chairs.* What have you to offer that meets ~~our~~ *these* requirements? Please quote *us* prices and give us ~~some~~ *an* idea of the time ~~usually~~ required for delivery after an order *has been* ~~is~~ placed and approved.

of bacon hanging from the ceiling. The floor was crowded with 48
barrels of sugar and flour. The shelves were piled high with 60
tins of coffee and canned foods, with cheese and crackers, 72
loaves of bread, and bags of dried fruits. It was a wonder 84
that so many things could fit into so small a shop, but there 96
they were. SI 1.20 97

11 Typists today find their work much more simple than did 12
those in the past. They can now do rapidly what they would 24
have found at one time to be a long and tiresome job. 35

There were many long years of hard and persistent work 47
on the part of those who wanted to make the job of a typist 59
easier and more pleasant. At that time they realized 70
that typists would one day make up a vital part of the 81
nation and they wanted just the right machine for the job. 93
The copier is one such machine that makes the typist's work 105
easier. SI 1.26 106

1 | 2 | 3 | 4 | 5 | 6 | 7 | 8 | 9 | 10 | 11 | 12

Topic 3 ACCURACY PRACTICE

When you wish to type with a high degree of accuracy, the best thing to do is slow down a little. This deliberate reduction in speed reduces tension and permits you to type with confidence and control.

Another way to improve accuracy is to analyze your errors and take corrective practice. You will find corrective drills for substitution-type errors on pages 74–78 in this section. In the Supplementary Practice section in the back of this book, there are remedial drills for every letter of the alphabet and punctuation mark.

ALPHABETIC SENTENCES

Each of the following sentences contains every letter of the alphabet. Type them more slowly than your normal rate and concentrate on each reach.

Directions:
60-space line. Double spacing.

1 Tomorrow we shall have our junior clerk type a list of expenses, 13
including prizes given at the banquet. 22

2 I am certain that a piece five or six inches square would be a good 35
size for a pocket on your jacket. 42

3 After briefly questioning the embezzler who stole the funds, the 55
banker rejected his vague explanation. 64

1 | 2 | 3 | 4 | 5 | 6 | 7 | 8 | 9 | 10 | 11 | 12 | 13

(Continued on next page)

may telephone for this service. Promptly on receipt of your order, we shall send you a confirmation card that shows the signature of the bonded driver who will call for your furs and the date on which you should expect him. Make certain that the driver signs the call slip and that you compare the signature with the one on the confirmation card. This precaution is taken to protect you against fraud or theft in transferring your furs. / Very truly yours

Exercise 2

Prepare a self-addressed postal card for enclosure with the letter in Exercise 1. Use the address shown at the right. Type the information given below on the message side. Leave enough space for the customer to fill in the required information.

Milwaukee Fur Company
Attention Fur Storage Department
809 Grange Street
Milwaukee, WI 53206

_____, 19__

Gentlemen

Please have your bonded driver call for my _____ within one week following receipt of this card. These furs are valued at $ _____.

_____
Name

_____
Telephone

_____
Street Address   Apt. No.   City, State, ZIP

Exercise 3

From the information below, prepare a list of fur storage rates for enclosure with Exercise 1. Give the table a title and use the current year. Type leaders between columns for ease in reading.

FUR COATS

Valuation	Rate
Up to $750	$ 15.00
$751 to $1,500	44.50
$1,501 to $3,500	51.00
$3,501 to $5,000	57.50
$5,001 to $6,500	67.00
$6,501 to $9,000	78.00
$9,001 to $12,000	85.00
$12,001 to $15,000	107.00
$15,001 to $20,000	137.00

STOLES

Valuation	Rate
Up to $1,000	$30.00

FUR-TRIMMED COATS

Valuation	Rate
Up to $300	$12.00

4 Without a doubt, many thousands have joined our organization 12 because of our quick exposure of the plot. 21

5 We recognize the justice of your claim for adequate damages, but 34 you are making charges that appear excessive. 43

6 An industrious worker of average ability frequently accomplishes 56 more at his job than one who is expert but lazy. 66

7 We require five dozen blue glass cups to replace the mixed 12 lot, damaged in packing, which we rejected last Friday. 23

8 We expect to keep the major portion of our heavy equipment in large- 35 sized storage vaults because of lack of floor space. 47

9 My cousin enjoys an inexpensive hobby; he likes building small- 60 sized models of railway equipment, made chiefly of matches. 72

10 A vast crowd at the banquet eagerly awaited the announcement of 13 the lucky exhibitor to whom the jury had awarded the prize. 25

11 The accountant required very little time to examine the journal and 38 find the errors which had so long puzzled the bookkeeper. 50

12 The superintendent of the factory developed a unique plan, with the 63 object of systematizing the work and eliminating excessive motion. 76

13 I recognized the handwriting of the Mexican in the journal that he 13 kept, which I had recently acquired with several other books. 25

14 Mr. Zimmer has been offering excellent values in mink coats; but 38 upon inquiry we find that the sale will be over in just a week. 51

15 The citizens joined in advocating a tax cut of a quarter of a million 65 dollars, but they did not know any feasible way of reducing expenses. 79

16 Another reason for advising you to patronize our store is that we 13 quickly exchange unsatisfactory goods and make liberal adjustments. 26

17 Some of the natives were paralyzed with fear; others, less excited, 39 ran back to join the king and queen and warn them of the danger. 53

18 The governor familiarized himself with every part of the text in the 67 appeal, so as to be prepared to make an equitable adjustment in the 80 case. 81

19 At the bazaar the children will present a musical skit or review in 13 which a five-year-old boy will play a banjo and a mixed quartet will 27 sing. 28

1 2 3 4 5 6 7 8 9 10 11 12 13

(Continued on next page)

Prepare a boxed table from the copy below. Figure the vertical and horizontal totals first. In the secondary title, use the date for Monday in the current week.

	WEEKLY SALES ANALYSIS			
	(Week of ———)			
	Hardware	Housewares	Linens	Total
Monday	$ 38.95	$ 56.80	$ 16.50	$ XXX
Tuesday	32.60	29.40	68.45	XXX
Wednesday	94.20	38.65	59.55	XXX
Thursday	73.85	43.82	48.16	XXX
Friday	25.15	18.25	89.00	XXX
Saturday	110.50	56.75	98.95	XXX
Totals	$ XXX	$ XXX	$ XXX	$ XXX

Project B-4

This project covers the preparation of:
1. Business letter
2. Self-addressed postal card
3. Table with leaders
4. Business letter with numbered insert

Review the general directions on page 394 before you begin.

This letter was dictated by Randall McKinney, Manager of the Milwaukee Fur Company's Fur Storage Department. Determine paragraphing.

March 19, 19— / Mrs. Alice Gardiner / 1482 Bay Road / Milwaukee, WI 53217 / Dear Mrs. Gardiner / If you value your furs, you will want to give them the protection they need. All furs should be put into storage for the summer, to avoid the drying effects of the warm air and the danger of damage by moths. Our storage service includes not only housing in vaults that are cold, dry, and completely free from moths, but also insurance against fire and theft, and a treatment that removes surface dust. We are enclosing a table showing our rates. We invite you to fill in and mail the enclosed form, postage free. If you prefer, you

(Continued on next page)

20 The crew disembarked from the vessel, the Queen Pat, in a light 41
drizzle, after an exciting journey that had taken them halfway around 55
the world. 57

21 Although the dealer had only a hazy idea of the current quotations 70
in woven textiles, he rejected the price they offered for the valuable 84
damask. 85

22 The woman was puzzled by the directions for operating the vacuum 13
cleaner and asked the salesman to briefly explain the adjustment 26
of the equipment. 29

23 The envelope contained a note politely asking for the loan of a razor 43
and a pair of pajamas, but not a word of explanation for this unusual 57
request. 59

24 By making an adequate gift to this organization, you may share the 72
joy of sending to camp next summer youngsters who very badly need 85
fresh air and sunshine. 90

25 The thousands who patronize our store unquestionably approve of 13
our good judgment in the choice of stock, our exceptionally courteous 27
service, and our reasonable prices. 34

26 As a consequence of the talk which exposed the fraud, a large group 47
of citizens demanded an investigation to establish responsibility and 61
bring the criminals to justice. 67

27 The members of the searching party returned quite exhausted but 80
happy, for in the maze of trees and bushes in the dark jungle they had 94
found the lost child, weary but alive and well. 103

  1| 2| 3| 4| 5| 6| 7| 8| 9| 10| 11| 12| 13|

PAIRED LETTER DRILLS

If you are making many errors, you may want to analyze your errors to see how many are substitution-type errors, that is, *m* for *n*, *i* for *e*, and so on. If you have this difficulty, the drills that follow will be helpful. Select and type those drills which are applicable.

Directions:
Type each line twice. 60-space line. Single spacing. DS after each pair of lines.

1 **a/s** assassin standards statements situation separate absenteeism
2 specials assaults assure assign shares arrest adjust surpass
3 We hope the bank will send our statement to our new address.
4 Speakers of all ages will be assigned to answer the charges.

5 **b/n** urban sensible balance nab knobs snubbing subpoena benefited
6 stubbornly rebellion probation mountable honorable crumbling

  1| 2| 3| 4| 5| 6| 7| 8| 9| 10| 11| 12|

(Continued on next page)

Project B-3

This project calls for:
1. Interoffice memo
2. Ruled table
3. Boxed table

Review the general directions on page 394 before you begin.

Exercise 1

Prepare an interoffice memo from the handwritten copy below. Use today's date.

Subject: Departmental Reports
To: J. Goodman, President
From: M. Niles, Sales Manager

The two enclosed reports provide the information you requested about sales in the departments under my supervision. I am sending them to you now to allow you time to examine them at your convenience before our next meeting.

Exercise 2

Prepare a ruled table from the copy below. Figure the amounts for the *Net Sales* column by subtracting the sales returns from the gross sales. Provide totals for each column.

ANALYSIS OF SALES RETURNS

Department	Gross Sales	Sales Returns	Net Sales
Cosmetics	$ 857.74	$ 12.18	$ xxx
Hardware	375.25	42.45	xxx
Housewares	243.67	76.55	xxx
Jewelry	375.25	10.25	xxx
Leather Goods	455.60	6.55	xxx
Linens	380.61	19.20	xxx
Sporting Goods	995.35	26.75	xxx
Totals	$ xxx	$ xxx	$ xxx

7   In the bank basement there was a bundle of bonds on a bench.

8   The husband was being stubborn, ungovernable, and maddening.

9   **c/d**   exclude idiotic deceased candid confidence deduction conduct

10   cardiac childhood educate decay cards handicap incident dice

11   Indicate on cards if the candidates are candid and decisive.

12   She decided that the accident was due to a cardiac handicap.

13   **c/v**   invoice vocation excavate conclusive advocate excessive vice

14   conserve evacuate conceive advance verdict collective active

15   A convict held Victor captive in a cavern below the convent.

16   Two vicious convoys advanced on the evacuated town of Vichy.

17   **d/e**   endure exceed extend eldest emerald evidence deathbed damage

18   deceased definite deferred delayed expedient explode educate

19   The college degree made a difference to the eldest daughter.

20   His case was deferred when new evidence was presented today.

21   **d/k**   thanked weekend worked stockades attacked keyboard crackdown

22   breakdown kicked liked provoked skilled backwards blackheads

23   I thanked the duke for the haddock and vodka I had Thursday.

24   After darkness the kid locks the stockade and looks skyward.

25   **d/s**   reside sardines scandals disorder decrease darkness sideline

26   deserve dress sandy dismissed describe despise dessert sides

27   He was dismissed speedily when a scandal showed he deserted.

28   Decreases in deposits caused considerable disorder in banks.

29   **e/i**   legitimate evidence hygiene implied leisure itemize receipts

30   indeed eliminate illegible imbecile impatient indicate irate

31   The differences in the itemized receipts require attention.

32   Either the irate children were impatient or they were tired.

33   **e/r**   effort concern charter reserve receipt recover elector reads

34   operate explore inherit engineer encircle rationale response

35   What concerns the engineer is the rationale of her argument.

36   Great pressure was exerted as the operator jerked the crane.

37   **e/t**   absent execute citizen credit deposit complete accept detect

38   expect attend matter excite interfere interest dictate tempt

39   The jet emitted exhaust fumes over the flowers in the field.

40   An executive ignited a cigarette before he dictated letters.

1   2   3   4   5   6   7   8   9   10   11   12

(Continued on next page)

Project B-2

This project covers:
1. Business letter
2. Tabulated price list
3. Telegraph message

Review the general directions on page 394 before you begin.

Exercise 1

This letter was dictated by Daniel P. Torres, Marketing Manager for Rally CB's. Determine paragraphing.

December 1, 19— / Norwood Electronics / 143 Snyder Avenue / Rochester, NY 14614 / Gentlemen / Why not offer your customers mobile Citizens' Band radios that have all the extras at prices they can afford? Let us put our Rally CB's on display for a week in your store. The enclosed leaflet illustrates and describes the five models in our line; the price list shows the profit margin you can expect on each one. We hope that you will take the time to examine both the leaflet and the price list carefully. If you are interested in our trial offer, a sales representative will be happy to bring a display CB of each type to your shop and demonstrate their many unique features. At the end of one week, we are sure that customer response will convince you to place an order. If you wish to have one of our representatives visit you, please call this office and ask for Lotte Simms. / Sincerely

Exercise 2

Prepare a table from this unarranged price list copy. Figure the last column by subtracting the cost price from the list price.

RALLY CB's / Price List

(Subject to Change Without Notice)

Model	List Price	Cost Price	Your Margin
68-P	$48.95	$20.00	$xxxx
69-P	$70.50	$45.50	$xxxx
70-T	$110.00	$89.50	$xxxx
71-C	$149.50	$99.50	$xxxx
72-C	$248.95	$198.00	$xxxx

Exercise 3

Type a record of this telegraph message submitted by telephone. (For review of this procedure, refer to pages 296 and 299.)

Night Letter / January 4, 19— / 4:50 p.m. / Charge Sender / Daniel P. Torres / Rally CB's / 4763 Crest Drive / Philadelphia, PA 19119 / (716) 422-6137 / CB's are selling well. Send following immediately: 4, Model 68-P; 5, Model 70-T; and 3, Model 72-C. Bill according to usual credit arrangement. / O. Lawler, Chief Buyer / Norwood Electronics

41 **f/d** field defeat friend defend fender definite confidence afford
42 afraid offend farmlands clarified difficult defended confide
43 It was difficult to defend Ford who benefited from the deal.
44 We offered food to my friend who fled because he was afraid.

45 **f/g** glorify fixing finger grapefruit foreign fights fidgety gift
46 fitting firebug frontage frightful goldfish foggy figure fog
47 I shall begin fixing my home or seek glory on a golf course.
48 A fragile gift arrived from a foreign land for a frugal man.

49 **f/r** refuse firm brief differ effort conform certify offer inform
50 familiar officer perfect ratify portfolio refrain profit for
51 Fred was afraid the firm could not afford the artful affair.
52 The kind officer refused to fire me from the firm for fraud.

53 **g/b** bigamy governable gamble baggage garbage beggars grumble big
54 grab bag agreeable bandage begrudge beg cabbage embargo bugs
55 I was flabbergasted at the gabby grumblings from the beggar.
56 With a meal of cabbage and gingerbread, he became agreeable.

57 **g/h** hedge ghetto fright thing change graph right weight hydrogen
58 length extinguish gather hanging foghorn haggard fights high
59 I was aghast at the frightened, haggard women in the ghetto.
60 We gathered at night to haggle over hamburgers and hot dogs.

61 **g/t** might regret greet sight suggest together struggle gentlemen
62 originate mortgage exaggerate integral sergeants recognition
63 The sergeant went abroad together with his teenage daughter.
64 It was a great night as recognition was given the graduates.

65 **i/u** antiques beautiful community inclusive illuminates ultimate
66 impurity inequity insulted requisition premium minimum build
67 The alumni inquired about equipment issuing in universities.
68 To correct injustices, audits are conducted by seven unions.

69 **k/l** nickel black booklet luck shakily likable cocktail blackball
70 leak bilk kill lifelike checklist bookshelf buckle blackjack
71 We will be lucky if we find a likable bricklayer with skill.
72 Chuckling, the lanky girls knelt beside the playful kittens.

73 **m/n** minimum names meeting nighttime mechanism manuscript numb
74 number machine magazine mailing maintain magnify namely name

1   2   3   4   5   6   7   8   9   10   11   12

(Continued on next page)

will be to implement, on a national level, the policies that have worked so well for us in the southeastern states. In her new position, Marianne will report to Chris Dahl, Vice-President, Marketing. David Santos is appointed Executive Vice-President. Most of you already know David and the fine job he has done as controller for the past nine years. As a direct result of the management controls that he instituted, corporate profits have enjoyed a steady growth for nearly a decade. In his new position, David will be reporting directly to me. Please join me in welcoming Marianne and David to their new positions.

Exercise 2

This memo is from Olga Ghequiere, Office Manager. It announces a temporary change in working hours to take advantage of daylight saving time. Date the memo April 15, 19—, and address it to all office employees. Determine the paragraphing.

Next month we will be adopting "summer" hours. Last year's response to this change was so favorable that we decided to make the change a month earlier. Beginning May 1, our working hours will be from 8:00 a.m. to 4:00 p.m., with 30 minutes for lunch. These hours will apply through the end of August. Anyone who finds that the new hours will create a serious hardship should see me personally before the end of this week.

Exercise 3

This memo is from Lee Anderson, Director of Marketing, and deals with a sales incentive program. Date it March 15, 19—, and address it to all field representatives. Copies are to be sent to Edna D'Or and Bill Capote. Determine paragraphing.

Last year was our best year ever. Sales were up a record 37 percent over the previous year. Those of you who had 12 months' service or more as of December 31 of the past year will share handsomely in this growth, as you will see when you receive your bonus checks later this month. Those of you who were not eligible to participate in last year's program will be pleased to know that, effective immediately, all field sales personnel will now participate in the incentive program from their date of hire. Not only has the incentive program for this year been expanded to include all field representatives, but it has been further modified to provide even greater rewards to those who surpass the budget targets set for their territories. By separate letter, each of you will receive full details of how this plan will affect the bonus you will receive next year. Some of the key points in the new program are as follows: 1. On sales that exceed budget by 10 percent or less, a bonus of one-quarter of one percent of the amount over budget will be paid. 2. On sales that exceed budget by 11 percent to 25 percent, a bonus of one-half of one percent will be paid on the excess over 10 percent. 3. On sales that exceed budget by more than 25 percent, a bonus of three-quarters of one percent will be paid on the excess over 25 percent. I look forward to our making this another record year. / LA

75 For a nominal sum, I can maintain many accounts in his name.
76 Many magazines were missing after going through the machine.

77 **o/i** objective offering office opening opinion opportunity option
78 optimistic inclusion organization import outline iron obtain
79 Opening bids on the stock options were low in their opinion.
80 His office is optimistic that the omission was not intended.

81 **o/l** follow pillow collection foreclose formerly accomplish close
82 tolerate toolroom allow overlook lower solve velocity fellow
83 Those boys have the only double allowances of the whole lot.
84 A couple of decades from now we will be low on domestic oil.

85 **p/o** opinions approve protest bishop hypnotize prompt dispose top
86 approximate popular compact apropos program cooperate oppose
87 Pat and Les prefer purple, compact cars imported from Paris.
88 Temporarily, a popular bishop was appointed to the top post.

89 **r/t** react truck treat third relate terrific tariff thrift report
90 return rotary repeat theater right tenure rebate rents ratio
91 I reacted hysterically when the truck accident was reported.
92 This is the third time I turned right on my new truck route.

93 **r/u** further incur culture frustrate construct accrue bureau turn
94 quarrel acquire absurd curve century argue mature pursue fur
95 Burty, a builder, has constructed some popular homes for us.
96 A true soldier was assured a furlough for the inaugurations.

97 **s/c** scene abscess checks access confuse excess obscene recession
98 facsimile sarcasm discount politics process sincere services
99 I remember picnics where we ate delicious and luscious food.
100 Do not discount reckless schemes by politicians on occasion.

101 **s/w** wash sweet west swell news guesswork towards whereas windows
102 renewals lawless disallow awesome twosome waste whose cashew
103 We saw hundreds of little brownish glowworms on the windows.
104 I wish the housewives would sew all the snowsuits very soon.

105 **u/y** young unity busily annually auxiliary budgetary buying unify
106 yule actually fully adequately equality quality nullify buoy
107 Usually the youthful Mr. Burgyman knows quality when buying.
108 Lucy carefully counted the number of boys beyond your truck.

1 2 3 4 5 6 7 8 9 10 11 12

(Continued on next page)

MINI INTEGRATED PROJECTS

The work of the typist who handles correspondence is not limited to just typing letters. Often, there are accompanying tables, schedules, business forms, or other information that must be typed also. Each of the following mini projects is designed to give you practice in following through on the preparation of the total package of typed materials that centers around a single transaction.

Directions for Series B

1. Prepare at least one carbon copy of each assignment.
2. Type envelopes as necessary.
3. Vary the letter styles from project to project.
4. Determine paragraphing before beginning to type exercises in which the paragraphs are not shown. Remember that a paragraph is a group of sentences that develops one central thought. A new paragraph should begin where an obvious change in thought occurs.
5. Use eye judgment as much as possible to determine the placement of each assignment.

Project B-1

This project covers the preparation of interoffice memorandums.

Review the general directions above before you begin.

Exercise 1

This memo is from John MacMillan, President. It concerns the promotion of two employees. Date it March 1, 19—, and address it to all members of the staff. Determine paragraphing.

I am very pleased to announce the promotion of two of our employees, effective March 1, 19—. Marianne Gilbert, formerly Media Manager for the Southeastern Region, will be joining us in Phoenix as Director of Advertising. Marianne brings to this position twelve years of experience in all phases of our corporate advertising. One of her first responsibilities

(Continued on next page)

Paired Letter Drills continued

109 v/b vibrating vagabonds brevity vocabulary bevels visible beaver
110   valuables avoidable verbal above beverages combative bravery
111   Beverly is well known for her brevity and verbal vocabulary.
112   In the vestibule of the house on the boulevard stood a vase.

113 w/e widower entwine eyebrow edgeways elsewhere wreckage bewilder
114   worthwhile whether eyewitness between newspaper white beware
115   We watched Eyewitness News and later read the old newspaper.
116   Whether it's worthwhile to remarry is up to the old widower.

117 y/t yesterday hypnotic typify ability analyst history rhythm toy
118   thrifty warranty validity technology synthetic treasury type
119   Try to type the story on the history of synthetic dyestuffs.
120   Yesterday a witty analyst with fifty yachts became a martyr.

121 z/a zodiac agonize sizable penalize jazz hazard serialize razors
122   quartz revitalize trapeze paralyze dazzle bizarre liberalize
123   Can you visualize a meal of zesty pizza accompanied by jazz?
124   A zealous zebra zigzagged, after a tranquilizer dazzled him.

1   2   3   4   5   6   7   8   9   10   11   12

ERROR CORRECTION DRILLS

Sometimes an error is triggered by the word preceding or following the word in which the error is made. Use the following six passages as practice copy for developing greater control over random-type errors. Follow the directions at the left for each passage.

Directions:
Type the paragraphs at the right at your own speed. When you make an error, stop and retype the preceding word, the word which contains the error, and the word immediately after the error. For instance, in the first line of the first paragraph, if you make an error on the word *job*, stop and type *right job can* and then continue. After previewing the paragraphs in this way, take a 3-minute timed writing. Your goal is no more than 3 errors.

60-space line. Double spacing. 5-space paragraph indention.

1   Getting the right job can make the difference between a happy, 13
successful life and a life of disappointment and failure. The right job 27
can mean good food and clothes and a comfortable home for you and 40
your family. 42

    It can mean time and money for recreation and vacations. It can 56
mean the respect of your friends. Today millions of men and women 69
are enjoying careers in clerical and sales work.   SI 1.46 79

2   Many of us have seen television programs in which people on the 14
street are questioned by the inquiring reporter. On one of these programs, 29
the question asked was whether people liked their work. The various 43
answers all pointed to the fact that if they did, it was probably because 58
they were good at it. 62

    There is a great deal of truth in this conclusion. You will not meet 77
experts in any trade or art who are not deeply interested in their work. 91

1   2   3   4   5   6   7   8   9   10   11   12   13   14

(Continued on next page)

Please ~~include~~ ^incorporate^ these two points when you draw up the formal contract. If you will then send the contract to us, we will forward it to our client for his signature.

                                    Very truly yours

Exercise 3

This letter was dictated by Elizabeth L. Hartley. It is to be sent to the address shown at the right. Send a copy of the letter to Walter S. Farley. (There are 143 words in the body.)

Municipal Transportation System
64 Penn Street
Madison, WI 53714

November 22, 19--

Gentlemen

My ^Our^ client, Walter S. Farley, reports an injury sustained by him as he was ~~in the act of~~ stepping off a No. 5F ~~southbound~~ (stet) bus operated by one of your drivers. The bus started suddenly, throwing ~~my~~ ^our^ client to the ground and ~~injuring~~ causing him to injure his back. ¶ The accident occurred last Monday (November 15) at about 5:30 P.M. at the northwest corner of Harvard Avenue and Day Street.

No doubt you have a complete report of this case, including ~~a copy~~ copies of the police and hospital records, and copies of the statements of three witnesses.

Before taking any legal action, we shall be pleased to consider an amicable ~~adjustment~~ settlement that will fully compensate Mr. Farley for ~~the~~ his suffering, medical expenses, and loss of ~~employment he incurred due to~~ earnings as a result of this accident. Please let us know when we can meet to discuss this matter with you and your attorneys.

                                    Yours very truly

People who excel at the work they are paid to do are certain to enjoy it 105
and are well on the road to a happy life. SI 1.33 113

3 A person who takes out a loan and does not repay it on time gets a 14
bad credit rating. If you are in high school, chances are you have not 28
taken out any loans and you have no large debts to repay. In terms of your 43
credit rating, that's an advantage. 50

On the other hand, chances are you do not have any record of good 64
credit either. Most likely, you have no credit rating at all. One bank mana- 80
ger says that she cannot automatically give loans to people with no credit 95
rating because that would be like saying it will be sunny all day when you 110
have seen only five minutes of the day. SI 1.32 118

4 I once asked a group of friends what work is. Most of them considered 15
the question a joke. One spoke of it as the only means he had discovered 29
of getting money. A second defined it as something she was paid to do by 44
someone who got more just for telling her to do it. A third said it is trying 60
to sell something to people who do not want it. 69

Still another took the question seriously. He said that by work we mean 85
using the labor of people in such a way that something is produced that 99
is needed or desired. That answer made me realize the true purpose of work. 114
SI 1.29

5 Sales work offers career opportunities for young people who have 14
not completed high school, as well as for those who have a college degree; 28
for men and women who like to travel and those who do not; and for 42
people who want salaried employment, as well as those who aspire to run 56
their own business. 60

Workers in this occupational group may sell for manufacturers, insur- 74
ance companies, and other producers of goods and services; for whole- 88
salers who stock large quantities of goods so that smaller lots may be 102
purchased and resold by retail stores; and for drugstores, dress shops, 116
and other retailers who deal directly with the public. SI 1.50 127

6 The real source of all the rivers of the earth is above our heads. A vast 16
amount of water is flowing into the many seas of the world and the flow 30
seems to go on forever. Every year fourteen of the largest rivers pour into 45
the seas five billion tons of water; yet the seas never seem to change 59
their level. 62

All rivers flow from the land to the sea, but they must return in another 77
form. When we look up and see masses of moving clouds, we are looking 91
at the constant flow of rivers back to the air. From the seas all over the 106
world, the sun turns water into vapor, which rises into the air until at some 122
time it falls again as rain to renew its ceaseless cycle. SI 1.29 133

| 1 | 2 | 3 | 4 | 5 | 6 | 7 | 8 | 9 | 10 | 11 | 12 | 13 | 14 |

with the terms of the court order by ~~then~~ that time, it will be

necessary to ~~apply for~~ request an extension of time in which to

settle the estate.

Please inform us immediatly whether you require

additional time. We must make formal application for an

extension at least (5) days prior to the final date set by

the Surrogate's (Ct.)

                              Sincerely

Exercise 2

This letter was dictated by Lloyd F. Gwynn. The letter is to be sent to the address shown at the right. Send a copy of the letter to Bradley Coombs. (There are 127 words in the body.)

Dodge & Bordeau
Building Contractors
206 Ryder Avenue
Madison, WI 53710

November 21, 19--

Gentlemen

We have examined the draft of the agreement between

you and our client, Bradley Coombs, that you sent to us last week. There are

two points that should be added before the contract is

signed.

~~In the~~ first place, no time limit for the completion

of the work is specified. ~~It is so important~~ that the

work ~~should~~ be finished by the end of the month, that our

client feels he cannot ~~put his~~ signature to any contract

that which omits ~~this provision~~ a stipulation. ~~In the~~ second place, no men-

tion is made of the repairs to the garage. Although they

are of a minor ~~importance~~ nature, they should nevertheless be

specified in the contract.

(Continued on next page)

Topic 4 NUMBER AND SYMBOL PRACTICE

KEY LOCATION REVIEW

Use Drills 1 and 2 to build your confidence in typing numbers and symbols by touch.

Drill 1
NUMBER REVIEW

These drills are designed to give you a review in typing numbers.

Type each line twice. 60-space line. Single spacing. DS after each pair of lines.

1 we 23 quo 179 yew 632 try 546 writ 2485 riot 4895 your 6974
2 to 59 wry 246 ewe 323 pup 070 quip 1780 tire 5843 rout 4975
3 up 70 yip 680 out 975 ire 843 quay 1716 tout 5975 yore 6943
4 wee 233 too 599 woo 299 putty 07556 error 34494 quite 17853
5 yee 633 you 697 root 4995 quire 17843 peep 0330 query 17346
6 pop 090 poor 0994 putt 0755 quote 17953 weep 2330 writ 2485
7 quit 1785 pipe 0803 wept 2305 purr 0744 tree 5433 poet 0935
8 rope 4903 were 2343 quay 1716 your 6974 pope 0903 ripe 4803
9 were 2343 joke 6983 inch 8736 tight 58465 moon 6997 box 592
10 pride 04833 stove 24953 quake 16183 zip 180 yuck 6738 cup 360

Drill 2
SYMBOL REVIEW

These drills are designed to give you a review in typing symbols on manual and electric typewriters.

Left margin at 15. Single spacing.

#	Symbol	*Manual*	*Electric*
1	$	fr4f fr$f f$f $4 $4	fr4f fr$f f$f $4 $4
2	/	;/; ;/; 1/3 3/4 4/5	;/; ;/; 1/3 3/4 4/5
3	%	f%f f%f 6% 7% 8% 9%	f%f f%f 6% 7% 8% 9%
4	-	;-; ;-; 3-cent 10-60	;-; .-. 3-cent 10-60
5	( )	191 1(1 ;0; ;); (9)	191 1(1 ;0; ;); (9)
6	'	ki8k ki'k k'k don't	;'; ;'; can't don't
7	"	sw2s sw"s s"s "go"	;"; ;"; 6'2" tall
8	_	j6j j_j <u>can't</u> <u>don't</u>	;-; ;_; <u>can't</u> <u>don't</u>
9	#	de3d de#d d#d #7 8#	de3d de#d d#d #7 8#
10	&	ju7j ju&j j&j 2 & 4	ju7j ju&j j&j 2 & 4
11	¢	;¢; ;¢; 20¢ 15¢ 38¢	j6j j¢j 20¢ 15¢ 38¢
12	@	;@; ;@; ;@; 7 @ 49¢	sw2s sw@s s@s 6 @ 9¢
13	*	;*; ;*; * (asterisk)	k8k k*k * (asterisk)
14	½	;$\frac{1}{2}$; ;$\frac{1}{2}$; 4$\frac{1}{2}$# 6$\frac{1}{2}$' 7$\frac{1}{2}$"	;$\frac{1}{2}$; ;$\frac{1}{2}$; 4$\frac{1}{2}$# 6$\frac{1}{2}$' 7$\frac{1}{2}$"
15	¼	;$\frac{1}{4}$; ;$\frac{1}{4}$; 7$\frac{1}{4}$# 8$\frac{1}{4}$' 9$\frac{1}{4}$"	;$\frac{1}{4}$; ;$\frac{1}{4}$; 7$\frac{1}{4}$# 8$\frac{1}{4}$' 9$\frac{1}{4}$"
16	=	;=; ;=; 9 = 8 A = B	;=; ;=; 9 = 8 A = B
17	+	;+; ;+; 21 + 3 = 24	;+; ;+; 21 + 3 = 24

interest in the house after your inspection of it last week, I wanted to notify you of the situation immediately. ¶There has already been a definite interest shown in the property by several parties, and I think you will have to act quickly if you want to purchase it. I know that the Carmines have already received one offer of $190,000. ¶I suggest that we get together on Saturday and sit down with Mr. and Mrs. Carmine to make them an offer of their asking price. I feel confident that they will accept a full-price offer.   (130 words)

Exercise 4

June 18, 19— / Boynton Pattern Company / 260 Purdy Street / Schenectady, NY 12318 / Attention Carl L. Boynton / Since you have informed us that you are looking for a new business location, we are writing to you about the Eliot Building at 300 North Berkeley Street. ¶We believe that this building, located in the heart of the commercial district, is particularly suited to your needs. It offers 30,000 square feet on the ground floor at a very attractive rate. ¶We suggest that you see it immediately. Please call me for an appointment.   (74 words)

Project A-5 LAW FIRM

You are working for the firm of Hartley, Gwynn, & Hartley, Attorneys-at-Law, 877 Madison Plaza, Madison, WI 53727. Each attorney dictates his or her letters and then has them transcribed in draft form. After the attorneys read the drafts and make necessary alterations, the letters are given to you to type. The name of the attorney who dictated the letter as well as the name of the firm must be included in the signature block of each letter. Use modified block style with mixed punctuation and 5-space paragraph indentions.

Exercise 1

This letter was dictated by Lloyd F. Gwynn, Attorney-at-Law. Note the subject line. The letter is to be sent to Mr. Jordan at the address shown at the right. (There are 94 words in the body.)

Mr. Richard T. Jordan
847 Highland Avenue
Madison, WI 53713

November 20, 19--

Dear Mr. Jordan

    SUBJECT:
  ∧ Estate of Mabel N. Jordan

    As administrator of the estate of Mabel N. Jordan,
        # granted   November 30
you were allowed until the end of this month by the Surrogate's Court to submit your Final Accounting and Distri-
                    are not (stet)
bution of the estate.   If you will not be able to comply

(Continued on next page)

SENTENCE PRACTICE

The purpose of this drill is to help you develop a smoother typing style when typing numbers and symbols in context.

Drill 3

60-space line. Single spacing. Type each line twice; DS after each pair of lines.

1 The Harvester Building is 176 feet high. It has 14 stories.
2 The Economy Market has turkeys weighing from 9 to 17 pounds.
3 Last week I interviewed 88 job applicants but hired only 25.
4 David says he is 5 feet 6 inches tall and weighs 147 pounds.
5 Ship them 18 boxes, each containing 25 dozen pairs of socks.

6 I have 5 pounds of sugar, 4 dozen eggs, and 6 bags of flour.
7 Traffic is eastbound on 178th St. and westbound on 179th St.
8 This 20-piece silver service provides four 5-piece settings.
9 Robby no longer wears a size 15½ shirt; he requires size 16.
10 Our ballpoint pens cost $2 each. Matching pencils cost 90¢.

11 On Monday, Atlantic Petroleum opened at 9¼ and closed at 8½.
12 The series of 5 broadcasts is entitled: FAMOUS NEW YORKERS.
13 I can supply you with worsted at $6 a yard less 2% for cash.
14 If I can deliver today, he will order a dozen of my $8 sets.
15 Though King & Lee ask $80 for the set, they may accept less.

16 Ling & Son have reduced their entire stock 20% for the sale.
17 "I'd like to be an executive secretary," said Suzie Jeffers.
18 "I studied English and typing; but I can't spell," she said.
19 Suzanne recognized her weakness (poor spelling) with regret.
20 I bought my oil stocks @ 8½ per share; Thursday they were 7.

21 Its value is still dropping! Will it ever zoom? I hope so.
22 Moral—don't gamble; sometimes you win but often you do not.
23 At 62, Hazel plans to apply for social security (not taxed).
24 Penn State University offered a 14-week session last summer.
25 Rooms were $9 per day—board extra. One freshman soon quit.

26 Was the 14-week experiment successful? Who knows? I don't.
27 I had 30 kids at the party. I expected all to obey quickly.
28 I'm a size 8. Jane's Dress Shop allows me a discount of 5%.
29 I send the dresses to her, c/o Mrs. Rite, with whom I board.
30 My grade was 99%; that's very good for me! What was yours?

31 Just ask me (but do it tactfully); I'll be quite reasonable.
32 Stay on Route #28 to get to Queens Town; attempt no detours.

(Continued on next page)

Project A-4 REAL ESTATE AGENCY

You are working for Laura Robbins Harwick, partner in the firm of Harwick & Moody, Real Estate Brokers, 210 Smith Street, Schenectady, NY 12315. Mrs. Harwick has given you four letters to type. She prefers that you use full block style, open punctuation. Mrs. Harwick uses her social title, Mrs., in the signature block of all letters. Supply the missing salutations and complimentary closings.

Exercise 1

A copy of this letter is to be sent to John R. Warren.

June 17, 19— / The Silver Pen Company / 466 Market Street / Schenectady, NY 12317 / Attention Cynthia Silver / In accordance with the agreement reached at the recent conference between your representative, Frank Baxter, and our representative, John Warren, we are submitting for your approval the enclosed draft of a three-year lease on the fifth floor premises at 411 Front Street. ¶ The terms and conditions of this lease have been prepared in accordance with Mr. Baxter's requests. They differ in some details from provisions usually found in agreements affecting the rental of business property. ¶ Please have the draft signed by an authorized officer of your company. Indicate on it either approval or the changes that you believe should be made, and return it to us. If the draft is substantially correct, we shall then promptly prepare the lease in final form. The original copy will be executed by us as lessors and the duplicate copy by your company as lessee. Upon completion, the two papers will be exchanged for signatures.   (152 words)

Exercise 2

June 19, 19— / Mr. and Mrs. J. P. Dorcas / 13 Carlysle Road / Scotia, NY 12302 / Last month you wrote to us asking whether we had in our listing file a six-bedroom house, Tudor style, on at least ten acres of wooded land. You stated at that time that you would be willing to pay up to $200,000 for the right place. ¶ Our agency is now negotiating to obtain the exclusive listing of a property that seems to be just what you have in mind. The owners, John and Paula Carmine, have agreed to my bringing you out to take a tour of the house and grounds at a mutually agreed upon time. Please call me if you are interested and I will set up an appointment. P.S. Some of the extra features of this property include stables, a swimming pool, and a small greenhouse.   (112 words in body; 18 words in postscript)

Exercise 3

June 25, 19— / Mr. and Mrs. J. P. Dorcas / 13 Carlysle Road / Scotia, NY 12302 / Our office has just received the exclusive listing for the Carmine property, and we will be moving quickly to secure a buyer. The listing price is $195,000. Since you had expressed such a great

(Continued on next page)

Drill 3 continued

33 If you are in doubt, ask, "How do I get back to Highway #28?"
34 Recipe for limeade: $1\frac{1}{2}$ cups of lime juice to $1\frac{1}{4}$ cups sugar.
35 Please ship it May 28 to our warehouse in West Philadelphia.

36 How could 54 men and 55 women use up 113 tickets so quickly?
37 Check on all orders numbered 41 to 1,265 as soon as you can.
38 A stalled engine delayed a train near the 125th St. station.
39 They employ 300 full-time workers and 190 part-time workers.
40 From May 4 to June 3, forward my mail to 68 East 9th Street.

PARAGRAPH PRACTICE

The purpose of the following drill is to give you practice in typing numbers and symbols more speedily and accurately.

Drill 4

60-space line. Double spacing. 5-space paragraph indention.

Note: Some of the numbers and symbols in these paragraphs would normally be used only in statistical copy. In standard copy they would be spelled out. They are included here only to provide practice on those keys.

1   Here's how we will help you with home improvements. We'll 13 give you suggestions; we'll show you samples; we'll demonstrate 26 methods—all without charge (we sell materials only). 37

2   We cordially invite you to come in and see our smart fall display 14 of men's suits and coats. Our store is open daily from 9 to 5 (open 27 evenings Thursday and Saturday until 8). 35

3   We are equipped with a complete line of custom-made ready- 13 to-wear clothes for men. Our credit terms of 4% discount if paid within 27 10 days or net in 90 days are the most liberal offered in the industry. 41

4   The only apartment still available in this building is on the 7th 14 floor. It has $4\frac{1}{2}$ rooms. The rent is reasonable for this type of luxury 28 apartment—$255 a month, with a month's rent in advance. A two- 41 year lease is required. 46

5   Do you enjoy boat rides? The steamer "West Point" (leaving from 14 Pier 52) makes daily trips up the Hudson; round-trip fares, $6. For 28 complete information, call us any day during the week between the 41 hours of 9 a.m. to 5 p.m. 46

6   When you buy corn oil, be sure to get Lorenzo's 100% pure corn 13 oil—the very best! Your salads will taste better; your cooking will 27 improve. Get it by the pint, by the quart, or by the gallon—in "the 41 can with the stars on top." 46

1   2   3   4   5   6   7   8   9   10   11   12   13

(Continued on next page)

issue us a new check for the amount of $156.21 to cover loan payment No. 19. Unfortunately, we must again assess a late charge of $6.54, which you may include with your payment or which we can add to your principal balance. ¶ In order to avoid future problems with your loan payments, may I suggest that you make them in person at the teller's window and have your loan book receipted. This will assure that your payments are properly recorded and credited to your account on the day they are made. If we can be of further assistance to you, please do not hesitate to write or call. / Sincerely   (492 words)

Exercise 4

This letter was also dictated by Paula Samson.

April 11, 19— / Mr. Harry Wells / Harry Wells and Associates / 384 Madison Avenue / New York, NY 10017 / Dear Harry / As we discussed in our telephone conversation last week, Central Savings and Loan is now well into the planning of its new accounts promotion. ¶ We would definitely like you to put together a series of newspaper and magazine ads, two 30-second radio and television commercials, and a four-color illustrated brochure. John Clementi, my assistant, will be in touch with you shortly to discuss specifications and content. ¶ We will require sample copy for each space ad and for each commercial. Once we have approved the samples, you will need to provide us with an estimate of the costs to develop and produce each one. The estimate should cover not only your fee, but all extra expenses such as fees for models and permissions. Also include an estimated schedule of the time required. For the brochure, please provide us with an estimate for printing in four colors in quantities of 25,000 and 50,000. ¶ I know you will do a fine job for us. Call me any time you want to discuss ideas or get feedback on the materials as you develop them. / Cordially / SPECIAL DELIVERY   (182 words)

Exercise 5

This letter was dictated by Thomas Smith, Accounts Officer. It is to be sent by registered mail.

April 12, 19— / Mrs. Kim Que Tran / 226 Cleeve Avenue / Jersey City, NJ 07316 / Dear Mrs. Tran / Your Regular Savings Account, No. 73625810, has been held inactive by our bank for a year. The last recorded transaction, made on April 11 of 19—, was a deposit of $250, which brought the balance of the account to $781.72. Interest at the rate of $5\frac{1}{4}$%, compounded daily, has increased the amount to $825.93. ¶ These funds, as of today, have been transferred from this branch to our head office, located at 280 Loreli Avenue. The funds will remain there for six years. If, at the end of that time, we still have no response from you, the funds will be transferred to the state. ¶ Please notify us of your intentions for the account. If you wish, you may instruct us to hold the account open indefinitely; or you may request that the account be closed and your funds withdrawn. We shall await your instructions. / Sincerely   (144 words)

7   Mother Emmy's Frozen Foods are the best you've ever tasted.   13
You can get them at Bee & Dee markets (and at many other stores).   26
Try them with this guarantee—if you feel they're not all that we claim,   40
send us the wrapper and we'll return your money.   50

8   Since May 1969 the Kilauea Volcano in Hawaii has produced   12
a total of more than 440 million cubic yards of lava. During one   25
eruption in December 1969, lava fountains reached tremendous   37
heights. Some witnesses claim they reached heights of 1,600 feet.   50

9   The famous cherry trees in Washington (a gift of the Mayor of   13
Tokyo) line the roadside for 2 miles in East Potomac Park. These   26
trees came from the original 3,000 trees which were propagated from   39
trees on the Arawaka River in a suburb of Tokyo. The first trees were   53
planted in 1912.   56

10   On May 2, 1927 Lindbergh took off from Roosevelt Field, Long   13
Island. The 25-year-old airmail pilot accepted the challenge to fly   27
solo in his plane, "The Spirit of St. Louis," nonstop from New York   40
to Paris—an act as daring in its time as any that can be imagined.   53
Lindbergh made the flight in $33\frac{1}{2}$ hours.   61

11   At the shareholders' 45th annual meeting in Boston, several   13
issues were discussed. The first was an amendment to the bylaws   26
to enable the company to hold its meetings in various cities. A two-   40
thirds favorable vote was required for adoption; the amendment   52
passed by a vote of nearly 98%. Were you present at the meeting?   65

12   The Washington National Monument is a tapering shaft, almost   13
556 feet in height. It is covered in white Maryland marble in 2-foot   27
slabs. Eight small windows, two on each side, are located at the 500-   40
foot level, where points of interest may be viewed. Set into the   53
interior wall are 190 memorial stones received from states, foreign   67
countries, and organizations.   72

13   The #7 train was due at two o'clock. The crowd that had as-   13
sembled to meet the ambassador—the hero of the moment—was   25
becoming restless because the train was 45 minutes late. Some were   38
heard to murmur, "Let's go! Why wait any longer?" Others com-   51
mented, however, "We've waited so long; why not wait a little longer?"   65
When the train finally arrived, the ambassador had vanished.   77

1   2   3   4   5   6   7   8   9   10   11   12   13

planning a major new accounts promotion campaign. We would like to inquire about purchasing 10,000 copies of your book, *Keep Your Money Working for You*, to offer as a premium to customers opening new accounts during the promotion period. ¶ If you agree to supply these to us, we will want a special cover showing various kinds of currency. We would supply the art for this, subject to your approval. However, we would ask you to obtain the required permission from the U.S. Secret Service to reproduce currency for this purpose. ¶ Please give us a price quotation for an initial purchase of 10,000 copies as well as a price for an additional 10,000 copies, f.o.b. our Jersey City office. We anticipate needing delivery of the first 10,000 copies in eight weeks. / Very truly yours   (140 words)

Exercise 3

Note that this letter will require two pages. It was dictated by Max Kosta, Manager, Consumer Loans.

April 10, 19— / Daniel R. Gallagher / 1411 Seward Avenue / Jersey City, NJ 07315 / Dear Mr. Gallagher / RE: Home Improvement Loan No. 128741 / I have your letter of April 4 in which you inquired about three late charges recently assessed against your home improvement loan. ¶ Our records show that payments Nos. 17 and 18 had both been received by us beyond the grace period allowed for loan payments, and that payment No. 19 so far has not been received at all. In your letter, you stated that all three payments had been made on time, and, therefore, no late charges should have been levied. ¶ Upon investigating the matter further, we found that loan payment No. 17, due on January 15, was not received until February 2, three days after the expiration of the fifteen-day grace period. Since this payment was not received in time to be credited on your monthly statement, a late charge of $6.54 was added to your principal balance. Although you state that you mailed the payment on January 21 and that poor mail service probably caused the delay in our receiving it, we cannot be held responsible for mail delivery. We regret, therefore, that no adjustment can be made for the late charge assessed against this payment. ¶ Our records concerning loan payment No. 18, due on February 15, show that it was received by our office on March 2, rather than on March 3, as shown on your statement. The late charge was erroneously assessed because the payment was not credited to your account until the day following its arrival. Accordingly, on the next monthly statement that you receive from us, this late charge of $6.54 will be shown as a miscellaneous credit, thus reducing the amount of principal balance owing. ¶ In regard to loan payment No. 19, due on March 15, as of the time of this writing, we have no record that it has ever been received by our office. Although you state that this payment was placed in our night depository box after closing hours on March 28, no trace of it can be found. Let me assure you that we have made a thorough check of the night depository box, and it is a complete mystery to us as to what might have happened to your check. May I suggest that you place a stop-payment order on the check to prevent its being cashed by another party and

(Continued on next page)

Topic 5 TIMED WRITINGS

Use the following 3- and 5-minute timed writings to measure your typing speed and accuracy. A measurement from time to time will show you the extent of your progress. It will also give you an opportunity to set new goals in order to reach the highest rate of speed and the greatest degree of accuracy of which you are capable. For additional selections use the Supplementary Practice section at the end of the book.

RATING TYPING ERRORS

Adapted from the International Typewriting Contest Rules.

1. Any change in a typed word from the printed copy is considered an error. Examples are: the misstriking of a letter or other character; a misspelling; a substituted, omitted, or transposed word; an added word or group of words; or a change in capitalization. An omitted line is charged as two errors.

2. Incorrect division of a word at the end of a line constitutes an error.

3. Errors in punctuation marks and in spacing following a word are considered errors in that word.

4. Faulty typing resulting from incorrect operating technique is charged as an error. Examples are: incomplete impression of a capital letter; crowded letters; irregular left margin or poor right margin; or faulty line spacing. However, a lightly struck letter is not charged as an error if the impression is visible.

5. Only one error is to be charged to a word, regardless of the number of errors it contains.

6. Failure to indent 5 spaces at the beginning of a paragraph is charged as an error.

Directions:
60-space line. Double spacing.

1   There are living forms in water that are known to have been in   13
existence through the ages. These tiny life forms, too small to be   26
seen by the unaided eye, are made up of only one cell. This one cell   40
at frequent intervals divides into two. Each time the cell divides,   54
the two new cells are complete living things. As this division can go   68
on and on, apparently without end, these one-celled forms may be   81
said to live forever—if they do not make a meal for some larger   94
creature. It is quite possible that there are some one-celled animals   108
living now that have already had a life of a million years.   SI 1.34   120

2   Just as there are different shades of beauty—one star differing   14
from another in glory—there are different degrees in our delight.   27
It is very pleasant to see the waving grain as the wind sweeps over   40
a wheat field, to sit idly by a stream and see it hurrying past, to lie   54
on the shore and look lazily at the tide coming in and at the gulls   67
sailing overhead. As we look longer and more intently, our delight   81
grows; what we see becomes clearer and takes on a deeper meaning.   94
We sense more vividly what we are looking at—the wheat field, the   107
stream, the tide and the gulls. As we look still longer, the scene   120
awakens memories.   SI 1.33   123

1 | 2 | 3 | 4 | 5 | 6 | 7 | 8 | 9 | 10 | 11 | 12 | 13

Exercise 4

Note the subject line. This letter was dictated by Mrs. Knight.

February 12, 19— / PERSONAL / Mrs. Wanda Anderson / Anderson Catering Service / 54 Market Street / Columbus, OH 43220 / Dear Mrs. Anderson / Loan Against Life Insurance Policy No. GS 26307614 / In reply to your letter of February 7, I am sending a loan application form that you will need to complete in order to borrow $5,000 against your life insurance policy No. GS 26307614. Your husband, as beneficiary under the policy, must also sign the form to show consent to the loan, since it will become a charge against any claim payable under the policy. ¶Once we have received the completed forms from you, we will process them immediately. If everything is in order, you should have a check from us within one week after our receipt of the forms. Interest at the rate of 6 percent per year will be billed to you annually on the anniversary date of your policy. / Cordially   (121 words)

Project A-3 SAVINGS AND LOAN ASSOCIATION

You are working in the general office of the Central Savings and Loan Association, 69 Hudson Boulevard, Jersey City, NJ 07322. As a member of a typing pool, you are required to type letters for a number of different executives. The firm prefers modified block style, mixed punctuation, with 5-space paragraph indentions.

Exercise 1

This letter was dictated by Roger T. Richman, Vice-President, Loan Department.

April 9, 19— / Froman & Sykes / 710 River Street / Jersey City, NJ 07317 / Gentlemen / We have received your application for a capital improvement loan to expand and modernize your warehouse facilities. ¶Before we can undertake to provide the financing you need, however, we must complete a review of your financial statements and your remodeling plans. To do this, we will require a certified copy of your firm's most recent income statement and balance sheet, and a detailed plan for the warehouse remodeling. Please send these to me at your earliest convenience. ¶In the meantime, we shall begin processing your application so that it will be ready for action when your statements arrive. / Sincerely   (98 words)

Exercise 2

This letter was dictated by Paula Samson, Advertising Manager.

April 10, 19— / Premium Sales Manager / Savoy Publishing Company / 61 Harbor Street / Roanoke, VA 24010 / Dear Sir or Madam / Central Savings and Loan is now in the process of

(Continued on next page)

3   Most Americans are well aware of how much the activity of   12
their daily lives is tied to the use of raw or processed goods that   25
have been made from minerals. Crude oil, for instance, is the source   39
of thousands of products that we use every day. The energy crisis   52
is but a part of a larger mineral supply problem; without a steady   65
supply of minerals, life, as we have come to know it, could not roll on.   79

Indeed, the whole world must face the challenge of a greater   92
demand for minerals in the years that lie ahead. With more and   105
more people adding to total demand, the strain on available supplies   119
could lead not only to shortages, but also to wars.   SI 1.39   129

4   Tides are a natural phenomenon. They are most visible at the   13
seashore as water rushes out to sea and then back toward land day   26
in and day out. This movement is caused by the gravitational pull   39
of the moon on the earth. As the earth rotates, exposing one side to   53
the moon, the oceans on that side bulge upwards, drawing water   65
away from the coastlands. And the tide goes out. As the earth com-   79
pletes its turn away from the moon, the bulge in the ocean subsides   92
and water flows back toward the land. And the tide comes in. Al-   105
though tides occur over all the earth, not just in water but in air and   119
land as well, the ocean tides are the most obvious because of   131
their size.   SI 1.31   133

5   You cannot dance to it. Nor can you boogie along with it. And   14
it does not attack you with a decibel power of an exploding dynamite   28
factory. As a matter of fact, there are many things it would not do   42
for you, but you are welcome to join in and sing along for the fun   55
of it. With folk music, that is. Unfortunately, folk music has been   69
labeled by many people as something you would listen to only if you   82
were in a one-horse town on a Saturday night and there was nothing   95
else open but a coffeehouse that had folk music.   105

People just do not associate folk music with having a good   118
time; it's too bad, because they are missing out on a lot of musi-   131
cal listening enjoyment.   SI 1.44   136

6   There is nothing like a busy street to give boys and girls an idea   14
of the working of the social machine. Let them see the various   26
tradesmen on their morning rounds. Let them look at the shops of   39
the grocers, the butchers, the bakers. Let them watch the street cars,   53

1   2   3   4   5   6   7   8   9   10   11   12   13

(Continued on next page)

day to and from your place of work. Other updating changes have also been made. Please refer to the enclosed Declarations Page for a complete description of the coverages now in effect. ¶As a result of all the changes made, your new premium to cover the policy period from February 13, 19— to February 12, 19—, was increased by $93.00. Please remit this amount no later than March 1, to ensure continuous policy coverage. / Very truly yours   (108 words)

Exercise 2

This letter was dictated by Mr. Dillon.

February 14, 19— / Ms. Roberta Vargo / 608 Cedar Avenue / Cleveland, OH 44112 / Dear Ms. Vargo / I have your recent letter requesting information about a policy to cover your cameras and recording equipment. ¶Our policies provide several forms of coverage for such personal effects, as described in the enclosed brochure. On page 3 you will see a policy that includes coverage for theft, loss due to carelessness on your part, and damage caused by someone other than yourself. Such coverage would apply no matter where the theft, loss, or damage occurred. ¶The cost of such a policy would depend on the value of the equipment being insured. However, the face value of the policy cannot exceed the current market value of the items. Any claims payable under the policy, therefore, would be based on the cost of the items less any depreciation for the time that you owned them. ¶I hope this information will answer your questions. If you require additional assistance in selecting a policy, please notify me and I will have one of our representatives in Cleveland call on you. / Sincerely yours   (166 words)

Exercise 3

Note the subject line. This letter was dictated by Mrs. Knight.

February 15, 19— / Mr. Louis Parten / Box 119 / Springville, CA 93265 / Dear Mr. Parten / Claim No. 62 5496 114 / I have your letter of February 8 and shall respond to each question in the order listed in your letter. ¶It appears that the seven items on your claim sheet totaling $225.00, while a result of the collision, are not covered under your policy contract. The one exception may be the tire that blew out at the time of the collision. This would be listed at $39.45, less any applicable depreciation. Please advise us as to the length of time the tire had been in use so that we may make the adjustment and reimburse you. ¶Regarding your second question, the adjuster who reviewed the tow bill deducted for the changing of the tire. However, it appears that you do have emergency road service coverage, which would have paid for this. Therefore, I am enclosing a draft for $5.25, to bring the reimbursement to the full amount you paid Smith's Towing. ¶Please feel free to call this office, and, if necessary, we will have an adjuster work with you to conclude the remaining items in your claim. / Very truly yours   (177 words)

the buses, and the automobiles carrying people to their appointed 66
tasks. In short, let them see the life of the street, and they will learn 81
that everyone must perform some work. 88

Through my morning and afternoon walks to and from school, 101
I developed an interest in people and in their work. As I grew older, 115
I gave up looking into shop windows, but I never lost my desire to 128
know what was going on in the busy world around me. SI 1.32 **138**

7 There are no workers more sought after or more independent 13
than top-rank skilled mechanics. They are persons with a trade, a 25
practical skill, a useful art. If I were a young person of twenty with 39
an ability to do mechanical work, I would try to get a job in a machine 54
shop. If I failed in that attempt, I would try for a job in a filling 68
station or work as an apprentice to a plumber or an electrician. I 81
would learn to work with my hands. 88

Training in manual skill is important, even if you plan to be a 101
doctor, a lawyer, or a business manager. Hand training is as essential 116
as mind training. The best equipped person is one who combines the 129
learning of books with the learning that comes from doing things 142
with the hands. SI 1.34 **145**

8 Home, to the average man or woman, means a house suitably 12
furnished, surroundings that please the eye, and perhaps a garden 25
in which to grow flowers or vegetables. It is a permanent retreat 38
that shelters its occupants from the world outside. 48

Most people would laugh at the idea that they might spend 60
their whole lives in a floating home. Yet there are hundreds of 73
thousands of men and women around the world who live on boats 85
either from choice or because of the way in which they earn their 98
livelihood. To them, home is a place that can be moved at will, at 111
any time. The hundreds of families that live and work on barges 124
on canals, for example, have a home in every sense of the word, 137
even though it is a home that is always moving from place to place. 150
SI 1.29

9 There are often occasions when you are faced with many dif- 13
ferent tasks, all of which seem urgent. When you undertake one of 26
them, you are troubled by the thought of a dozen other things that 39
you ought to be doing—things that cannot wait, you say. Or can they 53
wait? Of course they can; they have to wait. 62

| 1 | 2 | 3 | 4 | 5 | 6 | 7 | 8 | 9 | 10 | 11 | 12 | 13 |

(Continued on next page)

Exercise 2

A copy of this letter is to be sent to Mrs. Marilyn Flowers.

January 10, 19— / Mr. Frederick Homer / Convention Chairperson / Massachusetts Cosmetology Association / 814 Clarendon Street / Boston, MA 02115 / Dear Mr. Homer / I am pleased to learn that your association has selected our establishment for its annual convention next year. ¶ You will find our prices, service, meeting rooms, banquet facilities, and guest accommodations the best in the Miami area. We are especially proud of the number of repeat convention bookings we have from our many satisfied guests. ¶ Mrs. Marilyn Flowers, our convention coordinator, will be available to answer your questions about the arrangements and to help insure the success of your convention. / Very truly yours   (79 words)

Exercise 3

January 12, 19— / HOLD FOR ARRIVAL / Mr. and Mrs. Edward Tulbinski / Neptune Motel / 23 Ocean Boulevard / Virginia Beach, VA 23462 / Dear Mr. and Mrs. Tulbinski / One of our housekeepers turned in a baby blanket that was found in an unoccupied guest room today. In checking our records, we find that you were our last guests in that room. Since our records also show that you requested the use of a crib, we thought that the blanket probably belongs to you. ¶ If you find that you are, indeed, missing one of your baby's blankets, please telephone or write to my office and give us a description of the article. We will send the blanket to you as soon as we have positive identification. / Sincerely   (98 words)

Project A-2 INSURANCE COMPANY

You are working at the Empire Insurance Company, 644 Weldon Avenue, Toledo, OH 43608, as a typist for Marilyn E. Knight, Vice-President, and John Dillon, Assistant Vice-President. Either Mrs. Knight or Mr. Dillon has given you the following letters to type. Mrs. Knight prefers modified-block style with mixed punctuation and no paragraph indention. She also wants her social title included in the signature blocks of her letters. Mr. Dillon prefers full block style with open punctuation.

Exercise 1

This letter was dictated by Mr. Dillon.

February 13, 19— / Mr. Joseph Hawthorne / 216 Rainbow Road / Youngstown, OH 44515 / Dear Sir / Subject: Updated Automobile Insurance Policy No. TRN 34681919 / The following important change in your policy has been made since your last premium notice. ¶ We have updated the information on how your car is used to include business travel of fifty miles a

(Continued on next page)

Worry can never help you. It troubles your conscience and 75
distracts your attention from the work you are doing. Unless a real 89
emergency exists—and emergencies do come up—you must say to 101
your conscience, "Yes, that is important; but it must wait until this 115
more urgent matter has been disposed of. Then I will give it my full 129
attention." You will find that your conscience is easily satisfied if 143
you keep faith with it and really attend to each problem in its turn. 157

SI 1.32

10   Many typists today use special equipment and have job titles 13
that reflect their special duties. Unlike the clerk-typist who combines 27
typing with a number of other office chores, data typists and key- 40
board operators have no such general duties. They are highly skilled 54
people who produce typed copy free of error. How do they do it? 67
They use equipment that records data on magnetic tape or discs as 80
they type. If they make an error, they need only strike a correcting 94
key and the error is erased. Then they simply retype the correct word 108
or number as though no mistake had been made. In this way they 121
produce a tape or disc that is free from error. Later, the tape or disc 135
is run through a printer or automatic typewriter which can type the 148
finished copy at speeds no human could even approach.   SI 1.43 159

11   You will find that more and more business firms are developing 13
speakers' bureaus and urging their people to speak to outside groups. 27
If you need a speaker, call several firms to determine who could 40
provide a speaker for a particular topic. 48

After making your selection, invite the speaker by telephone or 62
letter and include such information as the date, time and place, type 76
of speech or subject, length of speech, question and answer period, 89
type of class, size of class, and description of your class. 101

Once the speaker has accepted, begin the process of making him 114
or her feel welcome. Write another letter to express thanks and give 128
detailed information on how to get to your school; find out what 141
props or equipment are needed; and ask for a brief description of 154
the proposed talk and the speaker's background.   SI 1.45 163

12   A watch needs attention if it is to give the best possible service. 14
Good watches are strong and will stand a certain amount of neglect 27
and abuse; but they will perform far better and last much longer if 40
they receive the care that they require. 48

| 1 | 2 | 3 | 4 | 5 | 6 | 7 | 8 | 9 | 10 | 11 | 12 | 13 |

(Continued on next page)

Project A-1 MOTOR INN

You are working for Frances S. Scully, Manager of the Good Neighbor Motor Inn, 212 Frasier Avenue, Miami, FL 33140. She gives you these letters to type for her. Ms. Scully prefers that her social title, Ms., be omitted from the signature block of each letter. Use a letter style of your choice, but use the same style for all letters in this project.

Exercise 1

January 9, 19— / League of Women Voters / 768 Magnolia Drive / Miami, FL 33144 / Attention Ms. Helen N. Hammond / Ladies / We wish to express our appreciation for your patronage in holding your annual business luncheon in our North Dining Room yesterday. We hope that you and your guests were completely pleased with the menu and the service. If you could spare a few minutes to write a note, we would appreciate your comments and criticisms. ¶As a service to the community, the inn is now making its Tower Room available, at a nominal charge, to civic groups that sponsor lectures and other educational programs. Coffee and other refreshments are included at no additional cost. We are now beginning to schedule events for February and March. Perhaps your group might want to book the facility for one of its upcoming programs. Please call me to discuss arrangements if you are interested. / Sincerely   (130 words)

A watch should be wound every day at about the same time. 60
It should be protected from jars and knocks, from dust and water. 73
Above all, it must never be dropped. It should be cleaned at regular 87
intervals, perhaps once a year; otherwise, its delicate parts may wear 101
away. Only an expert should ever be allowed to repair a fine watch; 115
an amateur handling it unskillfully may ruin it completely. 127

With proper care, a good watch may last a lifetime and may 140
even continue to give good service when handed down as an heir- 153
loom from parent to child. Many pocket watches made a century 165
ago still keep good time today. SI 1.40 171

13 A computer requires many specially trained operators. First, 13
the input data must be written in symbols that a machine can read. 26
Most often this is done by a keyboard operator who feeds the data 39
into the computer through a keyboard that is not a lot different from 53
that of a standard typewriter. 59

The number and kinds of employees needed also vary. A small 72
computer may need one or two employees; a large one may employ 84
ten or more. But regardless of size, each computer needs a program 97
to make it work. Those who write programs are in great demand 109
because of the key role they play. 116

Thousands of trained workers will be needed to fill new jobs, 129
both in firms that have their own computers and in service centers 142
that rent computer time to others. Even without growth, new 154
workers will be needed just to replace those who change careers or 167
leave the work force. SI 1.41 171

14 Success in any business depends on the people who work for it. 13
This is especially true in the retail business. Customers will return 27
to a store where they have received courteous and efficient service. 41
Although contact with customers is a part of all sales jobs, the duties, 55
skills, and functions of salespeople are as different as the kinds of 69
merchandise they sell. 73

In selling furniture, electrical appliances, or some clothing, the 87
salesworker's job is to create an interest in the products the store 101
has to offer. The salesman or saleswoman may answer questions 113
about the construction of an item, demonstrate its use, explain how 126
it is cared for, show various models and colors, and otherwise help 139

1 2 3 4 5 6 7 8 9 10 11 12 13

(Continued on next page)

SERIES **A**

TEMPA-TYPIST
EMPLOYMENT AGENCY

Temporary employment agencies have become a widely used source of employment in recent years, especially for people who have valuable clerical skills. Applicants who register with a temporary employment agency are tested in its office; then they are sent out on jobs with different companies on a day-to-day (or even a week-to-week) basis. The temporary agency keeps a portion of the employee's hourly earnings as its fee for the service of finding the jobs. Such temporary employment assignments can provide a variety of work experience that is invaluable for the beginning office worker.

Each project in this series is set in a different office environment. You are to assume that after being tested and employed by the Tempa-Typist Agency, you are sent to work in each of these different offices. In each new office you must quickly learn the names of the people for whom you work and their preferences for the ways in which their letters are typed. Of course, it is assumed that all of your work must be mailable. This means that you must proofread your work carefully and make neat corrections of any errors before presenting finished work to your employers.

Directions for Series A

1. Type each letter accurately. If the company prefers a particular style, use it. Otherwise, use an acceptable style of your own choice. If you need to review any aspect of advanced business correspondence, refer to Section 3, Part 2 (pages 235–313).

2. The number of words in the body of each letter is given to help you determine good placement. As you progress through the projects, however, try to use eye judgment to set up some letters. With practice, this skill will come easily.

3. Always use your own reference initials. Type an enclosure notation when a reference is made to an enclosure within the body of the letter.

4. For the first letter in each project, type a carbon copy and an envelope. (In actual practice, of course, every letter would require one or more carbon copies and an envelope.)

5. When you have typed a letter with a carbon copy and an envelope, it should be submitted to your employer for signature in the following manner:

   a. Put the original (ribbon copy) on top, so that it can be easily read and signed.

   b. Place the carbon copies underneath.

   c. Use the flap of the envelope to hold the package together. Place the envelope either at the top or along the side, as shown in the illustration on the next page.

the customer make a selection. In some stores, such as a hardware 152
store, special knowledge or skills may be needed to sell the store's 166
merchandise. But most stores don't require special skills or training. 180

SI 1.51

15   One secretary may type a great volume of letters in one day, 13
while another may type but a very few letters during the day. At 26
any rate, there is very little that is like a machine about their work. 40
There is no machine with the tact to soothe the ruffled feelings of 53
an important caller who must cool his heels while an equally impor- 66
tant one overstays her time with the boss. When the boss is absent, 80
no machine has the judgment to know which papers may be released 93
or which requests should be ignored. 100

A career as a secretary can give you great personal rewards. 113
Your workday and the conditions about you would be pleasant. 125
Your office is likely to be a comfortable one. If you work in a big 139
office, you will meet many people and make new friends. Your work 152
can put you in touch with men and women of achievement in many 164
fields. And no field of special interest is closed to the young person 178
who chooses this field as a career. SI 1.29 185

16   We all know that water runs downhill. In the course of time, 13
water running down a hill may have an effect on whatever is in its 26
path. If it meets a hard, large stone during its course, it breaks against 41
that stone and moves around it. If part of the stone is weak, however, 56
the water is sure to find that weak spot. In the course of years, per- 70
haps ages, the water will wear away the weak part until it can pass 83
through the stone. Stones have been found that are little more than 97
shells, because the water has made its way through a great hole in 110
what was once the heart of a stone. 117

The water also could break against the stone day after day, year 131
after year, until at last it cuts underneath it. Then it slowly makes a 145
new path for itself in the earth under the stone, through which it can 159
more easily pass. It may run under the ground this way, cutting a hole 173
hundreds of feet deep and several miles long, and then come to the 187
surface once again. SI 1.23 190

1   2   3   4   5   6   7   8   9   10   11   12   13

SECTION FOUR

Work Experience Simulations

The projects in this section offer exercises that integrate a variety of skills especially useful to students who are in the final stages of preparation for jobs as clerk-typists. The assignments simulate tasks typical of those performed on the job, giving students the opportunity to apply a wide range of skills, including English language skills. Work experience simulations will help students make the transition from classroom typing to on-the-job typing.

The projects are grouped into three *Series,* according to the complexity of the skills required to complete the assignments. In *Series A,* students work as clerk-typists for a temporary employment agency; their job is to type letters in a number of different business offices. *Series B* simulates the responsibilities given to clerk-typists who prepare business correspondence with supporting documents and enclosures. In *Series C,* students are expected to work more independently. They are given several different but related tasks and are expected to perform them without close supervision and direction.

PART 2

PREPRODUCTION SKILLS

Topic 1 ERASING AND CORRECTING ERRORS

Up to this point you have not been required to erase typing errors. This was done to minimize your concern, natural to beginning typists, about errors made on practice drills while you were developing your typing skill. As you begin to produce typewritten material (such as letters, envelopes, reports, and forms) that will be given to others to read, however, you must produce copy which is free of errors.

The first step toward producing error-free work is to *carefully proofread everything* you type. Develop this habit with all work that you type, no matter how easy it may seem to be. Spelling and punctuation errors, as well as letter transpositions, can occur even with the simplest material.

If at all possible, try to proofread your work while the paper is still in the typewriter to save yourself the trouble of aligning corrections. If your correction is at the bottom of the page, you may find it easier to roll the paper back to erase or opaque a mistake.

Since even the most experienced typists make errors while typing, it is important that you learn how to make neat corrections, avoiding the need to retype material completely. The most common methods used to correct a typing error are: erasing the error with a special typing eraser, and covering up the error with a chalky substance such as correction paper or correction fluid.

ERASING

If you are using a typewriter with a carriage, always move the carriage to the left or to the right before you begin to erase, so that the error you are erasing is as far as possible from the printing point. You want to avoid having the eraser crumbs fall into the machine because, as the crumbs accumulate, the keys will begin to stick.

When erasing, turn the paper up to a convenient position. Rub lightly in one direction to avoid making a hole in the paper. Keep your fingers off the typed copy as you erase the error. An *eraser shield* will help you make neat erasures. Use the following procedure to correct an error using an eraser:

Step 1. Bring the carriage as far to the right or left as necessary to prevent eraser crumbs from falling into the typewriter. Neatly erase the incorrect letter(s), rubbing lightly in one direction to avoid making a noticeable mark in your paper.

Step 2. Bring the carriage back to the printing point and type the necessary correction. Use a light touch when making the correction so that it will not appear darker than the surrounding copy.

Exercise 3
COMPOSITE LETTERS

Gulf Publications, publisher of a monthly magazine, uses a composite letter to reject unsolicited articles and stories sent to them for publication. The body of the letter is made up of three of the paragraphs shown at the right.

As typist, you are to send individually typed letters to each of the three persons listed below. Each person has submitted material for publication, but their materials are being rejected for different reasons. You are to complete the first paragraph of the letter with the appropriate information. You are to use only one of the three versions of the second paragraph (labeled A, B, and C), as indicated for each letter.

Supply a suitable complimentary closing, and include the name and title of Jerome S. Parker, Managing Editor, in the signature block.

Modified block style. Mixed punctuation. Use today's date. Note the enclosure.

Dear _____

Paragraph 1   Thank you for sending us your manuscript for _____.

Paragraph 2   A   As a result of marketing surveys that we conduct, our editors feel that the subject matter of your manuscript—although interesting and creative—will not appeal to our readership. We regret, therefore, that we are unable to consider your manuscript for publication.

       B   Our policy in recent years has excluded poetry from the materials which we publish in our magazine. We regret, therefore, that we cannot consider your poems for publication. This decision is in no way related to the quality of your work. If you are serious about publication, we suggest that you seek out a publisher of one of the more prominent anthologies.

       C   We have reviewed your material carefully and find it both interesting and well written. The story, however, does not meet with our requirements for length and scope of coverage. To assist you in making the necessary revisions, our editors have made notes directly on your pages to indicate where they feel additional work is needed. We encourage you to prepare another draft and resubmit it to us for possible publication.

Paragraph 3   Thank you for giving us the opportunity to look at your material. The manuscript that you submitted for our consideration is being returned to you with this letter.

Letter 1
A five-page article entitled "Nuclear Survival in the '80's" has been submitted for publication by **Douglas Schiefer, 424 El Dorado Drive, San Marcos, TX 78666**. Reply to him, using paragraph C as the second paragraph of the letter.

Letter 2
Send a reply to **Mr. John P. Wickersham, 11835 Plumed Eagle Court, Chesterfield, MO 63017**, who has submitted an article entitled "My Days in the Ghost Towns of Colorado" for publication. Use paragraph A as the second paragraph of the letter.

Letter 3
Three poems about wildlife animals have been sent in by **Mrs. Julie Malleau, 143 Hemlock Street, Fairfield, VT 05455**. Send her a reply, using paragraph B as the second paragraph of the letter.

CORRECTION PAPER

Backspace until the error to be corrected is at the printing point. Insert the correction paper (chalky side toward the error) in the *card holder* (No. 11, page 1). Retype the error. This will cover up the error. Then remove the correction paper, backspace to the required printing point, and type the necessary correction.

Study the following example and observe the procedure for changing *Francis* to *Frances* in this sentence:

He told Francis to send the telegram at once.

Step 1. Backspace until the letter *i* in the word *Francis* is at the printing point.
Step 2. Insert the correction paper under the card holder, chalky side toward the paper.
Step 3. Strike the letter *i* again.
Step 4. Remove the correction paper. The error should be completely covered with the chalk from the correction paper.
Step 5. Backspace to the proper point and type the correct letter *e* over the *i* which has been covered up.

CORRECTION FLUID

Turn the paper up to a convenient point. Carefully touch a *small* amount of the fluid over the mistake. Let the fluid dry and then return the paper to the required printing point and type the correction.

Drill A

USING AN ERASER

Type the seven sentences at the right exactly as they are are printed. Then, following the steps outlined, make the corrections indicated by using an eraser.

Half sheet. Left margin at 15. Double spacing. Begin on line 7.

1. We believe that we can leave early in June.
2. My address is: Hotel Venice, 14 Wyoming Street.
3. Mr. Thomas plans to take a trip next Monday.
4. Deli is the best typist in the office.
5. I gave my last dollar to Ron.
6. Linda was born on July 11, 1964.
7. Most business firms in this country are large.

CORRECTIONS

1 Change *June* to *July*.
2 Change *14* to *41*.
3 Change *Monday* to *Friday*.
4 Change *Deli* to *Dely*.
5 Change *Ron* to *Don*.
6 Change *11* to *25*.
7 Change *large* to *small*.

Drill B

USING CORRECTION PAPER

Type these sentences exactly as they are printed. Then make the corrections indicated by using correction paper. Use the same sheet of paper you used in Drill A.

Left margin at 15. Double spacing. Begin a triple space below Drill A.

1. The boy said he had nine.
2. She felt better after the vacation.
3. Fourteen members were present.
4. Don has a high clerical attitude.
5. I bought a color tv for my bedroom.
6. Can I borrow your class lecture notes?
7. Their winter home is in Florida.

CORRECTIONS

1 Change *nine* to *none*.
2 Change *the* to *her*.
3 Change *fourteen* to *thirteen*.
4 Change *attitude* to *aptitude*.
5 Change *tv* to *TV*.
6 Change *Can* to *May*.
7 Change *Florida* to *Georgia*.

Exercise 2

FORM LETTERS WITH FILL-INS

On the 20 copies of the letter reproduced in Exercise 3 (page 377), insert the date, inside address, salutation, and the missing words in the first paragraph from the information given at the right. Punctuate the insertions as necessary to match the letter style. Use the current date on all copies. Fold each letter to fit a window envelope.

Modified block style. Open punctuation.

1 Mr. Don J. Lee
   5109 Broadway
   New York, NY 10032
   Friday, May 12, 19—,
      at 8:45 a.m.

2 Ms. Irma Gold
   241 Park Avenue
   New York, NY 10040
   Tuesday, May 15, 19—,
      at 10:15 a.m.

3 Mr. Myron Volk
   4212 West 58th Street
   Yonkers, NY 10708
   Wednesday, June 3, 19—,
      at 9:00 a.m.

4 Miss Marian Colson
   54 Monroe Avenue
   New York, NY 10002
   Monday, June 1, 19—,
      at 11:15 a.m.

5 Mr. Stephen Luczek
   39 Washington Square
   New York, NY 10012
   Tuesday, June 6, 19—,
      at 2:30 p.m.

6 Mr. Ramon Guiao
   199 Lenox Avenue
   New York, NY 10026
   Monday, June 12, 19—,
      at 10:30 a.m.

7 Ms. Stella Cohen
   50 Mercer Place
   New York, NY 10013
   Friday, June 20, 19—,
      at 11:30 a.m.

8 Ms. Delia DiGregorio
   160 Central Park West
   New York, NY 10023
   Tuesday, July 1, 19—,
      at 9:00 a.m.

9 Mrs. Meredith O'Brien
   801 Sherman Avenue
   New York, NY 10011
   Thursday, July 8, 19—,
      at 11:00 a.m.

10 Mrs. James Burns
   50 Waterside Plaza
   New York, NY 10010
   Monday, July 15, 19—,
      at 3:30 p.m.

11 Mr. George Smirnoff
   121 Laurel Hill Terrace
   New York, NY 10033
   Wednesday, July 20, 19—,
      at 10:15 a.m.

12 Mr. John J. Falko
   243 Third Avenue
   New York, NY 10012
   Tuesday, July 24, 19—,
      at 9:15 a.m.

13 Dr. Ellen Goodman
   241 Dyckman Avenue
   New York, NY 10034
   Friday, July 30, 19—,
      at 10:00 a.m.

14 Mr. Norbert S. Gizinski
   399 West 42nd Street
   New York, NY 10009
   Tuesday, August 1, 19—,
      at 3:15 p.m.

15 Mr. Charles Bartley
   390 Edgecombe Avenue
   New York, NY 10002
   Wednesday, August 2, 19—,
      at 1:30 p.m.

16 Ms. Paula Iahn
   127 Fifth Avenue
   New York, NY 10003
   Friday, August 5, 19—,
      at 9:00 a.m.

Exercise 1

Type Sentence 1 at the right exactly as it is printed. Make the change indicated using the method of correction specified by your instructor. Correct Sentence 1 before you type Sentence 2. Follow this procedure to make corrections in the remaining sentences.

Half sheet. Left margin at 15. Double spacing. Begin on line 7.

1. The salesman will attend a conference.
2. The stenographer mislaid her notebook.
3. The hurricane will probably travel west tonight.
4. They averaged a little over twenty miles an hour.
5. Dinner will be served in the Blue Room.
6. Tomorrow will be too late; we must see you today.
7. Many typists are needed to complete the work.
8. Helen was at first employed as a clerk.
9. The lecture will begin at half past seven.
10. The boy refused to give up before he finished.

CORRECTIONS

1 Change *salesman* to *salesmen*.
2 Change *her* to *his*.
3 Change *west* to *east*.
4 Change *twenty* to *thirty*.
5 Change *Dinner* to *Supper*.

6 Change *we* to *he*.
7 Change *Many* to *More*.
8 Change *Helen* to *Alice*.
9 Change *seven* to *eight*.
10 Change *boy* to *man*.

Topic 2 REINSERTING PAPER

Although typewritten work should be read carefully to locate errors while the paper is still in the typewriter, corrections are sometimes necessary after the work has been removed from the machine. There may be typing errors or defects that you have over-looked, or you may wish to make minor changes in the copy. It is then necessary to reinsert the paper so that substituted characters can be typed in alignment with the old copy. There are other occasions, too, when the paper must be removed from the machine and later reinserted. For example, while you are typing one assignment, your employer may wish you to type some other material immediately. This makes it necessary for you to remove the work from the machine and reinsert it later to finish.

Before you reinsert paper and try to realign the type, study the following example to learn how to recognize proper alignment. Insert a sheet of paper and type this sentence:

I shall learn to reinsert my paper.

Notice how much space there is between the bottom of the typed line and the *aligning scale* (see arrow A). Memorize this space relationship because you will need it to find the writing line when you reinsert paper.

Now look at the individual typed letters. Notice how the vertical marks on the aligning scale line up with the letters (see arrow B). On most typewriters, letters like *i* and *e* are centered over the marks.

Remove your paper from the machine. Then reinsert it and find the correct alignment as follows:

Step 1. Turn the cylinder until the line of type appears just above the aligning scale. Use the *variable line spacer* (No. 12, page 1) and slowly turn the cylinder until you get the line in correct position above the scale.

Exercise 1

FORM LETTERS WITH FILL-INS

Use the 20 copies of the letter reproduced in Exercise 2 (page 377), and insert the date, inside address, salutation, and the missing words in the first paragraph from the information given at the right. Punctuate the insertions as necessary to match the letter style. Use May 17, 19— for the date on all copies.

Modified block style. Mixed punctuation.

1. Mr. and Mrs. Jerome Capretta
   3456 Union Road
   Cleveland, OH 44122

   son, Joseph

2. Mr. and Mrs. Donald Dobrowolsky
   19201 Leroy Avenue
   Cleveland, OH 44112

   daughter, Carol

3. Mr. and Mrs. Peter Gotfried
   702 St. Clair Avenue
   Cleveland, OH 44108

   son, Peter

4. Mr. and Mrs. Kenneth Lukas
   13415 Gainsboro Drive
   Cleveland, OH 44110

   daughter, Nancy

5. Mr. and Mrs. L. M. Mrozek
   2001 Reyburn Road
   Cleveland, OH 44115

   son, Larry

6. Mr. and Mrs. William Nelson
   13818 Emery Road
   Cleveland, OH 44111

   daughter, Sandra

7. Mr. and Mrs. Paul Rice
   2813 Silverdale Avenue
   Cleveland, OH 44109

   son, Steve

8. Mr. and Mrs. Richard Ramirez
   3168 West 40th Street
   Cleveland, OH 44106

   daughter, Carol

9. Mr. and Mrs. Gerald Rocco
   4604 Chardon Road
   Cleveland, OH 44133

   son, Vincent

10. Mr. and Mrs. Carl Swasey
    1011 Ashland Street
    Cleveland, OH 44168

    daughter, Rose

11. Mr. and Mrs. Terrance Winkel
    58475 Woodhill Road
    Cleveland, OH 44155

    son, Melvin

12. Mr. and Mrs. Louis Ziska
    3958 Fairhill Drive
    Cleveland, OH 44119

    daughter, Lueanna

13. Mr. and Mrs. Donald Hernandez
    1111 West 6th Street
    Cleveland, OH 44129

    son, Renaldo

14. Mr. and Mrs. Lionel Ratcliff
    340 Lake Shore Way
    Cleveland, OH 44109

    daughter, Marsha

15. Mr. and Mrs. Yung Fong
    19205 Arrowhead Drive
    Cleveland, OH 44130

    son, Lee

16. Mr. and Mrs. Allen Morales
    1835 East 97th Street
    Cleveland, OH 44144

    daughter, Alice

17. Mr. and Mrs. Casey Rasmussen
    13904 Liberty Place
    Cleveland, OH 44101

    son, Casey

18. Mr. and Mrs. Henry Smith
    1948 Kingston Avenue
    Cleveland, OH 44178

    daughter, Suzanne

Step 2. Select a letter whose center is easy to locate (such as *l*, *i*, or *m*) and compare its position with the vertical markings on the scale. If necessary, use the *paper release lever* (No. 7, page 1) and move the paper slightly to the right or left to get the letter into proper alignment with one of the markings on the aligning scale. Then restore the release.

Step 3. To check the accuracy of your alignment, set the *ribbon control* (No. 15, page 1) to stencil position and type a period over the period that was typed in the practice sentence. If the two periods coincide, your paper is correctly aligned. Reset the ribbon control and resume typing.

To test your alignment, space twice after the period at the end of the practice sentence and add the following sentence on *exactly the same line:*

I shall learn today.

Exercise 1

Type Sentence 1 at the right as it is printed. Remove the paper and erase the letters necessary for the correction indicated. Reinsert the paper and be sure it is properly aligned before you type the correction. Follow this procedure to make corrections in the remaining sentences.

Half sheet. Left margin at 15. Double spacing. Begin on line 6.

1. Late in the afternoon there was a hailstorm.
2. The men were promised a raise of 50 cents an hour.
3. A pupil in the fifth grade won the award.
4. We can prove that his signature is a forgery.
5. Few of the students passed the test.
6. I gave the beggar a nickel.
7. Sarah asked the guide for directions.
8. They wrote a short poem for the school assembly.

CORRECTIONS

1 Change *hail* to *snow.*
2 Change *50* to *65.*
3 Change *fifth* to *sixth.*
4 Change *his* to *the.*

5 Change *Few* to *All.*
6 Change *nickel* to *dollar.*
7 Change *Sarah* to *David.*
8 Change *poem* to *play.*

Topic 3 TYPING ON LINES

It is often necessary to fill in business forms and type on a printed line or to fill in a blank space. When you type on a printed line, try to have about the same amount of space between the type and the line as there is when type is underlined on a typewriter.

Practice locating the point at which to begin typing as follows:

Step 1. On a half sheet, type the underscore twenty times, left margin at 20.

Step 2. Remove the paper from the typewriter.

Step 3. Reinsert the paper. Use the variable line spacer to reach the line prepared in Step 1. Turn the cylinder so that the line is a little below the top edge of the aligning scale.

Step 4. Position the carriage so that the printing point is at the beginning of the ruled line.

Step 5. Type your name on the ruled line. Check to see that the letters in your name are slightly above the line, but not too far above it.

Topic 3 FORM LETTERS AND WINDOW ENVELOPES

FORM LETTERS

The cost of a business letter involves more than just the cost of stationery, postage, and the time spent in typing the letter. Someone must compose or dictate the letter, and that person's time could easily represent half, or more, of the cost of that letter.

To avoid the need to compose and type individual responses to every letter, some organizations use form letters to handle correspondence of a routine nature. Form letters may be used to answer inquiries, to follow up on customers who are overdue in their payments, to inform customers of their credit limits, and in general to handle any type of straightforward, routine situation. The chief advantage of a form letter is that once it has been composed and reproduced, the same letter can be used over and over for many addresses. The typist need only insert the date, inside address, salutation, and the variable information for which spaces have been left.

On some form letters, you must insert bits of information within the body of the letter. To do this, you must align the data to be inserted with the line of type in the letter. To review aligning, refer to Section 2 (pages 92 and 93).

Another type of form letter, sometimes called a composite letter, is made up by selecting appropriate paragraphs from a standing list prepared for that purpose. Each letter is then individually typed to fit the situation. With careful planning, composite letters can be as effective as those that are composed individually.

In many offices, word processing equipment is used to store form letters on magnetic tapes, cards, or discs. Through keyboard manipulation, the letters are located, revised if necessary, and typed automatically. A form letter prepared in this way is individually typed, making a good impression on the person who receives it.

FOLDING FOR WINDOW ENVELOPES

The task of addressing envelopes for business papers, form letters, and other correspondence is often eliminated by the use of window envelopes. A window envelope has a transparent section normally in the lower half, through which the inside address on the enclosed letter or business paper is visible.

The typist must fold the letter or business paper so that the address will appear in the transparent opening. Often, to guide the typist, the places for the inside address and folding line are indicated by printed dots or lines. The exact method of folding depends on the size of the paper and of the envelope. In all cases, however, the paper must be folded *back* so that the inside address is exposed.

To fold a standard sheet ($8\frac{1}{2}'' \times 11''$) to fit a No. 10 envelope, or to fold a note-size sheet ($5\frac{1}{2}'' \times 8\frac{1}{2}''$) to fit a No. 6 envelope:

1. Fold up from the bottom of the paper, bringing the bottom edge about $\frac{3}{4}$-inch below the inside address.
2. Fold the exposed upper part of the paper back along the line to which the bottom edge reaches.
3. Insert the paper into the envelope, making sure that the inside address faces the transparent space of the envelope.

Letter Folded for Window Envelope

SIERRA AUTO INSURANCE, INC.
24 El Paseo Drive,
South Lake Tahoe, California 95705
(916) 233-9630

March 29, 19--

Ms. Pamela Ungersoll
419 Snowpeak Road
South Lake Tahoe, CA 95705

Dear Ms. Ungersoll:

SIERRA AUTO INSURANCE, INC.
24 El Paseo Drive, South Lake Tahoe, California 95705   (916) 233-9630

Ms. Pamela Ungersoll
419 Snowpeak Road
South Lake Tahoe, CA 95705

Exercise 1

Type the lines printed at the right. When you type number 10, use the margin release and backspace once from the left margin. After typing all 10 lines, remove the paper from the typewriter. Following the procedures outlined on page 93, fill in the ruled lines with the material indicated for each line.

Half sheet. Left margin at 15. Double spacing. Begin on line 8.

1. Name *(Strike underscore 40 times)* _____

2. Street Address *(Underscore to end of line above)* _____

3. City and State _____

4. Birthdate _____

5. Social Security No. _____

6. Father's Name _____

7. Mother's Name _____

8. School's Name _____

9. Counselor's Name _____

10. Date _____

FILL IN

1 Your name
2 Your street address
3 Your city and state
4 Your birthdate (use words *and* numbers)
5 350-36-2179 (or, type in your own Social Security number if so instructed by your teacher)
6 Your father's name
7 Your mother's name
8 Name of your school
9 Mrs. Audrey Lester (or, type your own guidance counselor's name if so instructed by your teacher)
10 Today's date

Topic 4 CROWDING AND SPREADING

Sometimes after typing a line, or a whole assignment, you may find it necessary to substitute another word for one that you have typed. If the new word is not exactly the same length as the word already typed, some adjustment will have to be made.

CROWDING

If the new word is one letter longer than the space available, it can be *crowded* to fit. This is done by leaving less than the normal space before and after the new word. Practice crowding as follows:

Step 1. On a half sheet, left margin at 15, type the following two sentences. Space exactly as shown.

```
We left him at the park.
                DS
We left     at the park.
```

We left him at the park.
We left them at the park.

Step 2. To fit the word *them* in the space between the words *left* and *at* in the second sentence,

If your machine has a half-space key:

a. Move the printing point to the space following the word *left*.

The survey also indicated that the most popular methods of in-office duplicating are photocopying for short runs (ten or fewer) and offset for large runs. Decreasing sharply in popularity are the stencil and spirit processes. Among the reasons for the rapid growth in photocopying are the speed and ease with which copies can be made. In addition, advances in technology have led to steady improvement in the quality of copies, approaching that of a perfect original.

Exercise 2

COPY PREPARATION AND DUPLICATING

Type this letter on letterhead stationery or on a sheet of good-quality bond paper. Leave space at the top to insert the following items later: the date, inside address, and salutation. After the letter is typed, prepare a spirit, stencil, or offset master. (Another alternative is to have copies made on an office copier.) Run off 20 copies for use in the next topic.

Full sheet. 60-space line. Single spacing. 5-space paragraph indention. Begin on line 24.

The Third Annual Business Education Recognition Assembly will be held on Friday, June 2, 19—, at 8:45 a.m. in the auditorium of Sanger High School to honor your (*leave 20 spaces*). ¶This assembly serves a three-fold purpose: 1. To recognize those students who have excelled in the Intensive Office Education Labs and single-period Business Education classes. 2. To recognize those students who placed at the Regional and State Office Education Association's competitive events. 3. To recognize those students who have rendered outstanding services to the school and community by fulfilling the requirements of the Torch Awards Program. ¶In addition, we are trying to motivate our sophomores who may be considering Intensive Office Education classes for their junior and senior years. ¶We cordially invite you to attend this assembly and join us in congratulating those students who have excelled in their classes. Sincerely, Carolyn E. Thomas Department Chairperson Business and Office Education Ralph T. Krogh, Principal *xx*

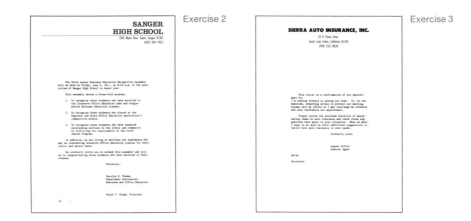

Exercise 2   Exercise 3

Exercise 3

COPY PREPARATION AND DUPLICATING

Type this letter following the instructions outlined in Exercise 2 above.

Full sheet. 50-space line. Single spacing. 5-space paragraph indention. Begin on line 27.

This letter is a confirmation of our appointment for (*leave 43 blank spaces*). I'm looking forward to seeing you then. If, in the meantime, something arises to prevent our meeting, please call my office so that I may rearrange my schedule and also reschedule our appointment. ¶Please review the enclosed checklist of money-saving ideas on auto insurance and check those suggestions that apply to your situation. When we meet, I hope to be able to offer additional suggestions to tailor your auto insurance to your needs. Cordially yours August DiVito General Agent AD:kp Enclosure

b. Depress *and hold down* the half-space key. The carriage will move forward a half space.

c. Type the *t* in the word *them* as you hold down the half-space key. Release the half-space key.

d. Continue depressing (and holding) the half-space key to type the remaining letters in the word *them*.

If your machine does not have a half-space key:

a. Position the printing point 2 spaces after the word *left*.

b. Depress the backspace key slightly so that the carriage moves back a half space (manual machines only). If your machine is electric, move the carriage or element carrier back by hand.

c. Hold the backspace key steady in this position and strike the letter *t*.

d. Release the backspace key.

e. Repeat this operation for each of the remaining letters in the word *them*.

At the beginning or end of a word, it may be possible to add an additional character which takes only a small space without erasing the entire word. Practice the technique of crowding without erasing as follows:

Step 1. Type the following sentence as shown here.

Today is Thursday May 17.

Today is Thursday May 17.
Today is Thursday, May 17.

Step 2. Add a comma after the word *Thursday*.

If your machine has a half-space key:

a. Bring the printing point to the position where the *y* in Thursday is typed.

b. Depress and hold down the half-space key as you strike the comma.

If your machine does not have a half-space key:

a. Bring the printing point to the space after the *y* in *Thursday*.

b. Depress the backspace key slightly and hold it steady as you strike the comma. (Or, push the carriage or element carrier back a half space manually instead of using the backspace key.)

SPREADING

If the word to be inserted is one letter shorter than the space available, the word is *spread* to fill the space. Practice spreading as follows:

Step 1. On a half sheet, left margin at 15, type the following two sentences. Space exactly as shown.

The price is too high.
DS
The   is too high.

The price is too high.
The cost is too high.

Step 2. Fit the word *cost* in the space left in the second typing of the sentence. To avoid leaving an obvious extra letter space as you fit the shorter word *cost* into the empty space, proceed as follows:

If your machine has a half-space key:

a. Position the printing point 2 spaces after the word *The*.

b. Depress and hold down the half-space key.

c. Type the letter *c* in the word *cost*. Release the half-space key.

d. Continue depressing the half-space key and typing the remaining letters in the word *cost*.

If your machine does not have a half-space key:

a. Bring the printing point to the third space after the word *The*.

b. Depress the backspace key slightly so that the carriage moves back a half space (manual machines only). The same effect can be achieved on some machines by moving the carriage or element carrier back by hand, instead of using the backspace key.

c. Hold the backspace key steady in this position as you strike the letter *c* in the word *cost*.

d. Release the backspace key.

e. Repeat the process for each of the remaining letters in the word *cost*.

3. Make corrections as follows:
   a. Remove or cover the carbon deposit with special correction materials made for this purpose. Otherwise, scrape off most of the carbon deposit with a razor blade. Then remove the remaining carbon with a soft, clean eraser.
   b. Place a piece of fresh carbon (carbon side facing you) over the area where the correction is to be typed.
   c. Roll back the cylinder to the proper position and type the correction.
   d. Remove the piece of carbon before continuing.

PREPARING STENCILS

Instructions will come with the stencil for the use of a cushion or a carbon sheet. Also, you may place a film sheet on top of the stencil to prevent letter cutout caused by a sharp type face. Follow these steps:

1. Clean the typewriter keys.
2. Disengage the ribbon by moving the ribbon control to stencil position.
3. Use the horizontal and vertical scales and guide lines to help you arrange the material attractively on the stencil.
4. Type slowly and evenly with a touch heavy enough to make a clear impression.
5. Make corrections as follows:

   a. Flatten the surface of the error by rubbing gently with a smooth, hard object. You may use a burnisher or the rounded end of a paper clip.
   b. Apply a very thin coat of stencil correction fluid. Allow it to dry for 15 to 30 seconds.
   c. Type the correction, using a lighter than normal touch.

PREPARING OFFSET MASTERS

In most offices today, an offset paper master is made by first typing an original. The original is then run through a special copier which generates the offset master from which copies will be printed. It is fast and easy to make a master in this way. However, when such a copier is not available, you can type the material directly onto the master. To do this, follow these steps:

1. Clean the typewriter keys.
2. Use a special typewriter ribbon made of carbon plastic or with grease-base ink.
3. To avoid getting grease or oil on the image area of the master, clean the cylinder, paper bail rollers, and your hands.
4. Use the horizontal and vertical scales and guide lines to help you arrange the material attractively.
5. Type more slowly than your normal rate. If you are using a manual typewriter, strike the keys uniformly. On an electric typewriter, set the pressure control at the lowest position.
6. Make corrections as follows:

   a. Use a special offset eraser to remove the error with a few light strokes. To prevent damage to the master, clean the eraser after each stroke by rubbing it on clean paper.
   b. Type the correction, using a normal touch.

Exercise 1

COPY PREPARATION

Type the bulletin at the right. Display the material attractively on a sheet of good-quality bond paper. Make sure it is letter-perfect and ready to be reproduced.

Full sheet. 60-space line. Double spacing. 5-space paragraph indention.

WHAT'S HAPPENING IN DUPLICATING?

Change is affecting office duplicating. Many companies have gone from stencil to offset, from multiple carbon copies to photocopy machines, from muscle power to electric power. Many of today's offices have a central copying center where sophisticated equipment is used to reproduce both small and large quantities of bulletins, letters, forms, lists, and other business papers.

A recent survey of 1,300 offices showed that they are doing more and more of their own duplicating rather than farming it out. As a result, duplicating department work forces have increased sharply.

(Continued on next page)

Exercise 1
CROWDING

Type Sentence 1 as it is printed at the right. Then make the correction indicated using the crowding technique. If your first attempt is not satisfactory, retype the sentence and try it at least once more before going on. Type and correct Sentences 2–6 in the same manner.

Full Sheet. Left margin at 15. Double spacing. Begin on line 10.

1. Jake's story was to fantastic for belief.
2. I now work in the boys' clothing department.
3. Our office is located on the fifth floor.
4. I must buy four pears for a fruit salad.
5. Mom was excited over my Special Honor Award.
6. I recently started taking piano lessons.

CORRECTIONS

1 Change *to* to *too*.
2 Change *boys'* to *girls'*.
3 Change *fifth* to *fourth*.
4 Change *pears* to *apples*.
5 Change *over* to *about*.
6 Change *piano* to *guitar*.

Exercise 2
SPREADING

Type Sentence 1 as it is printed at the right. Then make the correction indicated using the spreading technique. If your first attempt is not satisfactory, retype the sentence and try it at least once more before going on. Type and correct Sentences 2–6 in the same manner.

Full sheet. Left margin at 15. Double spacing. Begin on line 10.

1. The chorus is practicing for a concert.
2. We would appreciate anything you do to help.
3. The bowling tournament was held in June.
4. Make a right turn into the school parking lot.
5. You may want to add more sugar to the recipe.
6. My brother is a champion swimmer.

CORRECTIONS

1 Change *chorus* to *choir*.
2 Change *would* to *will*.
3 Change *bowling* to *tennis*.
4 Change *right* to *left*.
5 Change *sugar* to *salt*.
6 Change *brother* to *sister*.

Exercise 3
CROWDING AND SPREADING

Type the sentences at the right exactly as they are printed. Then make the corrections indicated using either the crowding or spreading technique.

Half sheet. Left margin at 15. Double spacing. Begin on line 6.

1. We were not aware of the error he had made.
2. The job will take at least four days.
3. The members of the club meet once a week.
4. I thought you were ready to take delivery.
5. Food prices usually rise in summer.
6. It cost two dollars.
7. They approve of our plan.
8. We shall be here soon.
9. We insist on early payment.
10. He was of course very surprised.

CORRECTIONS

1 Change *he* to *she*.
2 Change *four* to *forty*.
3 Change *meet* to *met*.
4 Change *you* to *they*.
5 Change *usually* to *seldom*.
6 Change *cost* to *costs*.
7 Change *approve* to *approved*.
8 Change *here* to *there*.
9 Change *early* to *prompt*.
10 Add a comma after *was* and *course*.

Exercise 6
FILE FOLDER LABELS

Type a label for each name in Exercise 4 (page 373). Type the name on the lower half of the label, 2 or 3 spaces from the left edge. Refer to the illustration on page 371 if necessary.

Exercise 7
MAILING LABELS FOR ENVELOPES

Type a label for each name and address in Exercise 3 (page 372). Center the name and address by estimating. *Use single spacing.*

Exercise 8
SHIPPING LABELS FOR PACKAGES

Type a shipping label for each of the first eight names and addresses in Exercise 2 (page 372). Center the name and address by estimating. Refer to the illustration on page 371 if necessary. *Use single spacing.*

Topic 2 DUPLICATING PROCESSES

When many copies of a letter, memo, or other papers are needed, one of three duplicating processes is used: *spirit* (or fluid), *stencil* (mimeograph), or *offset*. Choice of one process over another depends on the number and quality of copies required. Cost per copy is also an important consideration in deciding which to use. For just a few copies, of course, ordinary carbon paper or a photocopy machine is best.

After deciding on the process, the next step is preparing a *master*. A master is the original from which all the copies are reproduced. Learning to prepare good masters is the chief goal of this topic.

For the spirit process, the typist prepares a carbon-backed master. The master is then placed on a spirit duplicator so that the carbon side comes into contact with sheets of fluid-moistened paper. This method of duplicating is fast, simple, and economical. It is used for such items as menus, price changes, notices of meetings, and school lessons.

For the stencil process, the typist prepares a master on a thin tissue coated with a waxy substance. This is called "cutting" the stencil. The master is then stretched over the inked drum of a stencil duplicator. As the drum is turned, paper is fed into the duplicator and ink is forced through the stencil openings onto the paper. Stencil duplicating is relatively inexpensive and is used for newsletters, news releases, bulletins, and similar items.

The best-quality copies are made by the offset process. This is also the most expensive of the three processes. For offset, the typist prepares a "camera-ready" original, which is used to make a metal plate or a paper master. The kind of master used depends on the quality and number of copies wanted. When the master is placed on an offset duplicator, the image is transferred first to a rubber mat and then to the paper. The offset duplicator can produce thousands of uniform and high-quality copies. For this reason, it is often used to print catalogs, flyers, booklets, and forms.

PREPARING SPIRIT MASTERS

Spirit masters come in sets consisting of one sheet of master paper and one sheet of carbon fastened together along one edge. Between the two is a thin sheet of tissue. Remove the tissue before you begin to type. Then insert the set, open end first. Type directly onto the master sheet and observe these points:

1. Clean the typewriter keys.
2. Type more slowly than your normal rate. If you are using a manual typewriter, type firmly and evenly so that the impressions will be clear and uniform.

Topic 5 TYPING FROM ROUGH-DRAFT COPY

You may be asked to type a revised copy of typed material or printed matter that has been edited and corrected. The notations indicating the changes to be made in the revised copy may either be self-explanatory, or they may consist of special symbols. These symbols are called *proofreaders' marks* because they are commonly used to correct proof copy submitted by a typesetter. The most common proofreaders' marks are shown below.

PROOFREADERS' MARKS

Symbol		*Edited Copy*	*Corrected Copy*
ℯ	delete	a ~~very~~ short letter	a short letter
⌒	close up	in to	into
∧	insert	the ∧only child	the only child
#	insert space	may#be done	may be done
sp	spell out	one (hr.) sp	one hour
¶	begin new paragraph	He laughed. ¶ The next time we asked. . . .	He laughed. The next time. . . .
no ¶	run paragraphs together	It was done. no ¶ At dawn. . . .	It was done. At dawn. . . .
tr	transpose	recieve	receive
≡ cap	capitalize	Plaza hotel	Plaza Hotel
/ lc	lowercase	early in Autumn	early in autumn
stet	let it stand	the firm name	the firm name
ital	put in italics	The title Doctor	The title Doctor
∧	insert comma	clear∧forceful speech	clear, forceful speech
⊙	insert period	the time⊙ Now	the time. Now

⌐	move right	$137.50
		  3.10⌐
			$137.50
			  3.10

⌐	move left	Dr. A. M. Jones ⌐ Physician	Dr. A. M. Jones Physician

Exercise 5

OFFICE EQUIPMENT FILE

Type each of the eight items at the right on a 5″ × 3″ index card. Refer to Model 34 for correct placement of information. Arrange the cards in alphabetical order by item.

1 ITEM Calculator
   DESCRIPTION Elec. Printing
   LOCATION Payroll
   PURCHASED FROM Olivetti Corp.
   SERVICED BY Olivetti
   SERVICE RECORD 9/2/—
   DATE PURCHASED 5/3/—
   SERIAL NO. 5A346701
   NEW/USED New
   PHONE 873-6051

2 ITEM Transcriber
   DESCRIPTION Edisette
   LOCATION Personnel
   PURCHASED FROM Roach-Reid Co.
   SERVICED BY Dictating Equipment
   SERVICE RECORD 4/22/—
   DATE PURCHASED 12/1/—
   SERIAL NO. 35Z42110
   NEW/USED New
   PHONE 621-0733

3 ITEM Copier
   DESCRIPTION 3M
   LOCATION Advertising
   PURCHASED FROM Business Products
                   Sales
   SERVICED BY Business Prod.
   SERVICE RECORD 3/3/—
   DATE PURCHASED 7/15/—
   SERIAL NO. 427850
   NEW/USED New
   PHONE 741-6754

4 ITEM Calculator
   DESCRIPTION Elec. Printing
   LOCATION Accounting
   PURCHASED FROM Data Devices Inc.
   SERVICED BY Ohio Calc. Inc.
   SERVICE RECORD 9/11/—; 11/2/—
   DATE PURCHASED 7/21/—
   SERIAL NO. 23-41377
   NEW/USED New
   PHONE 252-4800

5 ITEM Acc't. Mach.
   DESCRIPTION NCR #36
   LOCATION Payroll
   PURCHASED FROM NCR
   SERVICED BY NCR
   SERVICE RECORD 2/15/—; 4/30/—
   DATE PURCHASED 6/10/—
   SERIAL NO. 56Z4110
   NEW/USED New
   PHONE 881-9500

6 ITEM Word Processor
   DESCRIPTION Royal CTS
   LOCATION Sales Dept.
   PURCHASED FROM Royal Typewriter Co.
   SERVICED BY Royal
   SERVICE RECORD 12/3/—
   DATE PURCHASED 10/3/—
   SERIAL NO. 3216A11
   NEW/USED New
   PHONE 621-8100

7 ITEM Typewriter
   DESCRIPTION IBM Cor. Sel.
   LOCATION Personnel
   PURCHASED FROM IBM
   SERVICED BY IBM
   SERVICE RECORD 4/3/—; 6/10/—
   DATE PURCHASED 2/4/—
   SERIAL NO. 20-61772
   NEW/USED New
   PHONE 347-9870

8 ITEM Duplicator
   DESCRIPTION AB Dick
   LOCATION Sales
   PURCHASED FROM Ace Office
                   Equipment
   SERVICED BY AB Dick
   SERVICE RECORD 1/25/—
   DATE PURCHASED 11/15/—
   SERIAL NO. 467189
   NEW/USED Used
   PHONE 775-1150

Exercise 1

Type the following sentences, including the sentence numbers, making all the corrections indicated.

Half sheet. Left margin at 15. Double spacing. Begin on line 7.

1. The Le gal Secretary must be accurate an typist.

2. My sister receives good grades in her english class. *es*

3. You will, of course need good skills ~~upon~~ when you graduate.

4. *Each* Our Spring ~~term~~ *our* baseball team recruits players.

5. My tpying class visited a Word Process ing center.

6. Learn to type is a ~~very~~ valuable skill.

7. Next week, we will begin to stduy Careers Clerical.

8. Miss Reed said, "learn today; earn tomorrow".

9. Accounting stu dents ~~in~~ usually begin with the bkkg. *sp* class.

Exercise 2

Type the following sentences, making the corrections indicated.

Half sheet. Left margin at 15. Double spacing. Begin on line 6.

1. At the end *of the year,* the firm gave each ~~worker~~ *employee* a generuos bon us.

2. You will find ti more conomical to let us buy the paper for y ou.

3. we never ~~no~~ *know* the worth of water *until the well runs dry.*

4. I can not be your freind and your flatter too. *er*

5. The botique is very expensive on Miller Ave. *sp*

6. Your party ~~was~~ a success and every body had a good time.

7. Please *return* the enclosed Form to us filled out and sign ed ~~properly~~. *properly*

8. When i lent I had a friend; but when I asked he was ~~not kind~~. *unkind*

9. Many schools now offer a place ment service to their students.

10. Annal wage ~~increaese~~ *increases* of 8% or more are not uncommon thise days. *sp*

Exercise 4

PERSONNEL FILE

Type each of the 12 items at the right on a 5″ × 3″ index card. Use the employee's name as the key word. Arrange the cards in alphabetical order.

```
Koenig, Frank

4893 E. 97 Street
Cleveland, OH 44114
Phone:  (216) 621-2380
Position:  Receptionist
Dept.:  Personnel
```

	EMPLOYEE NAME	ADDRESS	
1	Koenig, Frank	4893 E. 97 Street Cleveland, OH 44114	Phone: (216) 621-2380 Position: Receptionist Department: Personnel
2	DiMarco, Tony	3440 Virginia Avenue Parma, OH 44134	Phone: (216) 842-3651 Position: Programmer Department: Data Processing
3	Michalski, Alicia	251 Plymouth Street Bedford, OH 44146	Phone: (216) 232-8461 Position: Buyer Department: Purchasing
4	Clough, Debbie	1555 Hilliard Avenue Lakewood, OH 44127	Phone: (216) 521-6628 Position: Coding Clerk Department: Accounting
5	Koch, Joan	224 Van Aken Boulevard Shaker Heights, OH 44125	Phone: (216) 921-4261 Position: Accountant Department: Accounting
6	Krall, Ed	5281 Sunset Drive Berea, OH 44128	Phone: (216) 234-7745 Position: Manager Department: Personnel
7	Hendricks, Paul	2919 Park Drive Cleveland, OH 44130	Phone: (216) 321-8950 Position: Accounts Payable Clerk Department: Accounting
8	Fanelli, Judith	2832 Mayfield Road Terrace Park, OH 45174	Phone: (216) 321-8950 Position: Salesperson Department: Sales
9	Chin, Jim Lee	679 Fernway Drive Cleveland, OH 44111	Phone: (216) 784-0652 Position: Salesperson Department: Sales
10	Chuppa, Stella	4650 Fleet Avenue Cleveland, OH 44118	Phone: (216) 561-1158 Position: Typist Department: Word Processing
11	Harris, Dennis	5281 Superior Avenue Euclid, OH 44122	Phone: (216) 884-2432 Position: Secretary Department: Personnel
12	Nemeth, Patricia	45 Erieview Towers Cleveland, OH 44111	Phone: (216) 696-2930 Position: Manager Department: Advertising

Exercise 3

Type the following sentences, making the corrections indicated.

Half sheet. Left margin at 15. Double spacing. Begin on line 6.

1. A well-written telgeram must be breif, but it must also beclear.

2. The (GREATEST) of faults, I should say, is to be consciuos of none.
    lc

3. These chairs, made of fum oak and are strong and sturdy.
    are *ed* *d* *both*

4. When I do well, I heard it ne ver; when I did ill, I herad it ever.
    did

5. We are abound to for give an enemy, we arenot bound to trust.
    If *our* *ies* *#* *them*

6. [Merchandize must be shiped by parcel post, by freight, or by ex press.
    parcel #

7. You know, of course, that we expect payment with in too days.
    two

8. The even ing prreformance began at 8:00 and ended at 10:54.

9. Their is no thing so powerfull as truth--and often Nothing so strangle.
    There *lc*

10. The lamp is equpped with an Eye-Saver Shade (our own design).

Exercise 4

Type this short paragraph, making all the corrections indicated.

Half sheet. 2-inch side margins. Double spacing. Begin on line 8.

SMALL BUSINESS (Center title)

⟨TS⟩ Here Are cer tain facts about small businesses which a

person planning to go into busness for themselves should
business

know. ¶ A small business has certain faetures which make

it an important part of our economic life. It gives
#

indi viduals an opportunity to use all business talents
their

the operator of a small busniess, like the pioneer

farmwe, must be a jack-of-all-trades.
er

                    --Small Business Series ⌐

Exercise 2

MAILING LIST BY ZIP CODE

Type each of the 16 items at the right on a 5″ × 3″ index card. Use the ZIP Code as the key word. After you have typed the cards, arrange them in order by ZIP Code.

```
53401

Mr. Edward Ungers
631 Lincoln Drive
Racine, WI 53401
```

1	Mr. Edward Ungers	631 Lincoln Drive, Racine, WI 53401
2	Mr. Yung Koo	52 Morris Avenue, Fort Wayne, IN 46802
3	Miss Anna Yacobellis	8901 Harvard Avenue, Bay City, MI 48706
4	Ms. Carolyn Stinson	421 Case Avenue, Oak Park, IL 60301
5	Mrs. Lillian Wynn	782 E. 131 Street, Elkhart, IN 46514
6	Mr. Michael Voinovich	5600 Lander Road, Flint, MI 48502
7	Mr. Jerry Vittardi	344 Lake Shore Drive, Chicago, IL 60607
8	Ms. Doris Vollmer	831 Warner Building, Washington, DC 22013
9	Mr. George Trevino	475 Halle Drive, Corpus Christi, TX 78401
10	Mrs. Ralph Stokes	24 Regent Street, Macon, GA 31202
11	Mrs. Ruth Stein	1250 W. Clifton Drive, St. Louis, MO 63158
12	Mr. Tom Yamaha	3432 W. 25 Street, Cleveland, OH 44102
13	Ms. Linda Gray-Moin	753 Colorado Avenue, Palo Alto, CA 94306
14	Mr. R. H. Kocab	811 Ackley Street, Tulsa, OK 74111
15	Ms. Laura Donovan	3420 Lennox Drive, Albuquerque, NM 87101
16	Mr. Elvis Perkins	103 Triangle Court, Nashville, TN 38107

Exercise 3

CUSTOMER NAME FILE

Type each of the seven items at the right on a 5″ × 3″ index card. Refer to Model 34 for correct placement of information. Arrange the cards in alphabetical order.

	COMPANY	ADDRESS	CREDIT
1	Standard Construction Co.	14733 Grapeland Boulevard Floral Park, NY 11003 Account No. 76421	OK
2	Garcia Glass Works	26241 Pearl Road New Port Richey, FL 33552 Account No. 76502	Check Credit Manager
3	Hale Chisholm, Inc.	532 Bayfair Drive Passaic, NJ 07055 Account No. 76495	OK
4	Louis Gold & Sons	21 South Street Ellicott City, MD 21043 Account No. 76711	C.O.D. only
5	Oxford Iron Works	5521 Dalewood Road Allentown, PA 18105 Account No. 76552	OK
6	Matsumura Cycle Shop	2316 Bellfield Way San Jose, CA 95125 Account No. 76589	OK
7	Misch Electric, Inc.	4211 E. Sprague Street Huntsville, AL 35811 Account No. 76424	OK

Exercise 5

Type the short paragraph at the right, making all the corrections indicated.

Half sheet. 2-inch side margins. Single spacing. Begin on line 11.

Problems of a Small Business (caps)

Owners of small businesses have many problems. They must choose a location that customers can reach easily; they must get to know the needs of their customers and gain their good will. They must train their employees. They must plan store layout and make window displays, do their own recordkeeping and buying, and attend to numerous management details that, in a larger organization, would be handled by specialists.

Exercise 6

Type the rough-draft copy at the right, making all the corrections indicated by the proofreaders' marks.

Half-sheet. 1½-inch side margins. Double spacing. Begin on line 7.

Students who consider dropping out of high school will be at a serious disadvantage when they applying for the better paying jobs with better pay and chances for advancement. However, a high school diploma (or even a college degree) alone is not enough preparation for some occupations. There are many jobs require technical special training or work experience in a particular skill. Although the average college graduate does earn more, many better paying jobs do not require college. An important part of career planning is to decide how much and what type of post-high school education to acquire after high school.

LABELS

Names, subject titles, mailing addresses, and other items of information are often typed on labels. You may use these for identifying file folders, addressing bulk mailings, or addressing parcels and large envelopes.

Frequently labels are self-adhesive and are supplied in strips, sheets, or rolls with backing. As each label is typed, it is pulled off the backing and applied. To keep the remaining labels in place when typing, you should leave three or four inches of backing before the next label on the strip, sheet, or roll.

When typing on small labels that are not affixed to backing, try to avoid leaving only one or two labels at the end. These will be difficult to insert into the typewriter and will not stay in place. However, single large labels, such as those used for mailing or shipping, can be prepared following these steps:

1. Make a pleat across the center of a sheet of paper to form a pocket about 1 inch deep. (See the illustration at the left.) You may have to tape the edges of the paper to keep the folds in place.
2. Insert the paper into the typewriter and turn the cylinder until the top edge of the pocket appears above the aligning scale.
3. Place the label into the pocket and roll the cylinder backwards until the label is in typing position.

Mailing or Shipping Label

Moss & Skelton

733 Sycamore Street, Yakima, Washington 98902

TO: Mrs. Lillian T. Sacks
466 Pearl Street
Yakima, WA 98902

Perforated File Folder Label

Hartford, Brazen & Company

Self-Adhesive File Folder Label

Johnson & Mapes, Inc.

Exercise 1

MAILING LIST BY NAME

Type each of the 16 names and addresses at the right on a 5″ × 3″ index card. Refer to Model 34 for correct placement of information. If cards are not available, cut paper to size. After you have typed the cards, arrange them in alphabetical order.

1	Mr. Gerald Jaworski	11810 Lake Avenue, Sherman Oaks, CA 91403
2	Mr. Jim Chan	1375 State Road, Garden City, NY 11530
3	Mr. Michael N. Adamo	24 Siebert Avenue, Freeport, NY 11520
4	Ms. Anne Balogh	137 Tivoli Avenue, Flint, MI 48506
5	Mr. Joseph Cawrse	842 S. Green Road, Shaker Heights, OH 44120
6	Mrs. Roslyn Evans	2425 North Park Drive, Chicago, IL 60628
7	Mr. Tito Cavalaro	883 E. 144 Street, Austin, TX 78757
8	Mrs. Linda Deitz	511 South Spring Street, Los Angeles, CA 90013
9	Ms. Katie James	9515 Buck Road, Wilmington, DE 19808
10	Ms. Violet Fressler	1684 Avalon Drive, St. Louis, MO 63110
11	Mr. Irwin Fishman	25 Van Ness Boulevard, San Francisco, CA 94106
12	Mr. Rupert Manley	48 Fernald Street, Columbus, OH 43204
13	Miss Ruth Cendrowski	52 Akana Drive, Lahaina, HI 96761
14	Mr. Dominic Ferrito	3416 Warren Avenue, Reno, NV 89501
15	Mr. Robert Hughes	1358 W. 76 Street, Jackson, MS 34209
16	Ms. JoAnn Janka	3450 Russell Avenue, Des Moines, IA 50322

Exercise 7

Type this rough-draft copy, making all the corrections indicated by the proof-readers' marks.

Half sheet. 1½-inch side margins. Double spacing. Begin on line 5.

SEASONS ARE IMPORTANT?

How do Sales vary by months and seasons? Statistic show little season la variation in some lines; for exzmple, grocery stores and Drug store restaurants sales, too, are steady, expect for a great spurt before christmas. On the other hand, there is some great variation in other lines of business. For example automobile dealers are very much busier in the Spring months then they are in February and or September. Filling stations have their slack season in Febrary; they climb steadily to a peak in july and then graduually taper off. Ap parel stores, too have great variations.

--Small Business Series

Exercise 8

Type a copy of this notice, making all the corrections indicated by the proof-readers' marks.

Full sheet. 60-space line. Double spacing. Begin on line 16.

To All Sales Representatives:

We have just sent you under separate cover an additional supply of our special sales Report Forms. If your supply is insufficient, please let me know and additional copies will be sent to you. A number of you are not making full use of these report forms. I want to point out again the vital necessity of making fill out one of them for every call that you make. The information that we get from them is of great value to us me in planing replacements and in developing new materials. I urge you, therefore, to make out complete the reports regularly and get them to us me as promptly as possible.

James T. Harris

SPECIAL TYPING APPLICATIONS

Topic 1 INDEX CARDS AND LABELS

INDEX CARDS

Information of various kinds can be conveniently stored on index cards. Libraries, for example, keep card files of book titles, subject listings, and authors' names. You can check the card files to find a book you are looking for. In a business office, card files are kept so that information such as telephone numbers, addresses, and account numbers can be found quickly. Model 34, below, illustrates three different uses of index cards.

Index cards come in a variety of sizes: 5" × 3"; 3" × 2¼"; 6" × 4"; and 8" × 5". The size used depends on the nature or amount of information to be recorded. After the information is put on the cards, they are either stored in open card file trays or drawers or mounted on a wheel. When stored, the cards are usually arranged alphabetically, with the key words clearly visible at the top.

Here are some general guidelines for typing on index cards:

1. Type the key words (a name or a number) on line 2, about 3 spaces from the left edge. It is acceptable either to use solid capitals or to capitalize only the first letter of each important word.
2. Leave 2 or 3 blank lines.
3. Type all other data in block style, aligning each new line with the key words.

Follina, Peter

Follina, Mr. Peter
8249 Turney Road
Maple Heights, OH 44137

Mailing List by Name

ALLEN & CRAWFORD, INC.

2462 Dover Street
Raleigh, NC 27610

Account No.: 76490

Credit: C.O.D. only

Customer Name File

Item ____Typewriter____ Date Purchased ___9/16/--___
Description ___IBM Sel. II___ Serial No. _15-57345_
Location ____Sales Dept.____ New/Used ___New___
Purchased from _____Lakeshore Office Equipment_____
Serviced by _____IBM_____ Phone ___347-9870___
Service Record _3/21/--; 8/18/--;_____
_____

Office Equipment File

Model 34 *Index Cards*

Taking It For Granted ~~center~~ TS

All of us get many kinds of service~~s which~~ *that* are necessary for our personal comfort~~, and~~ to which we give little thought; *or* in fact, we generally take them as a matter of course. In the morning, we read our letters or our di*a*ly paper. We leave home at a certain time *each morning* to catch a bus or train to school or to work, and we expect the bus or train to be at our ~~station~~ *stop* at a ~~given~~ *definite* time. ¶ We turn on a faucet and are not surprised that water flows. If we turn on a light#switch and the light does not come on, we <u>are</u> surprised. ~~It's because we take these things for granted~~

No ¶ It is only when something goes wrong that we begin to think ~~at all~~ seriously about the services we usually take for granted. ¶ We expect our mail (to be on time), our newspapers, *and* our trains. When we pick up the phone and dia l a number, we ~~know that~~ *expect* our call ~~will~~ *to* go through. We depend on these and many other services to *help us* transact our business and keep (in order) our affairs.

In turn, we are expected to be at school or the office on time. If we are late to work, we may keep a customer or *a* co-worker waiting. If we arrive late for a doctor's appointment, other patients and the doctor may be inconvenienced. Being late wastes other people's time and delays work.

Many other people serve us, and we serve many other people (in this way). Through*ou* our lives, we depend on people in all parts of the world to do their work, to do it well, and to do it *on* ~~at the right~~ time, and they depend on us to do the same.

NATIONAL ANNUITY LIFE INSURANCE COMPANY

STATEMENT OF NET CURRENT ASSETS

June 30, 19—

CURRENT ASSETS:

Common stocks at market value	$133,963,387
Cash in bank	3,011,849
Commercial paper	23,919,350
Receivable for securities sold	1,777,682
Investment income receivable	390,301
Total Current Assets	163,062,569

LESS CURRENT LIABILITIES:

Payable for securities purchased	2,206,538
Balance due Company	27,576
Reserve for federal income tax	—

NET CURRENT ASSETS: $160,828,455

R. R. KLINGER, INC.

CHANGES IN FINANCIAL POSITION

Year ended December, 31, 19—

Source of Funds

	($000)
Funds provided from operations	131,744
Dividends from investments	10,149
Net proceeds from issue of securities	
Long-term debt	73,499
Common shares	870
	216,262

Use of Funds

	($000)
Additions to plant and equipment (net)	88,075
Arctic exploration project	5,495
Reduction of long-term debt	63,142
Purchase and cancellation of preferred shares	1,219
Purchase and cancellation of common shares	45,708
Other (net)	4,739
Increase in working capital during year	7,884
	216,262

Exercise 10
Type the following company bulletin,
making all the corrections indicated.
*Full sheet. 1-inch side margins. Double
spacing. Begin on line 11.*

Attention: All Employees   *TS*

    Fun is doing things. No matter what your job is or *what* your family life

may~~be~~ *#* , there are some forms of recreational activity in which you can take

an active
~~a~~ part. You can ~~play catch or~~ ride a bicycle, play a game of cards, or

play a musical instrument. All of these are "doing" activities. You might

d
choose one of these because it is ~~f~~ifferent from your job and allows you

muscles or
to use talents or interests other than those your job requires. You may

an activity
choose ~~something~~ because you are good at it. it may give you a chance to

match your skill against someone else's and maybe even to win. or you

may do it just because you think it's fun. The main point is that you are

time
using your ~~days~~, your thoughts and your energy in a way that is fun and

relaxing.
different from your work. You are ~~taking it easy.~~ You can often add

more interest and get more out of your recreational activities by doing

d
them in gr~~a~~oups rather than doing them alone. You coul~~d~~ take a class.

no
You could join a musical group and entertain young people's groups

or old. ~~P~~eople living in rest homes. Fun in groups wins you new friends.

Perhaps the most important reason that people like "doing" activities is

accomplished
the personal satisfaction they get from having something. Making a dress

repairing
or ~~fixing~~ a television set can be fun because you have something to show

for your work when you're done--something that you can be proud of.

one or more of
    Won't you join us in the many activities we have arranged for you.

l
Call me or my secretary for more information and an enro~~l~~ment card.

                Paul Simmons, so~~ic~~al director

Exercise 4

Full sheet. DS body. Spread center second line of title.

GREAT LAKES PIPELINES

SUMMARY BALANCE SHEET

(Thousands of U.S. Dollars)

ASSETS	1980	1979
Plant, property, and equipment	$362,317	$359,583
Less: accumulated depreciation	97,355	83,622
	264,962	275,961
Current assets	58,182	47,087
Deferred charges	262	392
	$323,406	$323,440

SHAREHOLDERS' EQUITY AND LIABILITIES		
Common stock	$ 50,000	$ 50,000
Retained earnings	27,761	30,079
First mortgage pipeline bonds	162,500	177,500
Current liabilities	67,972	60,284
Deferred credits	15,173	5,577
	$323,406	$323,440

Exercise 5

Full sheet. DS body.

TRANSWORLD INDUSTRIES

FINANCIAL HIGHLIGHTS

	1980	1979
	($000)	($000)
Operations		
Operating revenues	1,870,325	1,499,137
Operating income	142,761	134,932
Net income	86,183	79,635
Funds provided from operations	131,744	127,161
Dividends declared		
Preferred shares	7,786	9,960
Common shares	37,922	31,414
Net income per common share		
Basic	$2.01	$1.92
Fully diluted	1.95	1.79
Dividends declared, per common share	.97	.85¾

Topic 6 CONSTRUCTING NEW SYMBOLS

There are certain symbols for which there are no special keys on the standard keyboard. These symbols are made by using some of the characters on the standard keyboard in a special way or in a special combination. The table below lists some common examples. On some typewriters, the keyboard has additional keys for some of these symbols.

Symbol	How Made	Illustration
Ditto mark	Use quotation mark.	January 10 " 15
Fractions not on the keyboard	Use the slant to separate numerator and denominator. Leave a space before and after the fraction.	6 1/3 dozen
Minus sign	Use the hyphen. Leave a space before and after the minus sign.	6 – 4
Multiplication sign	Use the small x. Leave a space before and after the x. The x may also be used in measurements to indicate by.	3 x 2 a 9 x 12 rug
Division sign	Strike the hyphen, backspace, strike the colon. On some machines, it is necessary to turn the cylinder slightly before striking the colon in order to center the hyphen between the dots of the colon. Leave a space before and after the division sign.	6 ÷ 2
Degrees	Turn the cylinder down slightly by using the automatic line finder; strike small o.	32°
Feet and inches (after numbers)	Use apostrophe for feet and quotation marks for inches, each followed by a space.	6'5" tall
Minutes and seconds (after numbers)	Use apostrophe for minutes and quotation marks for seconds, each followed by a space.	Time: 2'4"
Exponents (raised numbers)	Turn the cylinder down slightly by using the automatic line finder; strike the desired key.	x^2
Chemical symbols (lowered numbers)	Turn the cylinder up slightly by using the automatic line finder; strike the desired key.	H_2O
Caret	Underscore the preceding letter; strike a slant in the space between words. Turn the cylinder down 1 line and center the word to be inserted over the slash.	good in/time
Brackets:		
Left bracket	Turn the cylinder back one line and strike the underscore. Turn the cylinder up one line; backspace twice; strike the slant. Backspace; strike the underscore.	∠
Right bracket	Turn the cylinder back one line; strike the underscore. Turn the cylinder up one line; backspace; strike the slant. Backspace twice; strike the underscore.	⌐
Roman numerals	Use capital letters (occasionally small letters are used). Key to Roman numerals shown: 1, 5, 10, 50, 100, 500 and 1,000.	I V X L C D M

MOLLY'S GIFT SHOPPE

Balance Sheet

December 31, 19—

ASSETS		LIABILITIES AND EQUITY	
Cash	$ 6,692	Notes Payable	$ 1,389
Notes Receivable	2,031	Accounts Payable	7,437
Accounts Receivable	9,930		
Merchandise Stock	26,500	Total Liabilities	8,826
Store Equipment	3,270		
Office Supplies	253	Owner's Equity	39,850
	$48,676		$48,676

FEDERAL FINANCE COMPANY
STATEMENT OF REVENUE AND EXPENSE
FOR THE YEAR 19—

Operating Revenues

Interest on Loans	$192,000	
Interest and Dividends on Securities	313,000	
Fees and Commissions	123,000	
Total Operating Revenue		$628,000

Operating Expenses

Salaries	244,000	
Taxes and Assessments	145,000	
All Other Current Expenses	153,000	
Total Operating Expenses		542,000

NET CURRENT EARNINGS $ 86,000

Exercise 1

Type the sentences at the right.

Full sheet. 70-space line. Single spacing; DS after each numbered item. Begin on line 13.

1. Week 1—The class average was 18 gross words, 14 net words.
   "   6— "   "   "   " 24 "   " , 20 "   "   .
   "   12— "   "   "   " 31 "   " , 24 "   "   .
   "   18— "   "   "   " 33 "   " , 29 "   "   .

2. The large box measured $8\frac{5}{8} \times 5 \times 4\frac{1}{8}$ inches. The small box measured $3 \times 2\frac{3}{4} \times 1\frac{7}{8}$ inches.

3. You should be able to give the answers to these examples without hesitation:
   $$12 - 9 = ? \qquad 8 \times 7 = ? \qquad 42 \div 3 = ? \qquad 35 + 6 = ?$$

4. The island was 44° 18′ 22″ north latitude.

5. If x^2 equals 36, then x must equal 6.

6. The lot is one hundred feet by forty feet (100′ $\times$ 40′).

7. The monument, when completed, will be 17′ 6″ high.

8. When the outdoor temperature is 30°C, is the weather cold or warm?

9. He said, "I like all of you." [Applause.] He added, "In fact, I love you all!" [Laughter.]

10. The chemical symbol, CO_2, represents carbon dioxide. The air you exhale contains CO_2.

11. The Magna Carta was signed in the year MCCXV. What year was that?

12. Although it is poor form to insert a word in typed matter by means of a caret, it may occasionally be unavoidable to do so. Example:
    $$\text{must}$$
    The wor\underline{k}/be completed today.

Topic 7 RULING LINES

You can rule a horizontal line in pen or pencil while the paper is in the typewriter. Find a notch or hole in the card holder, printing point indicator, or the ribbon guide. Place the tip of the pencil in the notch or hole, and hold the pencil steady. Depress the carriage release and move the carriage by hand from left to right, or from right to left. (Press lightly on the pencil so as not to make a ridge on the cylinder.) As you move the carriage, the line will be ruled neatly and easily. A double line may be made by turning the cylinder slightly up after the first line has been ruled and making a second rule.

To rule a vertical line while the paper is in the typewriter, use the automatic line finder to allow the cylinder to turn freely. Hold the pen or pencil steady at a convenient point and turn the cylinder using the cylinder knob. Press lightly to avoid making a ridge on the cylinder. Look at the illustrations on page 106.

Topic 4 FINANCIAL STATEMENTS

From time to time you may be asked to type tables that present financial data. Some of the more common forms of financial statements are presented in the exercises in this topic. Observe the following guidelines when typing them:

1. Center the statement title.
2. Single-space the body (although double spacing may be used occasionally). Leave a triple space before the side headings and a double space after them.
3. Align the amounts of money at the right.
4. Align the dollar signs at the top and bottom of a money column.
5. Double-space after a ruled line across a money column.
6. Type double rules under the final totals in a money column.
7. Single-space and indent runover lines.

Exercise 1
Full sheet. SS body.

THE ELITE LUGGAGE SHOP

BALANCE SHEET

December 31, 19--

TS

Assets:

DS

Cash	$ 1,450
Accounts receivable	2,750
Merchandise inventory	12,613
Store fixtures	2,500
Miscellaneous store supplies	58
Deposit on store lease	300

DS

Total assets	$19,671

TS

Liabilities and Capital:

DS

Accounts payable	$ 3,612
Notes payable	3,625
Unpaid expenses	74

DS

Total liabilities	7,311

DS

Capital	12,360

DS

Total liabilities and capital	$19,671

Ruling Horizontal Lines

Ruling Vertical Lines

Exercise 1

Practice ruling vertical and horizontal lines with pen or pencil without removing the paper from the typewriter.

Half sheet. 2-inch side margins. Begin on line 10.

1. Rule a horizontal line about 3 inches long by placing your pen or pencil as shown in the drawing above.
2. Space up ten lines and rule a second horizontal line the same length as the first.
3. Draw vertical lines to join the two horizontal lines at each end, forming a rectangle. Place your pen or pencil as shown in the illustration.

Exercise 2

RULING A FORM

With a pen or pencil, draw a form like the one shown at the right. Rule the 10 horizontal lines first, then draw the 5 vertical lines. Space the vertical lines so that columns 1 and 3 have 20 spaces each, and columns 2 and 4 have 15 spaces each.

Half sheet. Double spacing. Margins at 10 and 80 for elite type; 5 and 75 for pica. Begin on line 8.

Line 8 →

←——— 20 spaces ———→	←—— 15 spaces ——→	←——— 20 spaces ———→	←—— 15 spaces ——→

Exercise 3

Fill in the form you drew in Exercise 2. Center the column headings.

Name	Soc. Sec. No.	Name	Soc. Sec. No.
Margaret G. Abbott	333-62-1762	Frances P. Novak	169-83-5630
Carl C. Barret	748-05-2016	Nathan J. Nussbaum	481-89-0304
Ronald C. Blair	522-62-5443	Patrick T. O'Leary	801-76-5089
Dorothy S. Davis	243-08-7461	Ray D. Purcell	452-90-3055
Stanley J. Field	377-25-4793	Sigrid S. Raymond	117-89-8337
Mario L. Gonzales	807-98-2878	Michael F. Smith	729-36-9415
Adele R. Ingram	545-51-6073	Noboru Sumi	178-50-6259
Kevin W. Lang	557-84-6651	Mary L. Templeton	690-34-3614
Eleanor K. Little	932-81-5392	Susan A. Vaughn	944-98-6971

Exercise 7

LEADERS

Half sheet. DS body. Pivot right column.

SAM LINDSAY NEW CAR SALES

SAMPLE FINANCE PLAN

Suggested retail price	$6,195.00
Down payment (20%)	1,239.00
Amount financed	4,956.00
Number of payments	60
Annual percentage rate	10.75%
Finance charge	1,472.18
Amount of each payment	107.14
Total amount of payments	6,428.18

Exercise 8

LEADERS

Full sheet. DS body. Pivot right column.

THE CHRISTMAS PLAY

CAST OF CHARACTERS

Mother	Sherrita Hightower
Father	Kevin Pugh
Raymond	Habib Sri
Hallie	Charles Griffin
Evie	Bridget Corley
Christmas Fairy	Connie Embry
Christmas Elves	Patrick Webb
	Michelle Labat
Santa	Wendell Green
Mrs. Claus	Allison Knight

Exercise 9

LEADERS

Full sheet. DS body. Pivot right column.

TABLE OF CONTENTS

Preface	ii
Chapter	
I. The Early Days of Opera	2
II. Italian Opera	40
III. French Opera	71
IV. Wagnerian Opera	94
V. Russian Opera	122
VI. American Opera	134
VII. Other Operas	155
VIII. Famous Opera Houses	187
IX. The Future of Opera	200
Bibliography	215
Index	233

PART

HORIZONTAL AND VERTICAL CENTERING

Topic 1 HORIZONTAL CENTERING

To give an attractive appearance, typewritten material should be centered. Centering is achieved when left and right margins are approximately equal, and top and bottom margins are approximately equal. To center a line horizontally, follow these steps:

Step 1. Insert your paper with the left edge at 0 (zero) on the carriage scale.

Step 2. Since standard typing paper has a width of 85 *pica spaces* or 102 *elite spaces*, the center of the page is at $42\frac{1}{2}$ for pica typewriters and 51 for elite typewriters. For convenience, these are rounded off to 42 and 50 respectively.

Step 3. *From the center of the paper, backspace once for every two letters or spaces* in the line to be centered. Thus, the number of typed spaces on either side of the center point will be equal. Do not backspace for an odd letter at the end of a line.

Step 4. Begin typing at the point where you stopped backspacing.

Directions for Drills A–E Type the following drills to gain practice in horizontal centering. *Full sheet. Paper guide at 0. Tab at center.*

Drill A

Center the word, *SCHEDULE,* horizontally.

1. Move the carriage so that the printing point is at the center of your carriage scale (42 or 50).
2. Spell out the word silently to yourself, backspacing once for every 2 letters.

$$\widehat{SC} \ \widehat{HE} \ \widehat{DU} \ \widehat{LE}$$

3. At the point where you stopped backspacing, lock the shift and type *SCHEDULE* in solid capitals.
4. Space down 4 lines to prepare for the next drill.

Drill B

Center the word, *EDITORIAL,* horizontally.

1. Tab to center.
2. Backspace once for every 2 letters, ignoring the odd letter left at the end.

$$\widehat{ED} \ \widehat{IT} \ \widehat{OR} \ \widehat{IA} \ \text{(ignore L)}$$

3. At the point where you stopped backspacing, lock the shift and type *EDITORIAL* in solid capitals.
4. Space down 4 lines to prepare for the next drill.

Exercise 4

PIVOTING

Full sheet. DS body. 10 spaces between columns.

INTERSCHOLASTIC FOOTBALL LINEUP
November 9, 19—
Greenleaf High School vs. Brady Academy

Greenleaf	Position	Brady
Lustman	Left end	Mansville
Gasperi	Left tackle	Barbieri
Brunswick	Left guard	McGuire
Leddington	Center	Sachs
Corby	Right end	Meadow
Tomlinson	Right tackle	Westerfield
Taylor	Right guard	Millet
Kearney	Quarterback	Grosvenor
Cunningham	Left halfback	Burgess
Zaner	Right halfback	Raleigh
Campbell	Fullback	McKeon

Exercise 5

PIVOTING

Full sheet. DS body. SS and indent runover lines. 20 spaces between columns.

ACKNOWLEDGMENTS

		3
Honors Presentation Coordinator		7
	Mrs. Irma Vann	15
Class Sponsors	Mrs. Mary Kendziorski	27
	Anita Wessfann	33
	Theodore Lambret	40
Honors Presentation Speaker		44
	Wendy Laucks	51
Programs	Ms. Davida Cookes	60
Scholarships	Mrs. Irma Vann	68
Cover Design	Gerald Plett	75
Committee Chairperson	Ronald Drake	84

Exercise 6

LEADERS

Half sheet, inserted with short (5½-inch) side first. DS body. Pivot right column.

JOHN F. KENNEDY HIGH SCHOOL

SENIOR CLASS OFFICERS

19—

President . . . . Rudolph Carter
Vice President . . . . Kimberly Browning
Treasurer . . . . Inez Romero
Secretary . . . . Terry Mead

Drill C

Center the words, *MY FAVORITE STORY*, horizontally.

1. Tab to center.
2. Backspace once for every 2 letters or spaces:

   MY *space*F AV OR IT E*space* ST OR (ignore Y)
3. At the point where you stopped backspacing, lock the shift and type *MY FAVORITE STORY* in solid capitals.
4. Space down 4 lines to prepare for the next drill.

Drill D

Center horizontally the 15 lines at the right. You should be able to check your work easily!

Drill E

Center horizontally each item of information requested.

Double spacing.

DRILL D	DRILL E
To	Your name
your	The name of your school
skills	Your favorite class
now list	Your career choice
this skill	Your three favorite records
of centering	(Center each on a separate line.)
by backspacing	Your favorite movie
one for each two	The name of your local newspaper
items in every	Your favorite author
line or name	The oldest person in your family
or heading	Your favorite kind of ice cream
or title	The city where you were born
typing	A country you would like to visit
like	Your favorite TV show
so	The salary you would like to earn

SPREAD CENTERING

Sometimes it is desirable to *spread center* a word or phrase. This involves leaving 1 space after each letter.

T O D A Y

If two or more words are spread centered, 3 spaces are left between words.

S P R E A D   C E N T E R

Drill F

Spread center the words, *GRADUATION DAY.*

GRADUATION DAY

1. Center the carriage.
2. Backspace once for *every* letter except the last letter in the line and once for the space between words. Spell out the words and spaces as you backspace.
3. At the point where you stopped backspacing, type *GRADUATION DAY* leaving 1 space after each letter and 3 spaces between the two words:

   G R A D U A T I O N   D A Y
4. Space down 4 lines to prepare for the next drill.

Drill G

Spread center these phrases.
Double spacing.

MY BOOK REPORT

HONOR ROLL STUDENTS

BIRTHDAY PARTY

Exercise 2
PIVOTING

Full sheet. DS body. 14 spaces between columns. Spread center secondary title. TS before and after divider lines.

OEA CLUB AWARDS ASSEMBLY
P R O G R A M

Greetings   Ms. Phyllis Edwards
                                               Chapter President

****

AWARDS   Mr. S. Dixon

Musical Selection   Men's Glee Club

CLUB RECOGNITIONS   Mrs. A. Hatton

Musical Selection   Women's Glee Club

OUTSTANDING BUSINESS STUDENT AWARD   Mr. E. Taneka

****

Closing Remarks   Ms. J. Reed
                                                     Principal

---

Exercise 3
PIVOTING

Full sheet. DS body. SS indented lines. 14 spaces between columns.

METROPOLITAN HIGH SCHOOL

An Evening of Music

Sea Chanteys   Glee Club

   Blow the Man Down   Henry Faber, Soloist
   Codfish Chantey   Terry Plummer, Soloist
   Rio Grande   Sylvan Corbin, Soloist

Instrumental Music

   Selections from Tales of Hoffmann   School Orchestra
   Violin Solo—Estrellita   Helen R. Sebastian

Songs of the West   Madrigal Society

   Poor Wayfaring Stranger   Marie Tesorio, Soloist
   The Banks of the Sacramento   Ben Smith and Mike Fox, Duet
   The Cowboy's Lament   Eric L. Westholm, Soloist

Contemporary Show Tunes   Mixed Ensemble

   June is Bustin' Out All Over
   The Sound of Music
   Moon River

Closing Song

   America the Beautiful   Laura Rolls and Audience

Exercise 1

Type this notice of a club meeting, centering each line horizontally.

Half sheet. Double spacing. Begin on line 11.

ATTENTION O.E.A. MEMBERS

Office Education Association

IMPORTANT MEETING

Wednesday, April 20, 19—

Room 121

Period 6

Your name, Club Secretary

Exercise 2

Type a flyer announcing a dance club concert. Center each line horizontally.

Half sheet. Double spacing. Begin on line 11.

SPRING DANCE CONCERT

Presented by

Haley High School Dance Club

Friday, May 7, 19—

Matinee, 1 p.m., $1

Evening Show, 8 p.m., $2

Haley High School Auditorium

Exercise 3

Type a birthday party invitation. Center each line horizontally. Spread center the second line.

Half sheet. Double spacing. Begin on line 10.

Exercise 4

Type a title page for a school report. Center each line horizontally.

Full sheet. Line spacing as shown. Begin on line 15.

EXERCISE 3

You are invited to attend
A GALA BIRTHDAY PARTY
for
Your name
Sunday, *Your birthdate*, 19—
Your street address
Your city, state, and ZIP Code
RSVP *your telephone number*

EXERCISE 4

REPORT ON CLERICAL WORK
Space down 16 times
Your name
DS
Introduction to Business Class
Space down 16 times
Name of your school
DS
Today's date

Exercise 5

Type the flyer at the right. Center each line horizontally; spread center the third line. Make the corrections indicated.

Full sheet. Triple spacing. Begin on line 23.

MARYSVILLE BOY SCOUTS

lc PRESENTS A

P A N C A K E   S U P P E R

Friday, June 6, 19—

7 p.m.

Marysville Cafeteria

Tickets, $1

Bring the family!!

5. Type the second item in the left column (*Favorite color*).
6. Tab to the right margin. Then backspace once for every letter and space in the words to be typed (*S-h-o-c-k-i-n-g-space-P-i-n-k*).
7. Begin typing the words *Shocking Pink* where the backspacing ends. The words should end at exactly the same point where *Orange* ends.
8. Repeat this procedure with each additional line.

LEADERS

When there is a large space between two columns in a table, lines of alternating dots and spaces are sometimes used to connect the items in the columns. These are called *leaders* because they lead the eye across the space between the columns. The illustration below shows a table with leaders.

```
Main Floor . . . . . . . . . . . . . . . . $15.00
Balcony, first 6 rows  . . . . . . . . . .  12.50
Balcony, last 6 rows . . . . . . . . . . .   9.00
```

Follow these steps to type leaders between two columns:

1. Type the first item in the left column (*Main Floor*). Space once after the last letter.
2. Check the printing point indicator to see whether it is on an even or odd number. Remember which it is. Begin typing periods, alternating with spaces, from this point.
3. End the line of leaders with either 1 or 2 spaces between the last period and the beginning of the second column.
4. Begin each succeeding line of leaders so that the first period is always typed on either an even or odd number to correspond with the first line.

Drill A

Type this table, following the instructions for pivoting given on page 361.

Half sheet. Double spacing. Margins at 15 and 50. Begin on line 7.

```
Favorite fruit                     Orange
Favorite color             Shocking Pink
Favorite sport                 Ice Hockey
Favorite book                  Moby Dick
Favorite music         Country Western
```

Drill B

Space down 4 times after Drill A. Type this table following the instructions for leaders given above.

Half sheet. Double spacing. Margins at 10 and 65.

```
Main floor . . . . . . . . . . . . . . . $15.00
Balcony, first 6 rows  . . . . . . . . .  12.50
Balcony, last 6 rows . . . . . . . . . .   9.00
Second balcony . . . . . . . . . . . . .   7.50
Standing room  . . . . . . . . . . . . .   6.00
```

Exercise 1

PIVOTING

Half sheet. DS body. 10 spaces between columns.

RIVERVIEW CHARITIES, INC.

Board of Governors

January 1, 19— to December 31, 19—

President	Philip T. Westcott
Executive Director	Allan S. O'Hara
First Vice-President	Elvira A. Robertson
Second Vice-President	Herbert Hyde
Secretary	Andrew M. Trommer
Treasurer	Ida Modell

BLOCK CENTERING

Instead of centering *each line,* it is sometimes desirable to center a *block* of material. Block centering is most often used to type lists of items line for line. Poems, for example, are usually block centered.

To center a block *horizontally,* begin by moving both margin stops to the ends of the typewriter scale. Then, find the longest line in the copy. From the center of the page, backspace once for every two letters or spaces in that line, and set the left margin at the point where you stopped backspacing. Every line in the paragraph or listing (except the paragraph lines with indentions) will start at the point where the left margin was set. If there is a title, center it horizontally over the block.

Exercise 6

Type the following paragraph and its title. Use block centering.
Half sheet. Double spacing. Begin on line 7.

THE NEXT STEP
TS

    You may not have realized it, but your enrollment in a typing class was the first step toward preparation for earning a living. By practicing seriously, you should be able to reach the speed requirement for entry-level typing jobs. In addition to typing skills, employers will expect their workers to have general clerical skills such as filing and business telephone techniques. Ask your typing teacher to suggest other courses you could take next term that will allow you to gain these and other basic clerical skills.

Exercise 7

Type the following paragraph and its title. Use block centering.
Half sheet. Double spacing. Begin on line 7.

PROOFREADING TYPEWRITTEN COPY
TS

    Businesses are now using specialized typewriters which can type copy at much faster rates than a typist using the traditional typewriter. Typewritten copy is produced in order to communicate, so businesses cannot afford to send communications containing errors. Remember that just as correctly keyboarded data is being processed at high speed, errors that were missed in proofreading are being processed at the same high speed. Accurate proofreading, then, is a skill you will want to develop as you prepare for a business career.

Exercise 11
BOXED TABLE

Full sheet, inserted with long (11-inch) side first. DS body. SS runover lines. 6 spaces between columns.

PROJECT APOLLO
EARTH-TO-MOON MISSIONS

Date	Name of Mission	Significant Achievements	Hours on Moon	Mission Commander
July, 1969	Apollo 11	First manned landing; first moon walk	22	Neil Armstrong
Nov., 1969	Apollo 12	Second landing; two moon walks	31	Charles Conrad
Apr., 1970	Apollo 13	Explosion; mission aborted	—	James Lovell
Feb., 1971	Apollo 14	9-hour moon walk; craters inspected	$33\frac{1}{2}$	Alan Shepard
July, 1971	Apollo 15	Lunar roving vehicle; space walk	72	David Scott
Apr., 1972	Apollo 16	Lunar Rover inspects mountains and craters	72	John Young
Dec., 1972	Apollo 17	First scientist lands; last Apollo mission	75	Eugene Cernan

Topic 3 TABLES WITH PIVOTING AND LEADERS

PIVOTING

The appearance of some tables is improved if the items in the last column all align at the right. To accomplish this, a simple procedure known as *pivoting* is used. An example of a table with a pivoted right column is shown in the illustration below.

```
         Favorite fruit                       Orange
         Favorite color                Shocking Pink
         Favorite sport                   Ice Hockey
```

Follow these steps to pivot the right column of a table:

1. Type the first item in the left column (*Favorite fruit*).
2. Tab to the right margin. Then backspace once for every letter in the word to be typed (*O-r-a-n-g-e*).
3. Begin typing the word *Orange* where the backspacing ends.
4. Return to the left margin.

(Continued on next page)

Topic 2 VERTICAL CENTERING

A piece of typewritten material looks more attractive if the typist starts typing far enough down on the paper so that there are equal amounts of blank space left at the top and bottom of the page. This is called *vertical centering*. Center vertically by following these steps:

Step 1. Count the number of lines that will be used in typing the assignment. Include blank lines in your count. (Count 1 blank line when using double spacing and 2 blank lines when using triple spacing.)

Step 2. Subtract the total lines counted from 66, if you are using a full sheet, or from 33, if you are using a half sheet. The remainder is the number of extra lines left to be divided between top and bottom margins.

Step 3. Divide the remainder by 2 and add 1 to find the line on which to begin typing. Ignore fractions.

Study Drills A, B, and C to practice figuring beginning lines for vertical centering.

Drill A

Turn to Exercise 1, page 109. Use the copy given to see how the beginning line was figured.

Number of lines available for typing	= 33
Subtract number of lines in exercise	= 13
Number of lines remaining	= 20
Divide by 2	= 10
Add 1	= 11

Begin on line 11.

Drill B

Turn to Exercise 5, page 109. Use the copy given to see how the beginning line was found.

Number of lines available for typing	= 66
Subtract number of lines in exercise	= 22
Number of lines remaining	= 44
Divide by 2	= 22
Add 1	= 23

Begin on line 23.

Exercise 1

Type the announcement shown at the right. Set it up attractively, centering each line.

Half sheet. Single spacing unless shown otherwise. Center vertically.

Exercise 2

Type the menu at the right. Set it up attractively, centering each line.

Half sheet. Double spacing unless shown otherwise. Center vertically.

EXERCISE 1

BUSINESS TEACHERS' CLUB
DS
of
Metropolitan Detroit
TS
SPRING DINNER MEETING
TS
Friday, May 13, 19--
DS
6:00 p.m.
The LaSalle Room
DS
The Detroit Plaza Hotel
Renaissance Center
Detroit, Michigan
DS
RSVP 568-2001

EXERCISE 2

M E N U
TS
Assorted Relishes

Onion Soup

Salad Florentine

Roast Sirloin Tips of Beef

Baked Potato with Sour Cream

Seasoned Vegetables

Creme de Menthe Parfait

Bread and Butter

Coffee, Tea, Milk

Exercise 8

BOXED TABLE

Half sheet. SS body. 7 spaces between columns.

CHARLES WEBBER & COMPANY
Years of Employment of Sales Staff

Years	Number	Percent
Over 20	3	7
15–20	3	7
10–15	6	14
5–10	12	29
0–5	18	43
Total	42	100

POSTAGE AND HANDLING CHARGES

Total Material Ordered	Area 1	Area 2	Area 3	Area 4
$ 5.00 or less	$3.00	$3.00	$ 3.00	$ 3.00
$ 5.01 to $10.00	3.00	4.00	4.50	5.00
$10.01 to $25.00	4.50	5.50	7.00	8.50
$25.01 to $45.00	5.50	7.50	9.50	13.00
$45.01 to $75.00	7.00	9.50	12.50	19.50

Contact factory for charges on orders over $75.

Exercise 10

BOXED TABLE

Full sheet, inserted with long (11-inch) side first. DS body. SS runover lines. 5 spaces between columns.

COMPARISON OF REPROGRAPHIC PROCESSES

Process	Copies Expected	Error Correction	Copy Quality	Cost per Copy*
Carbon Paper	1–10	Difficult	Fair	Less than 1¢
Photocopier	1–10	Easy	Excellent	Up to 5¢
Fluid Duplicator	10–300	Difficult	Fair	Less than 1¢
Stencil Duplicator	50–1,000	Difficult	Good	Less than 1¢
Offset	50–5,000	Difficult	Excellent	Less than 1¢
Automatic Typewriter	1–10	Easy	Excellent	Less than 1¢
Facsimile Transmitter	1–5	Easy	Good	Up to 10¢

*Average cost of materials and equipment

Exercise 3

Type a membership roster of a school club. Use block centering.

Half sheet. Double spacing unless shown otherwise. Center vertically.

Exercise 4

Type a copy of the school song shown at the right. Use block centering.

Half sheet. Single spacing unless shown otherwise. Center vertically.

Exercise 5

Type a copy of a cheer for your school to be used at the next pep rally. Use block centering.

Half sheet. Single spacing unless shown otherwise. Center vertically.

Exercise 6

Type the list at the right using block centering.

Half sheet. Single spacing. Center vertically.

EXERCISE 3

MEMBERS OF THE PEP SQUAD
TS

Maria Portillo

Patrick Cotton

Sidney Johnson

Kristine Skorpen

Jeffrey Law

Patricia Brown

Penny Rosen

Kevin Johnson

Andrea Hill

EXERCISE 4

FALCONS FIGHT!
TS

Fight Falcons, fight, fight

Make your courage fine to see
DS

Go team, down the field

We will march to victory
DS

Raise high the red and blue

Let our colors always fly

To show the world that we will be

Ever loyal to Western High.

HEY, RAH!
TS

Our team is red hot,

Look and see what we've got.

We've got the coach,

We've got the team,

We've got the pep,

We've got the steam.

Coach, team, pep, steam—

Fifteen cheers for the whole great team.

Hey, Rah! Hey, Rah!

Hey, Rah, Rah, Rah! (Repeat five times.)

Well, all right!

Earning Your Driver's License (CAPS)
DS

The Road Test —
TS

Preparing to drive

Entering traffic

Lane use

Speed control

Turns

Stopping

Passing

Parking and backing

Exercise 6
RULED TABLE

Full sheet. DS body. 10 spaces between columns. DS before source note.

COMPARISON OF EARNINGS
OF BEGINNING COMPUTER PROGRAMMERS
BY SELECTED CITIES, 19—

City	Average Weekly Earnings
Detroit	$239.50
New York	239.00
Cleveland	238.00
Chicago	230.00
San Francisco-Oakland	229.50
Greenville-Spartanburg	201.50
Baltimore	193.00
Salt Lake City-Ogden	190.00
Chattanooga	185.00

Source: Bureau of Labor Statistics

Extend horizontal rulings 2 pica or 3 elite spaces past sides of table.

```
            MINIMUM SPEED REQUIREMENTS*
               (5-Minute Typing Tests)
                           DS
```

School	Term 1	Term 2	Term 3
Cushman	20	30	35
Northbridge	25	35	45
Hanover	15	25	35
Maynor	20	30	40
Ovington	18	30	40
Stafford	25	40	50
Whitlock	22	35	45

*Gross words per minute

Model 33

Boxed Table

Exercise 7
BOXED TABLE

Half sheet. SS body. 5 spaces between columns.

Type the boxed table shown in Model 33 on this page. Remember to make a pencil mark to indicate the midpoint between the columns. Then, turn the paper sideways and use the underscore key to type the vertical rulings.

Exercise 7

ROUGH DRAFT

Make the corrections indicated as you type this exercise. Use block centering.

Half sheet. Single spacing. Center vertically.

REASONS PEOPLE LOSE Jobs
(CENTER TITLE)

Carelessness

Unwilling to follow rules

laziness

Absence or tardy without cause

Making trouble

Lack of Too much attention to job outside interests

Lack of initiative

too little or Too much ambition

Disloyalty

Lack of adaptability

Exercise 8

Type this traffic bulletin on a half sheet with paper turned lengthwise. Use block centering. (To figure placement when the paper is inserted short end first, notice that 8½ inches equals 51 lines and 5½ inches equals 55 pica or 66 elite strokes.)

Half sheet. Double spacing. Center vertically.

TRAFFIC SAFETY RULES
TS

STOP — at the curb

LOOK — both ways

WAIT — until it's safe, then

WALK — across the street

Exercise 9

Type this title page for a school report. Center the material vertically and center each line horizontally.

Full sheet. Line spacing as shown.

A HISTORY OF THE VIOLIN
DS
(A Term Report)
Space down 13 times
Prepared by
DS
Jonathan H. James
Space down 13 times
Music Appreciation Class
SS
Mr. Adams, Instructor
SS
March 4, 19—

Exercise 3
RULED TABLE

Full sheet. DS body. 8 spaces between columns.

	Orchestra	Mezzanine	Balcony
Single Admission	$ 3.60	$ 2.40	$ 1.80
Any 4 Performances	13.00	8.50	6.50
Any 6 Performances	19.00	12.00	9.00
Any 8 Performances	25.00	15.00	11.50
Entire Series of 12	35.00	22.00	17.00

SHAKESPEARE FESTIVAL AT HAYDEN PLAYHOUSE — 8
Student Rates — 11
Friday Evenings, February 3 through April 21, 19— — 20

32
38
50
57
65
72
80
88
100

Exercise 4
RULED TABLE

Half sheet. SS body. 6 spaces between columns.

ADVENTURERS' ATHLETIC CLUB — 6
AFTER-SCHOOL PICKUP SCHEDULE — 12
April–May, 19— — 16

Day	Schools	Starting Date	Ending Date
Monday	McKenney, Lodge, Dow	4/17/—	5/08/—
Tuesday	St. Scholastica, St. Mary's	4/18/—	5/09/—
Wednesday	Holcomb, Burt, Cooke	4/19/—	5/10/—
Thursday	Emerson, Newton, Winship	4/20/—	5/11/—
Friday	Harding, Vetal, Dossin	4/21/—	5/12/—

TS — 30 / 33 / 38 / 52 / 61 / 72 / 82 / 92 / 101 / 115

Parents: Pack swimming and gym clothes. Buses will leave each school — 129
between 3:30 and 4 p.m. and will return between 6 and 6:30 p.m. Please — 144
arrange to meet your children at the main gate. — 153

Exercise 5
RULED TABLE

Half sheet. SS body. 8 spaces between columns. DS before footnote.

ACCESSORY LIST FOR FLOOR POLISHER — 7
GARWOOD MODEL NO. 100.7092 — 12

Key	Part No.	Part Name
93	691	Waxing and Scrubbing Brush
96	692	Polishing Brush
97	662	Rug Shampoo Brush
98	616	Buffing Pad
100	663	Wool Pad
107	666	Reconditioning Kit*

23
28
39
46
51
56
60
63
69
80

*Available on special order only — 87

THE CREATIVE TYPIST

In this textbook you will find advanced assignments similar to Exercise 10, below. They are intended to allow those who complete the basic practice exercises a chance to be creative. You are expected to use your own judgment and basic knowledge of typing to complete these exercises. The two requirements for acceptability in these exercises are that your typed work be accurate and that it be attractively placed on the page.

Exercise 10
TYPING A
GREETING CARD

1. Compose a message for a greeting card for a birthday, Christmas, Mother's Day, or a similar occasion of your choice. Limit your message to about 5 lines.
2. Fold a full sheet in quarters as shown. Do not tear the paper.
3. Open the folded sheet in half and insert it into the typewriter with the folded edge going in first.
4. Set a tab at the center point of the right-hand quarter.
5. Type your message on the right-hand quarter. Center each line horizontally and the complete message vertically.
6. Be even more creative and either draw or type an illustration on the cover of your greeting card.

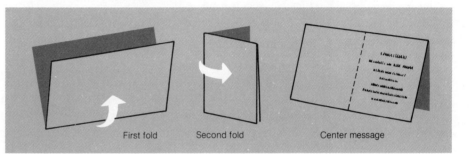

First fold   Second fold   Center message

Topic 3 SPECIAL DISPLAY TECHNIQUES

The exercises in this unit contain a variety of solutions to the challenges of displaying typed materials. These exercises require special spacing in addition to that usually necessary for vertical and horizontal centering.

Exercise 1
ARRANGEMENT OF
A SCRIPT

Full sheet. 1½-inch side margins. Single spacing, but DS between character parts. 15-space indention for dialogue (set a tab). Begin on line 10.

ANSWERING THE BUSINESS TELEPHONE
DS
A One-Act Production
TS

(Telephone rings)

V. Barnes	Murphy Products Company, Ms. Barnes.
J. Bulka	This is John Bulka of Uptown Radio. May I speak to Mrs. Murphy, please?
V. Barnes	I'm sorry, sir. Mrs. Murphy is out of the office. May I. . . . (Mr. Bulka interrupts).

(Continued on next page)

```
            RANDOLPH HIGH MOCK ELECTION RESULTS                    1
                                                                   2
                    Senior Class, 19--                             3
                            DS                                     4
    ───────────────────────────────────────────────────────       5
                            DS                                     6
    Category             Male                 Female               7
                            SS                                     8
    ───────────────────────────────────────────────────────       9
                            DS                                    10
    Best Dressed         Carl Ransom          Bernadine White     10
                                                                  11
    Class Clown          Kevin Smith          Regina Moreno       12
                                                                  13
    Class Cutie          Richard Roberts      Lesa Clarkston      14
                                                                  15
    Most Athletic        Carlos Ortego        Keisa Mitchell      16
                                                                  17
    Best Personality     Marathon Webb        Kim Vandenburg      18
                                                                  19
    Best Dancer          James Tammany        Kathy Murphy        20
                            SS                                    21
    ───────────────────────────────────────────────────────
```

Model 32

Ruled Table

The line count given at the right will help you determine the vertical placement of the table.

Exercise 1
RULED TABLE

Half sheet. DS body. 6 spaces between columns.

Type a copy of the table shown in Model 32 above. Use the line count at the right when planning the vertical placement of the table. Follow the spacing guides given above and below horizontal rules.

Exercise 2
RULED TABLE

Half sheet. DS body. 6 spaces between columns.

FIRST FEDERAL SAVINGS AND LOAN
March 1, 19—

Type of Account	Minimum Amount	Annual Rate	Effective Annual Rate
8-year certificate	$1,000	8.00%	8.24%
6-year certificate	1,000	7.75%	7.98%
4-year certificate	1,000	7.50%	7.71%
2½-year certificate	1,000	6.75%	6.92%
1-year certificate	1,000	6.50%	6.66%
90-day certificate	500	5.75%	5.92%
Regular (Daily Interest)	None	5.25%	5.35%

J. Bulka	Do you know when she will return? She asked that I call and quote her some prices on CB radios. I would like to speak with her today.
V. Barnes	Well, I'm not certain of the time she will return, Mr. Bulka. May I take a message and relay the information to Mrs. Murphy?
J. Bulka	On second thought, maybe that would be better. I may not get a chance to call her later today.
V. Barnes	All right, sir.
J. Bulka	Please tell Mrs. Murphy that we have a special 40-channel radio at a 20 percent discount.
V. Barnes	Yes.
J. Bulka	There will be a small difference in price of only $20 between the 23-channel models and the new 40-channel models.
V. Barnes	(Repeats information to verify accuracy of the message.) I shall be glad to give this information to Mrs. Murphy. How is your name spelled, Mr. Bulka?
J. Bulka	B–U–L–K–A.
V. Barnes	Thank you. I shall give Mrs. Murphy your message.
J. Bulka	Thank you. Good-bye.
V. Barnes	You're welcome. Good-bye.

Exercise 2

MINUTES OF A MEETING

Full sheet. 1-inch side margins. Double spacing unless shown otherwise. Begin on line 7.

Minutes of the Meeting

HOLLEY LANES JUNIOR BOWLING LEAGUE

October 19, 19—

TS

ATTENDANCE

Roll call was taken at 10:30 a.m. All teams were represented. League President Victor Clay presided.

TS

OLD BUSINESS

Minutes of the last meeting were read and approved as read. The treasurer reported that Team 5 has a shortage of $2.50, which must be cleared up before today's bowling begins.

TS

NEW BUSINESS

Our coach, Mr. McDonald, suggested that we purchase shirts with our league name and team names on them. League members agreed that

(Continued on next page)

Exercise 45
ROUGH DRAFT

Make all the corrections indicated by the proof-readers' marks. If necessary, review the symbols shown in the key on page 97.

Half sheet. DS body.

Crescent Furniture Exchange

Branch	Address	Telephone
Manhattan	321 East 108th Street	562-6011
Bronx	661 Front Street	927-1462
Jamaica	455 Hillside Avenue	866-3009
Newark	88 Grand Army Plaza	932-7411
Westchester	3211 Main Street	673-0776
Belleville	21732 Evans Road	735-2327
Cicero	9326 Telegraph Road	822-3670

Topic 2 TABLES WITH RULED LINES

Tables are often typed with horizontal and vertical rulings. The ruling can add to the attractiveness and clearness of the data presented.

RULED TABLES

Tables that have horizontal lines above and below the column headings and after the last line are called *ruled* tables. The underscore key is used to make these horizontal rulings. Look at Model 32 (page 357) and study the line spacing used before and after the typed lines in the table.

When a double horizontal ruling is required, follow these steps:

1. Type the first line of the ruling in the usual way.
2. Before typing the second line, use the automatic line finder and turn the cylinder until the first typed line can be seen slightly above the aligning scale.
3. Type the second line and then release the automatic line finder to restore the paper to the original line of writing.

BOXED TABLES

Term 1	12345	Term 2
20		30
25		35
15		25
20		30
18		30
25		40

Sometimes tables with horizontal lines also have vertical lines between the columns. These are called *boxed* tables. The horizontal lines in boxed tables extend ¼ inch past the sides of the tables. In planning a boxed tabulation, always leave an odd number of spaces between columns so that the vertical ruling can be placed at the midpoint between them. See Model 33, page 359, and the illustration at the left.

There is no special key on the standard keyboard for typing solid vertical lines. The vertical lines may be drawn with pen or pencil while the table is still in the typewriter. Refer to pages 105–106 for a review. Most often, though, the vertical lines are added after the table is typed, complete with its horizontal rulings. To do this, follow these steps:

1. Make a light pencil mark to indicate the placement of the vertical rulings;
2. remove the paper and reinsert it sideways;
3. use the underscore key to type the vertical lines between the columns.

Exercise 2 continued

this would be a great idea. A committee of five (Rose Lee, Tonya Adams, Russell Abdakar, Rosa Perez, and Anthony Williams) will investigate prices and make a report at our next meeting.

Sheila Jones suggested that it would be nice for the league members to visit a nursing home at Christmas time as a community project. It was decided to pursue this idea at our next meeting.

TS

ADJOURNMENT

The meeting was adjourned at 11:00 a.m.

Respectfully submitted,

Space down 4 times

Your name, Secretary

_____

Date Approved

Exercise 3

NEWS RELEASE

Full sheet. 1-inch side margins. Double spacing unless shown otherwise. Begin headings on line 13, at center.

N E W S
R E L E A S E

SOUTHEASTERN HIGH SCHOOL

Chicago, Illinois

Release: Immediately

From: Roger Mills, Club Reporter
         BOEC Club, Spartan Chapter

TS

BOEC SHINES AT STATE LEADERSHIP CONFERENCE

TS

SOUTHEASTERN HIGH, Chicago, May 14—With 38 members present, Southeastern had one of the largest delegations at the BOEC State Conference in Kankakee, Illinois, held May 7–9. With 104 financial members, Southeastern also has the largest total membership of all 89 BOEC chapters throughout the state of Illinois. In recognition of this, SE's delegation was allowed ten voting delegates—the highest number allocated any chapter.

On Friday evening at the conference, participants were entertained by BOEC members participating in the talent competition. Southeastern had two entrants in competition, April LaBeaux and Deborah Patrick.

The highlight of the two-day conference was the awards banquet held Saturday evening. At this banquet, winners of all competitions were announced. The Southeastern delegation was very proud when talent

(Continued on next page)

Exercise 43
ROUGH DRAFT

Make all the corrections indicated by the proofreaders' marks.

Half sheet. DS body. Block column headings. SS 2-line footnote.

REVISED TOUR RATES *
March 1, 19—

From	Canadian Rockies	Virgin Islands	Mexico
Boston	$480	$555	$575
Chicago	$450	570 500	[525
New York	475	545	570
Phila., SP	415	545	570
San Francisco	425	590	500
St. Louis	450	510	490
Washington, D.C.	475	545	570

* Rates include all charges for air fares transportation hotels accommodations and sight-seeing.

INDOOR PLANT DISTRIBUTORS
Retail price list

Name of Plant	Pot Size (inches)	Height (in feet)	Our Price
Croton	10	3	$17.95
Ficus Benjaminia	10	3½	15.95
Dracaena Marginata	10	3½	17.95
Pilodendron Selloum	10	3	14.95
Areca palm	10	4	14.95
Schefflera	14 10	5	25.00 17.50
Schefflera	17	12 11	75.00
Terradium Plants	3	¼	.50
False Aralia	14 10	5	27.50 19.95
Ficus Benjamina	14	6	38.50

Exercise 3 continued

competition winners were announced because April LaBeaux had danced off with first-place honors.

Southeastern was even more elated when Shelly Thornwell was elected as the BOEC State Treasurer for the coming year. BOEC members are already looking forward to next year's state conference.

Exercise 4

MEMORANDUM

Half sheet. 6-inch line. DS heading, SS body. Begin on line 7.

SUBJECT: Cap and Gown Measurement
TO: All Graduating Seniors
FROM: S. Thomas, Senior Sponsor
DATE: February 17, 19—

^{TS}

The Evans Rental Company will have a representative in our school auditorium on March 23 from 8 a.m. to 1:30 p.m. Measurements for caps and gowns will be taken at that time. Come prepared to pay a deposit of $2.50 when you are measured. Wear the height of shoes that you intend to wear at the graduation ceremony. An appointment is not necessary. You may go to the auditorium only before school, during your lunch period, or during a study period.

Your initials

Exercise 5

Compare the arrangement of the headings in this memo with those in Exercise 4. Begin right-hand headings at center.

Half sheet. 6-inch line. DS heading, SS body. Begin on line 7.

TO: Freshman Students   DATE: *Current date*
FROM: D. Kelly, Counselor   SUBJECT: Typing Classes

^{TS}

It is a good idea to learn to type while you are still in high school. Many students find themselves in college without having this skill. Most college professors insist that assignments be typewritten. Students who do not acquire typing skills may find it expensive to hire someone to type a term paper or report. Prices vary, but you may find you have to pay as high as $1 a page, depending on the formality of the paper. I think you will agree that learning to type while in high school is indeed a wise investment of your time and effort.

Former students have returned to our school to say that their typing skills were valuable because they were able to find better-paying part-time and summer jobs which require the ability to type a minimum of 40 words a minute. They have found work in government agencies, hospitals, banks, department stores, and in campus offices—the list of job opportunities is endless for students with typing skills.

Your initials

Exercise 41
ROUGH DRAFT

Make all the corrections indicated
by the proofreaders' marks.
Full sheet. DS body.

TEN TALLEST ~~TALL~~ BUILDINGS IN NEW YORK CITY

Center over both columns

Building	Stories	Height Feet	Meters
World Trade Center	110	1,353	412
Empire State Building	102	1,250	381 ~~375~~
Chrysler Building	77 ~~100~~	1,046 ~~1,406~~	319
Citicorp Center	46	914	279
40 Wall Street	71	851	259
RCA Building	70 ~~79~~	850	259
60 Wall Tower	66	826	252
One Chase Manhattan Plaza	60	813 ~~814~~	248
Pan Am Building	59	808	246
Woolworth Building	60	792	241

Exercise 42
ROUGH DRAFT

Make all the corrections indicated
by the proofreaders' marks.
Half sheet. DS body.

MERCYGROVE ADULT EDUCATION PROGRAM

Workshop schedule

Center column headings

Course	Date	Time	Fee
Home Decorating Clinic	October 16, 19--	9:30 - 3:30	$20.00
Knowing Yourself	Oct. 16, 19--	9:00 - 3:30	$20.00
Coming Alive	October 23, 19--	10:00 - 2:30	$25.00
So You Want How to Get A Job!	October 23, 19--	1:30 - 4:30	23.00
Fall Photography	October 12, 19--	9:30 - 3:30	35.00

Exercise 6

Copy the data sheet shown here. A data sheet is used by people seeking employment. It is sent or taken to potential employers to inform them of the job-seeker's background, education, and work experience. This is but one of several possible arrangements for a data sheet.

Full sheet. 1-inch side margins. Line spacing as shown. Begin on line 5.

PERSONAL DATA SHEET

TS

PERSONAL INFORMATION

DS

Name:	Rhonda Wilson
Address:	100 Abbey Road
	Phoenix, AZ 85026
Telephone:	(602) 322-4137
Age:	18
Health:	Excellent
Social Security No.:	324–60–2978

EDUCATION AND TRAINING

DS

School:	Kettering High School,
	Phoenix, Arizona
Major:	Business Education
Completion Date:	June, 19—
Degree Earned:	High School Diploma
Special Courses:	Office Cooperative Training

SCHOOL ACTIVITIES

Pep Club, JOTS Club, Thespian Club

INTERESTS AND HOBBIES

Bowling, Singing

WORK EXPERIENCE

Employer:	Top Hat Restaurants, Inc.
Address:	23645 Conner Avenue, Phoenix, AZ 85026
Telephone:	(602) 223-1976
Position:	Office Co-op Clerical Trainee (part-time)
Dates:	From June 9, 19— to present
Duties:	Checking extensions on invoices with an electronic calculator, figuring discounts, answering the telephone, typing letters and invoices, receiving office callers.

REFERENCES

Rev. James Browne, Minister; All Saints Church, 1100 Desert View Drive, Phoenix, AZ 85026.

Mr. John Greenburg, Neighbor; ABC TV, 395 Arroyo Seco, Phoenix, AZ 85023.

Mrs. Joan Bowers, Supervisor; Top Hat Restaurants, Inc., 23645 Conner Avenue, Phoenix, AZ 85026.

EDUCATORS' AUDIOVISUAL EXCHANGE
COMMUNICATIONS

Title	Time in Minutes	Medium	Recommended Grade Levels
To Communicate Is First	30	Motion Picture	9-12
Everyday Champions	22	Filmstrip	4-8
Words Are Wonderful	10	Filmstrip	1-4
Lasers Unlimited	30	Motion Picture	10-12
Survival of the Fittest	48	Motion Picture	9-12

SPECIAL
SELECTED RADIO PROGRAMS

FOR MUSIC LOVERS

Time	Radio Station (center)	Program (center)
10:30 a.m.	WNBC – AM	Madrigal Society
11:30 a.m.	WMCA – FM	The New Recordings
12:30 p.m.	WCBS – AM	Midday Concert
4:15 " p.m.	WQXR – FM	Symphonic Music
6:30 " p.m.	WHNE – FM	Dinner Music
7:30 " p.m.	WORF – AM	Holiday for Strings
9:00 " p.m.	WABC – FM	Boston Pops in Concert
10:00 " p.m.	WAAT – FM	Gilbert and Sullivan Songs

Exercise 7

This data sheet is arranged differently from the one in Exercise 6. Notice that the headings extend into the left margin. Use the margin release key and backspace five times to type each heading.

Full sheet. 1½-inch left margin. Line spacing as shown. Begin on line 7.

PERSONAL DATA SHEET

TS

PERSONAL

John Franklin
1345 Delaware Street
Chicago, IL 60611
(312) 833–1234

Birthdate: May 2, 19—
Citizenship: United States
Marital Status: Single
Physical Condition: Excellent
Height: 5′ 5″
Weight: 125 lbs.
Social Security No.: 313-03-1245

EDUCATION

High School: Miller High School, Chicago, Illinois

Degree: High School Diploma, June, 19—

Major: Business

Grade Average: B+

Special Skills: Typing Speed, 50 wpm
Shorthand, 90 wpm
Office Machines—training on mimeograph, fluid duplicator, and bookkeeping machine

SCHOOL ACTIVITIES/HOBBIES AND INTERESTS

Member of National Honor Society for two years

Member of Pep Club

Enjoy swimming and tennis

President of Youth Block Club

WORK EXPERIENCE

Delivered daily and Sunday paper for Chicago Sun-Times, July, 19— to August, 19—.

Clerk-Typist at Social Security Branch Office, 11327 Mack Street, Chicago, Illinois, Summer of 19—, NYC Summer Job, $3.20 per hour.

REFERENCES

Miss Jean Forest, Teacher, Business Education Department, Miller High School, 6101 Van Dyke, Chicago, Illinois 60605; (312) 921–1167.

Mrs. Emma Smith, Production Supervisor, General Electric Company, 600 5th Street, Chicago, Illinois 60610; (312) 921–5546.

Mr. James Williams, Branch Director, Social Security Office, 11327 Mack Street, Chicago, Illinois 60617; (312) 923–5567.

BRENNER PAPER COMPANY
Price List of Carbon Copy Paper, 19—

List Number	Color	Size	Price per Ream
21a	White	8½ × 11	$2.10
21b	White	8½ × 13	2.50
32a	Canary	8½ × 11	2.70
32b	Canary	8½ × 13	3.00
41a	Pink	7½ × 11	2.70
41b	Pink	8½ × 13	3.00

Line counts: 4, 12, 15, 27, 32, 37, 42, 47, 51, 56

REPUBLIC HIGH SCHOOL
Final Examination Results, Typewriting 1
June, 19—

Class	Register	Number Passed	Percent Passed
11	42	37	88
12	35	28	80
15	40	35	88
16	39	33	85
17	36	32	89

Line counts: 4, 12, 14, 17, 33, 35, 37, 39, 41, 43

OVEN TEMPERATURE ROASTING CHART

	Temperature (°F)	Minutes (per pound)
Chicken	300	30-45
Leg of lamb	300	30-35
Veal shoulder	325	30-35
Pork, loin	350	30-40
Ham	325	25-30
Beef, rib	325	25-30

Line counts: 6, 10, 21, 25, 29, 34, 38, 41, 45

SIMPLE TABULATIONS

Facts or figures may be presented in two different ways: (1) in the form of a paragraph, and (2) in the form of a table, which is referred to as a *tabulation*.

The two illustrations below give the same information in two forms. Refer first to Illustration A and then to Illustration B to answer the following questions:

- On what day of the week does the Economics Club meet?
- Who is the faculty adviser of the Mathematics Club?
- Of what club is Mr. Pierson the faculty adviser?
- Which of the two illustrations more readily provides the information requested? Why?

Illustration A

PRATT HIGH SCHOOL

Schedule of Club Meetings
September, 19-- to June, 19--

The Anthropology Club meets on Wednesday, with Ms. Montgomery as faculty adviser. The Dramatic Society meets on Friday, with Mr. Pierson as faculty adviser. The Economics Club meets on Thursday, with Miss Farrell as faculty adviser. The Chorus meets on Tuesday, with Mr. Bradford as faculty adviser. The Mathematics Club meets on Friday, with Mr. Conway as faculty adviser. The French Club meets on Monday, with Mrs. Frawley as faculty adviser. The Business Education Club meets on Tuesday, with Ms. Lavery as faculty adviser.

Illustration B

PRATT HIGH SCHOOL

Schedule of Club Meetings
September, 19-- to June, 19--

Club	Day	Faculty Adviser
Anthropology Club	Wednesday	Ms. Montgomery
Dramatic Club	Friday	Mr. Pierson
Economics Club	Thursday	Miss Farrell
Chorus	Tuesday	Mr. Bradford
Mathematics Club	Friday	Mr. Conway
French Club	Monday	Mrs. Frawley
Business Education Club	Tuesday	Ms. Lavery

Topic 1 TYPING IN COLUMNS

The drills in this section will give you practice in typing material in tabulated form. When typing items in columns, always type ACROSS the page, line by line. To reach the starting point of the second, third, and following columns, depress the tab key or bar. Repeat this procedure for each line in the table.

Directions for Drills A–I

1. Clear all old tab stops from machine.
2. Set only the *left margin* for the space line indicated.
3. Set tabs by spacing forward as indicated in the planning diagram under each drill.
4. Type each drill alone or as a class exercise from dictation by your teacher.
5. Use a full sheet and leave 3 lines between each drill.

Exercise 33

Be sure to align the program names in the last column.

Half sheet.

POLITICAL TALKS ON TV 4

Week Beginning Sunday, October 14, 19— 12

Channel	Day	Time	Program	
11	Sunday	11:00 a.m.	Open Forum	25 / 31
4	Tuesday	2:00 p.m.	The Candidates Speak	39
32	Thursday	4:00 p.m.	Opinions of the Press	48
7	Sunday	1:00 p.m.	Meet the Press	55
5	Sunday	2:30 p.m.	Issues and Answers	63

Exercise 34

Half sheet.

EXHIBITION OF PAINTINGS 5

Thornton Galleries 9

Catalog Number	Title	Artist	
417	A Rainy Day	John C. Renschler	11 / 22 / 29
443	Abstraction	Sophie A. Gordon	36
500	Treasure Hunt	Gerald C. Forrester	44
554	Portrait of a Lady	Charles N. Buchanan	53
611	The Winner	Leonard N. Pearson	60
662	Street Scene	Vera Newton	66
771	The Village Store	Martin Reilly	73
888	Self Portrait	Mabel H. Stewart	80

Exercise 35

Half sheet. SS body. Block column headings.

OUTGOING LUXURY LINERS 5

leaving New York City 10

Week of October 10, 19— 15

Ship	Destination	Departs	Arrives	
Olympia	Lisbon	Oct. 10	Oct. 23	33 / 39
Nordfels	Antigua	Oct. 12	Oct. 24	46
France	Naples	Oct. 13	Oct. 20	52
Jordeans	Le Havre	Oct. 15	Oct. 29	59
Mariposa	Athens	Oct. 16	Oct. 26	65

Drill A

40-space line. Double spacing.

Always	type	items
in	a	table
line	by	line
like	this	one

6	13	4	13	5

↑ Margin — Space forward 19 spaces — ↑ Tab — Space forward 17 spaces — ↑ Tab

PLANNING DIAGRAM

Drill B

60-space line. Single spacing.

an	be	he	it	of	to
am	by	if	me	on	up
as	do	in	my	or	us
at	go	is	no	so	we

2	10	2	10	2	10	2	10	2	10	2

↑ Margin — Space forward 12 spaces — ↑ Tab — Space forward 12 spaces — ↑ Tab — Space forward 12 spaces — ↑ Tab — Space forward 12 spaces — ↑ Tab — Space forward 12 spaces — ↑ Tab

Drill C

40-space line. Line spacing as shown.

act	ask	far	law	oil
age	big	for	low	one
air	but	has	may	out
any	car	her	met	own
are	day	his	nor	put
arm	end	how	not	red

3	6	3	6	3	6	3	6	3

Drill D

50-space line. Single spacing.

oak	pine	maple	laurel
elm	cork	aspen	willow
fir	plum	birch	linden
yew	pear	cedar	spruce
ash	lime	larch	almond
bay	palm	apple	poplar

3	10	4	10	5	10	6

In an office, you will often have to type material from handwritten and rough-draft copy. The following exercises will give you additional material to practice setting up tables from draft copy. If the draft copy has not been laid out in good tabular form, you, as typist, are expected to type the table in an acceptable style.

Exercise 31

Type the following table in an attractive style.

Half sheet.

DIRECTORY OF BRANCHES — 4
Globe Manufacturing Company — 10
January 10, 19— — 14

Branch	Address	Manager	
			27
Boston, Mass.	114 Bay Street	Mark C. Dixon	35
Detroit, Mich.	59 Howard Avenue	Laura Trenton	44
Tucson, Ariz.	87 Lee Avenue	Leonard A. Kraus	53
Dallas, Tex.	212 Blanchard Street	Charles L. Haight	63
Newark, N. J.	338 Seventh Street	Warren Liang	72
Philadelphia, Penn.	170 Sebastian Road	Eugene Quinn	82
Richmond, Va.	55 Rose Place	Henry A. Front	91

Exercise 32

Arrange in tabular form a list of degrees awarded by Lincoln University in June, 19—. Be sure to include totals for the columns that require them.

Half sheet.

Liberal Arts College: Bachelor's Degrees, 430; Master's Degrees, 85; Doctorates, 15
School of Business: Bachelor's Degrees, 120; Master's Degrees, 57; Doctorates, 8
School of Education: Bachelor's Degrees, 86; Doctorates, 12
School of Journalism: Bachelor's Degrees, 135; Master's Degrees, 34; Doctorates, 3
School of Engineering: Bachelor's Degrees, 260; Master's Degrees, 76
School of Nursing: Bachelor's Degrees, 114; Master's Degrees, 32
Totals: Bachelor's Degrees, 1145; Master's Degrees, 284; Doctorates, 38

Drill E

50-space line. Double spacing.

10	20	30	40	50	60
11	21	31	41	51	61
12	22	32	42	52	62
13	23	33	43	53	63
14	24	34	44	54	64

2	8	2	8	2	8	2	8	2	8	2

Drill F

50-space line. Double spacing.

555	666	777	888	999	000
515	616	717	818	919	010
525	625	725	825	925	025
121	232	343	454	787	898

3	6	3	6	3	6	3	6	3	6	3

Drill G

50-space line. Double spacing.

them	they	turn	down	work
form	world	their	town	angle
right	the	this	blame	man
and	that	she	did	both

5	6	5	6	5	6	5	6	5

Drill H

Notice that numbers in tables are aligned on the right. For numbers that have less than four digits (that is, those that don't take five spaces), space forward from the tab. To type *157* in column 2, for example, space forward twice from the tab.

50-space line. Single spacing.

1,205	1,003	2,208	3,103
1,290	157	412	368
51	67	64	46
1,639	1,464	1,294	2,121
415	1,337	507	694

5	10	5	10	5	10	5

Drill I

Notice that the dollar sign aligns with the largest amount in a column and that all decimal points also align.

50-space line. Single spacing.

$4.50	$11.80	$21.50	$ 4.20
6.00	8.75	11.70	21.22
6.90	13.70	7.25	35.00
4.23	5.45	78.43	6.99

5	8	6	8	6	8	6

Exercise 27

Half sheet.

MAIN TITLE	DURANT REALTY CORPORATION
SECONDARY TITLE	TRANSFERS, September, 19—
COLUMN HEADINGS	Premises / Seller / Purchaser / Price

440 Hoe Avenue, sold by Hoe Avenue Corporation to Jason Kemp for $52,500

101 Corbin Street, sold by Empire Realty Company to James Morelli for $80,000

221 Forest Avenue, sold by Oscar Walden to George Taylor for $38,200

198 Monroe Avenue, sold by William T. Schreiber to Madge Noyes for $32,500

244 Halsey Street, sold by James T. Randolph to Rita Sayre for $36,000

167 Clark Street, sold by Leonore Ransom to Clive Estates for $67,500

Exercise 28

Arrange in tabular form a record of the commissions shown for Gardiner Furniture Company for the month ended October 31, 19—. Use 4 columns to list the name of the salesperson, the commission earned, the advances paid against the commission, and the balance due the salesperson.

Half sheet.

John Alterman earned $1045 in commissions, received $800 in advances, and has a balance of $245 due.

Susan Baxter earned $750 in commissions, received $500 in advances, and has a balance of $250 due.

Robert Lever earned $625 in commissions, received $600 in advances, and has a balance of $25 due.

Maria Hernandez earned $590 in commissions, received $480 in advances, and has a balance of $110 due.

Peter Walton earned $545 in commissions, received $440 in advances, and has a balance of $105 due.

Exercise 29

From the information given, prepare a table entitled WHERE OUR MONEY WENT. Arrange the data in 3 columns and provide appropriate column headings.

Half sheet.

Employees' and Officers' Salaries amounted to 50% of the company's revenue last year; to 45% this year.

Material Purchased amounted to 25% of revenue last year; to 24% this year.

Replacement of Facilities cost 2% last year; 5% this year.

All Taxes amounted to 15% last year; to 14% this year.

Dividends to Stockholders amounted to 6% last year; to 6% this year.

Reinvestment in Business amounted to 2% last year; to 6% this year.

Total in each percent column: 100

Exercise 30

From the data given, prepare a table for the Gotham City Employment Agency, listing openings they have for office employment as of May 12, 19—. Provide the necessary column headings.

Half sheet.

Accounting Clerk, 40-hour week, 5 years of experience, $200 a week

Credit Clerk, 40-hour week, 2 years of experience, $125 a week

File Clerk, 35-hour week, 5 years of experience, $158 a week

Receptionist, 35-hour week, no experience required, $149 a week

Stenographer, 35-hour week, 1 year of experience, $171 a week

Secretary, 40-hour week, 5 years of experience, salary open

Clerk-Typist, 40-hour week, 1 year of experience, $160 a week

Junior Typist, 40-hour week, no experience required, $136 a week

Topic 2 HORIZONTAL PLACEMENT OF A TABLE

The preparation of a well-arranged tabulation requires careful planning. The typist must decide where to set the left margin and where to set tab stops. In the drills in Topic 1, the planning was done for you. In completing the drills and exercises in this section, you must do your own planning. You will learn how to figure the left margin setting and where to set the tab stops by using the backspace centering method. Follow these steps:

Step 1. Prepare the machine:

    a. Move margin stops to the ends of the typewriter scale.
    b. Clear all old tab stops left in the machine.
    c. Set the paper guide at 0 (zero).
    d. Insert a full sheet of paper. Space down to line 10.
    e. Move the carriage so that the printing point is at center.

Step 2: Prepare a planning diagram:

A planning diagram may be done on paper or it may be done mentally. A plan for typing the table shown in the left margin is described and shown below.

    a. Pick out the longest word in each column.

Column 1	Column 2	Column 3
Listen	tabulation	problems

The longest word in a column determines the width of that column. By counting the number of characters in each of these words, you know how wide each column will be.

Column 1	Column 2	Column 3
6	10	8

    b. Decide how many spaces you want to leave *between* columns. In this example, we will leave 6 spaces between columns. (The amount of space between columns will vary from one table to another depending upon the number of columns in the table and the width of the columns. For most tables, from 6 to 10 spaces works well.)

Column 1		Column 2		Column 3
6	6	10	6	8

Your planning diagram is now complete. You are ready to set a left margin stop for column 1 and tab stops for columns 2 and 3.

Step 3. Set the left margin:

With the carriage at center, backspace once for every *2 letters* and every *2 blank spaces* in your planning diagram. Spell out the letters and spaces in pairs as you backspace.

       Li st en *1 2 3 4 5 6* ta bu la ti on *1 2 3 4 5 6* pr ob le ms

Set the left margin at the point where you finish backspacing.

Step 4. Set the tab stops:

    a. Locate the tab stop for column 2 by spacing forward from the left margin. Strike the space bar once for each letter in the word *Listen* and for the 6 spaces that follow it. (Spell out the letters and spaces silently to yourself as you strike the space bar.)

         L i s t e n *1 2 3 4 5 6*
                  ↑Set the tab for column 2 here.

    b. Locate the tab stop for column 3 by spacing forward from the tab stop you set for column 2. Follow the same procedure as outlined above.

         t a b u l a t i o n *1 2 3 4 5 6*
                      ↑Set the tab for column 3 here.

Step 5. Prepare to type:

Pull the carriage back to the left margin and begin typing Drill A.

Listen	while	we
learn	to	prepare
a	planning	diagram
for	tabulation	problems

HAVE YOU A SAFE DEPOSIT BOX
TO PROTECT THESE VALUABLE BELONGINGS?

Legal documents	Trust agreements, contracts, deeds, mortgages, charters, leases, copyright papers. If legal papers are lost or destroyed, they may be impossible to replace; or replacing them may cost you many times the rental of a safe deposit box.
Important personal papers	Birth records, citizenship papers, income tax records, diplomas, marriage licenses, military discharge papers, wills. By keeping these papers in a safe deposit box, you will have them easily accessible for reference.
Insurance papers	Insurance policies and inventories of insured goods. Policies and related data kept together in a safe deposit box will be quickly available when needed.
Securities	Stocks and bonds. Securities need protection, especially if they are readily negotiable.
Valuable personal belongings	Jewelry, medals, heirlooms, rare stamps, valuable coins, treasured photographs. Valuable personal belongings kept in the home may be destroyed through fire, lost, misplaced, or stolen. Heirlooms are irreplaceable; other belongings may be replaced only at great cost.

Directions for Exercises 26–30

TABULATIONS FROM UNARRANGED COPY

The competent typist is able to plan tabulations from unarranged data. To give you practice in doing this, the copy for each of these exercises is given in unarranged form. Center each table attractively. Omit items in the body that are indicated or implied in the column headings. For example, in Exercise 26, the word *of* and the # sign are both implied in the column headings and should not be typed in the body of the table.

Exercise 26

Half sheet.

MAIN TITLE	LIST OF INACTIVE ACCOUNTS
SECONDARY TITLES	Atlantic Savings Bank
	December 31, 19—
COLUMN HEADINGS	Name / Address / Account No.

Charles N. Hoffman, of 62 Walnut Street, #11-440-0

Antoinette D. Hull, of 110 Johnston Street, #11-153-4

John H. Irvington, of 911 Marlowe Street, #11-336-6

Nicholas Lombardi, of 34 Wilson Boulevard, #12-271-1

Clinton S. McCloud, of 877 Pierce Avenue, #12-188-9

Hazel Pedersen, of 45 Tribune Square, #11-577-7

Gilbert A. Rondeau, of 776 West 15th Street, #11-478-8

Anita S. Savage, of 55 Coral Road, #12-378-9

Mary Wheeler, of 61 Exchange Place, #12-255-0

Directions for Drills A–N   *Full sheet. Leave 6 lines between drills. Center each drill horizontally. Begin on line 10. Continue on additional sheets if necessary.*

Drill A
Double spacing. 6 spaces between columns.

Listen	while	we
learn	to	prepare
a	planning	diagram
for	tabulation	problems

Drill E
Double spacing. 8 spaces between columns.

mailable	valuable	advisable
salable	unusable	dependable
adaptable	excusable	available
durable	desirable	comparable

Drill B
Single spacing. 10 spaces between columns.

receipt	receive	ceiling
perceive	deceive	their
freight	weight	conceive

Drill F
Single spacing. 6 spaces between columns.

if he did	and the	their work
the man is	when they	she did
it is the	if it is	they both

Drill C
As you are backspacing to figure the left margin setting, ignore odd letters at the end of your counting.
Single spacing. 6 spaces between columns.

relieve	review	relief
scientist	believing	cashiers
audience	variety	yield

Drill G
Double spacing. 8 spaces between columns.

may go	he did	for them
did they	and they	if they
he also	for it	turn it

Drill D
Single spacing. 10 spaces between columns.

so	sew	sow
new	knew	gnu
karat	caret	carrot
their	they're	there
flu	flue	flew

Drill H
Single spacing. 6 spaces between columns.

ring	rang	had rung
go	went	had gone
do	did	had done
be	was	had been
know	knew	had known

FDA   Food and Drug Administration—Safeguards the health of the nation by enforcing laws and regulations that prevent the distribution of unsafe foods, drugs and medicines, medical devices, cosmetics, and veterinary products.

FIC   Federal Information Centers—Function as clearing houses for information about the federal government.

FRS   Federal Reserve System—As the nation's central bank, regulates the flow of money and credit; also provides supervisory services to the public, the U.S. Treasury, and commercial banks.

FTC   Federal Trade Commission—Promotes free and fair competition in the marketplace by enforcing antitrust and other laws.

NLRB   National Labor Relations Board—Prevents or eliminates unfair labor practices.

OEO   Office of Economic Opportunity—Administers funds to programs that reduce unemployment and poverty.

Exercise 24
TABULATED LISTING
Arrange this material attractively.
Full sheet, inserted with long (11-inch) side first. SS body. DS between items.

GREAT NORTHERN COTTON MANUFACTURING COMPANY		10
Boston, Massachusetts		14
May, 19—		16
Information about Directors		21
Thomas H. Bailey, Jr.	President, Bailey & Lester, Inc., Hartford,	34
	Connecticut	36
Claire S. Gibbons	Chairperson of the Executive Committee,	48
	Lacey Cotton Mills, Springfield, Massachu-	56
	setts. Member of the Board of Directors,	65
	McPhail Threads, Portland, Maine	71
Hubert N. Grover	President of the Company	79
George A. LeClerq	Vice President of the Company. Member of	91
	the Board of Directors, Ralph Chalmers &	99
	Company, Boston, Massachusetts	105
Margaret C. Morgenstern	Chemist, Rand Corporation, Santa Monica,	118
	California	120
Martin L. Rivera	President, Jeffries Cotton Works, Boston,	131
	Massachusetts. Member of the Board of	139
	Trustees, James Benton & Company, Boston,	148
	Massachusetts	150
Clifford J. Robinson	President, Blockton Cotton Goods, Inc.,	163
	Atlanta, Georgia	166

Drill I

Double spacing. 7 spaces between columns.

MERCURY	VENUS	SATURN
MARS	JUPITER	EARTH
PLUTO	URANUS	NEPTUNE

Drill L

Double spacing. 5 spaces between columns.

1121	121	21	1
1232	232	32	2
1343	343	43	3

Drill J

Double spacing. 7 spaces between columns.

New York	London	Paris
Tokyo	Sao Paulo	Rome
Moscow	Cairo	New Delhi

Drill M

Remember to align numbers at right.
Double spacing. 8 spaces between columns.

10.1	20.2	30.3	40.4
500.5	600.6	700.7	800.8
9.9	1.1	2.2	3.3

Drill K

Single spacing. 8 spaces between columns.

negligible	feasible	forcible
admissible	incredible	audible
responsible	invisible	sensible
reversible	eligible	flexible

Drill N

Type in 3 columns.
Double spacing. 10 spaces between columns.

January, February, March

April, May, June

July, August, September

October, November, December

Topic 3 TITLES FOR TABLES

A table should always have a title that describes what kind of information it contains. The title should be as concise as you can make it. A title is usually centered and it is separated from the body of the table by 2 (sometimes 1) blank lines.

If a title requires more than 1 line, *each* line of the title is centered. The main title is always typed first and secondary titles are placed afterward. When you type the exercises in this topic, follow this style for the titles:

```
        MAIN TITLE

         Subtitle


Body of table    line 1
Body of table    line 2
```

1. Type the main title in solid capitals.
2. Type the secondary title (or titles) in lowercase, but capitalize the first letter of important words.
3. Double-space lines.

Exercise 21
LONG COLUMN
HEADINGS

Columns 2 and 3 have headings of more than one line. Center each line separately and single-space.

Half sheet. SS body. Center vertically and horizontally.

TEMPERATURES AROUND THE WORLD
June 6, 19—

City	Local Time	Temperature (°F)
Acapulco	7 a.m.	84
Antigua	1 p.m.	75
Casablanca	12 noon	68
Hong Kong	8 p.m.	81
London	1 p.m.	65
Madrid	1 p.m.	73
Moscow	3 p.m.	46

STEPS IN CORRESPONDENCE FILING
6

INSPECTING	The procedure of reading each piece of incoming mail	18
	to see that it has been marked for release to filing.	29
INDEXING	The procedure of deciding the name, subject, or other	42
	caption under which a paper should be filed. The main	53
	consideration here is how it will most probably be re-	64
	quested from the files.	69
CODING	The procedure of underscoring the caption selected in	81
	the indexing. (Whenever a paper might be called for	91
	under more than one caption, a cross-reference sheet	102
	must be prepared.)	106
SORTING	The process of arranging the material in order (alpha-	118
	betic, numeric, and so on) after it has been coded.	128
STORING	The process of inserting the papers into the files.	140

THE FEDERAL ALPHABET
(Government Department and Agency Abbreviations)

BLS	Bureau of Labor Statistics—Collects and analyzes data on labor economics.
EEOC	Equal Employment Opportunity Commission—Prevents or eliminates discriminatory practices in employment.
FCC	Federal Communications Commission—Regulates interstate and foreign communications carried on by radio, telephone, and telegraph; also regulates radio and television stations.

(Continued on next page)

Directions for Exercises 1–9

1. Center each exercise vertically and horizontally. (To review vertical centering, refer to pages 111–113; to review horizontal centering, refer to pages 107–110.)
2. Center the title of the table over the body.
3. Triple space after you type the title. (This will give you a 2-line separation between the body and the title.)

Exercise 1

Half sheet. Double spacing. 10 spaces between columns. Center vertically and horizontally.

```
          DEBATING CLUB OFFICERS
                     TS
Patricia L. Carlton          President

Gilbert Ramirez              Vice-President

Raymond L. Wayland           Treasurer

Samuel Law                   Secretary

Rosetta Morson               Editor
```

Exercise 2

Half sheet. Double spacing. 10 spaces between columns. Center vertically and horizontally.

```
        WESTVIEW NEWS EDITORIAL STAFF
                     TS
Anthony Beretti          Editor in Chief

Alma Rene Clark          Assistant Editor

Lloyd Hamilton           Executive Editor

Shelly Prillerman        News Editor

Alfred Monroe            Sports Editor

Thomas O'Brien           Social Editor

Claire Frankel           Clubs Editor
```

Exercise 3

Half sheet. Single spacing. 10 spaces between columns. Center vertically and horizontally.

WORDS USED IN APPLICATION FORMS	
Surname	Last name
Maiden Name	Name before marriage
Marital Status	Single, married, etc.
Signature	Written (not printed) name
Spouse	Husband or wife
References	Adults who know your abilities
Dependents	People you support
Soc. Sec. No.	Social Security Number
Occupation	Type of work you do
Residence	Where you live
Telephone	Home telephone number
Citizenship	Name of country
Surety Bonding	Insurance against company losses

Exercise 18

LONG COLUMN
HEADINGS

*Half sheet. SS body. Center
vertically and horizontally.*

COMMODITY RECOMMENDATIONS

Friday, June 8, 19—

Commodity	Today's Price	Recommendation
Wheat	$3.48	Hold
Corn	2.56	Buy
Oats	1.51	Sell
Lard	.29	Hold
Cotton	.59	Hold
Wool	2.10	Sell
Copper	.95	Buy
Lead	.48	Buy
Rubber	.66	Sell
Hogs	.47	Hold
Coffee	1.40	Sell

Exercise 19

LONG COLUMN
HEADINGS

*Full sheet, inserted with
long (11-inch) side first. DS
body. Center vertically and
horizontally.*

TOP MICHIGAN MANUFACTURING COMPANIES

Number of Employees, 19—

Company	Main Offices	Product	Employees
General Motors	Detroit	Motor Vehicles	797,000
Ford	Dearborn	Motor Vehicles	479,292
Chrysler	Highland Park	Motor Vehicles	250,833
Dow Chemical	Midland	Chemicals, Plastics	53,002
Bendix	Southfield	Auto & Aviation Equip.	80,006
American Motors	Southfield	Motor Vehicles	29,519
Burroughs	Detroit	Bus. & Electronic Equip.	51,295
Whirlpool	Benton Harbor	Household Appliances	23,573
Fruehauf	Detroit	Transportation Equip.	29,400

Exercise 20

LONG COLUMN
HEADINGS

Note that column 4 has a
2-line heading; center each
line separately and single-
space.

*Half sheet. SS body. Center
vertically and horizontally.*

HIGHEST MOUNTAIN ON EACH CONTINENT

Continent	Mountain	Location	Height in Meters
North America	Mt. McKinley	Alaska	6,193
South America	Mt. Aconcagua	Chile-Argentina	6,959
Europe	Mt. El'brus	Soviet Union	5,553
Asia	Mt. Everest	Nepal-Tibet	8,708
Africa	Mt. Kibo	Tanzania	5,802
Australia	Mt. Kosciusko	New South Wales	2,195
Antarctica	Mt. Vinson Massif	Antarctic	5,057

Exercise 4

PAIRED COLUMNS IN A TABULATION

When the relationship between two columns in a table is closer than between others, the spacing between columns is varied to show these relationships.

Full sheet. Double spacing. Follow the spacing shown in the planning diagram below this exercise. Center vertically and horizontally.

agcy.	agency	h.s.	high school
appt.	appointment	intvw.	interview
asst.	assistant	lic.	license
bkgd.	background	mo.	month
bus.	business	oppty.	opportunity
clk.	clerk	pd.	paid
coll.	college	refs.	references
dir.	director	sal.	salary
div.	division	secty.	secretary
eves.	evenings	sh.	shorthand
exp.	experience	swbd.	switchboard
ext.	extension	temp.	temporary
grad.	graduate	trnee.	trainee

5	6	11	16	6	6	11

Exercise 5

Half sheet. Single spacing. 16 spaces between columns. Center vertically and horizontally.

FREMONT HIGH SCHOOL
DS
Schedule of Football Games, 19—
TS

Oct. 12	McFee High School	At home
Oct. 22	Bayville Prep.	Away
Oct. 29	Fleer School of Business	At home
Nov. 5	Horace High School	Away
Nov. 11	Skelton High School	At home
Dec. 3	District Finals	Away

Exercise 6

Half sheet. Single spacing. 10 spaces between columns. Center vertically and horizontally.

VANDERWATER HIGH SCHOOL

19— Assembly Program Schedule

February 15	Current Events Club	Open Forum
March 1	English Department	Motion Pictures
March 15	School Orchestra	Musical Program
March 30	Glee Club	Easter Musical
April 27	Science Department	Demonstration
May 11	Counseling Department	Job Fair
May 25	Drama Club	A One-Act Play
June 8	Business Club	Awards Assembly

Exercise 15

LONG COLUMN
HEADINGS

Half sheet. SS body. Center vertically and horizontally.

ELBERT TOURS, INC.

Rate Schedule*

St. Martin from Pittsburgh, June 15–22

Hotel	Double	Single	Child**
Coralita	$479	$509	$250
Great Bay, ocean view	455	–	245
Great Bay, mountain view	429	479	245
Le Galion	399	459	230
Le Bay, garden	449	559	280
Le Bay, beach	465	599	300
St. Tropez, lagoon view	425	519	260
St. Tropez, ocean view	445	539	270

*Rates are per person. They include airfares and 6 nights' hotel accommodations.
**Ages 2 to 11.

Exercise 16

LONG COLUMN
HEADINGS

Full sheet, inserted with long (11-inch) side first. SS body. Center vertically and horizontally.

H. T. HARLAND COMPANY

Typewriter Inventory

Make	Model	Serial No.	Purchased
Adler	M-750	748-546	1975
IBM	Selectric	298-1646	1969
IBM	Self-Correcting	231-6658	1978
IBM	Executive II	191-8464	1969
Olympia	S-27	207-322	1977
Olympia	S-27	207-321	1978
Remington	EL-6	154-054	1974
Royal	J-300	869-1813	1974

Exercise 17

LONG COLUMN
HEADINGS

Half sheet. SS body. Center vertically and horizontally.

SUMMARY OF COMMON METRIC CONVERSION FACTORS

If you know	And you want	Multiply by
inches	centimeters	2.54
feet	meters	0.30
yards	meters	0.91
miles	kilometers	1.61
quarts	liters	0.95
gallons	liters	3.79
ounces	grams	28.35
pounds	kilograms	0.45

Exercise 7

Half sheet. Double spacing. Spaces between columns are 5, 15, and 5. Center vertically and horizontally.

BIRTHSTONES

January	Garnet	July	Ruby
February	Amethyst	August	Sardonyx
March	Bloodstone	September	Sapphire
April	Diamond	October	Opal
May	Emerald	November	Topaz
June	Pearl	December	Turquoise

Exercise 8

Full sheet. Double spacing. Follow the spacing shown in the planning diagram below this exercise. Center vertically and horizontally.

TWO-LETTER STATE ABBREVIATIONS

Alabama	AL	Montana	MT
Alaska	AK	Nebraska	NE
Arizona	AZ	Nevada	NV
Arkansas	AR	New Hampshire	NH
California	CA	New Jersey	NJ
Colorado	CO	New Mexico	NM
Connecticut	CT	New York	NY
Delaware	DE	North Carolina	NC
District of Columbia	DC	North Dakota	ND
Florida	FL	Ohio	OH
Georgia	GA	Oklahoma	OK
Hawaii	HI	Oregon	OR
Idaho	ID	Pennsylvania	PA
Illinois	IL	Puerto Rico	PR
Indiana	IN	Rhode Island	RI
Iowa	IA	South Carolina	SC
Kansas	KS	South Dakota	SD
Kentucky	KY	Tennessee	TN
Louisiana	LA	Texas	TX
Maine	ME	Utah	UT
Maryland	MD	Vermont	VT
Massachusetts	MA	Virginia	VA
Michigan	MI	Washington	WA
Minnesota	MN	West Virginia	WV
Mississippi	MS	Wisconsin	WI
Missouri	MO	Wyoming	WY

| 20 | 6 | 2 | 12 | 14 | 6 | 2 |

Exercise 12

LONG COLUMN
HEADINGS

Full sheet. DS body. Center vertically and horizontally.

WATCHING YOUR WEIGHT		4
"Junk" Food	Calories	12
Cake, chocolate iced	356	17
Cola beverages, 8 oz.	90	22
Hot dog	124	24
Hamburger patty, 4 oz.	331	29
Ice cream, chocolate	385	34
Cashew nuts, 8 to 12	94	39
Potato chips, 7 large	108	44
Popcorn with butter, 1 cup	100	50

Exercise 13

LONG COLUMN
HEADINGS

Some tables have no heading for the first column, as illustrated here.

Full sheet. DS body. Center vertically and horizontally.

FOOTBALL STATISTICS			4
Lawton High School vs. Marlin High School			12
Game of November 11, 19—			17
	Lawton	Marlin	24
First downs	14	15	28
Yards gained (net)	413	355	33
Forward passes attempted	33	18	39
Passes completed	15	9	43
Passes intercepted	1	1	47
Punts (number)	3	5	51
Average distance of punts (yards)	39	44	59
Yards penalized	38	67	63
Fumbles lost	2	3	67

Exercise 14

LONG COLUMN
HEADINGS

Remember to align the dollar sign with the longest amount in a column.

Full sheet, inserted with long (11-inch) side first. DS body. Spread center main title. Center vertically and horizontally.

S P E C I A L S U M M E R S A L E			7
SUNDECK REDWOOD FURNITURE			9
Week of June 1 Only			12
Item	Regular Price	Sale Price	29
Chair	$109.95	$ 99.88	33
Chaise lounge	149.95	124.88	39
Tete-a-tete	199.95	179.88	44
Coffee table	69.95	54.85	50
Ottoman	44.95	39.89	55
Rocker	119.95	99.88	59
Umbrella	89.95	69.88	64
Shell	9.95	8.88	68

Exercise 9

Half sheet. Single spacing. 8 spaces between columns. Center vertically and horizontally.

National Conference
Eastern Division

Dallas	Cowboys
Washington	Redskins
St. Louis	Cardinals
Philadelphia	Eagles
New York	Giants

Topic 4 TABLES WITH COLUMN HEADINGS

Column headings help a reader to understand the information in a table. A column heading may be centered over the column, or blocked, as shown in the illustrations below.

Blocked Column Headings

Instructor	Classes	Days
Mr. Cutting	Typewriting	Mon.–Fri.
Mrs. Shipworth	Clerk–Steno Training	Tues. & Thurs.
Ms. Rutledge	Data Processing	Mon. & Fri.
Margin 15	Tab 40	Tab 65

Centered Column Headings

Instructor	Classes	Days
Mr. Cutting	Typewriting	Mon.–Fri.
Mrs. Shipworth	Clerk–Steno Training	Tues. & Thurs.
Ms. Rutledge	Data Processing	Mon. & Fri.
Margin 15	Tab 40	Tab 65

SHORT COLUMN HEADINGS

A column heading that is blocked presents no difficulty in typing. Each heading begins at the point where the column starts. If the column headings are centered, however, you must first locate the midpoint of each column. The steps listed below describe how this is done for the table shown above.

Step 1. To find the midpoint of the first column:
    a. Move the carriage to the point where the column is to begin. The first column begins at a left margin of 15.
    b. Find the longest item in the first column (*Mrs. Shipworth*).
    c. Divide the longest item in half by spacing forward once for every 2 letters in it. This will place the carriage at the center point of the column.

Step 2. To type the column heading:
    a. With the carriage at the midpoint of the column, backspace once for every 2 letters in the heading of the column.

In st ru ct or

    b. Begin typing the heading at the point where you stopped backspacing.
    c. Backspace and underscore the column heading.

(Continued on next page)

Exercise 9
CENTERED COLUMN
HEADINGS

Half sheet. SS body. Center vertically and horizontally.

SCHEDULE OF PERFORMANCES

Grand Opera House

Fall Season, 19—

Date	Time	Opera
Saturday, November 15	8:00	Magic Flute
Wednesday, ˮ 19	8:00	Lohengrin
Saturday, ˮ 22	8:15	Il Trovatore
Wednesday, ˮ 26	8:00	Don Giovanni
Saturday, ˮ 29	8:00	Faust
Wednesday, December 3	8:30	La Traviata
Saturday, ˮ 6	8:00	Carmen
Wednesday, ˮ 10	8:15	Aida
Saturday, ˮ 13	8:00	Manon

Exercise 10
CENTERED COLUMN
HEADINGS AND
FOOTNOTE

Full sheet. DS body. Center vertically and horizontally.

MOODY PUBLISHING CORPORATION

White Plains, New York

BUSINESS TEXTBOOKS

Code	Author	Title	Price*
7114	Atkins, Adele	Office Practice	$7.65
7122	Bush, Ronald	Record Keeping	7.50
7125	Sobell, Richard	Elementary Accounting	8.65
7127	Sobell, Richard	Advanced Accounting	8.80
7131	Terhune, Edna	Learning to Typewrite	9.20
7137	Vann, Eva S.	Dictation Practice	7.85
7138	Vann, Eva S.	Transcription Practice	7.85

*All prices subject to a 25% discount on school orders

Exercise 11
LONG COLUMN
HEADINGS

Full sheet. SS body. Center vertically and horizontally.

SUFFOLK ELECTRIC COMPANY, INC.

Members of the Board of Directors, May, 19—

Name	Principal Occupation	First Elected
Julian V. Cohen	Attorney at Law	1972
Edward Dellman	President, Dellman Brothers	1965
Joseph F. Elson	Secretary, Budd, Inc.	1973
Victor Fehr	Treasurer of the Company	1974
Evelyn A. Mason	Attorney at Law	1967
Daniel T. Remson	President of the Company	1979
Helen H. Sugimoto	Vice-President of the Company	1971

Step 3. Repeat Steps 1 and 2 for centering the column headings in the remaining columns. The second column begins at a tab stop set at 40. The third column begins at a tab stop set at 65.

Step 4. Double-space after typing all the column headings and return to the left margin.

Step 5. Type the items in each column, typing across each line, and using the tab stops.

Drill A

Type the table shown here. Center the column headings following the procedure outlined above.

Instructor	Classes	Days
Mr. Cutting	Typewriting	Mon.–Fri.
Mrs. Shipworth	Clerk–Steno Training	Tues. & Thurs.
Ms. Rutledge	Data Processing	Mon., Wed., & Fri.

Margin 15   Tab 40   Tab 65

Drill B

Leave 10 lines after typing Drill A. Type the table shown here, centering each column heading over the column.

Player	Sport	School
Muriel Johnson	Tennis	Washington High
Richard Hamilton	Football	Northwestern High
Cecilia DuBois	Basketball	Peabody High

Directions for Exercises 1–8 Center each table vertically and horizontally. Center column headings unless instructed otherwise by your teacher. Decide how many spaces you wish to leave between columns. Generally, from 6 to 10 spaces between columns work well in most tables. Columns should not be so widely spaced that it becomes difficult to read across, nor so close that the table looks cramped.

Exercise 1

Half sheet. Single spacing.

BASKETBALL SCHEDULE
DS
Abraham Lincoln High School

(19— Season)
TS

Date	Opponent	Borough
March 22	Grover Cleveland High	Queens
April 12	George Washington High	Manhattan
April 24	Sheepshead Bay High	Brooklyn

Exercise 2

Half sheet. Double spacing.

FAMOUS AMERICAN POETS

(19th Century)

Name	Famous Work
Walt Whitman	Leaves of Grass
Edgar Lee Masters	Spoon River Anthology
Edwin Markham	The Man with the Hoe

Exercise 6

BLOCKED COLUMN HEADINGS AND FOOTNOTE

Begin each column heading at the point where the column starts.

Half sheet. DS body. Center vertically and horizontally.

CRAWFORD CONSTRUCTION COMPANY

Consultant Fees, Year Beginning January 1, 19—*

Consultant	Specialty	Amount
Lopez & Garretson	Attorneys	$8,000
Maurice Burgess Associates	Engineers	4,500
R. N. Carson & Company	Accountants	3,500
Herbert S. Schell	Tax Advisor	800
Patricia N. Galvin	Architect	1,500

*Only those amounts in excess of $500 are included.

Exercise 7

CENTERED COLUMN HEADINGS

Full sheet. DS body. Center vertically and horizontally.

UNITY DISCOUNT STORES

Branch Locations

Branch	Address	Phone
West Warren Area	20430 Van Dyke	893-6750
Madison Heights	John R. Flagg Shopping Mall	542-4961
Lincoln Park	4142 Dix Highway	386-7611
Pontiac	Tel-Huron Shopping Center	333-7594
Mt. Clemons	Gratiot at Camden	791-0460
Northville	Northville Plaza	348-9820
Southfield	Tel-Twelve Mall	836-2133

Exercise 8

BLOCKED COLUMN HEADINGS

Begin each column heading at the point where the column starts.

Full sheet. SS body. Center vertically and horizontally.

NEW YORK STATE DEPARTMENT OF COMMERCE

FIELD OFFICES

City	Post Office Address	ZIP Code
Albany	112 State Street	12207
Binghamton	66 Chenango Street	13901
Buffalo	908 Ellicott Square Building	14209
Elmira	327 Baldwin Street	14901
Kingston	442 Broadway	12401
Mineola	33 Denton Building	11501
New York	342 Madison Avenue	10017
Ogdensburg	321 State Street	13669
Rochester	45 Exchange Street	14614
Syracuse	351 S. Warren Street	13202
Utica	185 Genesee Street	13501
Washington, D.C.	1026 - 17th Street N. W.	20036
White Plains	148 Martine Avenue	10601

METRIC CONVERSIONS
Corresponding Units of Measure

Quantity	English	Metric
length	foot	meter
weight	pound	kilogram
temperature	Fahrenheit	Celsius
volume	quart	liter

KING SPORTING GOODS COMPANY
DS
165 Barnes Avenue
Seattle, Washington 98109
DS
S U P E R   S P R I N G   S P E C I A L S
TS

Equipment	Regular Price	Sale Price
Golf Clubs (Set)	$120.00	$75.00
Tennis Racket	25.50	15.00
Baseball Glove	32.75	17.50
Fishing Rod	19.00	12.50
Water Skis (Pair)	48.00	32.75
Backpack	60.00	49.90
Weight Bench	29.97	24.90

LECTURE SERIES
Executive Training Course
Summer Session

Date	Topics	Lecturer
June 10	Organization	James A. Ranedall
June 13	Public Relations	Marian Thomas
June 18	Personnel	Frank Saunders
June 21	Purchasing	Herbert Rawls
June 25	Market Research	Charles Meyers
June 16	Advertising	Burton Welding

Exercise 2
THREE-COLUMN TABLE

Half sheet. SS body. Center vertically and horizontally.

SALVADOR FOOD COMPANY 5

Canned Products 8

Grapefruit Juice	Apple Sauce	Beets	15
Lemon Juice	Blueberries	Carrots	21
Mixed Vegetable Juice	Grapefruit Sections	Peas	30
Orange Juice	Halved Apricots	Spinach	37
Tomato Juice	Sliced Peaches	Green Beans	45
Guava Juice	Fruit Salad	Asparagus	52

Exercise 3
TABLE WITH PAIRED COLUMNS

Give columns 1 and 2 and columns 3 and 4 the "paired" look by leaving extra space between columns 2 and 3.

Half sheet. SS body. Center vertically and horizontally.

PENSION BENEFITS FOR RETIRED EMPLOYEES 8

Ludlow Chemical Plant 12

January 1, 19— 15

Edith T. Burnham	$ 825	Philip Lustig	$1,025	24
Joseph R. Clarke	800	Alice T. Manning	900	32
Nils A. Ericson	1,100	John Miracolo	700	40
Foster Garner	770	Harriet P. Stillwell	1,110	49
Martha Zender	965	Charles Waite	850	56

Exercise 4
TABLE WITH PAIRED COLUMNS AND FOOTNOTE

Leave 2 blank lines between the last line of the table and the footnote.

Full sheet. DS body. Center vertically and horizontally.

TIME IN OTHER CITIES 4

When It Is Noon in New York City 11

Berlin	6 p.m.	Moscow	8 p.m.	16
Chicago	11 a.m.	Paris	5 p.m.	21
Hong Kong	1 p.m.*	Rome	6 p.m.	27
London	5 p.m.	Sydney	3 a.m.*	32
Los Angeles	9 a.m.	Tokyo	3 a.m.*	38
Mexico City	11 a.m.	Washington	12 noon	46

*The following day 50

Exercise 5
BLOCKED COLUMN HEADINGS

Begin each column heading at the point where the column starts.

Half sheet. DS body. Center vertically and horizontally.

COMPOSITION OF METAL ALLOYS 5

Alloy	Component Metals	
		18
Brass	Copper and zinc	22
White gold	Tin, copper, and antimony	29
Bronze	Copper and tin	34
Pewter	Tin and lead or copper or brass	41
Plumber's solder	Lead and tin	47
Steel	Iron and carbon	51
Lynite	Aluminum and copper	56

WELL-KNOWN BLACK WRITERS

Fiction	Poetry	Literary Criticism
Charles Chestnutt	Paul L. Dunbar	Alain Locke
Jean Toomer	James W. Johnson	Richard Wright
Rudolph Fisher	Fenton Johnson	Sterling Brown
Arna Bontemps	Claude McKay	James Baldwin
Langston Hughes	Jean Toomer	Darwin Turner
Richard Wright	Countee Cullen	Clarence Major
Ralph Ellison	Gwendolyn Brooks	Arthur P. Davis
Paul Marshall	Owen Dodson	Blyden Jackson
Frank L. Brown	Frank Horne	Richard Stern

BUSINESS DEPARTMENT AWARDS
Edison High School
June, 19—
Student / Subject / Award
Minnie Riggs / Stenography / Gold Medal
Jan Van den Bergh / Typewriting / Silver Pin
Willie Thomas / Bookkeeping / Gold Medal
Sarah Sykes / Office Machines / Silver Pin
Peter Dodge / Business Law / Silver Medal
David Knowles / DE Marketing / Gold Pin

JUNIOR LEAGUE CHARITIES
19— Distribution of Funds
Facility / Total / Paid / Due
Lincoln Hospital / $4,300 / $3,100 / $1,200
Home for the Aged / 3,300 / 2,500 / 800
Hill Family Home / 1,000 / 800 / 200
City Zoo / 2,000 / 1,500 / 500
Braille School / 750 / 600 / 150
Children's Hospital / 700 / 500 / 200
Salvation Army / 2,000 / 1,500 / 500

PART 4

ADVANCED TABULATIONS

Listings of detailed data are easier to read and more attractive when they are arranged in the form of tabulations. Before beginning these more advanced tabulation exercises, you may want to review the information presented in pages 120 to 133 of *Simple Tabulations* and pages 107 to 111 of *Horizontal and Vertical Centering*.

Topic 1 TABULATION PRODUCTION PRACTICE

With practice, a good typist will be able to use eye judgment to set up tabulated material. After you have typed several of the exercises in this topic, see if you can estimate machine settings and achieve attractive layouts.

Directions for Exercises 1–25
TABULATION REVIEW

Exercises 1–25 review all the tabulating procedures taught in Section 2, Part 4. Word counts are provided for many exercises so that you may measure your production rate. As you progress through the exercises, you will find that they become more complex and demand increasingly higher levels of skill.

Exercise 1

TWO-COLUMN TABLE

Full sheet. DS body. Center vertically and horizontally.

	HOTEL ATLANTIC	Words
		3
	Convention Schedule, Spring, 19—	10
March 21–23	Paper Manufacturers Association	19
March 30–31	National Organization for Women	28
April 2–3	National Council of State Garden Clubs	38
April 4–6	Society of Automotive Engineers	46
April 18–24	National Public Health Association	55
April 27–29	Midwest Trial Lawyers Association	64
May 14–18	Conference of Postal Women	71
May 21–24	Court Reporters Association	79
June 4–8	National Council of Social Studies	88

LONG COLUMN HEADINGS

When a column heading is longer than any other item in the column, use the column heading as the longest column item when you prepare a planning diagram for the table. Backspace to find the left margin and space forward to set tab stops in the usual way (refer to page 123).

Name of Student	Typing Class	Words Per Minute
B. Pierce	11-A	70
C. Hotl	11-B	65
R. Neys	10-A	58

In this table assume that you have completed a planning diagram. You have set a left margin stop and two tab stops. The tabs are set to allow for 5 spaces between column headings. After you type the column headings, follow these steps to center each column under the heading:

Step 1. To locate the center point of the first column: space *forward* from the left margin once for every 2 letters or spaces in the heading; select the longest item in the column (B. Pierce) and *backspace* once for each 2 letters or spaces in that item. Reset the left margin at this point.

Step 2. To locate the center point of the second column: move the carriage to the first letter of the heading; space *forward* once for every 2 letters or spaces; select the longest item in the column and *backspace* once for every 2 letters or spaces. Reset the tab for the second column.

Step 3. To reset the tab for the third column: use the same procedures outlined above. Now type the body of the table.

Drill C

Half sheet. Double spacing. 5 spaces between column headings. Begin on line 10.

Name of Student	Typing Class	Words Per Minute
B. Pierce	11-A	70
C. Hotl	11-B	65
R. Neys	10-A	58

Reset margin   Reset tab   Reset tab

Exercise 9

Half sheet. Single spacing. Center column headings. Decide on the spacing between columns. Center vertically and horizontally.

MAJOR LEAGUE PENNANT WINNERS

1970–1978

Year	National League	American League
1970	Cincinnati	Baltimore
1971	Pittsburgh	Baltimore
1972	Cincinnati	Oakland
1973	New York	Oakland
1974	Los Angeles	Oakland
1975	Cincinnati	Boston
1976	Cincinnati	New York
1977	Los Angeles	New York
1978	Los Angeles	New York

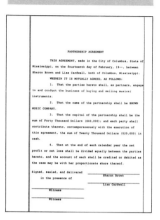

sum of Forty Thousand Dollars ($40,000); and each party shall contribute thereto, contemporaneously with the execution of this agreement, the sum of Twenty Thousand Dollars ($20,000) in cash. / 4. That at the end of each calendar year the net profit or net loss shall be divided equally between the parties hereto, and the account of each shall be credited or debited as the case may be with her proportionate share thereof.

Signed, sealed, and delivered
   in the presence of

_____   Sharon Brown
_____

Witness

_____   Lisa Cardwell
_____

Witness

Exercise 7
SUMMONS WITH HEADING

SUPREME COURT OF THE STATE OF NEW YORK / COUNTY OF KINGS / FRANK L. WARNER, / Plaintiff / vs. / JOSEPH C. COSTA, / Defendant / CASE NUMBER: 453,903 / JUDGE ROBERT C. RICE / SUMMONS / YOU ARE HEREBY SUMMONED to answer the complaint in this action and to serve a copy of your answer, or, if the complaint is not served with this summons, to serve a notice of appearance on the Plaintiff's attorney, within TWENTY (20) days after the service of this summons, exclusive of the day of service. In case of your failure to appear or answer, judgment will be taken against you by default for the relief demanded in the complaint. / Dated: March 12, 19—.

_____
Vincent L. Walsh
Attorney for the Plaintiff
603 Sulzer Street
Brooklyn, New York 11202

Exercise 8
ASSIGNMENT

ASSIGNMENT / KNOW ALL MEN BY THESE PRESENTS that I, Gerald Kates, residing at 2001 Reyburn Road, Shaker Heights, Ohio, in consideration of One Dollar ($1) paid by Donald Deal, residing at 135 Rugby Road, Cleveland, Ohio (herein called the "Assignee"), hereby assign to the Assignee all my right, title, and interest in the moneys due to me from Gent Blurtt, for services as a clerk performed by me, between May 1, 19—, and May 31, 19—, at the request of said Gent Blurtt, for the agreed sum of Five Hundred Dollars ($500). / IN WITNESS WHEREOF, I have hereunto set my hand and seal, this 5th day of May, 19—.

Signed, sealed, and delivered
   in the presence of

_____
Gerald Kates, Assignor

_____

Witness

Exercise 10

Full sheet. Double spacing. Center column headings. Decide on the spacing between columns. Center vertically and horizontally.

CENTRAL NATIONAL BANK

260 Market Street

Philadelphia, PA   19104

Mortgagor	Location	Loan Value
John Abbott	483 Main Street	$ 10,000
Acker & Smith	25 Wing Street	12,000
Hazel Arthur	316 Court Street	4,000
Henry Gorchakov	22391 Columbia Turnpike	10,000
Patrick Kelly	258 Main Street	9,800

Exercise 11

ROUGH-DRAFT COPY

Type the table, making the corrections indicated.

Half sheet. Single spacing. Center column headings. Center vertically and horizontally.

FILMS FOR IN SECRETARIAL Studies _CLASSES_

Sound--16 mm.

Title	Distributor	Time (Minutes)	Rental
The Office Day	Business Bureau	20	Free
The Expert Typist	Visual Aids, Inc.	15	$2.50
First Typing Lessons	Hugh A. Fiske & Co.	15	2.50 3.00
Stenographic Dictations	Visual Aids, Inc.	20	3.00
Applying for a Job	Hugh A. Fiske & Co.	23	3.50
Your Type writer	Business Bureau	20	Free
Office Duties	Central Films	20	3.00

Exercise 5
WILL

LAST WILL AND TESTAMENT / OF / KENNETH A. PARKER / I, Kenneth A. Parker, residing in Lakewood, Cuyahoga County, State of Ohio, do hereby make, publish, and declare this to be my Last Will and Testament, hereby revoking any and all former wills and codicils heretofore by me made. / FIRST: I direct my executrix, hereinafter nominated and appointed, to pay all my just debts and funeral expenses as soon after my decease as may be convenient. / SECOND: To my elder son, Jonathon T. Parker, I give, devise and bequeath my gold pocket watch, bequeathed to me by my father. / THIRD: To my daughter, Adria Parker Masters, I give, devise and bequeath my engraved sterling silver water pitcher, bequeathed to me by my mother. / FOURTH: To my younger son, David R. Parker, I give, devise and bequeath my set of golf clubs and my pool table. / FIFTH: All the rest, residue, and remainder of my estate, whether real, personal, or mixed, and wheresoever the same may be situated, or which I at any time during my life may be entitled to receive, I give, devise, and bequeath to my wife, Judy Parker, of Lakewood, Cuyahoga County, State of Ohio. / SIXTH: I hereby nominate, constitute, and appoint my wife, Judy Parker, executrix of this, my Last Will and Testament, without bond. / IN WITNESS WHEREOF, I have hereunto set my hand and seal at the City of Lakewood, State of Ohio, to this, my Last Will and Testament, consisting of two (2) typewritten sheets, this 4th day of August, 19—.

_____
Kenneth A. Parker, Testator

Signed, sealed, published and declared by Kenneth A. Parker, the testator aforesaid, in our presence as and for his Last Will and Testament; and we the undersigned at his request and in his presence, and in the presence of each other, did hereunto subscribe our names as witnesses thereto at the City of Lakewood, State of Ohio, the day and year aforesaid.

_____   Residing at _____
Witness

_____   Residing at _____
Witness

Exercise 6
PARTNERSHIP AGREEMENT

PARTNERSHIP AGREEMENT / THIS AGREEMENT, made in the City of Columbus, State of Mississippi, on the fourteenth day of February, 19—, between Sharon Brown and Lisa Cardwell, both of Columbus, Mississippi. / WHEREIN IT IS MUTUALLY AGREED, AS FOLLOWS: / 1. That the parties hereto shall, as partners, engage in and conduct the business of buying and selling musical instruments. / 2. That the name of the partnership shall be BROWN MUSIC COMPANY. / 3. That the capital of the partnership shall be the

(Continued on next page)

Exercise 12

Full sheet. Double spacing. Center column headings. Decide on the spacing between columns. Center vertically and horizontally.

(caps) Honor Roll
Term Ending June, 19--

Student	Counselor	Grade
Sue Ryan	Burke	12
Al Bijas	Vaughn	10
Tim Asher	Vaughn	11
Diane Sims	Lester	12
Shelley Green	Watson	10
Vicki Madoshi	Watson	11
Sidney Ryan	Burke	11
Charles Royal	Remus	12
Riley Roberts	Remus	12

Exercise 13

Full sheet. Double spacing. Center column headings. Decide on the spacing between columns. Center vertically and horizontally.

WEST HIGH BOWLING LEAGUE
League Standings
February 7, 19--

Team	Won	Lost	Total Pins
The Bombers	47	13	47,340
Lucky Ones	45	15	47,126
The Strikers	41	19	46,560
Charlie's Angels	40½	19½	46,240
The Group	40	20	41,040
Thunderation	38	22	40,260
Chocolate Chips	38	22	40,100
Friday Fools	37	23	39,660

Directions for Exercises 3–8

Type Exercises 3–8 on legal paper. If legal paper is not available rule the proper margins on a plain, 8½″ × 11″ sheet. You should have a double line 1½″ from the left edge and a single line ½″ from the right edge.

Exercise 3
POWER OF ATTORNEY

POWER OF ATTORNEY / KNOW ALL MEN BY THESE PRESENTS that I, Frank T. Haynes, in Dauphin County, State of Pennsylvania, do appoint Raymond Garland of the same place my true and lawful attorney, for me and in my stead, to take charge of my business as manufacturer and vendor of gas stoves; to purchase and to sell all such articles as he may deem proper in connection with said business; to sign, accept, and indorse notes, drafts, and bills; to collect or settle all claims due or to become due in my favor; and to adjust, settle, or pay all claims that now exist or may hereafter arise against me; and in general do all other acts which he may consider useful or necessary connected with my business and interests. I hereby give Raymond Garland, my said attorney, full power to do everything necessary to be done connected with the business as fully as I could do if personally present, with full power of substitution and revocation, hereby ratifying and confirming all that my said attorney shall lawfully do by virtue hereof. / IN WITNESS WHEREOF, I have hereunto set my hand and seal, this 14th day of July, 19—.

Signed, sealed, and delivered
in the presence of

_____
Frank T. Haynes

_____
Witness

Exercise 4
EXECUTION WITH HEADING

When typing the exercise at the right, set the heading up in correct form.

IN THE DISTRICT COURT OF THE STATE OF IDAHO / FOR THE COUNTY OF LUCAS / CIRINO RESTAURANT, INC., / Plaintiff / vs. / SAM HILL, / Defendant / STATE OF IDAHO / County of Lucas / CASE NUMBER: 486,910 / JUDGE SCOTT BRADY / <u>EXECUTION</u> / ss. / TO: SHERIFF OF LUCAS COUNTY, IDAHO: GREETING: / WHEREAS, on the 24th day of December, 19—, in the District Court of the State of Idaho for the County of Lucas, Cirino Restaurant, Inc., Plaintiff, recovered judgment against Sam Hill, Defendant, for the sum of $6,234.28 and court costs in the sum of $119.50. / THEREFORE, in the name of the State of Idaho, you are hereby commanded to seize the personal property of the said Sam Hill excepting such as the law exempts, and cause to be made by levy and sale, according to law, the amount of such judgment and disbursements and expenses that may accrue and of this writ make legal service and due return to me within sixty days from the date hereof. WITNESS my hand and seal of said Court. Dated: December 28, 19—.

_____
Clerk

Exercise 14

Half sheet. Single spacing. Center column headings. Decide on the spacing between columns. Center vertically and horizontally.

(caps) → Contests Open to High School Students
Spring, 19--

Sponsor	Type	Closing Date
Fire Department	Essay — Fire Prevention	March 12
TV Channel 4	Musical Composition	March 15
Parker Flour Company	Recipe Using Flour	March 31
The City Press	Editorial on Safety	April 10
Civic Opera House	Choral Music	April 20

Exercise 15

Half sheet. Double spacing. Center column headings. Decide on the spacing between columns. Center vertically and horizontally.

CARTER HIGH SCHOOL
D.E.C.A. Membership Roster

Name	Address	Phone	Dues Paid
Basil Willard	87 Hunter Avenue	893-4855	$5.00
Martha Dunn	12917 Ryan	366-7676	3.00
Evelyn Mason	19330 Edinborough	891-6913	1.50
Augusta Ellison	71 Vernier Road	882-5847	5.00
Daniel Remison	14230 Joy Road	772-0080	2.50
Richard Schmidt	23657 Hudson	565-9373	1.50

Bill of Sale

Know all Men by these Presents:

That we, JAMES R. PHELAN & COMPANY, of the Town of Babylon, in the County of Suffolk and State of New York------------------

the part_ies_ *of the first part, in consideration of the sum of* Fifty Thousand Five Hundred-- ($50,500) -- *dollars,*

current lawful money of the United States of America, to ----------us----------- *in hand paid by* Daniel F. Newmark, of Mineola, New York------------------------
----

*the part*_Y___ *of the second part, the receipt whereof is hereby acknowledged, do__ by these presents sell and convey unto the part*_Y___ *of the second part,* ------his-------- *executors, administrators, and assigns*

all the following GOODS, CHATTELS, and PROPERTY, to wit:

the gas and service station and automobile accessories business

now conducted by us at 475 South Shore Drive, Babylon, New York,

including the goodwill thereof, lease, stock in trade, fixtures,

and appurtenances, as per inventory schedule attached, and each

and every thing used by us therein.

To Have and to Hold *the same unto the part*_Y___ *of the second part,* ----his----- *executors, administrators, and assigns forever.*

And --------we---------- *do__ for* --------our--------- *heirs, executors, and administrators, covenant and agree with the part*_Y___ *of the second part,* ---his-- *executors, administrators, and assigns, to warrant and defend the sale of the said property, goods, and chattels, unto the part*_Y___*of the second part,* ------his----- *executors, administrators, and assigns, against all and every person and persons whomsoever lawfully claiming or to claim the same.*

In Witness Whereof *the part*_ies_ *of the first part ha*_ve_ *executed these presents the* 28th----------------- *day of* August-------------- *one thousand nine hundred and* eighty-two---------------.

_____
President

_____
Secretary Treasurer

Exercise 16

UNARRANGED COPY

Arrange this material attractively. Half sheet. Double spacing. Type in four columns.

MOTION PICTURE ACADEMY AWARDS

1971–1977

Year / Best Actor / Best Actress / Best Picture

1971 / Gene Hackman / Jane Fonda / The French Connection
1972 / Marlon Brando / Liza Minelli / The Godfather
1973 / Jack Lemmon / Glenda Jackson / The Sting
1974 / Art Carney / Ellen Burstyn / The Godfather, Part II
1975 / Jack Nicholson / Louise Fletcher / One Flew Over the Cuckoo's Nest
1976 / Peter Finch / Faye Dunaway / Rocky
1977 / Richard Dreyfuss / Diane Keaton / Annie Hall

Exercise 17

UNARRANGED COPY

Arrange this material attractively. Omit any words in the body which are indicated or implied in the heading.
Full sheet. Spread center the main title.

FINAL EXAM SCHEDULE

Greenwood High Business Department

June, 19—

Subject   Date   Time   Room

The examination in Bookkeeping 2 will be given on June 21 at 9 a.m.
    in Room 415.
The examination in Bookkeeping 1 will be given on June 21 at 9 a.m.
    in Rooms 419, 421.
The examination in Business Mathematics will be given on June 22 at 1 p.m.
    in Rooms 415, 417.
The examination in Business Law will be given on June 22 at 9 a.m.
    in Room 417.
The examination in Secretarial Procedures will be given on June 21 at 9 a.m.
    in Room 416.
The examination in Clerical Practice will be given on June 21 at 1 p.m.
    in Room 416.
The examination in Shorthand 1 will be given on June 22 at 1 p.m.
    in Room 421.
The examination in Typewriting 2 will be given on June 20 at 1 p.m.
    in Rooms 411, 413.

Exercise 18

THE CREATIVE TYPIST

Half sheet. Insert paper into the typewriter with the short (5½-inch) side first.

Type a copy of your current schedule of classes. Include such information as the class names, periods, rooms, and teacher names. Arrange the information attractively on the page.

𝕼𝖚𝖎𝖙𝖈𝖑𝖆𝖎𝖒 𝕯𝖊𝖊𝖉

𝕿𝖍𝖎𝖘 𝕴𝖓𝖉𝖊𝖓𝖙𝖚𝖗𝖊 *made the* 27th——————————— *day of*

August——————— *one thousand nine hundred and* eighty-one————————

𝕭𝖊𝖙𝖜𝖊𝖊𝖓

ELIZABETH ANN KOCSIS

the party____ of the first part,

and

WAYNE ROGER KOCSIS

the party____ of the second part,

𝖂𝖎𝖙𝖓𝖊𝖘𝖘𝖊𝖙𝖍: *That the said party____ of the first part, in consideration of the sum of*

Ten and 00/100 ($10.00)—————————————————— *dollars,*

lawful money of the United States of America, to ————her———— *in hand paid by the*

*party____ of the second part, the receipt whereof is hereby acknowledged, do*es *hereby release*

and forever QUITCLAIM unto the party____ of the second part, and to————his———— *heirs and*

*assigns, all th*at *certain lot* --, *piece* --, *or parcel* X *of land situate in the* City of

Lyndhurst——————————— *County of* Cuyahoga———————————

State of Ohio————————————, *and bounded and described as follows, to-wit:*

known as and being Sublot No. 193 in J. Marucik Co. Sunbay Subdi-
vision No. 1 of part of original Sunview Township Lot No. 9,
Tract 2, and part of original Sunview Township Lot No. 7, Tract
4, as shown by the recorded plat in Volume 36 of Maps, Page 98 of
Cuyahoga County Records, and being 50 feet front on the west side
of Cedar Road, and extending back of equal width 160 feet, as
appears by said plat, but subject to all legal highways.

𝕿𝖔𝖌𝖊𝖙𝖍𝖊𝖗 *with the tenements, hereditaments, and appurtenances thereunto belonging or appertaining, and the reversion and reversions, remainder and remainders, rents, issues, and profits thereof.*

𝕿𝖔 𝕳𝖆𝖛𝖊 𝖆𝖓𝖉 𝖙𝖔 𝕳𝖔𝖑𝖉 *the said premises, together with the appurtenances, unto the party____ of the second part, and to* --his--- *heirs and assigns forever.*

𝕴𝖓 𝖂𝖎𝖙𝖓𝖊𝖘𝖘 𝖂𝖍𝖊𝖗𝖊𝖔𝖋 *the party____ of the first part ha*s *executed this conveyance the day and year first above written.*

Signed and Delivered in the Presence of

_____ } _____

_____   _____

Topic 5 REVIEW OF TABULATIONS

The exercises in this topic emphasize spelling skills. The ability to spell is one of the most frequently requested skills in an employer's search for clerical employees. The increased use of word processing machines (automatic typewriter and transcription machines) demands excellent spelling from those who want to be clerk-typists.

A beautifully typed piece of work which contains even one misspelled word is unacceptable in the business world. Responsibility for the accuracy of the spelling in the final typed copy rests with the typist. The typist is expected to know the correct spelling of all commonly used words or to check the words he or she is unsure of.

The words used in the tabulation exercises in this topic are frequently misspelled in business correspondence. As you type these words, study the rules given and concentrate on learning to spell the particular words in the exercises. Spend extra time reviewing these drills at the beginning of class or at the end when you complete a day's assignment early.

If you will master the spelling of just the 100 words listed in the Master Spelling List that follows, you will be much closer to qualifying for a good job. Make time each week to practice typing some of these words from dictation.

MASTER SPELLING LIST—PART 1

1	absence	26	autumn	51	difference	76	noticeable
2	accept	27	beginning	52	disappoint	77	occasionally
3	accommodate	28	believe	53	discuss	78	occurrence
4	accompany	29	benefited	54	dyeing	79	omitted
5	accomplish	30	breathe	55	effect	80	opportunity
6	accuracy	31	brought	56	efficient	81	personnel
7	achieve	32	business	57	eligible	82	planning
8	acquaint	33	calendar	58	embarrassment	83	possession
9	across	34	cancellation	59	employee	84	precede
10	advantage	35	cannot	60	equipment	85	privilege
11	affect	36	character	61	equipped	86	procedure
12	aisle	37	choose	62	essential	87	receive
13	almost	38	committee	63	exceed	88	recommend
14	already	39	competent	64	existence	89	reference
15	altogether	40	conscious	65	facilities	90	remittance
16	analysis	41	consistent	66	familiarize	91	representative
17	analyze	42	controlled	67	forty	92	separate
18	answer	43	convenience	68	further	93	shipment
19	apologize	44	correspondence	69	genuine	94	similar
20	apparently	45	counselor	70	immediately	95	stenographer
21	appointment	46	criticism	71	incidentally	96	surprise
22	appropriate	47	customer	72	knowledge	97	their
23	arrangement	48	decision	73	loose	98	tomorrow
24	assistance	49	describe	74	maintenance	99	undoubtedly
25	attendance	50	develop	75	necessary	100	volume

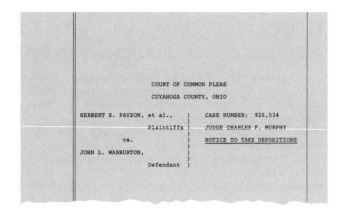

16. Legal documents that are used in court proceedings need formal headings. Although the documents may vary, there are some general rules for typing headings:
    - Center the name of the court 2 inches from the top of the page.
    - Type the names of the parties concerned at the left. The names are typed in solid capitals. The plaintiffs' names always appear first.
    - Type a line of parentheses as far down as the caption reads.
    - Type the case number, the judge's name, and the title of action in capitals at the right.

Look at the illustration of a heading at the left.

BACKING SHEETS

BACKING SHEETS   Sometimes a legal document may be bound in a cover, called a *backing sheet*. The backing sheet is slightly heavier and larger than the paper on which the document is typed. The document is inserted under a 1-inch fold at the top of the backing sheet and stapled.

ENDORSEMENTS   Sometimes information is typed on the backing sheet. This is called an *endorsement*. The information—such as the name of the document, the names of the parties, the date, and the name of the attorney—serves to identify the document.

FOLDING   Most legal papers are filed in the standard way, without being folded. But if a legal paper is to go into a safe-deposit box or a special file, it is folded to fit.

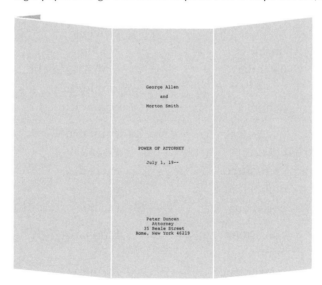

Exercise 1
QUITCLAIM DEED

Type the quitclaim deed shown on the following page. Use a printed legal form. If a form is not available, follow the procedures for typing the document in full given on page 332.

Exercise 2
BILL OF SALE

Type the bill of sale shown on page 335. Use a printed legal form. If a form is not available, prepare the document in fully typed form following the procedures outlined on page 332.

Exercise 1

Half sheet. Single spacing. Spaces between columns are 6, 12, and 6. Center vertically and horizontally.

WORDS FREQUENTLY CONFUSED
Learn to Use These Words Correctly

accept	except	lead	led
access	excess	lose	loose
advise	advice	patience	patients
affect	effect	personal	personnel
angle	angel	principal	principle
assistants	assistance	quiet	quite
choose	chose	recent	resent
council	counsel	stationery	stationary
course	coarse	than	then
dairy	diary	their	there
die	dye	to	too
forth	fourth	whether	weather
its	it's	whose	who's

Exercise 2

Full sheet. Single spacing. DS after each pair of similar words. 10 spaces between columns. Center vertically and horizontally.

COMMONLY MISSPELLED WORDS
List No. 1

Words	*Definitions*
accept	to receive
except	to exclude
advice	words of wisdom
advise	to give advice
assistants	those who give help
assistance	help
cite	to quote or refer to
sight	to see
site	a location
coarse	rough texture; not fine
course	direction of movement
choose	to select (present tense)
chose	past tense of *choose*
compliment	to praise
complement	to complete
council	an assembly to govern or advise
counsel	to advise; a lawyer
forth	forward; onward
fourth	*4th* spelled out

LEGAL DOCUMENTS TYPED IN FULL

Legal documents may also be typed in full, without the use of a printed form. When you type such a document, you must follow certain rules. Here are some general guidelines for typing legal documents in full:

1. Use legal paper that is 8½″ × 11″ or 8½″ × 13″. (Most courts require 8½″ × 11″ paper.) Legal paper has a double line at the left providing a 1½-inch margin, and a single line at the right providing a ½-inch margin.
2. Use pica type. For most legal documents, elite type is not acceptable.
3. Center headings between the vertical lines at the margins. To find the center, add the two numbers on your scale that fall on the vertical lines and divide by two.
4. Indent paragraphs 10 spaces.
5. Use double spacing, except for quotations, which are single spaced.
6. Triple-space after centered headings and titles.
7. Leave 2 inches for a top margin on the first page and 1½ inches on other pages. Leave at least 1 inch for the bottom margin.
8. Leave 1 or 2 spaces between the typing and the ruled lines along the margins. If you do not have ruled paper, leave a 1½-inch left margin and a 1-inch right margin.
9. Center the page numbers between the ruled margins and type them ½ inch from the bottom edge of the paper. Do not number the first page.
10. Do not erase important data, such as dates, figures and names. Unavoidable additions (written between lines) should be initialed by the signers of the document.
11. Express numbers in figures. However, important numbers, such as prices and measurements, should be spelled out, followed by numerals in parentheses.
12. It is customary to use solid capitals for certain expressions that appear at the beginnings of paragraphs. Some examples are: WHEREAS, IN WITNESS WHEREOF.
13. Spell names exactly.
14. Include dates either at the beginning or at the end of the document.
15. Make signature lines about 3 inches long and triple-space before and after each line. Signatures must never appear by themselves on the last page. At least 3 lines of text should appear above the signatures.

Exercise 3

Half sheet. Single spacing. DS after each pair of similar words. Spaces between columns are 4, 8, and 4. Center vertically and horizontally.

COMMONLY MISSPELLED WORDS
List No. 2

hear	to listen	principal	chief; school official
here	this place	principle	rule; general truth
know	to be familiar with	quiet	not noisy
no	opposite of *yes*	quite	completely
loose	not tight	their	belongs to them
lose	to mislay	there	that place
lead	heavy metal	too	in excess; or also
led	past tense of *to lead*	to	in the direction
passed	to go by	than	a comparison
past	a former time; beyond	then	at that time
personal	private	weather	the atmospheric state
personnel	employees	whether	alternative

Exercise 4

Half sheet. Single spacing. 6 spaces between columns. Center vertically and horizontally.

SIMILAR-SOUNDING TRIOS

to	too	two
quiet	quite	quit
cite	sight	site
counsel	council	consul
adapt	adept	adopt
holy	wholly	holey
clothes	cloths	close
martial	marshal	marital
loose	lose	loss
sent	scent	cent
rain	rein	reign
vain	vein	vane

Exercise 5

WORD-BUILDING PRACTICE

After typing this exercise as a tabulation, type the words in the last column from teacher dictation.

Half sheet. Single spacing. 4 spaces between columns. Center vertically and horizontally.

ANALYZING WORDS BY SYLLABLES
Five-Syllable Words

oc	occa	occasion	occasional	occasionally
rep	repre	represen	representa	representative
in	inci	inciden	incidental	incidentally
un	unnec	unneces	unnecessar	unnecessary
pro	pronun	pronunci	pronuncia	pronunciation
su	super	superin	superinten	superintendent

Topic 3 LEGAL DOCUMENTS

A typist in a law office must be familiar with certain typing practices unique to legal work. A typist in a business office also must occasionally type legal matter. You should, therefore, have a general working knowledge of the most common legal forms.

PRINTED LEGAL DOCUMENTS

Printed forms are available for many legal instruments. Here are some general guidelines for typing on printed legal documents:

1. Type insertions so that they align with the printed words on the line that you are filling in. To do this, use the variable line spacer or the automatic line finder.
2. Use hyphens to fill empty space that remains on either side of the item you type. This prevents alterations that might change the meaning of the document.

3. Leave 1 space between the inserted word and the printed word that comes before it.

4. Line up left and right margins with those on the form.

5. Draw a "Z" rule to fill in large blank spaces.

6. Leave no space after incomplete words that you, as the typist, are to complete. Type the fill-in letters close to the printed letter.

Top edges even   Insert into fold

7. Make the top edges of the original and carbon copies exactly even. In that way, the typing on the copies will appear on exactly the same lines as the printing. Cover the tops of the original and carbon copies with a folded strip of paper or an envelope. Then insert them into the typewriter. This will keep the papers even.

Exercise 6

WORD-BUILDING
PRACTICE

*Full sheet. Double spacing.
Decide on the spacing
between columns. Center
vertically and horizontally.*

ANALYZING WORDS BY SYLLABLES
Four-Syllable Words

ac	accu	accura	accuracy
ap	appre	appreci	appreciate
grad	gradu	gradua	graduation
ac	accom	accommo	accommodate
ex	expe	experi	experience
im	imme	immedi	immediate
un	undoubt	undoubted	undoubtedly
can	cancel	cancella	cancellation
fa	famil	familiar	familiarize
ac	acknowl	acknowledg	acknowledgment
ben	bene	benefit	benefited

Exercise 7

WORD-BUILDING
PRACTICE

*Full sheet. Double spacing.
Decide on the spacing
between columns. Center
vertically and horizontally.*

ANALYZING WORDS BY SYLLABLES
Three-Syllable Words

crit	criti	criticism
main	mainte	maintenance
sep	sepa	separate
sim	simi	similar
per	person	personnel
cus	custom	customer
dif	differ	difference
an	ana	analyze
com	commit	committee
dis	disap	disappoint
de	deci	decision
de	devel	develop
ex	exis	existence
ex	excel	excellent
de	descrip	description
con	conve	convenient

Exercise 8

Can you find the silent
letters in these words?

*Half sheet. Double spacing.
Decide on the spacing
between columns. Center
vertically and horizontally.*

TRICKY SILENT-LETTER WORDS

know	handkerchief	campaign	mortgage
anxious	often	answer	island
whole	sword	guarantee	autumn
straight	minute	column	listen
ready	debt	doubt	rhythm

Exercise 12
EXPENSE REPORT

NAME: James Cutre   WEEK ENDING: June 22, 19—

DATE	CITY AND STATE	LODGING	AIR	MEALS	ENTER-TAINMENT	MISC. EXPENSES	DAILY TOTAL
6/18	Grand Rapids, MI	48.70	68.42	60.00	15.40	6.00	198.52
TOTALS		48.70	68.42	60.00	15.40	6.00	198.52

ENTERTAINMENT EXPENSES:

DATE	ITEM	AMOUNT
6/18	Luncheon for Paula Briggs, President of U-STOR, Inc.	15.40
TOTAL		15.40

MISCELLANEOUS EXPENSES:

DATE	ITEM	AMOUNT
6/19	Registration fee for convention	6.00
TOTAL		6.00

EXPENSE SUMMARY:

TOTAL: 198.52   AMOUNT DUE EMPLOYEE: None

LESS ADVANCES: 225.00   AMOUNT DUE COMPANY: 26.48

Exercise 13
EXPENSE REPORT

NAME: Carol Barbour   WEEK ENDING: August 7, 19—

DATE	CITY AND STATE	LODGING	AUTO EXPENSE	MEALS	MISC. EXPENSES	DAILY TOTAL
8/1	St. Louis, MO	28.50	54.00	29.75	3.65	115.90
8/2	Topeka, KS	25.00	58.50	27.50		111.00
8/3	Kansas City, KS	27.25	15.80	24.20		67.25
8/4	Augusta, KS	22.40	12.65	18.90	5.22	59.17
8/5	Springfield, MO	25.00	18.40	20.55		63.95
TOTALS		128.15	159.35	120.90	8.87	417.27

MISCELLANEOUS EXPENSES:

DATE	ITEM	AMOUNT
8/1	Parking	3.65
8/4	Telephone Calls	5.22
TOTAL		8.87

EXPENSE SUMMARY:

TOTAL 417.27   AMOUNT DUE EMPLOYEE: 417.27

LESS ADVANCES: None   AMOUNT DUE COMPANY: None

Exercise 9

Be careful not to slur the vowels in these words.
Half sheet. Double spacing. Decide on the spacing between columns. Center vertically and horizontally.

WORDS THAT ARE OFTEN MISPRONOUNCED

arithmetic	probably	government	jewelry
separate	strength	athletic	family
across	library	length	empty
secretary	nuclear	generally	interest
quantity	treasurer	February	Wednesday

Exercise 10

Some word endings have a very similar sound. Take careful notice of the words listed at the right.
Arrange this material attractively on a full sheet.

WATCH OUT FOR THOSE WORD ENDINGS!

or	*er*	*ar*
administrator	messenger	grammar
ancestor	eraser	liar
doctor	consumer	scholar
visitor	employer	regular
distributor	subscriber	extracurricular
professor	manufacturer	calendar
collector	customer	collar
creator	receiver	peculiar

Exercise 11

Center attractively on a half sheet.

"UHBLE" ENDINGS

able	ible
changeable	invisible
agreeable	admissible
noticeable	terrible
unbelievable	responsible
usable	impossible
advisable	legible
comfortable	permissible
desirable	corruptible
probable	audible

Exercise 12

Learning one word ending can help you remember a similar one.
Center attractively on a half sheet. Don't forget to make a distinction in the spaces between the columns.

ANT/ANCE VERSUS ENT/ENCE

ant	*ance*	*ent*	*ence*
assistant	assistance	resident	residence
attendant	attendance	dependent	dependence
resistant	resistance	superintendent	superintendence
fragrant	fragrance	confident	confidence
reliant	reliance	correspondent	correspondence
radiant	radiance	prominent	prominence

EXPENSE REPORTS

Type each exercise following the style shown in Model 31. If forms are not available, prepare expense report forms similar to the one shown below.

Exercise 10
EXPENSE REPORT

Type an expense report using the information in Model 31.

Exercise 11
EXPENSE REPORT

Prepare an expense report using the information at the right. Then complete the expense summary, assuming no advances to the employee.

NAME: **Marilyn Franklin** WEEK ENDING: **June 8, 19—**

DATE	CITY AND STATE	LODGING	AUTO EXPENSES	MEALS	DAILY TOTAL
6/5	Duluth, MN	33.60	22.50	14.90	71.00
6/6	Duluth, MN	———	37.00	8.12	45.12
TOTALS		33.60	59.50	23.02	116.12

CORONA INDUSTRIES INCORPORATED

711 CHERRY STREET • ST. PAUL MN 55121
(218) 792-8450

EXPENSE REPORT

NAME ___Thomas Kessler___   WEEK ENDING ___May 13___   19--

Date 19--	City and State	Lodging	Transportation Air, Rail, etc.	Car Rental, Limo., Cab	Auto Expenses	Meals	Entertainment (See Detail)	Misc. Expenses (See Detail)	Daily Total
5/8	Chicago, IL	36 00	75 50	6 00		19 42		4 50	141 42
5/11	Baltimore, MD	64 65	92 70	11 40		36 50		15 00	220 25
TOTALS		100 65	168 20	17 40		55 92		19 50	361 67

NOTE: Attach all receipts.

ENTERTAINMENT EXPENSE DETAIL		
Date	Name/Place	Amount
TOTAL		

MISCELLANEOUS EXPENSE DETAIL		
Date	Item	Amount
5/8	Telephone call to home office	4 50
5/11	Laundry	15 00
TOTAL		19 50

EXPENSE SUMMARY		
TOTAL	361	67
LESS ADVANCES	325	00
AMOUNT DUE EMPLOYEE	36	67
AMOUNT DUE COMPANY	None	

Signature _____ _Date_ _____ _Department Head Approval_ _____ _Date_ _____

Model 31 *Expense Report*

REMEMBER "US" ENDINGS

<u>ious</u>	<u>eous</u>
cautious	courteous
curious	hideous
delicious	gorgeous
conscious	miscellaneous
gracious	simultaneous
religious	instantaneous

Exercise 16
There are only a few words with the "seed" ending.
Half sheet. Insert paper with the short side first.

STUDY LIST OF "SEED" ENDINGS

<u>sede</u>	<u>ceed</u>	<u>cede</u>
supersede	proceed	precede
	exceed	secede
	succeed	concede
		recede
		accede
		intercede

Exercise 14
Recognizing similar prefixes will improve your spelling.
Half sheet. Insert paper with the short side first.

STUDYING PREFIXES
For and Fore

<u>for</u>	<u>fore</u>
forget	foretold
forgive	forehead
forfeit	foreword
forbear	foreclosure
forward	forecast
forbid	forewarned

THE "EYES" ENDINGS

ise	*ize*	*yze*
advertise	criticize	analyze
supervise	apologize	paralyze
merchandise	familiarize	
surprise	equalize	
surmise	characterize	
devise	authorize	
advise	standardize	
revise	realize	

Exercise 15
These words have troublesome double letters.
Arrange attractively on a full sheet. Spread center title.

DOUBLE TROUBLE

collection	embarrassed	equipped	necessary
occurring	accommodate	address	misspell
across	accuracy	fulfill	appointment
recommend	cancellation	personnel	possess
questionnaire	omission	guarantee	business
immediate	accompany	cooperation	committee
especially	bookkeeper	remittance	apparent
acceptance	occupation	excellent	assistance

VOUCHER CHECKS

These voucher checks come from Glenwild Realty Corporation, Great Neck, NY 11023. Type each exercise following the style shown in Model 30. If forms are not available, prepare voucher checks similar to the one shown below.

Exercise 6
VOUCHER CHECK

Type a voucher check using the information in Model 30.

Supply an address from your own city or town for the payee of each check.

	VOUCHER CHECK NO.	DATE	PAYEE	DATE OF INVOICE	INVOICE NO.	AMOUNT
Exercise 7	0181	October 31	Best Landscaping	9/29/—	8942	512.92
Exercise 8	0183	November 3	Russo Bros.	9/2/—	7360	1469.40
Exercise 9	0195	November 19	Mays, Inc.	10/1/—	5289	367.85

GLENWILD REALTY CORPORATION
GREAT NECK NEW YORK 11023

No. 0179

1-7130
2260

October 27,   19 --

Pay to the Order of Shapiro & Associates, Inc. $687.12

Six Hundred Eighty-seven and 12/100--- *Dollars*

SCIOTO NATIONAL BANK
GREAT NECK, NEW YORK 11027

_____
TREASURER

⑊226071308⑊ 4038727⑊

DETACH THIS STUB BEFORE CASHING

No. 0179

TO

Shapiro & Associates, Inc.
781 Henry Street
New York, NY 10042

For payment of the invoice noted below:

Date	Invoice	Amount
8/15/--	6491	687.12

GLENWILD REALTY
CORPORATION
GREAT NECK, NEW YORK 11023

Model 30   Voucher Check

Exercise 18

Arrange attractively on a half sheet.

The Rule

I before e except after c or when sounded like a as in neighbor and weigh.

THE "IE/EI" COMBINATION

IE	EI	EXCEPTIONS
interview	ceiling	neither
believe	receipt	counterfeit
achieve	receive	foreign
fierce	sleigh	seize
niece	neighbor	height
convenient	weight	leisure
grievance	their	ancient
piece	freight	weird
achievement	eight	efficient
brief	vein	sleight

Exercise 19

Arrange attractively on a full sheet.

The Rules

1. Words ending in a silent e usually drop the e before a suffix beginning with a vowel.
2. Words ending with a silent e usually keep the e before a suffix beginning with a consonant.

THE SILENT FINAL "E"

To Drop or to Keep?

Rule 1	Rule 2	Exceptions
using	hopeful	acknowledgment
desirable	announcement	judgment
noticing	arrangement	noticeable
changing	immediately	changeable
encouraging	statement	manageable
writing	comeback	dyeing
coming	movement	mileage
advertising	carefully	ninth
typing	falsehood	wholly
closing	likeness	truly
deciding	management	argument

Exercise 20

Arrange attractively on a half sheet.

The Rules

1. Words ending in y preceded by a consonant usually change the y to i before any suffix except one beginning with an i.
2. Words ending in y preceded by a vowel usually retain the y before all endings.

CHANGING FINAL "Y" TO "I"

Rule 1	Rule 2	Exceptions
ordinarily	annoyance	paid
easily	attorneys	laid
heaviest	enjoyable	daily
cities	delaying	said
beautiful	buyer	ladylike
supplying	employer	shyness

3. Place the amount in Arabic numerals close to the dollar sign, leaving no space.
4. Make no erasures or alterations.

Here are some guidelines for typing expense reports: (Refer to Model 31, page 329.)

1. Use the variable line spacer to adjust the cylinder. The preprinted rule should be very slightly below the top edge of the aligning scale.
2. Type the dollar amount close to the vertical line at the right. Space once before you type the cents. Do not type the decimal point.
3. You may need to turn the cylinder by hand when typing on several printed rules. To do this, disengage the line spacing mechanism by using the automatic line finder

RECEIPTS

The following receipts come from the Glenwild Realty Corporation, Great Neck, New York 11023. Type each exercise following the style shown in Model 29. If forms are not available, prepare receipts similar to the one shown in Model 29.

Exercise 1
RECEIPT

Type a receipt using the information in Model 29.

	RECEIPT NO.	DATE	RECEIVED FROM	AMOUNT	PURPOSE
Exercise 2	196	July 2	Kollner & Budd	$450.00	Rent from 7/1 to 7/31
Exercise 3	274	Sept. 1	Frank Mancuso	$ 55.00	Office cleaning
Exercise 4	292	Oct. 15	Alice Kukar	$125.00	Typing services
Exercise 5	293	Oct. 16	C. J. Kolezynski	$376.50	2000 brochures

No. 148

GLENWILD REALTY
CORPORATION
GREAT NECK NEW YORK 11023

April 1, 19--

Received from Mayflower Dress Shop

One Hundred Eighty-five and 00/100--------------------- *Dollars*

Rent of store at 206 Main Street, from 4/1 to 4/30

GLENWILD REALTY
CORPORATION

$ 185.00

By _____

AGENT

Model 29   *Receipt*

Exercise 21

Arrange attractively on a full sheet.

The Rules

1. If a one-syllable word ends with a consonant preceded by a vowel, *double* the final consonant before adding a suffix beginning with a vowel.
2. If a two-syllable word, accented on the last syllable, ends with a consonant preceded by a vowel, *double* the final consonant.
3. If a two-syllable word, accented on the first syllable, ends with a consonant preceded by a vowel, *do not* double the final consonant.
4. If a word ends with two consonants, keep both consonants when adding a suffix.

DOUBLING THE FINAL CONSONANT

Examples of the Rules

Rule 1	Rule 2	Rule 3	Rule 4	Exceptions
stopping	beginning	labeled	dismissing	questionnaire
shipping	occurred	traveling	skillful	cancellation
planning	controlling	canceled	installment	transferable
baggage	regretted	profited	addressing	gaseous
putting	equipped	credited	embarrassment	reference
digging	referred	counseling	fulfillment	programming
manned	enrolled	editing	possessing	buses
ripped	forgetting	legalize	stiffness	conferee
running	remittance	marketing	blissful	kidnapped
fitting	recurring	budgeted	passable	boxing

Exercise 22

Supply the correct *ie* or *ei* combination as you type the words in this exercise. Check your work against the answers provided on page 149. Do not write in the book.
Half sheet. Double spacing. 8 spaces between columns. Center vertically and horizontally.

APPLYING THE "IE/EI" RULE

ch■■f	n■■ther	l■■sure
rec■■ve	th■■r	effic■■nt
ach■■vement	bel■■ve	for■■gn
w■■rd	p■■ce	conven■■nt
■■ght	h■■ght	rec■■pt
n■■ghbor	n■■ce	interv■■w

Exercise 23

Supply the proper word endings as you type this table. Check your work against the answers provided (refer to page 149.) Do not write in the book.
Half sheet. Single spacing. 6 spaces between columns. Center vertically and horizontally.

WORD ENDING REVIEW

List No. 1

"eyes"	"seed"	"uhble"
advert■■■	pro■■■■	terr■■■■
surpr■■■	con■■■■	imposs■■■■
critic■■■	re■■■■	justifi■■■■
anal■■■	suc■■■■	respons■■■■
real■■■	super■■■■	leg■■■■
familiar■■■	ex■■■■	dur■■■■
merchand■■■	pre■■■■	notice■■■■

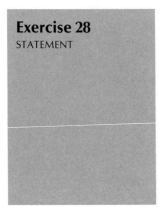

Exercise 28
STATEMENT

IN ACCOUNT WITH: **Batista Bookshop,**
Tribune Square, Lansing, MI 48911

DATE: **Jan. 30, 19—**

DATE	REFERENCE	CHARGES	CREDITS	BALANCE
Jan. 1	Balance			114.50
4	Invoice #5103	769.50		884.00
7	Invoice #5111	122.00		1006.00
9	Invoice #5120	205.00		1211.00
17	Payment		1000.00	211.00
22	Credit memo #682		70.50	140.50

Topic 2 RECEIPTS, VOUCHER CHECKS, AND EXPENSE REPORTS

RECEIPT After making a payment, an individual or company may be given a receipt. This acknowledges that the money has been received. This form usually contains such information as:

- Date and an identifying number
- Individual or company who paid the money
- Amount of money involved
- Reason for payment

VOUCHER CHECK A voucher check is used by businesses to pay for merchandise and services. This form usually contains such information as:

- Date and an identifying number
- Individual or company to whom the money was paid
- Amount of money involved
- Reason for payment

EXPENSE REPORT An expense report is an itemized account of the expenditures made by an employee in the course of employment. It is prepared after a business trip, or routinely, every week. This form usually contains such information as:

- Dates the expenses were incurred
- Lists of such items as lodging, transportation, meals, entertainment, and miscellaneous items, with amounts spent on each
- Place of departure and destination

Some forms may have space for additional information, such as the purpose of the trip, number of days away, and detailed explanations of certain expenses.

Here are some general guidelines for typing receipts and voucher checks: (Refer to Models 29 and 30, pages 327 and 328.)

1. Use the variable line spacer and the aligning scale to find the writing line. A small amount of space or "daylight" should appear between the typed material and the printed rules. To review how to type on ruled lines, see page 93.
2. Begin typing the amount of money in words at the extreme left. Fill in any space between the amount and the printed word *Dollars* with a row of hyphens.

Exercise 24

Supply the proper word endings as you type this table. (For answers, refer to page 149.)

Half sheet. Single spacing. 6 spaces between columns. Center vertically and horizontally.

WORD ENDING REVIEW

List No. 2

ance/ence	ious/eous	or/er/ar
attend■■■■	grac■■■■	gramm■■
depend■■■■	hid■■■■	calend■■
remitt■■■■	court■■■■	regul■■
superintend■■■■	delic■■■■	doct■■
exist■■■■	miscellan■■■■	administrat■■■
accord■■■■	consc■■■■	custom■■
correspond■■■■	relig■■■■	visit■■
fragr■■■■	cur■■■■	schol■■
confid■■■■	simultan■■■■	creat■■
radi■■■■	caut■■■■	messeng■■
resid■■■■	instantan■■■■	ancest■■
resist■■■■	gorg■■■■	coll■■

Exercise 25

As you type this table (both columns), read the definitions in the first column and supply the missing letters in the second column. Check your work against the answers provided (refer to page 149). Do not write in the book.

Center attractively on a half sheet inserted with the short (5½-inch side) first.

HOW DO YOU SPELL THAT WORD?

Definition	Word
unchangeable	p■■man■nt
means of support	main■■■ance
words of wisdom	advi■e
definitely	specifi■■ly
act of comparing	comp■■son
second month	Feb■■ary
nonpresence	ab■■■ce
help	assist■■■■
ownership	po■■e■■ion
thankful	gr■■■ful
alike	sim■l■r
without a doubt	undo■■■edly
chief; school official	princip■■
study carefully	anal■■■
lawyer	coun■■l
rough in texture	c■■rse

Exercise 24
STATEMENT

IN ACCOUNT WITH: The Place Furniture Company, Northfield Plaza, Knoxville, TN 37906

DATE: July 31, 19—

DATE	REFERENCE	CHARGES	CREDITS	BALANCE
July 1	Balance			26.40
16	Payment		26.40	00.00
18	Invoice #4690	886.00		886.00
20	Credit memo #461		30.00	856.00

Exercise 25
STATEMENT

IN ACCOUNT WITH: The Neighborhood Store, 56 Lucas Avenue, Cranston, RI 02910

DATE: July 31, 19—

DATE	REFERENCE	CHARGES	CREDITS	BALANCE
July 1	Balance			188.25
8	Payment		100.00	88.25
9	Invoice #4674	76.00		164.25
16	Invoice #4687	419.75		584.00
29	Credit memo #463		35.00	549.00

Exercise 26
STATEMENT

IN ACCOUNT WITH: Garrett Office Equipment Co., 800 King Street, Garrett, IN 46738

DATE: Aug. 28, 19—

DATE	REFERENCE	CHARGES	CREDITS	BALANCE
Aug. 1	Balance			2569.42
4	Invoice #4699	3055.00		5624.42
7	Payment		5000.00	624.42
13	Credit memo #464		122.20	502.22
18	Invoice #4723	1945.56		2447.78
23	Payment		2300.00	147.78

Exercise 27
STATEMENT

IN ACCOUNT WITH: Glenmore Arms, 406 Adams Street, Minneapolis, MN 55408

DATE: Sept. 29, 19—

DATE	REFERENCE	CHARGES	CREDITS	BALANCE
Sept. 1	Balance			50.98
5	Invoice #4701	203.00		253.98
15	Payment		200.00	53.98
22	Invoice #4786	462.53		516.51
28	Payment		500.00	16.51

Exercise 26

Concentrate on spelling as you type this table. Three different words appear on each line. One of the three words in each line is misspelled. Correct and underscore the misspelled word as you type each line. Do not type the numbers. (For answers, refer to page 149).

Full sheet. Double spacing. 10 spaces between columns. Center vertically and horizontally.

1	seperate	performance	development
2	writting	proceed	familiar
3	priviledge	unnecessary	government
4	loose	prosedure	possession
5	answer	maintainence	reference
6	questionaire	undoubtedly	convenience
7	specifically	shiping	description
8	confident	opportunity	greatful
9	grammar	necessary	secetary
10	ommission	criticism	practically
11	personnel	ocassionally	forty
12	governor	responsable	across
13	cancelled	disappoint	difference
14	Wednesday	strickly	extraordinary
15	Febuary	conscientious	assistance
16	beginning	similiar	omitted
17	judgement	representative	bankruptcy
18	experience	beneficial	imediately
19	prominant	existence	merchandise
20	probably	liesure	quantity
21	incidentally	library	surprize
22	apparent	gracous	analysis
23	mortgage	paralyze	athletic
24	rhythm	niece	forcast

CORONA INDUSTRIES INCORPORATED

711 CHERRY STREET • ST. PAUL, MN 55121
(218) 792-8450

DATE: June 30, 19--

STATEMENT

IN
ACCOUNT
WITH

Martin L. King High School
3842 Peachtree Street
Augusta, GA 30903

AMOUNT ENCLOSED

$ _____

PLEASE RETURN THIS STUB WITH YOUR PAYMENT

DATE	REFERENCE	CHARGES	CREDITS	BALANCE
June 1	Balance			500.42
5	Invoice #4583	175.89		676.31
11	Invoice #4589	342.50		1018.81
15	Payment		1000.00	18.81
20	Invoice #4594	2577.10		2595.91
25	Credit memo #439		125.75	2470.16
28	Payment		2300.00	170.16

PLEASE NOTIFY US PROMPTLY IF THIS STATEMENT DOES NOT AGREE WITH YOUR RECORDS

PLEASE PAY
LAST AMOUNT
IN THIS COLUMN

Model 28

Statement of Account

Exercise 23
STATEMENT

IN ACCOUNT WITH: Mrs. Susanne McGregor, DATE: Mar. 31, 19—
282 Ball Street, Fergus Falls, MN 56537

DATE	REFERENCE	CHARGES	CREDITS	BALANCE
March 1	Balance			25.80
10	Invoice #5205	125.32		151.12
26	Invoice #5221	43.21		194.33

Exercise 27

WORD DIVISION REVIEW

Refer to the word division rules (pages 53–54) before completing the next two exercises. As you type this table, complete columns 2 and 4. Insert a hyphen to show the first acceptable division point after the colored mark. Type the word without a hyphen if there is no acceptable division point after the mark. (For answers, refer to page 149.)

Full sheet. Double spacing. Follow the spacing shown in the planning diagram below this exercise. Center vertically and horizontally.

WORD DIVISION EXERCISE 1

Col. 1	Col.2	Col. 3	Col. 4
abs/ence		coul/dn't	
a/ccept		$31 .5/5	
acce/ptance		se/lf-interest	
accid/entally		begi/nning	
acc/ommodate		bu/siness	
accord/ance		canc/ellation	
ac/curacy		for/ty	
achie/vement		immed/iately	
ackno/wledgment		lo/ose	
ac/ross		t/he	
af/fect		occu/rrence	
Pete/rson		noti/ceable	
stra/ight		ge/ography	
co/ward		mea/sure	
a/wkward		repre/sentative	

14	3	15	6	14	3	15

Exercise 28

As you type this table, complete columns 2 and 4. Use a hyphen to show an acceptable division point after the colored mark in each word. (For answers, refer to page 149.)

Half sheet. Double spacing. Follow the spacing shown in the planning diagram below this exercise. Center vertically.

WORD DIVISION EXERCISE 2

Col. 1	Col. 2	Col. 3	Col. 4
expres/sed		descr/iption	
veri/fy		ali/gned	
th/eir		wal/ked	
su/rprise		pro/blems	
si/milar		si/tuation	
pla/nning		conve/nient	
ext/ension		addre/ssing	
buz/zard		pho/tographic	
cre/ative		pro/bable	
bea/utiful		suspi/cious	
U./S.A.		ra/dio	
all—a/round		lod/ging	
ad/ditional		fli/ghty	

10	6	11	10	12	6	13

Exercise 19
CREDIT MEMORANDUM

CREDIT TO: The Neighborhood Store,
56 Lucas Avenue, Cranston, RI 02910
NO.: 463

DATE: July 29, 19—
SOLD ON INVOICE NO.: 4687
YOUR ORDER NO.: 63421

QUANTITY	DESCRIPTION	UNIT PRICE	AMOUNT
1	Electric toaster, 4-slice	35.00	35.00

REASON FOR CREDIT: Short shipment on our Invoice No. 4687.

Exercise 20
CREDIT MEMORANDUM

CREDIT TO: Garrett Office Equipment Co.,
800 King Street, Garrett, IN 46738
NO.: 464

DATE: August 13, 19—
SOLD ON INVOICE NO.: 4699
YOUR ORDER NO.: 4228

QUANTITY	DESCRIPTION	UNIT PRICE	AMOUNT
			61.10

REASON FOR CREDIT: Wrong discount on our Invoice No. 4699.
Terms should read 4/10, n/60.

Exercise 21
CREDIT MEMORANDUM

CREDIT TO: Batista Bookshop,
Tribune Square, Lansing, MI 48911
NO.: 682

DATE: January 22, 19—
SOLD ON INVOICE NO.: 5103
YOUR ORDER NO.: 483910

QUANTITY	DESCRIPTION	UNIT PRICE	AMOUNT
1	Portable bookcase, #40	70.50	70.50

REASON FOR CREDIT: Returned—wrong color.

STATEMENTS

The following statements come from Corona Industries Inc., 711 Cherry Street, St. Paul, MN 55121. Type each exercise following the style shown in Model 28 (page 324). If forms are not available, prepare statements similar to the one shown in Model 28.

Exercise 22
STATEMENT

Type a statement of account for Martin L. King High School, as shown in Model 28 on the following page.

KEY TO EXERCISES 22–28

Exercise 22

chief	neither	leisure
receive	their	efficient
achievement	believe	foreign
weird	piece	convenient
eight	height	receipt
neighbor	niece	interview

Exercise 23

advertise	proceed	terrible
surprise	concede	impossible
criticize	recede	usable
analyze	succeed	responsible
realize	supersede	legible
familiarize	exceed	durable
merchandise	precede	noticeable

Exercise 24

attendance	gracious	grammar
dependence	hideous	calendar
remittance	courteous	regular
superintendence	delicious	doctor
existence	miscellaneous	administrator
accordance	conscious	customer
correspondence	religious	visitor
fragrance	curious	scholar
confidence	simultaneous	creator
radiance	cautious	messenger
residence	instantaneous	ancestor
resistance	gorgeous	collar

Exercise 25

permanent	possession
maintenance	grateful
advice	similar
specifically	undoubtedly
comparison	principal
February	analyze
absence	counsel
assistance	coarse

Exercise 26

1 separate	9 secretary	17 judgment
2 writing	10 omission	18 immediately
3 privilege	11 occasionally	19 prominent
4 procedure	12 responsible	20 leisure
5 maintenance	13 canceled	21 surprise
6 questionnaire	14 strictly	22 gracious
7 shipping	15 February	23 paralyze
8 grateful	16 similar	24 forecast

Exercise 27

Col. 2	Col. 4
absence	couldn't
accept	$31.55
accep-tance	self-interest
acciden-tally	begin-ning
accom-modate	busi-ness
accordance	cancel-lation
accu-racy	forty
achieve-ment	immedi-ately
acknowl-edgment	loose
across	the
affect	occur-rence
Peterson	notice-able
straight	geog-raphy
cow-ard	measure
awk-ward	represen-tative

Exercise 28

Col. 2	Col. 4
expressed	descrip-tion
verify	aligned
their	walked
sur-prise	prob-lems
simi-lar	situ-ation
plan-ning	conve-nient
exten-sion	address-ing
buzzard	photo-graphic
crea-tive	prob-able
beau-tiful	suspicious
U.S.A.	radio
all-around	lodg-ing
addi-tional	flighty

CREDIT MEMORANDUM

CORONA INDUSTRIES INCORPORATED
711 CHERRY STREET • ST. PAUL MN 55121
(218) 792-8450

NO. 439

DATE   June 25, 19--

CREDIT TO

Martin L. King High School
3842 Peachtree Street
Augusta, GA 30903

SOLD ON INVOICE NO.   4594

YOUR ORDER NO.   98102

WE HAVE CREDITED YOUR ACCOUNT AS FOLLOWS:

QUANTITY	DESCRIPTION	UNIT PRICE	AMOUNT
1	File cabinet, 4-drawer, letter-size, Model 415	125.75	125.75

REASON FOR CREDIT: Returned--damaged in shipment.

AUTHORIZED BY _____

Model 27   *Credit Memorandum*

CREDIT MEMORANDUMS

These credit memos come from Corona Industries Inc., 711 Cherry Street, St. Paul, MN 55121. Type each exercise following the style shown in Model 27. If forms are not available, prepare credit memos similar to the one shown above.

Exercise 17
CREDIT MEMORANDUM

Type a credit memo to Martin L. King High School for a file cabinet that was returned to Corona Industries. Use the information shown in Model 27 above.

Exercise 18
CREDIT MEMORANDUM

CREDIT TO: The Place Furniture Company, Northfield Plaza, Knoxville, TN 37906

NO.: 461

DATE: July 20, 19—

SOLD ON INVOICE NO.: 4690

YOUR ORDER NO.: 63413

QUANTITY	DESCRIPTION	UNIT PRICE	AMOUNT
6	Table, Model 601 MT20, 60″ × 30″ (Credit of 5.00 per item)		30.00

REASON FOR CREDIT: Erroneous quotation of 65.00 per item on our Invoice No. 4690; price should have been 60.00 ea.

PART 5

OUTLINES, REPORTS, AND MANUSCRIPTS

This part will teach you the basic skills and rules involved in typing outlines, reports, and manuscripts. There is a natural progression from one to the other of these three topics. A topical outline expresses the "skeleton" of ideas and sequence of a report or speech. Reports and themes follow certain forms to make them attractive and easy to read. Manuscripts are typed in generally the same manner as reports, with a few important differences.

Topic 1 TOPICAL OUTLINES

A *topical outline* is a series of main topics and subtopics that form the framework for a speech or report. An outline guides a writer or speaker in presenting the information in an orderly and logical way. It may also aid the reader or listener in reviewing and remembering the outstanding points of a report or lecture.

The outline must be well arranged and its parts clearly identified. Keep in mind the following rules when you type an outline.

1. Center the outline vertically and horizontally. Center the title of the outline and type it in solid capitals.
2. Use single spacing, but double-space immediately before and after a topic identified by a Roman numeral. A short outline may be double-spaced.
3. Use a combination of Roman numerals, Arabic numerals, and letters of the alphabet to identify different levels of topics. You may use six levels. In order of highest to lowest they are: I.
   A.
   1.
   a.
   (1)
   (a)
4. Put a period and 2 spaces after each numeral or letter, except those in parentheses. After a numeral or letter in parentheses, use no punctuation and leave only 1 space.
5. Indent each level of a new topic so that it aligns with the first word of the topic that precedes it. An a-level topic, for example, will align with the first word of a 1-level topic. Set tabs at the places where each new level of topics begins.

Exercise 14
INVOICE

SOLD TO: Garrett Office Equipment Co.
800 King Street
Garrett, IN 46738
INVOICE NO.: 4699

DATE: August 4, 19—
YOUR ORDER NO.: 4228
TERMS: 2/10, n/30
SHIPPED VIA: Amtrak

QUANTITY	DESCRIPTION	UNIT PRICE	AMOUNT
20	Book truck, Model WEP-20	41.25	825.00
40	Chair, with casters, Model 1A42	32.50	1300.00
30	Chair, with glides, Model 1A45	31.00	930.00
			3055.00

Exercise 15
INVOICE

SOLD TO: Batista Bookshop
Tribune Square
Lansing, MI 48911
INVOICE NO.: 5103

DATE: January 4, 19—
YOUR ORDER NO.: 483910
TERMS: 3/10, n/30
SHIPPED VIA: Conrail

QUANTITY	DESCRIPTION	UNIT PRICE	AMOUNT
5	Portable bookcase, tan texture, Cat. #40	70.50	352.50
2	Book truck, green, 36″ wide, 43″ high, Cat. #43-4	97.00	194.00
4	Magazine rack, tan texture, 21″ wide, 10″ deep, 36″ high, Cat. #36	55.75	223.00
			769.50

Exercise 16
INVOICE

SOLD TO: Mrs. Susanne McGregor
282 Ball Street
Fergus Falls, MN 56537
INVOICE NO.: 5221

DATE: March 26, 19—
YOUR ORDER NO.: 16025
TERMS: C.O.D.
SHIPPED VIA: UPS

QUANTITY	DESCRIPTION	UNIT PRICE	AMOUNT
1	Rubber link mat	6.00	6.00
16	Safety stair tread, brown	1.90	30.40
1	Sponge rubber mat	4.75	4.75
			41.15
		Sales tax	2.06
			43.21

6. If a topic requires more than one line, start the runover line under the initial letter of the first word of the preceding line.
7. Capitalize the first letter of each important word in topics that begin with roman numerals or the capital letters A, B, C, D, and so forth. Capitalize only the first letter of the first word in all other topics.
8. Use no punctuation at the ends of lines.

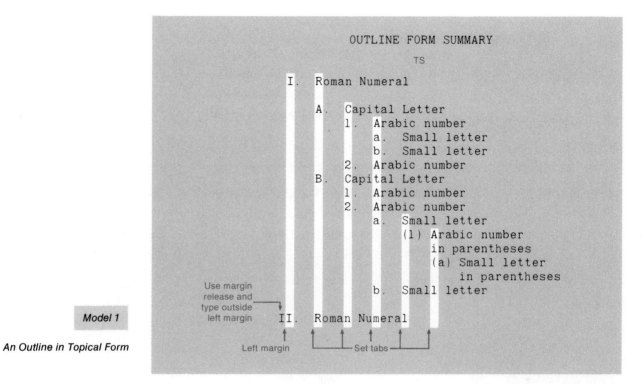

Model 1

An Outline in Topical Form

```
                    OUTLINE FORM SUMMARY
                            TS
          I.   Roman Numeral

               A.   Capital Letter
                    1.   Arabic number
                         a.   Small letter
                         b.   Small letter
                    2.   Arabic number
               B.   Capital Letter
                    1.   Arabic number
                    2.   Arabic number
                         a.   Small letter
                              (1) Arabic number
                                  in parentheses
                                  (a) Small letter
                                      in parentheses
                         b.   Small letter

          II.  Roman Numeral
```

Use margin release and type outside left margin →

Left margin   Set tabs

Before you begin Exercise 1, type Drills A–C to gain practice in aligning numbers. Remember that arabic and roman numerals align at the right. Repeat these drills if necessary.

Drill A

Half sheet. Double spacing. Align title at left margin. Begin on line 7.

Drill B

Half sheet. Double spacing. Block center the body. Center title. Begin on line 7.

DRILL A

```
                CHAPTER
                2 spaces
Left margin ─────→ I. ↓ One
Backspace once ─→ II.   Two
Backspace twice→ III.   Three
                 IV.   Four
                  V.   Five
                 VI.   Six
                VII.   Seven
               VIII.   Eight
                 IX.   Nine
                  X.   Ten
```

DRILL B

```
           ENJOYABLE ACTIVITIES
                2 spaces
Left margin ─────→ 1. ↓ Typing
                   2.   Swimming
                   3.   Bowling
                   4.   Reading
                   5.   Tennis
                   6.   Volleyball
                   7.   Skating
                   8.   Drawing
                   9.   Dancing
Backspace once ─→ 10.   Singing
```

Exercise 11
INVOICE

SOLD TO: The Neighborhood Store
56 Lucas Avenue
Cranston, RI 02910
INVOICE NO.: 4687

DATE: July 16, 19—
YOUR ORDER NO.: 63421
TERMS: 2/10, n/60
SHIPPED VIA: Yellow Freight Co.

QUANTITY	DESCRIPTION	UNIT PRICE	AMOUNT
5	Electric toaster, 2-slice	25.25	126.25
6	Electric toaster, 4-slice	35.00	210.00
3	Electric steam iron	9.50	28.50
1	Magic Mixer, 4-speed	55.00	55.00
			419.75

Exercise 12
INVOICE

SOLD TO: The Place Furniture Company
Northfield Plaza
Knoxville, TN 37906
INVOICE NO.: 4690

DATE: July 18, 19—
YOUR ORDER NO.: 63413
TERMS: n/30
SHIPPED VIA: Conrail

QUANTITY	DESCRIPTION	UNIT PRICE	AMOUNT
4	Credenza, Model 686 MC2D, 60″ × 19½″	86.50	346.00
6	Table, Model 601 MT20, 60″ × 30″	65.00	390.00
2	Table, Model 610 MT20, 72″ × 36″	75.00	150.00
			886.00

Exercise 13
INVOICE

SOLD TO: Glenmore Arms
406 Adams Street
Minneapolis, MN 55408
INVOICE NO.: 4786

DATE: September 22, 19—
YOUR ORDER NO.: 528198
TERMS: 2/10, n/30
SHIPPED VIA: Suppliers' Freightways

QUANTITY	DESCRIPTION	UNIT PRICE	AMOUNT
2	Arm chair, Model 64A	98.50	197.00
3	Arm chair, Model 60A	64.50	193.50
1	Desk chair, Model 5055	50.00	50.00
			440.50
		Sales tax	22.03
			462.53

Drill C

SIMPLE ENUMERATION

Type this agenda and align the items as shown.

Full sheet. 60-space line. Double spacing. Begin on line 13.

A G E N D A
Meeting of the BOEC Club
February 17, 19--
TS

A. Opening of the Meeting

   1. Roll call

   2. The BOEC creed and song

B. Old Business

   1. Reading of the minutes of the previous meeting

   2. Treasurer's report

   3. Report from the Membership Committee

C. New Business

   1. Planning for the State Leadership Conference

   2. Other new business

D. Adjournment and Socializing Time

Exercise 1

Type this topical outline using Model 1 (page 151) as a guide. Be sure to align numbers properly and set tabs for each series of indentions.

Full sheet. 50-space line. Center vertically.

MAKING BETTER USE OF YOUR TIME
TS

  I. Your Time at Work
     DS

    A. Organizing Your Day

      1. Planning what to do

      2. Avoiding interruptions

    B. Using Short Periods of Time
      DS

 II. Leisure Time
     DS

    A. Filling Mental Needs

      1. Learning to relax

      2. Selecting appropriate activities

    B. Filling Physical Needs

      1. Getting regular exercise

      2. Planning recreation

    C. Filling Social Needs

      1. Meeting people

        a. Group activities

        b. Parties

        c. Classes

      2. Building self-confidence

        a. Community service

        b. Hobbies

Exercise 9

PURCHASE ORDER

Note that the *Amount* column is not provided in this exercise. As you type the purchase order, supply the missing figures.

VENDOR: G. McGroarty Office Equipment Co.
25 Zacco Street
Kansas City, KS 66103

PURCHASE ORDER NO.: 7522

DATE: May 13, 19—

DATE REQUIRED: June 27, 19—

TERMS: n/30

SHIP VIA: Your truck

QUANTITY	CAT. NO.	DESCRIPTION	PRICE
2 ea	PN42	File cabinet, 4-drawer, letter-size	110.00
4 ea	PN48	File cabinet, 4-drawer, legal-size	120.00
4 ea	LM12	Secretarial desk, black top, #348	200.00

INVOICES

The following invoices come from Corona Industries Inc., 711 Cherry Street, St. Paul, MN 55121. Type each exercise following the style shown in Model 26. If forms are not available, prepare invoices similar to the one shown below.

Exercise 10

INVOICE

Type an invoice for the items sold by Corona Industries to Martin L. King High School, as shown in Model 26 below.

CORONA INDUSTRIES INCORPORATED

711 CHERRY STREET • ST. PAUL MN 55121
(218) 792-8450

INVOICE

NO. **4594**

DATE June 20, 19--

SOLD TO
Martin L. King High School
3842 Peachtree Street
Augusta, GA 30903

SHIP TO

SHIP TO ABOVE UNLESS OTHERWISE INDICATED HERE

YOUR ORDER NO. 98102	TERMS n/60	SHIPPED VIA Conrail		
QUANTITY	DESCRIPTION		UNIT PRICE	AMOUNT
1	Binding machine, Therm-A-Bind, Model 400		450.60	450.60
2	File cabinet, 4-drawer, letter-size, Model 415		125.75	251.50
25	Typing table (with bookrack), 20" x 42", Model 3800		75.00	1875.00
				2577.10

Model 26 *Invoice*

Exercise 2

Type this outline, using the proper spacing. (If you are in doubt, refer to Model 1, page 151.)

Full sheet. 50-space line. Begin on line 10.

A SYSTEMATIC JOB SEARCH PROCEDURE

I. Organizing Information for Employers

    A. Social Security Number

    B. List of References (minimum: three)

    C. Data Sheet with Summary of Work History

    D. Notepad, Pen, and Pencil

II. Limiting Area to Be Covered

    A. Industrial Areas

    B. Downtown Areas

    C. Shopping Centers

III. Doing Your Homework

    A. Learning About the Company

    B. Learning the Managers' Names

    C. Investigating the Types of Jobs Available

IV. Planning Your Arrival Time

    A. Travel Time

        1. Check bus schedules

        2. Select best route

    B. The Company's Schedule

        1. Lunch time

        2. Closing time

V. Presenting Yourself

    A. Grooming

        1. Cleanliness

        2. Conservative, neat clothing

    B. Success Tips

        1. Relaxed, smiling manner

        2. Clear, pleasant voice

        3. Good posture

        4. Arrive alone

VI. Filling In an Application Form

    A. Complete and Correct

        1. No lines left blank

        2. Check for spelling errors

    B. Neat and Clean

        1. Legible writing or printing

        2. No scratched-out corrections

Exercise 6
PURCHASE ORDER

VENDOR: The Colburn Company
811 Franklin Road
Long Beach, CA 90811
PURCHASE ORDER NO.: 7519

DATE: May 7, 19—
DATE REQUIRED: May 31, 19—
TERMS: 2/30, n/60
SHIP VIA: Conrail

QUANTITY	CAT. NO.	DESCRIPTION	PRICE	AMOUNT
12 ea	2010	Mattress covers, twin, #2632	9.35	112.20
6 ea	3050	Mattress covers, full, #2640	11.80	70.80
8 ea	3089	Mattress covers, queen, #2679	13.59	108.72
				291.72

Exercise 7
PURCHASE ORDER

VENDOR: Selby-Costa Fabrics, Inc.
365 Maple Avenue
Tucson, AZ 85719
PURCHASE ORDER NO.: 7520

DATE: May 12, 19—
DATE REQUIRED: June 16, 19—
TERMS: n/30
SHIP VIA: Norwall Truck Lines

QUANTITY	CAT. NO.	DESCRIPTION	PRICE	AMOUNT
12 rolls	2010	Fabric, cotton, Rosebud pattern, #3480	42.40	508.80
15 rolls	2042	Fabric, cotton, Laurel pattern, #3645	42.40	636.00
10 ctns	52	Buttons, brass color, ½″, #22Y	15.32	153.20
				1298.00

Exercise 8
PURCHASE ORDER

VENDOR: Fleming Metal Spring Co.
245 Lincoln Avenue
Scranton, PA 18501
PURCHASE ORDER NO.: 7521

DATE: May 12, 19—
DATE REQUIRED: July 1, 19—
TERMS: 2/30, n/60
SHIP VIA: Kaplan Express, Inc.

QUANTITY	CAT. NO.	DESCRIPTION	PRICE	AMOUNT
2000 ea	12A1	Coil spring, heavy duty, #6 size	.25	500.00
4000 ea	12A5	Coil spring, regular, #8 size	.21	840.00
4000 ea	12A6	Coil spring, regular, #9 size	.22	880.00
1000 ea	25B	Metal bands, 1″ wide, #367	.55	550.00
				2770.00

Exercise 3

Type this handwritten outline.

Full sheet. 50-space line. Proper outline spacing. Center vertically.

I. Introduction
   A. Purpose of Filing
   B. History of Filing
II. The Filing Process
   A. Preparing Letters for Filing
      1. Releasing
      2. Indexing
      3. Coding
      4. Cross-referencing
      5. Preparing follow-ups
   B. Filing Systems
      1. Basic systems
         a. Alphabetic
         b. Numeric
         c. Geographic
         d. Subject
         e. Chronological
      2. Special systems
         a. Terminal-digit (numeric)
         b. Soundex (alphabetic)
   C. File Drawer Contents
      1. Guides (Indexes)
      2. Folders
         a. Miscellaneous
         b. Individual

Exercise 4
PURCHASE REQUISITION

DELIVER TO: Chris Federico, Reception Room   REQUISITION NO.: 68421

CHARGE TO: Budget No. 4862   DATE: September 5, 19—

DATE REQUIRED: September 30, 19—

RECOMMENDED VENDOR: Parson's Office Supply, Kansas City, KS

ITEM	QUANTITY	DESCRIPTION	UNIT PRICE
1	1 bx	Rubber bands, # 16	2.70 bx
2	2 bxs	Paper clips, 50 per box, #3	1.39 bx
3	4 bxs	Paper clips, 100 per box, #2	1.19 bx

PURCHASE ORDERS

The following purchase orders come from the Kassor Mattress Company, 3642 Payne Avenue, Kansas City, KS 66106. Type each exercise following the style shown in Model 25. If forms are not available, prepare purchase orders similar to the one shown below.

Exercise 5
PURCHASE ORDER

Type a purchase order using the information in Model 25. Notice that the "SHIP TO" space is not filled in when goods are to be sent to the same address printed on the purchase order form.

Telephone: (913) 481-7723   **PURCHASE ORDER**   NO. 7518

DATE May 5, 19--

KASSOR
MATTRESS COMPANY
3642 PAYNE AVENUE • KANSAS CITY, KS 66106

TO Golubski Supply Co.
42 Truman Drive
Independence, MO 64051

SHIP
TO

SHIP TO ABOVE UNLESS OTHERWISE INDICATED HERE

DATE REQUIRED: June 5, 19--   TERMS: n/30   SHIP VIA: Yellow Freight Company

QUANTITY ORDERED	RECEIVED	CAT. NO.	DESCRIPTION	PRICE	AMOUNT
20 ctns		426A	Nails, $1\frac{1}{2}$", #38	4.52 ctn	90.40
10 ctns		113B1	Screws, $\frac{1}{4}$", brass, #42	6.40 ctn	64.00
3 ea		52B	Hammers, round head, claw-type, #6541	8.78 ea	26.34
					180.74

By: _____

Model 25   *Purchase Order*

SUCCEEDING ON THE JOB

I. Your Appearance

    A. What to Wear

        1. Conservative dress

        2. Simple accessories

    B. Grooming

        1. Suitable hairstyle

        2. Nails trimmed and clean

        3. Teeth cleaned and flossed

II. Your Speech

    A. Voice

        1. Pleasing tone

        2. Normal conversational level

    B. Correct Grammar and Choice of Words

III. Your Attitude

    A. Toward Work

        1. Alert

        2. Enthusiastic

        3. Willing to learn

    B. Toward Fellow Employees

        1. Considerate, helpful

        2. Courteous

        3. Cooperative

        4. Patient

        5. Cheerful

PURCHASE REQUISITION

KASSOR
MATTRESS COMPANY
3642 PAYNE AVENUE • KANSAS CITY, KS 66106

NO. 48162

DATE: May 3, 19--

DELIVER TO: Sam Salupo

DATE REQUIRED: June 5, 19--

CHARGE TO: Budget No. 4670

RECOMMENDED VENDOR: Golubski Supply Co., Independence, MO

ITEM	QUANTITY	DESCRIPTION	UNIT PRICE
1	20 ctns	Nails, 1½", #38	4.52 ctn
2	10 ctns	Screws, ¼", brass, #42	6.40 ctn
3	3 ea	Hammers, Lipstreuer & McGivern model with round head, claw-type, #6541	8.78 ea

Requisitioned by: _____   Approved by: _____

Model 24   *Purchase Requisition*

Exercise 2
PURCHASE REQUISITION

DELIVER TO: **Roberto Mendoza**
CHARGE TO: **Budget No. 4670**

REQUISITION NO.: **58164**
DATE: **Today's**
DATE REQUIRED: **Immediately**

RECOMMENDED VENDOR: **Jack's Tailoring & Upholstery Co., Kansas City, MO**

ITEM	QUANTITY	DESCRIPTION	UNIT PRICE
1	7 doz	"C" Clamps, 4"	2.10 doz
2	50 yds	Lining material, type 02	1.59 yd

Exercise 3
PURCHASE REQUISITION

DELIVER TO: **Shipping Department**
CHARGE TO: **Budget No. 4671**

REQUISITION NO.: **59057**
DATE: **Today's**
DATE REQUIRED: **Immediately**

RECOMMENDED VENDOR: **Parson's Office Supply, Kansas City, KS**

ITEM	QUANTITY	DESCRIPTION	UNIT PRICE
1	15 btls	Johnson's Glue-All, 8 fl. oz.	2.98 btl
2	10 rolls	Twine, extra-heavy, 500 ft. rolls	1.97 roll

Exercise 5

Type this topical outline, making the corrections indicated by the proofreaders' marks.

Full sheet. 40-space line. Proper outline spacing. Center vertically.

USE OF The BUSINESS TELEPHONE

I.   The sound of your voice

A. Distance from the Mouthpiece

     B. Clearness

         [1. Pronunciation

           2. Volume of sound

           3. Rate of speech

C. Manner and tone

II. Placing a call   #

A. Finding teh number

         1. Telephone lists

         2. Telephone directories

         3. ~~Information~~ *Directory assistance operator*

     B. Getting the connection

         1. Dial and push button phones

         2. Getting the person want*ed*

     C. Sepcial types of calls

         1. Long distance

             a. Direct dial

                 (1) Rate schedules

                 (2) When an operator can help

                     (a) Poor connection

                     (b) Wrong number   *c. Collect*
                                          d. Credit card

             b. Person-to-person

2. Emergency

[III. Receiving a call

A. Promptness *in* answering

     B. Preferred form of greeting

     C. Correct Procedure

     D, 1. Use of hold button

             a. Keeping caller informed

             b. Recovering from a cutoff

         2. Taking messages ~~properly~~

- Date the materials are needed
- Terms of payment
- Quantity and detailed description of each item
- Unit prices, extensions, and total

INVOICE   The vendor prepares an invoice (or bill) for the buyer. It is mailed at about the same time as the goods are shipped. An invoice shows the details of a sale and contains such information as:

- Name and address of the vendor and the buyer
- Buyer's purchase order number
- Terms of payment
- Method of shipment of the goods
- Quantity and detailed description of each item
- Unit prices, extensions, and total

CREDIT MEMORANDUM   When the goods arrive, the buyer checks them against a copy of the invoice. If there are any shortages, damages, or overcharges, the vendor is notified. Sometimes short or damaged goods are replaced. If they are not to be replaced, and the buyer requests credit, the vendor prepares a credit memorandum and mails it to the buyer. This indicates that the buyer's account has been credited for the difference. Credit memorandums contain information similar to that on an invoice, with the addition of a statement indicating the reason for the credit.

STATEMENT OF ACCOUNT   Usually, at the end of the month, the vendor mails the buyer a statement of account. Although statements are often prepared on data processing equipment, in smaller firms they are still typed. The statement contains such information as:

- Amount owed at the beginning of the month
- The purchases, credits, and payments during the month
- Amount due at the close of the month

Here are some general guidelines for typing purchase requisitions, purchase orders, invoices, credit memorandums, and statements.

1. Clear all tab stops and margin stops.
2. Set the left margin and tab stops so that they can be used for as many items as possible.
3. Line up the typing line with the bottom of the key words printed on the form.
4. Leave 2 spaces after a key word, such as *Date*.
5. In the body of the form, leave one blank line before you type the first line of data.
6. Set tab stops for the data to be entered in each column. For narrow columns, set a tab so that the longest item is roughly centered. For wider columns, set the tab 2 spaces to the right of the vertical rule.
7. If an item requires more than 1 line, indent the second and succeeding lines 3 spaces.
8. Double-space items when you have only a few; otherwise, single-space.
9. Omit periods in abbreviations of quantity units.
10. Omit dollar signs; align columns of numbers at the right.

PURCHASE REQUISITIONS

The following purchase requisitions come from the Kassor Mattress Company, 3642 Payne Avenue, Kansas City, KS 66106. Type each exercise following the style shown in Model 24 (page 316). If forms are not available, prepare purchase requisitions similar to the one shown in Model 24.

Exercise 1
PURCHASE REQUISITION

Type a purchase requisition using the information in Model 24.

Topic 2 REPORTS WITHOUT FOOTNOTES

The ability to type attractive and well-planned reports is one of the most useful typing skills you can acquire. Reports, whether long or short, are an important part of almost every business. You can also apply your skills typing reports for schoolwork.

The following general rules should be followed when typing school themes, speeches, business and technical reports, and camera-ready copy (typewritten material that will be photographed for offset printing):

1. Use white, good-quality, 8½″ × 11″ paper.
2. Use double spacing for the general text and single spacing for lengthy quotations. Occasionally, for special reasons (such as to reduce the number of pages), reports are typed using single spacing throughout.
3. Leave a 2-inch top margin on the first page and a 1-inch top margin on each succeeding page. If the report will be bound at the top, increase the top margin to 2½ inches on the first page and to 1½ inches on succeeding pages.

Left-Bound Report

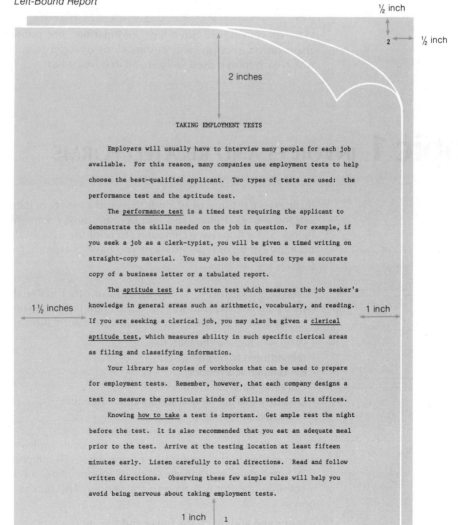

½ inch

½ inch

2 inches

2

TAKING EMPLOYMENT TESTS

Employers will usually have to interview many people for each job available. For this reason, many companies use employment tests to help choose the best-qualified applicant. Two types of tests are used: the performance test and the aptitude test.

The performance test is a timed test requiring the applicant to demonstrate the skills needed on the job in question. For example, if you seek a job as a clerk-typist, you will be given a timed writing on straight-copy material. You may also be required to type an accurate copy of a business letter or a tabulated report.

The aptitude test is a written test which measures the job seeker's knowledge in general areas such as arithmetic, vocabulary, and reading. If you are seeking a clerical job, you may also be given a clerical aptitude test, which measures ability in such specific clerical areas as filing and classifying information.

Your library has copies of workbooks that can be used to prepare for employment tests. Remember, however, that each company designs a test to measure the particular kinds of skills needed in its offices.

Knowing how to take a test is important. Get ample rest the night before the test. It is also recommended that you eat an adequate meal prior to the test. Arrive at the testing location at least fifteen minutes early. Listen carefully to oral directions. Read and follow written directions. Observing these few simple rules will help you avoid being nervous about taking employment tests.

1½ inches

1 inch

1 inch

1

PART 3

BUSINESS FORMS AND LEGAL DOCUMENTS

In an office, you will often type information onto printed forms, such as invoices, purchase orders, receipts, and various kinds of legal documents. Knowing the purpose for which each form is used will aid you in filling it out.

Topic 1 INVOICES AND RELATED FORMS

Businesses use forms of all kinds to record a variety of data in an organized manner. Transactions with customers and suppliers are most commonly recorded on the forms given below. Some firms have computers to print the data on the forms; but others still depend on handwriting or typewriting. If you have to type such forms, follow the guidelines on page 315.

PURCHASE REQUISITION   When supplies or other materials are needed, you may have to type a purchase requisition. This is then sent to the person responsible for ordering goods. The purchase requisition may contain such information as:

• Who is to receive the materials
• Department to be charged
• Recommended vendor
• Date the materials are needed
• Quantity and detailed description of each item
• Estimated unit prices

PURCHASE ORDER   After the requisition has been approved, a purchase order is prepared. This is mailed to the vendor (the person who sells the goods). Or, if the goods are needed in a hurry, they can be ordered by telephone. After a telephone order has been placed, a confirming order is mailed to the vendor. The purchase order contains such information as:

• Name and address of the buyer and the vendor
• Shipping instructions, including method of shipment

4. Leave 1-inch side margins and a 1-inch bottom margin. If the report will be bound at the left, increase the left margin to 1½ inches to allow for binding.

5. To avoid typing into the bottom margin, place a mark near the bottom of the page to warn you that the last line is approaching: Make two light pencil marks in the left margin, one at 1 inch and the other at 2 inches above the bottom edge. Don't forget to erase these marks before turning in your report.

6. Use Arabic numerals to number all pages within the body of the report. On the first page, the number is always centered in the bottom margin. (The first page of each major chapter or section is also numbered in this way.) If the report is unbound or bound at the left, other pages are numbered in the upper right corner. If the report is bound at the top, all page numbers are centered in the bottom margin.

7. Center the title of a report and type it in solid capitals. Triple space after the title. Type headings within the report at the left margin, underscore, or type in solid capitals. Triple space before each heading and double space after it.

8. Erase all errors carefully or use correction tape or fluid. If a report is to be photocopied or offset printed, the pages must be perfectly clean.

9. In multiple-page reports, avoid leaving fewer than two lines of a paragraph at the bottom of a page, and avoid carrying over fewer than two lines of a paragraph to the next page. Do not divide a word at the end of a page.

Exercise 1
ONE-PAGE REPORT

Full sheet. 2-inch top margin. 1-inch side and bottom margins. Double spacing. TS after title. 5-space paragraph indention.

TAKING EMPLOYMENT TESTS

Employers will usually have to interview many people for each job available. For this reason, many companies use employment tests to help choose the best-qualified applicant. Two types of tests are used: the performance test and the aptitude test.

The *performance test* is a timed test requiring the applicant to demonstrate the skills needed on the job in question. For example, if you seek a job as a clerk-typist, you will be given a timed writing on straight-copy material. You may also be required to type an accurate copy of a business letter or a tabulated report.

The *aptitude test* is a written test which measures the job seeker's knowledge in general areas such as arithmetic, vocabulary, and reading. If you are seeking a clerical job, you may also be given a *clerical aptitude test,* which measures ability in such specific clerical areas as filing and classifying information.

Your library has copies of workbooks that can be used to prepare for employment tests. Remember, however, that each company designs a test to measure the particular kinds of skills needed in its offices.

Knowing *how to take* a test is important. Get ample rest the night before the test. It is also recommended that you eat an adequate meal prior to the test. Arrive at the testing location at least fifteen minutes early. Listen carefully to oral directions. Read and follow written directions. Observing these few simple rules will help you avoid being nervous about taking employment tests.

cap com

ro

ab

ep

num

Community. Many of our social political and religious leaders participated in the NYSL as youngsters. ¶Your company can help us continue our work by sponsoring a team. All it costs is the price of shirts and trophies for your team you receive publicity when the youngsters wear the shirts with your co.'s name printed on them. This and more is all explained in the enclosed booklet, *NYSL Sponsorship*. ¶We have openings for sponsorship of both boys' and girls' tennis and volleyball leagues. Without sponsorship, these youngsters will be left out of this year's program. Can you please help. Call me at (208) 242-6177 any weekday before 5 o'clock, or write me at the address above. ¶On behalf of hundreds of area youngsters, thank you. *xx*   (141 words)

Exercise 23

This letter was dictated by **Janet Aiken, Public Relations Director** of **Morrell & Richardson Company**. The date of the letter is **March 18, 19—**.

num

com

col com

ab

Mr. Harold P. Hodge, President   Nampa Youth Sports Leagues   1927 Iris Street   Nampa, ID 83640   Dear Mr. Hodge   It would be our pleasure to sponsor a team in the Nampa Youth Sports Leagues. We regret that we have not done so already. ¶Our senior vice-president, Mrs. Barbara Holmes, played on 2 championship volleyball teams in the NYSL when she was a girl. Therefore we have decided to sponsor a girls' volleyball team. ¶I have read the booklet that you enclosed, but I will need your assistance with two questions What kinds of shirts do you require and where is the best place to purchase them? Do we supply first-, second-, and third-place trophies? We would appreciate talking to someone from the NYSL about these & other details. ¶Thank you for giving us this opportunity to support the youngsters of our community. *xx*   (124 words)

Exercise 24

In this letter, **Harold P. Hodge, President** of the **Nampa Youth Sports Leagues**, answers the questions raised by **Ms. Janet Aiken, Public Relations Director** of **Morrell & Richardson Company, 40 Granada Drive, Nampa, ID 83651**. The letter is dated **March 23, 19—**.

sp

frag

num ab

com

Dear Ms. Aiken   Thank you for your enthusiastic responce to our request for sponsorship. We hope the relationship between the NYSL and your company will be a long and enjoyable one. ¶The coach of the girls' volleyball team, Cindy Thorkelson, would be the best source of the information you need regarding the purchase of shirts and trophies. Phone number 877-0426. Ms. Thorkelson has all the girls' sizes, as well as catalogs and price lists. ¶The season starts the 3rd week of next mo.; so contacting Ms. Thorkelson promptly is vital. If we can be of help in any other way, please let us know. ¶Again thanks for your support. *xx*   (106 words)

THE OLD WOMAN AND HER MEMORIES

TS

The old woman sat by the fireside, thinking. Little by little, the light of day died away and the light given by the fire grew stronger until at last the room was full of its ever-changing light, a small haven of warmth and comfort cut off from the rest of the world. The few objects in the room, far from beautiful in the cold light of day, seemed to become lovely as the light of the fire touched them here and there. The old woman did not notice these changes. She was used to the room; she had lived in it for many, many years. She had lived there and she would die there if she had anything to say about the way of her going.

She was not thinking of dying just then, however. She was thinking of life, the most wonderful thing in the world. She was thinking of something that the young girl who lived next door had said that afternoon. The girl had come in, her face full of joy, eager to bring her happy news to the old woman. She was to be married next week. She was to marry a sailor, who was coming home from the seas. Her mother did not approve, for she said that the life of a young woman married to a sailor was a hard one; but the young girl said that old people know nothing of these things. She forgot that at that moment she was talking to a wise old woman who knew a great deal about such things.

The old woman continued to sit there, quite still, looking at the fire, but seeing other times and other people. The young always thought that the very old could know nothing and understand nothing; but she knew well what it was to be the wife of a sailor, sitting at home, waiting and waiting. She had been married to a sailor and she had three sons, and all of them in their turn had gone to sea. She remembered her husband as the young sailor she had first married—strong, light of heart, careless in the face of danger. Give him sails, he always cried, beautiful sails, and he would have nothing to do with the modern ships which were beginning to take the place of the sailing ships. He had lived, however, to see the change from the old sailing ships to the modern steamships and had learned to love them, too.

The old woman got to her feet with difficulty. The girl was right to be happy, she thought, for life was wonderful. She said to herself, "If I see the light of the morning tomorrow, I shall be ninety. Ninety years— a long time! I have often been lonely and sad. Yet I would gladly be as young as that girl and livē my life all over again."

A Theme by *Your Name* / Creative Writing 1 / *Your school* / *Today's date*

In the next five exercises, you are to supply any missing complimentary closings and enclosure notations as you type the letters. For each letter, address a No. 10 envelope and fold and insert the letter.

Exercise 20

This letter was dictated by **Frank H. Torrance, Business Manager, HOME TOOL DISTRIBUTORS.** It is being sent to **Mr. Robert J. Cranbrook, 8832 Baymead Drive, Duluth, MN 55814.** The date of the letter is **June 20, 19—.**

num

ab

ep

ww

Dear Sir   SUBJECT: Strongiron Wrenches, Lot No. 9774   We have received your letter of June 17th, in which you informed us of your dissatisfaction with your Strongiron wrench.   ¶Due to a crack in the manufacturer's mold for these wrenches, defective handles resulted in Lot No. 9774. We have been assured by the Strongiron Tool Corpor. that this mold has been replaced, and that inspections are being made frequently to prevent the recurrence of this problem   ¶Your retailer, Fred's Hardware Company, has been shipped replacements for these defective wrenches. If you will return your defective wrench to the retailer, he will be most happy to replace it with one from a resent, approved lot.   Yours truly *xx*   (105 words)

Exercise 21

The following letter was dictated by **Frank Penna, Advertising Editor, Household Magazine, Inc.** It is dated **November 1, 19—.** Be sure to add the notation for the enclosure mentioned in the letter.

ep sp

com

ww

sp

Mr. Albert T. White   White Household Appliance Company   474 Ward Street   Philadelphia, PA 19123   Dear Mr. White   Are you making full use of magazine advertising. Dealers have always reconized the value of the magazine market and many purchasers of your products are readers of our magazine.   ¶Won't you take a few minutes to look over this sample copy of HOUSEHOLD MAGAZINE? Since you deal in products that appeal to homemakers note how many articles are written especially for people who's interests lay in the home. Also note the advertisements —many of them for products of the same general type as yours.   ¶Don't you agree with us that an advertisement in HOUSEHOLD MAGAZINE would yeild substantial results? *xx*   (99 words)

Exercise 22

This letter was dictated by **Harold P. Hodge, President** of the **Nampa Youth Sports Leagues,** and is dated **March 11, 19—.** Note the enclosure.

Public Relations Director   Morrell & Richardson Company   40 Granada Drive   Nampa, ID 83651   Dear Sir or Madam   The Nampa Youth Sports Leagues (NYSL) help to build the characters of boys and girls in our

(Continued on next page)

A BOOK REPORT

by *Your Name*

<u>The Old Man and the Sea</u>
Ernest Hemingway

ABOUT THE AUTHOR

Ernest Hemingway was born July 21, 1899, in Oak Park, Illinois. He went to the public schools in Oak Park. After working as a reporter for the *Kansas City Star,* he was an infantryman and ambulance driver in the Italian Army during World War I. He was a war correspondent during the Spanish Civil War and in World War II. In 1954 he was awarded the Nobel Prize for literature. He died in 1961.

ABOUT THE STORY

This short novel (only 140 pages) is the tragic story of Santiago, a Cuban fisherman, and of the giant fish he kills and loses in the Gulf Stream. The old man's only real friend in the village is a very young boy, Manolin, who believes in the old man's ability as a fisherman when everyone else has lost faith in him. When the boy's parents finally tell their son that he must go out fishing in a boat with other fishermen, the old man goes to sea alone.

The major part of the story takes place on the sea as the old man is alone with his thoughts. In his loneliness, he talks to a bird, to the fish, and even to the big marlin he catches. It takes the old man two long days to finally harpoon the giant fish. Then, the blood of the fish draws sharks who eat the old man's prize catch. He fights them off as best he can, but by the time he gets back to his village, only the skeleton of the great fish is left. The old man is sad about his loss, but he is a hero to the villagers when they see the skeleton of such a huge fish strapped to his boat.

REACTIONS TO THE STORY

It is a sad story, told very simply. It is easy to understand the feelings of the characters because of the straightforward way in which the story is told. It seems cruel that the old man loses his prize fish after he has fought so hard and waited so long to get it. I enjoyed the way the author told the story by letting the reader "listen in" on the old man's thoughts. After reading the book, I understand why it is called a literary "classic."

Report for *English 4*
Today's date

June 14, 19— Fred's Hardware Company   210 Lorbury Street   Duluth, MN 55812

Attention: Ray Jackson

Gentlemen

SUBJECT: Complaints about Strongiron Wrenches

We are in receipt of your letter regarding the problems your customers have encountered with Strongiron wrenches. I have *cap* contacted the Company's customer service department in *sp* Cincinati with respect to your comments. Their representative informed me that they have received several complaints *com* about these wrenches. As a result the company has conducted an investigation of the manufacturing process for these tools. Evidently, a crack had developed in the mold for the wrenches, and this produced a defect in the handles *cap* of wrenches made under Lot no. 9774.

The broken mold has now been replaced, and the *sp* company forsees no recurrence of this problem.

I have been authorized by the company to replace all wrenches of Lot No. 9774 which we distributed to *num* retailers. Therefore, we are shipping a carton of 3 dozen wrenches, Lot No. 9832, to you today. This shipment will replace the wrenches of Lot No. 9774, which *sp* were shiped to you in April.

hy I trust that these steps will re-affirm your customers' faith in Strongiron products.

Sincerely yours

Frank H. Torrance   Business Manager   *xx*   (169 words)

BANKING IN A CHANGING SOCIETY

Banking has changed dramatically in the past twenty-five years. While society has evolved at what seems a breakneck pace, banks have tried, and I think succeeded, in keeping up. They have innovated and developed to meet the many diverse financial needs of their customers.

How has banking changed? Aren't banks still in the business of accepting deposits and making loans? Certainly, banks still fit this basic definition.

But in addition, the types of specialized savings, lending, and other services banks offer today have virtually exploded in number. There are more types of customers now than there were in the past and more types of services needed to accommodate them. In both appearance and outlook, banks have gone through a significant transformation.

Banks look different today. Modern architecture and design create a more open and inviting atmosphere for customers. The forbidding, barred teller windows are gone. Loan officers have moved out of the back rooms and right onto the bank floor. And banks have introduced special features, such as drive-in teller windows, 24-hour automatic cash dispensers, and bank credit cards. All of this has made banking easier.

The physical change in the appearance of banks is no mere cosmetic facelift. It reflects a fundamental change in attitude away from a nearly exclusive emphasis on commercial customers toward an increasing involvement with individual customers.

For many years, banks relied almost entirely on commercial depositors and borrowers for their business. Individual savings accounts and personal loans were relatively unimportant, and were not actively sought. One result was that a number of special-purpose thrift institutions developed, such as savings and loan associations, mutual savings banks, and credit unions. These thrift institutions were, and still are, oriented to the specific savings or borrowing needs of individuals.

But as individual purchasing and earning power surged after World War II, commercial banks realized the potential of individuals as customers. So they changed their way of doing business to serve this increasingly important source of deposits and market for lending.

Today, individual accounts make up the bulk of a bank's deposits. Individual lending, for almost every conceivable purpose, is a major portion of bank credit. Competition among banks, and between banks and other thrift institutions, has resulted in great benefits for you, the individual customer.

November 11, 19— Mr. Lincoln C. Rogers 728 Snyder Avenue Jersey City, NJ 07302

Dear Mr. Rogers

sp

In accordance with the preferance you have expressed we shall be pleased to have you call at our office next Monday afternoon to discuss the matter of financing your purchase of a home.

Either Mr. Frank Linton or Ms. Joanne Bartsch will be available to confer with you. Please ask for one of them when you arrive. I have given each of them a memorandum setting

ww

fourth the full particulars of the conversation we had last week, and since both Ms. Bartsch and Mr. Linton are specialists in home financing, they are, therefore, well qualified to advise you on the best procedure to follow.

ww

I am confident that with the sound advise they can give, you will be able to arrange a loan with a payment plan that meets your

sp

budjet requirements.

cap

Thank you for giving Central Savings And Loan Association this opportunity to serve you.

Very truly yours

CENTRAL SAVINGS AND LOAN ASSOCIATION Roger T. Richman Vice-President *xx*   (146 words)

The Legal Secretary ← center, caps

TS

One of the prized positions ~~jobs~~ in the secretarial field at the present time is the one held by the ~~law~~ *legal* secretary. The legal secretary has long been and *this* is likely to continue in very short supply. Like lawyers, this specialized secretary lives in a world of torts, contracts, and other legal matters. *Those in this position are* The person in the law office is first, of all, a skilled secretary *ies*. They type*s* about 60 words a minute, take*s* dictation at ~~speeds of~~ *rates up to* 120 words a minute, *and* understands basic office management procedures and principles. ←

In a small office, the legal secretary must be a versatile person. In a large law office, ~~the~~ on the other hand, the legal *secretary* may handle very special assignments. If we had to jo*t* down the main requisites for success as a legal secretary, accuracy would have to rank first on the list--lawyers just can't afford to have mist*a*kes on important legal documents. Other important *t*raits for a legal secretary are alertness, tact, honesty, ~~faith~~ and dependability. ¶ Since the legal secretary *ies* deals with a broad range of subjects involving human activity, it is helpful for them to have a good general education as well as formal study in such areas as economics, and literature. ~~But, it is imperative that the~~ ~~law~~ *legal* secretary *ies* have excellent stenographic skills.

Legal The ~~law~~ secretary *ies*, either by telephone or *on the* in the reception room is *office, are* the first person*s* whom the *lawyer's* clients meet. They are actually acting as a public-relations representative*s* of the law office ~~through these~~ contacts with clients, *legal secretaries*

Exercise 17
BUSINESS LETTER

December 4, 19— Mrs. Mary Kaufmann Eagle's Nest Ski Lodge Star Route 119 Jeffersonville, VT 05464

Dear Mrs. Kaufmann

I have spoken with the people in our shipping and production depts. in regard to the matter noted in your recent letter. As you are aware, the turnover rate among employees is quite large in the Fall, due to the replacement of "summer people" with "winter people." As a result, we have several new employes at the bakery.

I have impressed upon all our staff the need for better stock control. All day old products will be segregated and marked with a large "X" on the wrapper. There will be a 50% discount offered to those customers for whom same-day freshness is not important. All other customers will recieve only goods that are baked the same day as they are shipped.

I trust that these steps will assure the freshness of our goods upon your receipt. Please accept my sincere apologies for any inconveniences to you. Or to your guests.

Sincerely yours

Rex Peterson PETERSON'S BAKERY xx (152 words)

ab
·cap
sp
hy
ab
sp
frag

FINDING A JOB IS A JOB ⟵ *Center title*

TS

Now that you have acquired the skill of typing, you may feel that you are ready to use your skills in [*to find*] paid employment. Perhaps, you are considering summer or part-time work in an office. [*you should*] Be aware that finding a job might [*may*] not be as easy as you think unless [*if*] you do not use a approach that is systematic.

First, you must decide where you will go to apply. Check with your relatives and friends about openings # where they work. Many firms perfer to hire those [*people*] referred by their employees. Your school, church, and state employment offices are also excellent sources [*of job information*]. Ads in news- papers and professional publications will give you some good leads. Of course, larger business [*es*] and government offices [*agencies*] maintain a regular *(stet)* employment office [*s*] and welcome applicants every day.

Second, be sure that you are prepare [*d*] when you go to look for work. Take important papers with you, such as a [*your*] social security card and proof [*other*] identification of birth. Be ready to complete an application blank asking for the names of your [*the*] schools attended, your [*(stet)*] work experience, and your refer- ences. *(among other things)* It is a good idea to take a data sheet with you which has all this information typed out in a neat arrange- ment. ¶ Third, groom yourself [*dress appropriately*] for the interview. You want to make a good first impression. If you arrive for an interview late, unprepared and unkempt, you are stacking the cards against yourself.

Finally, remember that people rarely get the first job they inter- view for [*for which*]. Do not be disappointed and stop looking. *Think positively.*

November 28, 19 — Mr. Rex Peterson   Peterson's Bakery   14 Medusa
Road   Stowe, VT 05672

Dear Mr. Peterson

Until the past month, we were very pleased with the bakery goods which you have been supplying to our lodge. Since the first part of november, however, we have been recieving stale cookies, cakes, sweet-rolls and bread varieties. Many of the guests here have complained about the lack of freshness of these products.

I understand that you have had a large turnover in personnel recently; so perhaps you are unaware that shipments of stale bakery goods are being made. Or that your quality control prior to shipment is faulty.

Please advise me as soon as possible weather you will be able to supply us once again with the delicious products we have come to expect from your company.

Sincerely

cap

sp

hy

frag

ww

Mrs. Mary Kaufmann   General Manager *xx*   (118 words)

Exercise 7

REPORT FROM ROUGH-DRAFT COPY

Type this report in proper report form. Make all the corrections indicated by the proofreaders' marks.

Full sheets. Margins for a left-bound report. Double spacing. 5-space paragraph indention.

EARLY ART
DS
(A Report for <u>History of Art</u> Class)
DS
by Joanne Drew
TS

) *Center each line*

¶ When did ~~early~~ humans first show an interest in art? In those far-off days, was the first artist held in high reg*a*rd, as is the case today? These questions are not easy (o)t answer. It is possible to get a fairly satisfactory answer to the first, but it is difficult--~~herpahs~~ *perhaps* impossible--to answer the second.

No records exist to tell us about the attitude of other *s* ~~man~~ *ʼ* toward the artist. We can only guess. It seems probabl*e*y that the art *s* of making war and ~~art of~~ getting food were*ʼ* more highly valued than the art*s* of *cutting* ~~getting~~ figur*e*s out of stone or ~~the art of~~ painting pictures.

It is ~~however,~~ known, within limits, when art began. Experts be-le*ʼ*ive that the first artistic creations appeared about fifty thou sand years ag*a*o. It was a very simple form of *A*rt and for thousands of years it ~~litt~~ changed little. The earliest examples of art#that have been found are little more than great pieces of stone that were cut to *resemble* animals. They have no clear lines; they have only a rough general form. *Those ancient carvings* ~~It~~ represents*ʼ* the first attempts of ~~people~~ to copy what they saw around them (their in) daily lives.¶ In the next stage, *ʼ* there ~~will~~ were simple pictures of different animals. The details were poor, especially th*e* head and ~~the~~ feet*ʼ* but it is possible to recognize what the artist meant to paint.

(Continued on next page)

Exercise 13
BUSINESS LETTER

sp
cap
com
com hy

num

Today's date Mr. Edward Khan Eastern Food, Inc. 730 Royce Street Peoria, IL 61612 Dear Mr. Khan We are very much pleased with our customers' response to your products. Many of them allready know your line well and need no encouragement. Others try a box of eastern fruit or vegetables at our suggestion and then come back for more. We hope Mr. Khan that you will continue to supply products of the same first class quality and that you will add other varieties. ¶Could you please send us about fifty copies of your pamphlet, *Eastern Foods for Your Family.* Our previous supply was exhausted in less than 1 month's time. Cordially GOLDBERG & MONAHAN Ms. Laura P. Kopec Purchasing Manager LK:*xx* (93 words)

Exercise 14
BUSINESS LETTER

col ab
sem

ep
frag

num

April 21, 19— Mr. Samuel Morgan 41 Clark Street Brooklyn, NY 11212 Dear Mr. Morgan In answer to your question, we regret that we know of no store in your immediate neighborhood that carries our line of raincoats. You will, however, find a complete stock of our coats at the following stores, Baldwin Brothers' Shop, 1494 Swan Ave.; Smith Haberdashery, 128 D Street, and John's Downtown Store, 6940 Grove Street. We are certain that any of these stores will be able to fill your requirements ¶You may be interested to learn that these stores also carry our new models in polyester gabardine. Which are slightly above the price range mentioned in our advertisement. Sincerely yours ROGERS, LLOYD AND COMPANY Durwood Rogers, Sales Manager *xx* P.S. Watch for our annual clearance sale of raincoats, beginning May 1st.
(97 words in body; 11 words in postscript)

Exercise 15
BUSINESS LETTER

ab
cap
frag
col num
sem
sp

May 29, 19— Mr. and Mrs. J. P. Wylie, Managers Coastside Apartments 4017 Robertson Avenue Virginia Beach, VA 23451 Dear Mr. and Mrs. Wylie We are required by law to notify you in writing of the results of our recent fire inspection. ¶We were generally pleased with the condition of your apt. complex. We commend your concerned efforts to make coastside a safer place to live. However, there are a few hazards we would like you to eliminate. Before our next inspection on the 15th of next month. ¶These include a frayed wire on dryer #12 in the laundry room; broken smoke detectors in apartments 4B, 42D, and 19C, open paint cans in the storage shed; and a broken step on the fire excape for Building C. ¶When these problems are corrected, we will issue you a certificate of safety to present to your insurance company. Thank you for your cooperation. Sincerely Donald J. Wootten Fire Chief *xx* (126 words)

In the third stage—that is, about twenty thousand years ago—the pictures are masterpieces in attention to detail and in the clear outline of the stones figures.

You may ask how it is possible to judge the age of pictures and figures so many centuries old? The answer is to be found in the fact that these works of art are covered with a kind of protective covering stones that took thousands of years to form. From this covering, the expert can tell you, beyond doubt, the age of the picture or of the figures.

Topic 3 REPORTS WITH FOOTNOTES

Footnotes are used (1) to identify the source of a statement that is quoted in the text of a report, or (2) to include a thought or idea that the author of the report feels should be separated from the text. Remember the following general guidelines when typing reports with footnotes.

1. Footnotes are usually typed at the bottom of the same page on which they are referred to. They are numbered in order, using raised Arabic numerals. Type a divider line 1½ inches long at the left margin between the text and the footnote. Leave a single space below the text. Leave a double space after the divider line. (An alternative style is to type all footnotes on a separate page at the end of the report. This style is growing in popularity because it is much easier than the usual procedure.)
2. When typed at the bottom of the page, footnotes are single spaced. Double space between footnotes when more than one appears at the bottom of a page. Indent the first line of each footnote 5 spaces.

borders of China."[2] Then the Arabs captured some Chinese papermakers and from them the method was learned. Before this, the Arabs had used parchment, made from the skins of animals, but now they changed and used paper made chiefly from linen. They carried the use of paper to their colonies of Sicily and Spain. From these places it was carried to Europe. Early Europeans made paper of cotton and linen rags. When the great demand for paper and paper products created a

SS
——————————————— 1½ inch divider line
DS

[1]L. J. Vonderkraft, <u>Ancient Greek History</u>, 6th ed. (New York: Holt, 1976), pp. 60-61.

DS

[2]Campbell Shelby, "Our Marvelous Paper," <u>Paper Industry Journal</u>, vol. 4 (March 1973), pp. 78-80.

Exercise 9
BUSINESS LETTER

ab
hy
sp

com

ro

com

January 18, 19— N. A. Roberts, M.D. 4162 Wagner Street Pittsburgh, PA 15204 Dear Doctor Roberts A doctor requires an attractive waiting room and a comfortable, well appointed office. Furnishings in good taste play an important role in creating a pleasent atmosphere and insuring the comfort of patients. ¶We would be glad to have an opportunity to fill your requirements for new furniture draperies and floor coverings. Perhaps you would like us to refinish or reupholster your worn furniture. We have a large stock ready for immediate delivery our customer department will fill any special order you may have in mind. ¶Our consultant for interior decoration Lewis Vinings will be glad to call at your office to discuss your furnishing needs with you. Sincerely HALLIDAY & COMPANY Millard Wong Executive Director *xx* (107 words)

Exercise 10
BUSINESS LETTER

num

sem

ab
hy

Today's date Wilkins Food Products, Inc. 732 Birdwell Street Mobile, AL 36617 Ladies and Gentlemen On opening the first case of your recent shipment of canned peaches, we found 7 swollen cans. We cannot risk offering this merchandise to our customers. In fact, we feel doubtful about the entire shipment therefore, we have not opened the other three cases and we are returning the entire lot to you by freight today. ¶Please credit our acct. with this return shipment and inform us at once whether you can supply us with high quality goods. Sincerely yours HUGHES & RODMAN Walter Delapena, Buyer WD:*xx* (80 words)

Exercise 11
RECORD OF TELEGRAPH MESSAGE

Send this message as a direct telegram.

ww sp
com

October 27, 19— 11:07 a.m. Charge Sender Ramies Pharmaceutical Supplies, Inc. 1098 Maple Street Arlington, VA 22202 (703) 443-7070 Disregard message sent too you yesterday. Twenty-four cases of asprin arrived this morning and we no longer need the emergency order. Thank you. Cathy Dodge, Manager Save-More Pharmacy No. 17 *xx*

Exercise 12
INTEROFFICE MEMO

sp
frag

com ro

frag

SUBJECT Duluth Convention   TO Frank Gallina, Art Department FROM Frank H. Dreyer, President   DATE August 5, 19—   COPIES Patricia Gallagher, Marketing Manager I want to express my appreciation for your excelent exhibit of our company's products at the Duluth convention last week. ¶The booth was in a very desirable location. And everything was set up exactly as we specified. Many people stopped by to examine the exhibit make inquiries and pick up brochures we are hopeful this will result in increased business. ¶Your brochures, by the way, are beautifully designed. I believe they will do a lot to promote interest in our company. And in our products. Frank Dreyer *xx* (80 words)

3. Mark the bottom of your paper with a light pencil mark before you begin to type. As each raised footnote number is typed in the text, stop and make another light pencil mark approximately 4 lines above your last pencil mark. This will help you remember to stop typing in time to leave room for the footnotes and the bottom margin.

Often a report may include lengthy quotations and bibliographies. These items are handled in the following manner:

1. Lengthy quotations within the body of the text (more than 3 lines) are set off from the rest of the text by indenting them 5 spaces from both left and right margins. Such quotations do not need quotation marks since by setting them off you are already indicating that the material is a quotation. These longer quotations are single spaced.
2. A bibliography is placed at the end of the report on a separate page. The bibliography is an alphabetical list of books and articles that were referred to in the report or consulted by the author in preparing the report. Center the title, BIBLIOGRAPHY, in solid capitals on line 13 with a triple space after it. Single space within each entry in the bibliography and double space after an entry. The first line of each entry is typed at the left margin and the runover lines should be indented 4 spaces from the left margin.

These illustrations show the style used for a footnote and for a bibliographical entry. Note the order of the items and the punctuation in each example.

FOOTNOTES:

Author's Name (*first* name first), "Title of Article," Title of Book or Magazine, volume or series number, (Place of Publication: Publisher's Name, date), page numbers referred to.

BIBLIOGRAPHY:

Author's Name (*last* name first), "Title of Article," Title of Book or Magazine, volume or series number. Place of Publication: Publisher's Name, date, page numbers referred to.

Exercise 1

ONE-PAGE REPORT WITH FOOTNOTES

Type the first page of this report. (More copy is given here than will fit on the first page.) Type the footnotes, following the style shown in the example on page 165. For each footnote, make a warning mark 4 lines above your previous warning mark. When the text reaches a warning mark, roll the paper back and decide how many additional lines (if any) you will be able to type.

Remember to set off the quotation by indenting it 5 spaces from each side margin and by using single spacing.

Full sheet. 2-inch top margin. 1-inch side margins. Double spacing. 5-space paragraph indention.

THE STORY OF PAPER
TS

Paper serves us so constantly in our daily lives that it is difficult to picture a world without it. Most of our knowledge of the past comes to us on paper and most of our current information is printed on paper. Paper manufacturing today is a big industry which stemmed from a small beginning centuries ago.

The history of paper goes back to the time when history itself was first recorded. Vonderkraft states in his story of ancient times:

Our word *paper* comes from the Greek word *papyrus*, which is the name of a certain kind of tall reed. The story of papyrus goes back four thousand years. This reed, called *bullrushes* in the *Bible*, is a plant that grows along the banks of the Nile.[1]

Paper as we know it, made from fiber pulp, originated in China. In the first century, the Chinese made paper from such materials as silk and old linen. Shelby states, "For six centuries the secret of this art lay locked within the borders of China."[2] The secret became known when the Arabs

(Continued on next page)

Exercise 5
BUSINESS LETTER

hy sp
ww sem

ep

Today's date Joseph E. Silva & Company 381 Severn Street Jackson, MS 39204 Gentlemen We should like to know your wishes in regard to the method of payment for the shipment we made to you last week. ¶Some of our out of town customers preffer to have us draw a sight draft on them thorough their bank when payment is due, others favor sending us a check upon receipt of a monthly statement. Please let us know which of the two methods is suitable for you Cordially HOLLAND COMPANY, INC. Steven C. Dullas Credit Department *xx*   (72 words)

Exercise 6
BUSINESS LETTER

ww ro
ab

ep

June 9, 19— Highway Trucking Company 12000 Fedorovich Road Springfield, MO 65807 Ladies and Gentlemen My tire shop has thousands of old, treadless tires on the back lot. Their getting in the way, therefore, I would like them removed. ¶A recycling plant in Macon, Ga., buys old tires, and I know that trucks from your company make regular runs to Macon. Would it be possible for one of your trucks to haul the tires for us. Please write or call me with your answer or any questions. Thank you. Sincerely Morris Costello Service Manager *xx*   (74 words)

Exercise 7
BUSINESS LETTER

com
ww

ww com

Today's date Ms. Dorothy P. Henderson 408 Barnett Street Brockton, MA 02401 Dear Ms. Henderson We regret to inform you that the painting you wanted, "At the Fountain," has been sold since your visit to our gallery. We can however offer you another painting by the same artist, entitled "Brook Scene." It's price is about the same as that of "At The Water's Edge" ($250). It was painted at the same period of the artist's life and is in the same colors. ¶If your interested in this painting we hope you will come to see it soon. It is the only painting by this artist that we have, and is likely to be sold at any time. Yours truly G. Wellington Burke Gallery Director *xx*   (101 words)

Exercise 8
INTEROFFICE MEMO

frag
ww num

cap

sp
ab

SUBJECT Claim Against Our Company TO S. Hanover, Legal Department FROM Thomas Metz, President DATE *Today's date* I am attaching a letter received from Mr. Ronald Slater. Describing an accident involving his personnel automobile and 1 of our trucks. ¶Please take the appropriate steps (including getting an estimate of repair costs) to settle this claim. ¶Yesterday, I spoke with Mr. Ricardo, the district Manager at Liberty Insurance Company. Their representative will get in touch with you shortly to arrange for a meeting at a time conveneint for both you and Mister Slater. TM *xx* Enclosure   (75 words)

Exercise 1 continued

captured some Chinese papermakers and learned the method from them. Before this, the Arabs had used parchment, made from the skins of animals, but they soon adopted the Chinese art of making paper. They used chiefly linen. The Arabs carried the use of paper to their colonies in Sicily and Spain. From these places it was carried to Europe. Early Europeans made paper from cotton and linen rags. When the great demand for paper and paper products created a heavy drain on rag supplies, ways to make paper from wood pulp were discovered and made practical for mass production methods.

Footnotes to be typed with Exercise 1, "The Story of Paper"

[1]L. J. Vonderkraft, *Ancient Greek History*, 6th ed. (New York: Holt, 1976), pp. 60–61.

[2]Campbell Shelby, "Our Marvelous Paper," *Paper Industry Journal*, vol. 4 (March 1973), pp. 78–80.

Exercise 2

TWO-PAGE REPORT WITH FOOTNOTES

Type this 2-page report. Remember to place the footnotes at the bottom of the page where the raised numerals appear in the text. If a footnote falls on a partially filled page, place it at the bottom of the page with a divider line as you would if the text filled the page. Remember to indent the quotation.

Full sheets. Margins for an unbound report. Double spacing. 5-space paragraph indention.

THE BAT FAMILY

The bat flies, but it is not a bird; it is a mammal, similar to a mouse. Instead of wings, it has a thick membrane that connects its arms and legs and is spread when the bat is in flight. It flies as fast as a swallow, wheeling and darting about with remarkable skill, and without a sound. The bat guides itself by its sense of touch or of hearing, for it cannot see its way. Perhaps to make up for this lack of sight, its other senses are well developed. There is one species of bat that has ears so long that it folds them under its arms when it goes to sleep. All bats have very sensitive nerves that help them to avoid hitting objects as they fly.[1]

There are hundreds of kinds of bats, vastly different from one another. They vary in size from the common bat, which is as small as a mouse, to a huge bat that has a five-foot wingspan. Some eat fruit; others eat insects. They are found in many different regions—in the United States, in Europe, in India, in Egypt, and in Central and South America.

Vampire bats (which get their name from the vampire of old-time legends) are common to parts of Central and South America, but are never found in the United States.

At night the vampire bat goes forth in quest of its only food—the blood of defenseless animals sleeping in the open pasturelands or in

(Continued on next page)

Exercise 1
BUSINESS LETTER

sp num

com

hy

sp

September 4, 19— Mr. Calvin A. Hardy Advertising Manager Missouri Bus Company 82 Oakhurst Street St. Louis, MO 63104 Dear Mr. Hardy We have sent you under seperate cover approximately 20 sets of posters entitled "Appreciate St. Louis." If you find that you can make use of more we shall be glad to send you an additional supply. ¶We appreciate your co-operation. We would be pleased if you would forward to us any comments you recieve regarding the posters. Yours very truly ST. LOUIS BOARD OF TRADE D. Chu, Secretary *xx*   (56 words)

Exercise 2
BUSINESS LETTER

com

ro

frag

com sp

Today's date Stockwell Landscaping Company 438 17th Street Burns, OR 97720 Ladies and Gentlemen In keeping with the town's spirit of urban renewal we at Robey Brothers are considering remodeling the area around our building, the remodeling will include replacing the shrubbery and constructing a brick wall. Also, a small duck pool. ¶We have seen your work and are impressed. Would you consider doing our remodeling? If so mail us an estimmate based on the enclosed drawings. Sincerely ROBEY BROTHERS CORPORATION Steven Robey, President SR:*xx* Enclosures   (67 words)

Exercise 3
INTEROFFICE MEMO

cap

sp com

ww

SUBJECT Error in Shipping Order TO Supply Department FROM D. Bahr, Word Processing Training Supervisor DATE August 15, 19— We have just received twenty gross of no. 1 drafting pencils. We have no record of an order for these pencils. No one on our staff has any knowlege of such an order. In addition we would have no use for such pencils in this department. We use only the following—No. 1, No. 2, and special indigo blue No. 12. A mistake was made somewhere, probably in the shipping department. ¶Please check your order file and advice us on what to do with the pencils. D. Bahr *xx*   (86 words)

Exercise 4
BUSINESS LETTER

num sp

ab

cap

num

April 14, 19— Rudolph's Used Cars 747 Triumph Way Bloomington, IN 47401 Ladies and Gentlemen Would you like to double or triple your sales within 30 days? Our revolutionary new sales consept will help your company increase sales at an amazing rate while teaching your reps to properly account for commissions and to keep accurate records. ¶Send now for our book, *Rapid Sales growth,* or ask for the cassette tape series. Use the enclosed order form for prompt service. If your sales do not increase in 30 days, we will return your money. Sincerely Miss Margery Ritter, Vice President MR/*xx* Enclosure   (80 words) corrals. Vampires are dreaded by farmers because they spread disease among cattle and horses, which are their victims.[2]

When the bat rests it usually hangs head down, suspended by its curved claws. Each front foot has only a single claw; the hind feet have five each. The bones of the forefeet or hands are very long, in some species longer than the body. A bat can walk, though very awkwardly, on its hind feet and on the tips of its forefeet, first on one side, then on the other. The mother bat either carries her little ones with her when she searches for food, or she suspends them from a branch by their claws.[3]

Bats are the themes of many tales, and they are often introduced into a story to add an atmosphere of mystery or dread. However, when people find out the facts about bats and their habits, it becomes obvious that there is no need for fear.

Footnotes to be typed with Exercise 2, "The Bat Family"

[1]*Compton's Encyclopedia,* vol. 3 (1975), s.v. "Birdlike Animals That Navigate by Radar," p. 90.

[2]J. L. Ranft, "Vampire Bats," *Americas Magazine* (September 1974), pp. 32–35.

[3]*Compton's,* p. 91.

Exercise 3
MULTIPLE-PAGE REPORT WITH FOOTNOTES

Type this report, paying special attention to footnotes. Prepare a title page for the report. (Refer to Exercise 9, page 113.)

Full sheets. Margins for a left-bound report. Double spacing. 5-space paragraph indention.

UNDERSTANDING DATA PROCESSING

Information (data) has been processed since human beings first decided to keep written records of their possessions. Even cave dwellers who scratched crude marks and drawings on the walls of their caves can be said to have been processing data. With the invention of paper and the resulting paper explosion, it was just a matter of time before machines were invented to help with this burden of paperwork.

Whether the processing of data is done by hand (such as with a simple adding machine) or with a complicated electronic machine, there should be no mystery surrounding it. Data processing is "the restructuring of data by man or machine to increase its usefulness and value."[1] It is any method used to accomplish accounting, statistical, and reporting functions for business.

No discussion of data processing is complete without a discussion of the computer. In fact, some people believe, incorrectly, that the terms

(Continued on next page)

Exercise 7

June 25, 19— Dear Joyce It's been more than six months since your last dental checkup. Please call to arrange an appointment. ¶Dr. McCardle will be on vacation the month of August. Susan Brent, Nurse H.C. McCardle, D.D.S.

RETURN ADDRESS H. C. McCardle, D.D.S., 1947 West Pico Boulevard Los Angeles, CA 90034

ADDRESSEE Ms. Joyce Rothschild 3978 Sunset Boulevard No. 8 Hollywood, CA 90028

Exercise 8

Arrange attractively.

Association of Garment Manufacturers

New York, New York

The Time: Friday evening, May 7, 8 o'clock

The Place: Wagner Building, 644 Elm Street

The Purpose: Business meeting

    1. Annual election of officers

    2. Decision on meeting dates

    3. Plans for discussion topics

    4. Introduction of new members

Arthur T. Gross

Secretary

RETURN ADDRESS Association of Garment Manufacturers 383 Monroe Avenue, Suite 700 New York, NY 10031

ADDRESSEE Mr. Herbert N. Ferguson 63 West 49th Street New York, NY 10023

Topic 10 APPLYING ENGLISH SKILLS

The exercises in this topic will give you practice in correcting errors in spelling, grammar, and punctuation. Before you type an exercise, read it carefully to find the errors. The symbols in the margin of each exercise provide clues to the kinds of errors to look for. After you have identified each error in an exercise, make a list of the corrections. Then type the exercise in an acceptable business style. *Do not mark the book.*

The key below gives the meaning of each symbol. Three new symbols (marked with an asterisk) have been added to those used in earlier sections of the text.

KEY TO SYMBOLS USED IN EXERCISES 1–24					
*ab	abbreviation	ep	end punctuation	ro	run-on sentence
cap	capitalization	frag	sentence fragment	sem	semicolon
col	colon	*hy	hyphen	sp	spelling
com	comma	*num	number style	ww	wrong word

data processing and *computer* mean the same thing. Maniotes and Quasney state:

> A computer is simply a machine capable of accepting information, processing the information at high speeds, and providing the results of these processes in an acceptable form for the user.[2]

As computers have become more widely used in processing data for business, they have made possible a vast expansion in data handling.

Electronic computers have taken over many routine clerical jobs and have, understandably, caused a fear of the machine by people who do not understand it. Actually, computers have opened new career possibilities in data processing, creating job openings for an increased number of trained personnel on many levels. Jobs are now available in the field in seven basic categories: management, programming and analysis, clerical, maintenance, design and manufacturing, marketing and sales, and education.[3] Many of these computer-oriented careers in data processing did not exist even a few years ago.

A study of the role of data processing and computers is of value to everyone. There are few people who can get through a complete day without some form of data processing touching their lives. The checks we write, the bill receipts we return, even the letter envelopes we address have been adjusted to accommodate to being processed by the computer. Schools, courts, governments, banks, hospitals, police departments, industry—to name but a few—must all solve problems of processing the many names and account numbers to be handled each day.

Stories and jokes have been circulated portraying computers as monsters that may someday take over control of the entire world. But in fact, "without human direction the computer is quite useless."[4] Computers are only as capable as the men and women who program and maintain them.

Because of the volume of information to be handled and stored for reuse, more and more organizations are turning to the computer for help. We are fortunate to have the assistance of the computer in the job of processing data.

Footnotes to be typed with Exercise 3, "Understanding Data Processing"

[1]Gerald A. Silver and Joan B. Silver, *Data Processing for Business* (New York: Harcourt Brace, 1973), p. 5.

[2]John Maniotes and James S. Quasney, *Computer Careers* (New York: Hayden Book Co., 1974), p. 2.

[3]Ibid., p. 6.

[4]Ibid., p. 30.

Use the copy in these exercises to type the address and message sides of eight postal cards. Position the contents of the message side attractively. If you need to, refer to Model 23.

Exercise 1

Today's date Dear Mr. Babcock This is to notify you that the cleaning of your rugs has been completed. The rugs will be delivered to your home on Saturday. Yours truly T. Towers

RETURN ADDRESS Crawford Cleaners 177 Montrose Street Bridgeport, CT 06608

ADDRESSEE Mr. John T. Babcock 733 Barclay Street Bridgeport, CT 06607

Exercise 2

February 5, 19— Ladies and Gentlemen Kindly send me one gallon of Gerber Liquid Floor Wax at $8.98, as advertised in today's *Trumpet*. Charge to my account and send promptly. Muriel Joice

RETURN ADDRESS 17 Orville Square Largo, FL 33540

ADDRESSEE Gerber Brush Company 98 Carter Street Tampa, FL 33617

Exercise 3

Today's date Dear John Please note that we have changed our address to 189 Highbridge Road. Our new telephone number is 446-1004. ¶We hope to see you at our new store. Mrs. Elizabeth Brooks

RETURN ADDRESS The Antique Shop 189 Highbridge Road Utica, NY 13503

ADDRESSEE Mr. John C. O'Toole 511 Hutton Place Utica, NY 13521

Exercise 4

Today's date Dear Mrs. Parsons This is to acknowledge your contribution of $25 to the Wildlife Fund. We thank you in behalf of those animals you have helped by your generosity. Best wishes Barbara Taylor

RETURN ADDRESS The Wildlife Fund 448 Halloran Avenue Wichita, KS 67214

ADDRESSEE Mrs. Jacqueline Parsons 76 Cartwright Street Wichita, KS 67210

Exercise 5

July 2, 19— Dear Mr. Marsden Thank you for your subscription to our magazine. The first copy will arrive in about three weeks. Sincerely L. Clark

RETURN ADDRESS Modern Fiction Magazine 59 Hill Street Nashville, TN 37208

ADDRESSEE Mr. Dennis L. Marsden 322 Sumner Road Nashville, TN 37208

Exercise 6

December 31, 19— Dear Ms. Byrne The glassware about which you inquired will be ready for shipment next Saturday. It should reach you the following Monday. Regards J. Horton

RETURN ADDRESS Felix Hart & Company 201 Bard Street Flint, MI 48511

ADDRESSEE Ms. Alison Byrne 766 Hoyt Square Detroit, MI 48025

Exercise 4

BIBLIOGRAPHY

Type this bibliography. (For proper style, refer to page 166.) Type the heading in solid capitals. Use single spacing when typing each entry. Double space after each entry. If there is more than one work by the same author, do not repeat the name but indicate it by typing an 8-character under-score followed by a period.

Full sheet. 2-inch top margin. 1-inch side margins. Single spacing. 4-space runover indention (set a tab). Center the heading on line 13.

Exercise 5

REPORT WITH FOOTNOTES AND BIBLIOGRAPHY

Type this report with footnotes in the proper form. Type the bibliography on a separate page.

Full sheets. Margins for a left-bound report. Double spacing. 5-space paragraph indention.

BIBLIOGRAPHY

Campbell, William G., and Ballow, Stephen. *Form and Style: Theses, Reports, Term Papers.* 4th ed. Boston: Houghton Mifflin, 1974.

Carter, Colwell C., and Knox, James H. *The Complete Term Paper.* Reston, Va.: Reston Publishing, 1974.

Lester, James D. *Writing Research Papers: A Complete Guide.* 2d ed. Glenview, Ill.: Scott Foresman, 1976.

McMahan, Elizabeth. *A Crash Course in Composition.* New York: McGraw-Hill, 1973.

Manual of Style. 12th rev. ed. Chicago: University of Chicago Press, 1969.

Mulkerne, Donald, and Kahn, Gilbert. *The Term Paper—Step-by-Step.* Garden City, N.Y.: Doubleday, 1977.

Pierce, James F. *Organization and Outlining: How to Develop and Prepare Papers, Reports, and Speeches.* New York: Arco, 1971.

Taylor, Mildred G. *How to Write a Research Paper.* Palo Alto, Calif.: Pacific Books, 1974.

Turabian, Kate L. *A Manual for Writers of Term Papers, Theses, and Dissertations.* 4th ed. Chicago: University of Chicago Press, 1973.

_____. *Student's Guide for Writing College Papers.* 3rd ed. Chicago: University of Chicago Press, 1976.

BEES IN WINTERTIME

Bees have always been taken as the emblem of industry. No other creatures deserve better the title of "hustler" than do these restless little insects. They are never idle when conditions permit them to carry on their work. Even when the weather is too cold for them to leave their hives, they do plenty inside.[1]

Early in the winter, the queen—the mother of the hive—begins to lay eggs. These hatch into tiny grubs, or larvae, which are carefully fed. When twenty-one days have elapsed, the larvae have changed into full-grown bees.[2] They start to crawl out of the cells in which they were reared. At first they are weak and frail. After a few days they are full of the strength and energy of youth and are able to take up the work of the hive.

The queen continues to lay eggs, and what is called the *brood nest* grows steadily, but slowly, as the number of bees to look after it increases. The newly hatched bees devote themselves to the work of nursing and maturing the brood.

According to Rowland-Entwistle:

Apart from size and better development of the ovaries, there is not a great deal of difference between the worker bumblebees and their

(Continued on next page)

Topic 9 POSTAL CARDS

Postal cards are used for brief messages, such as announcements and notices, when privacy is not important. The card is usually 5½ by 3½ inches, and there are only 21 lines on the message side of the card. Since the message space is so small, the inside address and reference initials are omitted. The salutation and complimentary closing may also be omitted to save further space. Since postal cards often have the stamp printed on the address side, it is important to type carefully and not to waste cards.

Model 23 on this page shows the proper placement of the address and message on a postal card. Always use at least ½-inch margins on the message side, and type the message single spaced unless it is very short. Since you are limited to 21 lines, you will have to plan the proper spacing to arrange the contents of the message side attractively.

Before proceeding to the exercises, type Drill A to practice typing postal cards.

Drill A

Type the address and message sides of the postal card shown in Model 23. If no card is available, use paper cut to size.

```
Ideal Clock Company  ← Line 2
55 Devlin Street
Fulton, MO 65251

3 spaces

Set tab 5 spaces
left of center

        Mrs. Wilma Monroe  ← Line 12
        397 Bedrock Drive
        Fulton, MO 65251
```

Part A   Address Side

Part B   Message Side

```
                              March 14, 19--  ← Line 4
                                    TS
½-inch margin
    Dear Mrs. Monroe:                              ½-inch margin
        DS
        We have been unable to reach you by telephone.
    Repairs on your electric clock are complete.  Please
    call for the clock at your earliest convenience.
    Bring your receipt with you.
                                    DS
                                IDEAL CLOCK COMPANY
    Space down 4 times    D. Thomas

                                D. Thomas
```

Model 23   *Address and Message Sides of a Postal Card*

Exercise 5 continued

queen. There are size differences among the workers, however, and generally the larger bees go foraging, while the smaller ones tend the eggs and larvae.[3]

Honey is stored in the combs as a food reserve to be eaten during the winter and the spring, when nothing can be brought in from outside.[4] In winter the bees cluster together for warmth, eating only enough to keep themselves alive.

Early in the spring the bees fly about whenever the sun shines and the air is warm enough, although there are practically no nectar-bearing plants in bloom. You may well wonder what their object is. (Bees never do anything without a reason.) They have very important work to do outside. They need water, and plenty of it, at this time of the year. The older bees can get along with practically no water; but a great deal is needed to prepare the food for the young ones they are rearing in large numbers. Therefore, they must fetch all they can while the sun shines.

The young bees are fed on food prepared by the nurse bees from honey and pollen gathered the previous season. As both of these foods are highly concentrated, they are diluted with water before they are given to the larvae. That is why it is important to bring in plenty of water, and why the bees go out by the hundreds whenever the weather permits.[5] On every journey they bring back as much as their honey sacs will hold. In this way they store enough in the cells to last a few days.

Sometimes the weather becomes too cold for the bees to go out, and the water is used up. At other times the supply of honey in the hives runs short. Then the young are either destroyed or neglected.[6]

The bee benefits us more than any other insect does. It makes honey that we can eat; and in the process of making the honey, it helps farmers produce larger harvests of crops by serving as an excellent pollinator.[7]

Footnotes to be typed with Exercise 5, "Bees in Wintertime"

[1]Dorothy H. Patent, *How Insects Communicate* (New York: Holiday House, 1975), pp. 85–92.

[2]*The World Book Encyclopedia*, 1971 ed., s.v. "Bees: A Most Useful Insect," pp. 94–101.

[3]Theodore Rowland-Entwistle, *Insect Life: The World You Never See* (Chicago: Rand McNally, 1976), p. 93.

[4]Patent, *How Insects Communicate*, pp. 99–105.

[5]C. M. Larson and W. L. Gossett, "Some Facts about Bees," *Organic Gardening and Farming*, vol. 21 (May 1974), pp. 75–77.

[6]Ibid.

[7]*World Book Encyclopedia*, p. 103.

(Continued on next page)

Mailgram

November 12, 19—, 4:00 p.m.

Charge Sender

William S. Clapp
660 Bell Street
Jacksonville, FL 32202
(904) 622-9456

On return trip call on Norville Somerset, 22 Rand Road, Wilmington, DE. He wishes to see samples of our table-model radios.

B. Martin, Sales Manager

Albert Cortez and Company

Telegram
July 29, 19—, 1:00 p.m.
Charge Sender
Nicholas Aiken
Hotel Crosby
Meridian, MS 39301
(601) 667-9066
Change in coffee prices effective August 1. Continue taking orders at present prices through July 31. Customers will be notified by mail. New price list mailed to you today.
Henry Warden, Sales Manager
Griggs Wholesale Grocers, Inc.

Exercise 5 continued

Bibliography for Exercise 5, "Bees in Wintertime"

BIBLIOGRAPHY

Borror, Donald J., and White, Richard E. *A Field Guide to Insects of North America and Mexico.* Boston: Houghton-Mifflin, 1970.

Burton, Maurice, and Burton, Robert. *Encyclopedia of Insects and Arachnids.* London: Octopus Books, 1975.

Haguenoer, Michel. *World Treasury of Insects in Color.* New York: Galahad Books, 1975.

Klots, Alexander, and Klots, Elsie. *Insects of North America.* Garden City, N.Y.: Doubleday, 1971.

Larson, C. M., and Gossett, W. L. "Some Facts about Bees." *Organic Gardening and Farming,* vol. 21 (May 1974), pp. 75–77.

Patent, Dorothy H. *How Insects Communicate.* New York: Holiday House, 1975.

Romoser, William S. *The Science of Entomology.* New York: Macmillan, 1973.

Rowland-Entwistle, Theodore. *Insect Life: The World You Never See.* Chicago: Rand McNally, 1976.

World Book Encyclopedia, 1971 ed. s.v. "Bees: A Most Useful Insect."

Exercise 6

REPORT WITH TITLE PAGE, FOOTNOTES, AND BIBLIOGRAPHY

Type the following report in proper report form. Type a separate title page for the report (refer to page 113 for guidelines). For examples of title page arrangement and correct arrangement of text, footnotes, and bibliography, refer to the three illustrations at the right.

Full sheets. Margins for a left-bound report. Double spacing. 5-space paragraph indention.

PLASTIC SURGERY

Plastic surgery is the medical specialty that deals with the restoration of defects congenital, hereditary or acquired to improve both function and appearance. The basis upon which this branch of surgery rests is the transplantation of tissues.[1]

Introduction

Although generally regarded as something new, plastic surgery is actually ancient. In fact, it was used by the Egyptians over three thousand years ago to repair disfigurements caused by war.[2] Since then the specialty has progressed; new methods and treatments have been developed, facilitated by the advance of medical technology. At present, plastic surgery is more necessary than ever because of the after-effects of wars, and the high toll of automobile accidents.

(Continued on next page)

RECORD OF TELEGRAPH MESSAGE SUBMITTED BY TELEPHONE ◄————Center on line 13

TS

Class of service   Telegram

DS

Date/time sent   November 17, 19--, 10:15 a.m.

DS

Account charged   Charge Sender

DS

SS addressee's
name, address,
telephone number   Happy Home Furniture Company
370 Congress Street
Dayton, OH 45414
(513) 224-7612

DS

1½-inch margin   We urgently need at least 2 of the 12 cabinets ordered November 10.   1½-inch margin

Do not delay shipment until all are ready. Send as many as you can

DS message   immediately. Ship others as soon as possible. Wire dates we may

expect arrival of first shipment and final shipment.

TS

Dictator/title   C. Rutgers, President
Company name   Charles Rutgers & Company

DS

Reference initials   **xx**

Model 22   *Typed Record of a
Telegraph Message*

Exercise 6 continued

Procedures of the Plastic Surgeon

Contrary to the average point of view, there is nothing mysterious or occult about the procedures of the plastic surgeon. Deformities are diagnosed, photographed, studied, and corrected in much the same way as in any other surgical operation. For instance, the making of an entirely new nose is not difficult. The nose is formed from cartilage, taken from the hip or some other part of the body. Then flesh is removed from the scalp or forehead and grafted over the cartilage. When the operation is complete and the grafting has healed, no trace of the surgery can be seen.

Recent Advances in Plastic Surgery

The rising use of plastic surgery can be attributed to a number of factors. General medical progress has contributed much to its recent advance. For example, if there is a great loss of blood during the operation, blood plasma can be administered. The danger of infection has been reduced considerably through the discovery of penicillin. And because so much more is known about anesthesia than was known twenty-five years ago, facial disfigurements can be repaired in a relatively short time.

Although plastic surgery owes much to general medical progress for its rapid rise, most of its success is due to the experiments in the field of skin transplantation. Through the discovery of new methods and techniques in skin transplantation, the plastic surgeon has been able to do wonders with disfigured persons.[3]

What is needed to restore a disfigured human face, hand, or foot to its almost original appearance? A supply of skin tissue, cartilage, and the steady hand of an experienced plastic surgeon can be successfully applied to transform a disfigurement to a natural appearance. Thus, with cartilage as the basic structural material and skin as the covering material, the skilled plastic surgeon works "miracles of reconstruction."

Footnotes to be typed with Exercise 6, "Plastic Surgery"

[1]Arthur J. Barsky, *Plastic Surgery* (Philadelphia: W. B. Saunders, 1975), p. 17.

[2]S. L. Haas, "Rise of Plastic Surgery," *Newsweek*, vol. 13 (February 20, 1974), p. 34.

[3]A. Mazo, "New Faces," *Science Digest*, vol. 5 (May 1973), p. 9.

Bibliography for Exercise 6, "Plastic Surgery"

BIBLIOGRAPHY

"Army Organizes Plastic Surgery Service." *Hygeia*, vol. 20 (June 1972), p. 435.

Barsky, Arthur J. *Plastic Surgery*. Philadelphia: W. B. Saunders, 1975.

(Continued on next page)

Topic 8 TELEGRAMS

When a written message must reach its destination as fast as possible, a telegram is sent. A direct telegram offers the fastest service. The message is sent immediately and is usually hand delivered to its destination within hours. For faster transmittal, the message is telephoned to the addressee after it reaches the local telegraph office.

A less expensive class of service is the overnight telegram, or "night letter." A message sent at the night letter rate may be delivered to the telegraph office at any hour, but it will not be sent until nighttime when the telegraph lines are less busy. A night letter is delivered by messenger to the addressee on the day following its transmittal.

A third class of service is the mailgram. The message is wired to a post office near the addressee where it is electronically printed and then placed in the mail. A mailgram offers next-day delivery at less than half the cost of a night letter. Since rates vary considerably, you should choose the class of service carefully. The minimum rate for a night letter or mailgram is based on a 100-word message; but for a direct telegram, it is based on a 10-word message. Each additional word adds to the cost.

To send a telegram or mailgram, businesses most often call in their messages by telephone to a local telegraph office. This is more convenient for them than arranging for hand delivery of messages typed on standard telegram forms. Model 22 (page 299) illustrates how to set up a record of a telegraph message submitted by telephone. Study the model carefully, and reread the interoffice memo in Exercise 11 of Topic 7 (page 296). Then, do Drill A to gain practice in typing a telegraph message.

Drill A

Type the record of a telegraph message sent by telephone shown in Model 22. Follow the spacing instructions given there. Make 2 carbon copies.

Directions for Exercises 1–4

The telegraph messages in these exercises were submitted by telephone. Type them following the style shown in Model 22. Be sure to include the heading for each one. Make 2 carbon copies.

Exercise 1
Full sheet. 1½-inch side margins. Begin on line 13.

Telegram   July 19, 19—, 11:00 a.m.   Charge Sender   Atlantic Federal Bank   227 Morton Street Bangor, ME 04401   (207) 332-1788   Stop Check No. 10076 payable to Computer Service, Inc. written on our Account No. 3-035972-6. Check reported stolen from main office of Computer Service.   L. Benton, Accountant   SGS Investments   *xx*

Exercise 2
Full sheet. 1½-inch side margins. Begin on line 13.

Night Letter   May 24, 19—, 10:30 p.m.   Charge Robert Leahy Agency   3702 Gold Street San Francisco, CA 94107   (415) 359-5085   Margaret Hatcher   138 Sweitzer Avenue   Syracuse, NY 13213   (315) 531-3202   Please send remainder of art history manuscript immediately. Prince Publishers wants to see entire book. For reference, we have received Chapters 1 through 7, and are awaiting Chapters 8 through 10. Our art department is still waiting for slides that accompany Chapters 4 through 7. Must be complete for submission to publisher.   Lynn Wilson, Agent   R. Leahy Agency *xx*

Boon, A. R. "Human Faces Remodeled by Skilled Plastic Surgeons." *Popular Science*, vol. 124 (June 1974), pp. 24–26.

"Born with One Ear, Gets Another." *New York Times*, March 30, 1977, 44:3.

Brown, D., and Lumsden, R. "Surgery Heals the Scars of War." *Hygeia*, vol. 22 (January 1974), pp. 26–27.

Brown, James, and McDowell, Frank. *Skin Grafting of Burns*. Philadelphia: J. B. Lippincott, 1973.

Byars, L. T., and Kaune, M. M. "Plastic Surgery, Its Possibilities and Limitations." *American Journal of Nursing*, vol. 44 (April 1975), pp. 334–342.

"Cartilage Banks Urged for Face Injury Repair." *Science News Letter*, vol. 45 (March 18, 1974), p. 185.

Downs, W. "War Surgery for Sex." *Newsweek*, vol. 21 (February 8, 1976), p. 78.

Lewin, M. L. "Rehabilitation and Plastic Surgery." *Safety Engineering*, vol. 76 (November 1975), pp. 14–16.

Maisel, A. Q. "New Faces for New Men." *Science Digest*, vol. 13 (April 1973), pp. 28–32.

Maliniak, J. W. "Your Child's Face and Future." *Hygeia*, vol. 13 (May 1975), pp. 410–413.

———. "Plastic Surgeon and Crime." *Journal of Criminal Law and Criminology*, vol. 26 (November 1977), pp. 594–599.

Murry, M. "Turning a New Face to the World." *Reader's Digest*, vol. 31 (August 1977), p. 30.

Topic 4 MANUSCRIPTS

The procedures for typing manuscripts are essentially the same as those for typing reports. The differences lie in the fact that a report is a finished work to be read by someone seeking information, while a manuscript is more like a draft. It is read and corrected by editors. Then the edited manuscript is either retyped or set into type as the final copy.

Review the rules for typing reports (pages 157–158 and 165–166), noting these important differences for manuscript typing:

1. *All* copy must be double or triple spaced. *No* copy should be single spaced, including long quotations and footnotes. This is to make it easier for the editor to make corrections and to allow the text to be easily read by the typesetter.
2. Use generous margins to allow the editor to make notations or to write instructions on the pages. A 6-inch line with a 1½-inch left margin is desirable. Use right and bottom margins of at least 1 inch. Allow a 2-inch top margin on chapter-opening pages, and a 1-inch top margin on succeeding pages.
3. Do not underline subheads; type them in both capitals and small letters. Differentiate between different levels of subheads by their placement. For instance, the most important head may be centered; the next level subhead may be at the left margin on a line by itself; and a third level subhead may start a paragraph, followed by 3 spaces.
4. Number all text pages in the upper right corner, starting with Arabic numeral 1 and proceeding in order to the last page.

Exercise 12 continued

6. The addressee will type the reply on the bottom part of the copies received. The original copy is removed for the addressee's department files. The last carbon copy is returned to the sender.

These forms are very convenient and easy to use—not only for the sender, but also for the receiver. They eliminate the need to handle separate sheets of carbon paper. Also, they encourage prompt replies simply because of the way in which they are designed—the person responding to such a memo need only fill in the blank spaces. The process of writing a response automatically generates a copy for the sender's files. Carbon set memo forms, therefore, offer several advantages over standard memorandum paper. *xx*   (204 words)

Exercise 13
CARBON SET
MESSAGE FORM

Use a carbon set message form to type this memo. Follow the instructions given in the memo in Exercise 12. (After you have finished the message, you may remove the first carbon copy and exchange memos with another student before typing the response.)

If memo forms are not available, use a full sheet ruled across the middle. Type the headings in solid capitals. Make 2 carbon copies.

Message

TO D. Greene AT Personnel Department SUBJECT Employee Social Security Number DATE June 16, 19— We have received papers for a temporary summer employee, Rhonda Patterson, who has been placed in the Word Processing Center. We find, however, that her social security number was omitted from the form sent us. Please supply us with this number as soon as possible so that Ms. Patterson's check will not be delayed.   PLEASE REPLY TO—SIGNED S. Jenkins, Payroll Department

Reply

We are extremely sorry for this oversight. Rhonda Patterson's social security number is 382-77-3267. *xx* DATE June 17, 19— SIGNED D. Greene, Personnel Clerk

Exercise 14
CARBON SET
MESSAGE FORM

Type this message on a carbon set form. If a form is not available, create your own, following the directions in Exercise 13 above. For more detail, refer to Model 21, page 289.

Message

TO Joyce Kaplan AT Advertising Department SUBJECT New Logo Design DATE October 5, 19— As you know, our merger with Sandsdown Industries will be finalized in the next few weeks. I've been put in charge of developing new logo, letterhead, and business card designs. I could hire an outside designer, but the budget in this department is very tight right now. Any ideas? *xx* PLEASE REPLY TO—SIGNED G. Celli, Public Relations

Reply

George: Why not hold an intercompany contest for the design of the new logo? Our merged name—Albright-Sandsdown Industries, Inc.—makes me think of all kinds of possibilities. We have some very creative people here, too. We could offer $100 as a prize for the person(s) whose design is accepted. *xx* DATE October 6, 19— SIGNED Joyce Kaplan, Advertising

WORD PROCESSING CAREERS
TS

Exercise 1

MANUSCRIPT

Type this manuscript in proper form. If you make any typing errors, correct them as you go. Any remaining errors may be corrected by using accept-able proofreaders' marks in pencil. Remember to double-space footnotes.

Full sheets. 1½-inch side margins. 2-inch top margin and 1-inch bottom margin. Double spacing. 5-space paragraph indention.

Although the term *word processing* has been around since the mid-1960's, no one has yet come up with a universally accepted definition. Cecil defines it as "an efficient system of communicating one person's ideas to another in typewritten form."[1]

With the advent of word processing, a secretary need no longer work with only one executive. Now an "administrative secretary" serves a group of executives called "principals." In this new role, the secretary handles traditional secretarial duties, such as placing telephone calls, handling mail, and filing. In addition, he or she assumes more administrative-type duties—research, arranging meetings, and even dictation of routine letters and messages.

When there is typing to be done for the principals, the administrative secretary sends it to the supervisor in the Word Processing Center. There, a "correspondence secretary" is given the assignment. The correspondence secretary is an expert in using an array of transcribing, high-speed-duplicating, and electronic typewriters to produce perfect finished copy.

Not everyone will make a successful correspondence secretary. This specialist must have more than machine operation skills. He or she must also have a thorough knowledge of spelling, grammar, and punctuation.

Word processing has greatly altered career paths for clerical workers. A correspondence secretary with administrative abilities may want to switch to a job as an administrative secretary. An administrative secretary may want to make the switch to a position of correspondence secretary.

Today, the secretarial career has become increasingly specialized, opening up new possibilities in the word processing field for those with technical skills.

Footnote to be typed with Exercise 1, "Word Processing Careers"

[1]Paula B. Cecil, *Word Processing in the Modern Office*, (Menlo Park, Calif.: Cummings, 1976), p. 3.

Exercise 2

Use Exercise 1 (pages 166–167), "The Story of Paper," for additional practice in preparing typed copy for editing and printing. Retype the exercise, using the rules for manuscript typing. Remember to use wide margins and to double-space all lines.

Exercise 11

FULL-SHEET MEMO

When you type this inter-office memo, begin the numbered items at the left margin.

Full sheet. Memo form. No paragraph indention.

TO   A. Katz, Correspondence Secretary   FROM   D. Bahr, Word Processing Training Supervisor   SUBJECT   Procedures for Handling Telegrams   DATE *Today's date*   Telegrams are sometimes typed on printed forms supplied by the telegraph company and then delivered to the local telegraph office. However, like many businesses today, we find it more convenient to telephone our messages to the telegraph office. ¶To type a record of a telegraph message submitted by telephone, follow this procedure: 1. Use a full sheet of plain paper to make a record of the message sent. Type the message in triplicate. Use 1½-inch side margins. On line 13, center the title, RECORD OF TELEGRAPH MESSAGE SUBMITTED BY TELEPHONE. 2. At the left margin type the class of service used, a triple space below the title. 3. Double-space and type at the left margin the date and the exact time the message was sent. 4. Double-space and type at the left margin the name of the account to be charged. 5. Double-space and type at the left margin the addressee's complete name, address, and telephone number. Use single spacing for this address. 6. Double-space and begin the message, typing it in double-spaced form. 7. Triple-space after the message is complete and type at the left margin the name, title, department, and company of the dictator of the telegram. 8. Double-space and type your reference initials at the left margin.   DB   *xx*

(221 words)

Exercise 12

FULL-SHEET MEMO

Type an interoffice memo from the copy given at the right. Begin the enumerated items at the left margin.

Full sheet. Plain paper. No paragraph indention. Begin headings on line 7.

Memorandum   SUBJECT Using New QUIKIMEMO Forms   TO All Correspondence Secretaries   FROM D. Bahr, Word Processing Training Supervisor   DATE *Today's date*   Ms. Allen in our Purchasing Department has informed me that we now have a supply of QUIKIMEMO interoffice forms. These forms allow for two-way communication on a single sheet. They come in sets of three sheets, consisting of an original and two copies. QUIKIMEMO forms should be used instead of the regular half-sheet memo forms when messages are short and replies are required.

Follow these steps in using the forms:

1. Complete the top section, which calls for the name of the addressee, the location of the addressee, the subject, and the date.
2. Type the message on the lines provided on the top half of the form. Add your reference initials at the end of the message.
3. Type the name and location of the sender on the line marked "Please Reply To." Leave room for the dictator's initials or signature.
4. Remove the first carbon copy sheet and file it in our department files for follow-up purposes.
5. Send both the original and the last carbon copy to the addressee. Leave the carbon paper intact.

(Continued on next page)

TS

Chapter 1. Making Better Use of Your Time

Many of us complain that there is never enough time to do all the things we must do. Often we will find our situation greatly improved if we stop to be sure we are making wise use of the time we do have. Each of us has the same number of hours available in the day, yet some people seem to achieve so much more in those hours. Those of us who complain of lack of time will probably find that we have many hours of wasted time in our day that could be used more constructively with just a little bit of planning.

TS

Time on the Job

As a new employee, you will have to learn to organize work so as to make the best use of your time on the job. Employers pay for a certain number of hours' work from each employee. They expect that this time will be spent to produce the most work for the company.

Coming to work late and taking long lunch breaks are costly to employers, since an employee who wastes time cannot produce the expected quantity of work.

On most jobs there are short periods of time—just before lunch, break, or quitting time—in which there is not enough time to start a major project. During this time, however, you can be doing such jobs as changing a typewriter ribbon, cleaning file drawers, or getting fresh supplies. When these short periods are used constructively, there is more time available for major projects.

Leisure Time Must Be Planned

The use of free time away from your work is important, too. If you do not plan to make the best use of this limited free time, it will just slip away. Many of us "procrastinate" (put off things until another time). We waste much time in thinking about what must be done, instead of simply tackling the job. You can save time by making a list of the things that must be done—and then doing them.

Many of us waste time sitting inactively in front of a television set. Television has much to offer in the way of education and entertainment, but time you spend watching it should be planned.

Free Your Mind

On the job, you usually must work under the direction and supervision of another person. Your free time may be the only time that you

(Continued on next page)

Exercise 3

MANUSCRIPT WITH
HEADINGS

Type this manuscript in
proper form. Number all
pages on line 3 at the right
margin. Remember to make
light pencil marks at the left
margin 1 inch and 2 inches
from the bottom of the
page as a warning that you
are approaching the end of
the page.

*Full sheets. 1½-inch side
margins. 2-inch top margin
and 1-inch bottom margin.
Double spacing 5-space
paragraph indention.*

Exercise 10

ROUGH DRAFT:
FULL-SHEET MEMO

Type this interoffice memo,
correcting the copy as indicated by the proofreaders'
marks. Type your initials as
reference initials. Then
address an interoffice
envelope.

*Full sheet. Memo form. No
paragraph indention. Large
envelope.*

Sept. 10, 19—

To: N. Adams

From: Glenda Harrison

Subject: CO-OP Program

Copies: Mary Samuels, John Capistro,
Peter Matthews, Melanie Ames

At our recent ~~last~~ department Staff meeting, you spoke ~~of~~ to us about our company's proposed involvement in a cooperative program with our local school system.

~~As~~ Since I started my office career when ~~I began~~ by working in a Co-op while in high school, I am thoroughly convinced of the value of this type of program.

Please add my dept. to the list of those which ~~who~~ will participate in the program. Persons who ~~working~~ in my department ~~our offices~~ would require good typing skills, but speed is not as important as accuracy.

Please let me know further about the program as plans for it are developed and finalized.

Glenda Harrison

It would be ~~help~~ helpful if the Co-op students ~~they~~ also ~~have~~ had a basic ~~accounting~~ course in accounting.

(114 words)

Exercise 3 continued

have to do what you *want* to do. Remember that your mind needs to relax and be free from pressures at regular intervals. It is important to your physical and mental well-being that leisure time be planned to include pleasant activities. Group activities should be included in your plan, so that you have a chance to meet and talk with people in a non-work setting. Hobbies, too, are good leisure-time activities, because they build self-confidence.

Exercise 4

MANUSCRIPT—
HANDWRITTEN COPY

Type this handwritten copy in proper manuscript form. Use your judgment about the placement and spacing of the subheads.

Full sheets. 1½-inch side margins. 2-inch top margin and 1-inch bottom margin. Double spacing. 5-space paragraph indention.

SECTION I   PROBLEMS OF THE CREDIT MANAGER

COLLECTING OVERDUE BILLS

Collecting money from people who are not prompt payers is often a delicate, if not troublesome, matter. You must be careful not to offend. On the contrary, you must show the utmost courtesy, as some people are inclined to be sensitive. To collect bills from slow payers and still maintain their goodwill is a problem that calls for careful handling. Large firms handle this problem through their own credit departments. Small firms turn over their slow accounts to collection agencies that specialize in this kind of work.

In some cases, a tactfully worded letter will bring the response you wish. In other cases, you may have to send a series of short collection letters before the debt is finally settled. Sometimes a personal visit or a telephone call will solve the problem.

(Continued on next page)

her, and she will give you a draft for $200, together with the necessary forms to be sent with the draft to our London Branch.

Please bring this material to me as soon as you return, and I shall explain to you what I want done ~~you to do~~ with it.

(72 words)

Exercise 9
ROUGH DRAFT:
HALF-SHEET MEMO

Type an interoffice memo from this handwritten copy, and make the corrections indicated by the proof-readers' marks. Type your initials at the end of the memo.

Half sheet. Memo form. No paragraph indention.

July 10, 19—

To: Madge Kidd

Office Manager

From: Lawrence Werner

Supply Department Manager

Subject: Conserving Envelopes

At the present time, it is difficult to obtain the special paper used in the manufacture of our interoffice envelopes. ~~Therefore,~~ it is important, therefore, to ~~that you~~ avoid wasting envelopes, and ~~that you~~ to use a small ~~envelope~~ rather than a large ~~one~~ envelope, whenever a small ~~envelope~~ one ~~would~~ will serve the purpose.

Envelopes with the imprinted word RUSH are to be used sparingly.

L. Werner

(59 words)

There are extreme cases where any measure you may take short of legal action is a waste of time.

TAKING LEGAL ACTION

Legal action exacts a heavy toll in time, money, and effort. Business people, therefore, when confronted with debtors who fail to pay their bills on time, try to collect their debts by means of correspondence.

WRITING COLLECTION LETTERS

The ability to write good collection letters is rated highly in the business world. The story is told of a young clerk in a wholesale house whose salary was $115 a week. During the slack period, she was given the task of following up some small accounts that were regarded as hopelessly bad. In each case she sought out the facts and looked into the record of the debtor. Then she went to work on her letters. Within a month she had collected more than 60 percent of the accounts turned over to her. She was promptly rewarded by an increase in salary. Today she is a highly paid credit manager.

Exercise 5

Use Exercise 4 (page 170) for practice in preparing typed copy for editing and printing. Retype the bibliography exercise, using the rules for manuscript typing. Remember that all lines must be double spaced.

Accordingly, will you please address documentation for all such shipments to my ~~personal~~ attn.? In all cases, be sure to include the customer's purchase order number and the date on which ~~when~~ the goods were shipped. If a customer should pick up an order in person, ~~you must secure~~ obtain the customer's signature on the shipping ~~form~~ document. This will serve as proof that the goods were delivered.

When you ship parts, and wish to re-stock your inventory, please address your requisitions to me so that our inventory records can ~~may~~ be kept current. I shall make every effort to see that the part is shipped to you immediately ~~right away~~.

Whenever you prepay shipping costs on any order that you fill for customers, please send me the original ~~copy~~ of the freight bill receipted by the carrier.

xx   (174 words)

Exercise 8
ROUGH DRAFT:
HALF-SHEET MEMO

*Half sheet. Plain paper
No paragraph indention.
Begin headings on line 7.*

Type this interoffice memo from the handwritten copy. Make the corrections indicated by the proofreaders' marks. Use the standard headings, and arrange them in any order you prefer. The memo was written by **Oliver D. Church, Manager.**

May 19, 19—
Memo to ~~Mr.~~ E. D. Loring, Special Messenger, concerning an urgent pickups at City Bank. Copy for Ms. L. D. Morris

Please call at the foreign Exchange department of ~~the~~ City Bank this afternoon before ~~three~~ two o'clock. Ask for Ms. Morris, the exchange manager; Present your identification card ~~this note~~ to

(Continued on next page)

Exercise 6

MANUSCRIPT

Type the material at the right in proper manuscript form. Make the corrections shown in the copy.

Full sheet. 6-inch line. 1-inch top and bottom margins. Double spacing. 5-space paragraph indention.

BUYING MAGAZINES

Magazines, issued weekly or monthly, can take up a good part of our reading time. Although less lasting *in interest* than books, they can occupy our attention for a considerably longer period of time than the daily newspaper. No matter what your tastes or hobbies are, you can probably find something to satisfy you in one or more of the magazines on the market. As with books, you should know where and how to secure the magazines that you wish to read, *and the most economical way to purchase them for your specific uses.*

Newsstands

Newsstands display a wide selection of current magazines for those who want to buy individual copies. The annual cost of ~~individual~~ copies *purchased individually* can be more than twice that of a yearly subscription mailed to your home. On the other hand, if you do not have the time or desire to read a periodical every week or month, it will be cheaper *in the long run* to pay the newsstand price.

Subscriptions

As already noted, A yearly subscription is more economical if it suits your purpose. When you are sure that you will be a long-time permanent subscriber, you can save *a substantial amount of* money with a two-year or three-year subscription. Make certain, however, that you do not load yourself with more magazines than you have time to read, or that they do not consume time that would be better spent reading books.

Memo *sp* Center

Subject: National Fund Contributions

To: Dept. *sp* Heads

From: Warren McPherson, Public Relations

Aug. *sp* 2, 19—

The National Fund soon will be starting its annual fund-raising campaign. Once again, we are encouraging our employees to give to this worthy charity. ¶ Please inform Make sure the employees in your department are aware of the various ways in which make their they may contribute and sions. Discuss with them activities the many ways the National Fund sponsors to helps those in need in our community. ¶ A representative from the National Fund will visit appear at Plant 2 sometime during later this month. I will give you the more details on the date and time that later.

WM *xx* (88 words)

Memorandum

Date: November 5, 19—

To: All Branch Managers

From: B. Smith, Traffic Manager

Subject: Coordinating Invoices and Shipping Papers

From time to time we have make requested requests that you ship certain items to customers directly. Lately We have had difficulty in coordinating the invoices for these orders with the shipping papers. I have been asked to investigate and organize a plan for eliminating it this difficulty.

(Continued on next page)

PART **6**

PUNCTUATION AND CAPITALIZATION

The typist and transcription machine operator must know the basic rules of English grammar. This section reviews the most common rules of punctuation and capitalization. You can find a more complete discussion of these rules in a reference manual for typists and stenographers or in a standard handbook of English usage.

Topic 1 PERIOD

The period is used (1) at the end of complete sentences, (2) after abbreviations, (3) as a decimal point in writing numbers. This topic examines the use of the period at the end of complete sentences. Other uses of the period are presented in Section 3, Part 1.

Two serious errors commonly made in typing and transcribing are transcribing a part of a sentence (called a sentence fragment) as though it were a complete sentence; and transcribing two complete sentences as though they were one sentence (called a run-on sentence).

By learning and applying the following four rules, you can avoid these two errors.

SENTENCE FRAGMENTS

Rule 1.

A sentence must contain a subject and a predicate and must express a complete thought.

- *Fish swim.*
- *She will turn the page.*

- *Turn the page.*
  (Subject *you* is understood.)

Rule 2.

Words such as *when, if, since,* and *because* signal a dependent clause. A dependent clause that stands alone is a sentence fragment. To make a complete sentence, the dependent clause must be preceded or followed by an independent clause (a group of words that could stand alone as a complete sentence), and the sentence must end with a period. If the dependent clause precedes the independent clause, use a comma to

Exercise 4
FULL-SHEET MEMO

Type an interoffice memo from this copy and address an interoffice envelope.

Full sheet. Plain paper. No paragraph indention. Begin headings on line 7. No. 10 envelope.

MEMORANDUM   SUBJECT Stove Replacements   DATE   February 8, 19—   12
TO   S. Cornwall, Sales Manager   FROM   Paul F. Kenny, Production Depart-   25
ment   COPIES   K. Hodge, Repair Department   On several recent occasions,   39
we were informed that your salespeople had notified all customers that stoves   54
damaged in transit would be replaced with new ones. ¶This arrangement is   68
satisfactory only when damage is too serious to repair. When damage to a   82
stove is of a minor nature, the proper procedure is to use replacement parts   87
and make the necessary repairs. To replace all damaged stoves is much too   112
costly for the company. ¶We need your cooperation to make sure that all   126
claims are adjusted in our best interest. Although replacement is easier for the   142
salespeople, it is a much too expensive policy for the firm to follow in every   157
case. ¶Please bring this matter to the attention of the sales staff. Advise them   173
to use their judgment and to refrain from promising replacements of stoves   188
when repairs will serve the purpose. PFK *xx*   (141 words)   197

Exercise 5
HALF-SHEET MEMO

Follow the style of Model 17 to type this interoffice memo. Remember to type your initials at the end of the memo.

Half sheet. Memo form. No paragraph indention.

March 1, 19—
To: All Sales Representatives
From: Anthony D. Fanning, Sales Manager
Subject: Imperial Oil Sales
    It is very important that we make a concerted drive to boost the sales of the new Imperial Oil during March. Although each of us has written a few orders, sales, on the whole, have been disappointing.
    Because this new oil is such a superior lubricant, we produced a large quantity in the belief it would almost sell itself. In view of its quality and reasonable price, I am sure that an earnest effort will quickly result in an excellent showing for every one of you.

(85 words)

Rule 2 continued

divide them. If the dependent clause follows the independent clause, this comma is not needed.

FRAGMENT: *When you go to the store*
CORRECTED: *When you go to the store, buy bread and milk.*
FRAGMENT: *Because the train was late.*
CORRECTED: *She missed supper because the train was late.*

RUN-ON SENTENCES

Rule 3.

If there is a complete thought on both sides of a conjunctive adverb, such as *however, therefore, furthermore, consequently,* or *nevertheless,* use a period (or a semicolon—see Rule 13) to show the complete break.

RUN-ON: *Our teacher was absent, therefore we did not take the test.*
CORRECTED: *Our teacher was absent. Therefore, we did not take the test.*
OR: *Our teacher was absent; therefore, we did not take the test.*

Rule 4.

Watch for complete thoughts that run together without a conjunction, such as *and, or, but, for,* or *not.* Use a period (or a semicolon—see Rule 11) to separate the complete thoughts.

RUN-ON: *Do not be left out send in your application today.*
CORRECTED: *Do not be left out. Send in your application today.*
OR: *Do not be left out; send in your application today.*

Exercise 1
PERIOD

Review Rules 1 and 2. As you type the material at the right, make complete sentences by joining the clauses properly, or adding independent clauses as necessary.

Half sheet. 70-space line. Single spacing. Begin on line 13.

1. When you see my friend. Tell him to telephone me.
2. He lost his job. Because of poor attendance.
3. Having completed her work. She went home early.
4. I looked down. And found my lost pencil.
5. I read a new book. Which was most interesting.
6. If you are an accurate speller. Good jobs are yours.
7. Since she felt ill.
8. Before you begin to work.
9. When a letter is neatly typed.
10. Such as bowling and roller skating.

Exercise 2
PERIOD

Review Rules 3 and 4. As you type the sentences at the right, use periods to correct the run-on sentences.

Half sheet. 70-space line. Single spacing. Begin on line 13.

1. Accidents are caused they don't just happen.
2. I fell asleep on the bus I missed my stop.
3. The job was difficult nevertheless, we got it done.
4. I saw the movie however, I did not like it.
5. She practiced daily therefore, she was very expert.
6. We are having a party of course you are invited.
7. Try to remember names they are important to their owners.
8. Save your credit rating send us a check today.
9. Your business is appreciated we shall continue to serve you.
10. I couldn't mail the letter I lost my only stamp.

Exercise 1

HALF-SHEET MEMO

Type this interoffice memo following the style for the headings shown in Model 18. For the interoffice envelope, refer to Model 20, Style B.

Half sheet. Plain paper. No paragraph indention. Begin headings on line 7. Large envelope.

MEMORANDUM SUBJECT Customers' Complaints TO Louis E. Hastings 12
Manager, Sales Personnel FROM T. R. Vernon DATE *Today's date* Recently, 26
many customers have complained of poor service. Whenever a salesperson 40
was mentioned by name or number, I referred the matter to you to be dis- 54
cussed with the individual concerned. However, many complaints have been 68
general in nature. For example, there have been complaints that no sales- 83
person was available at the counter, or that two salespeople were engaged in 98
conversation and did not respond promptly to waiting customers. ¶Please 112
take this matter up with the sales personnel, and instruct the floor supervisors 128
to be alert to these problems. T. R. Vernon *xx* (87 words) 137

Exercise 2

FULL-SHEET MEMO

Refer to Model 19 before typing this memorandum. If a memo form is not available, use plain paper and type the headings. Address an interoffice envelope.

Full sheet. Memo form. No paragraph indention. No. 10 envelope.

TO Katherine S. Schultz Sales Manager FROM T. S. Armstrong Advertising 12
Manager SUBJECT Customers' Addresses DATE December 17, 19— Because 23
salespeople frequently omit customers' addresses on the sales slips, we are 38
having difficulty in compiling a customer card record for the purpose of 52
mailing circulars. ¶Please instruct all salespeople to fill in every customer's 68
complete address, even if it is not needed for credit or delivery purposes. This 84
will simplify our work and ensure that we are using current addresses. ¶We 99
shall probably have to send you, from time to time, some of your past sales 114
slips, requesting that you supply the customers' addresses from your own 128
records. At that time, please bring the omission to the attention of the sales- 141
people at fault. ¶This may seem to be a minor matter, but it is important in 156
assisting us to complete our records. We shall greatly appreciate your giving 171
it your careful attention. *xx* (133 words) 177

Exercise 3

FULL-SHEET MEMO

Type the memorandum at the right. Type headings like those shown in Model 18, page 286.

Full sheet. Plain paper. No paragraph indention. Begin the heading on line 7.

TO: All Sales Representatives FROM: Gladys Lahey, Controller SUBJECT: 15
Credit Cards DATE: January 27, 19— CC: Ronald Ritchie, Marketing Man- 30
ager In recent months our accounting staff has been having difficulty in 45
reconciling the company's monthly statement from Master Charge with the 59
items charged on your credit cards, as reported on your weekly expense 73
reports. ¶During the past three months there were 11 instances in which we 88
were unable to identify charges. In each case, we discovered that a sales 103
representative had misplaced or lost a sales draft and had neglected to include 119
the amount in his or her expense report. Without your copy of the draft, we 134
cannot identify a charge and have no means of knowing whether it is legiti- 149
mate. This forces us to ask Master Charge to send a copy of the draft to us for 165
verification. ¶We ask you, therefore, to treat your credit card purchases as 180
carefully as cash, and to be sure to attach copies of your sales drafts to your 196
expense reports. *xx* (148 words) 200

Topic 2 COMMA

The comma is the most used (and misused) punctuation mark. If you master its two chief uses, you will be much closer to writing clear sentences. These two chief uses are (1) to set off an introductory dependent clause, and (2) to set off words that interrupt the main thought of a sentence.

Rule 5.
INTRODUCTORY DEPENDENT CLAUSES

Words such as *if, as, when, because, since, before, after, unless, while, provided, whether,* and *although* introduce adverbial clauses. As mentioned in Rule 2, if these dependent clauses begin a sentence, a comma separates the dependent and independent (or main) clause. If the dependent clause follows the main clause, no comma is needed between them.

- *If you cannot be present, please notify me.*
- *Please notify me if you cannot be present.*
- *As I am sure you know, the store closes at five.*
- *When you finish your test, you may be excused.*

Rule 6.
PARENTHETICAL WORDS AND PHRASES

Use commas to set off all words and phrases that interrupt the main thought of the sentence.

- *I feel, therefore, that we should change our plans.*
- *Don't you think, Mr. Sanders, that the price is too high?*
- *He did not have the new orders, of course.*
- *Next Monday, January 6, is my birth date.*

Rule 7.
WORDS IN APPOSITION

Use commas to set off explanatory words or phrases within a sentence.

- *My neighbor, Ms. Fischer, owns a sailboat.*
- *We couldn't find Larsdell, the secretary who wrote the report.*
- *That tree, the redwood, fell during a storm.*
- *Our representative in your area, Ms. Shelly, will visit you soon.*

Rule 8.
SERIES

Use commas to separate items when three or more are listed in a sentence. A comma is usually used before the conjunction preceding the last item of a series.

- *I bought a tie, a coat, and a pair of shoes.*
- *I talked to her on July 1, July 3, and July 18.*
- *This summer I plan to read five books, fix my car, and plant a garden.*
- *Please close the windows, turn off the light, and lock the door when you go.*

Rule 9.
CONJUNCTION

Use a comma before conjunctions such as *and, or, but, for,* or *nor* when they join two completely independent statements. The comma is optional between very short statements joined by *and, or, nor,* especially if the two thoughts are closely related.

- *Rita attends Central High School, and she is a cheerleader.* (comma optional)
- *Rita attended Central High School between 1975 and 1978, and she was a cheerleader in her senior year.*
- *I have tried several new cars, but I am still not sure which one to buy.*

Rule 10.
OMITTED WORDS

If a word or phrase is obviously missing, use a comma to indicate the omission.

- *He was a fast, efficient typist.* (*and* omitted)
- *Bill sold two cookies; Sandra, none.* (*sold* omitted)
- *A cold, frosty shake is good on a hot, sunny day.* (*and* omitted both times)

Drill D

Type an interoffice envelope for each person addressed in the memo in Model 18. Follow Style B shown in Model 20. On each copy of the memo, check the name of the person to whom it is being sent. Then fold the memos and insert them in the proper envelopes.

Drill E

Type the memo in Model 21 on a carbon set message form. Include both the message and the reply. Follow the spacing shown. If no printed form is available, prepare your own on ruled paper with 2 carbon copies. Type the headings in solid capitals.

QUIKIMEMO

TO Grace Allen	AT Purchasing Department

SUBJECT Reorder of Interoffice Memo Forms	DATE March 4, 19--

We are now running very low on our supply of half-sheet size interoffice memo

forms. We need at least a ream of them immediately, since we use them daily.

Also, the form on which I am typing this memo was sent to me as a sample. I

think a supply of these forms would be very useful for all our departments.

xx

(The top half of the memo is completed by the originator.)

PLEASE REPLY TO   SIGNED
       D. Bahr, Word Processing *D. Bahr*

I am sending you today the ream of half-sheet interoffice memo forms that you

requested. I am also sending you a ream of the new carbon sets of QUIKIMEMO

forms. I received a sample at the same time you did, and I immediately

ordered a supply. Please instruct your typists in the proper use of these

handy forms.

(The lower half of the memo is completed by the receiver.)

DATE March 6, 19--	SIGNED Grace Allen, Purchasing Department *Grace Allen*

ORIGINAL

COPY 1

COPY 2

Model 21   *Carbon Set Interoffice Message Form*

Exercise 3

COMMA

Review Rule 5 and type these sentences, adding a comma after each introductory clause. *Do not mark the book.*

Full sheet. 70-space line. Double spacing. Begin on line 6.

1. As we began to assemble the pages of the long report we found that many of the pages were very difficult to read.
2. While it is not our usual practice to grant discounts in these cases we feel it is in the best interest of good customer relations to do so this time.
3. If you find you will not be able to keep our luncheon meeting on Friday please call my secretary before closing time on Thursday.
4. Because she attended night school to acquire specialized skills she was qualified for promotion to a job in the Data Processing Center.
5. After allowing the contestants a few minutes to read the directions the test monitor gave the signal for them to begin.
6. Since my recent move downtown to a high-rise apartment building I no longer have to face a two-hour commuter train ride each day.
7. Whenever you are not completely sure about how to proceed on a new job it is a good idea to ask questions rather than do the job incorrectly.
8. As we grow older we realize how little we know.
9. By the time the boat had left the dock it was already past midnight.
10. As soon as you feel you are ready to apply for credit at our store simply complete the attached application form.

Exercise 4

COMMA

Review Rules 6 and 7. Type these sentences and use commas to set off the words and phrases that interrupt the main thought of the sentence or add explanatory details. *Do not mark the book.*

Half sheet. 70-space line. Double spacing. Begin on line 6.

1. Our company for example handles over a million checks daily.
2. I suggest therefore that you make a special effort to see them.
3. We shall see you on Monday November 5.
4. I am happy to recommend my former assistant Karen Franklin for the job.
5. Return this card Mr. Davis to receive your free copy.
6. We understand Ms. Palmer that you will return tomorrow.
7. My assistant Mr. Jenkins will be delighted as usual to show you around.
8. His dog who is named Rover was lost last Monday.
9. We knew of course that she had no sales experience.
10. Our new brochure I do believe will be helpful to you.

Exercise 5

COMMA

Review Rules 8 and 9. Type the sentences at the right and insert commas, as necessary, within a series of items and before conjunctions. *Do not mark the book.*

Half sheet. 70-space line. Single spacing. DS between sentences. Begin on line 6.

1. Mr. Hammond was visited by his son a neighbor and his insurance agent.
2. The data sheet includes sections on personal information education work experiences and references.
3. He did not know shorthand but he was an excellent typist.
4. Ronald was very nervous but he won the contest.
5. It is a pleasure to have you for a customer and we hope to see you again soon.
6. We received your order but we are unable to fill it.
7. You are a good worker and we are sorry to lose you.
8. I went shopping and I bought a dress.
9. Typists must be accurate use good judgment and take pride in their work.
10. Nancy ran to the store bought some eggs and ran home.

Drill A

Type the memo in Model 17 on a printed half-sheet form. Follow the spacing shown. Notice that this memo is double spaced because it is so short. If no printed form is available, use a plain half sheet and type the headings in solid capitals and double spaced. Center the company name on line 5, and the words, INTEROFFICE MEMORANDUM, on line 7. Triple-space before typing the remaining headings. When typing your own form, remember to align the left margin of the body with the typed key words in the headings.

Drill B

Type the memo in Model 18 on a plain half sheet. Follow the spacing shown. Center the heading, MEMORANDUM, on line 7. Triple-space before typing the remaining headings. Type enough carbon copies to supply everyone addressed in the memo.

Drill C

Type the memo shown in Model 19, page 287, on a printed full-sheet form. If no printed form is available, use a plain full sheet and type the headings in solid capitals and double spaced. Center the heading, INTEROFFICE CORRESPONDENCE, on line 7, and triple space before typing the remaining headings. When typing your own form, remember to align the left margin of the body with the typed key words in the headings.

Model 20   Interoffice Envelopes

Exercise 6

COMMA

Review Rule 10. Type these sentences and insert commas in the proper places to indicate omissions of words or phrases. *Do not mark the book.*

Half sheet. 70-space line. Double spacing. Begin on line 8.

1. Rex lives 40 miles from the city; Eleanor 50.
2. If you call from Ohio, dial 876-3232; otherwise (800) 947-6543.
3. A large bright orange pumpkin sat in the window.
4. We saw an entertaining thought-provoking film.
5. I found the old dusty book in the attic.
6. My recipe requires three eggs; his four.
7. On last year's trip we arrived in four hours; this year in three.
8. The voters called for new revolutionary legislation to lower taxes.
9. Our downtown store closes at six o'clock; our mall store at nine.
10. It was a pleasure to see her sweet smiling face.

Exercise 7

PERIOD AND COMMA

This exercise is a review of Rules 1–10. As you type these sentences, *correct the punctuation as necessary. Do not mark the book.*

Full sheet. 60-space line. Single spacing. DS after each sentence. Center title on line 6 and TS after it.

PERIOD AND COMMA REVIEW

1. On July 1 however I will be beginning a new job.
2. If you want to be sure that your car is adequately protected against theft install our burglar-proof alarm system.
3. Come in Mrs. Jones and have a seat.
4. I received the magazine in April May and June.
5. I received a birthday card it was very nice.
6. Our manager Mr. Wallace will not be in until Friday.
7. I am returning your call of Friday July 1.
8. My brother felt ill so he stayed home from school.
9. Whenever you are looking for a quality restaurant where you can entertain important customers you will find our employees eager to serve you.
10. Before you spend time retyping labels for a mailing list you use often ask about copier labels.
11. I went shopping today and I saw a sale-priced chair that you would like.
12. You are a good worker we are sorry to lose you.
13. When you learn a new skill. You qualify for a better job.
14. If a word cannot be divided. Type it whole.
15. Our Boston agent Teresa Reed will call on you soon.
16. On Sunday our opening day there was a capacity crowd.
17. This will be an attractive comfortable costume for the beach.
18. In the meantime we have decided to purchase a new car.
19. Everyone wants to live long but no one wants to be old.
20. This is a suitcase sir that will give you excellent service.
21. We have received the copy of your canceled check, therefore we will consider the matter closed.
22. He was therefore not able to meet the deadline date.
23. Joe joined the union in 1961 and made big changes at first but he hasn't succeeded in changing the things he dislikes most.

Save-Rite Food Stores, Inc.

INTEROFFICE CORRESPONDENCE

Words

TO: All Employees ← Typed information is aligned horizontally with printed key words   DATE: March 4, 19--   6

FROM: Marcia Domino, Personnel Manager   13

SUBJECT: New Vacation Policy   17

TS

Left margin of body aligns with typed information above

The corporate personnel office recently issued a new policy on   30
vacations. Happily, this policy increases the vacation benefits   43
previously in effect. You will find a copy of the new policy   56
attached to this memo.   61

Briefly, the new policy provides the following: 71

1. Vacation time is earned on an anniversary-year basis. A   83
maximum of ten days' vacation time may be earned in the first   96
year of employment. (This has been increased from five days.)   109
This paid vacation time is earned at the rate of one day per   121
month, exclusive of the first two months of employment.   132

2. For the following four anniversary years of employment   144
(years two through five), vacation time is earned at the rate   157
of ten days per year.   161

3. For the sixth through tenth anniversary years, vacation time   174
is earned at the rate of 15 days per year. (This was a maximum   187
of ten days per year under the old policy.)   196

4. During the eleventh anniversary year of employment, and   208
thereafter, vacation time is earned at the rate of 20 working   221
days per year.   224

Of course, all vacation time is separate from paid holidays noted   237
in the Holiday Schedule.   242

I am sure you will all be pleased with these changes. If you   255
have any questions, feel free to contact me or any member of my   268
staff. This policy is effective immediately.   277

MD

xx   278

Model 19   *Interoffice Memorandum on a Printed Full-Sheet Form*

Topic 3 SEMICOLON, COLON, AND DASH

These three punctuation marks are used to indicate a partial stop in thought, as opposed to a period, which indicates a complete stop in thought.

SEMICOLON

Rule 11.

Use a semicolon between two complete statements where there is no conjunction. Without a conjunction or a semicolon you would have a run-on sentence. Remember from Rule 4 that a period may also be used, but use of a semicolon between two related complete statements prevents short, choppy sentences.

RUN-ON:	*Check your work carefully circle each typing error.*
CORRECTED:	*Check your work carefully; circle each typing error.*
RUN-ON:	*The play was very funny I could not stop laughing.*
CORRECTED:	*The play was very funny; I could not stop laughing.*

Rule 12.

Use a semicolon when one (or both) of the complete statements on either side of a conjunction such as *and, or, but, for,* or *nor,* contain other commas. The semicolon helps to separate the two statements.

- *It was a warm, humid day; and since we had air conditioning, we used it.*
- *Since we were hungry, we stopped to eat; but the restaurant was about to close.*

Rule 13.

Use a semicolon before a conjunctive adverb, such as *however, therefore, of course,* or *namely,* when there are two complete statements (related in thought) on both sides of the expressions. (Review Rule 3 regarding possible use of a period in such sentences.)

- *Time is limited; therefore, send your check today.*
- *Our supply is running low; of course, the price will increase.*
- *Students are excused on Friday; however, teachers must report as usual.*

Rule 14.

If the parts of a series are very long or contain commas, use semicolons to separate the parts.

- *I have lived in Detroit, Michigan; Cleveland, Ohio; and Chicago, Illinois.*
- *The boys amused themselves in the morning by taking walks; in the afternoon, by playing tennis; and in the evening, by playing cards.*

COLON

Rule 15.

Use a colon after the salutation in a business letter when mixed punctuation style (see Section 2, Part 7) is used.

- *Dear Mr. Freeman:*

Rule 16.

Use a colon to introduce a long quotation or a list of items. Some of the words that may signal the need for a colon are: *as, as follows, the following, thus,* and *these.*

- *I am taking the following subjects: physics, typing, bookkeeping, English, and history.*
- *Remember this: "The race is not to the swift, nor the battle to the strong."*
- *It was decided thus: You and I will both attend the meeting.*

An interoffice memo may be typed on a half sheet or a full sheet, depending on its length. Double spacing can be used for very short messages. When a memo is addressed to several people, list their names in a single-spaced column after the heading, TO. Sometimes people not addressed will also receive copies. List their names after the heading, COPIES. If there is no such heading, type in CC, and then list their names (single spaced). Make enough carbon copies to supply everyone. On each copy, place a check mark beside the name of the person to whom that copy is being sent.

When a memo is addressed to many people (an entire department, for example), the usual procedure is to type the memo either on a carbon-backed master (for spirit process duplication) or mimeograph stencil. The memo is then duplicated in the quantity needed.

Some dictators prefer to have their initials typed at the end of their memos. Others like to sign their own initials or names. Follow the dictator's preference. Type your reference initials at the left margin, leaving room for the dictator's signature, if necessary. Add an enclosure notation as required.

Many businesses use printed envelopes for routing their interoffice correspondence. See Model 20, Style A (page 288). These envelopes can be reused many times. If no printed interoffice envelopes are available, the routing information may be typed on a standard No. 10 envelope. See Model 20, Style B.

For speed and convenience, many offices use printed carbon set message forms that provide space for a reply. See Model 21 (page 289). These forms usually have 2 carbon copies attached. The writer of the memo sends the original copy and the last carbon copy to the addressee and keeps the first copy as a file copy. For more details, read the memo in Exercise 12 (page 296). Notice that these memos are double spaced.

	Words
MEMORANDUM ← Line 7	2
TS	
SUBJECT Personal Telephone Calls DATE November 1, 19--	13
TO Mr. G. Hollis, Sales Manager	19
Mr. R. Knight, Production Manager	26
Ms. B. Massino, Office Manager	32
FROM H. Olsen, Personnel Manager	39
TS	
We have received many complaints recently about employees who tie up the	54
telephone lines with private conversations. This creates costly delays	69
for those who must place business calls.	77
All employees, therefore, have been instructed to use only the telephone	92
booths in the main hall for personal calls. Company telephones may be	106
used for personal calls only in emergencies.	115
Please cooperate by enforcing this rule in your department.	127
DS	
HO	128
DS	
xx	129

Minimum 1-inch margins

Left margin aligns with typed headings

Model 18 *Interoffice Memorandum on a Plain Half Sheet*

DASH

Rule 17.　Use a dash to indicate a sharp change in thought or to set off an explanatory phrase. It is a more forceful punctuation mark than the comma, semicolon, or colon. Use the dash to make certain words or phrases stand out, but don't overuse it. To make a dash, type two hyphens with no space before or after.

- *Imagination is as good as many voyages—and how much cheaper!*
- *The six-foot sofa—not the eight-foot one—is on sale.*

Exercise 8

SEMICOLON

Review Rules 11–14. Type these sentences, inserting semicolons or replacing commas with semicolons as necessary.

Half sheet. 70-space line. Single spacing. Center title on line 5 and TS after it.

PUNCTUATION: SEMICOLON

1. Leonard likes his food very plain I prefer mine with salt and pepper and a variety of spices and herbs.
2. You pay nothing into your pension the company pays for it all.
3. Leslie has training in this area moreover, she has a wealth of experience.
4. Josephine was out of the office when I called so I left a message.
5. Our company did well last year, but of course, we will do better this year.
6. Our current low prices will not be repeated therefore come in today.
7. You will like our polite, friendly salespeople and you will like our merchandise, which is beautifully displayed.
8. John has worked in New York, in a furniture store, in Chicago, in a men's clothing factory, and in Springfield, in a hardware store.
9. My favorite classes are swimming, where I get exercise, typing, where I am learning a skill, and math, where I am forced to think.
10. An effective letter can build goodwill a poor one may lose a customer.
11. Occasionally, you will find employers who would like to hire you but they may not, at that time, have a job for you.
12. He was competent and hardworking however, he was not very good at dealing with people.

Exercise 9

Colon and Dash

Review Rules 15–17. Type the sentences at the right, inserting a colon or dash at the indicated points.

Full sheet. Center title on line 12 and TS after it. 70-space line. Single spacing. DS after each sentence.

PUNCTUATION: COLON AND DASH

1. Dear Mr. Johnson ■ (mixed punctuation)
2. The patient could have only the following visitors ■ his son, his wife, his mother, or his father.
3. Join our family of customers ■ you won't regret it.
4. Employers consider all of the following ■ your appearance, your attitude, your work experience, and your test scores.
5. Our tableware ■ china, crystal, sterling, and stainless flatware ■ are all open stock.
6. The dates of the lectures are as follows ■ August 3, August 10, August 16, and August 23.

(Continued on next page)

Topic 7 INTEROFFICE CORRESPONDENCE

Some of the dictation given to you to type will be correspondence from one employee to another. These communications are called *interoffice correspondence*. They are typed in a style different from that used for business letters. Note the following differences:

1. The salutation and complimentary closing are omitted.
2. Standard headings—TO, FROM, DATE, SUBJECT—are used, but the arrangement may vary.

Memo forms bearing the company name and printed headings are often available. (See Model 17, this page, and Model 19, page 287.) When these forms are used, the typed information is aligned horizontally with the printed key words in the headings. A triple space is used between the last line of the heading and the body of the memo. On printed forms, the left margin of the body of the message is aligned with the typed information in the headings.

When an interoffice memo is to be typed on plain paper (see Model 18, page 286), the headings must be supplied. These are typed in solid capitals, and are double spaced. Colons may be omitted after the typed headings. It is a good idea to begin with the SUBJECT heading, since it often requires the most information. Margins (top, bottom and sides) should be at least 1 inch, but may be increased depending upon the length of the memo. When memos are typed on plain paper, the left margin of the body of the message aligns with the left margin of the capitalized key words in the headings.

Spotless Dishwasher Company

INTEROFFICE MEMORANDUM

	Words
TO: M. Meadows	5
Sales Manager	8
FROM: E. Wheatley	12
Production Manager	19
SUBJECT: Electric Dishwashers	23

DATE: June 22, 19--

COPIES TO: R. Finley
            Warehouse Manager

TS

The dishwashers that you wanted rushed to Mr. Hargraves in Dayton will   37

be ready for shipment in two days. They should reach Dayton within a   51

week. Please notify Mr. Hargraves so that he will have someone on hand   66

to take delivery.   70

Space down 3 or 4 times

Ellis Wheatley

xx   71

Model 17 *Interoffice Memorandum on a Printed Half-Sheet Form*

7. Save 30 percent ■ in addition to our usual low prices ■ on your winter coat during our March sale.

8. This is your chance to try our TV set in your home ■ and with no obligation!

9. Drama, dancing, scenery, music ■ this movie has it all.

10. The judge finally gave the verdict ■ "Guilty as charged."

11. We raise money through projects such as these ■ car washes, candy sales, doughnut sales, and bike races.

12. All my good friends ■ John, Mary, Sue, and Fred ■ came to the party.

13. Remember this saying ■ "One enemy is too many, whereas a hundred friends are too few!"

14. Don't wait until tomorrow ■ do it now!

15. The winners of the typing contest are ■ Rosie, 77 wpm; Ronald, 75 wpm; Alisha, 70 wpm; and David, 68 wpm.

16. Swimming, bicycling, and jogging ■ these are my summer pastimes.

Topic 4 QUESTION MARK AND EXCLAMATION POINT

These two punctuation marks are used at the end of statements or sentences to indicate intent: questioning on the one hand, and strong emotion on the other.

QUESTION MARK

Rule 18.

Use a question mark after a direct question.

- *Are you going out for lunch at noon?*

Sometimes a statement is deliberately phrased like a question to make a demand seem more courteous. These statements may be punctuated with a period.

- *May we have your check by return mail.*
- *Will you please send me an application for the job.*

When you punctuate a courteous request with a period, you are not *asking* a question; you are making a polite demand.

Rule 19.

When the sentence starts out as a statement and ends with a short question, a question mark should be used at the end.

- *You will be in class tomorrow, won't you?*
- *You received our latest price list, did you not?*

EXCLAMATION POINT

Rule 20.

Use the exclamation point after a word, a phrase, or a sentence to express strong emotion.

- *We won!*   • *At last! It's our graduation day!*
- *What a wonderful surprise your present was!*

use of a company car for all business travel, and you will be entitled to participate in the company's stock option plan after six months' service. Complete terms of your employment will be set forth in your employment contract, which will be ready for your signature early next week. ¶Welcome to Olympic Industries. We look forward to seeing you on Monday.   Sincerely   Frank Evans   President   *xx*   (124 words)

Exercise 6

GOVERNMENT-SIZE
STATIONERY

Your letter should look like the one shown on page 282. Cut paper to size if stationery is not available.

Full block style. Open punctuation. 1-inch side margins. Begin on line 15.

October 19, 19— Mrs. Linda Jones 225 Woodland Avenue Middlesex, NJ 08846 Dear Mrs. Jones We can well understand the growing anxiety of the "survivors" as the phasing out of your center proceeded. However, we do not understand the distinction you draw between termination and layoff. Perhaps you use "layoff" to mean temporary suspension from employment rather than dismissal, as is more common. Even so, the prospects of reemployment with the company would appear very dim. ¶If you have lost your job, you should register at the nearest state employment security office for suitable work and file for unemployment compensation. Since employer taxes are affected by the number of former workers who draw compensation, the company may contest your claim. Their argument would be that you were let go for good cause—namely, failure to meet the quota. You would have the right to appeal an adverse decision. At that time, you could note that the newly imposed quota represented a change in job conditions. The fact that the staff has been drastically reduced according to a deliberate schedule would also, it seems to us, be a point in your favor. Sincerely Alexis Herman Director *xx*   (176 words)

Exercise 7

GOVERNMENT-SIZE
STATIONERY

Select suitable margins. Be sure to indent the paragraph insert.

Modified block style. Mixed punctuation. 5-space paragraph indention. Begin on line 15.

Today's date Lambert & Jarvis, Inc. 849 Wilson Street Newark, NJ 07107 Ladies and Gentlemen We wish to call your attention to Part 131 of the U.S. Postal Service Manual, which covers the classification of first-class mail: *(Begin insert)* Typewritten originals and carbon and letterpress copies will be accepted for mailing only as first-class mail. Facsimile copies of typewriting produced by computer-assisted printout, duplicating machine, printing press, multigraph, and so forth, shall be accepted as third- or fourth-class mail, provided they are being sent in identical terms to several people and have none of the characteristics of actual and personal correspondence. *(End insert)* ¶The computer-printed matter you mailed as third-class should have been sent first-class, since it contained inserts which personalized the correspondence. It was, therefore, returned to you for collection of the additional fee. Always, when mail similar to this is sent, the first-class rate shall be charged. ¶Whenever you have questions about postal services and regulations, please telephone the post office before sending anything. We can help you in working out programs for the most efficient and least expensive mail delivery system. Sincerely yours R. E. Wright, Postmaster *xx*   (175 words)

Exercise 10

QUESTION MARK AND EXCLAMATION POINT

Review Rules 18–20. As you type these sentences, supply the correct end punctuation marks.

Full sheet. 70-space line. Double spacing. Center title on line 6 and TS after it.

PUNCTUATION: QUESTION MARK AND EXCLAMATION POINT

1. Has the manager decided to include winter coats in the sale
2. Ride on over all obstacles, and win the race
3. Will you let us know your decision as soon as possible
4. May we have your answer soon
5. We will see you next week, won't we
6. Are you ready to take the test
7. Congratulations Your promotion is now official
8. What an experience that was
9. Why have you been ringing this bell
10. Will you please help me out of this predicament
11. Shouldn't the bill total $37
12. Ouch I hurt my hand
13. Mr. Jones is still our area representative, isn't he
14. Do your salespeople know how to make forceful presentations
15. Would you kindly return the enclosed sample before June 30

Topic 5 PARENTHESES AND QUOTATION MARKS

PARENTHESES

Rule 21.
Use parentheses for explanatory matter, for a reference, or for an expression that is not closely related to the main thought of the sentence.

- *Our check for the full amount ($35.00) is enclosed.*
- *The tools were used for scraping deer hides (Smith, 1971).*
- *Now (and forever, he hoped) he had the key that would unlock her heart.*

Rule 22.
Use parentheses to enclose letters or numbers before lists within a sentence.

- *Be sure to (a) read directions, (b) ask questions, and (c) work quickly.*

QUOTATION MARKS

Rule 23.
Use quotation marks around the exact words used by a speaker or writer.

- *"Have a wonderful time," she wrote.*

Rule 24.
Use quotation marks to enclose titles of such works as songs, poems, paintings, and articles within books or periodicals. Titles of books, newspapers, periodicals, films, record albums, and plays should be underlined.

- *Sharon had to memorize the poem, "Jabberwocky," from <u>Alice's Adventures in Wonderland</u> by Lewis Carroll.*

Exercise 2

HALF-SIZE STATIONERY

Select suitable margins.

Modified block style. Mixed punctuation. 5-space paragraph indention. Begin on line 8.

Today's date Mr. Charles Wikki 260 St. Helens Avenue Vancouver, WA 98602 Dear Mr. Wikki It is a pleasure to welcome you as a new credit customer. We know that you will enjoy the special store services that are now available to you. ¶Your credit card is enclosed. This card will make your shopping easier, quicker, and more convenient. All it needs is your signature. ¶Thank you, Mr. Wikki, for the confidence you have expressed in our store by opening an account with us. Sincerely Norman Avery Credit Manager *xx* Enclosure   (71 words)

Exercise 3

EXECUTIVE-SIZE STATIONERY

Your letter should look like the one shown on page 282. Cut paper to size if stationery is not available.

Modified block style. Open punctuation. 5-space paragraph indention. 1-inch side margins. Begin on line 14.

December 30, 19— Mr. Stanley M. Garrison 54 Market Street Nashville, TN 37225 Dear Mr. Garrison SUBJECT: Policy No. 4327 Your letter regarding dividends on your life insurance policy has been referred to me. ¶Our policies do not earn any dividends during their first year. Occasionally a dividend is paid on a first-year policy, but that is in expectation of its future earnings. At the end of the second year of coverage, however, you will be entitled to the dividends your policy earns during that year. Since no dividends are shared by policyholders their first year, special payments are sometimes made to them at the end of their fourth year of coverage. This occurs if the company accumulates an adequate surplus. ¶I trust that this explanation will provide a satisfactory answer to your questions. If any other problems arise, please contact me directly. Cordially Richard Palermo Executive Officer *xx*   (124 words)

Exercise 4

EXECUTIVE-SIZE STATIONERY

Select suitable margins.

Modified block style. Mixed punctuation. No paragraph indention. Begin on line 16.

Today's date Mr. James H. Carpenter 903 Webster Building 534 Spruce Street Reading, PA 19613 Dear Jim We find ourselves so absorbed in acquiring new customers that we wonder whether we neglect our old friends. So, we want to take time now to tell you how much we have appreciated your patronage over the years. ¶It has come to my attention that our sales representatives are sometimes late in making their calls because of their crowded schedules. If you experience any interruption in your service, please get in touch with me. I shall see that your needs are promptly taken care of. Best wishes Ralph Andrews Vice President *xx* (85 words)

Exercise 5

EXECUTIVE-SIZE STATIONERY

Select suitable margins.

Full block style. Open punctuation. Begin on line 14.

Today's date Ms. Annette Spear 627 Chester Street Tuckahoe, NY 10707 Dear Annette   I want you to know how pleased I am that you have agreed to accept the position of Vice-President, Research and Development, at Olympic Industries. Having considered many candidates, we are confident that you possess the qualifications and personal attributes most suited for this demanding position. ¶As we discussed yesterday, your starting salary will be $48,000 per year. You will be given

(Continued on next page)

Rule 25. Use quotation marks around words that need special attention called to them.

- *Mark's "new" car was really an old wreck.*
- *The lie detector disproved the "truth" of his statements.*

Rule 26. When quotation marks and other punctuation marks are used together, follow this order:

1. Type a period or a comma *before* the closing quotation mark.
2. Type a semicolon or a colon *after* the closing quotation mark.
3. Type a question mark or an exclamation mark *after* the closing quotation mark, unless it is a part of the quoted material.

- *"I hate to go," she said, "but my plane leaves at 5:30."*
- *"Parting is such sweet sorrow"; that was his reply.*
- *Who said, "I shall return"? (The entire statement is a question.)*
- *He asked, "When will you return?" (Only the sentence in quotes is a question.)*

Exercise 11

PARENTHESES AND QUOTATION MARKS

Review Rules 21–26. Type the sentences at the right and insert parentheses and quotation marks as necessary.

Full sheet. 70-space line. Single spacing. DS after each sentence. Center title on line 6 and TS after it.

PUNCTUATION: PARENTHESES AND QUOTATION MARKS

1. The topic of her article, English in the Typing Class, was interesting.
2. When the temperature reached 40°C 104°F, the plant wilted.
3. Our new offer mortgage life insurance will give your family security.
4. The lamp is equipped with a special shade our own design to give maximum light with minimum glare.
5. Quick action must be taken, Ms. Fleming said, on your nine pending bills.
6. The Drama Club will present the Balcony Scene from *Romeo and Juliet*.
7. We regret, the credit manager wrote, that we cannot make a shipment until the present balance is reduced.
8. The word pretty can have many different meanings.
9. Look for sheets and towels that are marked seconds.
10. Did he say, We are going to increase tuition next semester?
11. It is a good idea to 1 brush your teeth twice a day, 2 avoid sweets, and 3 see your dentist regularly.
12. The students were improperly labeled radical.
13. The abbreviation, C.O.D., means cash on delivery.
14. What an idea! said Mr. Brown.
15. Review the correct use of directional signals see page 23.
16. Live each day to its fullest, advised the old man.
17. Holding a second job is referred to as moonlighting.
18. Include a data sheet resume with your application blank.
19. If a letter is medium length 100 to 200 words, use a 5-inch line.
20. You will find the information in the encyclopedia volume 17.
21. The word re is sometimes used to start a subject line.
22. Feudalism began following the Roman Empire's collapse Kay, 1970.
23. There are some tricks-of-the-trade that can make the job easier.
24. Have you ever read Frost's After the Apple Picking?
25. The letter was marked Special Delivery.

Half-size stationery is best suited for short letters. Based on the length of the letter, the position of the date line may range from line 6 to line 13. The side margins vary from 1 inch to ¾ inches.

Side margins of 1 inch to ¾ inches are also used on executive-size stationery. The date line position may vary from line 10 to line 16, depending on the length of the letter.

The standard margin settings used for typing letters on 8½ by 11 inch paper may also be used for typing letters on these special sizes of stationery. The paper guide, however, will need to be adjusted for each size of stationery so that the sheet is centered at 50 (or 42) on the carriage scale.

On government-size stationery, 1½-inch to 1-inch side margins are used. The date line may be determined in the usual way or as directed in special government correspondence manuals.

Metric-size stationery is just slightly narrower than standard 8½ by 11 inch stationery. The same side margins can therefore be used as for 8½ by 11 inch paper. The main difference between the two sizes is the length. Metric-size stationery contains 70 line spaces—four more than 8½ by 11 inch stationery. Short to medium letters, therefore, are started two lines lower on metric paper. For long letters, no date-line adjustment is necessary. (No exercises are given in this topic for letters typed on metric-size stationery, since any of the exercises in Topic 1 can be used for such practice.)

Before you begin to type the exercises, study the three letters illustrated below. They show finished letters for Exercises 1, 3, and 6. If stationery is not available in the sizes called for in the exercises, fold or cut paper to size.

Half Size

Executive Size

Government Size

Exercise 1

HALF-SIZE STATIONERY

Cut paper to size if stationery is not available.

Modified block style. Open punctuation. No paragraph indention. 1-inch side margins. Begin on line 13.

April 1, 19— Mrs. Amy S. Sanborn 63 Marsh Avenue Tampa, FL 33616 Dear Amy We wish to express our appreciation to you for holding the Neighborhood Restoration Awards Banquet in our hall. We hope that the food and the service pleased you. We invite your suggestions and comments. ¶When you have occasion to plan another affair for your group, please call on us once again. Every consideration will be given toward making it a success. Cordially yours T. L. Hood, Manager

xx (61 words)

Topic 6 APOSTROPHE AND HYPHEN

APOSTROPHE

Rule 27.

Use an apostrophe with an *s* to show possession in a singular noun.

- *the student's notebook* • *William Shakespeare's plays*

Rule 28.

Use only an apostrophe to show possession in a plural noun ending in *s*.

- *my two aunts' children* • *the students' notebooks* • *the Jones' car*

Rule 29.

Use an apostrophe with an *s* to show possession in an irregular plural noun (one that changes spelling to form the plural).

- *men's clothing* • *children's toys* • *the alumni's newsletter*

Rule 30.

When two or more persons own one item jointly, add the apostrophe to the final noun.

- *Alice and Mary's house*
- *Alice's and Mary's wigs* (Both Alice and Mary possess their own wigs.)

Rule 31.

Form the singular possessive of an abbreviation by adding *'s;* form the plural possessive of an abbreviation by adding *s'.*

- *C.P.A.'s* (singular) • *C.P.A.s'* (plural)

The apostrophe is also used to form the plurals of numbers, letters, and words used as words.

- *four 5's* • *the three R's* • *too many and's*

HYPHEN

A hyphen is used to connect two words. Some expressions are always hyphenated, while others are not. If you are in doubt about whether to hyphenate any expression, check in a dictionary.

Rule 32.
IN COMPOUND ADJECTIVES

Hyphenate compound adjectives when they come before the noun they describe.

- *A slow-moving van entered the driveway* • *He is a well-known man.*
  BUT: *The van was slow moving.*   BUT: *The man is well known.*

Do not use a hyphen after adverbs (words ending in *ly*).

- *a completely fresh inventory* • *a poorly written book*

Rule 33.
IN A SERIES OF ADJECTIVES

Use the hyphen after each part of a compound adjective in a series of compound adjectives used to describe the same noun.

- *The flour is sold in one-, five-, and ten-pound bags.*

Rule 34.
IN NUMBERS

Use the hyphen in fractions (unless one of the elements contains a hyphen) and in compound numbers that are spelled out.

- *one-half* • *Thirty-three hundredths* • *twenty-one*
- *nine-sixteenths* • *One hundred forty-seven*

Exercise 4

AMS SIMPLIFIED STYLE

Following Model 16, type this handwritten letter in the AMS simplified letter style.

Today's date   City Council   City Hall   400 Main Street   Cedar Rapids, IA 52401

TREE PLANTING ALONG INDUSTRIAL PARKWAY

We heartily approve of your proposal to plant trees in the grassy strip along the sidewalks of Industrial Parkway. The trees will add long-lasting beauty to the area and make our neighborhood a more pleasant place to live and work.

Our office staff has volunteered to help with planting the trees and landscaping the area. Please let us know when you will want to do this work.

We appreciate your concern for our neighborhood.

MICHAEL ROLLINS, OFFICE MANAGER   (76 words)

Topic 6 LETTERS ON SPECIAL-SIZE PAPER

Most business correspondence is typed on standard (8½ by 11 inch) paper. However, four other sizes of stationery may also be used:

- Half size (5½ by 8½ in.)—sometimes used for miscellaneous, nonrecurring correspondence.
- Executive (7¼ by 10½ in.)—often used by top-ranking executives of an organization.
- Government (8 by 10½ in.)—used only by certain departments of the federal government.
- Metric (21 cm by 29.7 cm)—used by most foreign countries in all business letters.

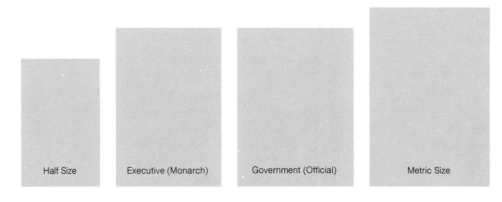

Half Size   Executive (Monarch)   Government (Official)   Metric Size

Exercise 12

APOSTROPHE

Review Rules 27–31. Type these phrases in two columns and add apostrophes where necessary.

Full sheet. Double spacing. 10 spaces between columns. Begin on line 10.

PUNCTUATION: APOSTROPHE

TS

1. several womens views
2. three authors books
3. both bicycles wheels
4. the insurers risk
5. Mrs. Smiths daughter
6. our neighbors believe
7. many students assignments
8. several days later
9. an M.D.s insurance policies
10. our ladies department
11. one companys stock
12. twelve companies stock
13. my mothers parents
14. his childs playmates
15. anybodys guess
16. a messengers luggage
17. a ladys husband
18. several ladies husbands
19. childrens clothes
20. my doctors office
21. our employees vacations
22. everyones favorite movie
23. Mr. Jones signature
24. Ron and Joans mother
25. the secretaries jokes
26. the bare trees
27. Rons and Joans mothers
28. his wifes club
29. my friends came
30. one hours sleep

Exercise 13

HYPHEN

Review Rules 32–34. Type the sentences at the right, supplying missing hyphens as necessary.

Full sheet. 70-space line. Double spacing. Center title on line 10 and TS after it.

PUNCTUATION: HYPHEN

1. The above mentioned report was mailed to you on Friday.
2. The letter was sent by first class mail.
3. A neatly typed letter of application will win the job.
4. I need eighty five dollars for my senior trip.
5. In class today we took one, three, and five minute timed writings.
6. Her term paper was clearly written.
7. Use the enclosed, self addressed envelope.
8. The woman was well dressed when she went for an interview.
9. Employers are impressed by a well groomed applicant.
10. He will soon reach his twenty first birthday.
11. One fourth of the students made the Honor Roll.
12. We use only up to date materials.
13. Be sure you maintain your self confidence.
14. He will be on vacation for a ten day period.
15. He always has a happy go lucky attitude.
16. The car has a finely tuned engine.
17. The long held notion that computers would completely take over and cause the loss of millions of jobs has not proven to be true.
18. More than three quarters of the report contained incorrect data.
19. She was recently promoted to a top level management position.
20. We will need shades for the first and second floor windows.

Exercise 1

HANGING INDENTED STYLE

Use the hanging indented style for the business letter given at the right. Follow the style shown in Model 15 for spacing.

Mixed punctuation.

October 14, 19— Mr. John A. Hembree 1802 Higby Drive Cincinnati, OH 45207 Dear Mr. Hembree Our organization, Consumer Advocates, is concerned about what you eat, drink, drive, see, and believe. We think that many of the foods and drinks Americans consume are bad for our physical health. We feel that much of the television we view and a great percentage of the advertising we see and hear are bad for our mental health. ¶In the last few years, greater emphasis has been placed on demanding more nutritious food, safer cars, and greater truth in advertising. Our group has been at least partly responsible for this greater awareness. But we must not be content with the changes already made. We must continue to make our demands known for a life-style that is safe, clean, and healthful. ¶We need your support! If you want to work to change the world in which you live, please call us at 328-5188. Our staff will let you know how you can help. Thank you for your concern. Sincerely Sheree Jansen District Coordinator *xx*
(152 words)

Exercise 2

HANGING INDENTED STYLE

Type this letter in the hanging indented style. Follow the spacing indicated in Model 15. Address a large envelope and fold and insert the letter.

Open punctuation. Large envelope.

Today's date Oklaco Corporation 700 Plaza Avenue Oklahoma City, OK 73127 Ladies and Gentlemen I'm sure that many of the letters you receive from station managers involve complaints and criticisms. This letter is different; I'm writing to thank you for the excellent service you have provided me through the years. ¶I have operated my Oklaco station here in Montpelier since 1946, and in all that time you have never treated me unfairly. The products and advertising posters have always been shipped promptly, and your truck drivers have been friendly and helpful. Whenever I've had a question or a problem, your representatives have provided thorough explanations. ¶I'm not the only one who has noticed the good service. My oldest son and his wife are so impressed with Oklaco that they are considering purchasing an Oklaco station in Nebraska. ¶I'm thankful to you for making my job easier and more pleasant. Keep up the good work. Respectfully yours Frank Carpenter, Station Manager *xx* (142 words)

Exercise 3

AMS SIMPLIFIED STYLE

For this exercise, use the AMS simplified letter style. Follow the spacing instructions indicated on Model 16. Check the placement points listed in the model carefully before you begin.

April 4, 19— Mark Klein, Distributor National Records 3000 Jackson Boulevard Los Angeles, CA 90012 SOARING SALES OF KING ALBUM The new album, *Across The River* by King, is selling at our store at a phenomenal rate. We sold more than 300 copies in just one week. It is the hottest album we have had in many years. ¶Please send us 1,200 more copies of the album as soon as possible. Also send us 100 copies each of King's two other albums, as well as 50 posters of the band. Any promotional banners or decals would also be appreciated. ¶I hope that National Records continues to produce albums as good as *Across The River* and to sign bands with the kind of appeal that King has. DENISE FRY, MANAGER *xx* cc: Jack O'Brien (106 words)

Topic 7 CAPITALIZATION

Words are capitalized to specify the actual name or title of a special person or thing. Opinions on proper capitalization vary, but the following capitalization rules cover problems most likely to be encountered in business situations.

Rule 1.

Capitalize the first word in a sentence.

- *They like ice cream.* - *Tomorrow is my birthday.*

Rule 2.

Capitalize the names (first, middle, and last) of persons. Also capitalize the personal pronoun *I* wherever it appears in a sentence. Capitalize geographic place names, the names of well-known landmarks, and the names of organizations.

- *John H. Jones*   - *Dallas, Texas*
- *The Grand Canyon*   - *Girl Scouts of America*

Rule 3.

Proper adjectives—words derived from the names of specific people, places, or things—should be capitalized.

- *Shakespearean play*   - *French cuisine*   - *American offices*

Because of frequent usage, some words originally derived from proper nouns are not capitalized. If you are unsure about a word, consult a dictionary.

- *french fries*   - *india ink*   - *pasteurized milk*

Rule 4.

Capitalize a title that comes immediately before a person's name. However, do not capitalize a title coming after a person's name except in the inside address of a letter. Capitalize a title used without a person's name only when the person is being directly addressed.

- *Mayor Brookes*
- *Ms. R. Roberts, president of the Historical Society*
- *The governor spoke at our luncheon.*
- *What do you think, Governor, of the chicken salad?*

Rule 5.

The first word of a quotation is capitalized when the quoted material is a complete sentence. But do not capitalize the first word of an interrupted quotation.

- *He told our group, "Two dogs fight for a bone, and a third runs away with it."*
- *"A bird in the hand," she quoted, "is worth two in the bush."*

Rule 6.

Capitalize the first and all important words in titles of books, plays, reports, periodicals, television shows, and so forth. The entire title may also be typed in solid capitals. (Refer to Rule 24, page 188, regarding quotation marks or underlining for titles.)

- *Practical English Handbook*
- *Reference Manual for Secretaries*
- *REFERENCE MANUAL FOR SECRETARIES*

Rule 7.

Capitalize the compass directions (east, west, north, south) only when they refer to sections of the country or of the world.
- *exploring the Old West*   - *go south on Parker Road*
- *Columbus sailed west in search of the Far East.*

Better Business Letters, Inc.

148 East Broadway, Manchester, N.H. 03102   (603) 922-1496

Words

January 4, 19--   3

Space down 4 times

Ms. or Mr. Word Processor   8
The Eastern Secretarial Association   15
1 Main Street   18
New Haven, CT 06525   22

TS

HAVE YOU HEARD?   25

TS

There's a new movement under way to take some of the monotony out   38
of the letters given to you to type. The movement is symbolized   51
by the Simplified Letter being sponsored by AMS.   61

What is it? You're reading a sample.   69

Notice the left block format and the general positioning of the   82
letter. We didn't write "Dear ----," nor will we write "Yours   95
truly" or "Sincerely yours." Are they really important? We feel   108
just as friendly to you without them.   116

Notice the following placement points: 124

1. All lines blocked at left margin   131
2. Triple space before and after subject line   140
3. Subject line replaces salutation   147
4. Complimentary closing omitted   153
5. Dictator's name and title in solid capitals   163

Now take a look at the enclosed suggestions prepared for you. Talk   177
them over with your boss. But don't form a final opinion until   190
you've really tried out the AMS simplified letter style. That's   203
what our secretary did. As a matter of fact, she finally wrote most   217
of the suggestions herself.   223

Our secretary is sold on the idea. We hope you'll have good luck   236
with better (simplified) letters.   243

Vaughan Fry   *Space down 4 times*

VAUGHAN FRY, RESEARCH & STANDARDS   250

DS

xx   251

DS

Enclosure   253

(Shown in Elite Type)

Model 16   *AMS Simplified Letter Style*

Rule 8.	Capitalize the name of a specific course title. Do not capitalize the name of a subject unless it is derived from a proper noun.

- *I am taking Typewriting II-A this semester.*   • *My English class is stimulating.*
- *I have taken typewriting.*

Rule 9.	Capitalize the first word in the salutation and the complimentary closing of a business letter.

- *My dear Mr. Evans*   • *Sincerely yours*   • *Very truly yours*

Rule 10.	Nouns followed by a number, either Roman or Arabic, are usually capitalized, except for page numbers. Examples:

- *Room 501*   • *Lesson 20*   • *Chapter II*   • *page 3*

Rule 11.	Capitalize the following: names of days of the week, months, holidays, races, religions, references to a deity, historical events, trade names of commercial products, and names of bodies of governments. Capitalize seasons only when they are personified, such as, "Old Man Winter."

- *Thursday*   • *November*   • *Fourth of July*   • *Vietnam War*
- *Asian*   • *Baptist*   • *God*   • *Kleenex*

Exercise 1

CAPITALIZATION

Review Rules 1–11. Type the sentences at the right, correcting any errors in capitalization.

Half sheet. 70-space line. Double spacing. Center title on line 6 and TS after it.

CORRECTING CAPITALIZATION ERRORS: ONE

1. The excelsior pen company has been in business for many years.
2. Avoid such high-calorie foods as french dressing.
3. Thank you, senator, for your interest in our efforts.
4. He said, "now is the time to learn all you can."
5. You will find this book, a trip through The Zoo, entertaining.
6. The new furniture we bought was made in the east.
7. I am doing well in English, Algebra, and Music.
8. Yours Very Respectfully,
9. Her class is located in room 780.
10. Our family always has a cookout on memorial day.

Exercise 2

CAPITALIZATION

Type these sentences, correcting any errors in capitalization.

Half sheet. 70-space line. Double spacing. Center title on line 5 and TS after it.

CORRECTING CAPITALIZATION ERRORS: TWO

1. I am taking a course entitled principles of art.
2. She works for a well-known Company.
3. We were told to read chapter 9 tonight.
4. We had to read only one chapter of the book.
5. We lost our hubcap traveling north on interstate 95.
6. I will be happy when old man winter is gone.
7. I am now enrolled in Nursing Training II in night school.
8. You will need to complete form 1040 for income tax purposes.
9. My dear Mrs. Masten:
10. Thousands of people telephoned the white house to speak to the president.

Columbia Appliance Repair Association

703 HERRICK STREET
COLUMBIA, SOUTH CAROLINA 29203
(803) 334-7880

	Words
December 12, 19--	4

Mr. David S. Sloan, Jr.   9
Victory Appliance Repair, Inc.   15
323 Jasmine Street   19
Columbia, SC 29212   23

Dear Mr. Sloan: 26

The Columbia Appliance Repair Association has a membership of more than   40
60 percent of the appliance repair businesses in this city and the   53
environs. Now, the association has set itself a membership goal   66
of 100 percent. We want you as a member. We hope that this letter   80
will convince you to join.   85

Reset left margin

With this in mind, we are asking you to consider these benefits. They   99
are just a few of the many the association will pass on to you as   112
a member: 114

Backspace 5 times to begin each paragraph

First: We have recently conducted an extensive advertising campaign   118
It has brought in many more service calls to all our members.   131

Second: This year, we established a business loan service for associa-   145
tion members at a very low financing charge. Many of our members   158
have already taken advantage of this new service.   169

Third: We send our members an assortment of current information. The   183
material describes up-to-date equipment and new techniques devel-   196
oped for improved appliance repair.   203

The membership fee is $150 a year, payable with the filing of your appli-   218
cation. If you prefer, you can pay three installments of $50 each.   232
Fill in the enclosed application form and mail it with your check   245
to this office. You will receive your membership card within a   258
week.   259

Very truly yours,   263

Roderick M. Aylesworth   271

Roderick M. Aylesworth   267
Secretary   269

RMA:xx   270

Enclosure   272

(Shown in Elite Type)

Model 15 *Hanging Indented Letter Style*

Exercise 3

REVIEW

The following sentences contain errors identified by symbols in the margin. Find the errors before you type a corrected sentence. *Do not mark the book.*

Full sheet. 70-space line. Double spacing. Begin on line 10 and continue on a second sheet.

KEY TO SYMBOLS		
	cap	capitalization
	col	colon
	com	comma
	ep	end punctuation
	frag	sentence fragment
	ro	run-on sentence
	sem	semicolon
	sp	spelling
	ww	wrong word

REVIEW OF SPELLING, PUNCTUATION, AND CAPITALIZATION

TS

com, sp	1.	To our surprise the city tried to acommodate our zoning request.
cap, frag	2.	The painters expect to return friday. And to complete the job.
sp, com	3.	When we listened to customer criticizm we avoided waste.
sp, cap	4.	After recieving the report, the Bank Manager rejected it.
sp, com	5.	The representive in our area Ms. Jones was most helpful.
ro	6.	My cousin has an expensive hobby he builds model trains.
com	7.	I could not understand his hazy inadequate reasoning.
com	8.	It was however an extremely painful injury.
frag	9.	I recognized his handwriting. Which I had seen recently on a check.
com, sp	10.	My friend Jane Quinn has a seperate checking account.
com	11.	My pearl necklace my jade ring and my diamond ring are in the safe—deposit box.
sem, com	12.	The mechanic is qualified for the job however there are several reasons why she was not hired.
ro, com	13.	Some of the children were afraid others luckily ran back to warn the rest.
ro, cap	14.	We are offering excellent values however, the sale ends monday.
sp, ep	15.	May we expect your remitance in a few days.
com, sp	16.	The plans were she felt quite similiar.
com	17.	Friday June 12 is the last day of the semester.
dash	18.	Bring the entire check with you not just the stub.
ww, cap	19.	My decision too study spanish was made slowly.
col, com	20.	The menu includes the following deviled eggs baked beans potato salad and hot dogs.
com, ep	21.	Good work Patty I knew you could do it.
sp, cap	22.	Are your children planing to attend camp this Summer?
com	23.	The woman was puzzled by the directions and she asked the
sp		salesperson to explain the equiptment adjustments.
com, cap	24.	Ms. Zimmer the Supervisor at our factory developed the plan.
ww	25.	It is quiet expensive to mail the brochure.

Use any acceptable style for this letter, but do not repeat the style used in Exercise 8. Opening and closing parts have been left for you to supply. Use today's date. The letter was dictated by **Edward A. Mitchell, Customer Service Representative**. A copy is being sent to **Earl Southwick**.

Mr. Nelson Barbrow Shipping-Receiving Clerk McNamara Hobby Shop 963 Main Street Hood, VA 22723 This letter will confirm our telephone conversation of this morning. ¶You asked that we place a tracer on the three cartons of camera equipment that were missing from the shipment you received yesterday. Our records show that the following goods are included in the missing boxes:

Quantity	Stock Number	Model	Unit Price
12	N3102T	Keystone 110	$49.88
24	N3110D	Electronic Strobe	27.98
12	N3107D	K-7 Instazoom	69.70

¶As is our usual policy, we will wait three days before putting a tracer on the shipment. It is very likely that the boxes will arrive by then. If they do not, please telephone us at our toll-free number, (800) 645-1322, and a tracer will be placed immediately.   (115 words)

Topic 5 LETTER STYLE VARIATIONS

This topic covers two additional letter styles that are used for typing business letters. The first one is the *hanging indented style,* illustrated in Model 15 (page 278). The second is the *AMS (Administrative Management Society) simplified style,* shown and explained in Model 16 (page 279).

To type a letter in the hanging indented style, set normal margins as indicated in the Letter Placement Chart (page 197). Type the inside address, salutation, and the first line of the body. Then, move the left margin 5 spaces to the right for the rest of the letter. To type the first line of each remaining paragraph, use the margin release and backspace 5 times.

Before proceeding to Exercise 1, type Drills A and B to gain practice with these two new letter styles.

Drill A

Type the business letter illustrating the hanging indented style shown in Model 15. For spacing, follow the style shown in the model. There are 209 words in the body.

Drill B

Type the business letter illustrating the AMS simplified style shown in Model 16. Follow the spacing instructions given in the model. There are 187 words in the body.

PART 7

NOTES, LETTERS, AND PERSONAL-BUSINESS LETTERS

In this part you will learn to type personal notes, personal letters, and personal-business letters. You will learn to center the typed message on the page so that it is framed by top and bottom margins that are approximately equal, and side margins that are approximately equal.

Topic 1 PERSONAL NOTES AND LETTERS

PERSONAL NOTES

A personal note is generally very short and written to someone with whom the writer is well acquainted. Because of its nature, a personal note is usually typed on short stationery ($5\frac{1}{2}'' \times 8\frac{1}{2}''$). It is usually single-spaced, although a message of only one or two sentences may be double-spaced in order to stretch it out on the page.

Look at Model 2 on the next page. Notice that the return address, the date, and the complimentary closing start at the center of the page. This arrangement is called *modified block style*. Also notice that a comma is used after the salutation and the complimentary closing. When punctuation marks are used at these two points but not in the other opening and closing parts, the style of punctuation is called *mixed*.

Exercise 1

Half sheet. Insert short side first. Margins at 13 and 58 for elite; 10 and 50 for pica. Single spacing. Set tab at center. Begin on line 16.

Type the short personal note shown in Model 2 on the next page.

Exercise 2

Follow the directions for Exercise 1.

Retype the note shown in Model 2 with the following changes:

1. Use your own street address, city, state, and ZIP Code.
2. Use today's date.
3. Write your own first name after the complimentary closing.

your plant until the time it returns. This ~~certificate~~ *coverage*
will ~~insure~~ *protect* your property against ~~these~~ *the following* risks:

<u>While in Transit</u>	<u>While on Exhibition</u>
Theft	Theft and Pilferage
Fire	Fire
Colision	Loading and unloading
Overturning	Malicious Mischief
Storm	Loss of Use of Space
Loading and Unloading	Strikes or Riots

The more exhibiters who take advantage of this coverage, the lower will be the premiums. ¶We hope that you will decide to purchase your insurance through us.

Please use the enclosed application and send it today.

No application can be considered after April 10.

                    Sincerely

John G. Newman Motorboat Committee *xx* Enclosure   (127 words)

Exercise 8
SPECIAL CHALLENGE
LETTER: NUMBERED
PARAGRAPHS

Type this letter in any acceptable style and supply the missing parts. The letter is dated March 28, 19–. It was dictated by **Jacqueline Masters, President, The Mutual Bank of Pittsburgh**.

Peter S. Murillo 68 Reading Square Pittsburgh, PA 15203 The United Bankers Association recently sent questionnaires to 5,000 Pittsburgh residents, asking them what services they most want from a bank. Three responses appeared on almost every questionnaire: free checking, longer hours, and credit cards. ¶The Mutual Bank is anxious to serve its customers better. Beginning May 1, we will offer the new services described below. *(Begin insert)* 1. Free checking will be given to holders of regular accounts maintaining an average monthly balance of $200. All checking and service charges will be dropped on special accounts with an average balance of $500. 2. Banking hours on Thursday and Friday will be extended to 6 p.m. The bank will also be open on Saturdays from 9 until noon. 3. We have made arrangements to offer eligible customers a choice of two major credit cards. The enclosed pamphlets explain what these credit cards offer you. *(End insert)* We pledge, above all, to give you fast, courteous service. We want to be your banker; so we are listening to you.   (165 words)

2
3
4
5
6
7
8
9
10
11
12
13

Tab at
center
↓

Return address   708 Main Street   16

                Buffalo, NY 14202   17

Date line   June 17, 19--   18

19

Space down 4 times   20

21

Salutation   Dear Alice,   22

                  DS   23

Indent 5 ——▶ Mother and I were very glad to learn   24

      of your success in winning a first place   25

      trophy in the fine arts display and con-   26

Body   test held recently at your new school.   27

      We knew you could do it!   28

                 DS   29

       We congratulate you and feel certain   30

     that there will be other happy occasions   31

     like this one.   32

                 DS   33

Complimentary closing   Cordially yours,   34

35

Signature   *Eleanor*   36

          ↑   37

       Tab at   38

       center   39

40
41
42
43
44
45
46
47
48
49

(Shown in Elite Type)   50

51

Model 2   *Short Personal Note • Modified Block Style with*
Mixed Punctuation and Indented Paragraphs

Exercise 5

NUMBERED LIST

Modified block style. Mixed punctuation. 5-space paragraph indention.

Today's date   Mrs. Eleanor Tsui   Western High School   8970 South Fort Street Detroit, MI 48217 Dear Mrs. Tsui I applaud your efforts to prepare your students for the difficulties of job hunting after graduation. As a personnel interviewer, I see many young people who fail to get the jobs they want. This is often because they lack skill in presenting themselves to potential employers. ¶In response to your query, I suggest that you include the following in your lessons on job-hunting techniques: *(Begin insert)* 1. The letter of application 2. The data sheet or resume 3. The job interview 4. The employment test 5. The importance of grooming. *(End insert)* ¶I hope this information will help you in counseling your students. I would be glad to come to talk to them if you feel it would be beneficial. Cordially Arthur J. LaRue   Personnel Interviewer *xx*   (119 words)

Exercise 6

TABULATED INSERT

Modified block style. Mixed punctuation. 5-space paragraph indention.

Today's date Mr. David Bonnington Imperial House 10785 Dearborn Avenue Ripley, OK 74062 Dear Mr. Bonnington The unbelievably small St. Clair calculator is finally available—at an unbelievably small price. Now you can carry a calculator in your pocket while you keep more money in your wallet. ¶You will be impressed by the specifications of this hand-held machine listed below:

Display:	8 Digits, Floating Decimal
Functions:	Add, Subtract, Multiply, Divide
Constant:	4 Functions
Power:	4 AAA Batteries
Weight:	$3\frac{1}{2}$ Ounces
Size:	$4\frac{1}{2} \times 2 \times \frac{3}{4}$ Inches
Warranty:	1 Year

¶If you would like to try the new St. Clair for seven days with no obligation, just complete and return the enclosed card immediately. This offer will expire at the end of the month. Very truly yours M. Fillmore Sales Representative *xx*
(109 words)

Exercise 7

ROUGH DRAFT: TABULATED INSERT

Full block style. Mixed punctuation.

March 12, 19— Atlas Boat Corporation 598 Seventh Street Boston, MA 02169

Gentlemen

We have secured a Master insurance policy ~~covering~~ to cover exhibitors at the Thirty-~~Second~~ Third Annual Motor Boat Show, to be held in the Sixteenth Armory. A certificate can be issued to cover your exhibit from the time it leaves

(Continued on next page)

Exercise 3

Half sheet. Insert short side first. Modified block style. Mixed punctuation. Margins at 13 and 58 for elite; 10 and 50 for pica. Single spacing 5-space paragraph indention. Begin on line 16.

Type a personal note from the copy given below. (The symbol ¶ means to begin a new paragraph.)

Your address / *Today's date* / Dear Frank, Our social club is meeting next Wednesday evening, and we are planning an hour of entertainment beginning at eight o'clock. ¶ We have invited three other people to provide entertainment. Several club members have requested that you play ragtime piano. Will you be good enough to play for us? Any selections you wish to play will be fine. / Sincerely, / *Your name*   (57 words)

Exercise 4

Follow the directions for Exercise 3.

Compose and type a short note to a friend or relative telling her or him of your new typing skill. Tell also about happenings at home or in school, your social activities, and so on.

PERSONAL LETTERS

The personal letter differs from the personal note in that it is generally longer and is addressed to a person with whom the writer may not be as well acquainted. It is a communication written by one private individual to another. In typing personal letters, two parts may be added which were missing from the personal note. They are: (1) the *inside address,* and (2) the *typed name of sender.* Study Model 3, page 198. These two new parts are optional if the letter is written to a close friend.

Letters are usually single-spaced on standard-size paper (8½″ × 11″). It is acceptable however, to double-space a letter which has fewer than 50 words in the body.

As with personal notes, personal letters should be arranged on the page to give the impression of a picture in a frame. The Letter Placement Chart given here will help you decide on margin settings for letters of varying lengths. Soon you should be able to judge the placement of a letter on a page without using the chart.

LETTER PLACEMENT CHART

Length of Letter	Actual Words in Body	Line Length Inches	Pica	Elite	Date Line
Short	Up to 100	4	40	50	20
Average	101 to 200	5	50	60	18–15*
Long	201 to 300	6	60	70	13
2-Page	300+	6	60	70	13

*Exact placement of the date line in average length letters, will depend on how close the number of words in the letter is to the maximum or minimum. The longer the letter, the higher the date line is placed on the page.

Exercise 5

Modified block style. Mixed punctuation. 5-space paragraph indention.

Type the personal letter shown in Model 3 (page 198). Note that the return address and date line, complimentary closing, and typed name of sender all begin at center. Refer to the Letter Placement Chart above to determine the correct margins and placement of the date line. There are 104 words in the body of the letter shown.

Exercise 2
QUOTATION INSERT

Modified block style. Open punctuation. 5-space paragraph indention.

December 14, 19— Ms. Dolores Gessler, Store Manager Corner Market 727 B Street Jacksonville, FL 32216 Dear Ms. Gessler As you know, there has been a rash of late-night robberies at area Corner Markets recently. The enclosed packet contains artist's sketches of two of the robbers, and a photograph of a recent robbery taken by a hidden camera. ¶The police asked me to pass along the following instructions: *(Begin insert)* Post the drawings and photograph in a place where your employees will easily see them. If an employee spots one of these persons in the store, he or she should not approach him, but should immediately call the police. *(End insert)* ¶We hope to catch these criminals soon and put an end to the trouble and fear they are causing. Your cooperation might be the key to apprehending them. Sincerely Peter J. Tomlivich District Supervisor *xx*

(120 words)

Exercise 3
NUMBERED PARAGRAPHS

Full block style. Open punctuation. Begin each numbered paragraph at the left margin.

September 11, 19— Mr. Joseph L. Bowden Factory Superintendent Specialty Suppliers, Inc. 408 Haddon Street Lansing, MI 48921 Dear Mr. Bowden We find it necessary to call your attention to various practices causing inconvenience to our plants. *(Begin insert)* 1. The East plant complains that parts are shipped in oily barrels. 2. Both East and West plants report receiving unrelated parts in the same barrel. An operator has to take time to sort these parts. In the process, some may go into the scrap barrels. 3. All plants find that the quantity of finished casters in some barrels is short of the number marked on the tickets. *(End insert)* ¶Please give your attention to these problems at once and inform me of the steps you have taken to remedy them. ¶With respect to item No. 3 above, it is preferable to run over the specified count rather than under it. Sincerely yours Lawrence D. Niven, Manager *xx*   (124 words)

Exercise 4
NUMBERED LIST

Modified block style. Open punctuation.

Today's date Charles N. Coffey 614 West 38th Street St. Louis, MO 63112 Dear Mr. Coffey You asked to be notified when we acquired any used office equipment in good condition. An insurance company, which recently closed its branch here, has sold us its complete installation of office furniture. Since the office had been open only a year, the furniture is in excellent condition. ¶The lot includes the following (all wood in walnut finish): *(Begin insert)* 1. Large and small flattop desks 2. Typewriter drop desks 3. Filing cabinets, sorters, and stools 4. Conference tables 5. Desk chairs and leather armchairs 6. Assorted portable partitions. *(End insert)* ¶Please let us know at once whether you are interested in purchasing any of these pieces. The furniture will be delivered to our warehouse on Franklin Street next Saturday. It would therefore be advisable for you to be there Monday when the selection will be best. Yours very truly Mrs. Frances C. Camden Sales Manager *xx*   (133 words)

Tab at
center   Words

Return address   397 Grand Street   3
                                  Boston, MA 02115   6
Date line   August 11, 19--   9

                          Space down 4 times

Inside address   Mrs. Eva L. Andrus   13
                    119 Hawthorne Street   17
                    Boston, MA 02115   20
                         DS
Salutation   Dear Mrs. Andrus,   24
                         DS
                        For the past two months our neighborhood has   33
                    been invaded by motorcycles that have been using   43
                    the streets as raceways during the evening hours   53
                    when most of us are trying to relax.   60

                        I believe we can put a stop to this nuisance   69
Body   if all of us who are affected would organize as a   79
                    group and make a formal complaint to the proper city 90
                    authorities.   93

                        On Tuesday evening, August 26, at 8 p.m., I   102
                    am holding a meeting at my home to discuss the prob- 113
                    lem and possible solutions. If you feel as most of   123
                    us do, I would be very pleased if you could attend   133
                    this meeting.   136
                                        DS
Complimentary closing   Sincerely,   138

Signature   *Rebecca Shaw*   Space down 4 times

Typed name of sender   Rebecca Shaw   141

                                   Tab at
                                   center

                                        (Shown in Pica Type)

Model 3   *Personal Letter • Modified Block Style with*
              Mixed Punctuation and Indented Paragraphs

North Star Stationers

7694 Twin Cities Parkway
St. Paul, Minn. 55110
(612) 572-2637

	Words
November 30, 19--	4

Mr. Walter T. O'Brien — 8
676 Hobart Boulevard — 12
Duluth, MN 55806 — 15

Dear Mr. O'Brien — 18

In answer to your inquiry of November 20, we are — 28
sending you under separate cover three samples of — 38
carbon paper we believe compare well with the sam- — 48
ples you sent us. The samples include: — 56

DS ── Set 3 tabs

Center table horizontally

10 Sheets	#8, Blue	Pencil Carbon	63
DS			
10 Sheets	#4, Black	Typewriter Carbon	72
DS			
10 Sheets	#6, Black	Typewriter Carbon	81

The No. 8 carbon comes packaged in envelopes of 100 — 91
sheets each; the No. 4 and No. 6 carbons are pack- — 101
aged in boxes of 100 sheets. — 107

We have made careful tests to match your samples, — 117
and we shall be glad to receive your comments after — 127
you have had an opportunity to test our selections. — 137

Very truly yours — 140

Rachel N. Perez

Rachel N. Perez — 143
Production Manager — 147

xx — 148

(Shown in Pica Type)

Model 14 *Business Letter with a Tabulated Insert*
Full Block Style with Open Punctuation

Exercise 6

Modified block style. Mixed punctuation. 5-space paragraph indention.

Retype the letter shown in Model 3 with the following changes:

1. Use your own street address, city, **state**, and ZIP Code.
2. Use today's date.
3. Type your own full name as the sender, and sign the letter.

Exercise 7

DRILL THE OPENING AND CLOSING PARTS

Modified block style. Mixed punctuation. 5-space paragraph indention. Begin on line 6. Fill the entire sheet.

Type Model 3 again, this time to see how far you can get in 3 minutes. Do not be concerned with speed and do not stop to correct errors. Instead, concentrate on the arrangement of the letter parts. Repeat this exercise until the arrangement of the opening parts of a letter in modified block style becomes automatic for you.

This time type Model 3, beginning with the last paragraph. Try to complete the closing parts of the letter in 2 minutes or less. Do not stop to correct errors. Compare your arrangement of the letter with that shown in the model. Repeat the exercise until the closing parts of this letter style become automatic for you.

Exercise 8

Modified block style. Mixed punctuation. 5-space paragraph indention.

Use Model 3 as a guide to type the following two letters. Refer to the Letter Placement Chart (page 197) to determine the margins and the date line.

Your address / Today's date / Ms. Ruth Elwood / One Florida Drive / St.	19
Louis, MO 63155 / Dear Ms. Elwood, My mother told me this morning that	33
she is taking me on a two-week trip. We are going to fly to Florida and	48
board a cruise ship to the Caribbean Islands. ¶As we are planning to leave	63
on Friday, I shall not be able to participate in the Piano Festival. The two	78
events have fallen in the same two-week period. I am sorry to have to dis-	93
appoint you. ¶I shall write you as soon as we return. Please let me know	108
about plans for the next festival. / Yours truly, / *Your name* (89 words)	120

Exercise 9

Modified block style. Mixed punctuation. No paragraph indention.

Your address / Today's date / Mel Wilson / P.O. Box 125 / Gary, IN 46410	17
Dear Mr. Wilson,	20
The class of 19— held its five-year reunion last Friday. After all the excitement	38
of seeing so many old friends for the first time since graduation, we realized	54
that one of our favorite teachers was not with us. ¶Our inquiries uncovered	69
the news that you were taken ill last July and have been confined to your	84
home now for several weeks. We are all extremely sorry to hear of this	98
and wish you a speedy recovery. ¶We took some photos at the reunion.	112
As soon as they are developed, I will send you a few of them.	124
Sincerely,	126
Your name (101 words)	128

EVANS PUBLISHING COMPANY, INC.

177 Buckwald Street, Stamford, Connecticut 06904 • (203) 746-1000

Raymond T. Patterson
Business Manager

December 21, 19--

	Words
	4

Dr. Rebecca D. Heymont, Dean   10
The Taylor School of Paralegal Studies   18
309 Myrtle Avenue   22
Stamford, CN 06901   26

Dear Dr. Heymont   29

    We welcome the opportunity of sending you an examination   41
copy of INTRODUCTORY PARALEGAL STUDIES. It is being mailed   53
today under separate cover.   59

    We hope that you will take the time to examine the book   70
carefully in order to see for yourself the many advanced ideas   83
and teaching methods it offers. We should like to call your   95
attention particularly to the following features: 105

Set tab ———⌐   DS

1. The book covers the basic subject matter taught   116
Reset margin ———   in standard courses of study. The material is   126
    logically organized; at the same time, it is   135
    graded, beginning with the simplest, most famil-   145
    iar cases and progressing to less common ground.   155

    DS

2. The writing is made as interesting as possible.   166
    For example, each new subject is introduced by   176
    a narrative history of an actual case.   184

    DS

3. The treatment of all issues is totally unbiased.   195
    Where differences of opinion exist, all sides   204
    are presented and the prevailing law explained.   214

    DS

    We should be happy to add your school to the many that are   226
now using the book. We also supply a Teacher's Guide without   238
charge.   240

    Yours truly   243

Raymond T. Patterson

Raymond T. Patterson   247
Business Manager   250

xx   251

(Shown in Elite Type)

Model 13   *Business Letter with Paragraph Inserts*
Modified Block Style with Open Punctuation

Exercise 10
ROUGH DRAFT

Modified block style. Mixed punctuation. 5-space paragraph indention.

Type this letter given in rough-draft form below. Use your own address for the heading and your own name as the sender. If you need to review proofreaders' marks, they are given on page 97.

Your address / May 1, 19— / Mr. Allen Fitzgerald / Alston Printing Co. / 755 Market Way / South Bend, IN 46614

Dear Mr. Fitzgerald,

Although it had been more than a year since we shared some very pl~~e~~sant *(a)* conversation on a cross-country fli~~l~~ght, I am hoping that you will still remember me. When we ~~left~~ *parted* eachother at the airport in Los Angeles, you gave me your *(business)* card and invited me to ~~visit you~~ *look you up* if ever I were to visit South Bend.

As it now happens, my company will be sending me ~~there~~ *to your city* in two week's time to attend to some business for them. ~~Being a stranger in the area,~~ I thought ~~how enjoyable it~~ *what a lucky opportunity* *this* ~~would~~ be for us to renew our short a~~q~~uaintance. *(c)* I will be in Su~~o~~th Bend for just ~~under a week~~ *three days*.

Please let me extend an invitation to you ~~for your~~ join~~g~~ *to* ing me for dinner one ~~night~~ *evening* in a restaurant of your choosing. I will call you ~~when I arrive~~ *at your office* at the Queen Anne Hotel on Tuesday, May 15. *afternoon #* I look forward to talking with you then.

Sincerely,

Your name   (159 words)

Exercise 11

Modified block style. Mixed punctuation. 5-space paragraph indention.

Compose and type a short letter of about two paragraphs to your high school principal asking for a letter of recommendation. You need the recommendation to receive a scholarship to a college in your state. You should mention the name of the college, the type of scholarship (athletic or academic), and the subject area that will be your major in college.

THE HARKNESS TV REPAIR SCHOOL

733 Nealy Street
Kansas City, Kansas 66117
(913) 651-2138

Words

July 10, 19--   3

Mr. Philip T. Amadeo   7
601 Fifth Avenue   10
Kansas City, KS 66102   14

Dear Mr. Amadeo: 17

Have your earning expectations in TV repair been realized?   29
Are you able to "spot" TV troubles quickly and accurately   41
and make expert repairs? What have you done to keep up with 53
the new developments in the electronics field?   62

Do these questions raise doubts in your mind? If so, you will   75
be interested in our advanced course in TV Theory and Repair.   87
Briefly, here is what the course gives you: twenty graded   99
lessons covering various phases of modern servicing, three   111
up-to-date textbooks, personal consultations with our coun-   123
selors on your individual servicing problems, and a certifi-   135
cate at the end of the course.   141

Mr. George Perry, TV service engineer, writes the following: 153

Reset margin———→   DS

After taking your course, I have been recommending   163
it to all my friends in the TV repair field. I   173
have found it extremely helpful in bringing me up   183
to the minute in modern servicing techniques. I   193
consider it worth many times the fee you charge.   203

Reset margin———→   DS

Read carefully the enclosed folder giving details about the   215
course. Then, if you wish to enroll, detach and mail the   227
application form.   231

                          Sincerely yours,   235

                          Randolph L. Harkness

                          Randolph L. Harkness   239
                          President   241

xx   242

Enclosure   244

(Shown in Elite Type)

Model 12 *Business Letter with a Quotation Insert*
Modified Block Style with Mixed Punctuation

Topic 2 PERSONAL-BUSINESS LETTERS

A personal-business letter, as its name suggests, is a business letter written by a private individual. Such correspondence could include letters to order merchandise, to apply for a job, to ask for a refund, or to handle any number of situations of a business nature.

Model 4 (page 202) is a sample of a personal-business letter. It is typed in modified block style, like that used in the preceding topic. Notice, however, that a colon rather than a comma is used after the salutation in a business letter. This style is still referred to as mixed punctuation.

SALUTATIONS   If a letter is addressed to a specific person in a company or an organization, use that person's name in the salutation. If the person addressed is a man, the salutation should be *Dear Mr. — —; if* the person addressed is a woman, the salutation should be *Dear Ms. — —, Dear Miss — —, or Dear Mrs. — —.* On some occasions, you may be unsure of the sex of the addressee. For example, a letter signed *J. R. Jones,* or *Terry Lorenz* does not indicate whether the writer is male or female. In response, you may address the person without using a social title: *Dear J. R. Jones* or *Dear Terry Lorenz.*

When a business letter is addressed to a company or organization and not to an individual person, a more general salutation is required. Two salutations are commonly used in such cases: *Gentlemen* and *Ladies and Gentlemen.* Sometimes a letter is addressed to the Sales Manager, Personnel Director, or other individual, but the name of that person is not known to the writer. In such cases, the salutation should be *Dear Sir or Madam.*

COMPLIMENTARY CLOSINGS   The complimentary closing for a business letter is largely determined by the preference of the writer. It usually indicates how familiar he or she is with the person being addressed. The most common closings are: *Sincerely yours, Sincerely, Cordially, Cordially yours,* and *Very truly yours.* More personal closings, such as *Regards, Best wishes, As ever,* and so on may be used at the writer's discretion.

ENCLOSURES   Quite often a business letter is accompanied by a check, a form, or some other document the sender wishes to enclose. In such cases, an *enclosure* notation is typed at the left margin a double space after the typed name. This notation serves three purposes: (1) it tells the person who receives the letter that the sender has enclosed something in addition to the letter; (2) it reminds the typist to enclose the required material when the letter is prepared for mailing; (3) it provides a record on the file copy that something was sent along with the letter.

CARBON COPIES   A copy of a business letter is very useful. The writer will often need to remember (sometimes weeks or months later) some facts included in the letter, such as the date, a price quoted, or an amount sent. For this reason you will be directed to make a carbon copy of letters in this topic. Although it is possible to obtain a photocopy of a letter, it is less expensive and less time-consuming to use carbon paper.

```
Jim's                          meet       the
day, and will be able to discuss his ideas with you at that
time.  I will be particularly interested to hear your opinions
on investing in commodities.


                              Sincerely,



                              Pat MacIntosh
```

Type enclosure notation
a double space below   Enclosure
typed name of sender

Topic 4 LETTERS WITH INSERTS

An insert may be included within the body of a business letter. It could be a long quotation, a list of items, a series of numbered paragraphs, or a tabulation. An insert is set off from the rest of the letter by a double space above and below it. It is usually indented 5 spaces from the left and right margins. Tables, however, are centered horizontally. If an insert consists of a list of short items, the items may be double-spaced. If the items are long, however, the insert should be single-spaced with a double space between items.

When you plan the placement of a letter that contains an insert, determine the margins and date line in the usual way. When necessary, refer to the Letter Placement Chart (page 197). The date line, however, must be raised to allow for the blank lines left above, below, and within the insert. For each 2 line spaces added, raise the date line by 1 line.

Study Models 12, 13, and 14 (pages 271–273). They show examples of letters with different types of inserts. Before proceeding to Exercise 1, type Drills A–C to gain practice in placing inserts in letters.

Drill A

Type the business letter shown in Model 12, which includes a quotation insert. Follow the spacing instructions given in the model. There are 179 words in the body.

Drill B

Type the business letter shown in Model 13, which includes a series of numbered paragraphs as an insert. Follow the spacing instructions given in the model. There are 174 words in the body.

Drill C

Type the business letter shown in Model 14, which includes a tabulated insert. Follow the spacing instructions given in the model. There are 106 words in the body.

Directions for Exercises 1–7

As you type these business letters with inserts, refer to Models 12, 13, and 14. Remember to reset the left margin when you start and finish an insert. For very short inserts or those that are in table form, use tab stops. Watch for the mention of enclosures in the letters and add the necessary notation.

Exercise 1
PARAGRAPH INSERT

Full block style. Open punctuation.

March 10, 19— Rothrock Homes 1717 Commerce Street Birmingham, AL 35217 SUBJECT: Fixtures Sale Gentlemen A builder needs to save money and still give quality. Morrison fixtures are the best quality you can buy. And now the price will help you save those precious construction dollars. ¶Because you are a bulk buyer of Morrison fixtures, here is what we will do for you: *(Begin insert)* We are offering you anything in our inventory at 25 percent off our regular price. This offer is good for one week only, April 8 through 14. It is being made only to you and a handful of our other preferred customers. *(End insert)* This is our way of saying "thank you" for being a faithful customer. Cordially Andrew Rux, Manager *xx* (104 words)

Tab at
center

Return address   1812 Overture Drive   4
                  St. Louis, MO 63117   8
Date line   March 18, 19--   11

Space down 4 times

Inside address   Personnel Manager   15
                  The ACT Company   18
                  2311 Wilson Drive   21
                  St. Louis, MO 63101   25

                  DS
Salutation   Dear Sir or Madam: 29
                  DS
                  Please consider this letter as my application for a job as a   41
                  clerk-typist for your company.   47

                  Queens School for Career Development

                  My graduation from ~~East End High School~~ will occur this June,   59
                  and I shall have completed a three-year business course. I am   71
                  able to type a minimum of 65 words a minute accurately.   82

                  30

Body   The enclosed data sheet gives more details of my high school   94
                  training, previous work experience, and references. Many of   106
                  my summer vacations have been spent working in offices, and I   118
                  have a genuine liking for this type of work. If given an oppor-   131
                  tunity, I am sure I shall prove an asset to your company.   142

                  I would appreciate the opportunity to come to your office for   154
                  a personal interview at any time that would be convenient for   166
                  you. You may reach me at the above address or by telephone at   178
                  592-7810.   180

                                                    DS
Complimentary closing   Very truly yours,   183

Signature   *Jane S. Paxton*   Space down
                                     4 times

Typed name of sender   Jane S. Paxton   186
                                          DS
Enclosure notation   Enclosure   188

                  Tab at
                  center

(Shown in Elite Type)

Model 4   **Personal-Business Letter · Modified Block Style with
           Mixed Punctuation and No Paragraph Indention**

Exercise 2 continued

shortly before Christmas. The envelope will be marked, "Do not open until Christmas." A few days later, the January issue of the magazine will be delivered in a special wrapper. Then, each month for a year, your friends will be reminded of your thoughtfulness by the arrival of another issue. It is an ideal Christmas gift. ¶Act now, while you have the opportunity to take advantage of this special offer. Yours sincerely Terry Pappas Subscription Department *xx* Enclosures P.S. Please notice on the enclosed price schedule that with gift subscriptions of ten or more, you receive an additional reduction of 33 percent off the already low Christmas rate. At this great price, you can hardly afford not to include all your friends. Why not get a subscription for yourself or your family as well?

Exercise 3
SPECIAL CHALLENGE LETTER

Type this business letter in any acceptable style, using either form of heading for the second page. Supply any missing parts. Address a large envelope. Don't forget to mark a 1-inch margin at the bottom of the first page. This letter was dictated by **Martha S. Wendell, President** of the **Wendell Real Estate Company.**

Today's date Mr. James F. Bancroft 604 Eustis Street Albany, NY 12206 I have your letter concerning the purchase of some property on Lake Champlain, where you wish to build a children's summer camp. ¶As it now happens, I have for sale an old estate covering 35 acres of level land on the western shore of the lake. The estate has a very beautiful large main house with 25 spacious rooms. This could easily be converted into a comfortable lodge for parents. The house is in an excellent state of repair and is very substantially built. The best materials and the finest workmanship went into its construction. ¶In addition to the main house, several other structures are situated on the property. There is a very large garage, fully equipped with a workshop. Several smaller buildings, which were formerly used as servants' quarters, are suitable for camper cabins. An old-fashioned artesian well adds an authentic rustic look. ¶The estate's lake frontage of more than 750 feet includes a beautiful white sandy beach. There is a well-constructed concrete dock and a two-story boathouse, large enough to hold 30 boats. ¶On the grounds are beautiful lawns and lovely old shade trees. A section of three acres, once used as a vegetable garden, could easily be converted into a ball field and tennis courts. The property is located about 25 miles from the airport at Burlington, Vermont. It is easily accessible by car over good roads. In town, it is possible for you to purchase all the supplies you will need for the camp. ¶I am of the opinion that this property would exactly suit your purpose. I am enclosing a recent set of photographs to give you an idea of the beauty and the layout of the estate. I think you will agree that the place is unusually attractive. ¶If Monday of next week is convenient for you, I should like you to meet me at my office at nine o'clock. We can drive over to the estate, and you may see for yourself how desirable it is. The price of the property and the terms of sale are open to negotiation. Cordially

(349 words)

TYPING WITH CARBON PAPER

The paper used for carbon copies is either a cheaper grade of paper (called a *second sheet*), or a thinner grade of paper (called *onionskin*). Carbon paper has two sides: a glossy side and a dull side. The dull side sometimes has the brand name of the carbon paper printed on it. The following steps will aid you in using carbon paper:

1. To assemble the carbon pack, place the sheet on which you will type the original facedown on the desk. Next, place the carbon paper on top, glossy side up. Then place the copy sheet (second sheet or onionskin) on top of the carbon paper. Avoid touching the glossy side when you handle the carbon paper. The coating may rub off on your hands, and your fingerprints may be transferred to the original copy.

2. Pick up the pack with the second sheet facing you and insert it into your typewriter. Use a folded strip of paper (such as the flap of an envelope) over the top edge of a thick carbon pack. This will help keep the papers straight as they are inserted into the typewriter. Avoid wrinkling the carbon paper; it creases easily. At the first sign of wrinkling, pull the paper release lever forward and smooth out your papers. After the carbon pack is in the machine and rolled into position, the dull side of the carbon paper should be facing you. Check for this.

3. Check the carbon pack before you begin to type to be sure it has been assembled properly. This will avoid the possibility of typing an entire assignment and then discovering a useless "mirror" copy printed on the back of your original.

4. When making several carbon copies, look at the last 2 or 3 copies before you go too far. Are they readable? On electric typewriters, adjust the impression control lever to make a stronger impression. On manuals, use a heavier touch, especially on capital letters.

5. To make an erasure when using carbon paper, erase the last copy first. Use a carbon eraser. Insert a strip of paper between the copy and the coated side of the carbon paper to prevent smudging as you continue to erase each copy until you reach the original. The strip of paper inserted should extend beyond the edge of the paper, so you will remember to remove it.

6. Use the paper release to remove the carbon pack from the machine. To remove the carbon paper, grasp the carbon pack on the upper corner, where the carbon paper is notched, and pull out the carbon paper.

7. If a typing error is discovered after the carbon pack has been removed from the typewriter, correct each copy and the original, one at a time.

Step 1	Step 2	Step 6
Original	Top edge	Top edge
Carbon paper (glossy side)	Second sheet	
	Carbon paper (dull side)	
Second sheet	Original Top edge	
Top edge		

Exercise 1
ROUGH DRAFT

Type the second page of a letter from the rough-draft copy given at the right. Refer to page 97 if you need to review the proofreaders' marks. Use Style A heading shown in Model 11.

Modified block style. Mixed punctuation. 1-inch side margins. 5-space paragraph indention. Begin on line 7.

Lucian Electric Appliance Company   2   *Today's date*

Night Beacon retails for $7.50. The cost to you is $4.00. You can make a profit of $4.50 with an installation charge of $1.00.

As there is no official distributor of the Night Beacon in your city, there are hundreds of possible sales waiting for you. We believe that you can increase your business considerably by carrying the Night Beacon. In fact, we are so sure that you will find this venture profitable that we are willing to give you an attractive window display without charge. We will also and to supply you with 25 units on 30 days' approval. You will not be obligated in any way if, after a trial period, of one month's you wish to return the merchandise.

On the other hand, if you decide to carry stock the Night beacon, as a permanent item of stock, we shall be glad to enter into a contract with you. The contract will give giving you the official agency in your city. We can then arrange credit terms to our mutual satisfaction.

Cordially,

NEWBOLD LIGHT FIXTURES, INC.   Frederick S. Newbold, President   *xx*

(158 words)

Exercise 2

Type the second page of a letter from the copy given here. For the heading, use Style B shown in Model 11.

Full block style. Open punctuation. 1-inch side margins. Begin on line 7.

Mr. Arnold Fenton Page 2 November 11, 19— letter is conveniently at hand, write their names and addresses on the order form enclosed. Then return the list in the stamped envelope we have provided for you. You may send payment now for your Christmas order, or, if you prefer, we can bill you later. ¶To each friend on your list, we will send an attractive Christmas card announcing your gift. Your name will appear on the inside fold. The card will be mailed so that it arrives

(Continued on next page)

Before you begin Exercise 1, practice the following drills to become familiar with handling a carbon pack and in making neat erasures on an original and carbon copy.

Drill A

Practice assembling and disassembling a carbon pack with one sheet of carbon paper. Repeat this several times. Follow the procedures outlined in Steps 1, 2 and 6 on page 203.

Drill B

Practice making an erasure. Follow the procedures given in Step 5.

1. Use the carbon pack assembled in Drill A.
2. Type the following sentence on line 15, exactly as it appears:

`Ms. Livingston is the President of the firm.`

3. Use the proper erasing technique to change the capital *P* in *President* to a small letter.

Drill C

Space down 5 lines from Drill B.

1. Type the following two sentences, exactly as they appear:

`I was happy to receive there good news.`

`The mills will remain closed for four weeks.`

2. Use the proper erasing technique to change *there* to *their* in the first sentence. In the second sentence, change *four* to *five*.

Exercise 1

Modified block style. Mixed punctuation. No paragraph indention. 1 carbon copy.

Type the personal-business letter shown in Model 4 on page 202. There are 141 words in the body of the letter. Use the Letter Placement Chart (page 197) to determine the correct margin settings and placement of the date line. Remember to set a tab at center when modified block style is used.

Exercise 2

Modified block style. Mixed punctuation. 5 space paragraph indention. 1 carbon copy.

Study Model 4 (page 202) which illustrates the use of the enclosure notation. Then type a personal-business letter from the copy given below.

Your address / *Today's date* / Mr. Joseph Sykes / Personnel Manager / Parke-Davis Company / 7 Riverside Drive / *Your city, state, ZIP Code* / Dear Mr. Sykes: The Placement Coordinator at my school, Mr. Borovsky, has informed me of an opening in your word-processing center for a Transcription Machine Operator. Please consider me an applicant for that position. ¶ My advanced typewriting class visited your center last semester. I was interested in what I saw, and I should like very much to work for you. ¶ My data sheet is enclosed; however, I believe a personal interview would give you a better chance to evaluate my worth to your company as an employee. I shall be very glad to meet the appointment time you set. My telephone number is (*insert your number*). / Very sincerely yours, / *Your name* / Enclosure   (102 words)

Line 7 → Heywood Associates   2   June 3, 19--   8
                    TS

discounts allowed on many brands, even some which are not listed here.   22
Please take advantage of the many savings available to you by shopping   36
through our catalog. We shall be happy to furnish catalogs and prices   50
upon your request.   54

                          Sincerely yours,   58

                          JOHN DALY & SONS   62

                          R. L. Daly

                          R. L. Daly   64
                          Vice President   67

xx   68

Style A

Words

Line 7 → Heywood Associates   4
         Page 2   5
         June 3, 19--   8
                    TS

discounts allowed on many brands, even some which are not listed here.   22
Please take advantage of the many savings available to you by shopping   36
through our catalog. We shall be happy to furnish catalogs and prices   50
upon your request.   54

Sincerely yours,   57

JOHN DALY & SONS   60

R. L. Daly

R. L. Daly   62
Vice President   65

xx   66

Style B

Model 11   *Second-Page Heading
of a Business Letter*

Exercise 3

Modified block style. Mixed punctuation. 5-space paragraph indention. 1 carbon copy.

Your address / Today's date / Ocean Airlines / 4000 Roche Boulevard / San 19 Diego, CA 92104 / Ladies and Gentlemen: My marketing class is currently 33 learning how to design window displays. Each student has been given a theme 48 for creating an individual display. My theme is Hawaiian travel. ¶ I've seen 63 your posters of Hawaii at the airport, and I'm impressed with your creativity 78 and bright colors. I believe a few of these posters would add the perfect touch 94 to my display. ¶ Will you be so kind as to send me three or four of your posters? 110 I will be glad to pay any handling or postage charge. Thank you for your help. 126 / Sincerely, / *Your name*   (92 words) 130

Exercise 4

Modified block style. Mixed punctuation. 5-space paragraph indention. 1 carbon copy.

Your address / Today's date / Ms. Carol Rhodes / IBM Corporation / 11676 18 Southfield Road / *Your city, state, ZIP Code* / Dear Ms. Rhodes: Thank you 32 for the time you spent with me this morning discussing the position of Mag 47 Card II Operator in your word processing center. I have given much thought 62 to the comments you made. ¶ This type of work interests me very much. I 76 believe my strong background in punctuation, spelling, and grammar will 90 greatly reduce the time it will take to train me on the equipment in your office. 106 ¶ I shall telephone you on Wednesday afternoon, as you suggested. / Sincerely 121 yours / *Your name*   (79 words) 124

Exercise 5

ROUGH DRAFT

Modified block style. Mixed punctuation. 5-space paragraph indention. 1 carbon copy.

Type a personal-business letter from the rough-draft copy given below. If you need to review proofreaders' marks, they are given on page 97.

Your address / Today's date / Mr. R. B. Price / 1836 Ryan Road / Gary, IN 46406

Dear Mr. Price:

Enclosed is my check to confirm my reservation for dinner at the Spring meeting of the Business Teacher's club, which is being held next Friday evening. I prefer to have menu featuring Lobster Newberg. ¶ I understand that since my reservation is being mailed late, I shall not receive my ticket in advance through the mail. Instead, I shall expect to pick up my ticket at the door on Friday night.

Sincerely yours,

Della Thomas / Enclosure   (71 words)

Today's date Barnett & Lowell 408 Manhattan East Orange, NJ 07019
Ladies and Gentlemen Subject: Your Purchase Order No. 02216 Please

sp notify us when you will be prepared to recieve deliveries at your new
warehouse. We are delaying shipment of your order for five cases of
continuous feed paper until we hear from you. After reading in your order

com that you wanted delivery this week we wondered whether we should hold

sp the merchandize until the warehouse is ready. ¶Since the goods are al-

sp ready packed, we would like to send them to you as soon as posible. We

sp would appreciate your sending us instructions immediatly. Cordialy

sp Ms. P. P. Froman Shipping Department Manger *xx* SPECIAL DELIVERY
P.S. Please verify the address of the new warehouse. Our records show it
as 37 Markland Drive, Paterson, New Jersey.

(80 words in body; 19 words in postscript)

Topic 3 TWO-PAGE LETTERS

Letters are often long enough to require more than one page. They are then continued on a second sheet of the same quality paper, but without a printed letterhead. Since the pages might become separated, each sheet after the first is headed with identifying information. This includes the name of the addressee, the page number of the letter, and the date. Study the two different styles of second-page headings shown in Model 11 (page 267).

When typing long letters of more than one page, remember to:

1. Use 1-inch side margins.
2. Avoid ending a page with the first line of a paragraph or with a hyphenated or divided word.
3. Mark the first page at least one inch from the bottom. This will remind you to stop in time to leave an acceptable bottom margin.
4. Carry over at least 2 lines of the body of the letter to the next page. This may require you to leave slightly more than a 1-inch margin at the bottom of the first page.
5. Begin the second-page heading on line 7. Triple space after you type the heading and then continue with the body of the letter.

Before you proceed to Exercise 1, type Drills A and B to gain practice in typing second-page letter headings.

Drill A

*Full sheet. Modified block
style. Mixed punctuation.*

Assume that you have typed the first page of a business letter and are ready to complete it on a second sheet. Type the copy given in Model 11, Style A, which shows one way to position the second-page heading. Repeat the drill until you can type this arrangement of a second-page heading without hesitation.

Drill B

*Full sheet. Full block style.
Mixed punctuation.*

Style B in Model 11 shows another way to arrange the second-page heading of a business letter. Type this letter several times until this arrangement of a second-page heading becomes familiar to you.

Exercise 6

Modified block style. Mixed punctuation. 5-space paragraph indention. 1 carbon copy.

Type a personal-business letter from the handwritten copy given below. Supply any missing opening or closing parts.

Your address / Today's date / Columbia Record Club / 55 Rochester Road / Columbus, OH 43215

For the past two years, I have been a member of your club. I have enjoyed receiving your monthly magazine and making my selections from your offerings.

I must cancel my membership at this time, however, because I am leaving the country for a year to participate in a student-exchange program in France.

I will write you when I return about reinstating my membership.

Your name   (65 words)

Exercise 7
ROUGH DRAFT

Modified block style. Mixed punctuation. 5-space paragraph indention. 1 carbon copy.

Type a personal-business letter from the rough-draft copy given below. Supply the missing salutation and complimentary closing.

Your address / Today's date / Alice Cohen, Director / Davis School of Art / 1120 Madison Avenue / New York, NY 10028

Since junior high school I have been interested in a career as an illustrator. I have decided that an education at a top-notch art school is the best course in the pursuit of my goal. My high school art teacher, Mr. Gregson, is a graduate of your school and highly recommends it. Will you please send me a catalog and an application for enrollment? In addition, I would appreciate any information you have concerning scholarships, grants, loans, work-study programs, or other types of financial aid. I look forward to hearing from you soon.

Your name   (96 words)

Directions for Exercises 16–19

Exercises 16–19 contain words that are misspelled. There are also missing commas in many of the letters. Before typing each exercise, find the misspelled word (or words) in each of the lines indicated by *sp* in the left margin. Make a list of their correct spellings on a separate piece of paper. Check each line that has the *com* symbol next to it and decide where on that line the comma (or commas) should go. Then type the letter in the style indicated with all the words spelled correctly and the missing commas in place. *Do not mark the book.*

Exercise 16

SPELLING CHECKUP

Modified block style. Mixed punctuation. 5-space paragraph indention. 2 carbon copies.

Today's date Mr and Mrs. David Lightfoot 372 Sand Street Youngstown, OH 44517 Dear Mr. and Mrs. Lightfoot We deeply appreciate your *(sp)* writting to us to express your satisfaction with our workmanship, and we thank you for the picture you enclosed. ¶We would like to have your *(sp)* permisson to show both the letter and the photograph to owners of *(sp)* houses who come to us with problems similiar to yours. ¶Also, we would like your permission to quote your letter and reproduce the picture in an *(sp)* advertizement we are planning to run in an industrial journal. If you prefer, we shall withhold your name. Sincerely yours RELIABLE HOME IMPROVEMENTS Charles B. Arnez, Manager *xx* cc A. Sands   (85 words)

Exercise 17

SPELLING AND COMMA CHECKUP

Modified block style. Mixed punctuation. 5-space paragraph indention.

Today's date Barton Printing Company 208 Dumont Street Decatur, IL 62506 Gentlemen Refer to: Purchase Order No. 02245 Three weeks ago *(sp)* we ordered some original printing plates that were shiped to the Springer Brick Company. The plates were later returned to you for some minor *(com)* changes. As we understood the contract an additional charge was to be made for the alterations to the plates. ¶We have not yet received a bill for *(sp)* the exact amount of the aditional charge. Please forward this informa- *(sp)* tion imediately so that we may submit our statment to the Springer Brick Company and bring the transaction to a close. Yours truly PETERS & DANZIG Jasper Austin, Director Accounting Department LBT:*xx*
(86 words)

Exercise 18

SPELLING AND COMMA CHECKUP

Full block style. Open punctuation.

June 9, 19— URGENT Craig Washing Machines, Inc. 555 Industrial Court Wilmington, DE 19809 Attention Mr. Joseph Stanski Manager *(sp)* Ladies and Gentlemen Last Wendsday we received a shipment of 32 *(sp com)* washers from your company. When we opened the crates we descovered *(sp)* that you had sent us the wrong models. Our laundrymat is schedualed to *(com)* open next month but we will be forced to move back the opening date unless you can quickly correct your mistake. We are returning the wrong *(sp)* modles with a copy of our original order. Please send the correct washers to us as quickly as possible. Sincerely DEL & FAYE'S WASH AND DRY Del Kanter *xx*   (77 words)

Exercise 8

Modified block style. Mixed punctuation. 5-space paragraph indention. 1 carbon copy.

Type a personal-business letter from the handwritten copy given below. Supply any missing opening or closing parts.

Your address / Today's date / Superintendent of Documents / Government Printing Office / Washington, D.C. 20402

I am presently enrolled in a class in which we are studying different careers. My teacher has assigned a term project which requires me to gather information on a career area of my choice.

I am interested in several occupational areas, so I would like to order one copy of each of the following reprints from the *Occupational Outlook Handbook*, Current Edition: No. 1955-5, *Clerical Occupations*; No. 1955-7, *Banking Occupations*; and No. 1955-26, *Small Business Occupations*.

I have enclosed a money order for $1.50 to cover the cost of the reprints. Thank you.

Your name   (93 words)

Exercise 9

COMPOSING A PERSONAL-BUSINESS LETTER

Modified block style. Mixed punctuation. 5-space paragraph indention. 1 carbon copy.

Compose a letter of application in answer to the following classified advertisement.

> **OPPORTUNITIES FOR CLERKS, CLERK-TYPISTS, SECRETARIES, AND STENOGRAPHERS**
> We have several openings from starting positions requiring no experience to secretarial positions requiring 2-3 years' experience. If you have had high school or business college training in office procedures, have excellent grammar and spelling skills, and can type at least 40 wpm, we would be interested in talking with you.
> APPLY BY LETTER TO: Box N-4420, Detroit News, Detroit, MI 48231.

Follow these guidelines when writing your letter:

1. State the purpose of the letter in the first paragraph. (Identify the exact job in question; tell where and how you heard about the job opening.)
2. Convince the employer that you are the one for the job by giving information about your education, training, experience, and skills which apply to the job.
3. List supplementary information about your special personal qualifications such as leadership roles in school, above-average grades, perfect attendance record, and so on.
4. Refer to a data sheet if one is to be enclosed.
5. Ask for an interview. (Supply necessary addresses and telephone numbers.)

Refer to the letters of application in this topic: Model 4 (page 202) and Exercises 2 and 4 (pages 204 and 205).

Directions for Exercises 13–15

SPECIAL CHALLENGE LETTERS

Before beginning these exercises, read the copy to decide on the placement of any parts that have been omitted and supply the missing parts. Use any acceptable style for each letter, but vary from one to the other. Use today's date.

Exercise 13
ATTENTION LINE, COMPANY NAME, AND MAILING NOTATION

Any acceptable letter style.

Address the letter to the attention of **Mrs. L. London.** The dictator of the letter is **Kale A. Sullivan, Sales Manager** of Atlas Containers, Inc. Include the company name in the signature block. The letter is being sent by certified mail.

Dickson Carton Corporation 730 Grand Street Omaha, NB 68102 The specifications of the large container that we submitted to you were intended only as suggestions. It is important to us to keep within the price limits given, because of the competition with similar products now on the market. ¶If you can suggest a satisfactory container in that price range, we shall be glad to consider it. Please send us some samples and price quotations as soon as possible. ¶If you find, after receiving the new adhesive, that you can produce the container we originally specified at an acceptable price, we would prefer it. In that case, we would like to see additional samples. Sincerely yours   (104 words)

Exercise 14
SUBJECT LINE AND POSTSCRIPT

Any acceptable letter style.

Include as the subject line: **Symphony Discount Tickets.** The letter was dictated by **Melvin Thompson, Ticket Manager.** Do not use postscript initials.

Ms. Georgia Templeton Cultural Resource Center 754 Comiskey Street Charlotte, NC 28212 Dear Georgia This year we will again be offering special discount tickets to performances of the Charlotte Symphony Orchestra. The discount is available to groups of 25 or more who purchase a block of tickets in the mezzanine section. Tickets normally costing $8 each cost only $5 under the special plan. ¶Your group may order tickets for any of the upcoming performances simply by phoning 364-5321. Thanks for your patronage. Cordially We hope to be able to offer this discount plan for the orchestra's next season. Our ability to do so will depend on this year's response.   (67 words in body; 26 words in postscript)

Exercise 15
ATTENTION LINE, AND ADDRESSEE AND CC NOTATIONS

Any acceptable letter style. Small envelope.

Use the addressee notation CONFIDENTIAL. Direct the letter to the attention of **Dr. Harold Fraser, English Department.** The dictator is **Dr. Leila Huff, Dean of English, Maryville State University.** A copy is being sent to **Dr. Leo Bonini, Counselor.**

Los Grande College 4000 Mindanos Blvd. Santa Fe, NM 87501 Tonya Godfrey, a sophomore student at your college last year, is transferring to our school for the coming academic year. While her grades and her attitude are fine, we are having difficulty placing her in our program because your curriculum is so different from ours. ¶I am sending you a list of requirements for a B.A. in English from our university. Would you please note the courses you believe are equivalent to the classes Ms. Godfrey took in your program? Your cooperation will be invaluable in helping us place Ms. Godfrey in our program. Sincerely   (95 words)

Topic 3 PREPARING LETTERS FOR MAILING

ADDRESSING ENVELOPES

The United States Postal Service now uses an automated machine called the Optical Character Reader (OCR) to speed the sorting of mail. The OCR can read printed or type-written envelope addresses and sort letters with more speed and accuracy than is possible with manual sorting. A few basic rules are necessary for addressing mail to locations in the United States in order to prepare it for machine sorting.

1. Use single-spaced, blocked format for address lines.
2. The sender's return address may be printed on the envelope or it may be typed in the upper left-hand corner. Refer to Models 5 and 6 below for the exact placement of the return address.
3. The street or box number must be shown on the next to the last line, just before the city, state and ZIP Code line.
4. The city, state, and ZIP Code must appear on the last line of the address. Only one space is required between the two-letter state abbreviation and the ZIP Code on an envelope. Example: Milwaukee, WI 53210
5. The placement of the receiver's address on the envelope should be roughly in the center of the envelope. Study the placement of envelope addresses in Models 5 and 6. The exact placement given in the illustrations will aid you as you begin to type envelopes. Soon you should be able to judge placement of envelope addresses without consciously counting lines.

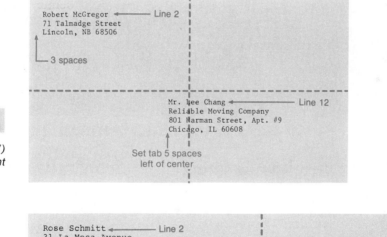

Model 5

No. 6 Envelope (6½" × 3⅝")
Showing Address Placement

Model 6

No. 10 Envelope (9½" × 4⅛")
Showing Address Placement

August 2, 19—   Mr. Randolph Gray, Vice President   C & T Grocers   408 Abbott Street   Kansas City, MO 64112

Dear Mr. Gray

SUBJECT : Printed ^Weekly Circulars

In reply to your letter ^of July 30, I am sending you some samples of our ~~work~~ ^printing in a separate package. ^With this letter I have enclosed a copy of our latest catalog, ~~that~~ ^which shows the different type faces and papers ^stocks we carry. ~~Also enclosed is~~ our current price list, good through September 30, is also enclosed.

We would be pleased to furnish ^you with estimates for printing your weekly circular. We guarantee completion ^of all work within three working days. On rush orders of 1,000 copies ^or fewer, we can provide 24-hour service.

If you have further questions we shall be glad to send a ^our sales ~~salesman~~ representative ⟨stet⟩ to talk with you. Please contact my office directly to make an appointment.

                    Yours truly

OFFSET PRINTING SERVICE   David L. Red Fox, President   *xx*   Enclosures

(120 words)

Exercise 1

Using slips of paper cut to size, or actual envelopes, type two copies of each envelope shown in Models 5 and 6.

Exercise 2

Use three small envelopes (No. 6), or slips of paper cut to size, and address one envelope for each letter given in Exercises 8–10 in Topic 1, pages 199–200.

Exercise 3

Use four large envelopes (No. 10), or slips of paper cut to size, and address one envelope for each letter given in Exercises 5–8 in Topic 2, pages 205–207.

Exercise 4

Address small (No. 6) envelopes, or slips of paper cut to size, for the addresses given at the right. Use your own return address.

1. Tudor Appliance Company / 719 Canal Street, Room 207 / New York, NY 10014
2. Gerald Yee / 308 Ingraham Street / Tulsa, OK 74151
3. Ms. Lydia T. Sobel / Ingersoll Metal Corp. / 57 Murray Avenue, Suite 7 / Evansville, IN 47706
4. Patricia St. John, President / Computer Professionals / 201 Convent Road / Minneapolis, MN 55405
5. Mr. Frank Carson / Hotel Shiawassee / 301 Court Street / Dallas, TX 75220
6. Lila's Boutique / 2764 Livonia Avenue / Warren, MI 48001

Exercise 5

Address large (No. 10) envelopes, or slips of paper cut to size, for the addresses given at the right. Use your own return address.

1. Mr. and Mrs. William B. Carroll / Roosevelt Apartments, #1305 / 191 Oak Street / Yonkers, NY 10707
2. Mr. David P. Cortez / Purchasing Department Manager / Lord & Gale / 67 Farley Street / Providence, RI 02906
3. Ms. Harriett Carstairs, President / American Air Conditioning / 149 Jackson Avenue / Dover, NJ 07801
4. Mr. Lawrence F. Kane / Kane Automobile Accessories Company / 1112 Lyman Street, Building B / Boston, MA 02108
5. Mr. Arthur M. Gordon / Hotel Westminster / 391 Clinton Avenue / Windsor, Ontario, Canada / N8X 1A7
6. Ms. Sandra T. Harrington / Apex Contracting Company / 830 Garfield Street / Bergen, NJ 07304
7. Ms. Julia Janowski / Manager, Production Department / Capital Radio and Television / 1108 Raynor, 5th Floor / New York, NY 10018
8. Spagna Brokerage Company / 183 Exchange Place / Shreveport, LA 71103
9. Mr. Michael Ulman / Standard Music / 39 Holly Street / Montreal, Quebec, Canada / H3X 3K6
10. Ms. Clara Barretti / Station WOMC / 12210 Jefferson Avenue / Detroit, MI 48215

items for office reception areas. We hope you will find something ~~to suit~~ *suitable for* your needs.

Cordially

PS   Please be sure to use the stock numbers when ordering items from our catalog. They will assure ~~you of~~ *your* ~~getting~~ *receipt of* the correct item*s*.

Mrs. Mary Ricker Product Supervisor *xx* Enclosure

(91 words in body; 23 words in postscript.)

Exercise 11
ROUGH DRAFT:
ATTENTION LINE, SUBJECT
LINE, AND MAILING
NOTATION

*Any acceptable letter style.
Large envelope.*

February 7, 19— Elite Window Designs, Inc. 64 Market Street   Milwaukee, WI 53205

Attention: Shipping department Manager

Gentlemen

SUBJECT: Return of Venetian Blinds

This will confirm my telephone conversation on Tues. with Mrs. Edmunds, ~~where~~ she *has* agreed to accept ~~us~~ *our* returning *of* the 230 Venetian blinds we ordered last Dec. Mrs. Edmunds ~~confirmed~~ *assured me* that you will be able to supply us with Roman shades (instead), as listed in our purchase order No. 0719 enclosed.

We will have the venetian blinds packed and returned ~~by~~ *to you* freight prepaid not later than ~~Saturday~~ *Friday*. To avoid *possible* confusion in our records, we would prefer ~~for~~ you to *that* issue us a credit for the Venetian blinds and bill us separately for the *Roman* shades.

Thank you for your co-operation in ~~this matter~~ *making this exchange for us*.

Yours sincerely

Calvin P. Ryder, President *xx* Enclosure CERTIFIED   (109 words)

FOLDING LETTERS FOR INSERTION INTO ENVELOPES

Letters should be carefully folded before being inserted into envelopes. The method of folding a letter depends upon the size of the envelope to be used.

To fold and insert a full sheet into a small envelope (No. 6), refer to the illustration below and follow these steps:

1. Lay the letter faceup on your desk.
2. Bring the bottom edge to within ¼ inch from the top edge of the page and crease the fold.
3. Fold the letter from right to left approximately in thirds. First, fold the right-hand third of the paper toward the left and crease the fold. Then, fold the left-hand third over the right so that the edge is within ¼ inch of the first crease.
4. Pick up the folded letter with the last fold facing you. The crease should be at the bottom and the open edge at the top. Insert the letter into the envelope in this position.

Folding a Letter for a No. 6 Envelope.

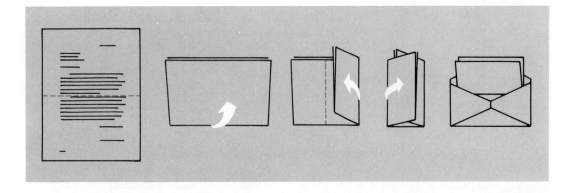

To fold and insert a full sheet into a large envelope (No. 10), refer to the illustration below and follow these steps:

1. Lay the letter faceup on the desk.
2. Fold the letter from bottom to top approximately in thirds. Begin by folding the bottom third of the paper toward the top and creasing the fold. Then, fold the top third down so that the edge is within ¼ inch from the bottom crease.
3. Hold the letter with the last fold facing you. The crease should be at the bottom as you insert the letter into the envelope.

Folding a Letter for a No. 10 Envelope.

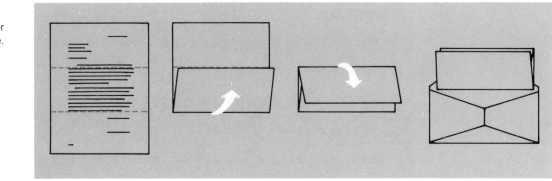

Drill A

Using either blank sheets or the letters previously typed in Topic 2, Exercises 1–4, (pages 204–205) fold them to fit a small envelope (No. 6).

Drill B

Using either blank sheets or the letters previously typed in Topic 2, Exercises 5–7 (pages 205–206), fold them to fit a large envelope (No. 10).

fund, is offering scholarships to women working to— 66

ward a career in accounting. ~I have~ Enclosed ~are~ several announce- 79

ments ~for~ of the scholarships ~being offered~ that we offer, and ask We hope 89

that you ~will~ post ~these brief announcements~ them on the 94

bulletin boards around your school. 101

Also enclosed is an application blank. We would 111

appreciate your dulpicating it to give to those stu- 122

dents who wish to ~have an application~ apply. Your coopera- 130

tion will be appreciated by us as well as by those women 141

who qualify. 144

Sincerely yours 146

Cecily Madison, Trustee   Mary Brookes Scholarship Fund   CM:*xx* 158
Enclosures   (87 words) 160

Exercise 10

ROUGH DRAFT:
ADDRESSEE NOTATION,
ATTENTION LINE, AND
POSTSCRIPT

Modified block style. Open punctuation. No paragraph indention. Small envelope.

Today's date   **PLEASE FORWARD**   Brown, Clawson, and Ott   444 Brinton Street   McAlester, OK 74501

Attention: Office Manager

Gentlemen

I trust that this letter will reach you at the new offices recently opened by your firm. ~It is in~

~regards to~ the plastic plants that you ordered for the re-

ception area were

No ¶ We have discontinued the particular line, but you

selected from our old catalog. We have several others

that are similar however and we highly recommend each

of them.

Enclosed is a current catalog containing illustrations and

information ~on each of~ about these new lines. It ~also~

includes in addition to plants, many other decorative

(Continued on next page)

Topic 4 PERSONAL-BUSINESS LETTER STYLES

So far, all letters in this part have been typed in modified block style. This topic introduces the *full block style* of typing letters. Look at the illustration on this page and compare the two letter styles. Notice that: (1) both styles have the same letter parts; (2) both styles follow the same placement rules for top, side, and bottom margins; (3) the two letter styles differ only in the placement of the heading and the *signature block* (which consists of the complimentary closing and the typed name of sender). Also, paragraphs are not indented in full block style. A letter typed in full block style, with *open punctuation* (no punctuation in salutation and complimentary closing), is shown in Model 7 on the following page.

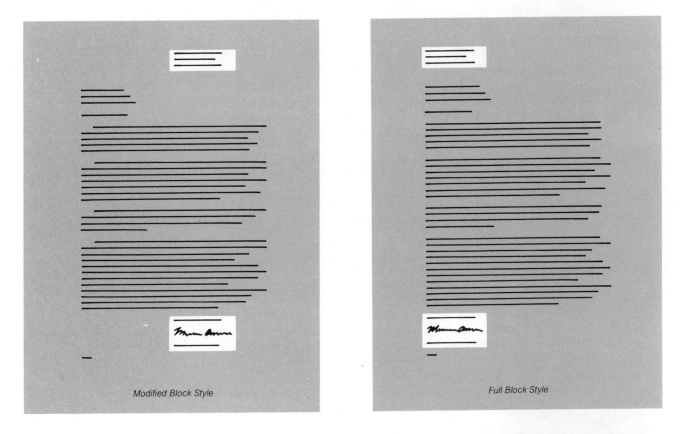

Modified Block Style   Full Block Style

Directions for Drills A–D	Type the letter shown in Model 7 (page 212) to practice the full block style and open punctuation in the following drills. There are 111 words in the body of the letter; use the Letter Placement Chart on page 197 to determine the proper margins.

Drill A	Begin typing with the return address and see how far you can type in 3 minutes. Repeat this drill several times.

Drill B	Begin typing with the word *committee* (third line of the third paragraph). Can you complete the letter in 2 minutes or less? Repeat this drill several times.

Exercise 8

SUBJECT LINE, CC AND MAILING NOTATIONS

Full block style. Open punctuation. Large envelope.

Today's date   The Modern Pharmacy   283 Main Street   Stillwater, MN 55082

Gentlemen

SUBJECT: Short Shipment

We have your letter reporting a shortage of two dozen bottles of aspirin in our recent shipment to you.

As you noted, eight dozen were packed, four dozen to a case, in one carton. According to our records, the remaining two dozen were shipped with other drugs later in the day.

Probably, at the time you wrote us, you had not received (or checked) the second shipment. We are certain that you will receive the full quantity indicated on the invoice. Please telephone our office immediately if you have further problems.

Sincerely yours

E. V. Mills   Shipping Department   *xx*   SPECIAL DELIVERY   cc: A. Kraft

(91 words)

Exercise 9

ROUGH DRAFT: ATTENTION LINE AND SUBJECT LINE

Modified block style. Open punctuation. No paragraph indention. Large envelope.

August 10, 19— Mt. Grove Business College   735 McNichols Road   Chicago, IL 60613   14 / 16

Attention: Financial Aid Director   23

Gentlemen   25

SUBJECT: Scholarships for Female Accounting Students   36

The Chicago Chapter of the Association of Women   46

Accountants, through the Mary Brookes Scholarship   56

(Continued on next page)

Begin return address
at left margin

139 Evergreen Avenue   4
Bethlehem, PA 18015   8
June 12, 19--   11

Harris & Sons   14
75 Howe Street   17
Bethlehem, PA 18015   21

Ladies and Gentlemen ◄——No punctuation after salutation   25

No paragraph ——► I am very happy to respond to your request for information   37
indention   concerning the character of Mr. William Peters.   47

Mr. Peters has been my neighbor and friend for more than ten   59
years. During that time he has participated in many civic and   71
community activities. He served as president of our community   83
association for four years.   88

In my dealings with Mr. Peters, I have found him to be loyal,   100
responsible, and trustworthy. I recommend him highly for the   112
committee appointment that you mentioned in your letter. I   124
can think of no person who is better qualified and more de-   136
serving of this recognition.   142

Do not hesitate to contact me if you need more information.   154

Begin signature block
at left margin

Sincerely ◄——No punctuation after complimentary closing   156

Charles J. Van Houten

Charles J. Van Houten   160

(Shown in Elite Type)

Model 7   **Personal-Business Letter**
Full Block Style with Open Punctuation

Exercise 5

ADDRESSEE NOTATION
AND POSTSCRIPT

Full block style. Open punctuation. Small envelope.

May 8, 19— PERSONAL Ms. Ann Hernandez Executive Secretary Danton 13
and LaFarge, Inc. 39 Franklin Street Boise, ID 83702 Dear Ms. Hernandez 27
Congratulations on your new job! From your letter, it sounds like a great 42
opportunity for you. And, I'm sure the company was pleased to find someone 57
with your impressive background. ¶I'm sorry I was not more help to you in 71
locating a position. Call me, if you can, in the next few weeks to let me know 87
how the job is going. By the way, many exceptionally good openings are 101
coming in every day. If you have friends looking for work, please refer them 116
to me. ¶Best of luck to you as you continue your career. Sincerely Paul Barry, 132
Placement Counselor *xx* PS If you decide at a future time to look for another 147
job, you can be sure I will do everything I can to get you the best position at 163
the highest possible salary.   (96 words in body; 33 words in postscript) 169

Exercise 6

SUBJECT LINE, BCC AND
MAILING NOTATIONS

(Note the use of REFER TO
in place of SUBJECT.)

Full block style. Mixed punctuation. Extra carbon copy. Large envelope.

February 18, 19— Mr. Raymond Speight 10938 Crandall Avenue Decatur, 14
GA 30031 Dear Mr. Speight REFER TO: Policy No. 637-033-039 I have 27
received important information from our company regarding your life insur- 42
ance policy as listed above. It is very urgent that I talk with you as soon as 58
possible about this important matter. ¶I have not been able to contact you by 73
telephone. Would you please call me at 354-8080, at your earliest convenience, 89
so that we may discuss this information. If you cannot reach me at that 103
number, please call me at home at 354-1695. Sincerely Jerome Ashley Sales 118
Representative *xx* bcc: T. Basker REGISTERED   (76 words) 127

Exercise 7

ATTENTION LINE,
COMPANY NAME,
AND POSTSCRIPT

Modified block style. Mixed punctuation. No paragraph indention. Large envelope. Supply the salutation.

November 28, 19— Security Department Nevada Coliseum Las Vegas, NV 13
89108 Attention Mr. Fred Falletti In reference to your letter of November 21, 28
ABC Security Systems can supply the extra security guards you will need for 43
the rock concert scheduled for the evening of January 5. ¶We need to know, 58
however, the exact number of guards you will require, their precise duties 73
and responsibilities, and the kinds of equipment each guard should have. 87
The sooner we have this information, the sooner we can draw up a formal 101
agreement to send to you. ¶ABC can also provide trained medical assistants. 116
Our past experience in handling large concerts has repeatedly shown their 131
usefulness. Please notify me if you are also interested in having any of them 146
on hand. ¶Thank you for contacting us. I am sure our well-trained employees 161
will do the kind of efficient job you want done. Sincerely ABC SECURITY 175
SYSTEMS, INC. Lorene Hughes Business Manager *xx* PS Since the 188
concert is just over a month away, please send me the needed information for 203
the agreement at your earliest possible convenience. 214
(133 words in the body; 24 words in the postscript)

Drill C

Type the entire letter in 8 minutes or less. (You can complete it even if you type less than 20 wpm.) Compare your copy with the model. Are all the parts placed properly on the page in the full block style?

Drill D

Type the letter again, this time with one carbon copy and correct any errors that you make. Address a small envelope, fold the original letter, and insert it in the envelope.

Directions for Exercises 1–9

Type the following personal-business letters. Use the Letter Placement Chart (page 197) to determine the correct margins and date line position for each letter. Fold and insert each letter into a properly addressed envelope.

Exercise 1

Full block style. Open punctuation. 1 carbon copy. Small envelope.

Your address / *Today's date* / Jewel Glassware, Inc. / 830 Eighth Avenue /   19
Glendale, CA 91209 / Ladies and Gentlemen / This is the third time I have   33
written to you concerning the set of monogrammed glasses which I ordered   47
from you four months ago. When I wrote you last, you said they were prob-   62
ably lost in transit; you promised to put a tracer on the shipment. That was   77
a month ago! I still haven't heard or seen anything of the glasses. ¶I have,   92
however, received the canceled check to show that you have received and   106
deposited my payment. I think four months is long enough to wait patiently   121
for a set of glasses. ¶Please cancel my order for the glasses and issue me a full   137
refund for the amount I have paid. I would appreciate your taking immediate   152
action on my refund. ¶ I am sorry that this incident has changed my formerly   168
good opinion of your company. / Yours truly / *Your name*   (137 words)   178

Exercise 2

Full block style. Open punctuation. 1 carbon copy. Large envelope.

Your address / *Today's date* / Mr. Gregory A. Hearn / Hearn & Slate, Inc. / 740 Emerson Avenue / *Your city, state, ZIP Code* / Dear Mr. Hearn / Last Friday I found that I had an immediate need for a pair of faucets I had ordered from you. I could not wait for the delivery of the entire order I had given you. I telephoned and explained the situation and offered to come by shortly after five o'clock for the faucets in question. You told me to ask for them in the shipping room where they would be ready for me. ¶When I arrived, only one clerk was in the shipping room. He said he had no package for me and had been given no instructions. When I asked him to see whether he could locate the package, he became very rude and offensive. I had no choice but to leave, and at considerable inconvenience, I had to get the faucets elsewhere. ¶I thought you should know of this incident. I cannot give you the name of the clerk (he refused to identify himself) but he was the only one on duty at the time. / Yours truly / *Your name*
(167 words)

Exercise 2

ATTENTION LINE AND CC NOTATION

Modified block style. Mixed punctuation. 5-space paragraph indention. Small envelope.

December 3, 19— Coloma Realty Company 5120 West Duneland Highway 13
Coloma, MI 49038 Attention: Clara DeSoto Ladies and Gentlemen As we 26
discussed last week, the rent increases for the apartments at Garden Manor 41
will be based on several improvements. These include installing new 55
showers, painting the living rooms, and remodeling the kitchens. ¶I have 69
engaged Mr. Anthony Harper, a local contractor, and he will call on you soon 84
to estimate the cost of the repairs. ¶I'd like to mention that I was very 99
pleased with the way the building looked. I feel you are managing it well. 114
Thanks. I appreciate it! Best wishes Delmont Kent *xx* cc: Anthony Harper 128

(85 words)

Exercise 3

ATTENTION AND SUBJECT LINES, AND CC NOTATION

Modified block style. Mixed punctuation. 5-space paragraph indention. Large envelope.

March 24, 19— McCullum & Fielder Accountants Suite 21 Dreyfuss Build- 14
ing, 231 Chase Drive Akron, OH 44310 Attention Wendy McCullum Ladies 28
and Gentlemen SUBJECT The Omni Account Some of your clients need 41
many banking services. Perhaps they now have several types of accounts to 56
take care of their different banking needs. Here is good news for them and 71
for you in your capacity as financial adviser. ¶The People's Bank has 85
developed a new account for customers with diverse banking needs. It is 100
called the Omni Account. The Omni provides every banking service our 114
institution offers for only one small monthly fee. ¶We think your company 128
should know about the Omni Account, since many of your clients do their 142
banking with us. The enclosed brochure describes the account in detail. If 157
you have any questions concerning the Omni, please call Mrs. Jennifer 171
Walker at our main office. Yours very truly Albert Santini Branch Manager 186
xx Enclosure CC Jennifer Walker (119 words) 192

Exercise 4

SUBJECT LINE, COMPANY NAME, AND MAILING NOTATION

Modified block style. Mixed punctuation. 5-space paragraph indention. Large envelope.

July 5, 19— Mr. E. D. Osgood Osgood & Rider, Inc. P.O. Box 27 Beverly, MA 15
01915 Dear Mr. Osgood SUBJECT: Construction of Factory Parking Lot 28
We have your letter expressing concern about the interruption in our work 42
on the parking lot of your new factory. Let us assure you that we will do 57
everything we can to meet the completion date agreed upon. ¶The con- 71
struction of the parking lot has been slowed by the rain and wind storms 85
during the past two weeks. In order to speed up the work, we will therefore 100
shift five men from another project to work with our crew at your factory. 115
With the additional crew, the job should be finished in three weeks, in accor- 130
dance with our contract. ¶Please do not feel that we are forgetting our agree- 145
ment with you. If you have further concerns, please call to discuss the 159
problems with me. Cordially yours ACME CONSTRUCTION COMPANY 171
Charles M. Floyd Vice-President *xx* CERTIFIED (131 words) 180

Exercise 3

Full block style. Open punctuation. 1 carbon copy. Small envelope.

Your address / *Today's date* / National BanKard Corp. / 156 New Portland / Memphis, TN 38107 / Ladies and Gentlemen / I have your letter requesting that I send you a financial statement on the form that you enclosed. ¶ I am very much surprised at this request. I can understand why you might desire such information from someone who is applying to you for credit when previous credit has not been established, or from a customer who wishes to have a credit limit greatly increased. ¶ I cannot understand, however, why anything of the sort is necessary in my case. I have dealt with your company for almost a year and have always met my obligations promptly when they became due. I consider your request unwarranted and can see no reason why I should comply with it. / Very truly yours / *Your name*   (115 words)

Exercise 4
ROUGH DRAFT

Full block style. Open punctuation. 1 carbon copy. Large envelope.

Your address / *Today's date* / Reader's Review / Treasurer's Office / Pleasantville, NY 10570

Ladies and gentlemen

Your invoice for $11 covering a three-year subscription to your magazine arrived today. This invoice is certainly in error since I am certain that I asked for a 1-year trial subscription. ¶ A copy of your invoice and my check for $4.57 are enclosed. This amount will cover my one-year subscription. please check your records and write me if you have any further questions.

Sincerely yours

Your name / Enclosures   (65 words)

Exercise 5

Modified block style. Open punctuation. No paragraph indentions. 1 carbon copy. Large envelope.

Your address / *Today's date* / Mr. Charles Floyd / Floyd Construction Company / 160 Third Street / *Your city, state, ZIP Code* / Dear Mr. Floyd / According to our contract, you were to complete the stone driveway from the public curb back to my garage in return for setting up your stone-crushing equipment on my property located at Sawyer and Third Streets. ¶ You have now had your machinery on my property for almost a year, you have completed the work you were doing in the area, and you appear to be preparing to leave. ¶ This letter is written to remind you of your part of the contract. Please write or call me to confirm when you will begin construction of my driveway. / Very truly yours / *Your name*   (97 words)

```
HOWARD GRAIN MILLS
275 Day Street
Milwaukee, Wisconsin 53208

CONFIDENTIAL                                           CERTIFIED



                   Hall Elevator Company
                   Attention: Mr. Anthony L. Weber, President
                   49 Tilden Street
                   Milwaukee, WI 53202
```

This illustration shows the preferred placement of special notations on an envelope. Note that the attention line is included as part of the address block; it is not placed in the lower left corner of the envelope. Since most mail is sorted by machines designed to scan the last two lines on an envelope, those lines should be reserved for the street address and ZIP Code. Addressee notations, attention lines, and mailing notations must, therefore, be placed in the upper half of the envelope where they will not interfere with machine sorting.

Letters that include special notations will require some adjustment for the placement of the date line. For each notation, the date line is raised one line above that indicated in the Letter Placement Chart on page 197. The number of words in a postscript must also be considered before figuring the date line placement. For each ten words in a postscript, the date line should be raised one line.

Drill A
TYPING MODEL 10

Type the letter shown in Model 10 (page 256). Assume that you are typing on letterhead stationery. Follow the spacing instructions given in the model. Determine the proper margins and position of the date line by referring to the Letter Placement Chart (page 197). Remember to count the postscript. Remember also to raise the date line one line for each special notation. Type your initials in place of *xx*. The body of the letter contains 156 words.

Drill B
OPENING PARTS OF MODEL 10

See how much of Model 10 you can type in 3 minutes. Use the same margin settings and date-line placement as in Drill A. Repeat the drill until you can type the opening parts of the letter without hesitation.

Drill C
CLOSING PARTS OF MODEL 10

Now start with the last paragraph of Model 10. Use the same margin settings as in Drill A. Try to finish the letter in 3 minutes or less. Repeat the drill until you can type the closing parts of the letter without hesitation.

Drill D
AN ENVELOPE FOR MODEL 10

Address a large envelope for the Model 10 letter you typed in Drill A. Copy the return address from the letterhead in Model 10. Add all the special notations from the letter that belong on the envelope. Then fold and insert the letter correctly.

Exercise 1
ATTENTION LINE AND SUBJECT LINE

Modified block style. Mixed punctuation. No paragraph indention. Large envelope.

Today's date Career Placement Office Eaton School of Management Training 29 Paint Street Circleville, OH 43113 Attention: Mrs. Sarah Ryan Ladies and Gentlemen SUBJECT: Job Applicants We want to thank you for sending two of your students to be interviewed for the administrative assistant's position available at DuPres Associates. Although their interviews and applications were very positive, we found someone whose qualifications better met our needs. We had many applicants for the position, and this decision was not reached easily. ¶We enjoyed meeting and talking with your students, and we wish them luck in their endeavors. Sincerely J. I. Krasnov Personnel Manager *xx*   (70 words)

Exercise 6
ROUGH DRAFT

Modified block style. Mixed punctuation. 5-space paragraph indention. 1 carbon copy. Small envelope.

Your address / *Today's date* / United Art Suppliers / 116 Hoyt Street / Duluth, MN 55811

Ladies and Gentlemen:

     Last week I sen~~d~~t you an order ~~for merchandice~~ which included ~~three dozen~~ *thirty-six* tubes of assorted oil paints. The goods arrived this morning. In the carton, however, I f~~i~~ound only two cases, each containing only eight tubes. There is, therefore, a shortage of *twenty* ~~20~~ tubes. ¶ Please send the additional tubes which ~~are in~~ *were* *indicated* ~~cluded~~ in my original order. Or, if you prefer, you may credit ~~me with~~ *my account for* the twenty tubes, as my # present supply will be sufficient ~~enough~~ until I ~~send you~~ *place* my next order. Yours truly,

Your name   (81 words)

Exercise 7

Full block style. Mixed punctuation. 1 carbon copy. Large envelope.

Your address / August 20, 19— / Metz Brothers / 491 South Street / Rochester, NY 14612

Gentlemen:

     Last month I was in your city for a convention. On July 24, a truck belonging to your firm and operated by your driver, Larry Steel, ran into my car while it was legally parked in front of Crompton Assembly Hall. I filed a report at that time with the Rochester Police Department.

     Since that time, I have had my car repaired at a cost to me of $387. However, my insuring agent at Coastal Insurance Co.

(Continued on next page)

HOWARD GRAIN MILLS

275 Day Street, Milwaukee, Wisconsin 53208

(415) 275-4030

Words

March 18, 19--   3

DS

Addressee notation   CONFIDENTIAL   6

DS

Hall Elevator Company   10
49 Tilden Street   13
Milwaukee, WI 53202   17

DS

Attention line   Attention: Mr. Anthony L. Weber, President   26

DS

Gentlemen: 28

DS

Subject line   SUBJECT: Elevator Inspection   34

DS

Since your company installed the elevators in this plant, the   46
service provided by your inspectors has been efficient and cour-   59
teous. However, I must call your attention to an incident that   72
occurred during the last inspection.   79

Prior to the inspection date, I had prepared a list of problems   92
that had arisen since the last inspection. Most of them were   104
minor and required only small adjustments to correct them. When   117
I handed the list to the inspector, he pocketed it without read-   130
ing it. I pointed out that my list would certainly save him time   143
and would assure us that the problems were corrected. He became   156
indignant at this and seemed to think I was interfering with his   169
work. Now, only five days after the inspection, we find that   181
several problems were not corrected.   188

Would you please schedule another inspection without delay. I   201
would appreciate your calling my office to confirm the date and   214
time your inspector will arrive.   221

Yours very truly,   225

DS

Company name in signature block   HOWARD GRAIN MILLS   229

John R. Rabin

John R. Rabin   232
Plant Manager   235

JRR:xx   236

Mailing notation   CERTIFIED   238

Carbon copy notation   cc: Carl Reese   241

Postscript   P.S. Our plant is available for your inspection only on Thursdays   254
and Fridays.   257

(Shown in Elite Type)

Model 10   *Business Letter with Special Notations*
Modified Block Style with Mixed Punctuation

has so far been unsuccessful in collecting this sum from you. The fact that your employee, Larry Steel, was using your truck to run a personal errand does not, in my opinion, relieve you of your responsibility.

I shall appreciate receiving your check for $387 without further delay. I think you will agree that settlement of this claim out of court would be better for both of us.

Yours truly,

Your name   (137 words)

Exercise 8

Modified block style. Open punctuation. 5-space paragraph indention. 1 carbon copy. Small envelope.

Your address / Today's date / Ann Riley, Credit Manager / Morales and Reiss / 1098 Maple Drive / Madison, WS 53705

Dear Ms. Riley:

I have your letter requesting information on the whereabouts of Patrick O'Connell, but I'm afraid I cannot help you.

It was a surprise to me to learn that Mr. O'Connell had listed me as a credit reference. During the seven months that he lived in my apartment building, I saw so little of him that I barely got to know him. You will want to know, however, that Mr. O'Connell was three months

(Continued on next page)

Topic 2 SPECIAL NOTATIONS

The opening parts of a business letter may contain any of three *special notations*. These notations are described below and are illustrated in Model 10 on page 256.

1. ADDRESSEE NOTATIONS. Special instructions are sometimes given for handling a letter when it arrives at its destination. These instructions include PERSONAL, CONFIDENTIAL, HOLD FOR ARRIVAL, and PLEASE FORWARD. Such notations should always appear on the envelope. They are typed a triple space below the return address. On the letter, notations for PERSONAL or CONFIDENTIAL may be typed at the left margin, in solid capitals, a double space below the date.

PERSONAL

CONFIDENTIAL

2. ATTENTION LINE   The word *Attention* is used to direct a letter to a particular person or department in a company. It may be typed with the first letter capitalized, and sometimes it is followed by a colon. The attention line is usually placed at the left margin, a double space below the inside address and a double space above the salutation. It may also be the second line of the inside address. The salutation *Ladies, Gentlemen,* or *Ladies and Gentlemen* is used, since the letter is addressed to the company, not to the person named in the attention line. On the envelope, the attention line is the second line of the address, immediately following the company's name, as shown in the illustration on page 257.

Attention: J. M. Ross

ATTENTION Carla Cortez

3. SUBJECT LINE   The word *Subject* is used to identify the main topic of the letter. (You might think of it as a title for the body of the letter.) Generally, it is placed at the left margin, a double space below the salutation and a double space above the body. Often, it is typed in solid capitals with a colon following it.

SUBJECT: Dental Care

Four other special notations are sometimes included as part of the closing of a business letter. They are shown here and in Model 10 on the following page.

4. COMPANY NAME IN SIGNATURE BLOCK   The firm name is included as part of the signature when it is necessary to emphasize that the signer is speaking on behalf of the company. It is typed a double space after the complimentary closing in solid capital letters.

Yours very truly,
HOWARD GRAIN MILLS

5. MAILING NOTATIONS   When a letter is sent REGISTERED, CERTIFIED, or SPECIAL DELIVERY, this fact should be noted on the letter and on the envelope. On the letter, the notation is usually typed in solid capitals directly below the enclosure notation (if any) or on the line below the reference initials. On the envelope, the mailing notation is typed below the stamp, as shown in the illustration on page 257.

REGISTERED

CERTIFIED

6. CARBON COPY NOTATION   The notation for carbon copy is used when a copy of the letter is made for someone other than the addressee. It may be typed either as cc, cc:, CC, or CC:, and it is followed by the name of the person who is to receive the copy. If the dictator does not wish the addressee to know that another person is receiving a copy of the letter, a *blind carbon copy* notation is typed in the upper left corner of the file copy. Either of the following forms may be used: bcc or bcc:, followed by the name of the person to whom the copy is sent.

cc: Eleanor Mennick

7. POSTSCRIPT   A postscript is typed at the very end of the letter as an afterthought or to give special emphasis to a particular point of information. Postscript initials may be typed either as P.S. or PS, followed by two spaces, or they may be omitted altogether. The postscript is typed in full block style or indented, following the style of the letter. It is always the last item on the page.

P.S. or PS

behind in his rent at the time he moved. All my attempts to collect his rent had failed, and I was, quite frankly, pleased when I discovered he had left.

Mr. O'Connell left no forwarding address. If you should succeed in locating him, I would appreciate your sending me his current address.

Sincerely,

Your name (130 words)

Exercise 9
ROUGH DRAFT

Full block style. Open punctuation. 1 carbon copy. Large envelope.

Your address / Today's date / Sun-Ray Solar Heating / 1700 South Serbin Street / Dallas, TX 75224

Ladies and Gentlemen

I picked up one of your brochures at the Home and garden Exposition in Cleveland last month, and I am impressed with the rapid technological advancement in your Solar Heating systems. I am seriously considering installing solar heating in my new house, but I still have a few unanswered questions. Will solar heating work well in areas where it is often cloudy? Do you provide long-term financing? Is it possible to add one of your systems to my existing blueprints or will I have to have new ones drawn? If possible, I would like one of your representatives to visit me and discuss these and other questions. feel free to contact me at (419) 282-5663 and make an appointment.

Sincerely

Your name (121 words)

sp on a person's abillity. Previous experience in
sp dealing with people is desireable.

We shall be very grateful for your prompt response so that we may reach a decision as soon as possible.

Cordially

Helen R. Cooke   Personnel Manager   *xx*   Enclosure   (131 words)

Exercise 36
SPELLING CHECKUP

Modified block style. Open punctuation. 5-space paragraph indention.

Today's date   Ms. Helen R. Cooke   Personnel Manager   Camp Woodland Asheville, SC 29416

Dear Ms. Cooke

sp   Jordan Drake was an assisstant in this office last
sp year from Febuary through August. In accordance with an understanding we had when he entered our employ, he left to return to school.

His duties in the office were fairly simple; he
sp acted as a receptionist and ocassionaly did some typing. His work was entirely satisfactory. He had a pleasing manner and was courteous, will-
sp ing, and cooporative. His duties were not of such a
sp nature as to give him much oportunity to show leadership qualities. However, he exercised good
sp judgement and got along well with our employees.

Had he again applied for the same position the next summer, he would have been hired
sp immediatly.

Very truly yours

Elizabeth Wolfe   Office Manager   *xx*   (114 words)

Exercise 10

Modified block style. Mixed punctuation. 5-space paragraph indention. 1 carbon copy.

Compose and type a short business letter to Mr. Isaac Goldberg, Editor, *The Daily Herald*, 3200 Lafayette Avenue, *Your city, state, and ZIP Code.* Use your own school address and today's date as the heading. Include the following information in your letter:

- You are writing as president of your senior class.
- Class members and class sponsors have suggested Mr. Goldberg as an interesting speaker.
- You have been given the task of writing to ask him to deliver a 10- to 15-minute address at your commencement exercises, which will be held on Wednesday, June 10, at 7 p.m. in your high school auditorium.
- Your class has budgeted an amount of $100 as a stipend to cover any expenses of the speaker.
- You would like Mr. Goldberg to address his reply to your graduating class sponsor, Mrs. Jewel Fischer.

Topic 5 LETTERS FOR REVIEW

Exercises 1–6 in this topic provide additional practice on the skills learned in the previous topics.

Exercises 7–14 contain errors in spelling, punctuation, grammar, and word usage. Each of these exercises contains *editing alerts* that provide clues to the errors you are expected to find. Locate the errors and list the necessary corrections on a separate sheet before you begin to type these exercises. *Do not mark the book.*

In all exercises where you are instructed to type letters, refer to the Letter Placement Chart (page 197), if necessary, to determine the proper margins.

Exercise 1
PERSONAL NOTE

Half sheet. Insert short side first. Modified block style. Mixed punctuation. Margins at 13 and 53 for elite; 7 and 47 for pica. Single spacing. Begin on line 12.

Your address / Today's date / Dear Sis, I'll bet you are surprised to get this note from me! Well, Dad was a little upset when our telephone bill arrived yesterday. He insisted that Mom and I begin to write more letters and make fewer long-distance telephone calls to chat. ¶Tell me all about your new lifestyle. It seems so exciting. I can hardly wait two more years until I can go off to college. ¶I am starting to save more of my allowance so I can afford to call you at least once every two weeks. Write soon. / Love, / *Your name*   (92 words)

Exercise 2
PERSONAL LETTER

Modified block style. Mixed punctuation. 5-space paragraph indention.

12076 Oakman / Dearborn, MI 48122 / *Today's date /* Dear Aunt Suzy and Uncle Don, I had so much fun during your visit. The only bad part was that you had to leave so soon. Perhaps you can stay longer next time. ¶Daphne finally had her puppies—nine days late. Yesterday, we found her and eight tiny, brown and white babies squeezed into that rag box that Mom keeps in the furnace room. I guess Daphne didn't like the nice basket we bought her. If you know anyone who would like a springer spaniel puppy, we have plenty. ¶I want especially to thank you for taking me to the baseball game. It was the first major-league game I had ever attended. I tacked the pennant you bought me to my door, and I think of you every time I look at it. / With much love, / *Your name*   (128 words) sp always payed his bills promptly. We have granted him credit to the extent of $3500.

sp We would not hesitate to give him a favorable recomendation. We believe you will find him a very desirable customer.

sp Let us know if we can be of further assisstence to you.

sp Sincerly

Philip F. Chandler   Business Manager   *xx*   (85 words)

Exercise 35
SPELLING CHECKUP

Modified block style. Mixed punctuation. 5-space paragraph indention.

August 23, 19—   Ms. Elizabeth Wolfe   Office Manager   Sherman, Spears & Company   4 Franklin Square   Charleston, SC 29408

Dear Ms. Wolfe

sp   Jordan Drake has submited your name as

sp a referance on his application for a position as trainee in our recreational camp. Will you be good enough to give us your appraisal of his

sp qualifications and charater ? We are enclosing our regular reference form. If you prefer to provide additional comments, we shall find that helpful also.

   A trainee in our camp is equivalent to an

sp apprentice councilor. The duties involve food service, receiving guests, and clerical work. Although these duties do not require leadership, we prefer to hire employees with ability in that direction. Camp work makes unusual demands

(Continued on next page)

Exercise 3
PERSONAL LETTER

Modified block style. Mixed punctuation. 5-space paragraph indention. 1 carbon copy.

Your address / Today's date / Mr. Richard Holley, President / National Association of School Secretaries / 51 Michigan Avenue / Grand Rapids, MI 49509 Dear President Holley: I was delighted to receive your kind invitation to serve as Recorder at the annual conference of the National Association of School Secretaries. I accept this invitation with great pleasure ¶If the NASS has made any special arrangements with the Hilton Hotel for accommodations and meals, will you kindly send me this information so that I may make reservations as soon as possible? I have attended many of these conferences, and I know that it is often difficult to secure reservations at the hotel serving as conference headquarters unless one applies well in advance. ¶Many thanks for your invitation. I am looking forward to seeing you at the conference. / Sincerely, / *Your name*   (109 words)

Exercise 4
PERSONAL-BUSINESS LETTER

Full block style. Mixed punctuation. 1 carbon copy. Small envelope.

Your address / Today's date / Dr. Janet Nottingham / 1670 Harper Avenue / Billings, MT 59101 / Dear Dr. Nottingham: / As you can tell from my return address, my family has relocated. I am now applying for a clerical position with medical offices in this city. ¶Since I worked part-time in your office for six months last year and received excellent training, I should like your permission to use your name as a reference. ¶I am enclosing a self-addressed postal card for your convenience in replying. Your approval would be greatly appreciated. / Sincerely, / *Your name* / Enclosure   (74 words)

Exercise 5
PERSONAL-BUSINESS LETTER

Modified block style. Mixed punctuation. 5-space paragraph indention. 1 carbon copy. Large envelope.

Your address / Today's date / Dr. Janet Nottingham / 1670 Harper Avenue / Billings, MT 59101

Dear Dr. Nottingham:

Thank you for allowing me to use your name as a reference. I am sure you will be pleased to learn that I have accepted a position at Mercy Hospital as a Ward Clerk. I shall begin work next Monday.

I appreciate your kindness, and I hope that someday I may have the opportunity to repay you.

Gratefully,

Your name   (57 words)

Exercise 32

SPELLING CHECKUP

Modified block style. Mixed punctuation. No paragraph indention.

sp

sp

sp

sp

sp

June 25, 19— Garner & Bruce Associates 41 Sother Street Brockton, MA 02045 Gentlemen Ms. Epstein has sent us the samples of carpet you chose for your new offices. ¶It is our oppinion that the carpets you chose are not apropriate for the daily wear and tear of an office. We feel you would do better to use a higher quality, more dureable material. This, of course, will be more expenssive now, but will save you money in the long run. ¶If you desire help in choosing carpeting, I will be in town next Tuesday. I will be glad to stop by to help you in your descision. Cordialy Mel Dantzler Sales Manager   (92 words)

Exercise 33

SPELLING CHECKUP

Full block style. Mixed punctuation.

sp

sp

sp

sp

sp

sp

Today's date Ms. Sylvia T. Bryant Superintendent Broderick Building 781 Henry Street New York, NY 10006 My dear Ms. Bryant We were glad to receive your recent letter. ¶We include in our services any and every kind of cleaning you desire, anywhere in the building. This even includes windows, both inside and outside. Our responsabilities cover hiring a crew of well-trained workpeople and providing all neccesary supplies and equipment. Our supervisers make daily checks of the work performed and submit reports and sugestions. ¶We cannot quote you any rates until we inspect your premises and determine the exact nature of the work to be done. We cheerfully furnish estimates without imposing any obligation on you. The cost of our service is usually considerably less than that of a self-managed staff. We sincerly believe we offer a practical and economical solution to all your cleaning needs. ¶Please fill out the enclosed postal card. We shall have our representative call imediately to give you an estimate. Yours very truly John M. McMurray, Manager *xx* Enclosure   (146 words)

Exercise 34

SPELLING CHECKUP

Full block style. Open punctuation.

sp

Today's date Ms. Eve L. Rivers Credit Manager Reliance Mortgage Corporation 183 Wharf Street Boston, MA 02118

Dear Ms. Rivers

We are pleased to comply with your request for confidential information concerning our business dealings with Mr. Robert T. Leyden.

Our records show that in the four years during which he has dealt with us, he has

(Continued on next page)

Exercise 6
PERSONAL-BUSINESS LETTER

Modified block style. Open punctuation. 5-space paragraph indention. 1 carbon copy. Large envelope. Supply any missing parts of the letter.

Your address / October 1, 19— / Barnett Auto Parts / 960 Carpenter Street / Jackson, MI 49280 / On July 6, I sent your company full payment for a pair of custom mud flaps for my MG. I received my canceled check on July 16, but I didn't receive my order until September 24, even though your catalogue promises delivery within four weeks. ¶When I opened the package, I discovered you had sent me a set of hubcaps for a Lincoln Continental. Not only that, I also received a bill for $78. ¶I am returning the hubcaps and the unpaid bill, and I want you to cancel my original order and return my money. Please do not take as long to return my money as you did to send me the hubcaps. / *Your name*   (114 words)

English Editing Alerts

Refer to page 194 for a list and an explanation of the editing alerts shown beside Exercises 7–14. Each symbol will give you a clue as to what kind of error is in that line. Read the copy carefully and locate the errors before you begin to type. *Do not mark the book.*

Exercise 7
PERSONAL NOTE WITH EDITING ALERTS

Half sheet. Insert short side first. Modified block style. Mixed punctuation. 5-space paragraph indention.

	Your address / *Today's date* / Dear Aunt Belle, It was very thoughtful of
com	you to remember my birthday. I thank you very much for the card the
com sp	novel and the good wishes. ¶I have allready started to read the book. It
cap	is most interesting. I am really enjoying it. / Yours Sincerely, / *Your name*

(41 words)

Exercise 8
PERSONAL-BUSINESS LETTER WITH EDITING ALERTS

Modified block style. Mixed punctuation. 5-space paragraph indention.

	Your address / *Today's date* / The Honorable Max Fentwick / House of
	Representatives / Washington, DC 20515 / Dear Mr. Fentwick: I am
	strongly opposed to the building of a new highway, through our congres-
com	sional district. The construction would be a waste of money and a terrible
sp	inconveniance to those whose homes would be destroyed to make way
	for the road. I think our tax dollars could be better spent on things such
	as improving present roads, building a new library, or adding a park. ¶I
sp	incourage you to speak out against this proposed highway. If I can help
cap	by writing to other members of Congress, Please let me know. / Sincerely,
	/ *Your name*. (89 words)

Exercise 9
PERSONAL-BUSINESS LETTER WITH EDITING ALERTS

Modified block style. Mixed punctuation. 5-space paragraph indention.

	Your address / *Today's date* / Kelley Pen Company / 400 Rosemary Circle
sp cap	/ Pittsburgh, PA 15230 / Ladies and Gentlemen: I recieved your model
ww	200 fountain pen for my birthday. Its a beautiful pen, and I was extremely
	happy to receive it. I had the pen in the front pocket of my white work
ro	uniform when the pen began leaking this made both me and my uni-
	form blue. My uniform is ruined, and I must buy another to replace it.

(Continued on next page)

Exercise 30
ROUGH DRAFT

Any acceptable letter style.

Mr. Gene M. Campbell   826 Doane Street   Sayville, NY 11782

Dear Mr. Campbell

We sincerely regret the mistake that was made, in your purchase order No. 7634. We appreciate your willingness to keep the cans shipped in error. Our truck will deliver to you this week the five two-gallon cans of White Premium Enamel that which you originally ordered. They will probably have reached you by the time you recieve this letter.

Enclosed is our invoice, No. 1288 for the two 5-gallon cans that which were shipped in error. Invoice No. 1253 (for five 2-gallon cans) you have already received.

Yours very truly

Sally F. Harris, Traffic Manager   *xx*   Enclosure   (86 words)

Directions for Exercises 31–36
SPELLING CHECKUPS

The following business letters contain words that are misspelled. Before typing each exercise, find the misspelled word (or words) in each of the lines indicated by *sp* in the left margin. Refer to the Master Spelling Lists on pages 138 and 230, and to a dictionary. Make a list of the correct spellings on a separate piece of paper. Then, type the letter in the style indicated, spelling all the words correctly. *Do not mark the book.*

Exercise 31
SPELLING CHECKUP

Modified block style. Open punctuation. 5-space paragraph indention.

Today's date   Clark Appliance Company   270 Bay Street   Boston, MA 02107   Ladies and Gentlemen   We have an application for credit from Mr.
sp   Robert T. Leyden of 44 Front Street. He has refered us to you concerning
sp   his record as one of your custamers. ¶He applied for credit with our company recently. At that time, we ran a credit check through Credit Data Bureau and received a negative report. Mr. Leyden states that the infor-
sp   mation contained in Credit Data's files discribing his payment history is
sp   incorrect. ¶We would be greatful for any information you can give us.
sp   We are especially intrested to know how much credit you have extended to him. We assure you that the information you give us will be kept in
sp   strict confidance.   Yours truly   Ms. Eve L. Rivers   Credit Manager   *xx*
(112 words)

Exercise 9 continued

com

¶Since the malfunction of your pen has caused this problem I believe that your company should reimburse me for my loss. The cost of the uniform was $37. I would appreciate your prompt attention in this matter. / Sincerely, / *Your name*   (97 words)

Exercise 10
PERSONAL-BUSINESS LETTER WITH EDITING ALERTS

Full block style. Open punctuation. 1 carbon copy. Small envelope.

sp
com sp
ro ww
com ww
ww
com

ep
sp

Your address / Today's date / Mr. Edmundo Oneggo / 1267 Clarity Way / Philadelphia, PA 19138 / Dear Mr. Onego / When I returned home from work yesterday I was surprized to find a package from you waiting for me I didn't expect you too be so prompt in responding to my request to borrow your camera flash unit, and lens. But the biggest surprise come when I opened the package and discovered you also sent me you best telephoto lens! Thanks to your generosity I know my school science project will be a success. ¶I will be sure to take good care of your equipment and return it promptly? I will also send you a few of the pictures from the project, and a leter telling you how everything turned out. Thanks again for your kindness. / Sincerely / *Your name*   (116 words)

Exercise 11
PERSONAL-BUSINESS LETTER WITH EDITING ALERTS

Any acceptable letter style. 1 carbon copy. Large envelope.

cap

sp

cap
sp ep
ww
sp

cap

Your address / Today's date / Mr. Larry Norman, program director / WARQ-TV / 44 Brock Building / Little Rock, AR 72207 / Dear Mr. Norman / Your station has always been exceptionaly responsive to the community's needs and wishes. I'm sure I speak for many when I say "Thank You." ¶Your latest action is a perfect example of responsiveness and ture concern for the public you serve, Dropping three programs because they are to violent or demeaning to certain groups shows responsibility, courage, and strong principle. I aplaud this action. ¶Your decision may stir protest among some, but I believe it will bring better quality television to the american people. / Sincerely / *Your name*   (84 words)

Exercise 12
PERSONAL-BUSINESS LETTER WITH EDITING ALERTS

Any acceptable letter style. 1 carbon copy. Large envelope.

cap
sp
ww cap
com ww
ww ro
sp
frag

Your address / Today's date / Ms. Dawn Mercer / Mercer Travel Agency / 518 Pierazzi Street / Tacoma, WA 98438 / Dear Ms. Mercer / My family and I are considering a vacation in your state in august and september. We are totally unfamilir with the area and would like to get some ideas fore an interesting trip. Our family is especially interested in american history swimming, and water skiing, so a trip to a recreational lake or a historical sight might be appropriate we are open to other ideas, however. ¶Please send us any information on tours or travel packages which mihgt suit our needs. Your prompt attention will be appreciated. Because we need to make our final plans within the next four weeks. / Sincerely / *Your name*   (100 words)

The Ryder Theater 710 Lane Street St. Joseph, MO 64506

Ladies and Gentlemen

If you are having problems with your present heating system, and are you tired of paying those high fuel bills each month? let Phoenix Solar Systems help you cut your heating costs!

During the past 12 months we have installed solar heating units in several public buildings, including motion picture houses. These units are designed to supplement existing conventional heating systems. The solar unit takes over whenever sunlight falls on the panels installed on the roof; then, it automatically shuts down your other heating system. Many of our customers have reported savings of more than 60 percent on their fuel bills this year — and that's in spite of two utility rate increases in the past eight months.

The enclosed phamphlet explains how solar heating works and describes our most popular units. If you would like more information, please fill out and mail the postal card at the back of the pamphlet.

Sincerely yours

Stanley T. Foxx, President *xx* Enclosure (147 words)

Typing for Vocational Use

Exercise 27
ROUGH DRAFT

Any acceptable letter style.

Mr. James L. Dalton   692 Fourth Avenue   Wilmington, DE 19808

Dear Sir

Since you have not yet received ~~it,~~ the watch that we re-paired for you ~~and~~ was mailed almost ~~2~~ two weeks ago, we must assume that it was lost in the mail. We have asked the post office to trace it. ¶ The watch was insured for ~~$60 dollars,~~ $60.00 (it's list price). If it is not re-covered, we shall send you a check for the ~~ammount~~ price of the watch less our repair costs. We hope this adjustment will be satisfactory.

Sincerely

Otis Simms, Manager   SMB/*xx*   (76 words)

Exercise 28
ROUGH DRAFT

Any acceptable letter style.

Miller Advertising, Inc.   42 West Jason Avenue   New York, NY 10064

Dear Mr. Miller

~~Along with~~ Accompanying this letter ~~are enclosed~~ is a summary of our first thoughts on ~~our~~ the "Keep Cool This Summer" ad campaign that ~~I already~~ we recently discussed with you. The ideas that we want to stand out have been circled in red ink. Since ~~it's your~~ you are the expert in knowing ~~business to know~~ what people find appealing, I leave ~~all the rest of~~ the design up to you.

When you have some rough sketches and prepared preliminary copy ready, please ~~give me a~~ call. Then ~~I can~~ confirm your ideas and give the "go-ahead" on the campaign. Since we ~~have~~ wish to run the first ads in ~~2~~ two weeks, there is ~~little time remaining~~ no time to waste.

Thanks so much.

Cordially

Penny Maxwell, Advertising Manager *xx* Enclosure   (103 words)

PART 1

TYPEWRITING STYLE GUIDES FOR BUSINESS

This section includes information on rules of English usage that are needed by typists, writers, secretaries, word processors, and anyone else who works with words. These rules are intended to cover only the problems most commonly encountered in nontechnical typing. For a more thorough treatment of typing style guides, refer to a good reference manual for office typing.

Topic 1 GUIDELINES FOR TYPING NUMBERS

Figures, rather than words, are generally preferred to express numbers in business typing. This is especially true in typing forms and tables. There are, however, many occasions when numbers are expressed in words to conform with accepted customs of English usage. The following rules cover the more common problems you will encounter in expressing numbers. For a complete guide to typing numbers, refer to a style manual for office typing.

Rule 1. Spell out exact numbers from zero through ten.

- *two desks* • *five pens*

Rule 2. When numbers less than ten occur in the same sentence with numbers greater than ten, use figures for all the numbers.

- *The secretary ordered 5 staplers, 12 desk calendars, and 24 typewriter ribbons.*

Rule 3. Spell out round numbers that represent an approximate quantity, but use figures for exact amounts.

- *Not even fifty people turned out for the meeting.*
- *The plant employs about five hundred workers.*
- *The stadium can seat 27,410 spectators.*

Exercise 25
SPECIAL CHALLENGE LETTER

Any acceptable letter style.

The date of this letter is **May 27, 19—**. The dictator is **Don Brody, Personnel Interviewer.** Address a small envelope and fold and insert the letter. Supply any missing letter parts.

Mr. James McCarthy 12047 Woodingham Gary, IN 46416 I received your letter and data sheet inquiring about job openings for clerk-typists in our company. We are now accepting applications from qualified applicants for entry-level positions that will be vacant in late June. These positions require no business experience. ¶Your clerical skills and the courses you have taken in the business curriculum seem to fit the qualifications needed for the jobs in question. You may be proud of your neatly typed letter and thorough data sheet. They prompted me to write to you. ¶If you are still interested in working here after you graduate in June, please telephone me at 556-1780, extension 114. I would like to arrange an appointment for you to come in to take our typing and clerical aptitude tests. You can also complete our job application form at that time.   (134 words)

Directions for Exercises 26–30
ROUGH DRAFT

As you type the next five business letters, make all the corrections indicated. If you need to refresh your memory of the proofreaders' marks, refer to the key on page 97. Use today's date for all the exercises, and include your reference initials. These letters are to be set up in any acceptable style, but be sure to vary the styles.

Exercise 26
ROUGH DRAFT

Any acceptable letter style.

Mrs. Isabel T. Johnson   80 Park Lane   Cincinnati, OH 54216

Dear Mrs. Johnson

We're sorry are that the table we sent to your home was delivered in such poor condition. All furniture manufactured by our firm is approved by our quality control inspection division (as indicated by the attached inspection tag) (note attached tag) prior to shipment. The goods are then and packaged with great care. The damage was probably caused by careless handling by the freight company which that delivered the table.

We will send an expert cabinetmaker to your home. who He will make the repairs to your satisfaction. There If you will call me at 891-7800, will be no charge for this service. I will personally make all the arrangements. My phone number is 891-7800.

Yours very truly

Loretta Berman   Sales Manager   *xx*   (105 words)

Rule 4.	Spell out a number when it begins a sentence.
	• *Twenty people applied for the job.*

Rule 5.	Spell out the smaller of two numbers that come together as part of the same construction.
	• *three 15-cent stamps* • *20 two-story buildings.*

Rule 6.	Spell out the hour when *o'clock* is used.
	• *eleven o'clock*

Rule 7.	Spell out numbers that represent periods of time.
	• *fourteen years* • *twenty minutes*

Rule 8.	Spell out ordinal numbers, except when part of a date.
	• *third fourth twentieth*
	• *12th of May* BUT: *May 12*

Rule 9.	Spell out simple fractions, but use figures for quantities made up of a whole number and a fraction.
	• *one-half mile three-quarters cup*
	• *6½ feet*

Rule 10.	Use figures: (1) to express sums of money when the dollar sign is used; (2) to express percentages; (3) with abbreviations and symbols; (4) to express measurements; (5) to express numbers in an address; and (6) to express numbers that identify buildings, rooms, pages, flights, documents, and so forth.
	• *I paid $8 for a front-row seat.*
	• *Ken owes me five dollars.*
	• *The interest rate on city bonds rose to 8 percent.*
	• *#3 12 doz. 7 a.m. 26¢*
	• *She is 5 feet 4 inches tall.*
	• *103 Russell Street*
	• *Passengers for Flight 9 should go to Room 405 for customs inspection.*
	• *Use Form 1053a to file the S.E.C. report.*

Exercise 1

NUMBER STYLE

Review Rules 1–10 on business style for typing numbers. These sentences show correct application of these rules. Type each sentence once.

Half sheet. 60-space line. Single spacing. Center title on line 7 and TS after it.

NUMBER STYLE GUIDE: ONE

1. Our office has eight new employees.
2. She has 24 tropical fish, 4 dogs, and 2 cats.
3. About five hundred members are expected to attend.
4. Four persons were on vacation in July.
5. You must pass 12 five-minute timings during the school year.
6. He will arrive at six o'clock this evening.
7. Roger studied piano for five years.
8. Your first payment is due on the 12th of the month.
9. The table measures $6\frac{1}{4}$ feet by $5\frac{1}{2}$ feet.
10. She formerly lived at 5900 Fifth Avenue.

Exercise 22 continued

new machinery, and enlarged our labor force. Now we are in a position to 72 produce a much larger quantity of hardcover and paperback bindings than in 87 the past. ¶Frankly, our problem is this: Until additional orders come in from 102 our increased staff of sales representatives, some of our machinery will be 117 idle. To meet this situation, we are offering a 25 percent price reduction on 133 orders placed within the next 30 days. ¶If you will send us your specifications, 149 we shall quickly submit quotations. Sincerely yours Ivan Stanislaus Sales 164 Manager *xx*   (114 words) 166

Exercise 23
Any acceptable letter style.

February 19, 19— Mr. Thomas S. Burke   11532 Meyers Street Allentown, PA 14 18141 Dear Mr. Burke I am pleased to announce a new program of personal 28 accident insurance. It will provide AUTOMATIC protection for all dues- 42 paying members of the Communication Workers of America, AFL-CIO (CWA). 56 Each member's coverage (at no additional cost) will be effective one month 71 following the date of membership in the CWA local. ¶Coverage of $5,000 is 86 provided against accidental death and dismemberment. An extra $5,000 will 101 be paid if accidental death occurs on a common carrier. The master policy 116 with details of the policy coverage will be on file at the national CWA office. 132 The insurance carrier is IMA Life Insurance Company of New York. ¶In order 147 to let you name a beneficiary on your policy immediately, we have enclosed 162 an enrollment form. Please complete the form and send it to your local 177 CWA office. Fraternally yours Kenneth J. Kagler Executive Secretary *xx* 190 Enclosure   (136 words) 192

Exercise 24
SPECIAL CHALLENGE LETTER

Any acceptable letter style.

Use today's date for this letter. The dictator is **Herbert L. Edmundson, President.** Note that an enclosure is mentioned in the first paragraph. Address a large envelope and fold and insert the letter. Supply any missing letter parts.

Bennett Engineering Works World Headquarters 30 Reynolds Circle Amityville, NY 11106 We are enclosing a folder explaining how our Fairview Lights meet all the requirements of modern lighting. ¶ The importance of lighting in factories and offices is being widely acknowledged today. It has an important influence on the health of employees and on the quality of work that they do. To be most effective, lighting must be of the right intensity and in the right position. Here, our expert knowledge can be of great value to you. ¶We suggest that you have one of our consultants survey your existing lighting system. The consultant can determine whether your system is the best one for your workers and the kind of work they do. Careful consideration will be given to such points as the location of machines, the position of the operators, and the kinds of work done. ¶We perform this consulting service without charge. Let us also assure you that any recommendations we make are offered in your best interests.   (158 words)

Exercise 2

These sentences show correct application of Rule 10 on business style for typing numbers. Type each sentence once.

Half sheet. 60-space line. Single spacing. Center title on line 7 and TS after it.

NUMBER STYLE GUIDE: TWO

1. She is 5 feet 2 inches tall.
2. Turn to page 7 in your textbook.
3. The charge on the shipment was 79¢.
4. The interest charge on extended payment accounts is 18 percent.
5. The suit now sells for $53.
6. That blender, Stock #7562, is on special order.
7. Janet saved thirty dollars on the carpet installation.
8. A check for $5.35 is enclosed.
9. The bank paid 5 percent interest, compounded daily.
10. We had to report for registration at 9 a.m.

Exercise 3

NUMBER STYLE

Type these sentences, inserting the number in parentheses in the space where the colored mark appears. Decide, according to Rules 1–10, whether to use figures or words. *Do not mark the book.*

Full sheet. 70-space line. Double spacing. Center title on line 13 and TS after it.

NUMBER STYLE GUIDE: THREE

1. I am the youngest of ▪ children. (3)
2. ▪ students went on the field trip. (60)
3. My favorite TV program begins at ▪ o'clock. (9)
4. The basketball star was ▪ feet tall. (7)
5. Our state has a ▪ percent tax on sales. (4)
6. This is her ▪ job in the past two years. (5th)
7. We drove ▪ miles on our vacation trip. (3,500)
8. Plan to return on the ▪ of July. (12th)
9. Please buy ▪ two-cent stamps. (35)
10. The stadium is only ▪ full. (2/3)

Key to Exercise 3

1. three 2. Sixty 3. nine 4. 7 5. 4 6. fifth
7. 3,500 8. 12th 9. 35 10. two-thirds

Topic 2 GUIDELINES FOR TYPING ABBREVIATIONS

For the sake of clarity, abbreviations should be used sparingly in business correspondence. When in doubt, spell out words. When you do abbreviate, use the standard forms listed in a dictionary. Be consistent in the abbreviations you do use.

There are some general rules you can follow when using abbreviations:

Rule 1.   Always abbreviate the titles Mr., Mrs., Ms., Messrs., and Dr. before a name. Spell out other titles when they are used with only a last name. Note that the title Miss does not require a period.

- *Governor Greene*
- *Mayor Mahoney*
- *Dr. Harriet Washington*
- *Ms. Yee*
- *Captain Hale*
- *Colonel McGuiness*

Exercise 20

Full block style. Open punctuation.

Today's date / Messrs. J. R. Tobin and P. T. Ford / T&F Equipment 13
Leasing / 1501 Jackson Street / Seattle, WA 98108 22

Gentlemen 24

We regret to inform you that we cannot accept 33
a cancellation of your order for 500 notebooks 43
imprinted with your company's name. 50
Inasmuch as the printing has been completed, 59
the notebooks are of no value to anyone else 68
except as scrap. We must, therefore, insist upon 78
your acceptance of them in accordance with 87
the terms agreed upon in our contract. 95
Cordially yours 98

K. S. Fields, Manager / *xx*   (60 words) 104

Directions for Exercises 21–25

Type the following exercises using a variety of acceptable letter styles. Note that in all exercise letters from this point until the end of Topic 1, line breaks for the opening and closing parts are not indicated. You are to decide yourself how these parts are to be set up.

Exercises 24 and 25 are Special Challenge Letters. You must supply the opening and closing parts. Remember to add your initials as reference initials.

Exercise 21

Any acceptable letter style.

October 12, 19— David Margulies, Manager Ko-Zee Motel 3610 Page Street 14
Beckley, WV 25801 Dear Mr. Margulies Three months ago, we shipped you 28
six dozen monogrammed bath towels and ten dozen hand towels. ¶On that 41
particular order, we had used a special material for making the monograms. 56
We would appreciate it if you would send us a note telling us how the material 72
has endured with constant use. In return for your sending us this information, 88
we will send you a set of six of our best-quality water tumblers. Thank you. 103
Sincerely Rick Davis, Marketing Manager *xx*   (75 words) 111

Exercise 22

Any acceptable letter style.

December 9, 19— Mr. Henry F. Akioto Van Dyke Publishing Company 1057 14
Walnut Street Salt Lake City, UT 84101 Dear Mr. Akioto We have a problem 28
that we think you can help us solve, and, by doing so, you can save your 42
company money. ¶We have recently leased additional floor space, installed 57

(Continued on next page)

Rule 2.   Do not abbreviate such words as *Street* or *Avenue* unless you must save space, such as on an envelope or in a list.

- *613 Grand Avenue*

Rule 3.   Spell out words indicating direction in street addresses, such as *East* or *West*. Abbreviations are acceptable on envelopes.

- *29 West Main Street*   • *8534 North Highland Parkway*

Rule 4.   Abbreviate academic degrees, professional designations, and *Junior* or *Senior* when they follow the name. (Be careful not to use two titles that have the same meaning. It is *incorrect* to write *Dr.* John V. Brown, *M.D.*)

- *Hedley J. Burke, Jr.*   • *Hilda J. Lyons, C.P.A.*   • *Jack Robbins, Ph.D.*

Rule 5.   Spell out names of localities, days of the week, and months of the year in formal writing.

- *October*   • *New York*   • *Wednesday*

Rule 6.   Abbreviate the word *Saint* when it is part of an address.

- *2976 St. Stephens Drive*   • *St. Paul, Minnesota*

Rule 7.   Abbreviate the words *Number* and *Numbers* when they precede a figure. See Rule 10 below for use of the number sign (#).

- *Model No. 880*   • *Model Nos. 880 and 881*

Rule 8.   Abbreviate words such as *Company, Incorporated,* and *Corporation* only when they are abbreviated on the company's letterhead.

- *General Motors Corporation*   • *Fearon Pitman Publishers, Inc.*

Rule 9.   Do not space after periods within abbreviations made up of the first letters of two or more words.

- *Ph.D.*   • *M.D.*   • *F.O.B.*

But, space once after the periods in the initials of a person's name.

- *Mr. R. M. Stone*

You may omit periods in abbreviations made up of initials that stand for a name.

- *USA   USSR   YMCA   TWA   NASA*

Rule 10.   Always use the two-letter state abbreviations in addresses on letters and envelopes. When an address occurs within a sentence, however, the name of the state should be spelled out. If the ZIP Code is also included in a sentence, one space should be left between it and the name of the state.

Rule 11.   Avoid using symbols and abbreviations in business letters and other general writing.

- *Use <u>percent</u> instead of %.*   • *Use <u>cents</u> instead of ¢*
- *Use <u>equals</u> instead of =.*   • *Use <u>number</u> instead of #.*
- *Use <u>hour</u> instead of hr.*   • *Use <u>pound</u> instead of lb.*

You may use symbols and abbreviations, however, in tables, in such business forms as invoices and purchase orders, and in technical writing when these units are used with figures.

Exercise 18

Full block style. Mixed punctuation.

March 14, 19— / Mr. and Mrs. Charles Olsen / 3057 Outer Drive / Saginaw, ⁣13
MI 48611 / Dear Mr. and Mrs. Olsen / Spring is indeed welcome this year, and ⁣27
we are already thinking about your lawn. First, we would like to thank you for ⁣43
last year's business. Second, we would like to include you in this year's pro- ⁣59
gram. ¶We are pleased to announce that our prices per treatment are the same ⁣74
as last year's. We have enclosed the monthly breakdown for your summer ⁣88
program. Your payment is due only as the monthly treatments are completed. ⁣103
You might, however, want to take advantage of the discounted prepayment ⁣117
offer. ¶Please sign the enclosed schedule and send it back in the self-addressed ⁣133
envelope. Then relax—your lawn-feeding and weed-control chores belong to ⁣148
us. / Sincerely / Miss Doris Ingram, President / *xx* / Enclosures   (111 words) ⁣159

Exercise 19

Full block style. Open punctuation.

Today's date / Mr. Ralph T. Furman / Assistant Merchandise Manager / ⁣13
L. M. Robbins Company / 68 Wakefield Road / Kansas City, KS 66104 ⁣25

Dear Mr. Furman ⁣28

    Andrew J. Rockland has applied for a ⁣36
position with our company as a clerk-typist. ⁣44
He has given us your name as a ref- ⁣52
erence. ⁣55

    We would like to have confirmation ⁣63
from you of the dates of his employment with ⁣71
your firm. In addition, we would be grateful ⁣80
for any comments you may have concerning ⁣89
his job performance, his abilities, and his ⁣99
character. We would especially like to ⁣107
know whether you found his work satis- ⁣115
factory and whether he had a good atten- ⁣124
dance record while in your employ. ⁣130

    Your reply will be kept in strict confidence. ⁣139

        Sincerely ⁣141

Carl Avery / Personnel Interviewer / *xx*   (95 words) ⁣148

Exercise 1

ABBREVIATIONS

Type this list of common business abbreviations.

Half sheet. Double spacing. Spaces between columns are 4, 8, and 4. Center vertically and horizontally. Center title on line 7 and TS after it.

SOME COMMON BUSINESS ABBREVIATIONS

acct., a/c	account	int.	interest
amt.	amount	inv.	invoice
bal.	balance	mgr.	manager
C.O.D.	cash on delivery	mdse.	merchandise
c/o	care of	Messrs.	plural of Mr.
cat.	catalog	misc.	miscellaneous
cr.	credit	mtg.	mortgage
dr.	debit	pd.	paid
dept.	department	recd.	received
F.O.B.	free on board	wt.	weight

Exercise 2

ABBREVIATIONS

These sentences show correct application of Rules 1–11. Type each sentence once.

Half sheet. 70-space line. Double spacing. Center title on line 6 and TS after it.

ABBREVIATION STYLE GUIDE: ONE

1. I saw President Carter when he campaigned in our town.
2. My summer address is 234 Lasher Street.
3. I recently moved to 76 North Maple Road.
4. His heir, William Ford, Jr., was present for the reading of the will.
5. The convention was held on the last Thursday in September.
6. She graduated from St. Gerard School in 1978.
7. Area No. 7 is our sales territory in Maine.
8. The clerical employees at Falvey Company are on strike.
9. My sister will receive her Ph.D. degree in June.
10. Send the bill to 12 Pine Street, Salem, Oregon 97302.
11. Eighty percent of the employees were female.

Exercise 3

ABBREVIATIONS

Type these sentences, inserting the information in parentheses where the colored square appears. Decide according to Rules 1–11, whether to use an abbreviation or spell out the word. *Do not mark the book.*

Full sheet. 70-space line. Double spacing. Center title on line 13 and TS after it.

ABBREVIATION STYLE GUIDE: TWO

1. Our manager, ■ Ryan, will retire in March.   (Ms.)
2. She went to visit her sister in Los Angeles, ■.   (Calif.)
3. I remember living at 37 Chestnut ■ when I was a child.   (Ave.)
4. My insurance Policy, ■ 113-467, will mature next year.   (No.)
5. There has been a 5 ■ increase in the price of silver.   (%)
6. Have you been to ■ Louis, Missouri?   (St.)
7. Gene King, ■, won the lottery prize last week.   (Sr.)
8. Wednesday, ■ 12 is our absolute deadline.   (Aug.)
9. She is manager of the Wilson ■ branch in Dallas.   (Co.)
10. ■ Millben will not run for office in this year's election.   (Gov.)
11. In one ■, the messenger will pick up the package.   (hr.)

Key to Exercise 3
1. Ms. 2. California 3. Avenue 4. No. 5. percent 6. St.
7. Sr. 8. August 9. Company 10. Governor 11. hour

Exercise 14 continued

the line of machinery you offer for use in wheel alignment and brake service 102
will be extremely helpful to us. We are open to all options, including the use 118
of rebuilt or used equipment. ¶Thank you for your kind assistance in this 133
matter. / Cordially / Andrew Jost / President / *xx*   (104 words) 142

Exercise 15

Full block style. Open punctuation.

Today's date / Manhattan Paint Company / 503 West 14th Street / New York, 14
NY 10009 / Ladies and Gentlemen / There was an error made on your recent 28
shipment to us. Our Purchase Order No. 7634 called for five 2-gallon cans of 43
White Premium Enamel. Instead, you sent us two 5-gallon cans. ¶We are able 58
to use the cans you sent; so we will keep them. However, please ship the five 74
2-gallon cans that we originally requested as soon as possible. A customer has 90
ordered them for a job he must begin shortly. / Yours truly / Gene M. 103
Campbell, Manager / *xx*   (75 words) 107

Exercise 16

Full block style. Open punctuation.

June 14, 19— / Mr. Howard Leyton / 711 Plaza Building / 834 Third Avenue / 13
Little Rock, AR 72201 / Dear Mr. Leyton / We shall, of course, comply with 27
your request to cancel your life insurance policy if you wish it. We urge you, 43
however, to reconsider. If you decide to take out another policy later, you will 59
have to pay a higher premium. You will also have to undergo a physical exam- 74
ination. ¶We hope you will be able to meet with our representative for your 89
area, Ms. Goldman. She can discuss with you the possibility of converting 104
your present policy into one that better suits your present needs. Ms. Goldman 120
will telephone you to arrange a convenient appointment. We hope that you 135
will consider her information carefully in making your final decision. / Yours 150
sincerely / Ms. Marilyn P. Young / Branch Administrator / *xx*   (108 words) 162

Exercise 17

Full block style. Open punctuation.

January 24, 19— / Drummond Brothers / 189 Linton Avenue / Scranton, 12
PA 18502 / Gentlemen / Since we always try to please our customers, we are 26
glad to make an adjustment such as you request. Since your present payment 41
date is not convenient for you, another arrangement can be made to our 55
mutual satisfaction. ¶ Unfortunately, we cannot vary our cash discount 69
period. The reason is that we feel it is only fair to give all our customers the 85
same time limit. We can, however, arrange to send your monthly statements 100
on the 15th of the month. They will cover all transactions from the 16th of 115
the preceding month. This will entitle you to our cash discount if payment 130
is made no later than the 25th. ¶Please let us know whether you wish us to 145
make this change. / Cordially yours / David L. Foster / Credit Manager / 158
xx   (108 words) 159

Topic 3 STYLE GUIDES FOR METRIC UNITS

The National Bureau of Standards has set standards to aid our transition to the metric system. The metric system is formally called the International System of Units. Our conversion to it will require some changes in the style we use for typing numbers. Here are the rules you are most likely to need in daily use of the metric system.

Rule 1.
CAPITALIZATION

a. Use lowercase letters for all metric units, unless they begin a sentence. Exception: a metric unit that comes from the name of a person is always capitalized. (Celsius, for example, was the person who created the metric unit for measuring temperature.)

- *They walked 25 kilometers.*
- *It was 18 degrees Celsius on graduation day.*

b. Use lowercase letters for most metric symbols.

- g *for gram*
- kg *for kilogram*
- mg *for milligram*
- m *for meter*
- cm *for centimeter*
- mm *for millimeter*

There are three exceptions to this rule: (a) Use a capital L to symbolize liter, since a lowercase l might be confused with the numeral 1; (b) capitalize the symbol for a metric unit that comes from the name of a person; and (c) capitalize the symbol for a metric term that stands for a million or more.

- L *for liter*
- C *for Celsius*
- kH *for kiloHertz*
- Mc *for megacycle*

Rule 2.
PLURALS

a. Use plurals only when the quantity expressed is zero, greater than one, or less than minus one.

- *0 degrees Celsius*
- *1 degree Celsius*
- *−5 degrees Celsius*

b. Symbols for metric units do not add *s* to form plurals.

- *250 mL for 250 milliliters (not mLs)*
- *15 kg for 15 kilograms (not kgs)*

Rule 3.
SPACING

a. Leave one space between a number and a metric symbol.

- *7 m   33.4 kg*

b. Leave one space—not a comma—between groups of numbers in the thousands, on either side of the decimal point.

- *7 540 321, not 7,540,321*
- *0.613 75, not 0.61375*

c. Do not leave a space between the degree symbol (°) and the symbol for Celsius (C).

- *20°C*

Rule 4.
PERIOD AND DECIMAL POINT

a. Do not use a period after a metric symbol, except at the end of a sentence. Examples:

- *15 cm   3 kg*

b. Use the dot (or period) as a decimal point within numbers. In numbers less than one, type a zero before the decimal point.

- *0.38*

Directions for Exercises 11–20

Following the letter style shown in Model 9, type the letters in these exercises in full block style. Use the Letter Placement Chart on page 197 to determine the proper margins and position of the date line. Substitute your own initials for the *xx* at the end of each letter.

Exercise 11
Full block style. Open punctuation.

March 10, 19— / June Gibson, Financial Manager / Good Heart Charities / Box 2000 / Concord, NH 03301 / Dear Miss Gibson / Our company is preparing tax returns and financial statements for Goetz Brothers Manufacturing of St. Louis. ¶In reviewing our records, we have discovered that you failed to send Goetz Brothers a statement of contributions for the first and third quarters of last year. We cannot complete our work until we receive those statements. Your prompt attention to this matter would be most appreciated. / Sincerely / Dennis Brendel / Accountant / *xx*   (63 words)

Exercise 12
Full block style. Open punctuation.

Today's date / Ms. Judith Nilsson / Computer Equipment Company / Housing Division / 305 Canton Road / San Diego, CA 92109 / Dear Ms. Nilsson / We are happy to submit a bid on installing a new heating and air conditioning system in your facility. The specifications you have outlined are receiving our careful attention. ¶We will want to send a representative to inspect the premises shortly, and we will call you to make an appointment. Our estimate will be completed within a week after the inspection. We can assure you that our materials and workmanship will meet the highest standards. / Cordially / Philip P. Logan, President / *xx* (75 words)

Exercise 13
Full block style. Open punctuation.

August 8, 19— / National Calculators, Inc. / 84 Cyril Street / Rochester, NY 14617 / Ladies and Gentlemen / Several weeks ago we purchased three dozen pocket electronic calculators from you. At that time, you offered us some attractive window posters. We did not believe that we could make use of them, and so we did not accept your offer. ¶We now find, however, that we have a place for two of these posters. Will you please send them to us as soon as possible? We are sure they will help to increase our sales of the calculators. / Sincerely / Ms. I. A. Golden / Store Manager / *xx*   (79 words)

Exercise 14
Full block style. Mixed punctuation.

February 10, 19— / Minnesota Machines / 4100 Simmons Road / Duluth, MN 55807 / Gentlemen / Until now, our small tire shop has specialized in the sale of tires exclusively. At this time, we are considering expanding our operations to include related services. We are especially interested in adding wheel alignment and brake service. ¶We would like a representative from your company to visit us or to give us a call at (218) 762-8196. A knowledge of

(Continued on next page)

Rule 5.
COMPOUND UNITS

a. Type square or cubic symbols with raised numbers.

- 8 cm^2 *for 8 square centimeters*   - 9 cm^3 *for 9 cubic centimeters*

b. Use the term "per" to form compound units spelled out. Use the diagonal to stand for "per" in the symbols for compound units.

- m/s *for meters per second*   - km/h *for kilometers per hour*

Exercise 1
METRIC STYLE

Type these sentences to gain practice in expressing amounts in metric terms.

Half sheet. 70-space line. Double spacing. Begin on line 6.

1. The small box measured 9.4 cm by 7.6 cm by 5.2 cm.
2. The lengths of the chains are 1.50 m, 2.20 m, and 3.50 m.
3. It takes a jet four hours to fly from Phoenix to New York, at an average air speed of 963 kilometers per hour (km/h).
4. Of this amount, $14 329 was spent for nonbusiness purposes.
5. What will the carpet cost if it sells at $14.50 per m²?
6. It's a hot day when the mercury hits 32°C.
7. The jug of milk holds 3 L; the container of butter weighs 0.5 kg.
8. The old saying now goes, "Give them a centimeter and they'll take a kilometer."
9. Sandra's prescription is for 200 milliliters of cough medicine.
10. Driving home, we traveled over 1 600 km in two days.

Exercise 2
METRIC STYLE

Follow the directions given for Exercise 1.

1. The cake recipe called for an oven setting of 160°C.
2. Using the Celsius scale, water freezes at 0°C and boils at 100°C.
3. The large size weighs 1.25 kg and sells for 99 cents.
4. The letter I mailed today weighed 28 g.
5. The living room measures 9 m by 5 m.
6. The cubic meter (m³) is the base unit for measuring volume.
7. The swimming pool is 15 m long, 9 m wide, and 3 m deep.
8. Soft drinks now come in 1-liter (L) bottles.
9. The measuring cup shows that 250 mL equal 8 fluid ounces.

Topic 4 REVIEW OF ENGLISH EDITING SKILLS

Study the words in this list in groups of fives or tens. Then type the words from dictation daily for a week. Take a test on them at the end of the week. Work to add this list of words to those you are able to spell accurately. Watch out for these words (and the words in the first spelling study list on page 138) as you type assignments that are given in unedited form.

A good command of spelling is an asset for any office worker. Equipment is constantly being improved to increase efficiency in processing paperwork; you, too, should expect to increase your skills steadily during your working years. If you have learned the basics of English grammar, punctuation, and spelling, you need not fear being replaced by a machine; there is always a demand for office workers who have good language skills.

ALBURY'S
WHOLE-GRAIN CEREAL, INC.
34 Virginia Avenue, New Orleans, La. 70122   (504) 525-3611

Words

Date line   February 17, 19--   4

Space down 4 times

Inside address   Mrs. Alberta Bonnard   8
                   109 Crippen Avenue   12
                   Baton Rouge, LA 70807   16
                        DS
Salutation   Dear Mrs. Bonnard   20
                        DS
                   We are pleased to send you a copy of our booklet, THE CARE OF   32
                   CHILDREN. It offers many practical suggestions to help you   44
                   in looking after the daily needs of infants and small children. 57
                        DS
Body   For more than thirty years, nutritionists have recommended our   70
                   whole-grain cereal as one of the first solid foods that babies   83
                   may have and as the hot breakfast cereal for every growing   95
                   child. Adults, too, find Albury's Whole-Grain Cereal nourish-   108
                   ing and delicious.   112
                        DS
                   We hope that you will try some of the excellent recipes sug-   124
                   gested in the booklet. They add welcome and healthy variety   136
                   to the daily menu and are easy and economical to prepare.   148
                        DS
Complimentary   Sincerely yours   151
closing

Signature   *Paul T. Daly*   Space down 4 times

Typed name and   Paul T. Daly, President   156
title of sender   DS
Dictator's and   MVT:xx   157
typist's initials   DS
                   Enclosure   159

(Shown in Elite Type)

Model 9   **Business Letter · Full Block
Style with Open Punctuation**

MASTER SPELLING LIST – PART 2

1	addresses	26	enclosure	51	interview	76	recognize
2	advertise	27	engagement	52	jewelry	77	referring
3	angle	28	enough	53	leisurely	78	regular
4	argument	29	especially	54	library	79	responsibility
5	association	30	exhibit	55	losing	80	restaurant
6	authorized	31	experienced	56	manager	81	secretary
7	bargain	32	familiar	57	marital	82	sincerely
8	bookkeeper	33	February	58	merchandise	83	specialize
9	calculate	34	finalize	59	mileage	84	specifically
10	career	35	financial	60	misspell	85	statistics
11	celebration	36	fiscal	61	mortgage	86	stepping
12	churches	37	foreign	62	ninety	87	strength
13	clerical	38	forward	63	ninth	88	studying
14	column	39	fulfill	64	paid	89	suggestion
15	conferring	40	gentlemen	65	pamphlets	90	superintendent
16	congratulate	41	government	66	permitted	91	supervise
17	consumer	42	graduation	67	physical	92	therefore
18	cooperation	43	grammar	68	probably	93	thirtieth
19	corporation	44	grateful	69	profited	94	thorough
20	criticize	45	guarantee	70	prompt	95	twelfth
21	definitely	46	happiness	71	quality	96	twentieth
22	desirable	47	height	72	quantity	97	using
23	dessert	48	incorporated	73	questionnaire	98	Wednesday
24	duplicate	49	individual	74	quite	99	weird
25	eighth	50	interest	75	receptionist	100	writing

Exercise 1
PUNCTUATION AND CAPITALIZATION REVIEW

As you type these sentences, make any necessary corrections in punctuation and capitalization.

Full sheet. 70-space line. Single spacing. Begin on line 6.

Comma

1. You want a comfortable home good food and time for recreation.
2. In another ten years in fact we shall be firmly established.
3. We know the shipment was wrong but we are puzzled about the error.
4. They complain of poor housing poor water supply and few stores.
5. I believe therefore that we are not responsible.

(Continued on next page)

M & R Trucking, Daniels Bottling, Ourston Auto Customizing, or Minkelson's Toys. Enclosed are copies of these and other logos we have created.

Many of the firms now using our logos have reported positive customer reaction to our designs. Several of our clients have written us letters to tell us of improved name recognition that has resulted from use of a logo.

We believe your business deserves the chance to get one step ahead of the competition. We will be glad to visit your office and explain the services we offer. If you prefer, you may visit our offices at any time to inspect our work firsthand.

Cordially

Rebecca LeBret / Art Director / *xx* / Enclosures   (129 words)

Drill D
TYPING MODEL 9

Type the letter shown in Model 9 on the following page. If letterhead stationery is not available, use a plain sheet. Follow the spacing instructions given in the model. Determine the proper margins and position of the date line by referring to the Letter Placement Chart. Type your initials in place of *xx*. The body of the letter contains 109 words.

Drill E
OPENING PARTS
OF MODEL 9

Type the beginning of the letter shown in Model 9 to see how far you can type in 3 minutes. Use the date line placement and margin settings determined for Drill D. Repeat the drill until you can type the opening parts of this letter without hesitation.

Drill F
CLOSING PARTS
OF MODEL 9

Type the letter shown in Model 9 starting with the last paragraph. Use the same margins you set for Drill D. Try to finish the letter in 3 minutes. Repeat the drill until you can type the closing parts of this letter without hesitation.

---

6. Our superintendent Mr. Walker graduated from Fisk University.
7. When your supply is low please telephone our order department.
8. She gave us some wise sound advice.
9. My newest book <u>Along the Way</u> is a novel.
10. Sgt. Riley Sgt. Holmes and Sgt. Fisher were promoted recently.

Semicolon

11. The neighborhood was poor the house was old the room was small.
12. The change has been beneficial for us it has also helped you.
13. We tried to explain the problem however, he refused to listen.
14. I arrived late nevertheless, I heard the entire sermon.
15. I have lived in Detroit, Michigan Chicago, Illinois and Akron, Ohio.

Colon

16. I need the following information name, date, age, file number.
17. I have one question to ask Why are you so eager for the change?
18. His reasoning was as follows he had never meant to stay there.
19. This investment has one great advantage it is absolutely safe.

Apostrophe

20. One hours sleep before midnight is worth three after.
21. Everybodys business is nobodys business.
22. The children were taught the three <u>R</u>s at an early age.
23. Mrs. Abbott spells her name with two <u>b</u>s and two <u>t</u>s.
24. My youngest brothers name is Harold.

Dash

25. You and I have a great heritage the heritage of a free democracy.
26. The piano was very large too large to fit into the room.
27. We rose bright and early or at any rate, early that morning.

Parentheses

28. That method trial and error was the only one she had ever tried.
29. That is the main purpose perhaps the only purpose of his visit.
30. He referred to the house our house as their legal property.

Hyphen

31. Our ready to wear dresses have been reduced for the sale.
32. Live so as always to maintain your self respect.
33. Our community was built by public spirited men and women.
34. Mail us the form in the enclosed, self addressed envelope.

to conduct himself properly. We do not excuse his action but are merely 85
explaining it. We have spoken to him about the matter and believe he sincerely 101
regrets his rudeness. ¶This employee did not know where your package was 115
because he had changed assignments with another clerk. It is most unfortu- 130
nate that these circumstances resulted in so much annoyance to you. ¶Here- 145
after, should arrangements be made for anyone to call for a package, we shall 160
leave it at the front desk. We trust you will have no further cause for com- 175
plaint. We want you to know we value your patronage and will do our best 190
to please you. / Yours very truly / G. A. Hearn, President / *xx*   (154 words) 201

Exercise 9

Modified block style. Open punctuation. No paragraph indention.

Today's date / Hoffman & Sons / 36 Water Street / Rochester, NY 14615

Gentlemen

We regret that we are unable to comply with your request for two posters advertising GOLDEN umbrellas. Since there was little demand for these posters, we did not re-order them when our supply was exhausted.

Perhaps you would be interested in purchasing copies of another poster we print. We are sending you, under separate cover, our latest catalog and a revised price list.

Sincerely

Mrs. M. W. Doss, Director / Public Relations Department / MWD:*xx*   (64 words)

Exercise 10

Modified block style. Open punctuation. No paragraph indention.

May 8, 19— / Mr. Gordon Hethcock / Hethcock & Parapoulos / 63 Dodge Street / Providence, RI 02907

Dear Mr. Hethcock

Our graphics firm specializes in creating eye-catching logos for businesses in this area. You may have seen the ones we designed for

(Continued on next page)

Quotation Marks

35. The prisoner cried, I am not guilty!

36. We began by singing The Star Spangled Banner.

37. She wanted to know the definition of a monopolist.

38. I asked, What time will the meeting end?

Capitals

39. Read chapter 6, page 115, of your english book.

40. Mr. Alexander, who is President of the company, works on satur-days and sundays.

41. I saw you driving West on Russell street last Spring.

Numbers and Abbreviations

42. Miss. Roberts was born May fourth.

43. Professor Joan Martin had to pay a ten-dollar parking ticket.

44. I found 3 valuable stamps in a store in Saint Louis, MO.

Exercise 2
COMMA REVIEW

Review Rules 5–10 on comma usage (refer to page 182).
Type these sentences, adding any necessary punctuation as you type. *Do not mark the book.*
Full sheet. 70-space line. Double spacing. Begin on line 8.

1. No two people look alike dress alike or work alike.

2. A personable efficient secretary is a valuable asset.

3. When you are looking for new office furniture let us know.

4. As we have not received your approval we cannot take any action.

5. It was a pleasure meeting you and we hope to see you again soon.

6. Thank you for the check to cover your water gas and telephone bills.

7. The school of course will pay all your expenses.

8. All you need do Ms. Gates is save a small amount each week.

9. When you apply for a job be sure to take a data sheet.

10. I lost my new typing textbook <u>Personal Typing</u>.

11. Frankly I find myself in an embarrassing position.

12. Our representative in your area Ms. E. Thomas will handle your problem.

13. Get a copy of our book <u>Using Your Hands</u> for complete directions.

14. You can therefore be certain of good service from us.

(Continued on next page)

7,500 books will be hardbound using a low-priced cloth. It will also be perfect bound, and the cover and spine will be imprinted. ¶Under separate cover, we are sending two sample books with bindings similar to what we want. Please use these in preparing the cost estimates. When submitting your estimates, let us know how soon you can make delivery after the order is placed. We would also like to see sample materials and some books you have done to these specifications. / Sincerely / Otto Q. Karman / Purchasing Agent / *xx*   (135 words)

Exercise 6
Modified block style. Open punctuation. 5-space paragraph indention.

August 19, 19— / Mr. Julius Watson / Watson and Lewis Contracting, Inc. /   13
42 La Salle Street / New Orleans, LA 70113 / Dear Mr. Watson / We are pleased   27
to inform you that we have accepted your bid for the construction of our new   42
warehouse. Even though some lower bids were submitted, management did   56
not choose the lowest bidder. Past experience in working with you has led us   71
to trust your estimates and rely on your ability to complete a job as agreed.   86
¶Our lawyer felt it necessary to make some minor changes in the terms of the   101
contract. It will be ready for your inspection early next week. If you would   116
like to meet to discuss any of the revisions, feel free to call me at any time.   132
You can reach me at 949-3112. Cordially / Baldwin Brooks / Financial Vice-   146
President / *xx*   (109 words)   148

Exercise 7
Modified block style. Open punctuation. No paragraph indention.

March 5, 19— / Miss Felicia Curtis / Edsel Ford High School / 14337 Rotunda   14
Drive / Dearborn, MI 48122 / Dear Miss Curtis / Thank you for your interest   28
in attending our typewriting conference to be held in Dearborn next month.   43
As you know, the authors of our newest typing textbook, *Modern Office Type-*   58
writing, will be on hand. They will make presentations and discuss the latest   74
innovations in typing instruction. ¶Your letter states that you will be able to   90
attend only the sessions held after the luncheon. Therefore, you need not send   106
in the registration form and the $5 fee. The fee is intended to cover the cost   122
of the luncheon only. ¶I am sorry you will not be able to be with us for the   137
entire day. However, I am certain you will find the afternoon sessions valuable   153
to you in your classroom instruction. / Cordially / Charles L. Lester / Regional   168
Manager / *xx*   (119 words)   170

Exercise 8
Modified block style. Open punctuation. 5-space paragraph indention.

November 1, 19— / Mr. Victor Stephens / Manor Plumbing Company / 40   12
Main Street / Ayer, MA 01432 / Dear Mr. Stephens / We deeply regret the inci-   26
dent about which you wrote us. We try to engage only courteous help, but we   41
do not always succeed. The people in our shipping room have little contact   56
with our customers. The man of whom you speak evidently did not know how   71

(Continued on next page)

15. When a data sheet is neat it makes a good first impression.

16. I lived in Detroit Michigan until the age of 17.

17. He made a great number of errors; however he made neat corrections.

18. Visit the Downriver Bank the friendly savings place.

19. I was happy to receive the shipment of Friday May 15.

20. It is you must admit a beautiful day today.

21. Because of its great value you should insure that package.

22. If you don't understand read the directions more carefully.

23. I will admit incidentally that I was very nervous.

24. He asked me when I worked last where I worked and why I left.

25. She is a bright conscientious student.

Exercise 3
CAPITALIZATION REVIEW

Review Capitalization Rules 1–11 (pages 192–193). Type
these sentences, correcting any capitalization errors as you
type.
Full sheet. 70-space line. Double spacing. Begin on line 13.

1. We are now located in the bradford building on lycaste street.

2. I would like to buy a set of turkish towels.

3. "Do you know," she asked, "what happened to my favorite fountain
pen?"

4. You will find the answers on page 75 of chapter 2.

5. My neighbors attend the chinese community church.

6. Our store's busiest season runs from thanksgiving to Christmas.

7. The frenchman spoke english with a strong accent.

8. An honest person is the noblest work of god.

9. The author of the book, My Holiday, has written a new book,
SURPRISE VISIT.

10. The painting "a visit to mars," shows vivid imagination.

11. The Olympia Cruise Ship sails on wednesday, July 18.

12. The secretary of state made an address at the meeting.

13. I prefer to wait and speak to president Lowell.

14. Mrs. Bahr, our school secretary, drove to florida on vacation.

15. I believe that Kensington park is located just east of us.

16. Many students still find mathematics a difficult subject.

17. The nurse put a band-aid strip on the child's finger.

18. I saw a joint session of the senate and house of representatives.

Exercise 2

Modified block style.
Mixed punctuation.
No paragraph indention.

Today's date / Mr. Albert Wheeler / 68 Elm Road / Rochester, NY 14605 / Dear Mr. Wheeler / We expect to open our new salesroom at 73 Hartford Avenue in about a month. ¶We have planned a private showing for our regular customers next Monday from 10 a.m. to 1 p.m. On display will be a number of new home appliances, which we are sure will interest you. ¶We hope you will join us and be our guest at a luncheon following the showing. / Cordially / Herbert Dean, President / *xx*   (66 words)

Exercise 3

Modified block style. Mixed punctuation. 5-space paragraph indention.

Today's date / Atlas Containers, Inc. / 481 Dalton Avenue / Omaha, NB 68106 /   14
Gentlemen / We regret that we cannot immediately submit samples of the   28
container for which you have sent specifications. As you have planned this   43
container, the manufacture will involve a very difficult gluing job. ¶We hope   58
to be able to send you a sample soon. We are awaiting delivery of a special   73
adhesive for a container ordered by another firm. We shall advise you as soon   89
as the adhesive arrives and we have had an opportunity to try it. ¶We doubt,   104
however, that we will be able to produce the container within the price limits   120
you mention. The expense involved in using the special adhesive will add to   135
the cost considerably. / Yours very truly / Samuel P. Lewis / Production   148
Manager / *xx*   (109 words)   150

Exercise 4

Modified block style. Mixed punctuation. 5-space paragraph indention.

January 6, 19— / Mr. Alvin Collins / Collins Furnishings, Inc. / 318 Washington   15
Street / Memphis, TN 38106 / Dear Mr. Collins / We are happy to have the   28
opportunity to explain our recent request for a financial statement. But first,   44
let us assure you that you have a most excellent credit rating. No reflection   60
whatever was intended by the request. ¶When revising our credit files, we   75
routinely send a standardized form to all customers—even those of long stand-   91
ing. That we have faith in your financial standing is indicated by the unlimited   107
credit we have extended you. We shall continue to serve you as we have done   123
in the past. Our service will not be affected by a decision on your part not to   139
furnish us a financial statement. / Cordially / Ms. Rachel Engel / Credit   152
Manager / BNL / *xx*   (107 words)   155

Exercise 5

Modified block style. Open punctuation. No paragraph indention.

Today's date / Mr. Norman L. Inman / Orville Book Bindery / 74 Raviolo Place / Auburn, ME 04210 / Dear Mr. Inman / We have two books in the process of being printed and are soliciting bids from several binderies. ¶Both volumes contain 432 pages and have a trim size of 6 by 9¼ inches. One lot of 10,000 copies requires an inexpensive two-color paper cover with a perfect binding. The second lot of

(Continued on next page)

Exercise 4

REVIEW

The following sentences contain errors identified by the symbols (see page 194) in the margin. Find the errors, then type the corrected sentence.

Full sheet. 70-space line. Double spacing. Center title on line 5 and TS after it.

TYPING FROM UNEDITED SENTENCES

com   1. If you agree we shall act at once.

ww, com   2. Weather you buy from us or not we desire to please you.

com, ww   3. If delivery is not made soon we will not except the goods.

ro, com   4. The road sloped gently downward on one side on the other side there was a steep drop.

com, sp   5. Our job is to produce better milk and we can suceed only with
ww   your corporation.

col   6. It takes the following two people to make a good photograph the
ep   one behind the camera and the one who makes the print

com, sp   7. An efficient well-planned road system is necesary for the progress of the country.

sem, com   8. We want our taxes to be low however we must pay for any Public Services that we want.

cap   9. Last Autumn we had to change the contract because no matter how
com, ww   hard we tried we found it impossible to meat the deadlines.

sp, com   10. We beleive you will find the material to be strong of good qual-
com   ity and reasonably priced.

ro, com   11. Supplies in our line will be limited for a few months we shall
com   therefore accept orders for future delivery only.

com   12. You deserve our thanks Mr. Evans for the way in which you have
sp   met the many dificult situations that have arisen during the
ww   passed year.

frag, com   13. When humans many thousands of years ago first learned to warm
ww   themselves and cook they're food.

com, sp   14. We hesitated to bring up this unpleasant matter but we dicided that you should be aware of the facts.

com, cap 15. Mary Drake our Committee Chairperson will make a favorable
cap   report at our annual meeting in the Fall.

cap   16. Our East coast branch is fully equipped to handle your export
sp   shipments just as soon as we receive your authorisation.

com   17. Last summer for the first time in more than five years we pro-
cap   duced a shakespearean play.

HOLT OFFICE EQUIPMENT AND SUPPLIES

320 Graham Avenue, Decatur, Illinois 62510 ■ (217) 964-1076

Words

Date line February 6, 19-- 3

Space down 4 times

Inside address
Mr. B. J. Elliott, President 9
Elliott Realty Company 14
504 Calvert Street 18
Decatur, IL 62512 22

DS

Salutation Dear Mr. Elliott: 26

DS

Body
As we discussed in our telephone conversation this 36
morning, my company is expanding very quickly, and . 46
it is likely that within six months it will double 56
its present stock. Consequently, we will require 66
additional warehouse storage space, preferably at a 76
location as near to our main store as possible. 86

DS

Since I will be out of town for a few days, I will 96
not be available until early next week to look at 106
warehouse properties. I'm sure you have among your 116
current listings some that you would recommend for 126
our storage needs. I will call you upon my return 136
to arrange an appointment with you to look at your 146
properties. 148

DS

Complimentary closing Cordially, 151

Signature *Paul Solomon* Space down 4 times

Typed name and title of sender Paul Solomon 154
Business Manager 155

DS

Typist's initials XX

Tab at
center

(Shown in Pica Type)

Model 8 *Business Letter · Modified Block Style with
Mixed Punctuation and No Paragraph Indention*

ADVANCED BUSINESS CORRESPONDENCE

Topic 1 BUSINESS LETTERS ON LETTERHEAD PAPER

Business letters typed on letterhead paper differ only slightly from the personal-business letters in Section 2. These differences are described and illustrated below.

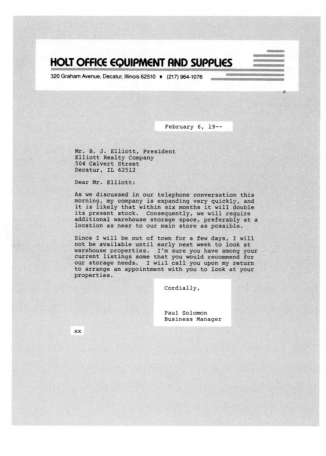

THE PRINTED LETTERHEAD   Businesses use special stationery printed with the company's name, street address, city, state, and ZIP Code and, usually, telephone number. Matching envelopes printed with the company's name and address are also used.

THE DATE LINE   Letters typed on letterhead stationery begin with the date line, typed a minimum of three lines below the letterhead information.

SIGNATURE BLOCK   This contains the signature, the typed name of the sender, and the title of the position held by that person. The sender's name is placed on the fourth line under the complimentary closing, as in personal business letters. The position title may follow on the same line, separated from the name by a comma. More often, however, it is placed on the next line, directly under the name.

REFERENCE INITIALS   These are the initials of the person who typed the letter. The typist's initials are placed at the left margin, in lowercase, a double space after the last line of the signature block. The initials of the person who dictates a letter are usually not included in the reference initials. However, if the person who dictates the letter is not the same as the person who signs the letter, then the dictator's initials should always be included. See Model 9 (page 242). Dictator's initials are typed in capitals at the left margin, and are separated from the typist's by a colon or a slash. All reference initials are typed solid without spaces or periods.

COURTESY TITLES   Use of courtesy titles in business letters poses a problem for the typist. The titles, *Ms., Mrs.,* and *Miss,* in the signature block are optional. If the letter writer prefers to include one of these, it is typed without parentheses in front of the name. (In the handwritten signature, however, the courtesy title is enclosed within parentheses.) The courtesy title, *Mr.,* is seldom used in the signature block.

In responding to a letter in which the writer has not used a courtesy title, it is acceptable to address that person in reply without a title. For example, a salutation might read *Dear N. Wilson, Dear Laura Martin,* or *Dear Earl R. Scanlon.*

The business letters that follow will cast you in the role of typist for the writers or dictators of the letters. Study Models 8 and 9 (pages 237 and 242) and notice the placement of the new letter parts. Then practice Drills A–F. Drills A–C should be mastered before you begin Exercise 1; Drills D–F, before you begin Exercise 11.

Drill A
TYPING MODEL 8

Type the letter shown in Model 8 on the following page. If letterhead stationery is not available, use a plain sheet and begin with the date line. Follow the spacing instructions given in the model. Determine the proper margins and position of the date line by referring to the Letter Placement Chart on page 197. Type your initials in lowercase letters in place of *xx.* The body of the letter contains 109 words.

Drill B
OPENING PARTS OF MODEL 8

Type the letter shown in Model 8 to see how far you can type in 3 minutes. Use the date line placement and margin settings determined for Drill A. Repeat the drill until you can type the opening parts of this letter without hesitation.

Drill C
CLOSING PARTS OF MODEL 8

Type the letter shown in Model 8 starting with the last paragraph. Use the same margins you set for Drill A. Try to finish the letter in 3 minutes. Repeat the drill until you can type the closing parts of this letter without hesitation.

Directions for Exercises 1–10

Following the letter style shown in Model 8, type the letters in these exercises in modified block style. Use the Letter Placement Chart (page 197) to determine the proper margins and position of the date line. Substitute your own initials for the *xx* given in each letter. (Note that these exercises, and those that follow throughout Part 2, do not include punctuation for the salutation and complimentary closing. This will give you practice in deciding the correct punctuation required in each letter.)

Exercise 1
Modified block style.
Mixed punctuation.
No paragraph indention.

Today's date / Bernard McKuen & Company / 146 Lewis Avenue / Knoxville, TN 37906 / Ladies and Gentlemen / This is in reply to your query about the signature on the delivery receipt for two boxes of letterhead stationery and envelopes. The delivery was made to your office last week. We find that only the initials of the person receiving delivery are indicated. They are not clear but appear to be either TSR or LSR. Our delivery person says that she left the package with the receptionist in the outer office. ¶If this information is not sufficient to help you trace delivery, let us know. We shall be glad to send a photocopy of the signed receipt for your inspection. / Sincerely / R. Thompson / Shipping Department / *xx*   (111 words)